# A PASSION FOR EXCELLENCE

Nancy Austin earned her MBA in 1977 from the Graduate School of Management at the University of California at Los Angeles, and was a management consultant for two years with Southern California consulting firms, including her own. She then spent four years at Hewlett-Packard, where she ran the company's management-development seminars. Now president of Not Just Another Publishing Company, a member of the Tom Peters Group, she is also the co-author of *The Assertive Woman*. She lives in the Santa Cruz Mountains in California with her husband, Bill Cawley, and their son Jeff.

Tom Peters, who was a partner at McKinsey & Co. during the research that led to *In Search of Excellence*, left halfway through the writing of that book, in 1981, to found his own companies. Now called the Tom Peters Group, they include the Palo Alto Consulting Center; A Center for Management Excellence, which conducts the intensive four-day seminars for top management (known to alumni as Skunk Camp); and Not Just Another Publishing Company, which, with its Massachusetts-based cousin Excel-Media Inc., is responsible for audio, video and print products. Tom and his family live in Palo Alto, California.

TOM PETERS AND NANCY AUSTIN

# A Passion for Excellence

## The Leadership Difference

HarperCollins*Publishers*

HarperCollins*Publishers*
77–85 Fulham Palace Road,
Hammersmith, London W6 8JB

This paperback edition 1994
3 5 7 9 8 6 4

Previously published in paperback by Fontana 1986
Reprinted ten times

First published in Great Britain by
Collins 1985

ISBN 0 00 637062 4

Set in Electra

Printed in Great Britain by
HarperCollinsManufacturing, Glasgow

*For Kate Abbe and Bill Cawley
and the Skunks*

In the following pages I offer nothing more than simple facts, plain arguments and common sense; and have no other preliminaries to settle with the reader, other than that he will divest himself of prejudice and prepossession, and suffer his reason and his feelings to determine for themselves; that he will put on, or rather that he will not put off, the true character of a man, and generously enlarge his views beyond the present day.

—Thomas Paine, *Common Sense*

# Foreword

PERHAPS FIVE MILLION people have bought copies of *In Search of Excellence*, including its fifteen translations, since its publication in mid-October 1982. If history is any guide, two or three million probably opened the book. Four or five hundred thousand read as much as four or five chapters. A hundred thousand or so read it cover to cover. Twenty-five thousand took notes. Five thousand took detailed notes. (Not all of this is speculation. After his many speaking presentations, Tom is regularly asked to sign books. The number with bent pages and heavy underlining is dispiritingly low.)

In the Introduction we will argue that a revolution is on, that managers in every field are rethinking the tried and, as it turns out, not so true management principles that have often served their institutions poorly. At the heart of revolutions, historically, there have been no more than a handful of people. Perhaps among them today are those five thousand who have underlined key points in *In Search of Excellence*.

But now it's time to enter another phase. The zeal to do something is clear. Video and audio cassettes on the new wave overwhelm the mind and the ad pages of airline magazines. A thousand seminars, all describing radically different approaches to managing, are in the air for the first time in memory. We ourselves have given hundreds of speeches and conducted almost five hundred seminars since 1982. Perhaps a hundred thousand to two hundred thousand people have gone through them. But the question remains: Who's *doing* much of anything differently? And that's not even the most important question. The most important is: How many have *sustained* the new "it"? *In Search of Excellence* disgorged no magic: it simply said, Stay close to your customers; wander around. The absence of magic—"Practice common sense"—turned out to be its biggest selling point. And its biggest source of frustration: no surefire formulas for productive wandering around, no ten-step guides, how to begin, how to learn, and above all, how to teach yourself to sustain success for decades. And how do you practice excellence if your first name isn't Chairman and his or her last name isn't Kroc or Watson?

*A Passion for Excellence* is a first step along the path to answering those questions. It is not a how-to book. It is not a book on theory. It is rather an avowed Whitman's Sampler of the passion for excellence observed and celebrated. The topics we've chosen emerged from experience at five hundred seminars. Each chapter tells paradoxical tales of obsession in pursuing both detail and a dream. Each has scores of examples, as well as suggestions for practical actions that you can start immediately. (As a respected colleague says with certainty, "If you don't get started in the next seventy-two hours, you ain't going to get started at all.") Each stands essentially alone, which means you don't have to read them in order. Our hope is that ten years from now you will be going back and checking your underlinings to see if you're still really doing the things you committed yourself to do.

Many of you are on the verge. You have the instincts, but you have been told for years that those instincts are all wet: "Get the heck back into the office and work on the ten-year plan." "Don't waste your time wandering around with customers. It's not statistically valid." "Learn to draw those charts better. You don't make much of a presentation." "Sure, listen to your people, but then you damn well better tell them how to do it right, to make sure they get it right." "Failure? Not around here; we don't tolerate it." You know that's nonsense. We hope that our accounts of people, in some cases toiling away in big organizations, will give you heart as well as practical, straightforward guidance to innovative new practices.

Who are we and where have we been? Nancy Austin learned about excellence at Hewlett-Packard, where she ran the company's management-development seminars for a uniquely tough-minded set of managers all around the world. She is also the co-author of *The Assertive Woman*, the first book written to help women take practical steps toward positive, assertive behavior.

Tom Peters was with McKinsey during the research that led to *In Search of Excellence*. He left halfway through the writing of that book, in 1981, to found his own companies. First came the Palo Alto Consulting Center, focused, with colleague Bob Le Duc, on serving a small number of bellwether companies—Apple Computer, People Express, Mervyn's (a Dayton-Hudson subsidiary). It soon became apparent that there was a great hunger throughout the nation—and the world, for that matter—to hear the message of *In Search of Excellence*. Hundreds of seminars followed. With them came the founding of additional companies aimed at spreading the message far and wide. Nancy Austin's company, Not Just Another Publishing Company, along with its Massachusetts cousin, Excel/Media, is responsible for audio, video and print products. A Center for Management Excellence conducts forty-person, four-day workshops a half dozen or so times a year; intense personal and organizational evaluation of the wellsprings of strategic competence is the object.

The whole endeavor is a kind of Skunkworks, Inc. Taken from the L'il Abner comic strip, skunkwork is a term that came to the world of business from the Lockheed California Company.* It denotes a highly innovative, fast-

---

*Where it is called Skunk Works, a registered service mark.

moving and slightly eccentric activity operating at the edges of the corporate world. As we see it, the movement toward developing a new managing approach for America is in its skunkwork phase. The term captures the very essence of what we and newfound colleagues far and wide—from Kuala Lumpur to Dublin to Sydney to Stockholm to Louisville—are up to.

This book is the product of classic skunkwork activity. In the Introduction we'll present twenty or thirty of the companies that have excited us most in the course of the last twenty-four months. They range from the highly visible People Express and Apple Computer to Perdue Farms, the chicken powerhouse, and Stew Leonard's, a one-store dairy operation, from Milliken & Company and Worthington Industries in, respectively, the battered textile and steel industries to BancOne, the highly innovative regional bank responding so aggressively to deregulation.

In corner after corner—of General Motors and Ford, in single-store operations, in schools, in Big Eight accounting firms—we've unearthed skunk after skunk. It's not that they are implementing what we are suggesting. They have been practicing it with passion for years, often achieving remarkable successes in arenas that others have written off as either inexorably declining, hopelessly constrained, or dull—or all three. And they continued to do it in the early eighties, during the worst economic recession since the Great Depression.

Many of us joined together in September 1984, for a seminal event, the First Annual Skunk Camp. Forty brave souls who have been going their own way met in California and swapped tales about the battles fought, the scars accumulated, and the personal and soul-satisfying experiences that have come watching their people become winners, serving their customers better, innovating constantly—and making piles of money for shareholders in the process (or improving the quality of life in their cities or education in their schools). This book is about those skunks. It is about their once lonely lives, and now their banding together. For this is their revolution, not ours.

—Tom Peters
—Nancy Austin
December 1984
Palo Alto, California

# Contents

# Introduction:
# A Revolution Is Brewing

AT A BREAK during a seminar in San Francisco one of the vice presidents of a giant oil company came up to Tom and said, "I bought your book a year ago, before it became fashionable. I didn't like it very much. I've come to listen to you. I find I don't like what you have to say very much either. But we haven't got a choice."

We think he gives the book too much credit. *In Search of Excellence*, and now *A Passion for Excellence*, do not constitute "the solution" to the problems of American management. But our friend has a point. We find that it is a rare American manager who is complacent these days. All are searching— school and hospital administrators, city managers, factory bosses and bank executives. Why?

We think it's fair to say that we have lived in a house of cards. It was, in fact, pretty difficult for management to mess up an American corporation during the twenty-five years immediately following World War II. William Morris, in *A Time of Passion*, concurs: "Only maligning incompetent management could have shut Americans out of the boom." Thus, in 1946 the United States was blessed with an intact industrial base and seventeen years' worth of unfulfilled consumer demand, pent up during the Great Depression and World War II. From 1946 until the early sixties we opened the spigots full bore, just to meet that domestic demand. The quality of what we made, frankly, didn't matter all that much. Tom remembers when his father bought his first car after World War II, in 1949. If Chevrolet had delivered it minus an axle, his dad probably wouldn't have taken it back, so excited was he at the prospect of having *any* car.

Then, as American demand lost its bloom in the early sixties, our enterprises discovered Europe, which was still not fully rebuilt. American corporations watched their profit-and-loss statements rapidly come to reflect 30 percent or more of sales overseas, and often well over half of their profits.

In the late sixties American management was touted by many, at home and abroad, as the primary asset that America could export to the world. And then came reality: OPEC, the Japanese, social and political unrest, changing concerns as represented by EPA, OSHA, EEOC and other federal agencies, an emerging work force with needs that were substantially different from those of the past. The vaunted American management mystique quickly turned out to be largely just that—mystique. The battering American business took in the seventies and during the 1981–83 recession (is there anyone who thinks the recovery means we're permanently out of the woods?) has humbled virtually every American manager. Nor have public-sector organizations been immune; their performance too has been problematic at best, and much of the reason is surely that their managers adopted, with sadly little reflection, the management techniques that were so highly praised in the industrial sector.

Out of those failures of our organizations, as evidenced by faulty microchips and tanks that can't handle dust, by declining SAT scores and garbage lying about, has emerged the beginning of a fundamental reexamination of managing per se. The landmark *Harvard Business Review* article by Bob Hayes and the late Bill Abernathy, "Managing Our Way to Economic Decline," is the piece that we think of as the cornerstone of the corporate revolution. It attacked the MBA/numbers-only mentality of American managers and the lack of concern in American corporations for such basics as manufacturing. Several other works would qualify as first alarms, including David Halberstam's examination of Vietnam in *The Best and the Brightest* and Daniel Patrick Moynihan's analysis of Great Society failures, *Maximum Feasible Misunderstanding.* All put the knock on mindless systems analysis and began the examination of a misplaced emphasis on paper rather than on people. More recent business books, aside from *In Search of Excellence,* that come to mind include Bill Ouchi's *Theory Z,* Richard Pascale and Tony Athos's *The Art of Japanese Management,* Terry Deal and Allan Kennedy's *Corporate Cultures,* Rosabeth Moss Kanter's *The Change Masters* and Ken Auletta's *The Art of Corporate Success.* Symposia are now regularly held on corporate/organizational cultures, on entrepreneurial revitalization inside and outside the firm and the like. Robert Reich's *The Next American Frontier* and George Gilder's *Wealth and Poverty* taken together—the two contain virtually the same diagnosis, albeit with very different conclusions—suggest that the left and the right are equally distressed.

So a revolution is brewing. What kind of revolution? In large measure it is in fact a "back to basics" revolution. The management systems, schemes, devices and structures promoted during the last quarter century have added up to distractions from the main ideas: the achievement of sustainable growth and equity. Each such scheme seemed to make sense at the time. Each seemed an appropriate response to growing complexity. But the result was that the basics got lost in a blur of well-meaning gibberish that took us further and further from excellent performance in any sphere. We got so tied up in our techniques, devices and programs that we forgot about people—the people who produce the product or service and the people who consume it. (We hasten to add that by "back to basics" we do not intend to bring to mind images of Henry Ford toting a gun, daring his people to go out on strike. When it comes to relations with one's work force, paying attention to one's people, really listening to them, acting on what one hears, and treating them as full-scale partners, we are decidedly not going "back" to basics—though, indeed, as discussed in *In Search of Excellence*, the IBM's and Procter & Gambles have been following these practices for many decades.)

What are the basics of managerial success? Two of the most important are pride in one's organization and enthusiasm for its works. A quick check of the twenty-five leading textbooks on management finds neither in any index. Nor does one find much about such concepts as "naive customer listening," customer perception of service/quality, employee commitment and ownership, internal corporate entrepreneurship (sometimes called intrapreneurship), championing of innovation, trust, vision or "leadership."

That last, the concept of leadership, is crucial to the revolution now under way—so crucial that we believe the words "managing" and "management" should be discarded. "Management," with its attendant images—cop, referee, devil's advocate, dispassionate analyst, naysayer, pronouncer—connotes controlling and arranging and demeaning and reducing. "Leadership" connotes unleashing energy, building, freeing, and growing. As Warren Bennis, a major figure in the current rethinking process, says, "American organizations have been overmanaged and underled." Yet the revolution *is* on, and everywhere we find islands of hope: we see those who have always done it well and have not been bamboozled by apparently inexorable external forces, and those, mounting in number, who have actually turned their organizations around—a clear result of inspired management (which is another way of saying leadership).

### At the Core: Paradox

An introduction is a place to deal with common misperceptions. One, concerning this revolution, stands out above all others: it is that we advocate a change from "tough-mindedness" to "tenderness," from concern with hard data and balance sheets to a concern for the "soft stuff"—values, vision and integrity. We have found that when it comes to achieving long-term success, soft is hard. The pressure to perform in the organizations we will describe— from Perdue Farms to the City of Baltimore—is nothing short of brutal: these are "no excuses" environments, where radical decentralization frees people to make anything happen, where training is provided, where extraordinary results are then routinely expected because the barriers to them have been cleared away. There is a certain militancy in the way values are protected and people are empowered to take possession of their own achievements.

The superb business leaders we use as models in this book epitomize paradox. All are tough as nails and uncompromising about their value systems, but at the same time they care deeply about and respect their people; their very respect leads them to *demand* (in the best sense of the word) that each person be an innovative contributor. Ren McPherson, former chairman of

Dana, went so far as to evaluate even those who held the most mundane jobs almost solely on the degree to which the person (secretary, clerk) contributed innovatively to the job. The best bosses—in school, hospital, factory—are neither exclusively tough nor exclusively tender. They are both: tough on the values, tender in support of people who would dare to take a risk and try something new in support of those values. They speak constantly of vision, of values, of integrity; they harbor the most soaring, lofty and abstract notions. At the same time they pay obsessive attention to detail. No item is too small to pursue if it serves to make the vision a little bit clearer.

We have been forced to deal daily with the central paradox of leadership. One set of attendees at our seminars beseeches us to provide more concrete data. We think we provide a bushelful of it, but they want much more. More practical examples. More details: "What do I do right now?" Another set, equally vociferous, tells us that such details are unimportant. The whole point, they say, is trust, integrity, care; given those, the details will take care of themselves. The paradox: both are *exactly* right. The difficulty: the vast majority of us—some 75 percent, we judge—understand (and live) one way or the other and thus resolve the paradox by avoiding it.

This we can no longer do. We must confront the paradox, own it, live it, celebrate it if we are to make much headway in achieving excellence. We must cultivate passion and trust, and at virtually the same moment we must delve unmercifully into the details. How do we do it, or at least make a beginning? That's what *A Passion for Excellence* is all about.

## The Players

*In Search of Excellence* used a broad brush to paint a picture of excellent performance on eight dimensions in forty-three very large companies. *A Passion for Excellence* etches a finer, bolder portrait of the sources of long-term distinction. And passion it is. Top-flight performance is not dry and deadly; it is spirited, it is emotion-filled. Nor is our focus limited to the chairman and the giant company; we include here managers at every "level," smaller organizations and divisions of larger companies. Our examples penetrate deeper to capture what we now call the "smell" of a customer-(or innovation-) oriented company. And a series of pragmatic questions and suggestions in almost every chapter lead you to analyze where you are, how you got there, and particularly what you might try to do now to construct the easy-to-specify, tough-to-execute, building blocks of excellence on your own turf.

In the last few years we've found excellence in every nook and cranny, overseas as well as in the United States. Here are a few of the friends we've made along the way:

One of the best is a single-store operation, **Stew Leonard's** of Norwalk, Connecticut. Stew does $85 million worth of business—in milk, cheese, rolls and eggs—out of one store. It's a treat to shop there. It's a celebration of imagination and excellence.

Stew's principal supplier is Frank Perdue, chairman of **Perdue Farms.** Perdue turned another commodity—chicken—into gold. Operating out of Salisbury, Maryland, on the economically depressed Delmarva Peninsula, he has built an $800 million enterprise and created seven thousand new jobs along the way. Quality, imagination—and profit—are the keys to his kingdom.

Service businesses have played a huge role in our adventure over the last couple of years. There were few in *In Search of Excellence*. They almost dominate this list. Stew Leonard's is one of them. **Domino's Pizza** is another. In just eight years Tom Monaghan has built a $300 million empire that has become the number two pizza company, right behind PepsiCo's Pizza Hut. It's a delivery-only business, with heretofore unknown levels of service—and an unbelievably turned-on group of young men and women on the payroll.

Talk about turn-on, talk about a fast-growing service company, and, above all, you're describing **People Express**, ranked by some measures as the fastest-growing business in the history of the United States. People Express may offer low airfares, but through the zest and enthusiasm of its young and vital (and wealthy, via share ownership) staff it also provides a service level that some of the "greats" don't match. Don Burr's People Express will be prominent in this book.

**Ryder System,** a Florida company engaged in truck leasing, also plays a part. The highly profitable and fast-growing $2.5 billion system has taken advantage of deregulation. Its higher value-added services have banished the word "commodity" from yet another business where price is generally considered the only variable.

Another service entrant comes from across the Atlantic. One of the most remarkable turnarounds we've ever observed was crafted by Jan Carlzon of the **Scandinavian Air System (SAS)**. In the middle of the 1981–83 recession that clobbered most airlines, Carlzon's company went from losing $10 million a year to making $70 million a year on over $2 billion in sales. The reason (good news, indeed): a return to old-fashioned service excellence, led by Carlzon's boundless spirit.

Retailing has come to intrigue us. What a fast-moving, tough game! It makes high technology look like child's play. The remarkably successful **Limited Stores** of Columbus, Ohio, will be visited in these pages. Les Wexner is providing his shareholders with a 35 percent return on equity and has become the definer of what can be done in specialty retailing. On the much more traditional end we find **Nordstrom,** a Seattle-based retailer. Their return on sales is at the top of the heap. Their formula? Plain, old-fashioned, exceptional service in its billion-dollar business, a decade after such service had been declared uneconomical by almost all others. Another star in the retailing world is **Mervyn's,** the winner in the all-around superb Dayton-Hudson organization. Mervyn's does in a week the total system remerchandising that its competitors take thirteen weeks to do. And interviews with new Mervyn's store people who have come from other chains almost always result in a variation of the same response: "It's like dying and going to heaven." Attention to service also marks a vast grocery store chain: **Giant Food** of Washington, D.C., which has by far the highest return on shareholders' equity among the publicly listed grocery companies. And talk about people and pride: you find both in **Publix**, a Florida-based retailer that, among other things, introduced across-the-board employee ownership long before it was popular to do so (it still isn't).

The United Kingdom is not thought to be the home of much excellence in management these days. But there are exceptions. Say the name of **Marks & Spencer** around a bunch of retailers in any land and they are silenced. Nobody has a better reputation. It's built upon people, and an under-control bureaucracy: that is, they've figured out how to keep the bureaucracy to a bare minimum. We'll observe a bit of their magic as we go along.

Real estate and banking are on this list as well. In banking, which was intentionally omitted from *In Search of Excellence*, we visit a giant star, **Citibank,** which keeps being rated by *Fortune* every year as the most innovative company in America. We believe it deserves the accolade. We'll examine some of the reasons why in our section on innovation. Banking is in the midst of turmoil because of deregulation. As is typical in all parts of the industrial scene, most of the innovation comes where it's not supposed to. **BancOne,** based in Columbus, Ohio, has been decades ahead of its time.

What is the association between warehouse leasing and love? None—if you don't know Trammell Crow and his colleagues. The **Trammell Crow** real estate organization is exciting, vital, fast-moving, based upon extraordinary service to customers—and, yes, love.

Excellence turns up everywhere. We'll talk about several San Francisco Bay Area companies. Take **Sunset Scavengers.** Employees own the garbage trucks. Yes, Sunset Scavengers is a garbage company—most say the best-run garbage company in America. Boss Len Stephanelli's secret: "I love garbage." And Tom Melohn's **North American Tool and Die** in San Leandro, California; Tom avers passionately that his $7 million company is based on caring. Zest and enthusiasm and really *caring* mark all the companies we've looked at.

Success stories found in certain beaten and battered industries provide magnificent examples of what can be done in the face of adverse economic conditions and other "external factors." Perhaps the most excitement we've had during our wanderings has been the time we spent in Spartanburg, South Carolina. Headquartered there is **Milliken & Company.** The $2 billion textile powerhouse has always been a technology leader. In 1980 they added an amazing quality-improvement program, moving from an authoritarian management structure to quality enhancement through participation in management. Has it ever worked! Tens of millions have been added to the bottom line, and factories have been kept humming as improved quality has led to new and bigger orders. (IBM's recently retired vice president for quality, John Jackson, calls Milliken's quality program the most advanced in the nation.)

Pursuit of excellence in steel led us back to Columbus, Ohio, home of BancOne and The Limited; there we also found **Worthington Industries,** whose return on shareholders' equity over the past five years—27 percent— is at the very top of the heap in steel.

Product "maturity" in main-line consumer businesses is a dominant theme of economists and futurists alike—and, we believe, all too often an excuse for premature pruning. We look at the once stodgy **Campbell Soup** and **PepsiCo.** Both are successfully fighting so-called maturity with programs for entrepreneurial revitalization that can serve as models for the rest of industry.

Nor is our focus always the strategies at the very top. In the beleaguered auto industry, we came across an operation that truly shines: **Phil Staley's Ford assembly plant** in Edison, New Jersey. Plant management in companies such as Westinghouse, Dana and GM are featured throughout.

And then some just plain gems, beyond categorization. **W. L. Gore & Associates** of Newark, Delaware: the quarter-billion-dollar company makes, among other things, the breathing synthetic fabric, Goretex. Bill and Vieve Gore's approach to managing people defies ten-word summations. Try the chapter on "ownership" for an exploration of it. **Herman Miller** is a superb office-furniture supplier based in Zeeland, Michigan. Max DePree's view of people will be prominently featured here; he's the Herman Miller chairman.

Bob Swiggett runs a high-tech company, **Kollmorgen.** High tech was a major focus in *In Search of Excellence* and receives less attention here. Swiggett's management style, however, and the path he followed to discover the values of radical decentralization are exactly appropriate for our message. Among our old friends, we've learned more, much more about the bases of customer service at **IBM** and constant innovation at **Hewlett-Packard** and **3M.** And no tour would be complete without featuring **Apple Computer.** Its products define "state of the art," to be sure; but its free-form organization and unbridled enthusiasm may well be the company's most lasting contribution to the U.S. business scene.

In this book we also venture outside the arena of private business. Our biggest foray took us to the Langley, Virginia, headquarters of the **Tactical Air Command, U.S. Air Force.** General Bill Creech thinks centralization and consolidation are the enemy. He has fought them—rapidly and successfully. We'll also talk about the turnaround in the city of **Baltimore,** whose flamboyant mayor, William Donald Schaefer, is a model of leadership and energy, and we'll take a quick look at the worlds of **education** and **health care.** Our conclusions are tentative and speculative, and not based upon the degree of expertise we wish we had, but we think it's important to test the water—and stick our necks out a little too.

So—this is a new walk. We can't wait to share it with you. Dig in. Sample. Cheer—weep. Pull the sheet over your head and privately examine your deepest biases. And, above all, try something—now, this afternoon!

---

### The 1,000 Percent Factor

Winners—even in mundane, declining, battered or regulated environments—don't do only a percent or two better than the norm. They do hundreds of percent better—at least.

In December 1983 Tom traveled to Burbank, California, to visit with Kelly Johnson of the Lockheed California Company, the man who brought the term "skunk work" to American industry.

Johnson and his determined band are responsible for an astonishing share of what flies in the sky. They developed the first of the military jets right after the end of the World War II, the YP- or F-80 (143 days from concept to first and successful flight); subsequently they turned out the F-104, C-130, U-2, SR-71 and others. That's quite a showing, but the output isn't the real story. What lies behind it is. In one instance Johnson got involved in an ailing satellite program. It was a couple of years behind schedule and way above budget; launch effectiveness ran 12.5 percent. While wandering around after taking charge, Kelly discovered, among other things, 1,271 inspectors working with a single subcontractor. In the course of the next year he trimmed that number to 35. He got the program back on schedule, and simultaneously improved launch effectiveness—to 98 percent. In another instance the Air Force demanded that an arch rival of Lockheed's visit with Johnson and his team. The two were working on projects of about equal magnitude and complexity. The competitor was years behind and hundreds of percent over budget, with 3,750 people involved. Johnson was on schedule and under budget, with 126 people. (A formal Rand Corporation study validated these extraordinary figures.)

Tom was so taken by Kelly Johnson's numbers that he took a little white card, calling-card size, and wrote "3,750/126" on it, and then had it plasticized. He keeps it in his wallet. It's a graphic reminder that no matter what he is up to—designing a product, thinking about marketing it, evaluating an addition to staff—that Johnson epitomizes what's possible. And, most important, what's possible is a function of *good management (read leadership)* alone.

The stories fill shelf after shelf:
• Frank Perdue earns a margin on a pound of chicken several hundred percent above the industry average; his share runs close to 60 percent, on average, in major urban centers: Norfolk, Richmond, Washington, Baltimore, Philadelphia, Boston and New York.
• Stew Leonard's sales per square foot, in his astonishing "Disneyland of dairy stores" are fully ten times the industry average.
• A. Ray Smith's Louisville Redbirds, in 1983, twenty-five years after the all too evident demise of minor league baseball, outdraw a quarter of the major leagues and exceed the all-time minor league attendance record (set in 1946) by over 100 percent.
• Mervyn's "remerchandises" a $1.25 billion operation a *dozen* times faster than its competitors.
• People Express typically opens a new station—e.g. Los Angeles—in ten days, including multiple government approvals, while the industry

giants tend to take twelve to eighteen months to accomplish the same task.

· Du Pont achieves a safety record 6,800 percent (68 times) above American manufacturing industry average.

· Mayor William Donald Schaefer wins reelection in Baltimore against a talented candidate by taking 94 percent of the vote (and every ward).

· The Tactical Air Command's Bill Creech takes a sortie rate (flights flown, a good bottom-line surrogate) that had been declining at a rate of 7.8 percent a year (average) for ten years and cranks it up 11.2 percent a year over the next five years, with no push from the budget or other external forces.

The stories we tell in *A Passion for Excellence* are decidedly *not* stories of organizations with 25 percent growth rates given to them from on high. They are stories of baseball diamonds that are the same shape for all competitors—stories of chicken, dairy products and soft goods, as mundane as they come. No outside factors can explain the extraordinary increments in performance. Superb management—leadership— is the only explanation left.

In the past two decades the most exercised part of the corporate body has been the pointing finger. If in doubt, blame it on OPEC, the Japanese, EPA, OSHA, EEOC, etc. Some didn't. Some looked to the talent they were given and seized the moment. They have outperformed the crowd by a long shot. That's the 1,000 percent factor. It's the challenge for all of us.

# ONE

## Common Sense

# 1

# A Blinding Flash
# of the Obvious

*"What's new?"*
*Nothing in particular.*
*"Then why read it?"*
*Because doing it isn't as easy as it sounds.*
*"Like what?"*
*Wandering around, for instance.*
*"What's so tough about that?"*
*Have you tried it?*
*"I haven't had the time."*
*That's what's so tough about it.*
*"What else is so tough?"*
*Listening to customers.*
*"You are right on that one; it is hard."*
*Glad to see you agree.*
*"Darn right. They just don't understand what we're trying to tell them."*
*Yeah, that's why listening is so hard.*

AND ON IT goes. It's now been four years since *In Search of Excellence* was written, and six since the research for it was begun. All involved have learned a lot, and yet we've learned nothing. We've learned nothing in that (1) there is nothing new under the sun, and (2) it was "all" covered in *In Search of Excellence:* customers, innovation, people.

But here's the issue. The highest praise we have received came from a colleague at the end of the third day of a four-day seminar for small-business presidents in late 1983. All were sitting around, working on a carafe of young white wine, and he blurted out, "You know what these three days amount to, so far? A blinding flash of the obvious." Right on! Nothing new under the sun, nothing new in *In Search of Excellence,* and nothing new since. Giving everyone in the organization the space to innovate, at least a little bit.

Answering the phones and otherwise behaving with common courtesy toward customers. Making things that work. Listening to customers and asking them for their ideas. Then acting on them. Listening to your people and asking them for their ideas. Then acting on them. Wandering around: with customers, your people, suppliers. Paying attention to pride, trust, enthusiasm—and passion and love.

It's common sense, isn't it? But then another good friend says, "I guess the obvious must not be so obvious, or more would practice it." That's right, too: we've often said, only half facetiously, that IBM's only magic is that IBM's people are the lone players in a quarter-trillion-dollar industry who bother to answer the phones consistently. That Disney seems to be the sole player in its big industry that has figured out how to keep a theme park sparkling clean. It turns out that the obvious is not so obvious—and it's a hell of a lot harder to do than we ever imagined!

## The Simple Scheme

Many accused In Search of Excellence of oversimplifying. After hundreds of post-In Search of Excellence seminars we have reached the opposite conclusion: In Search of Excellence didn't simplify enough!

In the private or public sector, in big business or small, we observe that there are only two ways to create and sustain superior performance over the long haul. First, take exceptional care of your customers (for chicken, jet engines, education, health care, or baseball) via superior service and superior quality. Second, constantly innovate. That's it. There are no alternatives in achieving long-term superior performance, or sustaining strategic competitive advantage, as the business strategists call it.

Obviously, the two courses of action do not constitute all that's needed. Sound financial controls are essential. Those without them fail, period. Solid planning is not a luxury but a necessity. Moreover, businesses can be temporarily or permanently set back by external forces, such as an overvalued dollar or the loss of access to natural resources. Nonetheless, these other factors are seldom, if ever, the basis for lasting distinction. That is, financial control is vital, but one does not sell financial control, one sells a quality service or product. The lemonade stand, the lemonade, selling and servicing efforts must precede the accountant who adds up the pile of pennies at the end of the day. One seldom sustains superior performance through mere access to natural resources; one sustains it through innovation in resource exploration techniques and subsequent market development. One is battered by an overvalued dollar, but one sustains performance by adding enough value to the product so that it is profitably salable despite international monetary variability. Likewise, in the school, efficient management of the budget is vital; yet a great school is never characterized by the remark, "It has a good budget." The superb school is superb only by virtue of its success in developing its ultimate customer: the student.

It turns out that neither superior customer service nor constant innovation—the two sustaining edges of excellence—is built upon genius in the executive suite, sleight-of-hand techniques or mystical strategic moves on a game board that allow one to gain a five- or ten-year advantage over one's competitors. Both are built, instead, on a bedrock of listening, trust and respect for the dignity *and* the creative potential of each person in the organization. Thus, customer courtesy means courtesy from the accounting department, from the purchasing department and the engineers, as well as from the sales people. Quality, too, is an all-hands operation. It means quality in all parts of the organization. The winners stun us not by their cleverness, but by the fact that each and every tiny aspect of the business is just a touch better than the norm.

So that is our model: care of customers, constant innovation, turned-on people. Yet one thing is missing, one element that connects all the others. It was a shadow over the pages of *In Search of Excellence*, but was seldom labeled, as many subsequently pointed out. It is leadership. Leadership means vision,

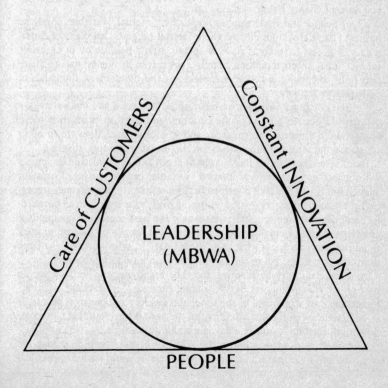

cheerleading, enthusiasm, love, trust, verve, passion, obsession, consistency, the use of symbols, paying attention as illustrated by the content of one's calendar, out-and-out drama (and the management thereof), creating heroes at all levels, coaching, effectively wandering around, and numerous other things. Leadership must be present at *all* levels of the organization. It depends on a million little things done with obsession, consistency and care, but all of those million little things add up to nothing if the trust, vision and basic belief are not there. It seems obvious, doesn't it?

## The Adaptive Organization

A regular criticism of *In Search of Excellence* was that it was focused internally (i.e., on management), and did not take into account changes and discontinuities foisted upon the organization by the outside world. It was a bum rap!

We repeat the "error" in *A Passion for Excellence*. That is, in this book you will find no litany of external forces that can affect the enterprise. Our "defense" is that the management practices we describe are aimed at ensuring that the organization is always externally focused, always sensing change and nascent change before it sneaks up.

True, people and leadership appear to be "internal" variables. And the hastiest glance at Akron, Pittsburgh, or Detroit suggests that many of America's past greats have come upon desperate straits because of an excessive internal focus. Internal politics, complacency driven by bigness and a "Members only" mentality led to severe problems and hundreds of thousands of permanently lost jobs.

Yet the two other variables we focus upon, customers and innovation, are external. Obsessive pursuit of the customer and constant innovation mean adaptation. To pursue the customer and to pursue innovation are to be in constant commerce with the outside world, listening and thus adapting.

But it's even better than that. As our in-depth look at people and leadership will suggest, even these two "internal" variables *can* be sources of constant adaptation. If you are asking for practical innovation from everyone—receptionist as well as designer—you are turning every employee into an outward-focused, adaptive sensor. And guess where the best sources of competitive analysis and assessment often lie: with the men or women on the loading dock or on the line who know what their friend Mary Jo, who works for the bank down the street, just got in the way of a new aid for check processing.

And leadership *can* be adaptive, too. The brand we propose has a simple base of MBWA (Managing By Wandering Around). To "wander," with customers (at least 25 percent of the time) and vendors and our own people, *is* to be in touch with the first vibrations of the new. It turns out that hard-data-driven information is usually a day late and *always* sterile.

The surviving organization is the adaptive organization. The adaptive organization is one that is in touch with the outside world via living data. All four of our variables—two that you would expect (customers and innovation) and two that are novel (people and leadership)—are focused on sensing change and adapting to it, not via great leaps and genius paper plans, but via constant contact with and reaction to people on the part of every person in the organization. Thus, we will begin by exploring our favorite topic—wandering, listening, staying in touch.

Raise the issue of marketing and the discussion soon becomes technical; no living, breathing customers and their whims intrude upon the heated but wholly sterile debate. Shift to innovation and the same thing is true. Hour after hour of chatter about "technology ramps" and changing demographics ensue; nothing so trivial as the way we continuously dampen the spirit of would-be champions through our questioning routines is raised. Talk of people and productivity and, again, often as not, the language is sterile and depersonalized. Labor intransigence is lamented. Trust and simple listening are never mentioned.

The topic of MBWA is at once about common sense, leadership, customers, innovation and people. Simple wandering—listening, empathizing, staying in touch—is an ideal starting point. Under the deceptively simple heading of MBWA lie the concepts that bring our whole scheme into clear relief.

# 2

## MBWA: The Technology of the Obvious

*We were pretty good geologists when we went down there. We found out we weren't nearly as good as we thought we were. . . . From the Brazos River east to the Mississippi . . . We saw bays and estuaries, channels and deltas and bars, lagoons, swamps, growth faults, salt domes. . . . We jumped in the water and felt with our toes the sand of a transgressive overlap.*
> —John Masters, president, Canadian Hunter Exploration, Ltd.

*The greatest problem American business faces is getting the boss back to work watching his customer and his product. Too many bosses are involved with long-range planning meetings. They are too busy playing golf, often to the point that they no longer know what the customer is saying, how he is being treated. They are not on the production floor enough to know how the product is being manufactured or how the buyers are stocking the stores. As a result, we have set ourselves up for a terrific pratfall.*
> —Stanley Marcus, former chairman, Neiman-Marcus
> (as reported in the Knoxville News-Sentinel, May 27, 1984)

*Get into the community and find out what their problems are. That's the best politics.*
> —The late Senator George Aiken of Vermont, in 1974,
> on his success at the ballot box

IN OUR WORK with groups of all sorts we have commented time and again that we can make a strong case, which boils down to this: the number one managerial productivity problem in America is, quite simply, managers who are out of touch with their people and out of touch with their customers. And the alternative, "being in touch," doesn't come via computer printouts or the endless stream of overhead transparencies viewed in ten thousand darkened meeting rooms stretching across the continent. Being in touch means tangible, visceral ways of being informed. It means a remarkably successful thirty-year veteran geologist/entrepreneur sinking his toes in the sand of a transgressive overlap, instead of totally depending on a computer's interpretation of sophisticated geophysical tools.

In *In Search of Excellence,* Managing By Wandering Around rated a subtitle in "A Bias for Action," the first of eight chapters on the attributes of excellent companies. We know it as the technology of the obvious, the method by which leadership becomes effective in any well-run school, hospital, bank, single-store operation or industrial enterprise.

## MBWA: With Customers

To listen is just that: to listen. Apple's Lisa computer (not a great commercial success, but the machine that spawned the wildly successful Macintosh) was noted for a breakthrough in the "user friendliness" of its operating system software (marked by the "mouse" and a revolutionary reduction in customer learning time). The developer of much of this software was John Couch, a prototypical engineer, with a Ph.D. in computer science from Berkeley, among other degrees. We asked John once about the genesis of his thinking. He was quick to reply: "I bought my dad a computer outlet. I worked in it, for the full two years of the project, at least one and often two days a weekend, doing a full shift on the floor, incognito. I learned about the fears and frustrations of the average first-time user and the more sophisticated one firsthand. I believe it was the single most significant source of what we came up with." Being in touch means just that—being in touch. Somehow. It usually has little to do with statistical surveys—Couch's experience didn't, certainly. But it *is* valid. Currently Apple prides itself on having gotten its entire executive staff (the senior officers) to volunteer for a regular stint of listening in on the toll-free 800 customer call-in number. Whenever an executive participates, she or he gets a commemorative Listening Certificate—with a gold star attached if the executive has the guts to actually *answer* one or more phone calls.

---

### *"Daily Dose of Reality"*

Three mornings a week, all executives of Castle find a 5″ × 7″ yellow sheet of paper on their desks. The title: "Daily Dose of Reality." Below is the name and phone number of a customer who bought a new piece of equipment from them (they make hospital sterilizers, surgical equipment) about six weeks before. (Better yet—the phone number is for the person who actually uses the equipment.) The routine is stated in full in an internal memo: "We will simply be asking our customers if they are satisfied with our product."

The objective is threefold: "to let our customers know they are important to us," "uncover problems before they become major irritants," and "give management a daily reminder of where the real world is—with our field reps and our customers."

"Naïve" customer listening. Raw impressions. They are not substitutes for computer printouts—but there are no substitutes for them either. Consider this analysis (in 1983) of the source of many of GM's problems by a Sloan student at Stanford from General Motors:*

> They [executives] drive down the highway outside Detroit. All the car company employees and suppliers are virtually required to buy American cars. He looks to his left, looks to his right. "Everybody's still driving American cars" registers at some level. Then he pulls into the company garage. His car is gone over from stem to stern for the next ten hours. When he leaves work he gets in, it starts like a charm: "And the damn things do work." All the tons of market research data that we have don't make up for the lack of *feel*. If even one of the companies or even one car-producing division had moved to California, they would have learned the bitter truth: Californians just don't like American cars anymore. These odd names—Honda, Toyota, Nissan—are all over the highways out here. Even I, and I consider myself pretty darned enlightened, didn't really "feel it" in the most important sense until I moved out to Palo Alto. I started subconsciously counting Japanese cars at intersections. I was incredulous. I'd tell my colleagues about it, back home. They didn't fathom what I was saying, as I hadn't before I came out here and lived it for myself.

If customer listening is the watchword, it should also be opportunistic. The president of Levi Strauss USA had a call, purely social, from a retailer who happened to be in San Francisco (the company's headquarters city). The man sat down and started to pour out his heart about some of the difficulties he had dealing with Levi Strauss (this was during the late 1970's, when the jeans craze led the company to fall behind in satisfying the demand for their product). To the Levi executive's credit, he cut the retailer off early in the discussion, invited him—begged him—to stick around for three or four hours, called in the video cameras and all of the marketing people who were in the headquarters building at the time. Everyone trooped over to the nearest auditorium, and while the audience sat in rapt attention and the video tape spun, this fellow unloaded and answered questions for a full four hours. A host of copies of the tapes was made, and sent throughout the system.

Now, Apple and Levi Strauss are among the most systematic collectors of market data. Yet none of these examples is very systematic. But, again, each is valid. Here's another, again from a senior executive at Levi Strauss: "We've begun to correct some serious problems, particularly in the service-to-retail-

---

*Stanford's and MIT's business schools run year-long programs (e.g., the Stanford Sloan Program) for about forty superfast-trackers, principally from big corporations and federal agencies. The programs were started with seed money from the Alfred P. Sloan Foundation; the student's company nominates and supports the student.

ers area, over the last couple of years [1983–84]. At the heart of it for me was a commitment I made, following an almost accidental first experience, to spend one Saturday a month on the sales floor of one of our major chain customers, one of my 'executive accounts.' I asked them if they would let me sell blue jeans one weekend. They were delighted. It was quite an eye-opener for me—to sell our own, to watch people decide to buy other people's jeans. We haven't burned the market research data, but I'll tell you it's a different view."

Campbell Soup Chairman Gordon McGovern hasn't burned the computer printouts either, to be sure. But he is going to even greater extremes than Levi Strauss to get in touch. It's a keystone to his effort to innovate based upon listening. *Business Week* (December 24, 1984) reports:

> McGovern recently convened his directors in the back room of a super-market for a board meeting, after which they roamed the store aisles probing shoppers for comments about Campbell's products. He regularly dispatches company executives to the kitchens of some 300 women across the country, to see how meals are prepared. And he insists that his managers do their own grocery shopping.
>
> McGovern himself can be found every Saturday in his neighborhood supermarket, stocking the family larder. "Gordon's made it his business to be out in the marketplace, getting to know his customers, whoever they may be," says Allen Bildner, president of Kings Super Markets Inc. in West Caldwell, N.J. With the entire food industry scrambling to meet America's changing tastes, McGovern's determination is the key to his dream of transforming Campbell into the nation's most market-sensitive food company—almost an about-face for the once-cautious food processor.

---

*Wandering with "Customers": Urban Government*

Mayor William Donald Schaefer of Baltimore has wandered with his constituents for years. Maintaining a feel for his city has long been at the top of his list of priorities. Richard Ben Cramer reported in *Esquire* (October 1984):

"I'm not pleased with this," he'd scolded them [members of the cabinet] many times. "That is NOT ... GOOD ... ENOUGH."

PEOPLE, he'd write on his easel. He picked the easel thing up a few years ago, thought it might get the message across. For greater weight, he'd write: PEE-PULL. Or: WHAT IF YOU LIVED THERE? He wanted the cabinet to have a feel for the citizens they governed.

Sometimes he'd decide the problem was they just couldn't goddam see. He'd be riding around like he does on weekends, with his driver and a cop riding shotgun, and he'd see the potholes, and

broken streetlights, caved-in trash cans, dirty parks, housing vio-
lations, abandoned cars, crooked traffic signs, dead trees, a missing
bus stop, trash at the curb. "What are the bastards doing with the
money?" he'd mutter aloud in the Buick. Then he'd get out his pen
and his Mayor's Action Memos and tear into the thing:

Get the g-----m trash off East Lombard Street. . . .
Broken pavement at 1700 Carey for TWO MONTHS. . . .
Abandoned car at 2900 Remington. Why?

Then the memos would be on their desks Monday morning, and
the trash, the pothole, the abandoned car had better be gone when
he drove by again. How'd it get there in the first place?

One time he popped them an Action memo: "There is an abandoned car . . . but I'm not telling you where it is." City crews ran
around like hungry gerbils for a week. Must have towed five
hundred cars.

That was NOT . . . GOOD . . . ENOUGH: Schaefer called in
his cabinet, the best municipal government in America. The
mayor held two fingers up, and he poked them at his own glittery
eyes.

"Do you know what these are? Do you? These are eyes." The
mayor was jabbing at his face now. They thought he might hurt
himself.

"I GOT TWO. AND YOU GOT TWO." Then he grabbed a
cabinet member and started menacing him with the fingers in the
eyes. The cabinet guy's head was burrowing between his
shoulders.

"So how come my eyes can see and a smart young fella like you
can't see a damn thing, huh? HOW COME?"

But today it's worse. He won't look at them. He is staring down
at the table. His head, in his hands, rocks back and forth in sorrow.
At his shoulder is the easel with the single word he'd written:
ERR-JEN-C.

## Bugging Customers?

Let's pick up on the phrase "They [customers] were delighted [that the Levi's
executive wanted to visit]." Often a rebuttal to our persistent suggestions for
customer MBWA is that "customers don't want to be bothered," "customers
don't want some damn vice president calling once a week to say 'How are
you'" (we actually got this comment from the vice president of a phone company in one session). But our experience on such MBWA's is crystal clear:
customers are, simply, always delighted by the attention.

Joe Baute, the president of Markem (a Keene, New Hampshire, maker of
packaging and labeling products), described a new and highly effective twist

to the company's annual top-management retreat in 1984: "The focus of the meeting was customers' concerns. We needed data, and decided to do something novel: Each attendee, at some point in the two weeks preceding the meeting, was to spend one full day with a customer, checking out his [the customer's] perception of us. Half our people thought it would be a waste. Several were certain the customers would feel imposed upon. To the contrary, without exception the customers loved it! And this even though we avoided the 'happy customer' problem—visiting only those most likely to tell us we were doing fine—by dividing the pile of candidates into good customers, bad customers and average customers. The debate at the meeting was informed by live impressions, for the first time in memory. Just about all agreed that it was the best meeting we've had. And follow-up has been terrific—and concrete."

An executive of AMP, the remarkably profitable ($1.5 billion in revenues) Harrisburg, Pennsylvania, makers of electrical connectors, tells a similar story. He brought in a dozen tough customers (and three or four AMP people: "We wanted 'them' to far outnumber 'us,' because the purpose was for us to be outnumbered, not for us to tell them why things were this way or that") for an intense weekend discussion. Again, several of his colleagues had argued that the customers wouldn't want to waste time on such an activity; and again, his experience was the converse: "To a man, they were flattered at the attention, and delighted to spend the time. You can't believe how much we learned."

After speaking to a bunch of hospital administrators, Tom had an interview with a new, local Cable TV group, this one specializing in communications with hospitals. As he walked toward the makeshift studio that had been set up in the auditorium, a fellow from the TV company grabbed him and started pumping his hand. It turned out that he was the marketing guy. His story: "I loved your book [In Search of Excellence]. The chapter on the customer in particular. As soon as I read it, I went out and started to call our customers, asking the major ones how they liked our programming. They told me! Boy, did I get an earful."

## "Naïve Listening"

"Naïve listening" is a term we ran across when talking with the chairman of Allergan, a highly profitable Irvine, California, subsidiary of SmithKline Beckman. About $100 million of the company's $200 million in revenues comes from a product family of ointments and the like aimed at helping contact-lens users. Chairman Gavin Herbert described the breakthrough that led to development of the product: "I've repeatedly argued that reading the data and talking to the ophthalmologists is not enough. In the pharmaceutical industry we're overwhelmed by data. All the prescription information comes in by the bushel, rapidly and neatly summarized. We have more than you need. But we miss the basic customer. I've always insisted that our people

stay in touch with the users, the patients. In the process of talking with contact-lens wearers, we kept coming across, in one form or another, the same
problem: 'itchy-scratchy eyes.' Now you know and I know that no ophthal-
mologist, after twenty years of professional training, is going to write down
as his diagnosis 'itchy-scratchy eyes.' It's just not professional language. Yet
it *was* the problem. We started working on coming up with something to
deal with itchy-scratchy eyes. That, plain and simple, was the genesis of this
immensely successful product line." (We find it interesting that the company
was founded by the current chairman's father, a practicing pharmacist. The
family, in fact, lived right over the pharmacy, and the current chairman put
in his time behind the counter too. Time and again we discover that the
hands-on companies are led by people who got their start in hands-on jobs.)

---

### "Black Box" versus South Bronx

The *Wall Street Journal* (December 12, 1984) reports:
  Westinghouse recently sent 30 hourly workers who produced sub-
  way generating equipment to New York to appraise their workmanship on the city's transit system, and underscore the need for
  reliability. "There's a difference between putting wires into a black
  box and riding the product through the South Bronx," contends
  Jack Geikler, general manager of Westinghouse's transportation
  business unit near Pittsburgh. Westinghouse workers say they see
  a big change in management's attitudes. "When I joined in 1968,
  just the notion that you went to see what you made was enough to
  send shivers up management's spine," recalls Harry Stauffer, a
  draftsman. Still, attempts to instill more pride-in-product at the
  workshop level won't necessarily land a contract. Westinghouse
  just lost a major streetcar contract in its hometown of Pittsburgh
  to a West German consortium. Nonetheless, asserts Westinghouse's Mr. Geikler, every little bit counts. "We see it as a survival
  issue. If we don't do these things, we're not going to make it."

---

Milliken and Company, the textile people, have taken the "naïve" idea and
are turning it into a strategic passion. Naïve listening is the source of literally
scores of programs. They include getting first-line people from Milliken factories in touch with first-line people in customers' factories. It turns out that,
first, "hourly to hourly" is a fine way to sell. (As a friend at Northrop says,
"Manufacturers are a helluva lot more credible to other manufacturers than
the sales people.") Second, both have clearer notions of the practical problems involved in the use of the product. Milliken is also opening a "customer
listening college." (Apple, to get its message through, is spending a huge sum
developing a "retailer's college," to teach the Apple way and Apple advantages to the retailing channel.)

Other parts of the Milliken strategy include an internship in manufacturing for all salespeople; a "stand-in-the-customer's-shoes" training program; a program to bring the customer to life (via videotapes of customers using Milliken products, etc.) for the service people—those in the PBX room answering the phones or on the loading dock;* sales training for all senior management (going through a not too shortened form of the normal sales-training program); training all Milliken people to understand customer manufacturing operations (in which so many of Milliken's products are used); inviting customers to come to the Milliken premises and present a history of their company's culture to Milliken people (including hourly people, so that all hands can get a "feel" for major customers); developing joint problem-solving teams with customers that include a heavy representation of hourly people from both Milliken and the customer's operations; having customers visit the specific factory at which their product will be made (and parading them through the factory so that factory people can see live customers);† showing visiting customers a film of the history of the Milliken Company (to give them a feel for what Milliken is all about in a tangible way). Milliken is also introducing extensive and detailed customer surveys through which customers will focus in particular on their perception of the way in which Milliken is responsive to them, and in which everything from phone courtesy through billing is included.

Of course, the heart of the matter is mind-set. Chairman Roger Milliken spends 80 percent of his time on the issue. That's right: eighty! An important customer on a visit finds him, once again, lecturing at the Milliken Customer Service Center in Spartanburg, South Carolina. "Who's minding the store while you and Tom [Milliken President Malone] are doing this?" the customer asks, somewhat incredulous. Roger doesn't answer directly. Instead he

---

*This is an extension of the whole MBWA idea. MBWA has become, for us, short-hand for "bringing business—customers, suppliers, etc.—to life," somehow, for all hands. A Texas bank is following the Milliken lead. Here are both the logic and the technique: a bank doesn't "lend money"; rather, it lends money so that others can productively employ it—e.g., build factories, restaurants. The bank's innovative program involved bringing the customer to life for the operations people (check processors, management information systems people, et al.) by shooting live footage of new construction financed by the bank, and then showing that footage (often beefed up by a brief interview with the customer) to all those distant from day-to-day contact with customers. The program, an officer reports, has been "a roaring success."
†Customer visits to plants is one of the debated issues. Some staunchly argue that it's "not right"—i.e., "they" will steal "our" secrets. We think they're more likely worried about a potential embarrassment: "They'll see our dirty plants!" None we know who are wholeheartedly committed to customers visiting plants have found any cause for alarm. All view it as an unadulterated plus. A Campbell Soup executive, who had spent his career in sales, was transferred to Pepperidge Farm manufacturing years ago. He said, "We were experiencing some quality problems. My first step was to invite our distributors [customers] into the plants. First, I wanted them to be joint problem solvers with us. Second, I wanted our plant people to understand that there were real customers out there. Some of them literally threw rolls at us. It worked, and fast."

says simply, "But what could be more important for me than to spend time with customers?" Roger Milliken is practicing customer MBWA with a vengeance. As he does, so does the company. (See chapter 16 for more on the importance of symbols.) As one Milliken manager, heavily involved in the new process, puts it: "A customer's problem is almost always solvable. It's up to us to see it as an opportunity. Put simply, the vendor who solves it gets the season's business." (He adds, to the naïve point: "We must constantly guard against the pitfall of being too knowledgeable.")

---

### Really Naïve Listening

In February 1984 Tom spent four days with Milliken's 450 principal officers at their annual top-management retreat. The sole subject was getting closer to the customer—with Tom's connivance, not just listening, but "naïve listening." About a month after the meeting was over, he received a letter from the marketing director (let's get it straight—*marketing* director, not a born-again accountant or lawyer) of the division that manufactures carpets for institutions such as schools and hospitals. In it he described how he is repositioning his product line, focusing on new features, adding some new products. The reason: right after the February meeting and making his commitment to "naïve listening," he had gone out and worked two weeks, on the swing shift, in a customer's hospital. As he said, "Getting close to the customer is a *winner!!* [his emphasis]. I just got back from my second week working in a major hospital as part of the housekeeping staff. What an experience ... to actually maintain your products (and competitive products) in the environment where they are used. Plus, it gave me an opportunity to do a lot of naïve listening while at this hospital. I worked the second shift (3:00 P.M. until midnight) and actually cleaned carpeting as well as hard-surface floors. I operated all the machinery they used daily, plus handled the same housekeeping problems that our customers face daily. I cleaned every stain from blood to urine, plus a few that I cannot even spell. To be honest, I was stiff and sore and worn out at the end of the two weeks, *but* I plan to do it again at least every six months. What did I learn? [At this point he goes on for about half a page talking about the features that really had come through in the "naïve" setting in which he had placed himself.] Now I can put together my trade advertising as well as my entire merchandising program based directly upon the needs of my customers as I observed them. No more SWAG (Scientific Wild Ass Guess) on what the market needs. I'm learning—from new-product introduction to maintenance of existing products—exactly what our health care customers require. We can now design products and programs that have a differential advantage for our customers plus get a fair profit for Milliken. ... I guess if we will just follow the Golden

Rule—'Do unto others as you would have them do unto you'—we will become more efficient in our dealings with all people, including our customers!! I know I'm on the road to answering 'Where's the beef?' for the health care market."

What a great story! There's only one nagging problem: How come stories such as this don't describe what *everyone* does naturally? Shouldn't it be like falling off a log, especially for the marketing guy, to go out and spend two weeks at a major customer site, working the swing shift?

## A Few (More) Ways to Keep in Touch

Oxford Software is a fine company, profitable, growing fast, with a solid outpouring of new products. At a celebration—a three-day meeting for all hands—of a recent success a secondary objective was to keep people from getting complacent. The chairman began the meeting with a speech. It included just one overhead transparency: a reproduction of a letter from a disgruntled (good, big) customer, telling the chairman that he thought Oxford had slipped of late, was resting on its laurels. Just one letter. Yet it had a truly galvanizing effect. When you eyeball it, see that the guy took the time to write, it's somehow different—very different. The picture is worth not just a thousand words, but more like a million.

Likewise, at People Express there's a highly visible bulletin board in each facility, located where almost everyone must pass by. Good-news customer letters are flaunted on the left side; the right side displays bad-news letters. Of course, the company systematically collects data on customer satisfaction—any sensible organization must. But the visible display of the real, unabridged words of the customer, on his or her letterhead, is compelling far beyond the numbers. It is life in a way that dry statistics can never be.

### Test Flying

GE's aircraft engine pioneer, Gerhard Neumann, is a longtime practitioner of customer MBWA. Here is his description from his book *Herman the German* (Morrow, 1984) of the unique approach he took, while a member of General Claire Chennault's World War II Flying Tigers, to improve the reliability of engine repairs:

I asked my squadron mechanics to "volunteer," if this was suggested by me, to test-fly in the single-seat fighter plane whose repair they had just completed. The pilot would sit on the crew chief's lap; neither would be able to sit on a parachute because the cockpit's canopy was not big enough. I had done this myself several times with my tall squadron commander, Major Robert Costello, sitting on my lap, to identify engine problems which showed up only at altitudes of 20,000 feet or higher. The pilots were enthusiastic about my plan. Consequent improvement in quality of workmanship was dramatic. Way past dinnertime, the airfield looked as if it were invaded by glowworms: the twinkling came from flashlights mechanics used to check—once more—the tightness of pipes or connections they had made, in case I might suggest that they "volunteer" to ride in their planes the next day.

Magazine publisher James E. Buerger reports the following in *Travelhost* (September 11, 1983):

Recently I had occasion to visit the national headquarters at Frito-Lay. They produce, among other things, Lays Potato Chips. In their national headquarters they have a large bowl of potato chips, and every one of those chips is perfect. They are literally hand-picked. They are not broken, burned or chipped. They are the finest potato chips that Frito-Lay manufactures. I found this very interesting, to find such perfect potato chips. They brought a point home to me: *that was their business.* [Emphasis ours.] They had brought together the very best that they could do. And because they did, people visiting their national headquarters would have an opportunity to sample the very best of their production. With that in mind, we started doing the same thing. I asked to have the finest magazines that we produce sent to our office each week. And the instructions were that these magazines were our potato chips. I didn't want the burnt ones, or the chipped ones, or the broken ones. I only wanted the ones that were the finest. At first, I was a little shocked. What I was shocked about was that the finest potato chips, the finest magazines, that we were producing were a little burnt and a little chipped. They didn't compare at all to the fine hand-selected potato chips that I had seen at the national headquarters at Frito-Lay.

Amen. Touch. Feel. Taste.

---

### MBWA with Customers:
### Some Questions—and Things to Do Now

• Do you regularly call your own company and competitors with a simple request (e.g., on product information)? What are differences in response, in detail—days to answer, completeness of answer, courtesy, etc.? Have five people do this with different requests and compare notes. (Less systematically, just make a habit of calling in to your company once every couple of weeks to judge responsiveness. A variation on this theme is to dummy up some stationery and, by letter, make a simple request of your company and competitors.)

• Do you have an 800 toll-free call-in number (even if you are a small company)? If not, why not?

• Must do: Call a minimum of *three* customers per week from a list of fifty or so good, bad and indifferent customers. And get a list of major sales made and lost in the last three weeks. Call one recently gained and one recently lost customer. Ask why it happened. (Have five to ten colleagues—preferably from different functions—repeat this exercise some week, and use the results as the basis for a half-day meeting.)

• Former Marks & Spencer Chairman Marcus Sieff had a simple ritual, reported by Walter Goldsmith and David Clutterbuck in *The Winning Streak* (Weidenfeld and Nicolson, Random House and the Tom Peters Group, 1985). Every Saturday at about 5:00 P.M., for years on end, he would call the heads of four or five stores, chosen randomly, and ask how the day had gone. Likewise, each week, call *three* of your operations that deal directly with customers (sales branches, service offices, retail stores) and ask how the day's business has gone.

• Do you bring customers to life (via video, visits, etc.) for the off-line departments—MIS, accounting, personnel? Do you have members of the off-line functions make occasional (but regular) customer visits, work on the retail floor, etc.?

• Do you conduct occasional intensive customer debriefings (à la Markem, AMP, Milliken) where customers are "called in" (invited in) for multiday "How are *we* doing for *you?*" sessions?

• Do you have set routines and visit patterns which are aimed at the "naïve" part of listening? (E.g., let the customer speak first at debriefings, à la Milliken; visit ultimate users rather than intermediaries, à la Allergan?)

• Do senior managers (and all managers) work in selected customer operations (in a regular job) on a quarterly basis? Do "technical experts" (R&D people, brand managers, designers) regularly visit *and* work in selected customer operations?

• Are customers regularly invited to visit virtually all facilities? Are people from all customer functions (e.g., manufacturers) invited to visit? Are there regular routines for debriefing (i.e., listening to) customers on these visits?

• Do visitations—ours to customers, customers' to us—go all the way down to the hourly level? And are they regular?

---

## Supplier as "Customer"

It seems that one of the half-dozen traits that we hear exemplify Japanese management (in contrast to management in the United States) is the long-term, almost familial relations between suppliers and producers. But there's no Japanese magic about it: it can happen in the United States—and does in many of the best companies. Again, our friends at Milliken are leading the way, doing virtually all the things we mentioned in connection with customers with their vendors as well, including swapping visits among hourly people from vendor organizations and Milliken organizations, and bringing vendor people into the Milliken operations to learn about things that the Milliken quality-improvement teams are doing.*

Milliken isn't alone. When Tom was in Sweden in 1982, he attended a meeting that included a presentation by Marcus Sieff of Marks & Spencer. Sieff commented on the exceptional family relationships that the company maintains with its suppliers. Tom expected the usual litany about a battalion of quality-control people, a tough legal-contracts section and the like. Instead Lord Sieff said, almost as an aside, "Well, of course, I and each of my [top 25 or so] executives make it a hard-and-fast point to visit a minimum of forty suppliers a year." Wow! So it isn't so mysterious after all. (Or is it? That's a lot of time and determination.)

There's a tough side to the M&S equation as well. They simply demand that their suppliers live up to their high standards. Walter Goldsmith and David Clutterbuck again, in *The Winning Streak:*

> M&S maintains a team of inspectors who visit suppliers' premises, ensuring that quality levels are maintained and making suggestions for improvements. It calculates that a one per cent reduction is faulty merchandise more than pays for all the support services it provides suppliers, including substantial help in areas of employee welfare. M&S reasons that good working conditions are a prerequisite for high-quality production. It lays particular stress on canteens, morale and hygiene, and provides free courses for suppliers on a whole range of employee welfare issues. A regular newsletter keeps suppliers up to date on developments that might improve quality directly or through employee motivation.
>
> "All our long-term suppliers are very profitable," claims Sieff, suggesting that that is a result of adopting M&S-sytle management.
>
> Suppliers who do not fall in line, fall out. A large meat supplier, for example, had very poor working conditions for its employees. "Our business with them was increasing considerably. But they had appalling canteens and lavatories and some of the walls were running with damp. I said I would give them three months to put it right. When I came back there was no improvement. They said, 'You'll never stop doing business with us.' One month later we gave them two weeks' notice."

*And again, the most common rejoinder we get on this point is "You're giving away your secrets to a potential competitor." Nonsense. The competitor—potential or otherwise—usually knows what you're up to. Besides, this kind of logic assumes that various segments of the channel are mortal enemies—and *that* assumption has gotten a good many of us into a mess. Both the vendors and the Milliken people benefit immensely from this exchange process, and the risks are minimal.

Only a couple of weeks after we met Marcus Sieff we visited Northrop, where we were doing some consulting, and where our friend Marv Elkin runs the purchasing organization. He's done a remarkable job of changing vendor-producer relationships for the better in the course of the past two or three years. We sat down to chat with him about it a bit, and mentioned Lord Sieff's comment about visits. Now, Marv's an animated fellow, and he leaped up halfway through our description: "That's it! That's it!" Yes, it was. It turned out to be *exactly* what Marv had been doing. He stated that over the past two years, in a program that departed remarkably from the company's previous adversarial relationship with vendors, he had visited over 150 suppliers. Equally important, his visits weren't thinly disguised opportunities to take whacks at the suppliers. They were open-ended, with no set agenda. He asked them to make a presentation on their company's history, their strategy, their work force, their quality programs: "It was just a chance to get acquainted, to learn about them, to show interest (which I desperately had) in them as a whole." It's a program that he's kept up, and gotten others of his own people thoroughly involved in as well. It's been a long first step toward reversing decades of adversarial and negative relationships, where the only senior contact came in the heat of battle and in response to pressing problems. And it came none too soon, because the quality programs that Northrop is having shoved down its throat by the Air Force are now requiring Marv to turn up the heat on his vendors. The groundwork, however, has been clearly—and expensively (in terms of time)—laid by his visits. Now all of them are in a position to work together.

Domino's Pizza Distribution Company (Domino's ingredients and equipment supplier) just says "Thanks." They regularly stage Vendor Appreciation Days. A horde of Domino's people will descend on a Wisconsin cheese maker or a California olive grower and shower the supplier with time and attention. Distribution executive Jeff Smith can't imagine it any other way. "They're part of the family, aren't they," he says, with surprise that anyone could conceive of a different position on the issue. (Interestingly, family relations with vendors are an explicit part of Domino's Distribution statement of its mission. Now, that is rare. But why not?)

That's really about the extent of the supplier-MBWA magic. Wandering around. Keeping in touch. Replacing theoretically adversarial relationships with garden-variety humanness, doing so at all levels of both organizations. And taking time to say thanks in more than a perfunctory fashion.

---

## MBWA with Suppliers:
### Some Questions—and Things to Do Now

• Do people with functions other than purchasing (e.g., manufacturing, marketing) regularly visit vendors? Do vendors regularly visit *all* your facilities—factories or operations areas, etc.? Does your chief purchasing officer spend

25 to 35 percent or more of his or her time with vendors at *their* locations dealing with other than brushfire problems?

• Pick three good (and long) and three rocky vendor relationships. Study them. Have an executive team select one good and one bad per person and visit with each for one to one and a half days. Ask the vendors how *you* are doing as people to sell to. Return and spend a full day analyzing the data. What do they perceive it's like to do business with you? What are the *ten* things that irritate them most about your practices? Can you fix three of the ten in the next sixty days?

• To what extent are vendors "part of the family"? Are they (small and large) regularly invited to strategy sessions, company celebrations (formal and informal)? If so, *who* is invited—just the person who sells to you, or members of the vendor's factory, Quality Control department (after all, your success depends on the vendor's QC people)? Is there any air of "can't share this with them because it's too confidential"? Do company newsletters, bulletins (annual reports, even) tell stories about vendors, vendor facilities, company-vendor joint-problem-solving successes?

• To what extent are you part of the vendor's "family"? Do your hourly or first-line shop supervisors attend vendor functions? Ever? Regularly? If not, have you ever asked for an invitation for your down-the-line people?

• Do you and vendors have numerous, ongoing joint-problem-solving teams that involve hourly people from both sides? If not, why not?

• More generally, check around with people in various functions, at various levels. Develop a five-minute questioning routine about vendor relations both in general and in specific terms. What does your little, nonsystematic survey suggest about the role of suppliers in your company? Are they seen as cherished, full-fledged members? Or as necessary nuisances?

---

## MBWA: Innovation

PepsiCo was a sleepy company a dozen years ago. Now it's aggressive. But while it spends extravagantly to get Michael Jackson on the tube as an advertiser for Pepsi-Cola in the ceaseless battle against Coke, it places its real bets on development of the likes of La Petite Boulangerie, a bakery chain with six stores in the San Francisco area that is expected to run to three thousand stores, nationwide, just five years from now. Growing new or small businesses is the PepsiCo technique. Its subsidiary Frito-Lay was a fine company with a large share. Yet in the mid-seventies it really began to take off. Changes in the size of the bag, a huge variety of new flavors—in short, innovation—marked the new Frito-Lay.

What's the magic of the PepsiCo transformation? Much of it stems from a form of MBWA, we'd contend. In particular, the unique form practiced by

PepsiCo's former chief operating officer, Andy Pearson. He was on the road a lot—probably 40 percent of his time. Much of that time was spent visiting subsidiaries. When he did so, the routine was standard. He ignored the executive suite at first, and headed for the office of the most recently hired members of the brand management staff. "What's up? What've you got going in the test market? How're they reacting to the new umpty-ump flavor?" And so on. Implicit (pretty explicit, come to think of it) was the message that *something* had better be going on. Under his and Chairman Don Kendall's stewardship the company took off like a jackrabbit. (They did the job so well that in 1981 Coca-Cola promoted the dynamic Roberto Goizuetta to chairman just to keep pace.)

To innovate is to pay attention to innovation. At Hewlett-Packard, each engineer leaves the project he or she is working with out on "the bench." Other engineers—including "retired" Bill Hewlett, who according to the old pros was always around and about—take a look at it, play with it, comment on it. More significant, even, is the tone set. Everybody leaves a device out. Everybody gets into the act and plays with everybody else's toys. (And you had darn well better be working on a toy, one that's fun enough and new enough to interest your ceaselessly wandering—and vociferously judgmental—peers.)

## MBWA: Problem Solving,
a Subset of Innovation

The Rockwell International engineer had a dubious distinction. He had been in charge of a large share of the space shuttle's misbehaving tiles (the ones that popped off during the stress of reentry in the troubled early days of the shuttles). After a discussion about MBWA a couple of years back, he came up to us and said, "I never had a label for it before. But that's it." The story he related was of the obvious—yet not so obvious—variety. It went this way: "Every Monday, it seemed, it would be the same. Another problem had arisen over the weekend. Another foul-up. And then the invariant ritual would begin. Twenty-four hours would pass. I'd arrive the next morning. Like clockwork, a fifty-page report would be lying prominently on my desk, from one of the engineering groups. The thrust of it was always the same: 'It ain't our fault. Two other engineering groups screwed up.' And then another twenty-four hours would pass. The next day's desk fare was also predictable: two more reports, this time numbering a hundred pages each, from the two offended groups [from the previous day] rebutting the accusations and blaming others, including (especially) the first group. We just didn't seem to get anywhere. Finally I had an idea. I started one Friday afternoon. I brought all the top people involved in the program to a cramped, sweaty conference room near my place. These people were from all over. It didn't matter where. After that, every week, on Friday afternoon, we'd sit there and thrash around, from early afternoon until the wee small hours if necessary. We'd go over every problem. We'd figure out what the heck it was each of us was going to do in the next seventy-two to ninety-six hours. We'd review where we'd been in the last ninety-six. It was just as simple as that. You know, it's a fact of human nature: you can bullshit people to a fare-thee-well with a two-hundred-page report, and you can pull the wool over their eyes pretty well with a twenty-five-page one. But it's damn hard, on a Friday afternoon, to do either when you're far away from home and the cigarette smoke has reached the 'can't-quite-breathe' level. It's real hard to sign up for an objective and then come back to that smoke-filled room like clockwork next Friday and report that you couldn't make it to the guy sitting four feet away across the table to whom you made the promise. Truth and honesty win out in such a setting with remarkable regularity. And that was our routine. Every Friday afternoon. And the things that began to occur! In a period of about ten weeks we made more progress than we had in the prior eighteen months."

Now, that's problem solving! No matrix reporting relations. No 16,000-bubble PERT charts. Smoke-filled room MBWA, instead. We'll see more of it when we talk later about Gerhard Neumann's skunkwork at GE.

---

### MBWA: Innovation
### Some Questions and Things to Do *Now*

• Given that concrete experiments are essential to innovation, how—specifically—does your *daily* routine reflect your desire to constantly test and try new things? Are you constantly, like Pearson or the HP people, out on the floor (of the lab, design rooms, MIS coders' space) asking "What's gone on in the last twenty-four (or forty-eight) hours?" (GE's Gerhard Neumann and Lockheed's Kelly Johnson never let more than twenty-four hours pass without thorough "What have you tried that's interesting?" probes of *all* hands.)

• Select two projects that are badly delayed, two that are on or ahead of schedule. (Alternatively, select two or three project managers who always seem to bring a job in on time, two or three who don't.) Analyze the information swapping and getting-the-people-together-for-problem-solving routines. Are there any parallels to the Rockwell story? If so, dig a layer deeper: look for fifteen to twenty-five ancillary "trivial" factors that enhance the problem-solving setting (e.g., physical setting, time of day, duration of meetings, record keeping re promises made). How commonplace is the use of the devices you unearthed? If rare, can you induce more widespread use—e.g., by writing up or otherwise communicating these "problem-solving success stories"?

---

### MBWA with Customers (yes, again):
### Innovation Source par Excellence

Go back to pages 13–17, where we introduced the concept of naïve listening. The term originated with the chairman of Allergan, in connection with the development of a new product—in other words, with innovation.

Listening/naïve listening. The studies continue to pour in. There are now over eighty that we have unearthed including those reviewed for *In Search of Excellence*. Virtually all of them say the same thing: the lion's share of new ideas comes from the users. (3M adds an important twist: a substantial share of their ideas come in response to the complaints of users. 3M sees the complaint per se as an unparalleled opportunity!) The Milliken people discovered that in virtually every division 50 percent or more of their product ideas came from users. And this was *before* they developed conscious, proactive "naïve listening" programs.

The power of listening: it borders on the bizarre. General Electric has radically increased its share of market in the railroad locomotive business against a tough competitor—the $80 billion General Motors Corporation. In 1980 customers were concerned that GM would achieve a monopolistic position. By 1984 they were again worried about a monopolistic position; only now GE was the worry. At the base of it was a division general manager hell-bent upon improving performance. He spurred a marketer to take on a semi-bootleg project with three engineers quietly borrowed from another operation. They hit the road, doing something that hadn't been done in a decade, talking, naïvely, with principal customers. They held workshops on customer premises. Walls were lined with butcher paper, and lists of desired features were divvied up: these are the features that we at GE will try to provide; this is what you the customer can best do. Out of it came the New Series Design, and then the remarkable new-order growth. The program was so successful that it has now allowed GE to invest over a quarter billion dollars in a new, highly automated factory in depressed Erie, Pennsylvania.

When you hear such stories you ought to be a bit skeptical. We were. But we did the best we could to check the information out, and it appeared to be valid. Then Tom had a unique opportunity to confirm it. He spoke at a luncheon meeting of San Francisco Bay Area business leaders sponsored by the chairman of the Stanford Board of Trustees. One present was Ben Biaggini, then chairman of the Southern Pacific Company. After relating this analysis, Tom turned to Ben, for the SP Railroad had been one of the companies that GE had purportedly "operated upon," and asked, "Is there any truth to this?" To his great dismay, Ben replied, deadpan, "Not a bit." Tom recovered and asked, "OK, what *is* the story?" Ben grinned, and paused for a second, then he proceeded: "To tell you the truth, Tom, it had been a lot longer than ten years since anybody had bothered to ask."

This theme rings especially true for the technology-based industries, where technical arrogance and a "This product will sell itself" mentality dominate many companies—and bring more than a few to their knees. Fred Cox, chairman of successful Emulex, a computer industry player, says, "So many lose because they come to 'own the market.' They start to *tell* the customer what he wants." In computers, Wang has the top growth rate (sales *and* profits) among the big, higher-end players. Their secret? For the most part it's better listening to the ultimate user. Sandra Kurtzig's ASK Computer, which makes software systems primarily for manufacturers, has gone from $0 to $100 million in no time flat. Almost all agree on the reason. ASK is well named: They ask *and* listen—and then adapt a product to the customer's needs. Digital Switch is a Dallas-based star in telecommunications switch gear. MCI chose it as a major supplier over Northern Telecom when both Digital Switch and MCI were small. The reason, according to one close observer: "NT [Northern Telecom] *told* MCI what they could have. Digital Switch *asked* MCI what they wanted."

3M is so committed to the idea of customer listening for innovation that they've made it their corporate theme/logo.*

## A Few (More) Tricks of the Trade

In many companies the best source of ideas is the sales force. Yet so few really listen to their sales force. The common wisdom is that "the sales force rolls over and plays dead in the face of every customer whim." To some extent, of course, that's true: that *is* what the salesman gets paid for, up to a point. But Chairman Bill Keefer of Warner Electric Brake and Clutch, running a highly profitable, $175 million company providing specialty industrial devices (such as clutches for Xerox machines), sees it differently. He knows that his future lies in the development of a large string of new, customer-induced, niche-oriented products (shades of 3M). And he knows that the people most likely to hear what's needed are his salespeople. So he has a boring routine. Each salesperson makes a monthly call report. Not so novel. As part of each call report, there is a requirement to submit the "best three potential product (new or line extension) ideas heard about on a customer premise." Now, this is a bit unusual. But the real novelty? The chairman spends almost a full Sunday each month *reading* those ninety reports. Furthermore, he has an unfailing routine of penning personal notes on thirty or forty of the individual suggestions—notes to people in engineering and manufacturing requesting concrete follow-up within, usually, a five- or ten-day period.

So much of the business of retailing seems to have come to focus on the centralized distribution function, the centralized computer-aided buying function. But there are exceptions. Mervyn's is the shining star in Dayton-Hudson's crown; it has a fine buying organization. Now, buyers these days (like package-goods brand managers) are typical of the hotshot, fast-tracking young men and women who don't have time for the boring task of learning the job on the retail floor. Mervyn's, to some extent, is no exception. Most of

---

*Sometimes our friends explicitly test our credibility when it comes to 3M. The president of a small bank had an idea for an adhesive to keep pothole plugs from popping out in the extreme cold. Having read about 3M's listening proclivity in *In Search of Excellence,* he called them and rapidly got through to a 3M technology executive. A week later, the fellow called our banker friend back to report that they were working on his idea. His comment to us, "By God, they really *do* listen."

3M hears you...

**3M**

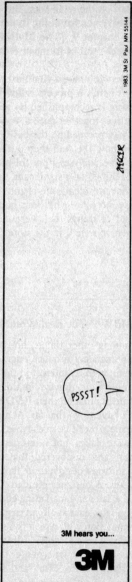

3M hears you...

**3M**

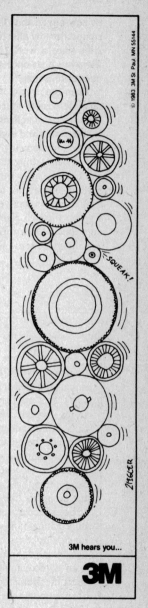

3M hears you...

**3M**

its new buyers didn't start on the retail floor. But Mervyn's stays ahead of its competitors by effectively remerchandising its entire billion-dollar-plus operation once a week (see chapter 9, "The Mythology of Innovation"); what Mervyn's does once a week most of its major competitors can barely do in a quarter of a year.

Then the people at Mervyn's take a vital next step. They keep in touch—tangible, visible touch. There's a process called Weekly Store Check. The fleet-of-foot merchandising is accomplished by getting their top hundred or so merchants and executives together once a week to redo things (i.e., create the Ad Supplement). They proceed on the basis of lots of written feedback, lots of data telling them how the stuff they pushed last week is selling this week. They have trend-line analyses from themselves and from their competitors' operations, too. But equally significant, they see it: that same cast of a hundred—executive vice presidents, merchants, buyers—troops together as a group through a single store for a full four hours once a week. They ask questions: "Does this set of things that we put next to that set of things actually make sense when you see it in the store's live format?" "What does it feel like?"

---

### MBWA: The Real-World Loop

MBWA means, among other things, not treating the innovator—designer/buyer/brand manager/product engineer—like a one-dimensional (and weird) being with no interest in the world Out There. Mervyn's gets all the innovators (buyers in this instance) out into the stores—weekly. 3M insists that all their R&D types make regular sales calls. But one doesn't have to go that far. At a seminar with a software company the usual issue arose: The sales types thought the prima donna software designers were flakes, not interested in the real world. We probed a bit deeper, and discovered that given the salespersons' *assumption* that "all software designers are flakes," they did in fact treat the designers like flakes. A designer pleaded: "How do you expect me to be excited about the sales and marketing end? You never give us any information on it—no sales data at all, no customer information except major glitches, in conjunction with which you simply run around calling us a bunch of 'impractical nerd assholes.'" It turns out that this sad tale is an all too common one. The sales types (or the president, who vowed to fix the problem instantly in this case—and did) act out their negative assumptions; thus the "far out" types are not brought into the real-world loop, and they become farther out as a result, with predictable effects on innovation.

### Customers and Innovation:
### Some Questions—and Things to Do Now

· Look at your last ten new products/services. What were the sources of the ideas? Look at key competitors' last ten new products/services. What were the sources of the ideas? (Our experience shows that 50 percent at least will come from customers, even if you aren't trying hard to tap this source. Does your evidence match this?) Have the customer-generated ideas led to faster (and more profitable) product development?

· Are all customers "hounded" for new ideas in all settings?

· Is there a specific and regular mechanism for salespersons to solicit customers' ideas? If so, is there a specific mechanism aimed at making sure that design/marketing/engineering/manufacturing pay attention to these ideas? Do nonsales functions (marketing, manufacturing or operations, accounting) specifically (alone or as part of a team) solicit customer ideas?

· Consider giving an award (sales, marketing, engineering) for "best idea garnered from a customer this month." Consider sales (marketing, engineering) contests focused on unearthing new ideas from customers. Consider adding manufacturers/operations people to this crusade (which must start by letting them visit the customers).

· Do you treat your designer/buyer types as well-rounded business people? Are they brought into the loop—the store, the factory, the customer's premises—in a way that makes them team members rather than the oddball "creative type"? If the answer is yes, then be specific: List 10 ways (or examples within the last 90 days) you've made the designers et al. part of the team.

· Are the "idea" people (engineers, brand managers, marketers, buyers) forced to visit customers or sales-floor operations regularly? Monthly? How about weekly?

## MBWA: People

Phil Staley has turned around an old Ford plant in Edison, New Jersey. We'll describe the process in some detail later. Here suffice it to say that every day he wandered the floor. And then he did more: He started barbecuing steaks for his people at one end of the plant. Then he more or less formalized it: he opened—on the floor—a shop of sorts, Staley's Steakhouse. He hangs out there a few hours a day, grilling steak, talking to people, listening.

Jimmy Treybig, Tandem Computer founder, thinks it's important to get people together. So he does. Everybody. Once a week. At every Tandem facility, from Santa Clara to Singapore, there is a "beer bust" once a week. No one is required to attend. But anyone can. And most do. Many say that more business is done in those couple of hours than during the rest of the week combined. The leader in the gene-splicing business, Genentech, a South San Francisco company, practices the same routine. Once a week. All hands. Free beer. (Free oysters the week that we were lucky enough to attend.)

We chat with executive after executive (and many nonexecutives). They brag: "Well, we get all our people together once a year. It's a big deal. It's an effort, but it's well worth it." Treybig wouldn't understand that; the Genentech people wouldn't understand it; Phil Staley wouldn't understand it. Hewlett-Packard insists that every division get all hands together, in a common setting, no less than once every two weeks. It's done. The cost—enormous. At least by some measures. It takes a lot of time, and a lot of energy. But how good are you? No better than your people and their commitment and participation in the business, as full partners, and as business people. The fact that you get them all together to share whatever—results, experiences, recent small successes and the like—at least once every couple of weeks seems to us to be a small price indeed to pay for that commitment and sense of teamwork and family. The "return on investment" is probably far and away the best of any program in the organization. Ask Victor Kiam: he started conducting regular all-hands meetings and sharing rituals as part of his turnaround program at Remington (the razor people) a couple of years back. He says it's the best investment he ever made. And if you don't believe him, ask his people.

There are, of course, numerous variations on this theme (we'll look at more of them in Part IV, "People People People"). Each serves to illustrate the imagination that can be applied to this underthought-about area of staying in touch. For instance, People Express has built an internal TV network, WPEX. A daily news show is taped (all "broadcasters" are regular employees—e.g., a pilot just finishing a flight) and transmitted to all the system's locations early the next day. Stock price, customer complaints and praise, and a hundred and one other activities are reported, and, we hear, avidly watched upon receipt. But here's our favorite (partially because it suggests that we *all* have the same problems). George Lucas, of LucasFilm (*Star Wars*, etc.) is just like you and us! His office people fight with his field people, and so on. Lucas has few rules, but one is this: on any LucasFilm softball team, there shall be no more than one person from any one department. Genius! When do you find out that people are human, not narrow-minded "functional bigots," as a colleague calls them? Much more likely over a postgame keg of beer than in a committee meeting.

---

### Boldness!

Most give lip service to getting people together. ASK, HP, Genentech, Dana and People Express put their time (and money) where others put only their mouths, bringing hundreds or thousands together, from far and near, weekly or monthly. S. C. Johnson & Son (Johnson's

Wax, etc.), the superb Racine, Wisconsin, company joins the list of the bold. Late in 1984, Chairman Sam Johnson observed that his British subsidiary apparently felt estranged from the Johnson "family feeling" he so cherishes. To rectify the situation, he chartered a 747 and flew all five-hundred employees of the British subsidiary to the United States for a full week! Three days were spent touring U.S. factories and attending a lavish gala in Racine put on by the U.S. work force; two more days were devoted to sightseeing in New York City.

## MBWA: People—
### Some Questions, and Things to Do Now

• How much time do you devote to walking the floor? Be specific: Collect some data for about twenty-five managers—all functions, all levels. How big is the variation? What's the low end: 5 percent? 10 percent? Are you surprised by the pattern?

• Wandering is a habit that starts close to home (i.e., the next office). Are the doors open or closed? Or, better yet, do you even have doors? Two examples: An officer in a mid-sized company has a favorite routine. Whenever he takes charge of a new area, he always begins by *personally* removing his door from his office. The message is clear. Another colleague one-ups him: he always moves his desk—again, personally—out into the secretarial bullpen area. More generally, do physical spaces enhance or thwart wandering? (At the highest level of generality, Mars, Inc., for instance, physically attaches *all* administrative facilities to manufacturing plants.)

• What is the frequency of "all hands" meetings? Why? Could you do more? We urge you to attend an all-hands session at Dana, Milliken, HP, Tandem or Genentech, for instance, if you can. "Seeing is believing" is probably uniquely applicable to this one.

• Can you readily list ten devices, à la LucasFilm, for *forcing* warring tribes into informal contact? If yes, can you list ten more—and put them into practice? This is a constant battle; there are never enough.

## MBWA: The Technology
### of Leadership

MBWA: the technology of the obvious. It is being in touch, with customers, suppliers, your people. It facilitates innovation, and makes possible the teaching of values to every member of an organization. Listening, facilitating, and teaching and reinforcing values. What is this except leadership? Thus *MBWA is the technology of leadership*. We will subsequently argue that leading (a school, a small business, or a Fortune 100 company) is primarily *paying attention*, and that the masters of the use of attention are also not only master users of symbols, of drama, but master storytellers and myth builders. All this can be accomplished only through means that are visible, tangible. The story of the senior manager's ten-minute visit with a neophyte salesman—in the field, in *his* territory—is relayed in minutes around a system spanning six thousand miles. Its effectiveness is many times that of the formal pronouncement, which is viewed by most as written by a committee of staffers.

---

### The Smell of MBWA

Is wandering encouraged or discouraged in your organization? (Look deeply at this. The *implicit* is *more* important than the explicit.) Do you give lip service to foster wandering, but then get angry and impatient when people take you at your word and are *out* of their offices—when you want something *now*? Bob Waterman reports a conversation with a long-time Arco executive about inveterate wanderer Chairman Bob Anderson: "If Bob would call you from the field, and if you happened to be *in*, you could detect noticeable disappointment in his voice." Sam Walton of Wal-Mart, too, shows ire when people are in their offices; and a P&G manufacturer reports, "The worst chewing out I got in my career came very early in my managerial days, when a visiting Cincinnati exec wandered by one morning and caught me in my office. He gave me hell and then some." These reports are exceptions. More common is a young brand manager we chatted with. We asked him if he got out to ride with salesmen once a month or so. His reply? "Once a *month?!* You're kidding. If we're not in the office, period, and ready to jump, with data in hand, on a split-second notice, we're in trouble. MBWA around here means bathroom breaks at most." His company's record, we'd add, is nothing to write home about. So, collect *good* data on this. By hook or by crook, get feedback you trust (especially from some entry level types): What is "OK" and "not OK" re wandering—how/how early is the message learned? What, direct and indirect, are the reinforcement devices?

Here are eight ways to fix the "smell," if it discourages wandering:
- Publicize the fact that *you* are out wandering 50% of the time, and that your colleagues are, too (if you and they are).
- Be meticulous in having meetings in other's offices/spaces rather than yours.
- Evaluate managers in part—and directly—on the basis of *their people's* assessment of how well/how frequently they are in touch.
- *Fire* a supervisor who doesn't know all his people's first and last names. (McPherson at Dana did this once; this fellow had been in the slot a half dozen years.)

• Hold meetings and reviews in the field (it gives a further signal that out-of-the-office is the norm).

• An especially tough one: When you're harried and need some information badly, and only Ms. X has it, and you discover upon calling that she's out on a field visit—*don't* call her in the field and tell her to rush back and get the answer. *Wait!*

• Start randomly popping into offices and asking the inhabitants why *they* aren't out.

• If, say, you're a manufacturing boss, make sure you have a second office on the shop floor. If you're an R&D V.P., make sure you have a second (non-headquarters) office in a lab. (S.I. Newhouse, who created the Newhouse publishing empire, never had an office or a secretary. He spent 100% of his time in his subsidiaries, roaming in unannounced and seconding an unimposing office to use for the day.)

MBWA pervades every level of the effective organization of every sort—which is to say that leaders exist at every level. We shall return to the subject again directly in the concluding section devoted to leadership. Indirectly it will permeate virtually every intervening page.

# 3

# Integrity and the Technology
# of the Obvious

"MBWA: The Technology of the Obvious" introduces you to our obsessions with integrity. The issue came clear in mid-1984. Tom read a book he had been asked to comment upon favorably. The words were terrific. They focused on listening, developing empathy for the person on the other side of the table. They emphasized the importance of traveling thousands of miles if necessary to see a person face-to-face, to watch the eyes. Tom, who takes pleasure in giving support for books he likes, demurred in this instance. Why? The book's implicit thrust was that these are *tools* anyone can use to gain immediate advantage over others. We're at a loss to describe the depth of our dismay. We believe in truly listening to the customer, taking the customer's view as *more* important than our own. We believe in truly listening to our people, taking their views as *more* important than our own. But the whole edifice tumbles if one doesn't deal off a base of integrity.

Thus what is not so obvious throughout this book is that virtually every device we suggest is doomed to be useless unless applied with integrity. Worse than useless, most of these devices, used without integrity, will expose you as a hypocrite of the first order.

Install a toll-free number, then don't "overtrain" your people or "overrespond" to customer call-ins. You'll find it won't work. The area code 800 numbers hum only for those who really believe in listening and responding, not those who are merely looking for a PR gimmick.

Paint out the executive parking spots, but treat your people with contempt, and you'll find you stand convicted of a kind of fraud.

Draw your organization charts "upside down" (customers or constituents on top, president or city manager on the bottom) and then provide the same careless service. It won't make an iota of difference. Except that you will become a joke.

In support of innovation, give speeches lauding failures that were good tries, and then demote or sidetrack the first champion whose head pops up; that's it for risk-taking, despite all the fine words.

We are especially at risk in the material we present here. There is little on formal organization structures, on planning or performance appraisal systems. Perhaps with these formal devices you can "get away with" a bit of inconsistency and, yes, lack of integrity, for the formal system is meant to carry the weight.

Not here! Each major element in our model is clearly underpinned by a thousand supporting devices, each insignificant but collectively grand. What gives them the collective coherence, the clarity of vision, is, simply, integrity. Each of a thousand customer-serving devices supports the passionate concern for customers at L. L. Bean. Each of a thousand devices to turn "employees" into owners and heroes at Apple and People Express is in direct support of the passion of Steve Jobs and Don Burr to create a whole new form of equitable organizations for their people.

We will remind you in every chapter that each example lives only as the leader's integrity (leaders at every level) lives within it. As you read on we would ask you to stop and pause, close the door and examine your deepest beliefs about people (and their creative potential and trustworthiness), about wandering, about the importance of the customer's perception, about failure. Especially when a suggestion makes your eyes light up. That's the time to pause. When, for example, you get excited about a listening device, when you want to install it *now*, start *now*, *today* (which is, after all, what we beg you to do).

Stop, nonetheless. Do you believe in it? Believe what it stands for? Believe that the people who will execute it are trustworthy enough to do so?

If you proceed through these pages simultaneously champing at the bit and reflecting, then we will have accomplished a major objective. And we hope you will have too.

We fight the same battle in our analysis that we are asking you to fight. We get excited at the excitement of Milliken president Tom Malone as he describes the details of his Fabulous Bragging Sessions, so integral to Milliken's quality-program success. But then we hesitate. We observe Malone carefully. We observe his enthusiasm, passion, excitement, genuine concern. When he talks of giving out awards personally, we write down the details of everything, including the way he frames them; and then we visualize him giving them out, and we know that he takes pleasure in handing the 157th award of the day to the receptionist or loading dock team. And across our mental screens run the other, all too familiar pictures of the stilted award givers who, from handing out award no. 1 to award no. 200, exude "I wish I were anyplace else but there."

A friend of ours, an outsider, joined us for dinner at our Skunk Camp, mentioned in the Foreword. She spent a half hour with Don Burr of People Express, and with Don Williams, managing partner of Trammell Crow. She knows their towering reputations. Yet her reaction (almost a stunned one, for she has attended far too many "corporate dinners"): "They are such good listeners. They focused on what I am up to, on my small business."

Ah yes, that's it. A million devices, each important—*and* integrity.

# TWO

## Customers

*I'd have to say that [before the events of the last four tough years] our culture in the Ford Motor Company said that there's one central objective in our business, and that's to earn a return on our investment. I think we've now learned there's something else that's central—and that profits will fall to you if you view this as central: Serve the customer. You have to have your costs right, quality right, all those other things that have to be done. But we must always think the customer is the middle of the thrust of what we're trying to do. I think that's what we've learned. I don't think it's much more complicated than that, and I would suggest it to you for your consideration.*

*—Edson P. Williams, vice president, Ford Motor Company general manager, Ford Truck Operations*

*Consumers are statistics. Customers are People.*

*—Stanley Marcus, chairman emeritus, Neiman-Marcus*

THE FIRST OF the two sustainable strategic advantages we have observed is an obsession with customers. Customers, not markets. Not marketing. Not strategic positioning (whatever that means). Just customers. A "market" has never been observed paying a bill. Customers do that.

Obviously there is a role for marketing, strategy formulation and the like. But ultimately, it all boils down to perceived, and appreciated, and consistently delivered service and quality to customers. Time and again we watch companies sharpen their market focus; we watch them work on quality issues. Progress is made. But it is either fleeting or a fraction of what it might be, because the customer has not become the obsessive focus of all hands—from the mailroom to MIS warren to the sales branch.

We've developed a term, after careful thought: *smell*. Does your company smell of customers? Do you listen to them directly (via MBWA), act on what you hear, listen naïvely (i.e., consider their *perceptions* more important than your superior technical knowledge of service or product)? Do you love your salespersons (i.e., listen to them), despite their efforts to strain your resources—and patience—in response to what you see as customers' whims? Do you look for the dozens (hundreds, really) of tiny bases for differentiation—i.e., a small but measurable difference that is the winning edge for superb cookie makers and aircraft engine makers alike?

IBM, Domino's Pizza, Stew Leonard's, Maytag, Perdue Farms—they seem to live for their customers. They are all good marketers. Or are they? They *appear* to be good marketers, masters of segmentation and strategic positioning, *because* they slavishly put the customer first—in every department in the business.

So the key words in our lexicon are simple ones, such as *courtesy, listening, perception.* We are (sorry to say) a bit self-congratulatory on this issue: that is, we are proud to have a full section in this book called, simply, *Customers.* Not many business or management books do. And all too often business performance reflects this lack of interest by writers, consultants and academics. Tom and Bob Waterman wrote a chapter on the subject of customers in *In Search of Excellence.* We now single it out for fully five chapters. It has become our preoccupation, our obsession. Surely it's obvious that everything necessarily starts with the customer. More specifically, with *common courtesy* toward the customer.

# 4

## Common Courtesy:
## The Ultimate Barrier to
## Competitor Entry

---

### Guests

At Disneyland and Disneyworld, every person who comes onto the property (the "set") is called a guest. Moreover, should you ever write the word at Disney, heaven help you if you don't capitalize the G.

---

MANY COMPANIES, FROM Hewlett-Packard and Du Pont to Big Eight accounting firms and banks or truckers newly faced with deregulation, seek to become more "market oriented." Often as not, management kicks off the effort by calling in a large group of marketing professors from Stanford or Harvard or Northwestern to teach market segmentation and the like. The companies love what they hear (the marketing jargon is as complex and scientific-sounding as their own technical jargon), and they go after applications of the new techniques with a vengeance. But not much happens or changes.

Why? We believe that long-term strategic advantage via "marketing orientation" comes principally from some commonsense traits: listening (see the discussion of MBWA with customers in chapter 2); common courtesy (or "uncommon courtesy," as we more correctly call it); slavish devotion to adding value to and differentiating the most mundane of so-called commodities; and superior service and quality. Those traits are, simply, not technique-driven. Moreover, they are not about "marketing." They are about customers. We strongly prefer "customer orientation" to "market orientation"; markets do not buy products, customers do. The distinction may sound pedantic. We think not. Before a sustained advantage can accrue from finely honed segmentation schemes, one must come to cherish the customer. Advantage comes not from the spectacular, or the technical, but from a persistent seeking of the mundane edge.

Portions of this essay were published under the title "Common Courtesy" in *Hospital Forum* and as "Service Excellence: It's Scarce" in *Florida Trend*.

We would even go a step further, beyond "customer orientation," to "culture," except that the term, which was discussed in *In Search of Excellence*, has rapidly become the focus of all sorts of gimmickry. And so, in this book, we have scrupulously avoided it. Thus, as mentioned, we chose to use the word "smell." IBM *smells* of the customer in a million tiny ways. So does SAS. And Stew Leonard's. And Perdue Farms, Trammell Crow. Others, despite the application of much marketing technique, do not smell of customers, do not obsessively seek advantages through enhanced closeness to their customers.

## T.D.C.: Thinly Disguised Contempt

On an all-night flight to Denver our plane stops briefly in Salt Lake City. It is on the ground for only about nine minutes, and then the Salt Lake passengers begin to board. As the new people begin to come down the ramp, the head stewardess turns to her associate and says, "Here come the animals."

A group of hotel company executives complain that they can exert no control over their franchisees, and wonder how McDonald's, operating under the same set of franchise laws, does it. We remind them, none too gently, of a conversation we had heard at a cocktail party the night before. Two officers of the company had stood around talking about the time they would have to "waste," during the next couple of days, meeting with the "franchisee bitch committee." They described it as a committee that "had been put together so the franchisees can blow off steam, can be made to feel that they're part of the company."

A sophisticated design engineer in a technology-based company plays a variation on the theme: "We designed a major fix to be applied in the field to one of our sophisticated machines. Then we engaged in a debate on whether or not we should send a letter out, along with the changes to the manual, explaining why we had done what we'd done. The vote was close to unanimous—'Don't confuse them out there; they're not all that bright.'"

Another engineering-based company, one that gets A pluses for its love of the product, gives their people what they call "product training"—everybody gets it—with great regularity. All are supposed to get a short course in sales. But, one officer explains, "Come hell and high water, the product training is done. If a budget crunch comes, though, we always defer sales training. It's implicitly considered 'soft stuff' and therefore expendable." And a receptionist at the same company adds: "Look, when an engineer comes to work here, they begin to train him further midway through the first week. I've been here going on four years, and I have yet to get my first day's training in telephone courtesy."

A few days before Nancy was to leave for a week's vacation in Mexico, she stopped by her favorite photography shop to pick up her newly repaired camera. The salesperson disappeared into the back of the store to look for it, but returned empty-handed, explaining that the camera was not there. Could she be mistaken? Was this really the store that repaired it? (A telephone call the previous day had confirmed that the camera was indeed repaired there and was indeed ready.) A second search ensued. No camera. Nancy finally asked for a loaner to take on vacation (a courtesy normally extended to customers). The salesperson hesitated, then remarked: "How am I to know that you don't already have your camera and are just trying to rip us off? I have to protect the store, you know. And since you don't have the service claim number, how can you expect me to find your camera—if it is here, which I doubt. You should have come in sooner, not just before you have to leave." Everyone's entitled to a bad day, but this was too much. A loaner was eventually granted. Two weeks later the missing camera was found (it had been "misfiled"). P.S. Nancy now has a new favorite photography shop.

---

### "Poor, Dumb Patients"

In *Verdict Pending* (Capistrano Press, 1983), Fredonia French Jacques, a patient representative for twenty-five years, writes about hospital care from the patients' (customers') point of view. Here, a patient speaks for himself:

"I'm brought into this hospital real sick and someone asks me a whole string of dumb questions. I tell them I feel like I'm going to faint and they say, 'I have to ask you a few more questions or else we can't admit you.' I faint and fall to the floor. I come to, and someone's saying, 'You can't lie here!' My wife starts to help me up. The voice says, 'You can't lift him!'

"They take my clothes away. My wife gets told to take home anything that's worth anything: my watch, my ring, my wallet. They say they can't be responsible. I put on this gown split down the back. It doesn't have buttons, and they make you wear it backwards. My backside's always hanging out or I'm clutching at my gown with my only arm. See, the other one has an IV in it and I have to push that pole along every time I get up to go to the bathroom or brush my teeth."

He continued: "They come in and say they're going to take my teeth out. Can't go to surgery with them. Trouble is that they take them out an hour before, so that when I kiss my wife good-bye, there's nothing to buck up against. I'm embarrassed, and they don't give them back until I'm awake, and who knows how many people gawked at me with my mouth hanging open."

---

In all these vignettes and comments we see one or another of the following: (1) casting aspersions upon the customer; (2) contempt for the franchisee, the field-service person, the receptionist, the people in the stores—that is, all the people truly responsible for the delivery of service to the customer/client; (3) writing off such things as phone courtesy as "obvious," as not requiring thoughtfulness or serious training; (4) "technical hubris"—a belief that technological superiority is the only thing that *really* counts.

We've come to call all these things, and many more, TDC—Thinly Disguised Contempt—for the customer. (And contempt for those who serve the customer, remember, is inevitably handed down to the customers themselves.) It's the biggest barrier to sustainable superior performance—in hospitals, schools, banks, among retailers and manufacturing companies.

The setting now shifts to a classroom at the Stanford Business School in 1983. A team is discussing Disney's obsessive commitment to park cleanliness and customer friendliness. "I've honestly never seen a scrap of trash in either park," a normally skeptical MBA candidate says. She polls the fifty-person class. All agree. Then the team playing the role of the "cynical consultants" rebuts the Disney presentation. They attribute the Disney parks' success to better locations and a couple of good real estate deals. The debate heats up. Many join in. A Sloan Program student, a fast-tracker from General Motors, heads the "cynical consultants" team. He turns serious now; this is no classroom exercise anymore. "*Anybody* can provide a clean park," he maintains. Therefore the explanation for Disney's success must be the real estate, the access to capital, pure and simple. And what about McDonald's? Might cleanliness and uniformly high standards of service have anything to do with their success? Again, "No." Why? "Anyone can do that." Tom, who has been observing this exercise in his professional capacity, is incredulous. He stammers, "Anyone *can,* but only McDonald's *does.*"

As IBM's Buck Rodgers, who retired as IBM's corporate vice president for marketing in 1984, correctly (unfortunately) observes, "It's a shame, but whenever you get good service, it's an exception, and you're excited about it. It ought to be the other way around." We agree. Common decency, common courtesy toward the customer ("Guest") is indeed the exception. Economists may not buy it as the ultimate barrier to competitor entry or as a crucial form of sustainable strategic advantage, but such disparate actors (and extremely successful competitors) as IBM and McDonald's certainly do.

---

### Good Show, Southwest!?

There were four of us in the two rows of seats. The Southwest flight was one hour 35 minutes late leaving Phoenix for San Diego on a Friday afternoon in October 1984. The 2:15 flight was posted on the screen for a 3:20 departure. It was now 3:15. The arriving plane was not at the gate. Tom asked, "When do you *really* think we'll leave?" The check-in counter clerk announced, "Oh, those posted numbers don't mean much. Think of it as within an hour of what they show." "What?" Tom stammered. "I didn't mean it," the clerk said. "Just a joke." Some joke when you're heading home to family on a Friday afternoon! Upon recounting this unpleasant experience once on board, Tom was one-upped. "That's *nothing*," a woman next to him boomed. "I was standing at the check-in counter in Albuquerque [the prior stop]. We had just been told of the first hour's dalay. One or two people behind me grumbled, sort of loudly. Right in front of me [she gestured strongly], the [Southwest] counter clerk turned to her colleague and said in a loud and clear voice, 'The passengers are behaving like idiots today.'" As we all chuckled mirthlessly at that, the ultimate one-upper chimed in. She, too, had been part of the Albuquerque delay. "Someone [a passenger] next to me exclaimed, not very loudly, 'This sure as heck makes my life difficult.' The Southwest employee nearest him shot back, 'What do you think it does to *mine?*' as though we passengers were to be blamed for fouling up *his* day." The woman concluded, "I'll be glad when America West [a new airline with a good service reputation] moves in. It'll give these jokers something to think about."

Only four people were part of this conversation. Three had horror stories. Schedule slippage, the lateness was not the point, all agreed. The flippant attitude and disregard for the passengers was. We've all suffered through delays. But being insulted when we express concern is too steep a price to pay.

### The Little Things—
### Making a Difference at the Margin

Without a doubt, Tom is a "rational man"—with two degrees in engineering, two degrees in business and a career principally as a business consultant/analyst. This rational man, Tom, flies Delta when he can. The reason? When you arrive at an airport for a connection, late in the day, say, and dragging, there's a living breathing body from Delta who smiles and says as he points, "Hope you had a nice flight. San Francisco is Gate 26, two down on the left." Tom believes *him*—and automatically disregards the CRT display. That's it—completely irrational. Tom, the rational man, is even a bit ashamed of such "reasons." But we've come to think they are critical.

In *Ten Greatest Salespersons*, Shelby Carter, past head of Xerox's sales force, describes the "Windex Man" in his life:

I'll give you a fine example of how a very small, seemingly insignificant thing influenced me as a customer. When our family had just moved into our new home—the whole gang, our six children and two dogs—it was the first day in the house and everything was in an uproar. The kids all poured into the family room, and the television set didn't work. I got out the Yellow Pages and called for a repairman, and he came right out Well, after he repaired the set, he asked me to come over and look at it

I stepped over the kids, our German Shepherd, the books, and instead of handing me a bill, as I expected, he took out a bottle of Windex spray and cleaned the glass. That impressed me, because he showed me how proud he was of his work and the product he served. From that day on, whenever we needed our TV fixed, I've said to my wife, "Honey, call the Windex guy."

Here's another Windex story. We stop by a local (Menlo Park, California) liquor store, Beltramo's, on Friday evening to buy a case of wine for our office party. At the counter we hand the clerk an American Express card. Amex must be busy in Phoenix or something, because it takes the clerk three or four minutes on the phone to get credit approval. Finally he does get it and hands the card back, and then he picks up a five-cent mint from an old-fashioned candy jar on the counter and drops it in the bag with an accompanying "Sorry for that delay. It was inexcusable. Hope it doesn't happen again. You know we value your business. Come back and see us again soon. And, oh, have a nice party." He's just bought our loyalty for *life!* We will shop with more determination than before at the "nickel-candy-man store." It wasn't the clerk's fault the American Express lines were busy. It was American Express's failing (too few phone lines at a peak hour). But the clerk took it on as *his* problem, not theirs. He didn't say, "Those SOB's at American Express always do this to me at rush hour." Instead he said, "*I* am sorry for the delay." Oh, we won't drive twenty miles out of our way to buy a single bottle of wine at Beltramo's, but, *at the margin*, we will go out of our way a *little* and pay a *little* more for that courtesy. Excellence is a game of inches, or millimeters. No one act is, per se, clinching. But a thousand things, a thousand thousand things, each done a tiny bit better, do add up to memorable responsiveness and distinction—and loyalty (repeat business) and slightly higher margins.

---

### "People's People Do an Awful Lot of Smiling"

An Eastern Airlines in-house newsletter (provided to us by a People Express employee) describes Eastern's discovery of the People Express secret; it turns out they are more than just a discount airline:

"People Express has replaced Eastern as New York's No. 1 airline."

The words, spoken by [Eastern] Miami Agent Pete Rogers to a crowd of fellow agents meeting for recurrent training, had the impact of a sledgehammer. How did Rogers, who isn't an instructor, find his way to the front of the class? And why a slide show about the company's biggest competitor?

The Communications Committee of Eastern's Miami Terminal

Employee Involvement group had discussed People Express but nobody knew very much about the low-cost carrier.

"The committee elected 2 people to go to Newark and ride back on People Express," Rogers explained.

Rogers and Deedee Welsh were the chosen couple.

To really test People Express, Rogers and Welsh would create a ruse—posing as newly marrieds on their honeymoon trip to Miami. [Eastern gets an A+ for practicing customer MBWA.]

The pair flew Sept. 14, [1984] on Eastern's Flight 6 to Newark, and put on a great act.

"Honeymooners are either subdued and quiet or confused," Welsh explained. "We chose to be confused. We went to Terminal C at Newark International. That's where People Express operates its international and transcontinental flights. We were directed to the North Terminal, where years ago Eastern began its passenger service."

Everywhere "Mr. and Mrs. Rogers" went they were treated with broad smiles and genuine friendliness. As Rogers told the agents, "People Express people do not look like professionals—but they show an interest in people and are always friendly. Everyone with whom we had contact helped us from the start of our trip to the end. They were polite.

"Deedee and I never expected to run across that sort of thing."

The newlyweds pressed home their case during the remainder of the slide show—showing pictures of People Express' facilities, their customer service managers, their in-flight managers. . . .

Aloft, the "managers" collect the fares and bag-check fees. They sell Cokes for 50¢, beer for $1 and drinks or wine for $2. A snack pack goes for $2. "And they don't care if you buy it or not. They just tell you that if you want something, put your tray table down. Nothing fancy. But the people are always smiling, making the atmosphere friendly," Welsh said.

Rogers explained how he told one of the People Express "managers" he had hoped for some honeymoon champagne once the flight departed. Sorry, the ground employee replied. People Express doesn't have champagne. "But the agent told me he'd take care of us," Rogers said. "When we arrived over Miami, the captain came on the P.A. and announced that the Rogers were starting their married life aboard People Express and thanked us and wished us luck. And the drinks and snack packs we had were complimentary.

"I thoroughly enjoyed the experience. People Express' people made it a fun trip I recommend to everyone in this room."

Welsh noted that new magazines refer to the Newark-based car-

rier's passengers as "back-packers." "Look at this picture," she said.
"What do you see. You don't see back-packers. Don't those people
look an awful lot like Eastern passengers?"

The room was silent.

"Most of those Miami-bound travelers were—*were*—Eastern
*passengers.* Now they are People Express *customers.*"

A Citibanker tells of a fifteen-minute effort to get a crisp new $100 bill for
an unknown customer who walked in off the street and wanted it to present
as an award that afternoon. Our Citibank friend made two phone calls, got
the bill, and put it in a little box with a "Thanks for thinking of us" note on
his card. The chance visitor soon came back and opened an account; in nine
months his major law firm had deposited $250,000 in Citibank's coffers. You
can't expect such things to happen often. That's not the point. But *at the
margin,* you increase the odds just a little bit with each such act.

Here's another. A friend's VW developed a mysterious clank, and he took
the car for repair to a local Shell station, which has a superb word-of-mouth
reputation. Well deserved, it turns out. The repairman called a couple of
hours after the car was dropped off: "Did you know this part is still under
warranty? I called the local VW dealer and he's ready for you right now."
Wow! From now on he gets all our friend's repair business—and ours, too.
We even stop there for gas, and pay at least a dime a gallon premium. (In a
subsequent transaction he talked our colleague out of buying a new battery.
No wonder he generally has a two-week queue for service—for which he
charges a handsome price.)

## The Source of Common Courtesy: Support People as Heroes

If common courtesy is the key, then the receptionist, service dispatcher and
switchboard attendant are the heroes, not the denizens of executive row.
That will be our "obvious" (again) conclusion in Section IV (People, People,
People). But the point is so vital to this chapter's argument that we will preview it here—using an unlikely setting as an example.

General Bill Creech led a remarkable turnaround of the U.S. Air Force's
Tactical Air Command. TAC has a clear peacetime "product," the sortie, in
which the weapon system (plane) and its pilot and support group are tested
as a unit in simulated combat conditions, and a peacetime "bottom line," the
sortie rate. When General Creech arrived at TAC in 1978, the sortie rate
had been falling for ten years at a compound annual rate of 7.8 percent. From
1978 through 1983, it rose at a compound annual rate of 11.2 percent. It used
to take about four *hours* on average to get a part to a temporarily inoperable
plane. In 1984 the average was eight *minutes.* Since the budget for spare parts
actually *decreased* along the way, and other "external" factors became more
adverse, the turnaround was a product of management, nothing else. At the

heart of it was a simple proposition: planes fly less often than they should because of some failure not of the pilots but of other people. Planes don't fly because, for example, the pickup truck transporting a critical part broke a U-joint in a long-unrepaired pothole while coming across the base. That is, supply and maintenance people and their on-the-job accoutrements (and support people and equipment in general) are at once the problem *and* the opportunity.

Or, as the president of a high-tech company put it to us once: "I'll teach you all you need to know about marketing in one easy lesson—in one easy sentence, in fact: the most important 'marketer' in our company is the man or woman on the loading dock who decides *not* to drop the damned box into the back of the truck."

Amen! And how did General Creech act on this indisputable fact? He motivated, celebrated and virtually canonized the typically unsung support people. He said, "The airplane is the customer for us." And he made heroes out of those whose mundane chores in fact most influenced his "customers'" productivity. (See chapter 14, on "ownership," for more on the turnaround at TAC.)

Like TAC under General Creech, the best customer-serving companies we observe—from Stew Leonard's to Marriott to IBM—overinvest in the welfare and morale of their support people. It turns out that a fire-eating spares department is the key to a truly exceptional Cadillac or Peterbilt (the truck people) dealership. A neglected and demoralized one is the sure sign of a mediocre outfit.

Attacking the problem (opportunity) requires some imagination. Designing measures, competitions, awards and devices for participation for salespeople (or designers, buyers, engineers) is fairly straightforward. It is more difficult to manage genuine (not phony) involvement and awards for customer-support people in the distribution center, MIS and the like. The critical "trick," we observe, is getting them involved directly with customers. Milliken, AMP and several others work to get direct and indirect support people on joint customer/company problem-solving task forces. Successful Davgar Restaurants (over a dozen Burger King franchises in South Florida, every one outperforming the local McDonald's) includes support people in all sales meetings and celebrations. Another route is even more direct: in chapter 14, on ownership, we talk of a bank that got everyone involved in soliciting new accounts at a time of crisis; interestingly, a motivated MIS team, rather than a team of lending officers, won the top prize for new business brought in. General Creech developed clever (and practical) measures of effectiveness for *all* support groups, induced intense and regular subsupport-unit versus subsupport-unit competition and gave numerous and lavish awards for top performances, including regular awards banquets for support people, which surpassed anything done for pilots.

That triggers a final thought. Though we could go on at length on this issue (and shall, indirectly, in the section called "People, People, People"), let us leave you with a question. Most have some familiarity with IBM's lavish off-shore Golden Circle galas for the top 3 percent of its sales force and with Mary Kay's spectaculars for her top saleswomen. Have you ever heard of an offshore bash of similar magnitude for the spare-parts departments, the distribution-center teams or the field-service gangs? If not, why not? There ain't a law that says it can't be done.

---

### Common Courtesy:
### One Thing to Do

• Commit yourself to performing *one* ten-minute act of exceptional customer courtesy per day, and to inducing your colleagues to do the same. In a 100-person outfit, taking into account normal vacations, holidays, etc., that would mean *24,000* new courteous acts per year. Such is the stuff of revolutions!

Good luck. (And *thank you* for reading.)

---

# 5

# No Such Thing
# as a Commodity

IN OUR SEMINARS, as common a question as any has been this one: "For the last decade or so we've heard about the joys of the experience curve [making more—selling more—at a lower price to gain share in order to achieve a barrier to competitor entry via lowest industry cost]. Recently it's come under heavy attack. You maintain that revenue enhancement is more important than cost containment. What's up?"

The senior regional sales manager from John Deere was wearing an odd tie tack. It was in the shape of a cross. The vertical letters spelled out DEERE, the horizontal SOQ NOP. When asked what the letters stood for, his reply was, "Sell on quality, not on price." He added, "It's my toughest job, in down markets, to make my own people realize that the objective is to sell the benefits, not just resort to price [as the only selling leverage]. I tell them a story. I was going after a sale [for Deere] some years ago. It came down to two final contenders. The fellow making the buy called me in to give me one last chance. His message in a nutshell: 'You're just too high on the price side. No hard feelings, and we hope we can do business with you again in the future.' I was about to walk out the door, unhappy to say the least. Then I had an inspiration. I turned around and said, 'Those are nice-looking boots you've got on.' He was a bit surprised, but said, 'Thanks,' and he went on to talk for a minute or so about those fine boots, what was unique about the leather, why they were practical as well as fine. I said to him, at the end of his description, 'How come you buy those boots and not just a pair off the shelf in an Army-Navy surplus store?' It must have taken twenty seconds for the grin to spread all the way across his face. 'The sale is yours,' he said, and he got up and came around his desk and gave me a hearty handshake."

The answer to the question posed at the beginning of this essay has been the subject of books, not a few anecdotes and pages of brief analysis. But let us begin by talking a bit about the sort of evidence that's been accumulated in the past few years. It speaks loud and clear to our point: People who find bases for differentiation and who produce for the higher ends of markets (not just Mercedes makers, but specialty steel makers, washing machine producers, chocolate chip cookie vendors and chicken sellers as well) tend to be winners over the long haul—i.e., the customer *will* pay a tidy premium for things that solve his or her problem and that work and are well serviced.

## The Systematic Evidence

(1) The focus for the *In Search of Excellence* research was on seventy-five companies in the United States and Europe. Five (e.g., Amoco) were in the resource-extraction business. For those companies, finding the substance for fewer dollars per barrel or cents per cubic foot may be an appropriate "first principle." Of the remaining seventy, fully sixty-five became and remained winners by focusing on what we now call "revenue line enhancement"—on *quality, service, courtesy, customer listening* and *nichemanship* (solving problems for tailored market segments).* Moreover, of the remaining five—those that fell into the "low cost at all costs" category—four had severe problems during the 1981–83 recession (including onetime darlings of the market—when demand was high—such as National Semiconductor, Data General and Texas Instruments; all three have recently restructured radically to focus on perceived quality, customer satisfaction, listening and, in general, a greater "market orientation"). In fact, the only one in the "low cost" arena that thrived was Emerson Electric. (And, arguably, the Emerson categorization is faulty. It could just as easily be called a company that often follows the "last player in the niche" strategy. In most arenas, they are a specialist producer.)

(2) The *In Search of Excellence* findings, circa 1980, were strongly reinforced in 1983 in a study that concentrated on a different part of the industrial base. An extensive study conducted by McKinsey and Co. for the ABC (American Business Conference)† focused on the management strategic practices among the forty-five top performers (on a financial basis) in this sector (which includes about fifteen thousand companies); surprisingly, the list was not entirely dominated by technology-driven companies: Dunkin' Donuts, A. T. Cross (the pen people) and Lenox (the china makers) were there along with Millipore, Loctite, Thomas & Betts, Wyle Laboratories. The study showed that management practice in most of these companies was to eschew a low cost–low end position, and instead to provide higher value added prod-

---

*We don't want to suggest that cost containment is unimportant to the sixty-five. It's *vital*. But the distinction we like (one not in the microeconomic texts, we'd quickly add) was made by a senior IBM manufacturing executive: "There is a vast difference between 'low cost' and 'competitive cost.' Your cost structure must be competitive. On the other hand, I've never known a company with a low-cost *attitude* that was a winner over the long haul."

†The ABC is a recently formed lobby representing America's "midsize growth companies," companies with sales between $25 million and $1 billion that have doubled or more in size in the most recent five years. (They also have the distinction of having created a huge share of the country's new jobs.)

ucts (often costing more to produce), for which they found ready markets. Astonishingly, in fully forty-three of the forty-five cases the following was observed: "Winners compete by delivering a product that supplies superior value to customers, rather than one that costs less. Most strategists have believed that business winners are those that capture commanding market share through lower costs and prices. The winner midsize companies compete on the value of their products and services and usually enjoy premium prices."

(3) These findings—from the research for *In Search of Excellence* and the ABC study—are wholly consistent with analyses made by the PIMS team, which has at its command the most extensive strategic information data base in the world.* PIMS has correlated literally hundreds of variables with long-term financial performance. The single variable far and away the most closely associated with good financial performance over the long haul is "relative perceived product quality." Technically the relative perceived product-quality "score" is deduced by a complex procedure that ranks the importance *to the customer and in the customer's terms* of various quality and service-delivery traits *(other than price)* among principal competitors in a market.

A sample of PIMS output: Those in the lower third on relative perceived product quality had an average ROI of 5 percent; those in the upper third averaged 30 percent. Winners "emphasize customer expectations," "research customer needs," "use customer-based quality performance measures," "formulate QC [Quality Control] objectives for all functions." Losers "downgrade the customer view," "make high quality synonymous with tight tolerances," "tie quality objectives to manufacturing flow," "formalize QC objectives for manufacturing only." The PIMS findings hold as tightly for both North America and Europe, for declining as for growing markets, in slow as in rapid inflation, for consumer as for industrial markets. In short, PIMS finds: "Customers pay more for better products."

Contrary to the conventional wisdom of the past fifteen years, PIMS data suggest that relative perceived product quality is much more positively related to financial performance than market share or relative market share (the latter had traditionally been the preferred variable of the Boston Consulting Group's widely used portfolio-analysis approach to strategy formulation). In fact, evidence from several quarters increasingly suggests that high market share is not an automatic winner. A 1984 *Harvard Business Review* article by Carolyn Y. Woo entitled "Market Share Leadership—Not Always So Good" reported on 112 market share leaders during the period 1972 to 1975. Seventy-one performed well financially (pre-tax return of 40 percent); their focus is on "high value added," "sales support," and "relative quality." Forty-one market share leaders, however, had an average pre tax ROS (return

---

*The PIMS (Profit Impact of Market Strategy) data base is managed by the Strategic Planning Institute in Cambridge, Massachusetts.

on sales) of less than 10 percent, and do not focus on the aforementioned traits.

(4) Another source of systematic reinforcement for the revenue-enhancement/high-value-added notion was the January 1984 *Forbes* "36th Annual Report on American Industry." Here is a small sample of the findings, focusing especially on flat or modest-growth industries, where one might least expect the HVA (high value added) phenomenon to appear.*

• *Chemicals.* Specialty chemical producers, as a group, did 40 percent better than diversified chemical producers. The former had a five-year (1978–83) return to equity of 15.8 percent, versus 11.6 percent for the diversified producers. (Perhaps even more to the point, and in support of the high-value-added, "Specialty people win" idea in general: specialty chemical producers did even better over the five-year period than *computer* makers as a group—15.8 percent versus 15.6 percent.) Among the "diversified producers" there's an interesting parallel. Following the 1973 OPEC energy price increases, Dow Chemical became the darling of the chemical industry analysts. It is primarily in "upstream businesses" (bulk building-block commodity chemicals), and almost immediately passed on the price increases to its customers. Du Pont, by contrast, took a walloping; Du Pont is more heavily concentrated in "downstream" (specialty/higher-value-added) businesses and, of course, had been a long-term winner in specialty chemicals, buttressed by its unparalleled research efforts. Now, ten years later, after the OPEC blip has been pushed thoroughly through everybody's system, Du Pont is once again, relatively speaking, the darling, and Dow, belatedly, is mounting a head-long catch-up effort to move a much larger share of its business downstream.

• In *steel*, the story is repeated. There are no separate "specialty"/ "diverse" categories, but the overall winners by a landslide are Worthington and Nucor—with mini-mills and specialty steels; their equity returns over the last five years are a whopping 27.6 and 23.9 percent (in contrast to a deficit for the industry as a whole). In fact, worldwide, virtually all the winners in the steel industry are in the specialty game. A 1983 trip to Sweden included a visit with Uddeholm's senior officers; they have mounted a substantial turnaround in the last three years, based entirely upon decentralization (increasing independent entrepreneurial units from 5 to 23) and a rapid push toward the specialty/higher-value-added ends of the marketplace.

• In the beleaguered *forest products* industry as well no specialty/diverse categories exist. Nonetheless, the two winners, among the big players,

---

*The findings are especially noteworthy, since they were published at the end of the 1981–83 recession and thus cover performance through the toughest of times.

by a country mile are specialty people: James River Corporation of Virginia, and Fort Howard Paper Co. in Green Bay, Wisconsin. Far above the herd is $2.4 billion James River, with a 26.7 percent equity return over the past five years (well ahead of IBM). The five-year industry average is just 5 percent. According to *Forbes*, the James River routine consists of "buying up numerous small mills that had become unsuited to the great economies of scale of the commodity grades, but were ideally suited to the much smaller markets of the specialty grades." (Among smaller forest products companies, none stands above Boise's $125 million Trus Joist. Driven by product technology, they have done well in even the worst of times. One industry securities analyst notes, "They made seven-figure profits at a time when more commodity-oriented competitors were drowning in a sea of red ink.")

• In the *foods* area, it was noted that brand-name foods were taking more and more shelf space (contradicting the conventional wisdom of a couple of years or so ago that all thinking Americans would soon be buying their staples out of big flour bins). This is entirely consistent with our observations in the industry. Campbell Soup, a high-quality but long-dormant company, is undertaking a major restructuring to radically decentralize and attack more specialty markets. Moreover, the long-term Campbell bias is reflected in the first two of the "six pillars" of the new Campbell corporate philosophy: (1) "We want to be in the quality business, first and only—if we can't produce quality, we get out of the category"; (2) "We want to have high-value products—we're not interested in the commodity business." PepsiCo, McCormick (best known for their spices) and others are doing the same: making small-unit entrepreneurial attacks on niche markets, instead of trading thousandths of share points selling "commodities." In the retail channel, analyses that leader Safeway has done suggest that long-term consumer loyalty is based upon the higher-value-added parts/higher-perceived-quality parts of the store— the produce and meat departments; the huge chain, whose CEO was voted one of the top CEOs of 1983, is now moving to a greater reliance upon branded products. In 1983 Giant Food was, as usual, tops among the forty-five publicly traded grocery companies, with a 23 percent equity return. An analyst comments: "[Chairman] Izzy Cohen sees Giant above all as a service company, which is why he isn't worried about the new warehouse supermarkets as competitors. 'You can't build business on price alone. Price will bring "shoppers" but not "customers,"' he says." (Even in fast food, the trend is toward the higher end. The main chains—Wendy's, et al.—are edging in that direction, and the emerging stars include, for instance, Fuddruckers, which features "gourmet hamburgers.")

• In *retailing* the "specialty" category, with a 17.7 percent equity return over the last five years, commands an edge of 40 percent plus over the "general" category, at 12.5. The big winner is The Limited, with a 33.2 percent equity return over five years. Even the tough shoes category has a real star: entrepreneurial U.S. Shoe, which calls itself "the sports car and convertible end of the shoe business." Among the general retailers, too, "higher value added through service" seems to pay—even in the 1980's. In 1983 the performance of Seattle-based soft-goods retailer Nordstrom led the way by a hefty margin. Nordstrom, with a strategy based clearly on superior service in an age of generally low service, earned a 5.1 percent after-tax return on sales in an $800 million operation. By contrast, the after-tax for the May Company, Federated and Dayton-Hudson was 3.9 percent; Nordstrom tops that by fully 30 percent. *The Wall Street Journal* reports, "Prices tend to be high at Nordstrom, markdowns infrequent. . . . but Nordstrom's has a sales formula: Coddle the customers, big and small."

• Among *airlines*, USAir and Piedmont share the winner's circle with a 20.9 percent equity return from 1978 through 1983 (in an industry in which the median was in the red during that troubled period). The USAir litany: Smaller is better. According to the simple and clear logic of President Edwin Colodny, "For the price of one big plane, we can have three small planes, and three small planes means three market segments." (Likewise in *trucking*, Miami-based Ryder System, now a $2.5 billion company, has responded to deregulation with a raft of high-value-added services. They will manage a customer's truck fleet, provide creative combinations of equipment, drivers [full or part time] and support on multiple dimensions. The result has been exceptional growth, profitability and a 1984 accolade as "Florida's best-run company.")

• And there are a raft of *miscellaneous specialty* companies that are absolute Cadillacs in their industry, and superb performers in general. A few, with their five-year equity returns in parentheses: Deluxe Check (20.9 percent), Snap-On Tools (21.8 percent), Maytag (23.7 percent), Kellogg (27.7 percent). On average the returns on equity of these four companies are 60 percent above their industry's average. Many others, of course, belong in this category, including several privately held firms, such as S. C. Johnson (makers of Johnson Wax, etc.).

Given the beating U.S. industry has taken in everything from cars to microchips—largely, make no mistake, as a result of the relatively poor quality of the American product and unwillingness to listen to the customer (industrial or consumer goods)—it would seem that the point we have been making wouldn't need to be belabored. The revolution now under way in American management involves a renewed focus, in virtually every industry in this country, on quality and quality products aimed at more or less specialized market niches. Gordon McGovern, the Campbell Soup chairman, makes it

abundantly clear: "Above all, we've got to teach our people to focus on quality first, cost second."

## From Chicken to Laundromats

Our favorite support for our emphasis on value added comes from oddball
corners of markets.

There's no better example than Perdue Farms. Frank Perdue has built a
three-quarter-billion-dollar chicken business in Salisbury, Maryland. Margins
are 700 to 800 percent above the industry average, and his market share
doesn't dip below 50 percent in his major markets, which are exceptionally
competitive urban areas, such as New York. He says it's simple: "If you
believe in unlimited quality, and act in all your business dealings with total
integrity, the rest (share, growth, profits) will take care of itself." Perdue,
then, quite simply believes that there's no such thing as a limit to quality—
even in chickens.

Stew Leonard is Perdue's biggest single-store buyer. Stew runs a dairy store
in Norwalk, Connecticut. Selling just a handful of items as compared with
typical grocery stores, Stew grosses $85 million in one location. Average gro-
cery store sales run a bit over $300 per square foot. Stew Leonard cashes in
at about $3,000 a square foot. The trick? He's made it a delight to shop for
chicken, cheese, eggs and muffins. He has a petting zoo for kids; the egg
department features a mechanical chicken, "the world's fastest egg layer." On
one wall there are over five thousand pictures of Stew's customers prominently displaying Stew Leonard's shopping bags. He happens now to have a
picture taken underwater of a customer with a bag on a deep-sea dive,
another of a Leonard regular atop the Great Wall of China and so on. Don't
tell Stew or his customer that food shopping is a bore!

---

*"Talk about Loyalty"*

Sept. 20, 1984

Mr. Stew Leonard
Stew Leonard's Dairy Store
Westport Avenue
Norwalk, CT 06851

Dear Mr. Leonard:

I am a funeral director . . . and am writing to tell you of an event which
happened recently.

An elderly woman passed away and requested that some of her most
cherished, personal belongings be buried inside a Stew Leonard's shop-

> ping bag within her casket. Her relatives stated that your store was her
> favorite shopping place.
>
> Being a patron of Stew Leonard's myself I have noticed the correspon-
> dence from your customers, and felt I should share this story with you.
>
> Sincerely yours,

Out in the West—Park City, Utah—Debbi Fields has a chocolate chip
cookie company, which is taking the country—in fact, the world—by storm.
Her secret? Over 50 percent chocolate content by weight in her cookies. The
profitability? About as high as the chocolate content.

Headquartered in the San Francisco Bay Area is rapidly growing Dreyer's
Grand Ice Cream, an $80 million producer, which, characteristically, buys its
Oreo cookies at retail (the only option) to put in its Oreo-cookie-based ice
cream. Its equity returns stay steady—in the forties.

The J. M. Smucker Co., in Orrville, Ohio, has stayed focused on quality
jams and jellies. They have top share, over 30 percent, and profits to match,
while competing against deep-pocket giants, such as Dart and Kraft.

Houston-based Sysco is a company in an even more mundane business—
wholesaling food to restaurants. Their motto, too, sounds as if it came from
the IBM book: "Don't sell food, sell peace of mind." Frito-Lay finds the dollars (paid back with a return on top) to have 10,000 salespersons servicing
accounts in their presumed low margin business. Sysco, with equivalent
audacity, has 2,000 and calls them "marketing associates"; they assure a service level of 98 percent same-day delivery—previously unheard of in the business. They have, literally, *created* a "new" industry segment: They discovered that a large number of customers, *at the margin,* are indeed service-
sensitive. They are a fast-growing, highly profitable ($2 billion) giant with
equity returns pushing 20 percent in a generally lackluster industry.

The fastest-growing sizable bus company in the nation, Jefferson Lines,
Inc., got that way by putting Pac Man on the buses and dreaming up bus-
plane/round-the-world tour packages. Says the boss, Donald Prins: "If we
could make buses into condominiums and have people live in them, I would
do that tomorrow."

Harry D. Oppenheimer, as reported in the *Wall Street Journal* (May 2,
1984), is the man to call if you want tents. He's a high-value-added specialty
producer who provided a gold lamé tent for King Saud of Saudi Arabia in the
sixties, and under whose tent Pope John Paul II preached in Chicago and
Washington. Says a competitor: "They don't do quick and dirty tents. If
we're all renting tents for fifty cents a square foot, Harry will get a dollar.
He's got a niche."

So, as shown by stars in businesses of every description—from Perdue
Farms to Mrs. Field's Cookies, from Dreyer's Ice Cream to USAir, from
James River of Virginia to Maytag, from The Limited Stores to U.S. Shoe to

Deluxe Checks—there is a sizable market for superior quality, especially quality targeted to a niche. Give the customer something worthwhile and she or he will pay. Mike Kami, an early pioneer of strategic planning at both IBM and Xerox, boils it all down to this: "What is it that makes you distinct and unique?"

As we pointed out above, some of the winners in *In Search of Excellence* were low-cost-at-all-costs producers and had used that strategy effectively. Lowest cost is, after all, a niche of sorts. The worst of all possible worlds is being neither fish nor fowl. A grocery-industry commentator noted at the end of 1983 that "The operators in the middle are extremely vulnerable, stores that have nothing major to distinguish themselves." That was, in fact, at the heart of Sears' problem in the mid-seventies. They gave away their quality-for-a-decent-price image, creating an incredible wedge for K-Mart and Wal-Mart to move in, but only ineffectively maneuvered into the higher end, at least at first. After two or three years of mucking about Sears was not credible at either end of the market, and their unexceptional results for several years reflected the loss of franchise—and uniqueness.

---

### The Floors Sparkle—in the Service Bays

SAS's Managing Director Jan Carlzon led the remarkable turnaround at SAS with this premise: "We don't seek to be one thousand percent better at any one thing. We seek to be one percent better at one thousand things." It's also the formula that has jacked Carl Sewell and Sewell Village Cadillac of Dallas to the top of the heap in customer ratings (of sales performance, service performance, and as a place you'd recommend to friends) among GM's Cadillac dealers. (In gross dollars, Sewell is number three nationally in sales, number one in service revenue.)

It begins with the look. It is thoroughly professional. The lighting on the showroom floor is sedate. A giant fresh-flower display, changed daily, is in the center of the floor. Office lighting is all from tasteful table lamps, and the waiting room is decorated with antiques. (Carl Sewell uses the same interior designer who did Trammell Crow's lavish Loew's Anatole Hotel in Dallas. Moreover, he is consulted on an ongoing basis by Stanley Marcus, the former chairman of Neiman-Marcus.) A room to the side of the showroom adds a special touch. Called the preview room, it's also decorated with antiques, and it's where you start your Sewell Village Cadillac experience: you begin by viewing a video tape that tells you a bit about Cadillac and a lot about the Sewell Village people and their service philosophy. In other words, you are welcomed to your would-be family.

The prospective buyer is virtually forced to visit the service bays. Had that buyer been dropped in from Mars, he or she would be likely to think the place was a Silicon Valley "clean room." It is no exaggeration to say that you could eat off the floors of the Sewell Village shop. Carl's service manager explains that it's not just for the benefit of customers: "If we want our service people to act like the well-trained professionals they are, we must provide professional working conditions."

Detail after detail mounts up. Sewell Village keeps on hand an incredible 150 "loaners" (cars to be loaned to customers who are having theirs repaired) at an annual cost of well over $500,000. Tom's introduction to the place offers another taste of the thousand "little" things that count. Tom arrived there on a chilly morning in November, 1984. All 225 employees had been invited to turn out. At 6:30 A.M., a popular bluegrass band began to play vigorously. At the ceiling of a temporarily cleared-out service area were thousands of balloons restrained by nets. The band stopped at 7:00 A.M., and Tom gave a speech to all hands, including the receptionist, sweeper, president. At the conclusion of the speech the balloons were released from the ceiling, as at a political convention, and it was off to work for everyone. Not exactly a ritual we've observed with any regularity at car dealerships in general! (And lest you think this was a special for Tom's benefit, the 7:00 A.M. "lecture" is a fairly regular occurrence at Sewell. The visitor before Tom had been Stanley Marcus.)

How do winners differentiate? That's how!

Ted Levitt, the dean of marketing thinkers and longtime professor at the Harvard Business School, opens one important chapter in his 1983 book, *The Marketing Imagination*, with the following: "There need be no such thing as a commodity." And, indeed, that's exactly what we observe. A while back we did a hasty, nonsystematic analysis to test this argument near its limit. The word "commodity" had seeped into the personal- and home-computer business by 1983, and what a disaster it was. Even small personal computers don't seem like commodities to us, and customer response to the relatively high-priced personal computers of reliable and service-oriented companies, such as IBM and Apple, suggests that they certainly needn't be. We wanted to make that point to the president of one sizable personal computer company that was about to head down market. He and Tom both had engineering degrees and were not pros in the world of mass marketing.

To test (make, we hoped) our point, we stopped in early 1983 at a local cooperatively owned grocery store in Palo Alto, California, and priced what any fool (any engineer, at least) would believe was clearly a commodity—one-ply toilet paper. The generic type, in a four-roll pack, was going for 79¢ at the time. Then we traveled just two blocks to the nearest 7-11. There we priced Procter & Gamble's Charmin entrant into the one-ply sweepstakes; the tag was fully $1.99. Within two blocks, an "upscale" service-delivery vehicle (7-11) and P&G's long-term devotion to product quality (and squeezability) had added $1.20 (value) to the price of four-roll package of one-ply toilet paper!* Needless to say, the returns to P&G and Southland (owners of 7-11) exceed those to most co-op stores and generic producers by a tidy sum. Value-added can indeed occur anywhere, as Professor Levitt says. (Another illustration comes from one of the fastest-growing businesses in the Midwest: coin-operated laundromats! More often than not, they are the eyesores of the neighborhood. But an enterprising group of high-value-added players has combined a corner laundromat and a *wine bar*. Their logo: "Try our suds while you wash your duds." Game, set, match, to Professor Levitt—and Harry D. Oppenheimer and Frank Perdue.)

We're so strongly in Levitt's corner on this that if we were allowed to be "business czars" for thirty seconds, our first act would be to remove the word "commodity" from the language of commerce. We despise it more than any other word in the business vocabulary.† The problem is that if we label something a "commodity," we often turn it into one. We listen to bankers describing the commercial loan as a commodity, to Big Eight accounting-firm partners calling the audit a commodity. When the label is used, it usually, or often, means that one big step has been taken toward "self-fulfilling prophecy." As a successful forest products wholesaler says, "If you view your product as 'no different from anybody else's' [i.e., as a commodity], then that's what it will somehow turn out to be." Stew Leonard, decidedly, doesn't think he's running "just another dairy store." Levitt, again, is instructive. He admits to an exception to his notion that there's "no such thing as a commodity." "The only exception," he says, "is in the minds of those who express that perception." Amen.

Of course, the closer one gets to the traditional notion of a commodity, the harder one must struggle to create differentiation. Says a DuPont chemical sales manager: "You've got to seek differences—delivery schedule, a snazzier paint job on the gas canisters, anything!" A Pfizer specialty chemical executive sings the same tune: "A lot of people think we're in the bulk chemical business. That's silly. Our objective is to differentiate and head for higher value-added plateaus. We don't want to produce commodities." An ICI (the British-based chemical giant) country boss concurs: "We've got to learn to think about creating differences throughout the distribution process, not about price as the only weapon."

---

### Real Estate, Too!

Trammell Crow has created a vast (and profitable) industrial real estate empire. A lengthy article by Joseph Nocera in the August 1984 issue of *Texas Monthly* chided Crow on the lack of external attractive-

---

*Interestingly, each point of differentiation contributed exactly 50 percent of the variation in price: i.e., the Charmin was tagged at $1.39 in the co-op store; thus 60¢ was added by P&G and 60¢ was added by 7-11.

†"Employee" (as opposed to, say "person") is a close second; see our "People, People, People" section.

ness of some of his buildings. At the heart of Crow's success, however, *is* attractiveness where it counts—the result of effective customer listening and differentiation in another of those mundane businesses—warehousing. *Texas Monthly* goes on: "From the start, elements of Crow's buildings set them apart from his competitors. First, they looked different. Crow intuitively understood that everyone prefers to work in pleasant surroundings, warehousemen included. So he radically reshaped warehouse buildings. Previously, warehouses had been built in long rows, each attached to the next, with loading docks in the front and executives' offices in the rear. Crow built his warehouses independently of each other, so that each stood on its own separate plot of land. Then he moved the unsightly loading docks to the side and put the offices—with windows, no less—in the front. Finally, he spent money on landscaping, which was unheard of at the time. Crow's warehouses were surrounded by trees and flowers and had neatly manicured front lawns. The people who worked in those buildings, unaccustomed to such touches, raved about them. Crow likes to say that one of the keys to his success was that he always followed the dictates of the market 'as we understood it,' and mostly that is true. But with his early warehouses he was doing something more: he was leading people to a market they didn't know existed. . . . Crow could work so fast partly because he refused to get caught up in details he considered unimportant. The exact placement of every window didn't matter, because the market he was trying to satisfy didn't much care where the windows were. But when it came to the inside of the building, to details like rugs and bathroom fixtures that he believed his tenants cared about, he could be quite demanding."

We linger over this point because it's proved to be significant to so many we work with. Several have attempted (with varying degrees of success) to expunge the word "commodity" from their language. Milliken, in textiles, has been a leader in doing so.* Thinking about the word, and then thinking about how we get beyond it in every market, is step one up the long climb to higher margins. And if it can be done in laundromats. . . .

## "Cost-Only" Mind-set

We've probably gotten our just deserts. In the grocery business, many consumers *have* been moved to buy things out of bins. In the clothing business

---

*And has it worked! Their effective quality programs, even in the core of their so-called (previously) commodity grade areas, have time and again led, for instance, to the unprecedented naming of Milliken as a sole source vendor for a product—to such tough customers as GM.

many *have* been buying off the piles in off-price stores. The chairman of the Hartmarx retail stores (formerly Hart, Schaffner & Marx), a profitable 260-store specialty business, provides an interesting hypothesis: "We've gotten exactly what we deserve. We let service deteriorate in our big department stores, and even in our specialty stores. So, naturally, the consumer went to the off-price store. He says, in effect, 'If I'm going to get rotten service, why not get my rotten service in a warehouse and save thirty percent.' That's the way I look at it too. The industry often gave no distinguishing service, and we reaped the reward—fed-up customers and, now, severe competition."

The evidence favoring differentiation and higher-value-added products and service (in any part of a market) is close to overwhelming. So why *did* we fall for the experience curve? Why did we come to act as if we believed that cost (and, derivatively, price) was the only variable we could manipulate? The reasons are doubtless numerous and will never be clear. We suspect, as we indicated in the Introduction, that, in some subtle respect, the relative historical ease with which the United States gained dominant market position worldwide after World War II is one culprit.* Institutions unintentionally took their eye off the service-and-quality ball;† the focus was simply on making a lot for every-hungry markets. And this led to any number of outcomes that added up to losing revenue enhancement as a primary strategy. One was a shift in the sixties and seventies to dominance of the executive suite by financially trained executive-administrators, and the exclusion of the people who were closest to the product (and thus to the importance of quality and service)—manufacturers, designers and salespersons.‡ The same type of people also came to dominate business schools, with the result that much of our current business-school logic is implicitly focused on just one variable: cost reduction. Look at Stanford, with its grand number one rank—in a vote by deans—in 1983. Courses in the accounting area outnumber the offerings in manufacturing and sales *combined* by a ratio of about seven to one! Jan Carlzon of SAS provides a personal view: "I said [in a speech], 'When confronted with any big problem, the businessman must either increase revenue or decrease costs. That's all I learned at school.' In response to my saying that, a former economics professor, who was in the audience, put up his hand and rebutted me: 'Mr. Carlzon, as I suspected, you weren't listening! We only taught you *one* thing at the [Swedish] business school—reduction of costs.'"

---

*The Japanese (and Germans) had no such luck. They were late arrivals to the party, and had to win grudgingly given respect via top quality.

†We are haunted by a discussion with a city manager. He came up after a speech in which Tom had been focusing on "living the quality message." He said, "My dad was the *head* of quality control for [a division in a Big Three car company]. He held the job for twelve years, and was only once visited by the division general manager in all that time." Talk about taking the eye off the ball!

‡A wonderful exception is IBM. It is now, and has always been, dominated by former salesmen—not accountants, not "marketeers" (though they call themselves the latter).

All of this in turn leads to that hard-to-describe but, we think, most important subject: *mind-set*. It's a central factor, squishy as it may appear to be at first glance. The negative results are all unintended: as one chief executive officer noted, "We act as if cost is the only variable available to us. In our hell-bent rush to buy share [via price cutting] to get costs down, we unintentionally give too short shrift to quality and service. So we wake up having, at best, bought great market share, but having, often as not, a marginal or lousy product or service. It's almost always a precarious position that can't be sustained. Somebody's gonna come at you sooner or later. They'll start by clipping away at corners of your market with a little tailoring, and soon they'll have you in full-blown retreat."

Now, this is vital: the experience curve makes exceptional sense *on paper*. Buy share (via one route: cutting price); therefore obtain a low-cost position (by taking advantage of scale economies provided by high share-driven volume); and then fend off the hordes (who won't need much fending off because of the capital required to match the leader's large-scale production facilities). It sounds terrific. *But* mind-set nails us. To gain the share, we discount like crazy in chicken (or watches, calculators and computers—ask an experience-curve-shell-shocked Texas Instruments). And we become "cost freaks," as a friend puts it. We zero in on creating a barrier to competitor entry through more and bigger low-cost production facilities. Controllers are both king and crown prince. Paper-clip counting becomes the most valued (and promotable) skill. Manufacturing and sales types are viewed as crybabies and second-class bumpkins. Service and quality invariably, albeit *unintentionally*, suffer.

"Unintentional" is the key word. No one is for poor quality or service. All wish their people would treat customers with courtesy and would care about making a fine product. But it's jolly tough to get a big business (or a small one, for that matter) to do even one thing right. J. Willard Marriott, Sr., still reading complaint cards after fifty-seven years, *still* doesn't think he's got the service right. So the management that focuses obsessively on cost usually ends up, albeit unintentionally (i.e., through omission—a lack of focus), *not* building a "quality fetish" or a "service fetish." That's the harsh reality of big, dumb companies and, as it turns out, of small ones too—inhabited as they all are by that most intractable of all creatures: people in groups.

PIMS comes at the "mind-set" issue in a slightly different fashion, but it nonetheless speaks to the heart of the conundrum with a strong statement on the cause-and-effect chain that constitutes the most effective path to success. It is in direct and explicit contradiction to conventional experience-curve wisdom.

The experience-curve chain of causality says, in effect: (1) Cut the price so as to (2) buy share. Increased share, in turn, allows you to (3) take advantage of economies of scale and thus (4) reduce costs. You eventually (5) obtain a low-cost position which (6) constitutes an effective barrier to competitor entry. PIMS evidence doesn't refute in any sense the desirability of eventually achieving a low-cost position. (Nobody sensible fights a low-cost position.) But the PIMS paradigm is diametrically opposite to the experience curve *from a cause-and-effect standpoint:* It says, *First* achieve a "relative perceived product-quality" edge over your competitors. If you do so, you will gain share. (I.e., there are only *two* ways to gain share: first, the conventional approach of late—rapidly, via murderous price discounting, if you don't screw up the whole market permanently; and, second, more methodically via better relative quality and service.) By gaining share (via relatively higher perceived product quality) you can, indeed, *then* take advantage of economies of scale as appropriate, and achieve low-cost distinction.*

The difference is radical. By the PIMS logic, you *start* from quality and achieve low cost as a result. According to the traditional experience curve approach, you buy your way in with low prices, achieve low cost, and may or may not have acceptable service and quality. If you don't have them, then you're constantly vulnerable to any higher-quality attacker who comes your way; the edge you scrambled so hard for is not likely to be sustainable. We call the distinction "earning your way in" (via quality and service) versus "buying your way in" (via heavy discounting). Only the former, it would appear, is sustainable.

We still think of P&G as prototypical in this regard. Often their dominant position allows for maximum-scale economies (and attendant low cost), yet that position is *always* achieved through "earn in" from higher quality. David Ogilvy, in his marvelous *Ogilvy on Advertising*, argues against competing with P&G. Why? Because of their cost position? Big ad budget? No. The would-be competitor's problem, he says, is that "they [P&G] make better-quality products." Hear, hear!

The cost-only mind-set also seems to lead to an unintentional denigration of innovation. There's something about overly formalized systems, systems run by accountants, that are simply inconsistent with a sea of skunkworks or the highly decentralized environment of Hewlett-Packard, Johnson & Johnson or 3M. We believe, for instance, that the excessive focus on the experience curve (and on the disciplines necessary to exploit it) at Texas Instruments, both in the consumer electronics business and in the "commodity" merchant chip business, led *directly* to the loss of the commanding innovative edge TI once enjoyed. (See the chapter 11, "The Context of Innovation," for more on this theme.)

Another, related mind-set problem is that we tend to get conned by the goings-on in the bottom 10 percent of the marketplace, where, indeed, there *is* usually a ready consumer for generic toilet paper, flour out of a bin, or dirt-

---

*All this, we must urgently add, ignores a point that we've made persistently: these economies of scale at the end of the rainbow add up to *the* most overrated variable in the economist's variable chest. Paper economies are seldom realized in the harsh, cold real world. Smaller, more highly focused and motivated units outperform the larger time and again, in any industry you might choose to review. (Even the popular press is finally picking this up. A major *Business Week* article in October 1984 focused on "Small is beautiful in the factory.")

cheap (albeit often unreliable) home computers. There is a "commodity buyer," a person who will buy on the basis of price no matter what, a person who is willing to (or by poverty forced to) settle for close to junk, as long as it's cheaper. It may be 2 percent of the market, or it may be closer to 20. But whenever such a buyer becomes active—in the purchase of toilet paper, groceries, menswear, audits, computers—it seems to drive salespersons, in particular, crazy. They assume that the whole game is lost, the whole market is going to the dogs. Many believe (who among us who've sold for a living doesn't at some level?) that this activity proves that there really is only one variable—price. They don't remember the seemingly effortless wins, garnered on the basis of numerous tiny service edges or as a product of a carefully nurtured continuing customer relationship; all that's recalled is a recent dramatic loss because of a bid a nickel too high. There is often overconcern, then, about the need to "shore up the fences" at the bottom. Whatever the reason, it leads many companies at some point to go after the true bottom end. And then we sadly note yet another self-fulfilling prophecy grabbing hold. Our simple observation is that no company—even one that operates through disparate, highly autonomous divisions or groups—can maintain a "quality and service fetish" (of the P&G/Maytag/Marriott sort) in one part of the company and make marginal stuff in another.* The reduced-quality-and-service focus in a given area tends to seep through the company as a whole. A senior brand manager from an old-line European package-goods company once regaled us for an hour with tales of the pernicious side effects of his company's decision to make just a few private-label products, which were not quite up to the business's long-term quality standards. "Somehow," he said, "a lax attitude toward quality began to infect the rest of the company." Ken Melrose, dynamic young chairman of Toro (the lawn-mower people) tells a similar but even more dramatic tale. "When we'd run [in the factory] the other [private-label product], an odd thing would happen. Long after the run, our branded Toro line would be affected. Errors would go way up. We couldn't figure out why to save ourselves." Toro finally decided to get out of the private-label business as a result of the intractable problem. Is there anything to this "mind-set" stuff? Ask Ken Melrose.

Yet another aspect of the experience-curve mind-set is our preoccupation with size and centralization, which is abetted by the dominance of financial officers who focus on paper studies of investments rather than on people. The

---

*Which is not to say that a company can't cover a fairly wide range of a market. For years General Motors went from Chevy to Cadillac; even the low end, though, was a fine car, not at the very bottom of the total automobile market by a long shot. The issue is much more serious and subtle than the little we've said suggests. We've had many vociferous debates about "How far down is too far?" The consensus is, to oversimplify, that there is a "too far," that it's probably not quite as far down as you think, and that no amount of organizational and managerial separation will protect your "Maytag/Perdue Farms end" from way down, bottom-end, marginal quality/service pollution.

United States in the past opted for the biggest plants—in automobiles, in steel, in forest products. Yet the evidence is clear. Top quality—and, ironically, lower cost, as it often turns out—tend to come from smaller units.* So we now see a headlong plunge by automobile companies, as well as the steel makers with their mini-mills and the forest-products vendors, toward the smaller productive unit. It's always been a way of life for Emerson, Dana, 3M, Hewlett-Packard, Milliken.

The truth of the matter is that the analytic models we use are simply not neutral. Analysis always comes down on the side of the big unit and cost control. But as Charles Tandy (founder of Tandy Corp.—Radio Shack, et al.) says, "You can't sell from an empty wagon." Wally Kalina, former chief operating officer at Mervyn's, adds, "Turnover ratios win trophies. Revenue leads to profits." And Bill Andres, recently retired chairman of Dayton-Hudson, notes that if you let the accountants, with their (always) more systematic analyses, win the day, "You'll end up with zero inventory—and, unfortunately, zero revenue." A longtime Macy's follower suggests that their good fortune stems from the same solution: "Overstocking is one of the major reasons for Macy's success."

George Gilder in *Wealth and Poverty* argues that you have no choice but to proceed on "faith" with the new. 3M officers agree. J&J says big productivity gains come, first and foremost, from building small, charged-up decentralized units. Brunswick and Campbell Soup are forgoing a stodgy past to try the 3M/J&J formula, and are loving the early results. The analytic, pro-centralization, economies-of-scale models are not neutral; their result is an excessive focus on cost that seldom fails to generate a reply of no to innovative proposals.

The experience-curve notion is a terrific one—looked at after the fact, and on paper. Even in reality, there's no doubt that market dominance combined with lowest industry cost is nice if you can achieve it. But quality is the driver; it must come first. You simply make the very best product or provide the best service you can in any category you wish to attack. That, in turn, far more often than not, is what wins customers by the bushel—which in turn allows you to reap whatever benefits there may be in economies of scale.

---

### A Few Questions— and Things to Do Now

. Conduct a casual or systematic analysis of your own industry. Who have been the winners over the long haul? Have "low end" people, though darlings for a while from time to time (and usually a different darling each time),

---

*See the powerful discussion of the focused factory in Steve Wheelright and Bob Hayes's 1984 *Restoring Our Competitive Edge: Competing Through Manufacturing*.

become long-term winners? (Consider inviting the Strategic Planning Institute—PIMS—people in for a seminar.)

• Do you call any products or services "commodities"? Take two or three closest to that categorization. Look in every corner—factory quality to delivery to follow-up—for differentiation factors and uniqueness. Study the market leaders in detail. This is obviously a major effort, but well worth it. Involve people from all functions; have each conduct detailed customer visits and competitor assessments. (This is vital. Each area provides numerous potential sources of differentiation. True—and sustainable—differentiation seldom comes from a single or a few big-bang advantages. It's always—witness Marriott, Disney, IBM—from a thousand things, each done a little better; that's why it's ultimately so hard to beat.) Think about starting with a detailed study of Levitt's The Marketing Imagination, Chapters 4, 5 and 6: "Differentiation—of Anything," "Marketing Intangible Products and Product Intangibles" and "Relationship Management."

• Do you accept commodity-ish/"no different from" language? (Remember our forest-products friends: "If you don't think it's any better, then it won't be.") Do your people, in any function, accept it? Do people on the line—back-room operations, factory, distribution center—accept it?

• Remember Gordon McGovern of Campbell Soup: "We've got to teach quality first, cost second." A colleague did a survey of a growth company recently. The leaders all knew that their success had come from superior quality. Yet the message had been taken for granted of late (the leaders erroneously assumed that "of course everyone knows quality comes first"). The survey revealed that most, down the line, thought that, at the margin, "ship the product to make monthly numbers" was more important than "unwavering adherence to quality standards." How about you? What really comes first, where and when it counts—on the loading docks on the very last day of the quarter? How do you know? How often do you test your knowledge? (E.g., IBM samples its first-line people quarterly to see if they think IBM is living up to its superior-service promise.)

• How wide a range of products do you offer? Is there evidence that your lowest-end offerings interfere with higher-end quality standards? (Is there any hard, longtime evidence that more than 5 to 10 percent of any part of the market will go to low-low-end players? If the answer is yes, try again. We are skeptical.)

---

### "Marketing" According to an Iconoclastic Master

Ted Levitt is dean of the marketers, sitting in a senior position on the Harvard Business School faculty. His 1983 book, The Marketing Imagination, rings bell after bell:

All energies should be directed toward satisfying the consumer, no matter what. . . . The purpose of business is to get and keep a customer, or, to use Peter Drucker's more demanding construction, to *create* and keep a customer. . . . To do that, you have to do those things that will make people *want* to do business with you. All other truths on this subject are merely derivative.

Cyrus McCormick pioneered the whole idea [of adding service] putting demonstration salesmen to work on wheat farms and providing repairmen in the field. Du Pont pioneered with applications specialists in the textile and garment industry. In all these cases, the "product" that was offered by the "salesman" consisted less of what was manufactured in the factory than of what was provided by way of practical help and advice in the field. "Service" was the product and still today in many situations it remains more *the* product than meets the eye. Customers don't buy things, they buy tools to solve problems.

There is no such thing as a commodity. All goods and services can be differentiated. Though the usual presumption is that this is more true of consumer goods than of industrial goods and services, the opposite is the actual fact. . . . Though it is true that on the commodities exchanges, dealers in metals, grains, pork-bellies and the like trade on totally undifferentiated generic products, what they "sell" is the claimed distinction of their execution—how well they make transactions on behalf of their clients, how responsive they are to inquiries, the clarity and quickness of their confirmations and so on. In short, the "offered" product is differentiated, though the "generic" product is identical. . . . The usual presumption about so-called undifferentiated commodities is that they are exceedingly price-sensitive. A fractionally lower price gets the business. That's seldom true except in the imaginary world of economics textbooks. In the actual world of real markets, nothing is exempt from other considerations. Even when price competition is virulent. The fact that price differences are, prima facie, measurable becomes the usual, and usually false, basis for asserting their powerful primacy.

A product is, to the potential buyer, a complex cluster of value satisfactions. The generic "thing" or "essence" is not itself the product. It is merely, as in poker, the table stake, the minimum necessary at the outset to allow its producer into the game. But it's only a "chance," only a right to enter play. Once entry is actually obtained, the outcome depends on a great many other things.

It is precisely when the buyer has become less dependent on the technical help or brand support of the originating buyer, that greater attention may be beneficially focused on a systematic program of finding customer-benefiting and therefore customer-keeping augmentations. It is also a time when increasing efforts should be focused on possible price and cost reductions. Thus arises the irony of product maturity: Precisely when price competition gets more severe and therefore price reduction becomes more important is when one is also likely to benefit [the most] by incurring the *additional costs* of special new product augmentation.

Though a customer may "buy" a product whose generic tangibility (like the computer or the steam plant) is as palpable as the primeval rocks, and though he may have agreed after great study and extensive negotiation to a cost that runs into millions of dollars, the process of getting it built on time, installed, and then smoothly operational involves an awful lot more than the generic tangible product itself. What's more crucially at stake are usually a lot of complex, slippery, and difficult intangibles that can make or break the "product's" success. . . . So it makes sense to say that all products are in some crucial respect intangible. . . . Even tangible, testable, feelable, smellable products are, before they are bought, largely promises. . . . The more complex the system, and the more "software" it requires (such as its operating procedures and protocols, its management routines, its service components) and the longer it takes to implement the system, the greater the customer's anxieties and expectations. *Expectations are what people buy, not things.* [Our emphasis.]

The sale merely consummates the courtship, then the marriage begins. How good the marriage is depends on how well the relationship is managed by the seller. . . . The natural tendency of relationships, whether in marriage or in business, is entropy—the erosion or deterioration of sensitivity and attentiveness. . . . A healthy relationship requires a conscious and constant flight against the forces of entropy.

# 6

# "Mere Perception": On the Irreducible Humanness of Customers

WE SPENT FOUR long days with the thirty top managers of a $1.5 billion capital-goods manufacturer. We scrutinized sales problems, marketing problems, manufacturing problems, people problems. When it came time to summarize, six were thought to merit top-level follow-up. However, in five of the six it was noted that persistently the approach was: "We're OK. It's only a perception problem." Finally, Tom had had enough. Stepping far beyond the bounds of what's good and proper for a visitor, he virtually shouted, "A perception problem is an engineer's way of saying, 'We've got the right solution, if it weren't for the damned people who invariably get in the way of implementation.'"

A "mere" perception problem. The real problem is that *perception is all there is*. There is no reality as such. There is only perceived reality, the way each of us chooses to perceive a communication, the value of a service, the value of a particular product feature, the quality of a product. The real *is* what we perceive. As the First Commandment of the formal, written Customer Philosophy at a successful forest-products retailer says: "Feelings are facts." Or, in the words of Rothchild Venture's Arch McGill (formerly the youngest vice president in IBM's history): "The individual [customer] perceives service in his or her own terms." (We always add to McGill's line: " . . . in his or her own *unique, idiosyncratic, human, emotional, end-of-the-day, irrational, erratic terms.*")

## Perception Kills

Ignaz Semmelweis, the father of modern surgical sterilization techniques, committed suicide. Why?

In 1848 Semmelweis, working in a clinic, came up with a simple technique: having a physician wash his hands in a chlorine solution prior to delivery of a baby. It reduced, immediately, the maternal mortality rate in the clinic from 18 percent to 1 percent! Twelve years later, in 1860, in the same clinic, 35 out of 101 mothers died. What happened? Why didn't it take? Semmelweis was perceived as a flake, a disrupter, someone who had extreme political views; he and his unassailable results weren't heeded. Physicians didn't take him seriously, so nobody listened. In June 1865 Semmelweis, in despair, was duped into entering a mental sanatorium, where he killed himself two weeks later. It was another two decades before Lister and Pasteur came along. They apparently wore the equivalent of three-piece suits and otherwise fit the current establishment's mold: they were listened to. Their sterilization techniques were adopted rapidly, and remarkable improvements occurred. The credit and the fame accrued to them. The Semmelweis tragedy is the result of the erroneous "mere perception" of a human being by other human beings. The fact that the field was hard science and that one out of three mothers needlessly died for decades longer than necessary as a result of "mere perception" is simply an indication of its power.

## Computer Customers Are Human, Too

At a seminar for executives of companies that make scientific instruments, the wife of the president of one company (she is fully involved in its operations) related this tale. A friend of hers was about to buy a washing machine; she recommended that her friend buy Brand X. The reason was simple: in her long experience with Brand X machines, she had never had a problem. Her friend, also part of a die-hard engineer/"rational" family, said unequivocally, "No." She was going to buy GE, as she had always done. "Why?" "Well," said the friend, "when they've broken down in the past, GE repair people have arrived immediately." The recommender of Brand X replied, "Yes, but mine has never broken down!" Her friend's last word (after all, she was the buyer): "I don't care. It might."

The above could be written off as "housewives" arguing over washing machines. However, a conversation we overheard on the subject of a principal competitor (call it "B") of IBM offers an almost word-for-word parallel. The product was multimillion-dollar systems, and all the people involved were senior technology types. An executive of a third company, Company A, was talking about Company B: "The people at B have really gone overboard on this self-diagnostic stuff. It's efficient, but all human contact is lost. We're not going that route. We're going to show the flag." We reflected on our experience in chatting with IBM customers (versus all other customers). We know both IBM and "Company B" quite well. Company B, according to hard-nosed, third-party measures, has better service ratings in several categories than IBM, but it has a less than sparkling service reputation (a reputation, in particular, for arrogance), while IBM's reputation, of course, is great. Why is this so? The answer lies in Company B's highly articulated process for responding to customer problems. People stored away in little cubbyholes, hundreds of miles from the scene, follow a precise manual and escalate their response according to the manual's definition of the customer's need. The only problem is, they never *tell* that customer just how hard they're working for him or ask him if the response meets *his* definition of the need. As we've gotten to know IBM even better in the years since the research for *In Search for Excellence* began, we've become more impressed by their difference in this dimension. They must have a giant stash of little brass bands. When they begin the fix, they tell you. They call you ("The service truck is heading down the driveway right now"). The branch manager takes you to lunch to remind you what they did for you (and how fast they did it). A 3M executive who used to run 3M-Italy describes an IBM "overresponse" to a minor problem. A banker in Minneapolis does the same. A financial-services executive in Columbus, Ohio, tells a similar tale. Yet another service industry executive laments his inability to toss out IBM. "Sometimes they're damned overbearing," he says. "But then my guys say, 'Yeah, but you can count on them.'" In every instance the customer responds to the "humanness" of IBM's response. IBM people, en masse, show up—quickly and with banners unfurled. Telephone calls are immediately made by IBMers to senior people. Often, because of the technical realities, these calls will result in no enhanced practical outcome. But they do show that live bodies at IBM are tracking the difficulty and paying close attention. In fact, many people point out that IBM uses these problem situations as selling opportunities; IBM suggests (seldom without warrant) that the problem may have come about because the wrong machine was being applied to a new or modified application.

---

### Call Him at Home

The tradition of "overresponse" has deep historical roots at IBM. Tom Watson, Jr., speaks of it in *A Business and Its Beliefs*: "In time, good service became almost a reflex in IBM, and Father loved to show what the company could do. In 1942, an official of the War Production Board gave him a perfect excuse to do it. The WPB man called him late on the afternoon of Good Friday to place an order for 150 machines, challenging him to deliver the equipment by the following Monday in Washington, D.C. Father said he would have the machines there on time. On Saturday morning, he and his staff phoned IBM offices all over the country and instructed them to get some 150 machines on the road that Easter weekend. Just to make sure his caller got the point, Father instructed his staff to wire the WPB man at his office or home the minute each truck started on its way to Washington, giving the time of departure and expected time of arrival. He made arrangements with police and Army officials to escort the trucks, which were to be driven around the clock. Customer engineers were brought in and a miniature factory set up in Georgetown to handle the reception and installation of the equipment. There were a lot of sleepless people at IBM—and the WPB—that weekend."

Watson goes on, underscoring the importance of the story: "These are not small things. The relationship between the man and the cus-

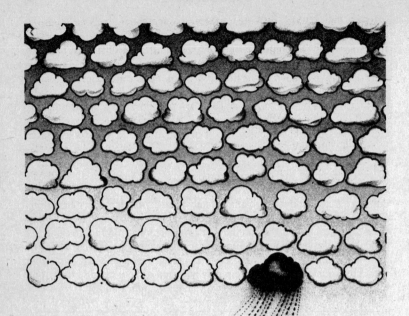

## If your failure rate is one in a million, what do you tell that one customer?

Millions of parts go into the machines we build every year. At IBM, we work hard to make sure that everything we make is defect-free, from the smallest circuit to the finished product.

But if an IBM computer or office system ever needs service, we provide our customers with an experienced and widely skilled service organization.

IBM customer service people are on call every day of the year for large companies that have many of our machines and small businesses that may have only one.

Our service people can call on computerized data banks where solutions to thousands of hardware and software problems are stored and instantly available to them.

They also work directly with IBM engineers at our laboratories to help design products that need less service and are easier to maintain.

It's all part of our commitment to deliver fast and reliable service to every customer, every time.

Because when it comes to service, we treat every customer as if he or she is one in a million. **IBM**

> tomer, their mutual trust, the importance of reputation, the idea of put-
> ting the customer first—always—all these things, if carried out with real
> conviction by a company, can make a good deal of difference in its
> destiny."

So everything IBM does is "wrong": they don't use the most efficient techniques, they try to sell you more in response to a problem. Yet it works out
beautifully. IBM is paying attention—palpable, human attention. And what
is the number one "demographic attribute" of the customers system's buyer?
You got it in one. He or she is a human!

Humanness. Let's look at another variation. There is a classic tale from the
annals of marketing. A fine company introduced a cake mix that worked like
a charm: Pour the mix into the pan, add water, stick it in the oven and, voilà,
a beautiful cake! It bombed in the stores. The reason? The cake-making had
been taken out of cake-making. So the product was reintroduced. It was pur-
posely made complicated: now the user had to add an egg (i.e., participate in
the cake-making). The reintroduced product took off like a jackrabbit. Ah ha,
you say again: the housewife phenomenon. Yes, but. But a major software
company, selling IBM compatible software at the highest systems level, also
just reintroduced a major product. The problem? The first version of the
product had been "too good." The new launch was titled, "A Step Back into
the Future." Here's the issue: The first version was so good that the ultimate
users (in, say, the customer's manufacturing operation) could develop their
programs with virtually no assistance from the customer's MIS people. The
MIS bunch, who controlled (and bought!) the software, said, in effect, "No
way." They didn't like (or buy) the product. The reintroduction essentially
took a step back from the state of the art and complicated the product on
purpose, so that there would still be a major consultant's role for the friendly
people in the customer's MIS department. Now all is well. The product's
relaunch is exceeding plan.*

---

### No Plastic Wrappers, Please!

Stew Leonard, Jr., of Stew Leonard's, describes an apropos experience, which surfaced at one of Leonard's many customer-focus group
meetings, as shown in Sam Tyler and John Nathan's 1985 PBS film, *In
Search of Excellence:* "One of the ladies stood up and she said, 'I'll tell
you what I don't like.' She said, 'I don't like your fish,' and we said,
'What do you mean, you don't like our fish?' She said, 'Well, it's not
fresh. I like to go to a fish market and buy fresh fish.' The fish guy was
there, and he stood up and said, 'What do you mean it's not fresh? We

---

*And then there are the tough-minded engineers who can't see the need to peddle
game software for their personal computers. After all, real men don't eat quiche.

get it fresh every morning from Fulton Fish Market, and we get it fresh from the Boston piers every morning.' He said, 'I guarantee you it's fresh!' She said, 'But it's packaged. It's in a [plastic wrapped] supermarket package.' So what we did was to set up a fish bar with ice in it. And we did that right after that meeting. Now there's wrapped fish in one place, but some people like to buy it fresh right off the ice, so it's available across the aisle at the same price off the ice. Our packaged fish sales didn't decrease at all, but we doubled our total fish sales. We were doing about fifteen thousand pounds a week; now we're doing thirty thousand pounds a week."

---

### "Computer Customers":
### Some Questions—and Things to Do Now

• Look at two or three new products or services that recently failed or required an inordinate amount of time to get established/take off. Assess the ways in which they were used by early/trial adopters, the classes of customers who used them first. How (in detail) did actual use vary from that projected by marketers/designers/focus groups/market research? How did you go wrong on attractive features/properties, usability/reliability, etc. (in the customer's eyes)? How could these surprises have been prevented? Did you track early use in enough detail to pick up such issues right away? If so, did you move fast to react?

• Take two or three mature or main-line products/services. Do you really know why people repeat purchase (is it the quality of your service à la GE, or something else)? What is the basis/frequency for monitoring your organization's characteristics as *perceived* by those who deal with you?

• What role do you perceive service to play in the sale of two or three major products? How do you *know* that your perceptions match the customer's perceptions (i.e., are you doing regular *in-depth* debriefs with major customers at all levels in the user organization—e.g., purchaser, accountant, ultimate user such as first-line person in the factory, intermediate user)?

• To what extent does response to problems feature in your thinking? What does response mean? How/how rapidly do you personalize it? Does the customer know how hard you are working for him/her (via what mechanisms, how assiduously practiced)?

---

### Unfair!

Ah yes, it is an unfair world in which we ply our trades. Don Burr, chairman of People Express, agrees. He notes, "Coffee stains on the flip-down trays [in the airplane] mean [to the passengers] that we do our engine maintenance wrong." How right he is! In fact, we've often argued that the only real distinction of IBM, McDonald's, Disney, Frito-Lay and Marriott is that they are the world's greatest wipers-up of coffee stains; they will not allow you to see a coffee stain and because of it make unfair assertions about the engine maintenance.

Most of our engineer (banker, accountant, manufacturer, designer, whatever) friends unfailingly make some variation on the following response when confronted with Don Burr's statement: "Oh, what a world, in which we must sell our wonderful, marvelously designed, beautifully crafted products and services to *unappreciative people*." Another—equally plausible—response would be to say, "Wow! What an opportunity!" For the upside of the perception issue is as high as the downside is low. Our colleague Jack Zenger addresses Don Burr's comments about coffee stains: "I've been skiing for over four decades. I've probably been in every resort worth the name in the world. At just one, in the Sierra in California, there's a Kleenex dispenser at the head of the lift line, right before you hop on the chair lift. You can grab a Kleenex and wipe your goggles on your way up the slope." He pauses. "I just can't tell you how many of even my sophisticated friends refer to the place as the 'Kleenex-box resort.'" It's really a superb metaphor. Virtually all business people agree that the be-all and the end-all of business (or ballet or baseball) is repeat business—which only comes as a result of long-term customer satisfaction. *And what's the secret to long-term customer satisfaction? From fast food outfits to department stores; from tentmakers to mainframe computer manufacturers and Boeing's 767, it's the customer's cumulative memory of a long string of "Kleenex-box experiences."* Contrariwise, customer satisfaction soon becomes nil after an all too short string of negative "coffee-stain experiences."

The president of a large technical company, another rational man (with fifteen years of background at IBM), recently ranted and raved in our presence about General Motors. He'd gotten into a Cadillac limousine on a business trip, and forty-five minutes later, emerging from the car, had ripped a finger on a protruding piece of metal near the door. "Damn it," he shrieked, "can't those bastards in Detroit do anything right?" It's not fair: Maybe he would have ripped his hand on a Japanese or German car door, too. But the problem is, he (we) has come to expect tiny problems in large numbers from GM/American cars.

It's not fair. And yet it *is* fair, because *whatever* a customer feels is, by definition, fair. The customer alone pays the freight (or doesn't) for whatever reason or collection of reasons he or she chooses. Period. No debate. No contest.

Here's another story we've become particularly fond of—a "Kleenex" story with a vengeance. Major corporate turnarounds are few and far between. A remarkable one is surely that at Scandanavian Air System (SAS), which was accomplished in just three years, and in the midst of the 1981–83 recession-depression. How was it done? SAS's managing director, Jan Carlzon, focused attention not on buying new $35 million aircraft but on the "mundane" (read "cost-effective") items that would vault SAS into the number one position as the European businessman's preferred airline. He painted the planes, spruced up the interiors, intensified the customer-service training of personnel, bought more de-icing trucks to put the on-time departure rate at the top of the heap. Carlzon describes his view this way: "SAS has ten million passengers a year. The average passenger comes in contact with five SAS employees. Therefore, SAS is the product of the ten million times the five. SAS is fifty million 'moments of truth' per year. Fifty million, unique, never-to-be-repeated opportunities to distinguish ourselves, in a memorable fashion, from each and every one of our competitors. My job is simply to manage the dickens out of the fifty million moments of truth!" He adds, "SAS is the contact of one person in the market [customer] and one person at SAS. *That* is SAS."

## Impersonalness: The Ultimate
## (Perceived) Discourtesy

We chided a bunch of Pacific Telephone senior managers a while ago. In California (alone, we understand) when you dialed information (411), you'd get a whiny (could be that it only comes across as whiny) canned message: "You *really* can save money on your phone bill if you'll just look it up. . . . " After the message, the information operator invariably answered on the first ring. We said to the telephone folks, "Look, you probably spend billions of dollars to get 'first-ring answering.' But it's all down the drain, because we're so darned annoyed by that dinky little message that we ignore all your technological wizardry and go away mad."

It makes a human being happy to hear the live voice of another human being. That's why we love the Delta Airlines people—the people who point. They may not be any more efficient than a taped message or CRT display, but they're alive. A Pacific Gas & Electric experience provides corroborating evidence. In the midst of storms that knocked out electric service throughout Northern California in 1982, PG&E used to have a taped message that described what was going on in the system—where the repairmen were, estimated time to repair and so on. It was changed regularly, and was in fact quite up-to-date. Complaints, however, were frequent. Then the company changed the routine. A live human being started answering the phone. In reality, the live human being was not as up-to-date and had less specific information than the regularly adjusted taped message. But PG&E got rave notices! People need other people, especially in the midst of uncertainty. It's the difference between calling to get the weather report every day (here the taped message is expected and therefore OK) and trying to get information in an emergency.

American Airlines president Bob Crandall is emphatic on the subject. There had been many complaints about American's response to lost baggage. It turned out that if it wasn't working hours in the locale where a bag was lost, the aggrieved party, upon dialing the lost-baggage number, was confronted with a taped message asking that he or she call back the next morning. So Crandall arranged to have any phone call to the lost-baggage number from any location at any hour answered by a live service rep at a center manned around the clock. The reality was that the live person didn't know any more than the taped message did, and also in effect told the bereft passenger to call back in the morning. But the *real* reality (reality as perceived by the customer) was the sympathetic response that the living person provided—a degree of comfort no tape machine could match.

## Long Memories

Oh, the length of the trail we leave behind! Is the memory trail one of Kleenex boxes? Or of coffee stains? Or of but a single coffee stain, *long, long* ago? After a presentation a while back at which Tom had gone through his analysis, a solid candidate for "prototypical rational man" came up to him. He is the senior officer in research and development at the $6 billion pharmaceutical company, Johnson & Johnson, and he had an example of his own to contribute to the discussion. A dozen years before, he had bought an analytic instrument from a fine company. A couple of months after buying it he had a problem with a $2.95 component. The company's response? "First, they mustered their top engineers to try and prove that it was my fault, and that I abused the part and busted it. They were unconscionably tardy in answering my correspondence. They were actually rude over the phone on more than one occasion. Today, fully a dozen years later, I still tell my people, 'Don't you buy equipment from those guys.' Now, I *know* it is not rational, that it is emotional, but it is *life*." Ah, yes. The little memories—the "mere perceptions"—that pollute forever!*

And of course the flip (positive) side is available for (active) examination. Among a hundred or so presentations during the last eighteen months before trade associations or user groups, in which Tom has been joined by officers of various companies as co-presenters, on only four occasions has a company officer begun his or her speech as follows: "Thank you. I want to thank those of you in the audience who are our customers. We sincerely hope that we will continue to deserve your business in the future." Is it only a coincidence that all four executives were from the IBM company, that IBM thought to say those two lovely words, "Thank you"? More: IBM opened a users' meeting Tom attended in Vancouver, B.C., in typical IBM fashion—with a film clip. About 110 companies were represented in the 500-person audience. The film clip consisted of footage shot at the headquarters location of *each* of the

---

*A Maryland utility executive laments that many of his industry's problems in Congress were caused by Montana Senator Lee Metcalf, who was still angry because his mother's service was cut off in mid-winter in 1913!

customers, with the company's logo prominently displayed. "Mere fluff?" One big technology company vice president says so: "Tom, that's just pat-on-the-back marketing!" Our response: "Yeah. Forty-seven billion pats a year called revenue dollars, seven billion of them after taxes. We'll take it." Memories are made of such stuff.

### And How Long Will This Be Remembered?

During our 1984 visit to Ireland an executive passed this on:

**HARRODS LIMITED**

**Knightsbridge   London   SW1X 7XL**

Telephone 01-730 1234   Telex 24319   Fax 01-581 0470
Registered Office 87/135 Brompton Road, London SW1X 7XL
Registered in London No 30209

Mr P J Dineen                                              19.8.80
EIRE

Dear Sir,

We are always seeking to improve upon the despatch of goods by sea and air freight, although standard freight rates leave very little margin for competitive charges. Often freight rates are increased without warning, and this leads to a loss.

On occasion we are able to bulk shipments or obtain a concessionary commodity rate, and, should a saving occur we believe our customers should benefit. I am very glad to be able to enclose a cheque for £217.00 which constitutes the total saving made on a recent shipment, and I hope that we may have a further opportunity to serve you very soon.


Yours sincerely


I G Drummond
Manager
Shipping Office

---

## "Unfair!:
## Some Questions—and Things to Do Now

• Look at your own buying habits at home with respect to, say, an airline, a department store, a plumber. Look at your purchasing habits in your corporate life with respect to a few key suppliers. Sit around as a group and try to figure out why—over the long haul—you sustain a relationship. Likewise rerun three or four home/corporate relationships that you have severed. What are the *perceptual* attributes of your decision to buy/sustain/leave? (Specifically take *one* long "best" relationship, and list a minimum of twenty to thirty attributes of dealing with the supplier that are attractive. Do the same for *one* recently severed relationship. Now, switch the game: On the dimensions/traits that surfaced in the above, how do you rate as a supplier? For a sample of products/services, what are the top ten "coffee stain" irritants you regularly subject your customers to? The top twenty "Kleenex boxes" you provide? Are you actively in search of "Kleenex boxes" to add? "Coffee stains" to clean up? How do you measure yourself/keep up with the above? Especially perceived deterioration? (P.S.: How well did you do in answering the question? Did you have a firm enough grasp of the data to do so?)

• *Stop!* Commit *ten full days* in the next two months to checking out your "coffee stain"-"Kleenex box" image. Pick *four major customers* and spend one full day with each—in a remote location for at least two of the four. Pick *eight* minor customers and spend one-quarter day with each. Spend one day with *three recently lost accounts*, another day with *three accounts recently gained from a competitor*. Spend the remaining two full days with a group of colleagues from *all* functions, *all* levels (about ten to fifteen people); invite two longtime customers to attend. What is the "coffee stain"-"Kleenex box" story that emerges? How surprised are you?

• Track a routine customer transaction with you, cradle to grave. How many "moments of truth" are involved? Make sure to cover all functions—PBX room, reception, manufacturing, contracts, accounting, delivery, follow-up. Are you actively managing your "moments of truth," especially relative to the "nonmajor" (i.e., nonselling) functions?

• Do a "mere fluff" (small signs of courtesy) check. What do you, and your function/company, call customers? Do you have a term? Do you "police" your language? Do you talk about customers regularly in your communications? What is your "Thank you" quotient? Your "logos/pictures" quotient (i.e., to what degree—very specifically—do you go out of your way to personalize the trappings of your customer contacts)? Review customer/user meetings. Are they first rate, the very best in the industry show (especially relative to the "mere fluff")? What is the very best user meeting you've ever been to as a customer? What are the twenty-five "little things" you find most attractive? Can you/do you replicate all of them for your company?

Note: All of the above will be hard slogging. Increasing your awareness of the "Kleenex box"–"coffee stain" attributes of a series of transactions is not easy. Keep at it, keep digging. When it looks as if you bought something for "price alone," try again, especially hard. You probably disqualified ten to twenty potential suppliers for "coffee stain" reasons before you reached the list of the last three.

---

## Complaints CAN Be Golden

Joe Girard, the premier car salesman, appeared in *In Search of Excellence.* For ten years in a row he sold over twice as many cars as the number two dealer in the world. He said the key was that he *cared.* Fine. Then Joe stretched it just a bit too far: "I want to sell you a lemon. Then I'll show you just how well I'll perform for you with the service department." We laughed when a seminar participant pointed out that line in a Girard article, a line that we'd missed, frankly. And, then, upon some further reflection, we quit laughing. We thought back to the last ten (senior corporate) slavish IBM devotees we'd chatted with. Surprisingly, not one had very much nice to say about IBM. They pointed out, instead, problems! *But,* they always added that whenever a problem had arisen, fifteen IBM people—eleven of them by parachute—had descended on them within three hours. And they always got the machine up just as the first streak of dawn was about to mark the sky. IBM doesn't want to sell you a lemon, for sure, but if they do, they make darned sure you know that they are very, very sorry.

---

*And Watson's Assistant Was Already There*

We talked to a Hewlett-Packard executive who spent over a dozen years at IBM. He regaled us with story after story. For instance, there was the time when a Union Carbide machine crashed and Mr. Watson, Jr., was going to call on the president of Union Carbide at 8:00 A.M. the following Monday morning for a report on it. Our friend recalls the bus ride at midnight with twenty-two colleagues, heading for the trouble spot, deep in the West Virginia hills. They drove for three hours in blinding rain, snaking through the mountains, in order to arrive at the Union Carbide site in time to get the machine up before Mr. Watson made his in-person call. When they arrived at 4:00 A.M., Mr. Watson's executive assistant was miraculously waiting there to greet them. Where had he come from? How did he get there? Heaven only knows. (Levitation?) But he did. It's the IBM way.

All of the above has led us to broader speculation, to the supposition that there are two kinds of companies. The first, the most typical, views the complaint as a disease to be got over, with memory of the pain rapidly suppressed. The second, exemplified by IBM, views the complaint as a luscious, *golden opportunity*. As the president of IBM's Entry Systems Division (maker of the PC), Don Estridge, says: "A live customer on the line. Wow! What an opportunity! What an opportunity to turn him, and make him into a lifelong friend." He adds, "It's the ones who *don't* call that worry me."

The logic behind the IBM view of the "joy of complaints" (live customers on the line) is evident in the words of one retail executive: "For every complaint you get, remember, fifty people walk. They don't even bother to tell you they're mad." We've heard the numbers 10, 25, 50 or 150 in this regard. We suspect it varies by industry, though it doesn't really matter. Whether 10 or 2,000 "walk" before picking up the phone, complaints are clearly important. And we are astonished, as are all the business people that we chat with, at just what a *small* world it is. Joe Girard (our car-salesman friend) made the point that each angry person has 250 friends, 100 will hear from him about the rotten experience he had with you. And 50 percent of them, in turn, will tell their 150 friends. A Digital Equipment service executive adds: "There's no such thing as a *small* customer. The least of customers, especially angry customers—and it almost seems inevitable—*always* lives next door to the chairman of the company you've been trying unsuccessfully to sell to for the last fifteen years."

Yet another issue when it comes to complaints is the blithe assessment, "This one is an anomaly." True, at some level each complaint is unique. On the other hand, in our experience in working with companies on this issue and in running our own small business, there is no such thing as a unique complaint. If you get a complaint about a lack of phone courtesy that you can readily explain away as having been caused by a "uniquely busy day," the odds are very high (about 99$\frac{44}{100}$ percent) that there are a lot of "uniquely busy days," and that the apparently anomalous complaint is but the tip of an iceberg. Technically (the engineer's/financial person's pristine logic again) each one *is* different; in reality a "pattern of one" invariably turns out to be, sad to say, just that—a pattern.

The availability of information about complaints is vital as well. How easy do you make it for the customer to complain? How rapidly is the whole system made aware of complaints? L. L. Bean, the superb Maine sporting-goods store, updates its product-by-product complaint/problem file *daily* and makes the output available to all hands. People on Nissan's production line in Smyrna, Tennessee, have displays at each workstation, updated regularly, of customer and dealer comments. Caterpillar Tractor and Deere ceaselessly *beg* customers to complain, and then pass on the information about problems with lightning speed. Most, however, make it bureaucratically tough or socially awkward to complain, and they do little with the information once received, on the indefensible basis that it's "too sensitive [i.e., useful to competitors] for widespread dissemination."

There is a last, ought-to-be-obvious point to be made on this subject. If you decide to handle complaints by, say, installing a toll-free 800 "hot line" complaint number, then you'd damn well better follow through, with near perfection! One fellow described an atrocious event to us. Had we not known him fairly well, we wouldn't have believed it. An $800 million high-technology company installed an 800 hot line for customer complaints. But then, our friend says, "They changed the 800 number every three months. That way you'd have to call information and get the 303 area code number. Then you'd have to pay for the subsequent call." In many instances we've come across, people who have installed an 800 number have not realized the substantial degree of training that is necessary for truly effective responses. Milliken & Co. is developing a Milliken Customer College. A principal reason is to train the people who deal with 800 number call-ins and the like on how to respond to customers. The hot line is a magnificent idea, and today's (let alone tomorrow's) telecommunications technology makes it easy to have one—and almost irresponsible not to have one.

We observe time and again that even after a big foul-up you can turn that foul-up into something positive; the disgruntled customer can become a top customer and better friend than ever just by your calling back and saying you're sorry. Astonishingly enough, that's usually all you need to set yourself far apart from (ahead of) the pack.* It's a constant source of amazement to

---

*While making revisions on this manuscript, Tom was on a flight from Dallas to Detroit. At 11:37 P.M. the plane arrived in Detroit. An overzealous pilot took a corner too sharply. The plane ran off the runway by a couple of feet; it got stuck because of a recent glut of rain. Bad enough. But to make a bad situation worse, the passengers were left on board for thirty-five minutes (until after midnight) while efforts were made to blast the plane's way out, thereby using up all the fuel, and the passengers were cast into darkness. Then the bus shortage hit. The airline rounded up one van with an eight-person capacity and proceeded to unload a full plane, one row at a time, for more than two hours. Meanwhile, never *once* in the three hours did the pilot emerge from his cocoon, in person or via the PA system, to say the two

us: Simple common courtesy, such as a personal call after a foul-up, makes you special. It shouldn't (it should be boringly commonplace), but it does.

---

### Have You Gotten Our Letter Yet?

A colleague, Pat Townsend, reports an example of Perdue Farms' response to a customer (remember, this is a three-quarter-*billion*-dollar company): "A friend of mine mentioned last week that he once bought a Perdue chicken that, he discovered after getting home, was all dry and nasty. He took it back to the store and got an immediate refund. Then he decided to write Frank—having seen him on TV—and tell him that he had bought one of his damn quality chickens and it was all dry and nasty. By return mail he got a letter from Frank that not only included profuse apologies and a certificate for a free chicken but also enlisted his help to make sure it never happened again by asking a whole list of specific questions: Where did he buy it? When? Exactly what was wrong? What did he think had happened? What *exactly* did the store say when he returned it? Etc., etc. Two days later an executive of Perdue Chickens *called* to make sure he'd gotten the letter, to make sure that all was well, and to ask some more specific questions. My friend will never buy anything but Perdue Chicken."

---

### "Golden Complaints":
### Some Questions—and Things to Do Now

• Pick three customers you lost after a botched transaction (or series of transactions). Spend time with them on the phone, or, if possible, interview them. To what degree did the loss come from the foul-up per se versus the post-foul-up response to the problem?

• What is your *exact* method of responding to a complaint? Is it formalized? If so, is there exact adherence to the procedure? How soon and under what circumstances do senior people get involved? How is your personal concern

---

simple words, "I'm sorry." (The story presents a golden opportunity to emphasize a point we made before. When we talk of "superior customer service," we don't mean expensive frills à la Regency Air; we *do* mean the apparently all but lost art of saying "I'm sorry.")

A recent seminar participant recounted an episode in stark contrast to the story above. She had lost some luggage needed for a meeting, instantly. Instant retrieval wasn't physically possible, but she was treated with such courtesy and concern by the airline that she wrote the president a positive letter about the whole event. Thus there was a foul-up and, further, even the thoughtful response failed to result in a fix; nonetheless, the outcome was a big net plus for the company and the customer.

transmitted? How do you handle, if at all, postresponse follow-up ("How'd we do?")?

• How easy is it to get in touch with you/your company about a complaint? Do you make it a lead-pipe cinch: big posters with the 800 call-in number very easy to see and with fill-in complaint cards; random sampling of customers 30, 60 and 120 days after a big sale to see "how we're going," spot calls after a sale to check on same, spot calls/visits to nonmain functions in the customers operation (how do the first-line operators in the factory like the printout format on the new analytic instrument, was the patient's billing handled well?). Do these samples include seeking out complaints from big, good customers: "I know you haven't called, but we just modified our billing procedure, and I wanted to check." "We just issued a new manual for the 4261xx; how do your operators like it?"

• How is your response to complaints perceived? Spend a fair amount of time on this. IBM, for instance, unabashedly does 10 to 100 things to generate the perception of "overkill." Can you say the same? Sample ten complaints. Within how many hours/days did you promise a fix? How many times did you beat the deadline? Does the customer know it? (I.e., did you tell him? How many times, and how, in the process of the fix, did you get in touch to say, "We're working on it," or "We just got X done"?)

• Sample 20 complaints from small customers. Do your small accounts get the same level of perceived service as the large? If so, is it by conscious choice?

• If you sell various levels of service packages, do you have a "low end," which, in retrospect, ensures that certain customers—albeit as a result of their own characteristics—will be underserviced (and therefore angry, their "fault" or not)?

• Do you have an 800 call-in number? If not, why? If so, (a) is it widely publicized? (b) is it more than adequately manned? (c) are the people involved "overtrained"?

• What do you do with complaint information? Are copies of complaint letters, 800 call-in transcripts, etc., circulated to all levels? Is the nature of complaints instantly tallied and summarized (the L. L. Bean approach)? Do you do multifunction, multilevel post hoc analysis of complaints. If so, how regularly?

• How many new products/services or extensions thereof can you attribute directly to follow-up on a single complaint? Or as a response to a pattern of complaints? If the number is small, why? Are there mechanisms for turning the complaint/complaint pattern directly into a new or modified product/service?

• Specifically, take the last five complaints you've been involved with. Have you rationalized any of them as attributable to "special circumstances" (e.g., "a 36-day month"), or have you treated the solo complaint as a likely "pattern"?

• Are you a *fanatic* about this subject? Is anybody in the industry/segment better? If so, is it an advantage for them?

---

## Do You Measure Satisfaction?

A final issue related to customer perception came to a head in the midst of a four-day seminar with forty company presidents (members of the Young Presidents Organization). We had spent fully a day and a half on the subject of customer perceptions of service and quality. At the end, we evaluated the importance of these ideas, even formalized it with a ballot. Forty out of forty agreed that long-term, total customer satisfaction (and repeat business) was clearly priority number one, the be-all and end-all for any organization in fields ranging from wholesale forest products to fast food franchises, from the manufacture of computer hardware and software to thread making. Then we returned to a discussion we'd had of the IBM measurement process. A large share of IBM's marketing force (all varieties: service, reception, sales, marketing staff) and many nonmarketing people are *directly* evaluated (compensation, bonus, promotion, annual performance review) on the basis of hard-nosed, quantitative, external/third party and in-house developed measures of customer satisfaction. (*Not* market share or other surrogate indicators, but "straight satisfaction.") We stuck the two ideas together—hard-nosed measurement and the unparalleled importance of the issue. We then asked the obvious question: "How many of you measure *any* of your people directly on a third-party or impartial, quantitative in-house measure of long-term total customer satisfaction?" The answer? Zero. Thus, forty out of forty say the issue is far and away the most important; yet none of the forty does anything about it.* We suspect it has a lot to do with the idea of "mere perception."

Fred Cox, chairman of the highly successful Emulex Corporation in Southern California, a computer components maker, spoke to the same issue in early 1984 in addressing technology executives: "We all know and agree that customer satisfaction is the prime reason for being in our businesses. But look at the measures I ran across. I just discovered one called 'return on net capital employed.' Now, what the hell does that mean? I've never seen *any* strategy, *any* plan, *any* annual report that includes a *direct* measure of customer satisfaction. Why?" Why, indeed? We don't happen to be quite the enemy that Fred is of return on net capital employed, but we surely agree otherwise with his comment.

---

*The day after we wrote the initial draft of this section we tried again, this time only with an audience of 132 (94 of them presidents of small or medium-sized companies). The results? Ditto—all 132 rated long-term customer satisfaction tops in importance; none measured it for purposes of compensation and evaluation.

## Did Anything Bug You?

Domino's Pizza Distribution Company, the dough makers and equipment suppliers for Domino's Pizza's over 1,200 franchises, *do* measure service systematically—and *weekly*, to boot—in their Ideal Service Survey. They make an extensive phone survey of their customers to ask them how the service and product quality were. The survey not only covers quantitative/technical issues—e.g., response time—but also qualitative ones; "Did *anything* we do bug you?" Monthly evaluation and compensation for all hands (up through the president!) are predicated on the results, which are instantly summarized and made available to everyone; in fact, they are publicly and prominently posted in *all* facilities. President Don Vlcek explains the logic behind the survey: "We believe customer satisfaction is an advance indicator of swings in market share. Why wait for the P&L's?"

### Domino's System

Many can see the usefulness of measuring customer satisfaction. However, most in our experience have difficulty taking the next step and tying it to compensation and evaluation. Domino's Pizza Distribution president, Don Vlcek, provided us with a description of the process he uses; read it in the context of an extensive weekly survey system, in which quantitative satisfaction scores are developed on numerous parameters from the lumpiness of the dough to pepperoni freshness to whether the driver closed the franchisee's freezer door at the conclusion of the delivery. Here's Don:

> *Tying the survey results into the TIPO (Team/Individual Performance Objectives) system:* The purpose of the TIPO system is to try to make the monthly bonus be in direct relation to people's and team's performance for that given period. Other purposes are to help the team and people know their priorities and their expected level of performance, which ranges from "crisis level" to "exceptional level." The process is: First, Key [satisfaction] Indicators are developed for each unit and each specific job and are stated in quantifiable terms. Then points are distributed amongst the key indicators in a manner showing how much priority each key indicator has at the present time. The expected level of performance is then determined. If that level is attained, the Team Member receives 80% of the points in that category. Also figured are the level of crisis performance, which would allow the Team Member to receive [a maximum of] 20% of the points available in that category, and the level of exceptional performance, which would result in 100% of all points in that category.

A score of 100 on the national [survey] would set aside 4% of profits for a given period, which goes into a pool to be disbursed amongst Team Members. In that way, a month of high profits in which we have fallen off in customer service might result in having lower bonuses even though the company is making more money; or the reverse. This determination of the pool is done strictly on the performance of the entire team (all divisions of the company).

Individual performance is determined the same way. Every individual has a set of key indicators developed with his or her Team Leader. Their score determines the percent of available bonus they actually receive.

Some jobs are hard to quantify, but not impossible. It must be done to ensure everyone knows his or her priorities, expected level of performance, and how it will be determined. For example, the accounting department exists to perform services for others. We've developed a "rating" system where the users of these services grade them on a scale of 10 and comment. No grades can be given without comment. I've noticed this is a great method to motivate peers to get together to coordinate rather than asking their leader for help. Delegation by osmosis!

The expected performance for the Ideal Service Survey is reviewed every six months and set slightly above the average for the last six months. This tends to motivate people to be slightly better every six months. We set the crisis performance at the lowest score received during the last six months, and the exceptional performance at the highest score during the last six months.

Measuring satisfaction is nifty. As you can tell, we are fans of it. But we don't mean to scare you off by our enthusiasm for such highly articulated arrangements. After a talk at a late 1984 seminar, the president of one small company said, "Look, I attended a seminar of yours a year back. After that I forced myself to adopt the simple habit of calling, religiously, three or four customers a week to ask, 'How are we doing for you?' The result has been nearly revolutionary. They tell me, in no uncertain terms, exactly how we're doing. And then I do something about it." We agree with all but one aspect of his "simple habit." It sounds deceptively simple and therefore commonplace, but he's oh so rare!

---

### "Measurement":
### Some Questions—and Things to Do Now

• Do you regularly and extensively measure customer satisfaction? by internal surveys? by third-party surveys (e.g., mystery shoppers, regular externally administered surveys)? by third-party or in-house hard measures (e.g., comparative response times—(yours vs. those of competitors)? by in-depth customer debriefings (e.g., a two-day, three-person team *not* directly associated with the account doing top-to-bottom, multifunction interviews, partly structured, partly open-ended)?

• Do you widely *publicize* satisfaction measures (e.g., in company magazines, on bulletin boards, in annual reports)? Do you set objectives based upon them? Do you *directly* base any part of compensation/evaluation/promotion on them? Do you celebrate satisfaction-measure successes?

• Does *every* department or function have "customer satisfaction" measures? (E.g., do the accountants survey their users/"customers" on various aspects of satisfaction?) Note: Developing the notion of "customer" is hard work for internal groups, but it can be done and is worth the struggle.

• Do you have any "simple" rituals, like our colleague's weekly calls to ask "How are *we* doing for you?"

• *Backtrack a moment:* Are you sure you know what customer satisfaction is for *you*? Look ahead to the story of Todd Fraser on p. 96. He wasted two years by first designing *their* (his customers') satisfaction in *his* terms; then he belatedly asked, and got it right!

Note: The process of developing measures that are appropriate and stable is not easy. Try various measures in various locations; experiment for sixty days. Update, revise and hone. It will probably take a year before you are comfortable enough with the nature/validity of a measure to start using it to affect evaluations/compensation.

---

## But You Can't Give Away the Store

Perception is all there is. That's no surprise. All business, from potato chips to washing machines to jet engines, is about people selling to people, whether it's a 17¢ transaction or a $10 million one.* There is only the cumulative memory, the pattern, the perceived consistency, the perceived level of concern and care and attention and responsiveness.

Seems obvious, doesn't it? But, oh, the rejoinders we get! One important part of total customer satisfaction, we argue, is adapting the service or product to a specific customer's needs. And the wolves howl. They say, "Yes, that's exactly what *all* salesmen want. Redo the product to meet *each* custom-

---

*The latter figure is not chosen lightly. GE just won at least that much business in aircraft engines away from Pratt & Whitney. P&W, most say, had the technology edge. GE won on service warranties and spares policy, and because of P&W's hardheadedness (i.e., rudeness and arrogance, it's said, in prior dealings with the Air Force).

er's need. We'd have a jillion products—and a totally confusing product line and a wildly noncompetitive cost base." That's not the point at all! Take a $2 million project. Paint the box brown to meet the customer's needs. You win. The situation is so bad (or, conversely, the opportunity so good!) that a *tiny* step in the direction of responsiveness sets you *way* ahead of the pack.

Once we got a question concerning our negative comments about over-doing self-diagnostics in the analytic-instruments world. A company president said, "You mean we shouldn't use self-diagnostics? We shouldn't allow our customers to plug into a modem and diagnose their own problem?" Before we could respond, the president of another (highly successful) company leaped in: "No, that's *not* what they mean at all. The point is the need for human, eyeball-to-eyeball contact—somehow. Maybe not at that time. But you've gotta be in touch. You've gotta press the flesh. You've gotta show the flag. Somehow. Self-diagnostics are fine. But being out of touch is bad news." We couldn't thank him enough. Our sentiments exactly.

---

### "Give Away":
### Some Questions—and Things to Do Now

• Do discussions of service endlessly bog down in cost-of-service issues? Take three or four recent major sales or extensions of contracts. To what extent did you modify product/service traits to meet the customer's perceived needs? Did it take a lot to give the impression of flexibility? Take three or four lost sales: Did you fail to be perceived as flexible in any instance? Could you have gone one-quarter step and have been perceived as forthcoming?

• Take one or two particularly pleasing or displeasing experiences with suppliers from whom you buy (or your experience as a consumer, e.g., dealings with a phone company, washing machine purchase and installation). What sorts of flexibility/tailoring-of-package have impressed you? What sorts of inflexibility have irritated you? In the "good news" cases, has the tailoring been expensive to the vendor? Have you paid a premium for the flexibility?

• In pursuit of automation (e.g., of distribution, service), has the human touch been degraded? If so, what countermeasures are you taking, if any, to keep the human/personal link in transactions? regularly or on a planned but irregular basis? Are any competitors doing it better? What devices are they using?

---

### Learn to Love your Salesperson
### Even If It Hurts

The perception issue. It goes so deep. Feelings are facts. Arch McGill is clear on another point: "Marketing is an *art*," the art of selling the benefits of your product and, by contrast, making it clear that your benefits are more relevant than the competitor's. The heart of marketing is not computer-based segmentation. Much as we seem to have ignored it in the last twenty-five years, the heart of marketing is selling. Selling is a fine thing! We love salespersons! We continue to believe that a good candidate for the single most significant strength of the all-powerful IBM Company is the fact that it has *always* been run by former *salesmen*.* Salespeople are *people* talking to other *people*. They are people who, in our experience, always live with the certain knowledge—call it terror—that they are going to lose *every* customer between now and tomorrow morning; thus, they take a very different view from ordinary folk of "mere perception" problems.

An interesting discussion with a Citicorp vice chairman and McGill led us to think about the issue of people selling to people. We said we wondered why salesmen have always been so denigrated. (In Tom's old consulting firm, McKinsey, about the worst thing that could ever be said about a consultant was, "He's a bit of a salesman"—it was said about Tom once). The Citicorp vice chairman agreed that "selling" was looked down upon in his world (at least prior to deregulation). But selling, of course, is where the perception issue really comes to the fore.

---

### The Branch Manager as King

IBM, much as we love and respect it, is a pretty darn bureaucratic company, truth be known. And on many dimensions it's quite centralized, at least within the context of a typical several-billion-dollar division. Yet its customer responsiveness—with nearly four hundred thousand on the payroll—is legendary. How do they do it? At the heart is the autonomy of the (sales) branch manager. It is, simply, his or her responsibility to make things happen for the customer, and break whatever china (i.e., rules) it is necessary to break in the process. There will be no recriminations for a branch manager who moves heaven and earth, and steps on countless toes in the process, to get the customers satisfied.

But heaven help that branch manager who says, "I could've done it, *but* . . . " And heaven help the field service manager or other support person who says of the branch manager, "I would've helped him or her, *but* . . . " Neither is long for IBM's world.

IBM is a bureaucracy, to be sure, but there is a pecking order. And the branch manager, responsible for customer satisfaction, is indisputably at the top of it.

---

Selling—and advertising. Many are as contemptuous of most advertising as they are of salesmen. Many consider it to be "mere fluff"! Most of our

*IBM is alone in this regard among major participants in its industry.

technical (and banking, etc.) friends hate it. (Actually they resent the *need* for it. "It should be obvious to any fool that the benefits of this management service [of ours] are overwhelming," is the sentiment just a millimeter below the surface.) They look at it not with thinly disguised contempt but with wholesale contempt. And yet, *is* there a product whose benefit is known before it's been broadly and effectively communicated (i.e., effectively advertised)? Clearly not.

Let's look at it another way. Whether one is a staunch, left-of-center Democrat or far-right-of-center Republican, it would be hard not to agree that President Reagan has done a masterly job of selling his programs and philosophy to America. A *New York Times Magazine* cover story (October 14, 1984) went a long way toward explaining it. It said that Reagan spent "merely" 20 percent of his time formulating programs, and 80 percent "communicating" and—horror of horrors—"selling" them. Communicating, implementing, selling—the bases for changing and establishing perceptions (positive or negative)—are the heart of all dealings with customers (constituents, patients, students). Mr. Reagan simply happens to be the first person in the Oval Office in a while who understands that. Superior leadership, make no bones about it, is pure selling, selling in the best sense of the word—i.e., establishing the *perception*, the feeling, the picture, that your view is right, that you listen, hear and understand, that you are worth listening to and following (or buying from).

Furthermore, the *only* great product, by definition, is one that sells (just as it's mandatory to win the election if one is to be considered a candidate for "great president" or "great alderman"). Seldom if ever—and despite, again, the protestations of our technocrat (banker, accountant, etc.) friends—does a product "sell itself" on the basis of its "clear technical merits." The history of innovation is particularly supportive of this point. Many a company has gone down the drain because it has consistently been too far ahead of its time. Varian Associates, the early pioneer in electronics, had, prior to 1983, a dozen bad years. In a speech to security analysts, a Varian executive blamed the largest share of the company's troubles on the fact that Varian engineers have traditionally been about a decade *ahead* of their customers. Mr. Birdseye invented the flash-freezing process in 1912; it didn't garner a profit until 1952. It took fully *forty* years to change the eating habits and food-buying and distribution habits of the nation to prepare us for the benefits of (and need for) flash-frozen products. A product sells only when it fits all elements of the customer's "real time" (i.e., today's) need and context.

---

### "Love Your Salesperson":
### Some Questions—and Things to Do Now

• Do you honor your salespeople (beyond compensation and the annual-awards gala)? Talk to a friend at Tupperware, or Mary Kay Cosmetics, or The Limited or IBM. Review, *in detail*, the nature and frequency of salesperson celebration. How do you stack up?

• What's the *language* surrounding salespeople? Are they seen as second-class citizens? Is "mere salesmanship" the implicit message? Are former salespeople represented to a substantial degree in the ranks of top management? Do all would-be kings or queens do a two-year stint (or more) in sales on the way up? Do top managers still sell (e.g., take a regular turn on the retail floor, do store calls, have assigned accounts)?

• What is the role of advertising? Is it seen as a necessary evil or is it exploited to the hilt? Is "overspending" to support the winner brands/services/products the norm? Do you outspend, per sales dollar, the industry/your three top competitors? If not, why not?

• Do you *ceaselessly* work on the simple message of product benefits? (David Ogilvy explains, and our experience strongly supports his, that most ads simply fail to communicate—or sometimes even mention—the top one or two [at most] major benefits.) Does every form of communication reflect this? Do any competitors do it more clearly? If so, how? Are benefits in tune with— i.e., not *too* far ahead of—the customer's perceived needs?

---

## Emotion and Feel: Being Human

It's all about being human. The irritation of a tiny incident of rudeness colors dealings a dozen years later. A simple and genuine "I'm sorry" can make up for a massive (and expensive) technical error.

And it's also about managing by wandering around—MBWA, as we've said before. Yet we shouldn't need to do MBWA, should we? With computer printouts generated in seconds by $250 machines, staying in touch *should* be a simple matter of reading, via electronic spreadsheet, the outcomes of attitude surveys and summaries of market research data. (With two touches of the finger to the HP-150's screen you can instantly turn spreadsheet output into a seven-color pie chart!) And yet we go wrong time and again because we do rely on the numbers and printouts and transparencies alone, and lose our "feel." The only way to enhance feel is to be there. Feel may not constitute statistically significant data by University of Chicago Ph.D. board standards, but what can match the human being in operating in the visual, tactile spheres?

Procter & Gamble exemplifies sophistication in analysis of market data. Yet the biggest payoff from the toll-free "complaint" number the company has placed on all its packages probably did not come from the brand managers' analyses of the phoned-in comments themselves. It probably came when senior vice presidents agreed that they themselves would listen in on the line at least three hours a week. "I can't tell you exactly what I do differently as a result of answering the phone," says one, "but I can tell you that no decision is made quite the same way." Similarly, the deputy director of health in Pennsylvania sent all those who reported directly to her out of the office to work four hours a week in a local service bureau. This is pointedly not a "show the flag" visit by a senior officer; rather, the director insists that each of her people sit on the other side of the glass window and process would-be service recipients, answering complaints and dealing with the same forms that her first-line people have to deal with. "We can sit here talking about too much bureaucracy, too many complex forms, until the cows come home," she notes. "But until you've really been there, regularly, really seen how ridiculous it is to collect this kind of data or that, seen how you're wholly unable to answer the simplest questions because of the bureaucratic procedures that must be followed in order to answer them, until you've done that, until you've felt the frustration, you haven't really begun to get a feel for the situation."

"Mere perception." "Mere communication." "Mere listening." Or should we say, "merely human"? In Chapter 2 we discussed Milliken & Company's development of a revolutionary approach in dealing with its customers: a vast number of commonsense efforts aimed at "getting close to the customer" are being tested and refined. None of their programs is very exotic. Yet a senior—twenty years plus—Du Pont marketing executive, who was a guest at the annual top-management retreat in February 1984 when Milliken people presented those programs, got up spontaneously and said, "In all my years in so-called marketing jobs, I've never seen the likes of this." And all of it is just good common sense. Each device simply *humanizes* the relationship between the seller and the customer.

---

### What Is a Customer?

A Customer is the most important person ever in this office . . . in person or by mail.

A Customer is not dependent on us . . . we are dependent on him.

A Customer is not an interruption of our work . . . he is the purpose of it. We are not doing a favor by serving him . . . he is doing us a favor by giving us the opportunity to do so.

A Customer is not someone to argue or match wits with. Nobody ever won an argument with a Customer.

A Customer is a person who brings us his wants. It is our job to handle them profitably to him and to ourselves.

(A poster that is prominently displayed all around L. L. Bean, in Freeport, Maine)

---

In a perfect world, where robots would make the product and sell the product via computer network to other robots in the purchasing organization, none of this would be important. But we're a long way from that. In fact, we'll never reach it. Because any organization, the $45 billion IBM company or Stew Leonard's incredibly successful single store, is purely human, too. The perceptions of human beings are all there is. Let's come to grips with this—it's the essence of managing and marketing. And leading.

---

### Glad He Asked!

Todd Fraser [not his real name] is in a mundane business: plumbing supplies. He has about forty locations in the Southwest. In the last couple of years he's added 50 percent to his revenues, in a no-growth market, and is able to charge premium prices—1 percent to 2 percent above his competitors, a remarkable edge in a very low margin game. How has he done it?

Several years ago Todd was determined to become the "best service company" in his business. To figure out what that meant, he asked his forty branch managers—a sensible enough idea, or so it seemed at the time. They told him: Offer more brand-name products, spruce up the looks of the branches, hire a higher-caliber (and more experienced) salesman, answer the phones more efficiently—*and lower the prices*. It sounded good. Todd did it all. And then waited. And waited. Nothing happened.

A couple of years later his frustration reached the boiling point. Then he got an idea that he now says is "so obvious it's impossible for me to think that I hadn't done it before," and proceeded to carry it out with all his energy. He simply visited his customers and asked them what they wanted, what was bugging them. He patiently devoted a full year to carefully visiting the "bad" as well as the "good" customers of every single branch.

Turns out the branch managers had been out of touch. Some had, literally, he found, not visited a single customer on the customer's own premises in up to five years! Here's what Todd heard: Price was *not* it. Even answering the phones was not it. The problem for the plumbers was the cost of the labor they wasted waiting for an order from Todd (or one of his competitors) to arrive. So Todd promised one-hour service, where the local industry standard was (then) one-half day. He promised a 90 percent "fulfillment factor" (i.e., he guaranteed that 90 percent of the parts ordered would be available instantly), where the standard was 75 percent, and that the remaining 10 percent would be delivered within a day—also far better than his competitors' average. (This last is key: a plumber might be held up several days, while paying his laborers, because of the absence of one little 75-degree bend in an otherwise complete 175-item order.) He promised a maximum wait of fifteen minutes for service fulfillment if the plumber came to the branch. Giant fifteen-minute timers were installed in every branch; if more than fifteen minutes elapsed, the order was filled free of charge. In sum: time is money for the plumber, who turns out not to be all that part-price-sensitive, after all.

The results are history. Todd Fraser did his customers the rare courtesy of "naïvely" asking them what they wanted. And they told him. And then he did something about it. His business was truly revolutionized as a result. Says Todd of the process: "'Best service' doesn't mean a darned thing. It's best service *in the customer's terms* that counts. And I don't know for the life of me why it took so long to figure that out."

# 7

# Quality Is Not
# a Technique

*There is a central quality which is the root criterion of life and spirit in a man, a town, a building, or a wilderness. This quality is objective and precise, but it cannot be named.*
　　　　—Christopher Alexander, The Timeless Way of Building

*I was brought up by a father who was difficult to satisfy because he always felt something could be made or done better. He was never content with success. . . . It does take eyeball. I'm afraid as great as computers are, they cannot tell you about the quality of your product. The profitability, yes, but not the quality. The human eye, the human experience, is the one thing that can make quality better—or poorer.*
　　　　—Stanley Marcus, former chairman, Neiman-Marcus

WE SOMETIMES THINK that the average American manager, post *Theory Z* and Phil Crosby's *Quality Is Free*, has a slot directly behind his or her right ear, and in it is a 3½-inch floppy diskette. Say the word "quality," and the manager, seemingly by rote, spits out: "Quality circles, statistical quality control, CAD/CAM/CAE, robotics . . . " And, yes, quality circles can be grand. Statistical quality control is invaluable. Automation is essential. Yet none of the three or a vast array of earlier devices—e.g., job enrichment—is what quality is all about.

This is a short chapter—perhaps surprisingly so. But in fact this entire book is about quality. Because quality, above all, is about *care, people, passion, consistency, eyeball contact* and *gut reaction*. Quality is not a technique, no matter how good.

Any device to maintain quality can be of value. But all devices are valuable only if managers—at *all* levels—are living the quality message, paying attention to quality, spending time on it as evidenced by their calendars. And if managers, at all levels, understand that no matter where the technology leads, quality comes from people (starting in the mail room) who care and are committed. Finally, quality comes from the belief that *anything* can be made better, that beauty is universally achievable—in the collection of garbage, in the services provided by Federal Express or UPS, in the raising of chickens and the making of potato chips, pizzas or French fries, in the design of a retail store or a piece of software or the bypass air intake mechanism of a jet engine. Quality involves living the message of the possibility of perfection and infinite improvement, living it day in and day out, decade by decade.

Ray Kroc once visited a Winnepeg franchise. It's reported that he found a single fly. The franchisee lost his McDonald's franchise two weeks later.

Frank Perdue invested a quarter of a million dollars in "the world's biggest blow dryer, powered by a 727 engine." The reason? Frank thinks the most obnoxious thing in the world is the eight hairs that stick up on a typical chicken wing when it is barbecued. With his new blow dryer, he is able to fluff up the hairs and burn most of them off before the chicken is delivered to the stores. But he is not finished. The new technique on average reduces the eight hairs to two. Frank doesn't think it is enough.

Williams-Sonoma is a very successful gourmet-cookware distributor. Its major business comes via catalog. Bringing in the world's best photographers to take the pictures, Williams-Sonoma puts exceptional efforts into development of the catalog. In 1983 the cover for the Christmas edition was to feature a piece of quiche in a new piece of cookware that Williams-Sonoma had imported. The shot cost tens of thousands of dollars and took a full day. Late in the evening, founder Chuck Williams came upon the scene, then being dismantled. He picked up a fork that was lying about and sampled the quiche that had been featured. The taste wasn't quite right. Without so much as a twinge, he threw out the photography. It wouldn't have occurred to him to have a Williams-Sonoma catalog cover featuring a piece of quiche that didn't *taste* right.

Story after story—from IBM, Hewlett-Packard, the Marriott Corporation, Disney, Mayor Schaefer of Baltimore, Milliken & Co., Stew Leonard's, Trammell Crow, Domino's Pizza, L. L. Bean, Delta Airlines, et al.—has the same theme as that from McDonald's, Perdue Farms and Williams-Sonoma: senior and middle managers alike who live the quality message with passion, persistence and, above all, consistency. Attention to quality can become the organization's mind-set only if *all* of its managers—indeed, all of its people—live it.

Living it means just that. You can't pay attention to it 80 percent of the time or even 95 percent of the time and let it lapse now and then. The only thing that will do is obsession. Tom Watson of IBM understood the connectedness of it all. One of the three principles in IBM's philosophy is excellence in execution in *all* we do. On paper, perhaps, inconsistencies can thrive. But not in sizable human organizations. You can't allow typos in internal memos and then turn around and demand perfection in client reports. There is no such thing as being perfectly conscientious part time.

The stories, apocryphal or not, that circulate in an organization reveal its devotion (or lack of it) to quality, and serve to inspire its people to live (or

*"Unless I'm misinterpreting the signs, gentlemen, we are approaching the end of the golden age of shoddy merchandise."*

•    •

Drawing by Weber; © 1983
The New Yorker Magazine, Inc.

not to live) the quality message. Are the stories in your organization about spending $250,000 to cut the chicken-wing hair count? About making sure there isn't a single fly on a food preparation table? Or are they stories like this: "The old man's in favor of quality twelve weeks a quarter. The thirteenth week, though, it's 'Ship the product,' and send it to Australia if we can; the returns take longer"? Or, "Of course the old man's for quality. But he's for everything else, too. I mean, he's never said he's against quality. It's just that he doesn't make a distinction between quality, filling in the forms or [production] line speed"?

## Strong Words on Quality Circles

Tom did an unconscionable thing. In early 1984 he was the lunchtime speaker in Logan, Utah, before an audience of seven hundred. Bill Mohr, a respected colleague from Hewlett-Packard, who, with his wife Harriet, had just published a superb book, *Quality Circles: Changing Images of People at Work* (Addison-Wesley, 1983), was presenting a seminar later that afternoon at the gathering. In front of the seven hundred, with microphone in hand, Tom said, "I notice Bill Mohr of Hewlett-Packard is giving a seminar on his book on quality circles. I think what he is doing borders on the *immoral*." Strong word! He added, "Of course the darned quality circles work at Hewlett-Packard. Ever since Dave Packard and Bill Hewlett opened their fabled garage in 1937, they and their successors and colleagues have, above all, had a bone-deep belief in the ability of *everybody* in the organization to contribute creatively to the betterment of the quality of the products. Given that bedrock, getting HP's quality circles to work is like falling off a log." And then the conclusion: "I come from the so-called human-ized/humanistic Silicon Valley. I'm here to tell you that in six out of seven companies that I visit in that valley, Mecca of twenty-first-century management, the average worker wouldn't attend his or her next quality circle meeting if it was the last day on earth. They see it for exactly what it is: another way for management to jerk labor's chain."

Bill and Harriet Mohr's book *is* superb. We heartily recommend it to all. At the same time, we are in dead earnest in our objection. The heart of quality is not technique. It is a commitment by management to its people and product—stretching over a period of decades and lived with persistence and passion—that is unknown in most organizations today.

Quality is about passion and pride. Sometime back Tom spent two days in a series of seminars with managers of a major retail chain. In the course of the meeting the subject of affordable levels of service came up continually. At one point Tom was well launched on a bit of a diatribe about the rotten level of service in retailing in general when an executive vice president, in front of forty of his peers and subordinates, got up and interrupted him: "Tom, sit down and calm down. Or get off our case. It's a changing and complex and highly competitive world. We are no worse than anybody else." We had our graphics people draw up a little logo that illustrated what this fellow was talking about (see page 102). It's a long way from there to L. L. Bean (see page 103)!

Quality is about people. We will not delve here into the messages dis-

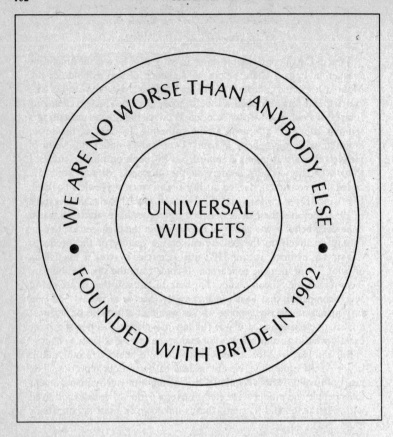

cussed in the section called "People, People, People." It is enough to say at this juncture that quality is a function of commitment—from all hands—on the loading dock, at the receptionist's desk, in the design spaces. Without that commitment—and only human beings can give it—you will not get top quality.

W. Edwards Deming taught quality, as it's known today, to the Japanese. He is also thought of as the father of statistical quality control. The principal reason he believes it's important is that the techniques of statistical quality control lead to hugely increased self-inspection (control) by the people on the line. Deming believes, after all is said and done, that quality is primarily a function of human commitment. In a 1983 lecture to college-level business students at Utah State University, he said:

> Some of you are students of finance. You learn how to figure and how to run a company on figures. If you run a company on figures alone you will

# L.L.Bean®
## Outdoor Sporting Specialties

# THE GOLDEN RULE OF L.L.BEAN

"Sell good merchandise at a reasonable profit, treat your customers like human beings and they'll always come back for more." Leon Leonwood Bean started a company 72 years ago based on this simply stated business philosophy. We call it L.L.'s Golden Rule and today we still practice it.

Everything we sell is backed by an unconditional guarantee that never wears out. We do not want you to have anything from L. L. Bean that is not completely satisfactory. Return anything you buy from us at any time if it proves otherwise.

All of our products are regularly tested by us in the field, as well as in the lab. Each product continues to be made with the best materials, construction and design that we think are appropriate to the needs of our customers. They represent a solid value and deliver a fair return for the money.

The L. L. Bean Customer Service Department operates on L.L.'s belief that "A customer is the most important person ever in this office, in person or by mail." Telephone representatives are available 24 hours a day, 365 days a year for customer assistance and order taking. Your order is shipped promptly, accurately and **L. L. Bean pays all regular postage and handling charges.**

Send us the coupon below or call 207-865-3111 Ext. 39.

1984 L. Bean Inc

Send for a FREE
Christmas 1984 Catalog

Name_____

Address_____

City_____

State_____ Zip_____

L. L. Bean, Inc., 169 Casco St., Freeport, ME 04033

go under. How long will it take the company to go under, get drowned? I don't know, but it is sure to fail. Why? Because the most important figures are not there. Did you learn that in the school of finance? You will, 10 or 15 years from now, learn that the most important figures are those that are unknown or unknowable.

What about the multiplying effects of a happy customer, in either manufacturing or in service? Is he in your figures? What about the multiplying effect of an unhappy customer? Is that in your figures? Did you learn that in your school of finance? What about the multiplying effect of getting better material to use in production? What about the multiplying effect that you get all along the production line? Do you know that figure? You don't! If you run your company without it, you won't have a company. What about the multiplying effect of doing a better job along the line?

People all over the world think that it is the factory worker that causes problems. He is not your problem. Ever since there has been anything such as industry, the factory worker has known that quality is what will protect his job. He knows that poor quality in the hands of the customer will lose the market and cost him his job. He knows it and lives with that fear every day. Yet he cannot do a good job. He is not allowed to do it because the management wants figures, more product, and never mind the quality. They measure only in figures. The factory worker is forced to make defective products, forced to turn out defective items. He is forced to work with defective material, so no matter what they do, it will still be wrong. The worker can't do anything about it. He is totally helpless. If he tries to do something about it, he might as well talk to the wall. Nobody listens.

I can take you to spots, an entire factory with 2,000 people, where conditions have been cleaned up by the management. All the factory workers there are proud of their work. They are turning out almost no defective material. These are happy people. Happy doing a good job.

A dean of a school of business wrote to me to complain that I was a little rough in a speech that I gave to 2,400 purchasing managers in New Orleans. It was a meeting of the International Benevolent Protective Order of Purchasing Managers. They could hear what I was saying. The acoustics were good in the auditorium. There was just one difference between me and the dean. I get around to see what materials come in; he does not. Teamwork is needed between the purchasing department and production and sales. They won't get it, though, because the mandate handed down from management to the purchasing department is to get the lowest price. Top management has to learn something about the entire company. They can no longer play solos or be prima donnas. There has to be teamwork, but the annual system of rating destroys teamwork. How could someone in purchasing get a good rating for paying a higher price? Even if it saves 10 times as much in production, you do not get a good rating by paying a higher price.

The foreman better not stop the line. He'll hurt production if he does, and he may not be here tomorrow. Fear governs almost everybody. Only perhaps one in 200 are not governed by fear. A millright, feeling a bearing, informed the foreman that it was getting warm. He suggested that they stop and take care of it before the bearing froze up and scored the shaft. If that happened, they would be down for sure. The foreman knew that the proper thing for the company to do was to stop and work on the bearing. His answer was, "We can't stop now, we must get these castings out today." He didn't make it. The bearing froze and scored the shaft. The line was down four days, but the foreman did his job.

So quality is an all-hands-on proposition. Period.

Let us conclude where we began—with a return to Stanley Marcus's comment on the role of the schooled human eyeball in producing superior quality. In a word, we observe that a disproportionate share of the most effective leaders/managers we've met who have induced a pervasive sense of quality throughout their organizations develop that sense by growing up around the product. They have great gut feel, are tinkerers, tweekers. IBM lives customer service—quality of customer service—with a passion. As one graduate of their eighteen-month sales boot camp put it, "The word 'customer' was heard so frequently that you soon began to dream about them." 3M, too, lives customers and quality. Virtually everyone in 3M's senior ranks grew up with extensive tours in the factory and selling the product. Gerhard Neumann, GE's aircraft engine entrepreneur, was a miracle worker when it comes to quality, service, and speedy design and implementation. His background includes a two-year "dirty nails" stint as a master mechanic's apprentice in Germany. Neumann attributes a great deal of his subsequent success to superior feel developed during that apprenticeship. Ed Carlson turned around United Airlines after moving from the presidency of Westin Hotels to the airline (UAL owns Westin). We attribute a lot of Carlson's success, which focused on cleaning up the bureaucracy and returning to the basics of service and delivery, to the way he got his start: as a bellhop. Dave Thomas has performed miracles in creating the Wendy's organization and making it grow. His formal schooling is limited, and he began his career as a busboy. He says he learned as a busboy that there is no limit to the quality that can be produced in the "meanest" job. Marcus Sieff, chairman of Marks & Spencer, calls himself "a simple third-generation shopkeeper." In sum, it's hard to imagine an organization with a truly exceptional record of quality where a large share of the senior team did not grow up and around the product.

(As usual, we must go briefly on the defensive and state that we do not consider such reliance on "the eyeball" to be "soft." One more time: We think the concepts of "soft" and "hard" have gotten badly fouled up. Most seem to believe the "eyeball" is "soft," and that computer output is "hard." Both can be soft, both can be hard. But if our life depended on it, and we had to cast a vote on the "hardness" of Dave Thomas's [Wendy's] "eye" for quality versus ten pounds of MBA-and-electronic-spreadsheet-produced analysis, Thomas would get the nod, no doubt about it.)

So what do you do if you haven't sold or designed or made or serviced the product or delivered the service? Our advice is at once very pragmatic and very abstract. The pragmatic: Get back in touch. MBWA, period. And lots of it. Start now, whether you're chairman or accounting supervisor or assistant sanitation department head in a town of 19,000. The abstract part? Learn, if you can, to trust your gut, to respect passion and enthusiasm and pride. What do you *feel* for your product(s) or service(s)? (And this is as valid a question for an MIS department supervisor as for a Fortune 100 CEO.) There's no winning, no hope of constant improvement, for you or your people, unless there is involvement. You must love (or learn to love) what you do, or else excellence remains an elusive target. Loving what you do or produce is not the exclusive domain of Silicon Valley computer designers, Bloomingdale's buyers or Carnegie Hall harpsichord soloists. During a stay at the Hotel Del Coronado near San Diego, the front entrance was being repaired. We interrupted (rudely to others involved, we're afraid) a busy schedule to spend twenty-five minutes watching a bricklayer at work—because he was an artist, with an artist's passion, and because the quality of his product reflected that.

So measure it, by all means. Reward it. Celebrate it. That love will be readily transmitted. So, sadly, will its absence—even more readily. There is no other route.

# 8

# The "Smell" of
# the Customer

"SMELL": NOT "MARKET ORIENTATION," but *living* for one's customers. How do you know you're moving in that direction? Or when you've arrived? We have sorted out twenty-two aspects of a true customers-first orientation.* Almost all are missing from most management and even marketing texts. The list is not meant to be exhaustive. It is simply intended to spur you to ask "Why not?" time and again. Indeed, why not? None is exotic. Each is merely sensible.

1. Company bulletins, annual reports and all other forms of printed matter feature stories about working with customers. In particular, joint company/customer problem-solving activities mark all printed material. Customer contact by "noncustomer" functions—R&D, manufacturing, personnel, accounting, MIS—is stressed. Stories about customers, by actual count, occur far more often than any other type. Special bulletins dealing exclusively with customer service exist, from all parts of the company, and are issued regularly (i.e., at least *weekly*). Individual facilities (e.g., each store, each distribution center) are encouraged to develop regular customer bulletins.
2. In a host of ways, unique respect for *salespeople* is demonstrated. A disproportionate share of salespeople are promoted to general management. Celebrations for salespeople are special and taken very seriously (e.g., they are *lavish* and attended by almost all of general management). When the salesperson talks, the engineer, manufacturer or MIS person jumps—i.e., failure to "overrespond" to a simple request from sales is a moral sin. (This is rare, surprisingly. Yet it is arguably the key to the success of the top companies— from Frito-Lay to P&G, from Domino's Pizza to IBM.) Salespeople fill, even dominate, the top executive ranks (a minimum of 50 percent of, say, the top 50 managers have spent a substantial share of their career in sales). Early in

---

*No one company we know, not even IBM or Marriott, lives all twenty-two with equal intensity. Thus the package of traits form an idealized portrait, though each has been derived from empirical observation.

their career, young men and women on the move clamor for an opportunity to be in sales. The company's "hall of fame"—ten past heroes about whom stories are most frequently related—consists principally of salespersons (or perhaps marketers).

3. Customer support people are showered with attention. "Excessive" training is aimed at receptionists, people who answer the 800 toll-free call-in number, the "minor actors" in the service delivery effort (e.g., dispatchers, people on the loading dock). Major celebrations for these people are common, with awards focusing directly on tiny acts of meritorious service to customers. (This is in marked contrast to the normal "technical" focus on manufacturing or engineering/buying/lending in other institutions. In such institutions, the supporting cast tends to be given short shrift.)

4. The importance of the customer pervades every function of the organization. The customer is "alive," through displays of letters (good and bad), film clips and visits, and what-have-you in MIS, accounting, personnel and legal, as well as in the main-line and direct customer support functions. Moreover, the indirect support function members (e.g., in MIS, personnel, accounting) are *required* (not just encouraged) to go out on sales and service calls, serve on joint company/customer problem-solving teams and otherwise engage in *regular*, results-oriented customer activities.

5. There is a special (and friendly/respectful) language associated with customers (à la "guest" at Disney, "customer" rather than "passenger" or "pax" at People Express). In particular, contemptuous language is simply not permitted.

6. Reviews and reports of all kinds have a disproportionate share of their content aimed at customers and revenue-enhancement activities. Almost every report (manufacturing, MIS, etc.) *begins* with an analysis of the direct impact of any proposed action on the customer. The absence of such a clear tie is an almost sure knockout factor.

7. Visits with customers are exchanged regularly, at *all* levels in the company and customer organization. Customers are invited in to visit all facilities, especially plants or back-room operations. Manufacturers, MIS people, et al. are out visiting customers with some degree of regularity. Customers are invited to many company meetings (both celebrations and policy meetings) and are vigorously encouraged to present their views. Almost no facility is off limits to customers. Factories are open at all times for their visits, which are actively encouraged *and* subsidized (for all levels—i.e., shop floor as well as executive—and functions of the customer operation).

8. Hallway discussions, celebration of heroes—minor and major—overwhelmingly (again, by actual count) focus on support for the customer. Moreover, the customer support stories are invariably *personalized*. They are about particular people and circumstances. That is, the customer is treated as a unique person, *not* as a statistical abstraction.

9. Devices abound for customer listening. Surveys (of customers and our people's views of our customer support skills) are conducted regularly—i.e.,

at least monthly. Specific training in "naïve" customer *listening* is provided to R&D people, engineers, manufacturers, accountants (as well as sales and service people). Numerous formal and informal customer feedback devices exist, are used, and are paid attention to. "Iron laws" about time-to-respond (e.g., eight to forty-eight hours) to customer requests and information from customers' feedback surveys are religiously enforced; the response "system" is intrusively overseen by top management.

10.  Devices exist to ensure that connections are made (and then acted upon) between sales and engineering and manufacturing. That is, suggestions collected by salespersons from customers are viewed not as "merely the natural tendency of salespersons to snap to attention in response to every customer's whim," but as the tangible rewards of *listening*.

11.  Customer satisfaction is measured frequently—monthly at least, and perhaps as often as weekly. Sampling is extensive. Surveys are quantitative as well as qualitative (i.e., response time and feelings count equally); the measures are taken very, very seriously. They are reviewed unfailingly by top management: the development of such measures is taken as seriously as the development of budgetary measures of product-reliability measures. Evaluation of people in all functions at all levels is significantly affected by the satisfaction measures. Special, intense "customer satisfaction reviews" are regularly layered on top of the regular evaluation procedures.

12.  "Overkill" complaint response mechanisms are firmly locked in place. Unfailingly, they include an "excessive" (as viewed by the rest of the industry's standards) focus on immediacy and personalization of the response. Foulups with big or small customers are not tolerated; even minor glitches are brought swiftly to the attention of top management. Top management, in turn, gets directly involved both with the customer and with correcting what went on. There's a well-documented feeling throughout the company that *anything* untoward that happens to a customer is "somehow" known in the executive suite within minutes (or sooner).

13.  Promises to customers are kept, period, regardless of cost in overtime. Achievable delivery dates are set to begin with, and then met. Missing a promised date, no matter how small the customer or order, is the subject of intense top-management scrutiny and severe sanctions. (Every one of our better performers agrees that setting unrealistic delivery times is madness, even if it costs the company a particular job—or even several—to a competitor who promises the moon. Over the long haul, customers respect, above almost all other vendor traits, the ability to keep promises.)

14.  The calendars of executives at all levels and in all functions reflect their insistent focus on customers. Visits to customers and time spent with them never run less than 30 percent for senior line management, and not less than 10 percent for indirect function management—accountants, manufacturers, MIS people.

15.  Quality and reliability of product and service is an obsession throughout the organization, reflecting virtually the same intensity as that directed to the

customer per se. Stories of tiny quality improvements and celebrations of those who brought them about are abundant. The product or the service-in-use is prominently and "excessively" displayed. Almost all in the company use the product themselves, if possible. Samples are always around for all to see (and use, if possible). An array of T-shirts and caps featuring the product or service, especially a new or enhanced product when it's launched, is in evidence—in every corner of the organization.

16.   Every element of the organization actively looks for ways that it can specifically contribute to differentiating the product or service. Even ideas that add only minuscule improvement in performance (especially as it's *perceived* by the customer) are the subject of endless reviews, bragging sessions, awards and ceremonies in accounting and personnel, as well as in sales, service, marketing and manufacturing.

17.   Manufacturers (or operations people in service companies) are deeply involved in customer activities, especially selling (*directly*) and joint problem-solving teams.

18.   The customer's *perception* is what's viewed as most important, rather than a so-called hard-nosed view of reality. We remember well a letter from an executive in a company focusing entirely on manufacturing. Tom had described the IBM approach to disputes with customers, and a respondent was dumbfounded. "You *really* mean that when you're *right* and the customer is way off base you will nonetheless respond to the customer's view—even when it costs you a substantial amount of money?" The very idea that there *is* such a thing as "right," "factual" and "real" is the number one problem we encounter in the technically or financially driven company.

19.   There is an explicit philosophy statement, part of or an adjunct to the corporate philosophy statement, that deals with "the way we perceive and treat customers." It is widely distributed and constantly (and explicitly) reinforced in almost every setting, from the Fourth of July picnic to the annual performance review.

20.   Executives (and managers at all levels) from *all* functions regularly spend time *performing* all primary customer-support tasks—e.g., working on the loading dock, at the dispatch center, in the spares department, at the distribution center. About a week a quarter is a minimum. At least one visit is in depth—e.g., at least two full days performing the task, for a full shift.

21.   Executives in all functions keep track of and manage the bureaucratic (e.g., paperwork) load that gets in the way of customer-contact time for all customer-related functions—e.g., reception, sales, field service, dispatch. "Time in front of (or in direct support of) the customer" is guarded and tracked jealously/measured religiously.

22.   The number one "it" is a *passion* for *tiny* customer-related improvements in every department. Accounting people are hell-bent on improving ease of billing. MIS people are determined to improve customer-related information. There is an obsession in every department, in every nook and cranny, to do things just a tiny bit better.

So these are the characteristics we find in companies that truly "smell of the customer." Above all, when we observe these traits in action, we notice that they are lived with intensity, as a matter of reflex. Many, if nost most, companies devote some time and attention to developing many of them; the truly distinctive customer service companies are obsessive in pursuit of the least of them. The discourtesy of a single receptionist in Podunk, even in a 150,000-person operation, is cause for top-to-bottom alarm, discussion and decisive action. (Usually such ameliorative action is *not* the disciplining of the receptionist but the disciplining of management—two, three or even four levels above her or him—plus the design of corrective programs aimed at cutting off at the pass an incipient system-wide problem.)

Does your company/organization smell of the customers?

---

### Redefinition of the Mundane

Remember Todd Fraser, who learned that price is less important than 100 percent order-fulfillment in the plumbing supply business? He redefined his highly competitive, low-margin industry in a two-state area. One thousand tiny things vault Stew Leonard (dairy products), Tom Monaghan (pizzas), Carl Sewell (Cadillacs) and Jan Carlzon (airline seats) to the very top of highly competitive, previously-deemed-commodity heaps. Each has won big where it couldn't be done—in theory—by redefining what can be done for the customer.

None is a lavish spender. You can't be if your game is plumbing supplies or dairy products. Each has applied imagination (better yet, the imagination of all his people) to serving the customer better—more personally (via service and product tailoring), with better quality—and each has created virtually a new industry (or a new definition of an old industry). The great mayors (à la Schaefer of Baltimore) and educators (à la Sybil Mobley at Florida A&M—see page 411) have done the same. Each has proven that the customer *can* be served in today's highly automated world where impersonalness has been the all too frequent norm.

We have tried, along the way, to share a little of our emotion. A visit to Stew Leonard's, Perdue Farms or Sewell Village Cadillac redefines forever what *is* possible in a striking and dramatic fashion. We'd conclude by urging every reader to begin his or her own forays to observe superior quality and customer service. Thinly Disguised Contempt is found everywhere. But so, although more rarely, are florists, restaurants, barbershops, machine tool companies that can show us what can be done, and done profitably. We urge you: Become an expert, don't delay. (And then reread this section!)

## Some (More) Good Reading on Customers

There is, of course, lots written on marketing. As one would expect from our discussion, there is little written on our point of focus—customers. Nonetheless, two recent jargon-free books stand out at the top of our "must read" list in support of the points in this section. The first is David Ogilvy's *Ogilvy on Advertising* (Crown, 1984). Ogilvy writes delightfully on the whole issue of bringing products to the marketplace and selling them; on the subject of product differentiation and maintaining client relationships, there is no better work than Ted Levitt's book, from which we extracted heavily, *The Marketing Imagination* (Free Press, 1983).

Robert Shook's *Ten Greatest Sales Persons* (Harper & Row, 1978) at first looks like another garden-variety "how to" book. It's not. Shook writes well and provides biographies and long interviews with Joe Girard, the world's greatest car salesman; Buck Rodgers, former head of marketing at IBM; Shelby Carter, former head of Xerox sales (and a former IBMer as well); Edna Larson, the world's top Avon salesperson; and so on. The message—"Serve the customer" and "The sale doesn't begin until after the sale"—comes through loud and clear, and we often use the book in our seminars.

Mere perception: nowhere else is it dealt with so beautifully as in Fredonia Jacques's *Verdict Pending: A Patient Representative's Intervention* (Capistrano Press, 1983). The odyssey of a hospital patient representative, it has implications far beyond the health care setting. It is about professional human beings dealing with "customers" (patients, in this case); the stories of unimagined "minor" slights that leave irreparable memories are staggering.

We recommend no texts on quality as such; our subject, after all, is not quality per se but its relationship to leadership. Quality itself will always be in the eye of the beholder. Thus the most constructive book on the topic for both of us continues to be Robert Pirsig's *Zen and the Art of Motorcycle Maintenance* (Morrow, 1974). A much more practical look comes from Stanley Marcus (chairman emeritus of Neiman Marcus) in his *Quest for the Best* (Viking, 1979).

# THREE

## Innovation

*The project reminded me of the Flying Tigers in China . . .
undermanned, overworked, and successful.*
> —Gerhard Neumann, on the development of the successful GE
> Variable Stator Experimental Engine

*The best leaders are apt to be found among those executives who
have a strong component of unorthodoxy in their character. Instead of
resisting innovation, they symbolize it.*
> —David Ogilvy, Ogilvy on Advertising

*The reasonable man adapts himself to the world: the unreasonable
one persists in trying to adapt the world to himself. Therefore all
progress depends on the unreasonable man.*
> —George Bernard Shaw

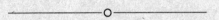

INNOVATING REGULARLY, at all levels, in all functions, is the second basis for sustainable strategic advantage. Our story here is analogous to that of the preceding section, on customers; namely, that traditional management thinking misses the point. For the most part, management writing, and typical discussions even among practicing managers, focus on structures, monetary incentives and planning techniques (e.g., technology forecasting). Our observations—from Stew Leonard's to Trammell Crow to 3M—suggest the emphasis is badly misplaced.

The most significant issues are, again, those concerning "smell" ("smell" of innovation, this time). Is inaction tolerated or not? That is, what's the most commonly asked question in your bank/school/public works department/ retail operation? Is it "Why don't you form a task force to look into this?" or is it "So what have you gotten done in the last twenty-four hours?" Are skunks (champions) and skunkworks encouraged or suppressed (in a host of almost always subtle ways)?

The real world of innovating is serendipitous and passion-filled, whether the object is a new banking service or a pharmaceutical miracle derived from basic chemistry. "Managing" it involves MBWA—paying attention to innovation, talking it up, wandering the design spaces, and celebrating the emergence (and even some of the failures) of champions—in a ten-person accounting department or a sluggish $10 billion science-driven company.

So—we beg you to sit back and kick up your feet on the table before delving into this section. The customer section may well have elicited an "Ah, ha, common sense." This will be a tougher take. "Restrain the oddballs [i.e., would-be champions]" has been conventional wisdom for so long that it may be tough to come to grips with the central message here: Champion/skunks, and skunkworks are a must, not a luxury, if constant innovation is truly sought.

# 9

# The Mythology of Innovation, or a Skunkworks Tale

POST-IT NOTE PADS have become a staple in the American office—and a $200 million winner for 3M. The notion originated with Art Fry, a 3M employee who sang in a choir; the bits of paper he used to mark the hymns kept falling out of the books, and he yearned for an adhesive-backed paper that would stick as long as necessary but would leave no trace when removed. From the labs of 3M, the home of Scotch tape, a prototype soon became available. "Great success story," you say? Not quite yet. Major office-supply distributors thought it was silly. Market surveys were negative. But 3M executives and secretaries got hooked, once they actually *used* the little notes. The eventual breakthrough: a mailing of samples to the secretaries of the CEO's of the Fortune 500 under the letterhead of the secretary of the chairman of 3M, Lew Lehr. The time lapse between the germ of the idea and its commercial fruition? Almost a *dozen* years.

The above anecdote would amount to little more than just a charming story were it not similar to stories from Citicorp and Bell Labs, from companies making jet engines or computers, from surgicenters and accounting firms. The course of innovation—from the generation of the idea through prototype development and contact with the initial user to breakthrough and then to final market—is highly uncertain. Moreover, it is *always* messy, unpredictable, and very much affected by the determined ("irrational"?) champions, and that is the important point. It's important, because we must learn to design organizations—those that are public as well as private, banks as well as software developers—that take into account, explicitly, the irreducible sloppiness of the process and take advantage of it, rather than systems and organizations that attempt to fight it.

Unfortunately, most innovation management practice appears to be predicated on the implicit assumption that we can beat the sloppiness out of the process if only we can make the plans tidier and the teams better organized. Experiments and skunkworks, the zeal of champions, the power gained from

Portions of this chapter were published under this title in the *Stanford Magazine.*

exploiting the innovative user (customer) as partner are thought of as fit only for those who aren't smart enough to think far enough ahead and plan wisely enough. As a friend at General Electric says, "When you go through this inordinately messy, sloppy, fouled-up, mucked-up seven-year process of bringing a new product to market, you say to yourself at the end, 'Any idiot could have done it better than that! Let's get organized for the next round.' And in that single phrase, 'Let's get organized for the next round,' lie the seeds of subsequent disaster."

We propose the following (see the chart on the facing page): It *is* a messy world. We hope to demonstrate that. *If* it is a messy world, the *only* way to proceed is by *constant experimentation:* "Don't just stand there, *do* something." *If* constant experimentation is the *only* antidote to a messy world, then we need experimenters—or champions (skunks). And if we need champions, we must realize that the most effective environment for champions is almost always an abundance of *skunkworks*, those small off-line bands of mavericks that are the hallmark of innovative organizations. Finally, and this is the $64,000 issue: *if* the messy-world-experiment-champion-skunkwork paradigm makes sense, then we need to *create a climate* that induces all the above to occur—a climate that nurtures and makes heroes of experimenters and champions.

· Datapoint executives insist that a farmer in Arkansas, running an outfit called Chicken Pride, constructed the software that was crucial in the early development of their intelligent terminal business. He reprogrammed some primitive software cassettes and called in seeking additional advice: "What do I do next?" Datapoint engineers were dumbfounded by what he had done already.

· More Datapoint, from founder Victor Poor: "There have been surprises, particularly in the way customers apply our products. They use them in ways we never expected when we designed them. The 2200 programmer terminal device, for instance, would emulate any number of terminals. The customers paid no attention to that and started using it in stand-alone computing operations. . . . Very few companies will admit that this is the way products get developed—really. They always tell you their product was planned."

· The "technical specs" for a major new Hewlett-Packard test instrument consisted of a picture of an old instrument cut out of an HP catalog, with a hand-drawn sketch stapled to it. The division general manager's response to his engineer's primitive approach: "Do it."

· With United Technologies, General Electric, Westinghouse and IBM in the fray, the first "intelligent mobile robot" nonetheless comes from a company that is hardly a household name, Denning Systems, Inc., of Washington, D.C.—the classic "three persons in a garage" operation.

· The *Nobel Duel* describes the twenty-one-year-long bitterly fought race between Andrew Schally and Roger Guillemin that led to the 1977 Nobel Prize in medicine (divided between them) for the discovery of a brain hormone release mechanism. Others in the field had retired from the fray years

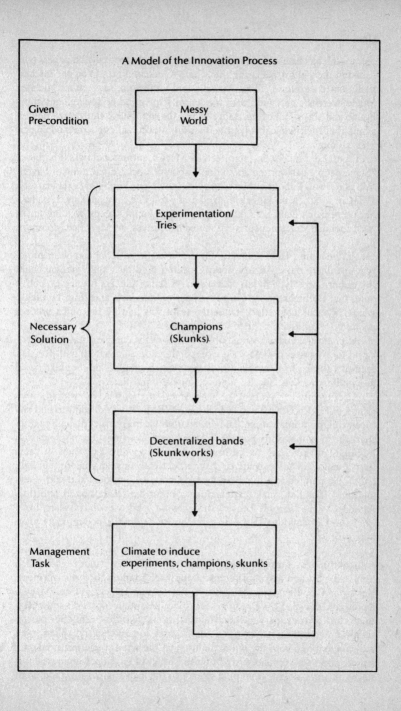

A Model of the Innovation Process

Given
Pre-condition

Messy
World

Necessary
Solution

Experimentation/
Tries

Champions
(Skunks)

Decentralized bands
(Skunkworks)

Management
Task

Climate to induce
experiments, champions, skunks

before (the mechanism had been fully described, theoretically, in papers published in the 1940's), declaring the Schally-Guillemin race to be an "intellectually barren exercise." Thus, Schally and Guillemin, says author Nicholas Wade, were the only ones with the tenacity to "grind up the millions of pig brains and sheep brains necessary to get the job done." Both prize holders admit that their work involved neither an intellectual nor a methodological breakthrough.

• From Ed Finkelstein, architect of Macy's entrepreneurial turnaround: "Some people get worried about duplication of stocks, duplication of buyers. We don't worry about either." And from the New York Times (January 17, 1984), in an article on Finkelstein and Macy's: "[The company] insists on having no research staff, no strategic planners. It simply keeps building up its 'well rounded, entrepreneurially minded executives,' as Mr. Finkelstein puts it."

• Commodore's Jack Tramiel built the first Vic personal computer prototype in ninety days. Adam Osborn, angered by others' fluffy designs, built the Osborn prototype in just four weeks. A senior GE gas turbine executive notes that the breakthrough on a major current product came from an intense sixty-day small-team effort—after the team was told by the unit's product planning committee that their idea was a loser.

• After several embarrassing public failures of the complex, state-of-the-art, liquid-fuel Vanguard, NASA (in a desperate effort to catch up with Russia's Sputnik), turned to Wernher von Braun's much simpler "off-the-shelf" solid fuel military rockets. Success followed almost immediately.

• After twenty-five years of studying American industrial innovation, Brian Quinn of Dartmouth's Tuck School said of IBM: "It was difficult to find any successful major innovation that derived from formal product planning rather than the championship process." After years of using Quinn's line with hundreds of audiences, we've heard a demurring voice only once. It came from a senior AT&T executive: "Nonsense. I know it's not true for the [Bell] Labs." He pointed to a highly respected Labs vice president and said, "You tell him." The Labs man scratched his chin for ten seconds or so, and then replied, "Well, I've only been at the Labs for a bit over thirty years, but I can't think of anything that ever came directly from the new product planning process."

Breakthrough. Optimization. Systems analysis. Technology plan. Such terms are part and parcel of the usual approach to innovation management. Yet from GE, IBM and HP, from Citibank and Mervyn's, from Macy's, Apple, and Raychem, we hear instead about persistence (passion and obsession!), lots of tries, perverse and unusual users, five- to twenty-five-person skunkworks sequestered in dingy warehouses for ninety days, plans gone awry, inventions from the wrong industry at the wrong time for the wrong reason, specs for complex systems on the backs of envelopes. Innovation, it seems, in areas ranging from pure science to the industrial organization, from health care to accounting, just doesn't occur the way it's supposed to. Time and again we roll out the Manhattan Project to illustrate that the concerted effort, well planned, is the only one that wins the day. But it is the Manhattan Project that turns out to be the anomaly.* The computer or financial service prototype—or locomotive(!)—in the garage turns out to be closer to the norm. What's up?

Here we will explore ten popular myths (five "major myths," five "sub-myths") about innovation management. Our case will not be balanced or unbiased. (We've yet to meet an unbiased analyst.) Our objective is to give credence to the sloppy side of innovation, lest the powerful images of the Manhattan Project or the "well-organized" MITI (Ministry of International Trade and Industry)† lead us to fall prey to the myths of rational innovation planning. (Such myths have already damaged many companies, including such stalwarts as GM, U.S. Steel, GE, Xerox, Bell Labs/Western Electric, Sylvania, Westinghouse, RCA, Singer, Texas Instruments.)

We hope we will persuade you to allow for the inherent sloppiness of innovation—indeed, *to take advantage of it.* And if we don't, we do hope you'll at least occasionally scratch your chin and think, They may have a point. The myths we'll examine are these:

1. Myth: Substantial strategic/technological planning greatly increases the odds of a "no surprises" outcome.
Counterpoint: Though you must be thoughtful in order to be in roughly the right arena, **innovation in business (and nonbusiness is highly unpredictable,** and the context and configuration must be predicated on uncertainty and ambiguity.

2. Myth: Complete technical specs and a thoroughly researched market plan are invariant first steps to success.
Counterpoint: You must move as rapidly as possible to real tests of real products (albeit incomplete) with real customers. That is, you must **experiment** and learn your way toward perfection/completion.

3. Myth: Time for reflection and thought built into the development process are essential to creative results.
Counterpoint: "Winners"—e.g., successful **champions/skunks**—are, above all, pragmatic non-blue-sky dreamers who live by one dictum: "Try it, now."

---

*And even that's not clear. Upon publication of some of the material that appears in this chapter, we received several lengthy notes from participants arguing that the Manhattan Project was a classic form of what we were describing: multiple competing groups, crazy champions, skunkworks within larger systems, etc.
†This image, too, is under attack, as in David R. Henderson's "The Myth of MITI," *Fortune*, August 8, 1983. More practically, our friend Ken Ohmae, managing director of McKinsey's Japanese offices, states, "The Japanese [company] winners look more like survivors of a demolition derby than meticulous strategic planners."

4. Myth: Big teams are necessary to blitz a project rapidly, especially a complex one.

Counterpoint: Small teams—e.g., **skunkworks**—can be many times more efficient than large ones, and can often accomplish the lion's share of even the most complex tasks in a fraction of the time that a large team takes.

4a. Related myth: Strong centralized functions (and, consequently, functional organizations) are imperative if the would-be innovators (from R&D, engineering, merchandising) are to get a fair hearing.

Counterpoint: Commercially viable innovation, though not as orderly, is more likely to occur in radically decentralized organizations. **Smashing engineering, manufacturing and marketing functions together** in outcome-oriented, small-scale groups overcomes the most important source of delays in innovation.

4b. Related Myth: Big projects are inherently different from small projects—or, an airplane is not a calculator.

Counterpoint: Some projects are indeed much bigger than others. Yet the most successful big-project management comes from a **small within big** mindset, in which purposeful "suboptimization" is encouraged.

4c. Related Myth: Product line/product family (and interproduct line) compatibility is the key to economic success.

Counterpoint: Compatibility is vital, but **gaining the last 2 percent in compatibility often costs you the market.**

4d. Related Myth: To win big you must strive to optimize.

Counterpoint: **Optimization** always wins on paper, and **loses in the real world.**

5. Myth: Customers only tell you about yesterday's needs.

Counterpoint: While "average" customers may reflect yesterday, **lead users**—i.e., forward-looking customers—are usually years ahead of the rest, and are the best source of leading-edge innovation.

5a. Related Myth: Technology push is the cornerstone of business (and presumably American) economic success.

Counterpoint: The "marketing push"—"phony-demand generation," as some see it—versus "technology push" argument has been overplayed. **Listening to the market is the winning approach,** but it need not mean forgoing sophistication in design.

### Myth No. 1: Solid Plans Mean "No Surprises"
#### Counterpoint: Learn to Live with Uncertainty and Ambiguity

These days attacks on strategic planning are in vogue. It's been too rigid, too bureaucratic, "everyone" says. Let's at least decentralize it, "everyone" agrees. General Electric and Westinghouse, early pioneers, are doing just that. A few have suggested maybe we should even get rid of it. But wait—even as we do it, do we really mean it? The new "in" terms are "innovation" and "production." Now "manufacturing strategy" and "innovation strategy" are proffered as *substitutes* for (additions to?) strategic planning. But wait, again—we're *in favor of* strategic planning, strongly so, but we're not so sure about "innovation strategy." Before industry heads off down this new trail in search of a cookbook panacea, let's at least look at the record of new product and service forecasting. It's hardly spotless.

Anecdotal evidence awaits us by the bucketful. "*We do not consider that the aeroplane will be of any use for war purposes,*" said the British Secretary of War in 1910. The United States lost most of its aircraft early in World War II because we perceived the threat from ground-based saboteurs to be greater than that from heretofore unused sea-launched aircraft (even though we knew full well that the Japanese had carriers), and bunched our planes on the ground accordingly. The French invested billions of dollars (in 1930's money) on the Maginot Line, which was flanked in a matter of hours by the flexible German tank strategy, as the young Charles de Gaulle had predicted.

Go back and look at the first projections for sales of the mainframe computer, developed in the late 1940's. The market was estimated to be a dozen (!): a handful each to the Census Bureau, Bell Labs, Lawrence Livermore Labs. Similar early studies of xerography suggested that a maximum of one thousand machines might be placed. Ironically, these thousand machines were to take on the high-end offset printing market; over twenty years later, Xerox and its competitors still have not decisively beaten that market. (We will accept, tongue in cheek, one variety of success in forecasting: Two wrongs can occasionally make a right. When Xerox introduced the big 9200 machine, it predicted first-year lease placement of about 70,000 units. Scores of market researchers took years to develop the estimate. The actual first-year placements were about 7,000, an error by anyone's standard! However, there's a saving grace: the damnable, idiosyncratic users made twice as many copies on the 7,000 as had been estimated to come from the full 70,000.)

What do such anecdotes prove? A little, but not much. You can doubtless match them with your own collection to prove the positive value of forecasting. Ours versus yours. Good laughs. But there's more, lots more.

## A Systematic Study

As is often the case, where there's smoke, there's fire. A half-dozen or so thoughtful studies of the process of invention all add up to the same story: the lion's share of invention comes from the "wrong person" in the "wrong place" in the "wrong industry" at the "wrong time," in conjunction with the "wrong user." Perhaps the most systematic analysis is *The Sources of Invention* by John Jewkes and colleagues. At the heart of it are extensive case studies of fifty-eight major inventions, a sample systematically chosen from twentieth-century Europe and America. The fifty-eight range from ballpoint pens and self-winding wristwatches to penicillin, the continuous casting of steel and the digital computer. Jewkes's evidence suggests that at least *forty-six of the fifty-eight* occurred in "the wrong place": they were invented by an individual not in any company, by a very small company, by an individual in an "outgroup" in a large company, or by a large company in the "wrong industry."

Typical among the forty-six is Kodachrome, invented by two musicians. A watchmaker fooling around with brass casting came up with the process for the continuous casting of steel. Dye-making chemists developed synthetic detergents—after soap-making chemists turned the project down as uninteresting. The manufacturers of reciprocating aircraft engines thought the jet engine was useless; the individuals who developed it were finally able to peddle it not, as they "should have," to *engine* makers but to air*frame* makers. The diesel engine was developed solely to haul cars within railyards; all the experts agreed it would *never* be capable of pulling trains long distances.

One of our favorite stories, rather typical of invention in the wrong place, involves the venerable Alfred P. Sloan of General Motors. GM, early in their history, had developed two important new chemical components: freon, the refrigeration agent, and tetraethyl lead, the substance that reduces engine knock. During the 1920s the same researchers wanted to investigate synthetic rubber. Because the inventions had come from the General Motors labs and not one of the expected chemical companies, Du Pont's president wrote to GM, skeptical about their new interest. John Jewkes, et al., who tell this tale in *The Sources of Invention*, quotes the correspondence:

> [GM and Du Pont at the time had substantial joint ownership]: "I wonder if it is a wise expenditure of money on the part of GM to go into synthetic rubber investigation. A great deal of work has been done on this subject by very competent people and well-organized research groups. I understand that the GM chemical department is neither well-organized for this purpose nor is the personnel such as would likely prove successful. The same line of thought has so far kept Du Pont from a general investigation of the subject, and we think that Du Pont is better equipped for this purpose than General Motors." Mr. Sloan replied as follows: "You say that General Motors Chemical Department is neither well organized nor is its personnel such as is likely to prove successful. This statement may be right or it may be wrong. Frankly, I do not know which it is, but I think that if I had told you six or seven years ago that General Motors Research was working on some chemical scheme whereby we could inject some quantities of some unknown material into gasoline to enable us to increase the compression and produce a fuel of antiknock qualities, you would have said exactly the same thing and would have thought that we were very foolish in mixing up with something that was purely of a chemical or fuel character and had

nothing to do with the primary manufacture of motor cars. Then after we had discovered the material you would very likely have questioned the ability of our research department to develop methods of making the material itself in a practical way, yet that was accomplished too. . . . "

In Jewkes's thorough canvassing of the evidence he does come across one study of one industry in which the majority of the innovations is attributed to the right groups at the right time—plastics. But after describing the study in some detail, Jewkes proceeds, in a carefully documented analysis, to challenge it. His conclusion? There is no industry group where very much innovation occurred as or when it was supposed to.

## An Exception?

We sometimes are told that the principle of invention in the wrong place at the wrong time, by somebody else, does not and cannot hold for pharmaceuticals, where you have a fifteen- to twenty-year development and approval cycle. And we agree that certain stages of the drug development and testing process must be highly systematic. *Invention*, however, particularly in the case of so-called miracle drugs, appears to be just as "messy"—a numbers game, champion-driven and skunkwork-driven—as in the rest of the world. Among the top sellers on the market today is SmithKline's Tagamet, an ulcer drug. The invention of Tagamet embodies the very essence of messiness. The Tagamet team was apparently told to stop working on its area of science three or four times (or five or six, depending on whose version of the story you hear, and we've heard at least a half dozen). One reason, says an informant: the developer was a "disrespected, simple scientist from Glasgow." (He adds, with a touch of awe in his voice, "The same simple fellow subsequently went on to develop the Beta Blocker.") Moreover, the sales potential of the drug, according to a couple of sources, was woefully underestimated at $25 million to $50 million.* It rapidly became a billion-dollar-plus drug (suggesting, as do so many of our examples, that its current description as a "home run" was created *long after the fact* rather than as the result of a preplanned swing for the fences).

## Convoluted Paths

Jim Utterback, at MIT, who has studied innovation for over a decade, talks about the special role of *early users*. He concludes that "the initial use and vision for a new product or service is virtually never the one that is of the greatest importance commercially," and he recounts the path to success of

*Similarly, Upjohn's head of research, Jake Stuki, reports that the ibuprofen family of drugs (Motrin et al.) was at first thought to have little potential: "Market surveys told Upjohn to forgo development before they were ever named, let alone developed."

invention after invention to support his point. Typical is the case of incandescent lighting. It was first installed in the late 1870's aboard ship, which in retrospect is natural enough. It's dangerous there, in an unstable environment (tossing sea), to have open gas lamps or other forms of flame. Thus the incandescent lamp found a first home, to use Utterback's terms, in a "highly specialized end-use niche." (Likewise, transistors were first used for missile guidance systems; consumer use lagged by twenty years.) And then, in a move that every market research department would have readily predicted, incandescent lighting spread to night baseball! From there it moved to neighborhood lighting, and only fifteen years later did it begin to seep into the home.

Lowell Steele, a GE R&D executive, describes a slightly different twist—the unexpected complications involved in creating the *infrastructure* required to turn a "compelling idea" into a mundane, commercial reality. Here, for instance, is his account of the history of frozen foods (we referred to it briefly earlier): "Clarence Birdseye had his flash of insight in 1912, but his development of a satisfactory, quick-freezing process was only the first of an excruciatingly drawn out series of steps. Dietetic information had to be developed on the properties of different foods, and new methods were needed for gathering produce. These changes, in turn, required the location of processing plants closer to sources of supply; new techniques and equipment for transferring, storing, and displaying frozen foods; and willingness on the part of both retailers and homeowners to buy adequate storage systems. Even so, the real catalyzing event was the government's decision after World War II to de-control the price of frozen foods before that of canned goods. In all, it took some *forty years* [our emphasis] before all the pieces were in place for a major new technology to flower!"

In *Patterns of Technological Innovation*, Devendra Sahal has developed a useful term: "technological guideposts." By this he means that some fairly mundane products have become bellwethers for a whole generation of sustained development. He finds that these "super products" that trigger so much subsequent development are seldom from the top tier of exotic technology. Rather they are the *culmination* of many exotic technological advances in a product that is right and *practical for its time*. For example: "A great many advances were centered around a single type of aircraft, the DC-3. Yet it is interesting to note that from a strictly technical view, the DC-3 was not the most advanced aircraft of its time. It was *singularly lacking in novelty*." Sahal adds: "The technological guidepost lies in the culmination of prior advances. It is seldom a matter of radical breakthrough." (We think of the Apple II as a more recent product of exactly that sort. It was the right product at the right time. It was a sound product which incorporated advanced but not exotic state-of-the-art technology. Moreover, because of its initial popularity, it attracted any number of effective software writers. Indeed, several have commented that the core of the machine's success was the electronic spreadsheet, first developed by Visicorp. Visicalc—as much as the hardware—really turned the hobbyist's home computer into an effective tool for large numbers of people.)

The path to widespread adoption of an invention, then, is almost always unpredictable—and often lengthy.* Few Hewlett-Packard instrument users did with the instruments what Hewlett-Packard engineers had planned. Scotch tape became a household word only after an enterprising salesman—on his own, at home, during his off hours—invented the desk-top dispenser for a previously narrow-use industrial product. Our strategies for innovation must, then, be based upon *acceptance* of this convoluted process rather than the false hope that "better planning" can magically straighten the maze.

## It's Worse than You Think

The evidence is actually frightening. Picking up Utterback's trail again, we find that there is apparently a tendency inherent in organizations to do *exactly* the wrong thing. Following a rigorous study, Utterback concludes: "In 32 of 34 companies, the [challenged market] leader *reduced* investment in the *new* technology in order to pour even more money into buffering up the *old*." Not only, then, does the leader not embrace the new, but he actually—in absolute and relative dollar terms—reduces his investment in the new in order to hang tight to the old. Utterback's analysis of the turn-of-the-century lighting industry, again, provides a marvelous example. Following the introduction of incandescent lighting by small firms, the then leaders spent fifteen years polishing the old technology apple in gas lighting. And they made big bucks at it, because the old technology had not been under challenge and thus yielded big improvements when subjected to renewed scrutiny. In the meantime, however, they *reduced* their investment in the new incandescent lighting. We have seen the phenomenon much more recently. Kueffel and Esser, the premier slide-rule makers (who among engineers didn't carry their K&E with pride?), were not participants at all in the hand-held calculator business. "No names" of the time, such as TI and HP, took the play away from K&E. The Swiss watchmakers' response to digital microchip technology is an instant replay.

## Technological Hubris

The problems are manifold. Technological and engineering hubris—the engineer-buyer knows best, he or she can predict the use of the product best. Marketing hubris—could all those data on the Edsel be wrong? The issues are organizational, political, habitual, cultural. And they're individual as well.

---

*There is an interesting paradox here. Because of the fact that the path to adoption is uncertain (and often lengthy), one must respond by short-time-frame experiments. That is, the uncertainty is reduced only by constant, rapid tries and adaptations.

The potential lost from not listening to would-be champions because they wear the wrong-color suit is a phenomenon of the ages. It goes back hundreds of years, at least. A recent study by William Broad and Nicholas Wade focuses on several giants of science who weren't listened to at the time (and for many subsequent decades—or centuries) because they were not of the then establishment's "right stuff." Ohm (of electricity fame) was disregarded because he was a mere "Jesuit math teacher." Mendel (the pioneer geneticist) was ignored because he did his work at "a little experimental plot in a rural abbey." We mentioned Semmelweis in chapter 6. Even the most inventive have blind spots, in their own back yard, too. Edison did. He fought against the use of alternating current. Marconi, father of radio, fought against wireless telephony. And recently, the wildly creative Nolan Bushnell, then at Atari, could see no value in Steve Jobs's ideas for a new computer, and failed to support it with even a few bucks. Steve, of course, packed up his ideas and (along with Steve Wozniak, similarly unloved at HP) founded Apple.

The causes run deep. Human beings seem to have a need to explain, to write tidy stories. Professor Jewkes puts it this way: "Successful inventors contribute to the romantic aura. . . . It is much more agreeable for them to think of their achievement as the outcome of a flawless chain of brilliant decisions and deliberate planning than as the result of desperate groping and frequent backtracking. . . . Subsequent writers, possessing more complete records of the lucky strokes than of the more numerous failures, and searching for a tidy story rather than a muddled one, carry on the building up of legends."

Are we opposed to central planning? Are we opposed to a central R&D activity? Many have asked that. The answer is no, and yes. One *does* need to make bets on general directions for innovation—the difference, say, between north and northwest. That's great. What's not sensible (it's actually counterproductive) is trying to specify far in advance whether a given course should be 343 degrees or 346 degrees. We also support central research as a good place from which divisions can *steal* ideas. More often than not that's what people at HP, 3M et al. see it as. Finally—another HP view—central research is a marvelous place from which product divisions can *steal* people. And, of course, every now and then, a new product really will come according to plan or from central R&D.

In no sense do we believe we have "proved" that new product or service forecasting is impossible or not useful. If we were in a position to order it done, we'd do so. We just wouldn't bank on it. We'd cover our bets with a bit of eclecticism. Procter & Gamble has done that with its intensive and substantially overlapping brand-versus-brand competition. Mervyn's, Macy's and Bloomingdale's do it with buyer-versus-buyer competition. Smart hospitals are beginning to do it by encouraging internal entrepreneurs to create off-premises walk-in clinics that compete directly with the hospital's service. 3M, Mars, HP, Raychem, Johnson & Johnson, Campbell Soup and others allow several divisions to do about the same thing. Duplication and competition, starting very early in the development cycle, are a hallmark, as well, at IBM.

---

### Never Too Small

These ideas—duplication, purposeful seeding of competing skunk-works, eclecticism, and the like—are often seen by the smaller company, $5 to 100 million, as not workable for them, as only available to an IBM. However, our most successful friends in Silicon Valley, and in banking and in retailing, reject such talk outright. Duplicative development can start in the $5 million company. Experimentation can start in the $200,000 enterprise. In fact, it had better! "Where's the second product or service coming from?" is almost always a burning issue. So you got lucky, hit a home run (or at least a ground-rule double) with the first product or service. It's not enough. Too many founders assume that because they did it right once, they'll likely do it right again, that they are among the chosen few who can hit consecutive home runs. We don't see that happen very often. The true geniuses—the institution builders—start to split their company up, break it into pieces, foster eclecticism, skunkworks and the like at the $5 million mark at the latest (and the $200,000 mark if they are really wise).

---

### "Live with Ambiguity":
### Some Questions—and Things to Do Now

• We believe it's vital to senior managers—in all businesses in enterprises of all sizes—to become "expert" on this topic beyond this brief anecdotal analysis. We suggest that you occasionally read biographies of scientists and inventors, or tap the repertoire of Dartmouth's James Brian Quinn or the innovation group at MIT's Sloan School.

• More specifically, gather a group of ten to fifteen for a one- to two-day meeting. Include line executives, designers/buyers/engineers and marketers. First review the industry—historically and over the last ten years. Look at both minor and major innovations. Evaluate the source. (If you can't muster enough evidence, you might even try this on a multicompany basis.) Then on the second day repeat the exercise for your own company. Inviting retired pros in can add immeasurably to the process, we find. Do the results square with what we've presented here?

• Repeat the process above for various functions—MIS, manufacturing, accounting. Same story?

Instant results from the above may be limited. It is simply our observation that one needs to examine the process and history thoroughly to gain personal and group commitment to these notions. Otherwise, the response to most "horror stories" about innovation will be "That's an anomaly" or "You don't understand." Our bet is that the "horror stories," upon semisystematic investigation, will add up to a clear and normal pattern.

---

### Myth No. 2: We Must Begin with a Sound Set of Specs, Mustn't We?
### Counterpoint: Experiment and Move Fast

---

#### Innovation in Banking!

*Forbes* (January 28, 1985) reports:

[Richard Braddock, Citicorp's new top U.S. consumer banker] seems to be coming up with a new product every day or so: a personal computer banking service, insurance centers in branches, a credit card and checking account package. "It's not going to get any less confusing," Braddock says wryly of his myriad new business targets.

A shotgun approach! "Sure," says Braddock, "let the consumer pick the winners. The more things we can try in the marketplace, the better," he says, "as long as we can afford them."

---

### Home-Run Mentality vs
### Wee Willie Keeler Approach

We call it the "two path" theory. Path One constitutes the "home run mentality." A bright idea is rapidly turned into a $2 million, six-month study—a paper study. The paper evaluation of the study by various interested parties takes another three months. Some sort of a design go-ahead is then given, and technical spec writing, at a cost of another $3 million, takes another six months. The specs are evaluated by several groups during the following four-month period (we're now $7 or 8 million and a year and a half or so into the project). At this stage, a prototype is finally built. It costs $5 to 10 million and takes four to six months. And guess what? In all of history, it seems, from French-fry seasoning at McDonald's to IBM's System/360 computer, the first *and* second prototypes *don't work*. Never! But on Path One, you've invested so much time (and so much money) that competitors are catching up, or have leaped ahead.

So now you enter the "Ignore the misfit data and make the damn thing work" stage. Careers by this time are on the line. And a lot of bucks. And a lot of psychological investment in *the* "one best design." So ignore some of those data that suggest it doesn't work. And as for the rest? Well, competitors

have introduced three or four new products or services in the two years
you've been at it. Each has several new features. As time went by you got
further and further behind. So you have to complicate the product or service,
make sure it has every imaginable feature, get it *exactly* right. Remember,
this is going to be *the* home run to end all home runs. So you enter the "Make
it work" phase. It probably goes on for six months and costs $10 to 15 million
more. The whole process has now taken three years and cost $30 million.
You'll never scrap it now. You say, "The market's shaking out. It's now or
never." The future *always* looks more complicated (and dire) than simplistic
reconstructed models of the past. So you think, We must get *all* the features
on *this* version or the competitors will steal the market—for good. Falling
into this trap is the surest way to bring about exactly the gloom-and-doom
result you are trying to avoid. And as you delay and delay in order to craft
your home run, six bunt singles and two walks, several by unknown new competitors, put you out of the game for good or cripple you. In the end you
finally get to the marketplace with a camel invented by a committee and
including every feature known to humankind. It works poorly because of the
very fact that so many bells and whistles have been tied to it. But by now it's
so late that you *have* to introduce it—whether it works well or not.

In contrast to the home run mentality is Path Two, or the "Wee Willie
Keeler" approach. Wee Willie Keeler was a baseball player who played from
the 1890's to the 1910's, a consummate opportunist, who said, "Hit 'em where
they ain't." He made it into the Hall of Fame stroking only thirty-four home
runs in a career that lasted over twenty years.

The Wee Willie Keeler approach is practiced by 3M, Hewlett-Packard,
Raychem, Mervyn's, Wang, PepsiCo, Citicorp et al. to a T. How does it
work? Start by spending $25,000,* even up to a quarter of a million. Develop
a prototype, or a big hunk of it, in sixty to ninety days. Whether your product
or service is a digital switch, a new aircraft or a computer—or a new health
service or a financial instrument or a store format—our evidence suggests that
*something* can always be whacked together in that time.

Then evaluate the prototype; that takes another sixty days. (Also, even at
this early point, support—explicitly or tacitly—a second team or skunkwork
doing roughly the same thing.) You're already playing with something *tangible*, or a piece of something that's tangible, or, say, a large hunk of primitive
software code. Now you take the next little step. Maybe it costs a little more,
for a more fully developed prototype, or the beginning of a second prototype.
Let's say it costs $100,000 to $500,000. But again you build it fast, in the next
ninety days. And this time you can probably get it, or part of it, onto the
premises of a user (customer)—not an average user (that *is* a bit away), but a
"lead user" who's willing to experiment with you, or at least an in-house lead
user (a forward-thinking department). And on the process goes: slightly larger

*Or $1,500 to $5,000 for a small business.

investments, time frames that never run more than sixty to ninety days. It's the "learning organization" or the "experimenting organization."

At each step you learn a little more, but you have harsh reality tests—with hard product/service and live users/customers—very early. If it doesn't work, you weed it out quickly, before you have career lock-in and irreversible psychological addiction to the "one best design." Most generally, our experience suggests that the Wee Willie Keeler approach to product or service development, with a sizable dose of duplicate development thrown in, can cut the time it takes to complete the development cycle by 50 percent or more. And more products and services ensue. They're not always home runs (or even doubles). Usually, in fact, they're singles or sacrifice flies. And, true, all the potential features don't get loaded on the first product. Instead, you introduce another, and another, and another. But you do get there.

## Chicken Test!

Here are a couple of Path One "Swing for the fences" examples. First, the Chicken Test. Aircraft engines have to contend with the possible ingestion of flocks of birds. So one of the important things you do to test an aircraft engine is go out at some point to your local chicken farm, buy several gross of chickens, put them into the barrel of a huge (several feet in diameter) "chicken gun," and fire them at the engine. It's the ultimate pragmatic test. Now consider this: Rolls-Royce spends several years and about a quarter billion dollars on a new graphite-based engine, then it fails the Chicken Test. Reworking costs them a big share of a volatile market.

And more of the same: Xerox was determined to get it "exactly right." A twenty-nine-story tower full of MBA's at Rochester armed with powerful multi-hundred-variable models to score would-be product attributes generated and revised marketing study after marketing study in the mid-seventies. Debates raged endlessly. Machine families were going to be perfectly rationalized: Machine A simply was not going to cannabilize Machine B. Now, maybe this was a fine strategy for a de facto monopoly with patent protection. But as the analyses continued to be churned out, and as product development continued to lag—and to be continually complicated—competitors took upwards of 50 percent of Xerox's market away. (It took fully ten years—and substantial decentralization—to stem the decline.)

The Wee Willie Keeler approach, or the experimenting approach, is precisely aimed at getting your inevitable "Chicken Test(s)" out of the way early: in the first year, maybe even after the first ninety days, maybe sooner. Every new product fails a Chicken Test or two (or twenty-two) along the way. The burning issue is "When?" At the end of two or three years, by which point there's a whole array of competing products on the market? Or at the end of ninety days, or a hundred and eighty, when damage is still containable, when the design can still be changed?

### Eight Per Week/In Just Five Days/
### A Week versus Thirteen Weeks

Hewlett-Packard, it is said, introduces substantially new products at the rate of eight per week. They are the consummate singles hitters, and sometimes they turn out doubles and triples, even home runs. (Ironically, numerous singles often set in motion a series of developments that become de facto home runs; few home-run swings result in getting on base at all—see Myth No. 1, on the sloppy course of invention.) But HP thinks it has problems: it views its already remarkably short product-development cycles as too long. So the watchword at HP in 1983 became "QTP" (Quick Turnaround Projects). The major instrument whose genesis we mentioned above—the one that emerged from a catalog illustration and a hand-drawn sketch—took, from conception to development and debugged prototype, just seventeen weeks. (Remember that Kelly Johnson's development of the first jet aircraft, the YP-80, took 136 days from concept to flying prototype.)

Raychem is another company that does Wee Willie Keeler's kind of work. Raychem is a highly profitable ($700 million) maker of sophisticated products based on materials science. On the occasion of the company's twenty-fifth anniversary, in 1982, Chairman Paul Cook estimated that 200,000 products had gone through the Raychem product line! The company's idea of a winner is a 100% market share, with a 90 percent operating margin, in a $5 million market. It listens to customers, and builds what the customer wants. It comes as no surprise that its motto is "Raychem in Response." Typical was this example we stumbled across. A Raychem field engineer got word of an undersea leak at an offshore oil platform in the North Sea. Within 120 hours (just five days) Raychem had shipped in researchers from Menlo Park, California (headquarters), and Swindon, England (European R&D headquarters), put up a field site on location, developed an honest-to-gosh state-of-the-art new product, prototyped it, debugged it and installed it. (It's now a $10 million or so business; as usual, its ultimate market bore little relation to its first use.) The contrast between Raychem and most of the rest of the "real world" was aptly captured by a participant in a recent seminar: "In our company, at the end of those five days, you'd have been darned lucky to have gotten your travel orders cut to get out of California."

---

#### New Ventures Strategy

Allen Michels rapidly built Santa Clara–based Convergent Technologies into a $400 million company. His secret? He started spinning off mostly independent ventures (usually three-person teams) at a very early stage. At the heart of this new ventures strategy, he declares, is the "Try it" orientation. His primary advice: "Think small." "Make decisions and don't contemplate." "Review the day every day and move ahead." Above all, he adds, "Engineers need decisiveness. They mustn't allow themselves to be hung up in pursuit of perfection." In fact, he says, the overarching management challenge is to "nurture rapid decisive activity in a disorderly environment."

Far from the world of HP, Raychem and Convergent Technologies is Mervyn's, the winner by quite a margin in the fine Dayton-Hudson family of retailers. Their winning formula? They accomplish in one week what it takes their prime competitors thirteen weeks or more to do. Every Wednesday morning at 7:00 A.M., fifty-two weeks a year, a hundred Mervyn's people— the president, the executive vice presidents and almost all the merchants (buyers) in the company—march into a giant auditorium. Before them, up on a huge wallboard, are about thirty or so big blank spaces. For the next six hours they will fight, scrap, pull, tug, tear hair. They will assess and interpret the last week's successes and failures. They will turn the blank spaces into the contents of a thirty-page booklet listing items they want to have featured next week in the hundred or so Mervyn's stores in the billion-dollar-plus system. They are developing the *Ad Supplement*. Less than a week later it will be mailed out to approximately fifteen million people! In sum, Mervyn's remerchandises their sizable operation once per week; others are lucky to manage it in 10 to 15 weeks. The magic? None. It's simply what Mervyn's does for a living. It's their (boring? obsessive? passionate?) equivalent of "Raychem in Response."

## Turn It to Tin

Howard Head, inventor of Head skis and the Prince tennis racquet, says, "We try to get a prototype made as soon as possible. I want to see an idea. I want to hold it and touch it." That's what it's all about. Such products— early prototypes, even the final products of a Wang or a Rolm—often aren't as "pretty" as the Western Electric or Xerox product. In Tracy Kidder's *The Soul of a New Machine*, about Data General's remarkably quick construction of a super minicomputer needed to compete with DEC, the outcome was described by various DG players as "a wart on a wart on a wart" or "a bag on the side of the Eclipse [the predecessor machine that was being revolutionized]." No, it wasn't pretty. But it was quick, and it got started without muss and fuss.

At HP some R&D managers jokingly argue that a new rule should be instituted: "Anyone developing technical specs more than three pages long will be summarily fired, without right of appeal." (In contrast, a Texas Instruments executive considers some of their recent failures: "[The] number one mortal sin is excessive quantification of the imponderable.")

The late Fred Hooven, holder of over thirty major patents, one-time student of Orville Wright and former senior R&D manager at Ford, used to go on at length about the necessity of getting something built quickly. He talked about the reluctance to experiment and some of the silly reasons he'd heard for failing to do so: "My favorite was when they told me, 'We can't put the engineers and the model shop together because it'll get the drawings dirty.'" He'd argue that getting on with it, doing the next live test or mocking up the next piece would often "take half an hour, whereas sending it 'upstairs' for formal drawings and specifications will take at least four months." That's what we're really talking about: the difference between half an hour and four months! The difference *is* that great.

The phenomenon holds for far more than product development. In process development the experimental way is critical too. An article by Joseph Limprecht and Robert Hayes, "Germany's World-Class Manufacturers," in the November–December 1982 issue of *Harvard Business Review*, argues, for instance, that the American fixation on the home run is a major factory/process issue: "As the auto, steel, and machine tool industries grimly attest, Americans have not been as zealous [as the Germans] in making incremental improvements in mature technologies.... American companies put too much faith in the possibility of breakthroughs." As we review the Milliken, or Perdue Farms environment, for example, we find the contrary. Process breakthroughs are hoped for, but the major management effort is aimed at making, non-stop, the small improvements in performance that inch productivity along.

## Analysis I versus Analysis II

The case adds up, on another dimension, to what we call Analysis I versus Analysis II. Analysis I is abstract. It depends on market reports, lengthy technical specs. Analysis II is all about immersion: *Touch. Feel. Do. Try. Fix.* As John Masters, head of Canada's most successful oil and gas wildcatter firm says, "This is so simple it sounds stupid, but it is amazing to me how few oil people understand that you only find oil and gas when you drill wells. You may think that you're finding it when you're drawing maps and studying logs, but you have to drill." We are adamant about labeling this pragmatic immersion process "analysis," because in many quarters today only the abstract stuff is viewed as "analysis." But the scientific method rests foursquare on empiricism, which is to say, the experimenting mentality, not the home-run—on paper—mentality. Get *hard* data. Get it quickly. That's the key. Get market data, of course, but market data from *trying it* with a user as soon as possible. Get technical data, of course, but from *building* a prototype and *handling* it as the real world does, not keeping it bottled up forever in the pristine, sterile, temperature-controlled, dust-free lab or test kitchen.

## "Experiment":
## Some Questions and Things To Do Now

• Take two recent new product or service (or business) introductions that succeeded. Take two that failed or were inordinately delayed. Analyze them in some detail. Are there any differences consistent with the experimenting ideas presented here? Was "test it now" as opposed to later more the mark of the successes? (Assuming that the failure cases were marked by a lack of experimentation, what were the reasons? E.g., lack of coordination between warring functions? delays to get specifications "exactly right" before prototyping? List 10 typical blocks, and what you can do to remove them.)

• Repeat the analysis above for the industry as a whole, reviewing the practices of two industry leaders, two laggards, then three or four of the most recent innovations. Did they come from people who move fast? Or from massive, well-planned, multiyear efforts?

• Are you willing to gamble on putting a product into a partial test market (e.g., two stores) quickly? Or to seek out a potential "lead user" before the design is finalized? Is such behavior the norm or the exception? (Again, review systematically a handful of successes and failures to aid this analysis.) As a live test, see if you can *halve* the planned time to put two new (under development) services or products into the hands of lead users/test markets. (Remember that there are all sorts of levels of test-market effort. Long before full scale test-market launch you can conduct numerous quick-and-dirty five-person samples to test reaction to bits or pieces of prototypes.)

• Most generally, is this—honestly—a "Try it, test it" environment? In new product design? Manufacturing? Operations? MIS? Do most people (the young especially) think that "to get ahead you've got to be constantly trying stuff" or "keeping your nose clean is what *really* counts around here"? Are you sure you can answer this accurately (i.e., from *their* perspective)?

• Can you, looking ahead, pinpoint four or five places where you can *test* the experimenting notion? Push a new product team (or factory process improvement team) to try something faster, to cut the bureaucracy and get on with a practical experiment? (If you come up empty on this, get five to ten of your people together for three or four hours. Our experience is—unfailingly—that you'll come out of it with twenty to thirty practical ideas in the next 15 to 30 days.)

## Myth No. 3: Creativity (Innovation) Follows
### from Reflection
### Counterpoint: Champions/Skunks a Necessity

Home-run swings take muscle-bound athletes. If innovation took powerful "thinkers," we would expect to find that those thinkers would regularly climb to a mountaintop retreat to look out over the pines and accomplish the necessary breakthroughs (and then return, presumably on schedule). If, on the other hand, the Wee Willie Keeler paradigm is the norm in innovative organizations, as we claim it is, one would expect to find bleary-eyed folks staring at CRT's or test tubes or mucking about with a nutty fashion designer in forgotten corners of basements and lofts. Instead of tweeds and meerschaum pipes, one would expect torn dungarees and a determined cast to the eye.

### Champions Everywhere—Passion a Must

It turns out that the bleary eyes have quite a role to play. If an endless series of practical experiments is the "norm" of the truly innovative enterprise (remember *The Nobel Duel:* Grind more pig brains), people called champions are a necessity.

We've become collectors of stories like these. Formal in-house studies of research project successes at IBM always unearth the presence of a champion. National Science Foundation studies suggest that the champion's role is crucial in pushing an idea to fruition. MIT's Ed Schon argues most generally, "The new idea either finds a champion or it dies. No ordinary involvement with a new idea provides the energy required to cope with the indifference and resistance that change provokes." John Masters of Canadian Hunter, looking back on successful projects (and reminding himself of the need to support lonely champions), adds, "A really new idea at first has only one believer." Brian Quinn, previously cited, concludes that "fanaticism is crucial." And Peter Drucker, looking back on fifty years' experience in all walks of life in *Adventures of a Bystander*, remarks, "Whenever anything is being accomplished, it is being done, I have learned, by a monomaniac with a mission." Thomas Edison's premier biographer concluded, "What set Edison apart was that, with all his boundless exaggeration, he conveyed the feeling that he would succeed. No matter what the obstacles, he would pound away until he had demolished them." A successful consumer-goods manager argues that one of his prime criteria for promotion within the brand manager ranks is that the successful candidate be "a thug"—i.e., determined to beat down any barriers in his path. A study of Nobel Prize winners suggests that they often give away a few IQ points relative to the rest of the researcher colleagues on top of the heap. Time and again, they are said by their peers to have instead such traits as "peasant toughness," "a streak of brutality" and "killer instincts," and to be "good finishers."

There are crucial implications here. In the halcyon days of Organizational Development in the 1960's and 1970's, cooperation and conflict-smoothing were considered the most desirable traits for any human being working in a sizable enterprise. Our champions, however, are usually not the souls of sweetness and light. As Jewkes puts it: "The most inventive spirits have confessed a constitutional aversion to cooperation." In fact, the people who are tenacious, committed champions are often royal pains in the neck (except to their immediate team members, who would often go over the hill for them).

Egotistical. Competitive. Passionate. Persistent beyond belief. These are the most universal traits of those who withstand all the inevitable rebuffs (occasionally personal) and get their "it" to market. (Or get their change in an accounting procedure accepted by the factory managers.) They must be fostered and nurtured—even when it hurts a little (or a lot)—if regular innovation is to flourish.

## Failure Goes Hand in Glove

A crucial corollary is that the organization that would nourish champions *must* also tolerate, even celebrate, failures. General George Doriot, the godfather of development along Route 128 in Massachusetts, said in an address to Digital Equipment (one of the first companies he wisely invested in), "If failure can be explained, and it's not based on lack of morality, then to me failure is acceptable." The best of the companies we've looked at explicitly support failures in the sense that they admit that failure along the way is normal. Their philosophies say so, and tolerance for it is fostered through war stories. Setbacks—not sloppy foul-ups, but thoughtful missteps along the way—are considered to be normal. The winners are seen as people who persist. People who fail, sometimes in rather big ways, may get demotions or lateral transfers—but the ranks of corporate vice presidents are densely peppered with those who have *returned* from "Siberia" to bring a critical product to the market or contribute in some other important way. Even egregious failure is thus seen as a natural way-stop on the path to eventual success.

---

### "Champions":
### Some Questions—and Things to Do Now

• Take *twenty* projects that succeeded—small (mainly) and large, process (all functions) and product (or service); likewise, take *twenty* failures. Are the successes marked more by naturally emerging champions than are the failures? This analysis should best be discussed in a group of five to fifteen, each of whom has done a similar homework assignment (again from all functions).

• If champions do mark the successes, how were they nurtured? Was a godfather running interference? Or was grabbing their own territory without aid more commonplace? (We find that all environments, innovative or not, spawn at least a few champions. The most innovative are marked by more champions, nurtured consciously by a *network* of past champions-godfathers. The *fewer* champions among the less innovative are lone rangers who broke out without godfathers.)

• Take four terrific middle-aged champions. Where did their championing start? Usually the answer is "Very early in their careers"; if so, is championing being encouraged today in the lower levels of the organization? (Incipient or full-blown atrophy is best observed as the absence of champions among the young.)

• Be more specific. Evaluate your career—alone or with four or five colleagues in a half-day off-site session. Are you all or some of you former champions? If yes, how did it come about (the role of your godfather, etc.)? If no, why/how was your championing thwarted?

• Look, specifically, and in a separate exercise, for champions at *lower levels* in *non*-line functions: Are they popping up in MIS? Accounting? Personnel? If not, why not?

• How is the word (and idea) of *failure* treated by you and your colleagues? Positively (given that it was a vigorous, well thought out effort)? Or negatively? Take a project or two you're *most* proud of. Are numerous small failures a part of it? If so, do you tolerate (encourage, in the best sense) such failures by others? One service company marketing vice president says, "We need to fail more quickly around here (i.e., get the inevitable failures out of the way faster)." (Also see a more extensive discussion of failure in chapter 11.)

---

### Myth No. 4: Big, Formal Groups Are Essential
### Counterpoint: Skunkworks as the Norm

Giant projects require giant well-integrated groups, it's said. Is the BOF (basic oxygen furnace), by which Japan and MITI, supposedly with malice aforethought (read central planning), battered the U.S. steel industry, a big project? Is GE's entry into plastics and aircraft engines big? The IBM System/360? The Polaris submarine? Of course each is, and yet we'll observe that each was spearheaded by a "skunk" (bootlegger, scrounger) working at the far edges of the traditional corporate structure.

Kollmorgen, Raychem, Convergent Technologies, Macy's and J&J are really nothing more than collections of skunkworks: tiny to modest teams in realtively small divisions performing numerous off-line activities.

Even massive IBM: its Personal Computer (PC) came from one of no fewer than a half-dozen parallel development teams. (Don Estridge's winning team initially consisted of twelve somewhat discredited people working in a run-down facility in Boca Raton, Florida.) And the company's current move toward Independent Business Units (IBU's)—close to twenty have been created in the last two years—is yet another of their continuing efforts to certify non-bureaucratic bunches. To similar purpose were the senior Mr. Watson's constant lauding of Wild Ducks and, more formally, establishment of fifty IBM Fellows, each with a five-year carte blanche to stir things up. Another senior IBMer talks, with relish, about $500,000 that "slipped away." He knew about it, he says, and then again he didn't. The end result was a major new memory device created by a small skunkwork in about 150 days. (Larger groups had been wrestling with the project—unsuccessfully—for years.)

*The evidence rolls in: when a practical innovation occurs, a skunkwork, usually with a nucleus of six to twenty-five, is at the heart of it.*

Bootlegging marked each step (from the initial technical triumph to the organizational form of the exploitation group) on the way to GE's spectacular successes in aircraft engines and engineering plastics. Their first locomotive and their first off-highway vehicle both got their start from bootleg projects. In fact, every major internally grown business success at GE, from high-tech turbines to the GE Credit Corporation (GECC) and GE Information Services Company (GEISCO), came through a passionate champion, working within a skunkwork operation, always at or slightly beyond the periphery of GE's formal policies and central systems. Then, in the seventies, "planning" was centralized—with deadening effect. When young (just forty-five at the time of his promotion) Jack Welch became chairman in April 1981, and an early act was to dismantle two-thirds of the central (corporate) strategic planning staff. The reason wasn't antipathy to strategic planning (they still do it well in the trenches). Welch had concluded that a return to technological preeminence demanded inducing more entrepreneurial skunks and putting them to work.

Find an industry, look at its principal accomplishments, and you'll invariably find a trail of skunks. Relatively small L. M. Ericcson spurts to the top in the international digital telecommunication switch competition. The origin of the LME product? Twenty disaffected engineers, angry at their bosses, who banded together (within the corporation, but barely) and built the AXE switch—cowing in the process such giant stalwarts as the plodding Siemens. The about-to-be-industry-standard UNIX operating system was created at AT&T/Bell Labs as a hobbyist project using spare computer capacity to build a language to meet the needs of a small group (of two!). (The absence of corporate oversight, says one knowledgeable observer, led to development of a language that "lacked the many compromises and complexities that inevitably afflict large team efforts.")

Name your industry! Mercantile Bank, a highly innovative regional bank headquartered in Dallas, has exploited telecommunications and computer technology much more rapidly than 99 percent of the banking community. It has a vital, high-fee service-producing 600-bank network now. Where did it come from? A big, well-planned, centrally funded MIS-department-driven project? No! One fellow had the idea, and George Clark, the bank's president, had the good sense to let him run with it. The fellow worked on it principally *at home*; it took him about three months and cost but $200,000. His system was simple, practical and to the point. John Fisher, another champion with an effective executive champion protecting him, vaulted BancOne of Columbus, Ohio, to the fore in fee service businesses. With a small supporting cast, he has time and again worked miracles developing, for example, the support system for Merrill-Lynch's revolutionary cash management scheme.

And yet . . . "Sure, Bill Hewlett did it with the hand-held calculator. You can readily imagine someone putting that in his or her pocket, or carrying it home in a brown paper bag. But what about the big stuff?" Well, the GE locomotive is a classic case in point. GE had been building subassemblies. A group wanted to build the whole thing. They were flat out told—not once, but four times—to knock it off. Apparently that was exactly the spur they needed. They *"bootlegged" a locomotive* in an underutilized facility in Erie, Pennsylvania. Locomotives decidedly don't fit in vest pockets.

Let's get even more ridiculous. Consider the development of the basic oxygen furnace (BOF). It turns out not to have been a meticulously planned ten-year 100,000-milestone effort inspired by MITI. BOF technology emerged from Nippon Kokan, then the third largest steel company in Japan (now second, approaching first). And within that steel company, it came from the second and far less respected (disdained, if the truth be known) group of technologists (Thomas rather than Open Hearth engineers). Moreover, within that least respected group, a young fanatic was at the core of it. Pretty much against his superiors' wishes, he went off to Austria to learn about their early experiments with BOF. He came back, commandeered some outdated equipment (an old ladle), carried on BOF experiments "off line." The story is, of course, more complex, especially when we get to the final exploitation of the technology in Japan (a half-dozen to a dozen years ahead of the Americans). But essentially it is, clearly, a skunkwork tale: a small group competing against a stronger and more respected technological group in-house, against bigger companies in Japan as a whole—and led, as is so regularly the case, by a fanatic champion.*

Furthermore, we find the same skunkworkish activities at the heart of *process* improvement as well as product development. Far from being the result of the meticulously planned activities of industrial or systems engineers, they usually occur incrementally, as the result of the efforts of four or five disgruntled machine operators or central MIS users who commandeer a couple of industrial engineers or programmers on Saturdays and at nights and redesign a part of a line, or a machine, or a flow process.

---

*We picked up along the way a case even harder to believe: a breakthrough in aluminum production (at Kaiser Aluminum). A whole pilot plant was built off line, without senior management's explicit awareness.

## The Time It Takes

What are these bunches of six to twenty-five people—these skunkworks—all about? First, most seem to do things in an exceptionally short period of time. Allen Michels of Convergent Technologies talks of regularly telescoping four years' work into one. GE's Gerhard Neumann (aircraft engines) and Lockheed's Kelly Johnson (airframes) regularly reduced development time 50 to 90 percent below the norm—on giant projects. Tom West, Data General's computer project leader, suspects that the crucial breakthroughs in microcoding occurred during the course of a week, and probably a very long weekend. At Hewlett-Packard, the hand-drawn sketch we mentioned earlier was translated into hard product in only seventeen weeks, a year or so less than "normal." Bell Labs executives, recalling the development of the digital switch, refer time and again to "breakthroughs" that took place in the home basements of individuals over a single weekend. Many Xerox executives talk lovingly of the East Rochester skunkworks (a ten- to fifteen-person group sequestered since 1978 in a "leaky third-floor loft" in a deteriorating eighty-year-old building): product after product pours out, often after only a few weeks' effort (one 28-day project has now generated $3 billion in revenue), while hundreds at the main lab are stymied, often for years.*

In sum: when big groups are at their wit's end, they turn to the skunkworks, and near-magical results start to occur in only three or four weeks, or less. Why? Surely one reason is that in such groups there's no passing the buck. The pressure is on. The deadlines can't be evaded, even if they're not entirely real: some of West's colleagues at Data General did chide him for going out of his way to "create dramatic events." West is in good company. Thomas Edison, it is said, had a habit of announcing a product to the press and only afterwards bothering to go about inventing it, while putting himself under the pressure of an absurd self-inflicted deadline.

## The Matter of Quality

But what happens with a "quick and dirty" skunkwork product? Isn't the quality lower? Does it ever fit with the rest of the product line? Indeed it does! In fact, the stuff from skunkworks is usually of *higher* quality, even though it was invented in a tiny fraction of the so-called normal time. What's the reason? Under the pressure of ridiculous deadlines, and suffering limited staffing, the skunkwork seldom reinvents the wheel. A while ago Tom was involved in some "reverse engineering" of a high-technology product. The client's manufacturing costs were about $1,400 a unit, while the Japanese competitors' cost was about $800. It had already been determined that most of the difference was not "better" Japanese technology or cheaper Japanese labor. Tom and his colleagues decided to look at some little part of the

*Others speak less lovingly, for exactly the same reason.

machine, such as a small electric motor doing a mundane task. The unit cost ran to an egregious $60. What had happened? The engineers had gone and reinvented the electric motor (in 1980) to get it exactly right for their need. The Japanese, to accomplish the same task, had gone outside to a vendor who supplied a garden variety $2.95 motor; to that they had added twenty-five cents' worth of resistors to change the motor's operating characteristics. The "garden variety" $2.95 motor was developed in about 1940; its reliability is unsurpassed.

Big groups tend to reinvent the wheel, start from scratch with every activity. Small groups *must* improvise—and the improvisation is usually an adaptation of a standard item that's been manufactured flawlessly for years. The IBM PC group went outside to get a disc drive—the first IBM group to do so. And Lockheed's Kelly Johnson insists that one of the fourteen "golden rules" of skunking is the ability to go wherever is necessary—including going to direct competitors—to purchase components.

## Small Is Beautiful

Still, we must ask: What is the source of the skunkwork's power? What drives the skunks to success when larger groups founder? We think that it is, above all, a sense of *ownership* and *commitment*. West describes the phenomenon to author Tracy Kidder in *The Soul of a New Machine:* "There's thirty guys out there who think it's their machine. I don't want that tampered with." We'll go into it in some detail in chapter 14, "Ownership"; the point to be emphasized here is the importance of smallness. The small group is, simply, crucial to innovation. Recent studies by the National Science foundation put the optimal size of a research group at about seven. Convergent Technologies says the maximum size of a development team should be two or three; Raychem says five; HP says about six; 3M, no more than eight or ten; Digital, fifteen to twenty. West's team had about thirty. Jewkes observes that the optimal number appears to be under fifty, even for complex projects like aircraft, though Kelly Johnson did go up to one hundred twenty-five, and Gerhard Neumann went even a bit higher. But regardless of what the number is exactly, it is surprisingly small.

## The Role of Competition

Also crucial to innovation because of the sense of ownership and commitment it engenders is competition. In the Data General case, competition was encouraged at all levels. It was West's team *versus* the industry (Build the best damned 32-bit minicomputer), *versus* Digital (the hatred rival that had gotten there first), *versus* corporate (who had cut off the funding for West's project, forcing it into bootleg status) and, above all, *versus* North Carolina (the large, central, well-funded development group). And finally there was mini-group *versus* mini-group competition within the team (the hardware people *versus* the software people), and occasionally, even one individual versus another (Who would get the debugging done first?). The objective in West's words: "to get a machine out the door with your name on it."

Formal recognition of the value of internal competition may have originated at GM in the 1920's, with Alfred E. Sloan's purposeful creation of division overlap. P&G instituted brand-versus-brand competition way back in 1931. As a fairly small company then, they felt that their innovative juices would dry up unless brands were allowed to engage in "no-holds-barred competition." Yes, such competition did (and does) lead to duplication. Yes, it did (and does) mean cannibalization of other P&G products. Yes it did (and does) entail costs. But the positive outcome, making sure that the next product comes from P&G rather than by a competitor, was thought then—and is still thought—to outweigh by far the more readily calculable "downside" costs. 3M states adamantly that they always want the "second product in the category to come from a competing 3M division, rather than from a competitor." Mars' sixty divisions follow the same rule, with virtually no limits: for example, a U.S. division having problems in its own markets shifts its efforts to Australia, where it competes with a Mars subsidiary with a huge share there. Perkin-Elmer, a top performer in the instrument business, talks about "two-site" management: at least two wholly independent centers must be working on anything important. HP divisions, too, compete with one another. The result? An HP computer group introduces products that "should have" come from the hand-held calculator group, and vice versa.

Internal competition is darned difficult to manage. There are a great number of subtleties and traps that come with it. A term that we've developed to encompass the opportunity (and focus on the problem) is "(ED)IC"—(Externally Directed) Internal Competition. Internal competition at Data General—West's "fight" with North Carolina—was aimed at developing hard product to fill a gap in Data General's product line; it did not involve the marketers' view of a product versus the designers' view versus the view of finance staff, in "wars" waged via paper studies with the prime, albeit unspoken, objective of "getting the other staff." True, West wanted to "get" North Carolina, but the only way he could do so (or they could "get" him) was by inventing something that worked or didn't in the real world. On paper, internal competition is not only not necessary but downright wasteful. But in the real world and over the long haul it is the engine of sustained success.

## A Pain in the Neck

How do you manage "collections of skunkworks"—duplication, internal competition, fanatics? In Search of Excellence referred to "leaky systems," a term that comes from Tait Elder, president of the internal venture group at Allied Corporation and formerly of 3M. Tom West of Data General comments that "there are a lot of people pretending this [computer] project doesn't exist." Talk with HP, IBM, 3M, Citicorp, American Express managers about managing bootlegging and their eyes suddenly glaze over. Their response is an important clue. Managing under these conditions involves staying constantly on top of things—but at the same time, one "sort of" (a term we've come to cherish) pretends it's not there. That's also essential, to foster the all-important sense of ownership without which a skunkwork ceases to exist (again, see chapter 14).

Nothing we can say will reduce the agony of managing champions and skunkworks. We cannot tell you how many you need as a function of the size of your company or its position in your industry's life cycle. We cannot tell when you've cut them off too late, when too early. We are most pleased when a seminar participant tells us he's "trying one" or "at least my instinct is not to chop one off if I see it springing up." We are only sure that skunkworks are vital to innovation, whether you are running a 12-person accounts receivable department, a 25-person sanitation department in a small town or chairing a Fortune 500 company. And we do have some ideas about how you can create an environment where skunkworks naturally emerge. Turn to chapter 11, "The Context of Innovation," for those ideas, but be forewarned: they involve very little managing in the traditional sense.

The turned-on band seems to be at the heart, then, of innovation of all sorts—big *and* small, new product (or service) *and* process improvement. Even when big teams are necessary, as for the final assembly and the launch of, say, the IBM System/360 or, surely, a missile system, look for help to a skunkwork when a crisis arises (see Myth 4B Counterpoint: Small within Big). And in sales too: GE managers, HP managers, 3M managers, Citicorp managers all talk about taking new territory with skunkwork sales development operations, calling on "unapproved" segments of markets.

---

### Ten Quick Questions (and Ten Quick Answers) about Skunkworks

1. Can you "appoint" or "designate" a skunkwork?

Yes. Experience from Convergent Technologies, Mercantile Bank, Raychem, Apple Computer, Monarch Marking (Pitney-Bowes) and IBM, among others, suggests you can. On the other hand, the desired end is to achieve an innovative climate from which they "emerge naturally, somehow, at roughly the right time," as a GE manager puts it.

2. *How many people in an ideal skunkwork?*

The evidence suggests a number ranging from 2 to 125, with 5 to 25 surfacing most regularly. (P.S.: Even at the level of 2 to 3, extensive multifunctional experience—manufacturing and marketing as well as design—is a *must*, according to the pros.)

3. *Can you have a part-time leader or part-time members?*

3M would say no. So would we. Ownership and commitment are "it."

"Part-time ownership" is a non sequitur (you're either "on the bus" or "off the bus," as Ken Kesey used to say).

### 4. Who's the best leader?

Clear agreement on this: a "tinkerer" with an urge to act, *not* a "blue sky" type. Effective skunkworks have a dramatic outward and pragmatic (customer, action) thrust.

### 5. Are there no rules?

Yes, there are rules and controls. Kelly Johnson insisted, though, that they be extraordinarily simple and to the point, as did GE's Gerhard Neumann. Michels says milestones are great and vital, as long as they don't exceed four or five in number ("and I'm not talking about PERT charts," he adds with emphasis).

### 6. Should we expect the quality to suffer?

No, it will likely be better. But compatibility may suffer a bit. A 5 percent "cost" in lost compatibility (or confusion from partial duplicating) is usually a more-than-fair price for a possible 200-300 percent speedup.

### 7. What do we do if they (skunkworks) fail?

Most will. The Raychem/3M/HP trick is that there's always a next place/project to go to. If there is no pad/fall-back, you won't get many volunteers. (Which is not to say that you should look with favor upon someone who lopes from failure to failure.)

### 8. Do you have to offer a big monetary incentive?

No. HP and 3M, best of the (big) bunch, don't. As Tom West explained in *The Soul of a New Machine*, people do it so they'll get to play "pinball" again: "You win with this machine, you get to build the next" (i.e., participate in an even tougher future assignment).

### 9. Do you allow the internal competition between skunkworks to be "unbridled," as P&G calls it?

No. P&G lies! The powerful P&G quality standard is always adhered to. HP is the same. The P&G/HP constraints on competition are twofold: (1) external focus—Do "it" with live customers, not on paper; (2) the "it" must be of unsurpassed quality, not a cheap low-end product/ service aimed at knocking off one of our own high-end market leaders.

### 10. What else?

Kelly Johnson says the skunkworks must have purchasing authority, be allowed to buy components on the market, if necessary, rather than from one's own divisions, which may produce a component at a higher price, or one that is more complicated, or too late.

11. (Bonus) *When should I expect results?*

Expect tangible outcomes (not finished products) in sixty to ninety days. If you don't get them, forget it.

---

### "Skunkworks":
### Some Questions—and Things to do Now

· Personal exercise: Go back at least as far as college. Assess the *five* things you are most proud of—being on an athletic team that turned around and surprised everyone, a literary endeavor, a sale to a new major customer. How many of the five were a product of a-"skunkworklike" organizational arrangement? (Most find the answer is either "All" or "A majority.") Assess the conditions that lead to the turned-on team/skunkworks creation; the kind of things that fostered high performance. Does the analysis have applicability to your current organizational setting (i.e., do most of the preconditions for effective skunking exist or not)?

· Look at the last *ten* innovations (small or large, process or new product/service). How many originated in or were abetted by skunkworks? (If the "winners" have been marked by skunkworks, how—*in detail*—were they started/sustained?) Look at five recently stalled or failed projects: Is there an absence or presence of skunkworks? Look at two *failed skunkworks*. What went wrong? (*No* full-time, volunteer champion? No early customer contact? No freedom to purchase outside? Too much money and thus not enough pressure? Premature corporate intrusion once it started to look like a winner?)

· Become a historian! Collect ten great skunkwork tales, from the founder (if applicable) to today. Tell them. Video-tape the stories, if the protagonists are still around. In this and other ways, begin to get "skunking-as-normal-procedure" into the air.

· Sit down with a stalled project team in the next ten days. Listen to them—for a full day perhaps. Look for opportunities to get a one to three-person band to go off and do a quick subproject (semi-skunkwork) to break the logjam. (Such partial and guided starts underpin shifts to more entrepreneurial climates.)

---

### Related Myth 4A: Only Strong Functions Spawn
### Concern for Innovation
### Counterpoint: Smash Functions Together

"Engineers/designers lose out to operations and finance people in divisional organizations." "The division is only interested in short-term profit." "Only a strong functional monolith will keep the engineering/designer/buyer/brand manager (and innovation) at the forefront." So runs the conventional argument. It's a fine argument on paper, but it doesn't hold much water in practice. The functional monolith is, almost by definition, bureaucratic, not commitment/small team/skunkwork/action-oriented.

## Division Equals Being Adaptive

For constantly innovating companies—Hewlett-Packard, 3M, Johnson & Johnson, PepsiCo, Raychem, Emerson Electric, Mars, Rolm, Kollmorgen, Citicorp—the division is the solution (and the strategy). J&J constantly creates new divisions. Its corporate watchword is "growing big by staying small." Says J&J chairman Jim Burke: "Decentralization causes creativity, which in turn leads to productivity. That form of productivity [creativity-driven] is giant leaps ahead of all other forms." Likewise PepsiCo prides itself on being "the [world's] biggest small-company environment." IBM people use exactly the same language.

The structure, for these companies, drives and shapes not only their strategy but even the specifics of their product offerings. In fact, for them, the structure *is* the strategy. A Rolm executive speaks to the point eloquently: "The insides of our CBX's [Computer Branch Exchanges] look like us [as a company]—just a bunch of microprocessors on a board talking to each other. [Those of a particular competitor] look like them—inflexible and hierarchical architecture."

Today we are seeing a new wave of radical decentralization aimed directly at increasing innovative vitality. the first such wave—we call it Round no. 1—lasted from about 1950 to 1970, and was generally superseded by the matrix forms of organizations designed to control the giants that American corporations had become as single divisions grew larger than the original company was when it divisionalized. This one—"Round no. 2"—is coming largely from mature industries, with major moves at places like Campbell Soup and Brunswick leading the way. Interestingly, these two have turned their backs (explicitly) on portfolio theory. Rather than pigeonholing people and products, they are giving all hands in any division the freedom to create new markets, in any product area, on the J&J/3M/HP model.

Round no. 1 decentralization was *not* always accompanied by "leaning up" the corporate staffs. In fact, it was often accompanied by the growth of central staff and the addition of a "group executive" layer of management. Round no. 2 is invariably accompanied by paring down central staffs. Brunswick's Jack Reichert, for instance, has cut corporate staff, so far, from 560 to 230. He has completely removed the group executive layer; he has also given each division "six-figure spending authority" (up from a tiny amount). The result, in part: "Decisions that once took weeks or months now take hours or days." Round no. 2 is marked as well by a move toward much smaller divisions, and eschews many paper economies of scale (usually unrealized) on both the marketing and the manufacturing/operations sides.

## Linking Functions

A vital advantage of the small team/small division approach to organization is the ability to manage, with less muss and fuss, the "pass-off" interfaces (e.g., design to manufacturing or operations) that, we'd judge, account for 75 percent of the delays in the development of new products and new services—in every business from high technology to banking. At HP, the principle of the "triad" development team ensures that the manufacturer and marketer (as well as the design engineer) are full-scale (i.e., full-time) partners in the development process starting very early in the design phase. (A former student of Tom's from IBM went so far as to call the Triad "HP's most distinctive positive [relative to IBM] trait.") 3M follows the same principle, putting a full-time manufacturer on the team long before a full-time body can be warranted theoretically (on paper). The enhanced manufacturability and increased effectiveness of the pass-off to manufacturing is huge.

John Masters of Canadian Hunter brought about much of his success with a similar routine—getting the geologists and petroleum engineers to communicate: "We expand the horizons of our engineers and geologists by constant association, by osmosis. We have lunch meetings, management meetings, social occasions. We provide the environment for them to rub together, then let nature take its course. Suddenly an engineer starts to think like a geologist and vice versa."

Interestingly, Ford is taking the same tack. The company now systematically solicits input from all functions, including hourly workers on the line, very early in the design process. First-line people comment on the manufacturability of various parts and are full-scale members even of advance design teams. Said a senior Ford executive in 1983: "We've used the process on our last two new product launches. It's only taken two. Results have been exceptional. I don't think there's a person in the company who would go back to the old way." He also quantified the results: hourly workers provided over seven-hundred *implemented* design changes in one Ford truck (the successful Bronco)!

Milliken Customer Action Teams (CATs) follow a like principle. Salespersons and marketers were regularly bedeviled, in the manufacturing-driven company, by a "we can't stop the line to run new product samples" mentality. Now, the institutionalized reaction is to create a CAT at the drop of a hat. It consists of four or five Milliken people (from sales, marketing, design, manufacturing, accounting) and a handful of customer people. With typical determination, Milliken mounted 1100 (!) teams in the first 15 months of the process, exploiting many untapped market opportunities, and cutting sample delivery time from months (on average) to eight or ten *days*.

It's important that we bring to the surface the prime objection we get to this point: "Won't the 'creative' skill (e.g., geology) suffer if we put these experts on a [short-term results-oriented] business team?" We have, if truth be known, little patience with this one. Of course, the answer is in part yes.

Only a pure functional organization will maintain purity of skill. But the "real world" answer is just as clearly "no." Human nature weighs on the side of the discipline: your people want to write papers and be heroes at discipline-based conventions (just as, it's said, most ad copywriters are writing primarily to show off to their peers, not their clients' customers). You don't have to worry about that. The management objective, however, is to deliver real new products or services in a hurry—and most speedup occurs when you allow the real world (e.g., manufacturing) to intrude very early, even if the designers' dreams of grandeur are roughed up a bit.

---

### "Smash Functions Together":
### Some Questions—and Things to Do Now

• Assess the performance of your decentralized elements—intentional (e.g., small divisions) and unintentional (e.g., skunkworks that have arisen, crash-project team efforts). Specifically, review in depth a half-dozen occasions when decentralized units have pulled the bacon out of the fire. Contrast these occasions—very specifically—with the performance of your more centralized elements. Is there a pattern of performance in favor of the decentralized unit?

• Review your divisional (factory, store) structure. Have you *unintentionally* abrogated authority, in a thousand subtle ways, since instituting a "clean" structure perhaps three or four, or ten, years ago? Don't take *your* word for it! Ask the leaders in the field. Make them *demonstrate*—via the accumulation of manuals, etc.—that it is *not* any worse than "x" years ago. (In other words, reverse the normal "goodness" assumption. *You* should assume that you *have* been fouling them up. Make *them* prove to you that you have *not!* Ten gets you one that you lose.)

• Take three or four development projects. How many have been delayed because of manufacturing scale-up, hopelessly unrealistic financial-needs assumptions, etc.? At what point do manufacturers (or operations experts), financial planners, etc., get added to teams? Can you speed up their introduction to the teams? Take one team and try it. (Caution: We mean—à la 3M, HP, Ford—*full time* support from the other functions; moreover, support where the "helper's" evaluation is based upon how well the team does, not how zealously he or she guards his or her function's integrity. The point is that the ancillary cast members must be committed to the project, not called in as part-time, dispassionate "experts.")

---

### *Related Myth 4B: Big is Different*
### Counterpoint: Small Within Big

"Hold on a minute," you say. "Maybe I buy in—at Bloomingdale's or Macy's, or for HP's hand-held calculators or a Raychem connector. And you did unearth that story of the GE locomotive. And even Nippon Kokan's BOF success. But what about the 'real stuff'? The truly big projects? The space program? The invention of the transistor at Bell Labs? The MX missile? The Boeing 767? Surely it's different for the giant ones."

### Look Again at "Breakthroughs"

First of all, we doubt that big breakthroughs have much to do with development at all. "Big" and "breakthrough," as we discussed earlier (Myth no. 1) are often after-the-fact constructs (even with miracle drugs). Even when we write about relatively "small" big inventions, like Howard Head's metal sandwich ski, with Head as the hero, we are aware that there must have been twenty-five people (more like two hundred fifty, we suspect) who contributed the advances in materials science during the prior two decades that made it possible for Head to conceive of the solution as he did and when he did. The world of computers is similarly indebted to hundreds of important developments from the hardest sciences, from polymer chemistry and surface physics to optics. Evolutionary accidents ("breakthroughs") do occur (which wouldn't negate our point, anyway), but most advances are incremental, and most "breakthroughs" are the so-labeled post hoc results of cumulative innovation. In fact, according to a recent analysis of the space shuttle (and even the moon shot!), no truly monumental technological advances were required to pull it off. Development was, instead, one hell of a task of implementation, of putting known technologies in a new wrapper! (See another parallel in *The Nobel Duel*.)

### Big, Yes!/Small Within Big

Even if we assume that there are big projects, that not all "breakthroughs" represent the results of cumulative innovation, we want to suggest that these, too, can be treated to a substantial degree as collections of skunkworks. In particular, the principle we call "small within big" turns out to be "optimal."

The Bell Labs' digital switch and IBM's System/360 were *not*, at first glance, built in skunkworks. That is, each was the organization's main project at the time. Nevertheless, a close look reveals that they were, in fact, thoroughly skunked. That is, most of the "breakthroughs" in the development of each came from champions operating off line, alone or with small teams. At IBM, time and again a 25-person group would go off-site for ten days, usually to a motel ($29.95 per room), and break a logjam that had been holding up the multihundred-person main group for months. Similarly, according to our informants at Bell Labs, the development of the digital switch is replete with tales of breakthroughs that occurred in basements. An executive in Honeywell's successful controls business puts it nicely: "I believe in project planning. It's just that I think of the major project map as a sort of Christmas tree on which I hang skunkworks like ornaments."

Or, consider Boeing's development of the air-launched cruise missile (ALCM). The system was complex. It should have been developed "all at once," undoubtedly with the aid of a 100,000-bubble PERT chart.* It wasn't. The missile was broken down into seven major pieces. Teams of modest size were assembled around the seven substantially autonomous tasks. To outsiders the tasks decidedly did *not* look autonomous. There was a lot of connectedness on paper. However, and this is precisely the point, Boeing *made* the tasks semiautonomous by fiat. Each had a champion. Each was in competition with all the others on several speed and quality parameters. The result? Each of the tasks was accomplished in a remarkably short period of time, relative to the norm. Not all came up roses. When the seven pieces were whacked together, they didn't fit exactly right. So the teams had to spend some more time, up to a few months even, getting the interfaces right, despite the effort that had already gone into interface specification. (Boeing hadn't ignored this issue. There had been twice-a-week meetings of a "tiebreaker" group that had sorted out a good many of the interface issues along the way.)

Now many bridle at such "sloppy" retrofitting. And it is true that once the interfaces have been "Rube Goldberged" together, the final design usually isn't as technically "beautiful" as theory-on-paper suggests is possible. But multiple passes usually take much less time, and result ultimately in the development of simpler (more reliable), more practical (if less "beautiful") systems than the single "Get it exactly right the first time" blitz. (The Boeing ALCM was delivered over a year ahead of schedule and well under budget.) That is, using the "multiple pass" route on a "big" project, you wind up with a handful of quickly done, relatively simply designed hunks. Let's say it takes six months to reach that point. Then you take two months to fix the interfaces. Then the five or ten teams go back to work again and polish their individual apples, at the cost of another three months. Then another two months are needed to get the interfaces fixed one final time. You've made two complete "passes" through the system in, say, thirteen months. You probably have a reliable if not "optimal" (beautiful-on-paper) system. The "single pass" (everything depends on everything else), "Get it exactly right the first time" approach is likely to involve a two-year effort to start with—first full pass— and then the damn thing won't work anyway and will likely be too complex, at which point the "all at once" retrofit—which is equally complex—sucks up another couple of years.

---

*If you discern in our attacks on 100,000-bubble charts the zeal of a convert, you're reading correctly. Tom once drafted the world's most complex PERT chart, he thinks. And his ancient master's degree in engineering featured a then-state-of-the-art treatise on combining probabilistic time distributions in multitask PERT (Program Evaluation and Review Technique) design. To repeat a by now familiar refrain: It isn't that *milestones* are bad. It's just that we're in complete accord with the point of view of Allen Michels of Convergent Technologies that we stated in part before: "A group should have maybe four or five milestones. But I'm *not* talking about PERT charts. I'm talking about four or five unassailable things that you sign up to get *done* by a certain time. More complex than that and it doesn't mean anything."

#### "Small Wins"

Our friend Karl Weick wrote a lovely academic paper titled "Small Wins" (*The American Psychologist*, January 1984). It speaks directly to the "small within big" issue:

A series of small wins is also more structurally sound than a large win because small wins are stable building blocks. This character istic is implicit in [Nobel laureate Herb] Simon's analysis of "nearly decomposable systems" and is illustrated by a fable:

Your task is to count out a thousand sheets of paper, while you are subject to periodic interruptions. Each interruption causes you to lose track of the count and forces you to start over. If you count the thousand as a single sequence, then an interruption could cause you, at worst, to lose count of as many as 999. If the sheets are put into stacks of 100, however, and each stack remains undisturbed by interruptions, then the worst possible count loss from interruption is 108. That number represents the recounting of the nine stacks of 100 each plus the 99 single sheets. Further, if sheets are first put into stacks of ten, which are then joined into stacks of 100, the worst possible loss from interruption would be 27. That number represents nine stacks of 100 plus nine stacks of ten plus nine single sheets. Not only is far less recounting time lost by putting the paper into "subsystems" of tens and hundreds, but the chances of completing the count are vastly higher.

Small wins are like short stacks. They preserve gains, they cannot unravel, each one requires less coordination to execute, interruptions such as might occur when there is a change in political administration have limited effects, and subparts can be assembled into different configurations.

Yes, big *is* different. The hand-held calculator and the MX missile are *not* the same. The Boeing 767 and a change in the store format at Mervyn's are *not* the same. On the other hand, championing, the small group, the value of the overtight deadline, internal competition and commitment are keys to all.

---

#### "Small Within Big": Some Questions—and Things to Do Now

• Analyze your two or three biggest projects. All stall from time to time. When you've broken out of a slump, what's been the cause? A skunkwork that emerged? Were your two best big programs marked by some form of "small within big," à la the Boeing case?

• Look at your two worst big project fiascoes. Were they beset by overcomplexity and "all at once" thinking?

• If your analyses in both questions above are congenial with our conclusions, can you do something about it—e.g., break down one big stalled project to get past a hurdle? Now?

• What's the nature of the discussion around this issue. Do many (particularly, technical people) pooh-pooh the analysis as "defeatism" (i.e., "What we really need are *better* PERT charts—and better managers!")? If so, can you muster more convincing evidence or begin an experiment right away, aimed at defusing the skeptics or testing the "small within big" view?

---

### Related Myth 4C: Compatibility Drives All
### Counterpoint: Last 2 Percent May Cost You the Market

A good plan violently executed right now is far better than
a perfect plan executed next week.
—General George Patton

Product release is held up another three months. And then another two. And then another forty-five days. "We've got to make sure that the software is *totally* compatible with *all* the rest of the product family," the logic goes. We buy it—up to a point. Product compatibility *is* important, particularly in products related to higher technology systems. But sometimes the last 2 (or 3) percent takes twelve (or eighteen) months. In the meantime ten competitors have approximated the solution, and gotten theirs into the marketplace faster and first. (At Data General, Tom West wrote these lines on the Magic Marker board in his office: "Not everything worth doing is worth doing well.")

IBM announced the System/360, and then they decommitted many of its most important compatibility features in a sequence of a half-dozen separate announcements. Incompatibility still bedevils IBM today, but the System/360 is legend. The Intel 8080 chip, a landmark, was put into the marketplace with many fewer features than had been planned (and promised). Hewlett-Packard engineers, marketers and salesmen lament the incompatibility (and partial overlap) among some products. But another computer maker, which held up production of a product for over six months, saw a major competitor come out with a product that was 75 percent as good (in the area of the principal new feature) and steal the march on an important niche. Several major manufacturers have been delaying products for months while trying to enhance networking and manufacturing interface compatibilities. Meanwhile, a company that is not exactly a household name, On-Line Software International, has introduced a decentralized software product to allow most personal computers to talk to corporate data bases.

In 1982 the Apple III was introduced before compatibility with IBM had been fully worked out—a major error, some said. Only a short while later software packages were developed independently by Base Two, Core Technology, Ergonomic Software, Mesa Graphics, Microlink NESTAR Systems, Protocol Computers, Viking, Soft-Tronics, Softwestern Data, Teksim—to name just a few—to make the Apple III substantially compatible with various IBM systems. Our colleague Bob Waterman went to a major computer systems bazaar at Brooks Hall in San Francisco in late 1982. In his words, "There were fifteen hundred people displaying. Seven hundred fifty of them were turning Apples into IBMs, and the other seven hundred fifty were turning IBMs into Apples."

We're not against compatibility, certainly. But particularly in the extremely fast-paced markets associated with computers, data handling and telecommunications, there are literally thousands of entrepreneurs who will (and do) fill in the spaces, do for you the last 2 percent (and very rapidly at that). Those who wait, trying to get the last percent of compatibility, may well go by the boards.

The same phenomenon, we might add, holds in many other markets, too. That's the reason Proctor & Gamble, 3M, Mars and Johnson & Johnson are so insistent about spurring competition among their divisions and brand managers. Bloomingdale's does the same thing among buyers and for floor space in its stores, and Macy's has done extremely well emulating the practice. In most markets, new things are being developed all the time and the lion's share of this activity is virtually invisible. You frequently don't see it until it's too late. The only way to fight it is to get something out there—now— even if it's not exactly tidy in terms of a perfect game plan.

A warning note is in order on this point: premature new-product release can be (and frequently is) disastrous. So when we talk about early release in connection with the last inch of compatibility and newly surfacing competitor products, we're limiting "early" to that—the last inch of compatibility; we're not talking about overall quality or the stocking of supporting spares. All too often a product hits the marketplace with the bugs not ironed out or spares not available, with the result that its technical or fashion advantage is blunted by rotten quality and reliability or insufficient support. Things that get out there ought to work, and ought to have some new features that give you good position in the marketplace. But getting that last possible feature, that last degree of complexity (read overcomplexity), that last degree of compatibility, may cost you more of the market than you would have gained by moving out smartly.

It's never an easy call. In our experience, however, the clear tendency—in all industries—seems to be to err far too much on the side of the optimizers, the perfectionists, the last quarter-percenters, who tend to win around the boardroom table; their case unfailingly looks great on paper, and they always use the argument, "And besides, it will only take another thirty days"; unfortunately, those last 30-day activities always seem to take 120 days—if you're lucky.

## "Last 2 Percent May Cost You the Market":
### Some Questions—and Things to Do Now

• Look at five projects where competitors have gotten the jump on you in the last six to eighteen months. Have you in any instance had the response waiting but on hold while you tried to make it 2 percent (or 1 percent) better? Could you have released it earlier, while maintaining quality standards? Look at three good-news examples, when you have beaten a competitor to the punch. What did you do to speed up release while maintaining quality? Could you do this more often? What are the ingredients? Run an experiment on one or two projects, over the next ninety days, to see if you can noticeably speed up release time.

---

### *Myth No. 4D: Optimize!*
### Counterpoint: Optimization Loses in the Real World

Oh, if it weren't for people! Ten-thousand-person groups would be the most efficient. Oh, if it weren't for people! One-hundred-thousand-bubble PERT charts and "all at once" execution would be most efficient. Oh, if it weren't for people! Huge amounts of money put into technical forecasting would anticipate competition, customer and technological surprises. Oh, if it weren't for people. De novo invention of every bit of machine innards would be the best way to assure quality. Oh yes, if it weren't for people.

What's optimal? We find that the so-called suboptimal is most often truly optimal (caveat: in the real world). Two "passes" through the system, the second to patch up sloppy boundaries among the skunkworked pieces (e.g., the seven pieces of the Boeing missile), are, it turns out, a heck of a lot faster *and* cheaper than the "optimization" route, and the results are of higher quality, too. Getting 95 percent compatibility and letting the Darwinist marketplace do the rest turns out to be optimal, not suboptimal, since getting the last 5 percent may well cost you 50 percent of the market. TI's Mike Lockerd says the key is "intense dedication to what you do, and if it's convenient, be synergistic." (Or, as we rephrase him: Champions/Skunkworks - 1; Matrix/fractionalized responsibility - 0.)

The real problem is the word itself, and our training, especially of engineers and financial/administrative types. When we use the word "suboptimal" to describe a skunkwork, we are implicitly suggesting that the optimal is *possible* in the real world. But what's optimal in the real world is the product of a skunkwork—one that's simple, friendly, timely, fills a practical need and works. Optimal to us is the group that goes outside to buy, off the shelf, highly reliable parts; the group that gets a task that usually takes fifteen months done in fifteen weeks. Optimal is, in sum, the *practically obtainable*

*optimal combination* of technical and people resources applied over a finite—
i.e., *competitively plausible*—time period. In other words, "suboptimization"
is "optimal," what we observe when an organization is really humming.

Let's take an example far from U-2's and super minicomputers. A former
Unilever brand manager pointed out a surprising fact about Procter & Gamble, the master consumer-goods advertiser. He said, "You know, P&G basically uses just one measure of ad effectiveness: whether or not the ad will be
remembered after twenty-four hours—'the twenty-four-hour recall'. The
marketing journals serve up a new measure [of ad effectiveness] every month.
At Unilever we used each one as it came along. We'd debate endlessly, and
the reality was that each new one was pretty good. But when the measures
are shifting all the time, most of the debate and discussion ends up being
about the measures rather than the ad, and then you're not getting anywhere.
The P&G measure may not be the world's best, but they've used it for years.
They have developed a feel for what a good ad (or a bad one) is based on that
invariant measure." P&G, per our friend's analysis, is following a "suboptimal" procedure—arriving at the true (maximum plausible) optimum. Technically, twenty-four-hour recall may only explain as much as 70 percent of
what goes on. But twenty-five measures that explain 90 percent are humanly
unmanageable and virtually meaningless. Everyone loses "feel" with so much
complexity. There's no time to worry about ad copy because you're so worried about shifting post hoc measures of ad effectiveness. The suboptimal is
optimal for P&G; the optimal is suboptimal for Unilever.*

---

### "Optimal Loses in the Real World": Some Questions—and Things to Do Now

. We simply propose that you think back to the last three of four extensive
paper studies you've reviewed of savings from centralization, integration,
matrixes. Of precision gained from ten more measures of something or other.
Of certainty accruing from another four-month delay to collect "all the data."
We suspect you'll find that the large majority of such delays or "complexifi-
cations" failed to pay off. That in the meanwhile successes that did accrue
came from passion-driven, "too small," "underfunded" bands from odd corners of your world. Reflect on all that when next you sit down to review a
gee-whiz proposal for a state-of-the-art mega-plant/mega-system/mega-
project.

---

*Nobel Prize–winner Herb Simon invented the word "satisficing" to describe the
real-world process of decision-makers reaching a satisfactory solution to a complex
issue. Many have glommed onto it, and would say that's what we're talking about
here. We disagree and take exception to "satisficing" because it hints that we *could*
do better, and that it's "just good sense" to settle for the "satisfactory." Our point is
that the joint technical/human/market "suboptimal" combination is truly optimal
*within the context* of a real-world competitive environment.

*Myth No. 5: Customers Tell You about Yesterday*
**Counterpoint: Lead Users Are Years Ahead**

As we observed in our discussion of MBWA and innovations, we've been able to unearth about eighty studies of sources of new-product ideas. They cover perhaps thirty industries, from bulk commodity chemicals to computers to shoes. In only one instance does the product development department seem to provide the lion's share of the ideas: in a study of bulk commodity chemicals. Analysis after analysis shows, in fact, that the great majority of ideas for new products come from the users. Our own research confirms it, not just in high technology but in the banking, health care and hamburger business as well.

An executive close to the aircraft industry provided a classic example, in this case in the fast-moving area of CAD/CAM (Computer-Aided Design/Computer-Aided Manufacturing). He works with McDonnell-Douglas. Their CAD system was the leader by a mile in the late seventies. But McDonnell-Douglas decided that it was so good that they'd keep it proprietary, and thus hold on to their advantage. Our colleague also works with the Lockheed CAD system. Lockheed came late to the marketplace and, positioned well behind McDonnell-Douglas, decided to take a different tack—in effect, to let users do most of the development for them. Instead of keeping their system proprietary, they sold it. Over a three-year period they garnered 250 commercial customers. (We refer to them as 250 "free development centers.") In just a couple of years, the very-late-to-the-market Lockheed system leapfrogged the McDonnell-Douglas system, thanks to the input of new ideas from those 250 users.

The computer industry is rife with such cases. Much of the money for applications development in the field has come from MIT, Carnegie-Mellon, Penn State, Michigan and Bell Labs, and all have been prime prototype test sites. Carnegie-Mellon is now serving as the lead user for a whole new concept of network architecture that IBM is testing for the 1990's. The ferocious fights between IBM and GE (when GE was still in computers) for user sites—i.e., Bell Labs—in the early days of decentralized computing demonstrate the crucial importance of the lead user. ASK Computer has given HP (and others) fits in its heartland—designing computer software for manufacturing systems. ASK's essential edge is low technological hubris—and a high "naïve" listening IQ among lead users.*

The key word is *lead user*. The diagram on page 00 describes the phenom-

---

*There are some downright amusing stories in this arena. A classic "lead user" was a housewife whose husband worked for Corning. One night he brought home a new glass container for a certain laboratory acid. She needed an extra pan to put in the oven, so she used the acid container. It didn't break, as ordinary glass would have. Thus Pyrex was invented.

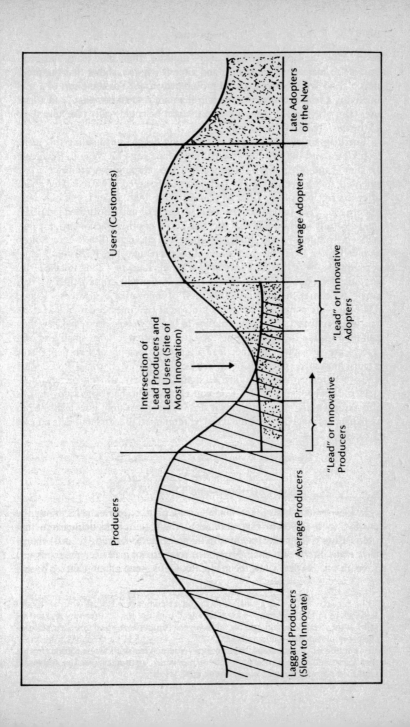

enon. After-the-fact analysis for every industry, from blue jeans and hamburgers to mainframe computers and aircraft engines, shows that the products of 1995 will be invented and prototyped ca. 1985 as some sort of a trial involving a *lead producer* (more often than not a small company) and a *lead user* (also often small), someone who thought he could really take advantage of the new, untested technology.*

The diagram also points up an interesting debate surrounding this issue. Bob Hayes and the late Bill Abernathy ("Managing Our Way to Economic Decline") and others have suggested that U.S. corporations are too market-oriented, not driven enough by technology. We agree, *if* we're talking about after-the-fact polls to find out what users want; then, indeed, you only hear about *yesterday's* tastes from the *average* user. But in sophisticated industries (and *all* really are!) we find that users, like a lot of other phenomena, are normally distributed. At the "front" tip of the bell curve are those who are often as much as ten to fifteen years ahead of their average peers (GM and Boeing, for example, were that far ahead in CAD use). They're willing to take a risk in return for a new invention. Similarly, the lead producer (particularly if he's small) welcomes the lead user. The best of innovative companies—Wang, 3M et al.—are constantly out there probing at that intersection of lead users and lead producers. They pay attention to their own lead users, and how they can better serve them; moreover, they pay attention to what small lead producers are providing to other lead users.† (*In Search of Excellence* rails against most forms of acquisitions. Yet we find that 3M, PepsiCo, P&G, Mars and others regularly acquire *tiny* "lead producers" as a window on new products and technology.) MIT's Eric von Hipple, who has been studying this process intensely for years, sums it up: "Market research, now chartered to seek data and analyze it, would [best] be reoriented to search out data on *user prototypes.*"

---

### "Lead Users Are Years Ahead:"
### Some Questions—and Things to Do Now

• Have every unit analyze the source of new product/service ideas during the last two to three years. (The more detail, the better.) How many come from users? How systematic are your listening devices (debriefing reports, annual debriefing interviews, etc.)? Name five *new* listening devices/programs you have installed in the last eighteen months. Get a group of ten to fifteen people

---

*The success strategy of a small forest product company we work with is to offer themselves to all (legitimate) comers as a lead-user site for new technology. In that fashion they stay several years ahead of bigger competitors—*and* get their state-of-the-art-plus stuff dirt cheap to boot!

†The lead-user phenomenon pops up everywhere. The *Wall Street Journal* reports that Campbell Soup keeps in touch with several "impresarios of the restaurant world" in an effort to keep ahead of changing tastes.

together for a day. Go over the data and form a "next-30-days-action plan" for better "naïve" listening and follow-up. (Incidentally, this can profitably, readily and effectively be done by internal functions—e.g., MIS—with the lead users being certain departments within the company.)

• Repeat the above for the industry as a whole. Go back *ten* years, if you can. (If you can't do the exercise, even that's good news: You've learned something about your ignorance in this area!)

• Do you seek out "lead users" (especially small, innovative companies) as test sites for *all*(!)/some/a few of your new programs? If not, why not? (By "seek out" we mean on a regular, knee-jerk basis, *very* early in the development cycle.)

---

### Related Myth No. 5A: Technology Push Is the Secret
### Counterpoint: Listening Is the Winning Approach

"More scientists in bigger labs" seems to be the watchword, with "better planning, better tools." Massive funding for huge R&D projects to help the United States retain its competitive edge. We expect such an approach won't work very well, not only because it precludes skunking but because the product that looks best on paper is not always or even often what the customer wants.

We've quoted Arch McGill: "The individual perceives service in his own terms." The customer wants to "feel good" about the product, no matter what it is. A bank chairman in Ohio apologetically admitted that he had bought an IBM system instead of "a much lower priced, technologically superior" Amdahl system. He said, "I simply feel better with IBM." The good feeling can come from the right sort of design, one that incorporates scores of details to enhance user friendliness, to make maintenance easier. It might even come simply from the shape of the package. (For instance, superior package design has long been a closely managed attribute at Raychem, approved in detail by Chairman Paul Cook.)

The point is that all this "stuff" ("stuff" or "fluff"—too many of our technologist/financially trained friends call it the latter) ought to be an up-front part of the *innovation process.* (We are, in fact, making another plea for the skunkwork. A skunkwork often has a much more "holistic" view of the product it's creating. It tends to view it more pragmatically, and out of necessity, in the customer's terms.)

---

### "Listening Is the Winning Approach":
### Some Questions—and Things To Do Now

• Does your design process have a large dose of "mundane user friendliness" infused into it from the very *start?* (To test the usefulness of this idea, can you point to five recent past examples where a competitor has "unfairly" trumped you by paying attention to little, friendly attributes rather than bigger technologically advanced features? Or where you, inadvertently or intentionally, have trumped a competitor this way?)

• Does every function in the company (i.e., purchasing, accounts receivable, MIS, as well as the more obvious functions) view itself as part of the innovating, new-product development process, with a role to enhance the "friendliness" of every tiny attribute of the product or service as it is presented to the customer? Do you celebrate (and reward) "customer friendliness innovations" from the service, accounting and purchasing departments as enthusiastically as you do those from marketing or design? If not, why not? Can you mount, right now, a contest for innovation success in every department, in general or relative to a specific new product?

---

# 10

# Three Skunks

THE LIFE OF skunks is seldom chronicled. Most fail. Many are fired. (As IBM's Don Estridge' puts it, "You can always tell the pioneers. They're the ones lying face fown in the path ahead of you with an arrow in their back.") We've come across three especially good ones, in print and in real life: Tom West of Data General, Kelly Johnson of Lockheed and Gerhard Neumann of GE. To help you understand these three, we want to provide (1) some excerpts from Tracy Kidder's *The Soul of a New Machine*, which talks about Tom West's successful thirty-person band at Data General, (2) a letter Tom received from a fellow who worked with Lockheed's Kelly Johnson for years (which was consistent with our interviews with Kelly and other of his former colleagues), and (3) a brief look at the management practices of GE's Gerhard Neumann, gleaned mainly from his fine 1984 autobiography, *Herman the German*.

## *Tom West*

No one tells the story of a skunkwork better than Tracy Kidder in *The Soul of a New Machine*, an account of the creation of Data General's MV/8000 computer (the Eagle Machine) by the Eclipse Group, at the time a maverick team of engineers, championed by Tom West. The Eagle was to be an enhancement of the existing machine, the Eclipse. The following excerpts trace West's work with the new machine, and his relationships with the young creators (the Hardy Boys and the Microkids), his managers, Ed Rasala (the hardware designer) and Carl Alsing (the software designer), with whose description of West we begin.

> West's never unprepared in any kind of meeting. He doesn't talk fast or raise his voice. He conveys—it's not enthusiasm exactly, it's the intensity of someone who's weathering a storm and showing us the way out. He's saying, "Look, we've got to move this way." Then once he gets the VP's to say it sounds good, Tom goes to some of the software people and some of his own people. "The bosses are signed up for this," he tells them. "Can I get you signed up to do your part?" He goes around and hits

people one at a time, gets 'em enthused. They say, "Ahhh, it sounds like you're just gonna put a bag on the side of the Eclipse," and Tom'll give 'em his little grin and say, "It's gonna be fast as greased lightning." He tells them, "We're gonna do it by April." That's less than a year away, but never mind. Tom's message is: "Are you guys gonna do it, or sit on your ass and complain? It's a challenge he throws at them. . . .

There was, it appeared, a mysterious rite of initiation through which, in one way or another, almost every member of the team passed. The term that the old hands used for this rite—West invented the term, not the practice—was "signing up." By signing up for the project you agreed to do whatever was necessary for success. You agreed to forsake, if necessary, family, hobbies, and friends—if you had any of these left (and you might not, if you had signed up too many times before). From a manager's point of view, the practical virtues of the ritual were manifold. Labor was no longer coerced. Labor volunteered. When you signed up you in effect declared, "I want to do this job and I'll give it my heart and soul." It cut another way. The vice president of engineering, Carl Carman, who knew the term, said much later on: "Sometimes I worry that I pushed too hard. I tried not to push any harder than I would on myself. That's why, by the way, you have to go through the sign-up. To be sure you're not conning anybody." . . .

Ed Rasala allowed that West made life in the corner of the basement more dramatic—"Definitely more dramatic"—than it usually had to be. . . .

West kept final authority over the circuit designs. But he loosened control over most of the management of their creation. How did the Hardy Boys invent the general plan for the hardware? "Essentially," said Ed Rasala, "some of the guys and I sat down and decided what elements we needed." Over in the Microteam, though never explicitly told to do so, Chuck Holland took on the job or organizing the microcoding job. Holland and Ken Holberger mediated the deals between the Hardy Boys and the Microkids, but in general the veterans let them work things out for themselves. The entire Eclipse crew, especially its managers, seemed to be operating on instinct. Only the simplest visible arrangements existed among them. They kept no charts and graphs or organizational tables that meant anything. But those webs of voluntary, mutual responsibility, the product of many signings up, held them together. Of course, to a recruit it might look chaotic. Of course, someone who believed that a computer ought to be designed with long thought and a great deal of preliminary testing, and who favored rigid control, might have felt ill at the spectacle. Criticism of that sort flattered West. "Show me what I'm doing wrong," he'd say with a little smile.

In fact, the team designed the computer in something like six months and may have set a record for speed. The task was quite complex. . . .

That fall West had put a new term in his vocabulary. It was *trust*. "Trust is risk, and risk avoidance is the name of the game in business," West said once, in praise of trust. He would bind his team with mutual trust, he had decided. When a person signed up to do a job for him, he would in turn trust that person to accomplish it; he wouldn't break it down into little pieces and make the tasks small, easy and dull. . . .

Above all, Rasala wanted around him engineers who took an interest in the entire computer, not just in the parts that they had designed. He said that was what was needed to get Eagle out the door on time. He wanted the Hardy Boys to bind into a real team, and he spoke with evident frustration of engineers who were reluctant to work on boards that someone else had designed, who felt comfortable only when working on their own. . . .

Holberger runs into a problem—he needs to reprogram a PAL. To do that he needs the services of a functioning computer. He hurries to his cubicle and turns on his terminal, which is hooked up to the Eclipse called Woodstock. But a message appears on his screen saying that the program will not run, he'll have to wait—too many other engineers are using Woodstock now. But Holberger can't wait. So through his terminal he broadcasts an EMERGENCY WARNING MESSAGE. Throughout the basement, on every screen of every terminal using Woodstock at the moment, this message now appears. It says, in effect, "Shut down your terminal at once because the system is crashing." From his terminal Holberger can watch the various responses to this false alarm. Some engineers just go on working, he notes with amusement. "The cynical and jaded," he thinks. But enough other users shut down their terminals for Holberger to run the PAL program.

Holberger grinned. "I have the feeling that's the kind of behavior West approves of." . . .

When they had time on their hands to look up from the machine, some saw that they were building Eagle all by themselves, without any significant help from their leader. It was *their* project, theirs alone. West was just an office out of which came "disconnected input and outputs," said one Hardy Boy. He shrugged. It didn't matter. "West may be acting as a real good buffer between us and the rest of the company. Or maybe he's not doing anything."

Alsing listened, and sometimes he smiled. "When this is all over, there are gonna be thirty inventors of the Eagle machine," he predicted. "Tom's letting them believe that they invented it. It's cheaper than money." . . .

They didn't have to name the bigger game. Everyone who had been on the team for a while knew what it was called. It didn't involve stock options. Rasala and Alsing and many of the team had long since decided that they would never see more than token rewards of a material sort. The bigger game was "pinball." West had coined the term; all the old hands used it. "You win one game, you get to play another. You win with this machine, you get to build the next." Pinball was what counted. It was the tacit promise that lay behind signing up, at least for some. . . .

Maybe in the late 1970's designing and debugging a computer was inherently more interesting than any other jobs in industry. But to at least some engineers, at the outset, Eagle appeared to be a fairly uninteresting computer to build. Yet more than two dozen people worked on it overtime, without any real hope of material rewards, for a year and a half; and afterward most of them felt glad. That happened largely because West and the other managers gave them enough freedom to invent, while at the same time guiding them toward success.

West never passed up an opportunity to add flavor to the project. He helped to transform a dispute among engineers into a virtual War of the Roses. He created, as Rasala put it, a seemingly endless series of "brush fires," and got his staff charged up about putting them out. He was always finding romance and excitement in the seemingly ordinary. He welcomed a journalist to observe his team; and how it did delight him when one of the so-called kids remarked to me, "What we're doing must be important if there's a writer covering it."

Engineering is not of necessity a drab, drab world, but you do often sense that engineering teams aspire to a bland uniformity. West was unusual. Alsing, who might have traveled anywhere, but whose life had been largely restricted to the world of engineering, responded most strongly to him. "West," said Alsing, "took a bag on the side of the Eclipse and made it the most exciting project in the company, the most exciting thing in our lives for a year and a half. West never bored us."

---

### Kelly Johnson

H. S. "Blackie" Shanlian worked for decades with the original Kelly Johnson Skunk Work at Lockheed. He wrote Tom about the experience:

Sunnyvale, CA 94089
July 25, 1984

Dr. Thomas J. Peters
505 Hamilton Ave., Suite 201
Palo Alto, CA 94301

Dear Dr. Peters:

It was with great interest that I read your book *In Search of Excellence*. Since I've been in supervision and management at Lockheed for some forty years I saw myself in the many good and some not-so-good situations that you described. . . . The experimental division "Skunk

Works" was the brainchild of Clarence L. "Kelly" Johnson. He organized the division in 1943 to design, build and prove the first tactical jet fighter in the United States, XP80. This plane was designed, built and flown 143 days after the project was started. The reason that this project and numerous others following succeeded so well was that Kelly practiced the principles you have analyzed in your book. . . .

First of all, the application of the term "skunk works" to Lockheed's experimental division was on the part of several engineers who were griping about the lack of normally accepted organization in the small group. In the course of time the gripers disappeared but the name stuck. I was one of the charter members of Kelly's team and worked with him for twenty years and so the following comments are from personal observation.

Kelly organized his original team by choosing the best man to be found in each skill, discipline or craft. Each person was told why he had been chosen, He was the best one to be had! Whether it was absolutely true or not, each one believed it and did his darndest to live up to it.

Kelly was the great motivator. He offered to take all 75 employees to see the first flight of the XP80 if the plane was ready to fly in less time than the six months he had quoted the Air Force. When his enthusiastic crew beat his estimate, Kelly kept his word and took everyone to Muroc to see the wondrous first flight of an airplane without a propeller. Milo Burcham, the test pilot, was so impressed by the responses of this first take-off and landing that he then took off and gave the most thrilling exhibition of aerobatic flying that we had ever seen.

Kelly encouraged each person to give all that he could contribute to the program in spite of his job description. At one time I was a shop supervisor in charge of some 25 fabricators and assemblers. Besides supervising my crew I did all the planning, procuring, record keeping, liaison engineering and coordinating with the design engineers. In addition I was the timekeeper, safety man, security man and employment representative and I loved every minute of it.

Kelly practiced positive reinforcement. He gave credit to whom credit was due. We strived to do more than was expected of us so that we could get Kelly's nod of approval. So we became molded into a team that had a common goal.

Kelly advocated the simple solution whether it was in respect to design or keeping of records or in solving problems. Paper work was kept to a minimum. Even Air Force requested forms and reports were minimized. He issued no volumes of procedures or policies. He reiterated his basic philosophy, "Do the best possible job in the simplest way, at the cheapest cost in the quickest time." The application of this philosophy resulted in meeting or beating difficult schedules and in returning monies to the customer because we had been able to do the contracted job cheaper.

Kelly believed in having a minimum staff. There were only two levels of supervision between the vice president and the lowliest hourly paid employee. There was no need for an organization chart. Each one knew to whom he reported, what his job was and when it had to be done, and he did it.

Kelly communicated directly with all of his team, not with just one or two managers. He told all of us his goals, his joys, his fears and his pride in us. After one of his meetings there was nothing that any one person would not do. He not only talked to us but he listened and often accepted our suggestions when they were worthwhile. We respected him and he respected us. It was a pleasure and an honor to be a member of Kelly Johnson's team.

Sincerely,

H. S. "Blackie" Shanlian

---

### Gerhard Neumann

Gerhard Neumann was a guiding force in establishing GE's dominance in jet aircraft engines (against sound, entrenched competition from United Technologies' Pratt & Whitney). His recent (1984) autobiography confirmed stories about him we'd heard for years. It also reinforced our perceptions about the role of skunkworks and passionate champions.

| Our perceptions | Neumann |
|---|---|
| Small groups are an advantage. | "The project [to create the Variable Stator Experimental Engine] reminded me of the Flying Tigers in China. . . . undermanned, overworked, and successful!" |
| Big time savings. | "Normally the job takes 24 months. . . . I was given one year." |
| Importance of integrated teams. | "All of us were one team: workers, managers, foremen, and engineers." |
| Isolate team for esprit. | "I insisted this area be painted snow white, in stark contrast to the customary unattractive dark factory gray. Anyone working in the white area could not help but get a feeling of care and importance." |
| Drama, pizzazz. | "Each morning I stood on top of my desk and got the attention of my [120] associates by ringing a Swiss cowbell. . . . One Friday we ran into |

a problem whose solution called for
a miracle. 'Isn't there anyone who
can pull a rabbit out of a hat?' I
asked. Under the table in my hat
resting on my knees was a live
rabbit. I slid the hat into the middle
of the round conference table and
pulled the astonished bunny by his
ears out of the hat. We *did* find a
solution that afternoon."

No frills for the boss.

"I moved out of my private office to
sit with the troops. . . . I refused to
have a rug in my office or a private
john next to it—both seemingly
essential for all executives in
American big industry."

Daily review.

"I updated the assembled team on
what we had accomplished during
the past 24 hours, what problems
had arisen, how many days we had
before the next milestone. . . . We
held design reviews several times a
week. . . . I established [in a bigger
group] an IOI (Items of Importance)
system: A daily, typed, single-page
memo covering the main events of
the last 24 hours was mandatory,
from everyone reporting to us. (To
delegate the writing of an IOI was
verboten.)"

MBWA.

" . . . my nightly walks through the
plant . . . informal discussions during
first, second, and third shifts became
routine."

Allow team to purchase
components, etc., outside.

"I began to encourage competition
by outside manufacturers with our
own shops."

Importance of "feel."

"My career was helped by my
having been fortunate to remain in
my professional field of mechanics
and aircraft. I thus had an
opportunity to develop a superior
*feel* for technical 'go' or 'no go'

designs in the real world, regardless of theory or computers."

Obsession.

"Every bit of available time was invested in reading the daily IOIs, studying reports, walking the shops. I will not answer here the question, 'Would you again?'"

# 11

# The Context of
# Innovation

*My father's real gift and value to U.S. Shoe is not in 'properly
segmenting the market'; rather, he has created a beautiful corporate
culture which rewards risk taking, which supports rather than
punishes those who have a bad year or two, which allows ideas to
percolate upward.*

—Michael Barach, responding to
a Fortune article about U.S. Shoe

THERE ARE SOME fabled (and somewhat crazy) champions around: Steve Jobs
and Steve Wozniak at Apple, Howard Head, Barney Oliver at HP, Ken Stahl
at Xerox, Tom West, Gerhard Neumann, Kelly Johnson. But while of great
importance, these people are not the heart of the matter for the continuously
innovative firm, except as real-life symbols of what can be done. The heart
of the matter is turning the crowd in the top 10 percent (if not the top 30
percent) into champions, continually reeling off practical innovations, small
and large, in accounting as well as in product development. Such is the magic
of Schlumberger (its field engineers), The Limited (its store managers), Citicorp (its country managers), Macy's and Bloomingdale's and Mervyn's (their
buyers), 3M and Raychem and HP (their product developers), PepsiCo (their
brand managers), Trammell Crow (its entrepreneurial associates). The tenacious inventor of the Post-It Note Pad at 3M, the developer of Doritos at
Frito-Lay, Marriott's entrepreneurial property manager who created a big
win at their Rancho Los Palmas resort in Palm Springs, California, are our
models: "ordinary" people turned into vigorous, enthusiastic experimenters.
The environment that transforms them into champions is the context of innovation, the subject of this chapter.

## The Visit

The meeting with the division general manager has been scheduled two
weeks before. He runs a $40 million division, and has a lot on his platter,
starting with endless corporate committee assignments. So it takes about that

long for a mid-level engineer to get in to see him. The hour arrives, 10:45 A.M. precisely. You march up to his office. His perfectly coiffed, slightly graying executive secretary silently motions you to take a seat. Aggressive young staffers shuttle in and out of his sanctuary over the next twenty minutes. Each seems to be carrying a thicker set of briefing papers than the last. Finally it is your turn. You are ushered into the cavernous 30-by-30-feet office. His desk is in the back corner, spotless, even dust-free. It's a beautiful old mahogany desk, rumored to have been used by the company's founder over sixty years ago (sometimes you think the wood must have come from the *Mayflower*). He sits there, perfectly poised, vest buttoned and in a dark blue suit coat despite the August heat. He's tapping his Cross pen lightly on the desktop and talking to his secretary via the intercom, checking on his next meeting, to be held in exactly twenty-five minutes.

Somehow it seems most unlikely that you'd traipse into this Presence and have a little chat about an "interesting screwup" at the lab bench or a vendor's shop or in a preliminary test market. Here you had better have something darn concise to say. And it had best be the good news he wants to hear.

Unfortunately, we find that this scenario comes all too close to the mark most of the time, in big and even small organizations. It stands in stark contrast to the gist of a discussion we had in late 1983 with a group of eight or ten senior people at a major pharmaceutical house on the subject of "nurturing champions." One fellow's name kept cropping up again and again as a prime candidate for Hall of Fame nurturer. He had been the "executive champion" for an extraordinary share of successful new products and new-product champions over a period of decades. He wasn't a genius. Not a brilliant planner. In fact, he had none of the conventional attributes of a "star" performer. But a score of other attributes eventually surfaced, such as the following.

• "It didn't matter what had gone on. It didn't matter how bad the news of the day was. Whenever you walked into his office, the first thing he invariably asked was, 'Are you having fun? Are you up to something that's giving you some kicks?'"

• "It was interesting. He had a cramped office, with samples of every product he'd ever been associated with scattered about. Also prominently displayed were some of the more egregious failures that he had worked on, and some that a few of the champions he had sponsored had worked on. There was even a plaque, BONEHEAD OF THE YEAR, prominently displayed. And then there was the centerpiece—his pride and joy. His chair. It was—now, get this—an old-fashioned barber's chair! When you'd come in, he'd wander over to it and, with a bit of fanfare, hop in. He'd look you in the eye: 'Now tell me something interesting that's going on.'"

There was no question about whether or not this champion of champions was a tough character. He was: "You wouldn't want to go see him unless you had *something* to chat about. He was no fan of sloppiness or shoddy work. But you felt this guy had been there before. You felt that he understood, that he knew, really *knew*, the inherently messy process associated with innovating." You could see right away, they added, that he loved interesting experiments, and was almost as happy with those that failed as with those that succeeded—as long as you had *learned* something from the failures. In fact, one fellow notes, "I think he really liked the failures *better* if he and you learned something interesting. He always wanted to know exactly what you learned, whether it had taken you a step further down the pike toward dealing with the problem that you had set for yourself. In a way, he considered success to be boring. He wanted you to hurry through your successes, and push up against another stumbling block, defined, really, as a failure. The new barriers were the gist, to be puzzled over, thought about. Then you'd discuss the things that might make sense to move on to next. In a hurry."*

## The Entrepreneurial Environment

In the years since *In Search of Excellence* was written, we have gotten to know the 3M Company better. 3M was featured in a chapter on autonomy and entrepreneurship in that 1982 book. Tom was frankly proud of that section, feeling that it went far beyond the usual discussion of innovation. It was not about "technology strategy planning," and barely touched upon organizational structure. Instead it talked about the unique composition of a 3M product team and, for instance, the way its members were rewarded and promoted as a group. It was a fine discussion as far as it went. But what we have observed since is much more subtle—and arguably much more important. Let us try to give you a bit of a sense of the context of innovation at 3M.

Sometime ago, Tom visited with a large group of 3M salespeople in the western part of the United States. In preparing for such visits, we routinely ask the organizations involved to send along in advance some information about what they are up to. Usually the most recent annual report is forwarded. Sometimes there will be a statement of philosophy, a recent speech by the president to the security analysts, and occasionally a truncated strategy document. The 3M packet arrived. It must have weighed close to two pounds. What was it? A catalog of every product that the company sold in this area (the health care sector), complete with specifications, and featuring extensive literature on the new ones. New products are "in the air" at 3M. If you want to know about 3M, you've got to get to know their products! They're "into" their products.†

---

*A 3M manager in Sydney, Australia, reacted strongly to this story. He said this fellow sounded like a carbon copy of the man responsible for an "unfair share" of a whole sector's products at 3M. In fact, he thought that was whom we were talking about before we identified the company as a pharmaceutical house.
†3M's was the first product catalog we'd ever received. In July 1984 we received our second. It was from the Raychem Corporation, a 3M clone in terms of innovativeness. Actually, Raychem topped 3M; they came to our office and, unsolicited, gave our staff a product demonstration—of a sophisticated thermal sensor!

Then it was off to the meeting, the monthly "rally" at which the 3M sales force gathers to talk about their products. Part of a program adopted in the last few years, it's aimed at getting the various sales forces (3M has about fifty specialized sales forces) to learn about one another's products. In this instance, it featured a half-dozen or so sales forces in the health care products area. If it had been a big 3M user conference, the sort that the computer industry has, we'd have understood the extensiveness of the displays. But this was just a routine monthly meeting. And yet what a show! Table after table of displays, with all the new products. The feeling went far beyond that, but the inadequacy of our skill at description limits our ability to transmit it to you (and what a contrast to most settings it represents). The "smell" of innovation lies in such tiny things! Everyone was actively testing the products, fiddling ceaselessly with this, that and the other. Everyone was genuinely interested. Getting any of them into the conference room was painful—they preferred playing with products.

Things were going well for them, a good year. Yet they're not in some astounding 40 percent-a-year-growth arena. In fact, the introduction of standardized reimbursement schemes in the health care sector is a bit threatening to high-price players in the field such as 3M. So if they had no reason to be unhappy, they had no reason to be ecstatic either. And yet they seemed genuinely to be having fun. One of the newer groups in the area had garnered enough sales to be automatically elevated to the status of division, in accordance with 3M rules. There was loud cheering when that was announced. Tom was surprised. In most companies such things as achieving divisional status according to a rule don't happen, period. If they were to happen, only the very senior people or executives on the division's payroll would take much note. It would hardly be an occasion for all-hands interest, as was the case here. Another oddity: Products are regularly transferred from one sales force to another with little fanfare (and without the bloody, destructive, demoralizing product-transfer battles we routinely observe). Presentation after presentation, made by senior and junior salespeople alike, focused on that: "We just inherited the blankety-blank product from the blankety-blank division. This is what we are going to try to do with it." Yet another oddity: Tom began his speech with a fairly flippant remark: "It's always a pleasure to talk to the 3M Company. Things are in such disarray. It's the most screwed-up company in America. And I think that's great." Call most groups of people "screwed up" and smiles would turn to frowns; there would be stony silence. Here a cheer went up. 3M people know they're screwed up (in their wonderful fashion), and take great pleasure in the fact.

All small things. For another 3M meeting, this one the 1984 retreat for the company's top 150 managers (the theme was "Commitment to Innovation—what else?"), we were thumbing idly through the agenda, some two or three pages listing various presentations. We were struck by the fact that unfailingly first names were used. Chairman Lew Lehr's presentation was labeled "Lew's Speech." That was the formal designation! Small thing? No, not in our opinion. (Just for the heck of it, we went back and rummaged through our files on other corporate meetings and randomly pulled—from files on banks and insurance companies and pharmaceutical houses—fifteen similar agendas. Five referred to each speaker as Mr. or Ms. such and such. Nine used initials: B. L. Smith, C. N. Jones. The fifteenth used last names alone. None of the fifteen had a first name in it.)

We have also had a chance in these last few years to share the podium with 3Mers at various events. In all settings they own up to (i.e., preach) the messy world of innovation. One speech, made by an executive vice president, Ken Schoen, began this way: "You've got to begin with the unassailable premise: Innovation is a very untidy process." He went on to talk about the value of "gut feel for the customer's needs," which he said "is worth a ton of market research." Further along in his speech, there was another telling off-hand remark: "This week, when we created a new division ... " The tone was "If it's Monday, there must be a new division." In most companies, creation of a new division takes years and is marked principally by political hassle. On another occasion, Ken joked about having once had to hire a lawyer for his division—in the midst of a head-count freeze, no less—for the express purpose of fighting a corporate lawyer over a product issue. Can you imagine that in most settings? Heresy is not too strong a word. Yet at 3M, that's the way a division manager is *supposed* to act. Nothing, *especially* corporate, is supposed to get in the division's way. It's up to the general manager to make sure it doesn't.

In just this brief discussion, several variables have surfaced: the role of informality, the physical feel of the innovative place, all-hands involvement in new products, having fun, creation of new divisions and shifts of product responsibility as the norm, the role of the general manager as a corporate beater. The language, the feel of a 3M setting, suggest more than a bit about the context of innovation.

Let us now switch abruptly to another extreme case, one that supports our overall point, but which, frankly, scares the daylights out of us. It scares us because it suggests just how big (and deep) the chasm is between the innovators and the noninnovators. Innovating is *the* priority at Hewlett-Packard (as it is at 3M). We were talking to a group of executives who manufacture analytic instruments about the unique HP approach they call the Triad Development Process (see pp. 147–148). At issue was the way the more innovative companies have come to grips with the tough issues of manufacturing scale-up. An HP division general manager who was present came up during a break and said that we'd been right on the mark. He then proceeded to tell a story that suggested we'd missed that mark by a country mile at *least*. We had talked about the need for design engineers to have access to manufacturing from time to time. He said, "Damn it, they did it to me *twice* last week!" "What?" we asked. "Two times my plant manager *shut down the line*, in the middle of an important product run. In both cases, the engineering guys needed some part of a new-product prototype they were working on tested with some important factory equipment." Our reaction: "Holy smokes!" Why? Because, in 99 out of 100 companies (at least), if a new-product engineering guy asked a plant manager to disrupt an important run, he'd be thrown out on his ear. (In nine out of ten companies, the new-product people don't talk regularly to the manufacturing guys, period. Don't live in—or even near—the same home.) Here it was *natural.* Moreover—and most important—it was the *expected* response by the manufacturer. The general manager put on a ritual show of anger at what had gone on, but he knew it was futile as he said it. In the most important sense, he was delighted. Innovating, experimenting, testing things in manufacturing areas—at any time, at almost any cost—simply comes frist at HP. It would never occur to manufacturing *not* to accede to the engineer's request. That *is* HP. You don't short a salesman at Frito-Lay or P&G. You don't get in an engineer's way at HP. And that's that.

---

### "The Entrepreneurial Environment": Some Questions—and Things to Do Now

• We will be more specific in the pages ahead. But at this time we suggest you reflect on the "visit" and the "entrepreneurial environment." Pick, in your mind, two or three innovative departments in your company, or an innovative company you've worked with. Then pick two or three noninnovative spots. Think about the involvement of management in products and innovation in the two sets of examples. Can you "feel" the difference? Try a walk through an innovative group, a noninnovative group (either can be an accounting department as easily as a design department). Does one "look" different from the other? Try to list 10 to 15 "trivial" points of difference in language, physical trappings, etc.

• Reflect on the HP "Stop the line" example. To what degree do all functions in your organization "live for innovation"? Could the HP event have happened in your company? Ever? Routinely? Are you sure you can answer (try to collect some hard data around the issue)?

• As a first action step, sit with a half-dozen colleagues, preferably from multiple functions, and discuss your findings from these reflections. Be tough on one another: that is, are you really sure that's the way people respond?

---

### Language, and the
### Tales You Tell

The parallels between HP and 3M are striking, especially in their language; Peters and Waterman (Tom judges) flat out missed it in *In Search of Excellence.* Sit down with a bunch of senior HP people. A couple of executive vice presidents could be present or not. It doesn't matter. Invariably, and usually rather quickly, the talk turns to new products. The undertone is irreverence: a division takes pride in getting a product (often a partial duplicate of a product made by some other division) to the marketplace *before* corporate has figured out whether or not they even want it. Senior management is often the butt of jokes. Publicly—in the very best sense. The message is clear: "Don't wait for the fogies; do it."

Listen to young HPers; the talk is similar: "You learn the first week that you're *nothing* around here until you've been on a successful product development team." Constantly the chatter reinforces the idea that "getting on with it, by hook or by crook, is the way to do things around here." In most companies such bull-in-the-china-shop behavior doesn't occur frequently (especially when youngsters are involved). If and when it does, it's a well-guarded secret, not the subject of constant and public banter among respected elders "designed" to cause emulation by the young.

The openness is vital. We talk to companies with poor records of innovation. We persuade them to discuss in detail a new product that has been brought in. It turns out that the story in the stodgy company is *exactly* the same as in the innovative company: a mess. Experiments. Lucky breaks. A determined (to the edge of irrationality) champion. Bootlegging (products or pieces of products being built off-line). Projects costing $100,000 being done as a series of a hundred innocuous authorizations of a thousand dollars each. So innovation occurs in the same way in the great innovative companies and the not so great. But at the great ones—Raychem, HP, 3M, Citicorp, Macy's, PepsiCo—the language suggests that this sloppy, semi-illicit way of doing things is the *norm*, to be tried by all, to be cherished.

At Bank X (the norm) the bootleg project is a well-guarded secret. At Citicorp, if you're *not* out bootlegging, you're a second-class citizen. And if you're not bragging about it, it's surprising. At Package Goods Company Y (the norm), a test market failure is a closely kept secret. At PepsiCo, the response is: "So what. What the hell are you going to do to fix it? *Now.*" The difference is that the open chatter directly induces the huge number of rapid tries that are *essential* for bringing in a constant stream of winners.

---

### "Language of Innovation" Some Questions—and Things to Do Now

• Interview ten junior people in development, manufacturing sales and service; talk about ongoing or recent projects. Also sit in on two or three meetings of such people (yes, your presence will change things). Is the talk openly marked by discussions of failures, acknowledgment of the failures of the planning process? Is it marked by juniors' *irreverence* (even with you there, assuming you're a "boss"—second-line supervisor, vice president, etc.) toward *everything*, especially delays? Are illicit/semi-illicit responses (bootlegging, skunkwords) talked about *openly* as *normal* solutions to conundrums? Repeat the process with *very* junior/entry-level people (some with 90 days' experience or less). Does the language of bootlegging, scrounging, sur-face (it would at HP/Raychem/PepsiCo/Citicorp within a week of hiring!)?

• If you are dissatisfied with the results of the above, the *only* way to fix it, we believe, is to purposefully and systematically introduce irreverence into your casual and formal chats, especially with the *very* new. More formal vehi-cles, such as workshops on innovation that analyze past successes and failures and home in on the role of (and expectation of) scrounging, will help.

---

## Honor Thy Cheaters—in Public

We were talking about the goings-on in innovative companies with a col-league in a not-so-innovative company. He said, "The trouble is, when they get to the top [here], they forget what got them there. Namely, 'cheating.' They become the paragons of virtue, beholden to the controller." In fact, he was talking about a specific boss. And we chatted with the boss subsequently. We reviewed together his five or six most successful projects, those that had led to various promotions. It turned out that every one had involved "cheat-ing," lots of it. By cheating, we don't mean stealing or behaving in an immoral fashion. We do mean bringing people and resources and, often, customers together more rapidly than the bureaucratic rules would allow. Well, it turns out that this boss is an inveterate cheater! The trouble is that he doesn't admit to it or tell anybody about it. And by not telling anybody about it, he fails to inspire emulation of the process that brought him success. He doesn't signal that "this ['cheating,' scrounging] is *the* way." Rather, his words and standard bosslike behavior induce people to follow the petty rules and be good bureaucrats. (We regularly use this experience as a jumping-off point for an exercise. We've gone through it, taking up to half a day, with groups of fifty or sixty: bankers, MIS people, retailers, software-company types. The result, under probing, has been exactly the same everywhere, whether the place is innovative or not. Behind every promotion is a win or two. Behind every win is "cheating," in the best sense of the word.)

In stark contrast to the above, at Raychem the language in an interview with a general manager is peppered with remarks like "Everything takes a champion." . . . "Business plans exist, but they are bullshit." . . . "There's nothing you can't get done overnight." . . . "There's not a damn thing wrong with failure. It's erasable!" Openly and explicitly, people at Raychem *honor* cheating. Demand it, really. A middle-management interview yields similar paydirt: "It's a magic place." . . . "Write your own ticket." . . . "It's a moving target." . . . "Structured people can't survive here." . . . "Anybody can present an idea to [Chairman Paul] Cook." . . . "There is always something going on." . . . And best of all (wouldn't you love to have your people saying this about your group?): "People believe they can make *anything* happen."

An executive in Honeywell's controls group put it well: "I don't tell or order anybody to cheat. Of course I don't do that. What I do is make it a regular point to drop by and chat with the development teams, the marketing guys, the engineers, especially the young ones, some of the manufacturing people involved in new products. I talk about what I used to do when I was their age. I talk openly about some of the shenanigans that I pulled, squirreling away resources, not telling someone I was finished with one project so that I could get time to work on a bootleg job, and so on. I don't demand that they do the same thing. I just tell them what *I* did, and then I get up quietly and leave." Another colleague, a consultant with a major firm, puts it almost the same way:" "I don't sanction it [cheating]. It's just that when people tell certain kinds of stories [about bootleg activity, skunkworks, and the like], I smile a lot. Sort of knowingly."

It's exactly such stories that are at the heart of the innovating—i.e., "Get on with it," "Try it"—process. The best of the innovative companies seem to have vast oceans of tales about how innovation was *really* done. Instead of stressing the buttoned-down attributes, they stress the sloppy attributes, and thus the need to get on with it.

There can, of course, be a more public side to it. Domino's Pizza Distribution Company will honor an innovation/cheater by naming an award after him or her—e.g., the "Dennis Collins Award." The one so honored personally gives out the award when next granted, and the picture of award winners go permanently into a Hall of Innovation.

Another variety of stories leads us to see yet another dimension of the language equation. We call them "big-end-from-small-beginnings stories," a line that we first heard, in fact, from 3M's international president. In chapter 2 (pp. 22–23) we spoke of the transformation of PepsiCo into an innovative entrepreneurial company. Four or five times recently we've listened to PepsiCo senior managers make speeches (inside and outside the company). They all talk, regardless of the topic of speech, about the need to find small entrepreneurial activities to grow. They invariably recount the history of the Frito-Lay and Pizza Hut start-ups, emphasizing that each grew out of a $500 loan from a mother to a son! Obviously, the notion being touted is that future winners will as likely come from the $5,000 or $50,000 ideas as from the well-planned $10 million development projects.

The lesson from all this is compellingly simple. If you *want innovation, you have got to talk—incessantly—about innovation.* If you want skunkworks, you've got to talk about skunkworks. If you want people to "cheat," you have to talk about the rewards (and honor) of "cheating." If you want people to devote energy to seeking out small, risky ventures instead of merely attaching themselves to today's big-team effort (in the spotlight now), you must tell stories that suggest that the heroes of today were risk-seeking entrepreneurs inside the company who started small and poor, not big and safe.

It boils down to associating yourself regularly with certain kinds of activities as opposed to certain others. In his column in the Spring 1984 issue of

*Chief Executive*, Robert W. Lear, former chairman of F&M Schaefer (and now a professor at Columbia), reinforces the point:

> In many companies, at many times, the CEO must be the devil's advocate and play a calculated, negative role. There are periods when he must avoid catastrophe, minimize risk, and play the waiting game. A danger is that it can become his management style to be negative. The CEO can come to envision himself as the answerer of tough questions, the insister on compliance with procedures, the setter of high hurdle rates. He can too readily punish those who have tried and failed, too easily reward those who took no risks at all. . . . Product championing by the CEO can be done with a sense of humor. [Admiral] Chester Nimitz, when he was chief executive officer of Perkin Elmer, told me about attending a product development presentation. At the end of the show, he said to the management group, "I hope you have seen me sidling over to stand beside this new product suggestion. I like the idea so much that I want to be identified with it when it becomes successful." How much better that is than "viewing with alarm" and theorizing pitfalls.

So add "sidling over" to your vocabulary. A senior IBM finance person says, "I know where all the bootleg project money is hidden—sorta." Add "sorta" to your vocabulary, too! In *The Soul of a New Machine,* author Tracy Kidder speculated on whether or not Data General CEO Ed de Castro knew about Tom West's skunkwork. The answer? Of course he did—sorta! Said West: "There's a lot of people pretending that this project doesn't exist." Add "pretending" to your vocabulary! This isn't very precise language, but it's key. How often do you use cheat, sorta, sidling over, pretending—or fail?

---

### Sloppy But Not Shoddy

We must stress one caveat here: the fact that sloppiness is one of the essential attributes of innovation decidedly does not imply sanction for sloppy or shoddy thinking or action. To say that 3M honors the sloppy process is to say they respect the irreducible need to try, try, test, test, in order to confront, as rapidly as possible, the numerous roadblocks that always bar the path to a successful commercial product. Paradoxically, this sloppy procedure requires you to know—*exactly*—what you hope to learn from each new iteration or partial iteration. *The more the chaos of the natural world is honored, the greater the discipline required to confront the mess and move forward with alacrity.* Thus, on net, the more innovative the company, the more tough-minded we find management to be: PepsiCo, Mervyn's, Macy's, HP, 3M, Bloomingdale's, Convergent Technologies, W. L. Gore, Kollmorgen and Raychem surely qualify as places for the faint of heart to avoid like the plague. On the flip side the companies that live by a belief that the 100,000-bubble PERT charts will conquer uncertainty and ambiguity are the patsy institutions. There "checking off the boxes," rather than actually doing something, is often acceptable behavior.

### "Honor Thy Cheaters":
### Some Questions—and Things to Do Now

• Did you "cheat" to get to where you've gotten? Do you admit it? In public? Do you get specific? With pride? To junior subordinates? Regularly? How about your peers (same seven questions—try it with five peers from five different functions)? If you think you "pass" on this, test your assumptions with very junior people. Do *they* think of you as a "scrounge" or as a "good bureaucrat"? Ask them bluntly! Sit with a half-dozen colleagues: Bring up the last *five* times, specifically (date/place), you "bragged about your bootlegging skills"—past or present. Do you have to go back more than *thirty* days? (If so, you've probably got a problem.)

• Are there written stories about the company's bootleg-strewn past? Are there stories of young, nonsenior champions around? Are *all* functions (MIS, accounting, manufacturing, as well as engineering, design, merchandising) covered by your historical sketches of champions? Do your stories *stress* "big ends from small beginnings"? (Are you sure, and if so, are they effective? Causally survey ten people: Would they rather have an ancillary role on a big, visible project team—where they *perceive* they are being more closely watched—or a more central role on a small team?)

• Discuss, for a full half day, the words "sorta," "pretend," "sidle over," etc. The language surrounding successful bootlegging is delicate. Do you consciously manage it?

• Take several of the phrases from Raychem (e.g., "Everything takes a champion," "Structured people can't survive here," "People believe they can make anything happen"). Construct an "agree"/"disagree" questionnaire using these phrases. Try it, with guaranteed anonymity, on a half-dozen people in three functions (e.g., design, MIS, manufacturing) and at three levels (entry, first-level supervision, department head). What's the result? How does it match with what you think it ought to be?

## Focus on Failure

We think of the people who are supporters of the "Good tries that fail are OK—even normal" school. The best personalize. They personalize by focusing, openly and in public, on *their* past failures. Pete Thigpen is dealing with the troubles that have arisen at Levi Strauss. To grow into the future they need to try a host of new things. To try is tough. To test is to fail, repeatedly. They need, in Pete's words, to "increase the failure rate" (i.e., get the inevitable—necessary—missteps out of the way as rapidly as possible). A major tool he uses to induce this is relating in every imaginable setting—when he teaches at Stanford, at in-house meetings with marketing staff—and in grim and gory detail stories of his own foul-ups (and he's got a doozer or two). The implicit (darn near explicit) message is "You can foul up, learn from it, and eventually get to the top." Your boy can chop down a cherry tree and grow up to be President, too!

Bill Smithburg, the new chairman of Quaker Oats, is trying to shake up and revitalize that company, a fine but somewhat stodgy institution. He gives a similar high visibility role to failure. He talks regularly about his own failures, and he talks about the failures of all of his colleagues in the senior executive ranks. He adds, "It's just like learning to ski. If you're not falling down, you're not learning."

Even bankers! Ron Terry, chief executive of innovative First Tennessee, says, "Admitting I make mistakes is my greatest strength." He's in good company. Thomas Alva Edison, the peerless inventor, once said, "I failed my way to success." So did Mary Kay Ash, founder of Mary Kay Cosmetics.

Some have included the notion of failing explicitly in their company philosophy. Our favorite is from a small, very successful computer peripherals company, brought to our attention by our colleague Jim Kouzes. One of just a half-dozen points in their formal written philosophy is this: "We tell our people to make at least ten mistakes a day. If you are not making ten mistakes a day, you are not trying hard enough." Depending upon whether you are in retailing or in jet engines, that number may vary from two to forty. But we think that directionally it's right on.

Two points need emphasis here. First, just as sloppy does not mean shoddy, to be a supporter of failure is in no way to be a supporter of slipshod performance. We're talking about good tries that fail, well-planned good tries from which one explicitly learns something quickly. Second, we'd add that there are absolutely no limits to this notion. We've gotten snide asides from time to time: "I certainly don't want my pilot to fail ten times a day!" Well, we would just as soon not have our pilot foul up either. Since we're probably as frequent fliers as anyone who will read this book, it is more important to us than to most. But—and it's no small point—we want that person in the front seat of our plane to have screwed up in every way known to man, and to have come back from it. We want his or her career to have been marked by a close call from time to time, so that he or she would have learned indelible lessons from each and every one of them. We feel exactly the same way about the surgeon who does open heart surgery or takes out a gallstone. We want that knife to have slipped a number of times, so that he would have had to come back from every one of the boo-boos to save the patient. And if he couldn't come back a couple of times, we want him to have learned a lesson. (The notion of thinking about failure in terms of surgeons was introduced to us by a European executive of a pharmaceutical company. Tom had gotten sidetracked in a questionable beauty-of-failure argument, and the man came up afterwards: "Listen, the attack on you was nonsense," he said. "Do you want to know what's the most experimental business around? It's surgery. When has surgery made its most rapid advances? In time of war. The extremity of the cases provides an unending stream of 'hopelessness,' where every technique in the world has been tried—and most of the new ones invented. Most of the rest of the learning occurs analogously on patients whose prognosis is worse than grim. 'Try something' is the dictum. Find me a new surgical technique that wasn't learned the hard way, via trial and many an error, and you're a better person than I.")

We have devoted considerable time to the failure issue because we think it is merited. Constant tries are the simple watchwords of innovating. Most fail. And yet, implicitly or explicitly, failure (even tiny) is a dirty word in most settings. We don't talk about it, and we cover it up. Both responses (silence/cover-up) directly impede speed of action and the learning process.

---

### Is It Tough to Tolerate Failure?
### The Art of Purposeful Impatience

Some of the most renowned "tough bosses"—Walter Wriston, former Citicorp chairman, Jack Welch at GE, Andy Pearson, former PepsiCo president, and Ed Finkelstein at Macy's—are the most vociferous advocates of "failure-as-normal," even "failure-is-to-be-rewarded". So how come they're so tough? They reserve unlimited contempt for those who have tolerated inaction. To fail, learn and try again *quickly* is seen as normal. To sit and wait for "all the data" to come in is unconscionable. To utter, "I would have gotten it done, *but* ... [purchasing wouldn't cooperate, accounting couldn't get the numbers]" is contemptible. Each believes that you get paid to make things happen, regardless of the charts and boxes or the rules and policies that they themselves may have written.

A story is told of Welch. He had asked some purchasing people to work on some tasks. Weeks later he met with them to review progress. To his dismay, they had none to report, only weighty analyses and half-completed efforts at coordination with various departments. Welch was furious. He called the meeting to an abrupt halt, then ordered it reconvened only four hours later. The agenda? To report on progress. He got it, too. More was done in those four hours than had been done in the several weeks preceding them.

To some, all this purposeful impatience may seem a small matter. Our experience suggests that not only is it not small, it is perhaps *the* biggest distinction between the winners and the losers. Among the losers: (1) a "good presentation" counts as much as a report of concrete action, (2) good logic and lots of data substitute for action, (3) the explanation that it couldn't get done "because" of budget or an inability to get certain people or departments together is considered adequate as long as there is "evidence" demonstrating that "we" tried and "they" were recalcitrant, (4) you "need more staff work," or "need more expensive data," or "should form a committee" (the typical disposition of nine out of ten agenda items at the department, division, corporate or board level). It all adds up to trappings and audit trails being more important than doing.

To what extent do you and your colleagues, team, group, company meet the profile above? Do you accept "I couldn't because . . . ," etc. Or do you demand action, *now?* If you're seeking to move in the latter direction, we'd only remind that to do so will be impossible unless the tolerance for the good try that fails goes hand in glove with *your* program of purposeful impatience. Impatience matched with an abiding fear of the tiniest failure is a design for madness (or high turnover). We've seen it all too many times. It's not pretty.

---

## "Failure":
## Some Questions—and Things to Do Now

• What do you think about failure? First, reflect on the above analysis by yourself, and then with a small group of peers. If you think it's natural (in the best sense, as described here), do you talk about it, and if so, do you personalize your talk (i.e., describe in gory detail some of your own debacles)? Suppose you come out, in your own mind, OK on this score. Is the message getting through? Far down the line? (I.e., for starters, can your direct reports recall, unaided, five specific stories about your foul-ups that you have owned up to?)

• Are *tiny* mistakes hidden (and thus allowed, inevitably, to fester into bigger ones) or are they rapidly owned up to? (This is a *very* tough issue to get at. You desperately need "hard facts" to deal with it. You might begin with a handful of case studies of recent major foul-ups. Should the information about the problem, when it was small, somehow have surfaced? If it didn't, why didn't it? Try a success case or two: a minor problem turned aroiund *before* it festered: was there a different sort of openness in the department/group when the minor problem was brought to the surface in a timely way and fixed? You also might try an anonymous survey on the subject—this topic is a big deal and well worth the energy; if you do, make sure you collect specific data about specific cases as well as scores on various questions.)

• As a fix, you can mount your own campaign of "failure story-telling." Try to induce your colleagues to do so, too. Moreover, consider a public awards program (with weekly awards) for the "failure brought to the surface most rapidly." Do it for all departments. Post a weekly list of your own "five best" failures each week (indicating what *concrete* things you learned from each). Postweekly "this is what we learned from mistakes" bulletins for each new product or project group. Consider a "failure Olympics"—the fastest learning from a neat little experiment that failed. (Again, try to get all departments involved.)

• The above is directed at "rapid good tries—failures—from which we learn." There are also "dumb" failures, which need to be brought to the surface rapidly to avoid the snowball phenomenon. Start a quiet campaign of *writing thank-you notes to two or three people a week* who have had the courage to bring uncomfortable information to the surface early. (Try to solicit the participation of colleagues in the campaign, too.)

---

## The Look of Innovativeness

The *physical* attributes are hard to overemphasize. We've talked of a barber's chair in contrast to an elegant, spacious office. We've talked of the 3M fetish for using and displaying the product, and Hewlett-Packard's "next-bench syndrome," in which everyone has whatever project he or she is working on out on top of the bench, for everyone else to look at, play with and comment on. Most companies have the obligatory picture of their product in the entrance hall (some don't even have that); fewer have the product—or the pictures of the product—lying about all over the place: in the mail room, on the loading docks and in the MIS department, as well as the design spaces.

These simple practices may seem bizarre (or irrelevant, or "trivial"). "You mean HP engineers really leave their products out for others to play with?" the president of one small company said to us once, incredulously. "My engineers are afraid somebody will steal their ideas. I simply can't conceive of what you're saying. How do they *do* it?" Unfortunately, our lame answer was that "they do it because that's what they've always done." Of course, it's much more than that. The "gold stars" at Hewlett-Packard go to people who cooperate and assist others, not to those who showboat to their own advantage. In fact, one of this fellow's major problems, it turned out, was too much of a push for "grand slam home runs." He gives out irregular $25 to $50,000 awards, and not enough regular $100 prizes. (We'll return to incentive schemes in a moment.)

Another physical attribute of innovative organizations: the engineer, marketer and manufacturer are together in a single location at Hewlett-Packard, from the inception of the project onward. The same holds at 3M. Monarch

Marking, a $100 million subsidiary of Pitney Bowes, decides to develop a skunkwork. Boss Bob Vanorek rents an old restaurant, across the road from the company's main facility, and converts it unabashedly into a skunkwork. It is an untidy cubbyhole, which is part of the company (close by) but also slightly separate (not too close). Allen Michels of Convergent Technologies likewise believes that the skunkwork, by definition, must be physically isolated, and sends forth his little teams accordingly, setting them up in separate, Spartan sites.

We talk about this particular trait with many, and the consensus seems to be that the activity should be close enough to get succor from the parent organization and separate enough to induce a feeling of team spirit, a bit of "us against them," and isolation from the bureaucracy. This was a part of the trick with Tom West's group at Data General. His team of Young Turks was squirreled away in a dingy basement far from the direct view from corporate—a setting in marked contrast to the Taj Mahal at the Research Triangle in North Carolina and where the formal development group worked (in competition with West's bunch). And, it's interesting to note, the West team's extraordinary esprit started to unravel when a long-requested (and, previously, long-denied) appropriation came through: individuals were given offices with walls, and the basement hangout was spruced up. The "us against them" spirit was dented a bit by the formalizing changes.

Isolation is important. But so is proximity—in a very special sense. The textile industry is not well known for its R&D. The prime exception is Milliken and Company. Roger Milliken has a passion for constant experimentation in his production facilities. One clear signal of his concern is that Roger's office is in the middle of the splendid Milliken Research Park. Moreover, a prototype shop where manufacturing techniques are tested regularly is right outside Roger's window; and he's proud to declare that when he built the prototype facility he was considered a bit crazy by both his own people and others in the industry. Often as not, you can find Roger wandering through that facility, checking on the latest tests. You can then see Roger's closeness to innovation. While, on the one hand, substantial isolation is good for the skunkwork, on the other, proximity (or not) of the main lab to the boss is a highly visible symbol of the importance (or lack of it) attached to innovation in general. Talking to the president of a small division of a pharmaceutical company reinforced the point. Several years ago he had spent two long days in the central research facilities of a big company with which his own firm was working on a joint venture. The research facilities had been recently moved from the corporate center to a sterile hilltop location twenty-five miles from headquarters. At the end of the two days he paid a call on the company's chief executive officer. "After only two days I knew more about their research than he [the CEO] did," he said. "If you're separated, you just don't quite get around to it." It's no coincidence that this fellow has extreme views on the significance of physical location as a symbol of what's important. You'd better believe his R&D facility is well within a pebble's throw of his office.

## "Look of Innovativeness": Some Questions—and Things to Do Now

• Do you prominently display the product? In all function areas? Are all hands familiar with the products or services? Especially new products or services? Do you *regularly* have demonstrations and films about new products and services for *all* levels and *all* functions?

• Within engineering/design/buyer areas, are new products out and around for all to get involved with, to comment on? Do you have lots of internal meetings where people bring their peers up to date on their projects. (I.e., is sharing or squirreling away the norm?)

• Do you pay careful attention to the physical settings of small development teams, focusing in particular on semi-isolation and the Spartanism that helps bring teams together? On the converse side, are design/engineering spaces given prominence in a way that symbolizes directly your (boss, division manager, etc.) strong interest in the design function?

---

### Networking

Silicon Valley is essentially a grand collection of skunkworks, a few of which have become very successful. And their highly visible successes have fueled the flames: The best have in turn expelled many of their best and brightest (as a result of stodginess that invariably accompanies success—even in electronics), a handful of whom are now working on their third or fourth successes (or failures). The Silicon Valley message is a message about the role of critical mass among experiments, champions and skunkworks. With critical mass, networks arise and a near-perpetual-motion machine is possible (e.g., HP, J&J, 3M). Without critical mass—that is, without a certain volume of experiments, champions and skunkworks—the possibility of continuing innovation collapses.

In 1984 Ev Rogers of Stanford and Judith Larsen of Cognos Associates published *Silicon Valley Fever: Growth of High-Technology Culture*. It provides a good model for the individual company as well as a description of the Valley; "networks" are the subject of a full chapter, and the role of "spas"—slightly upscale hamburger joints—is critical. The availability of venture capital is the subject of another chapter; again the critical mass phenomenon plays a vital role, providing a large number of places within the company to "shop." (It's akin to 3M's prodding would-be product champions to try to sell their idea to any division that will listen.) Competition between different companies in the Valley plays a major role as well, of course.

Rogers and Larsen contrast critical mass conditions in the Valley on a vast number of individually "trivial" dimensions—e.g., the number of restaurants—with the absence of same in other places:

> The close networks that characterize Silicon Valley give the region an advantage over other areas. Nolan Bushnell [then of Atari] illustrated this point: "There's a tremendous amount of networking here in Silicon Valley, unmatched anywhere else. I recently visited a group of engineers in London who were working on a new product in competition with a group here in Silicon Valley. Both started at the same time, but the Silicon Valley team got the jump by six months. Our group included an engineer who had a friend working at Intel. He smuggled out a couple of prototypes of a new chip that was just what they needed. The chip was soon to be on the market, but it wasn't yet in the catalogue. Intel was very happy because there were some immediate buyers. Just that six months shows that we have tremendous advantage here. That's why Silicon Valley is always ahead." Indeed, a Federal Trade Commission report said that the unique strength of the U.S. semi-conductor industry derives from its firms' rapid copying of others' innovative chips.

And:

> The equivalent of the Fairchild-Atari old-boy network in the micro-computer industry is the Home Brew Computer Club. This unique organization had its first meeting in March 1975 in the garage of microcomputer enthusiast Gordon French in Menlo Park. Twenty-two [!] microcomputer companies have since been launched by club members, and twenty of them are still in operation. Many are, or were, leading companies in the microcomputer industry: Apple, Cromemco, and North Star, just to name a few. Some of the Computer Kids in Home Brew pioneered in computer software, others like Paul Terrell and Boyd Wilson launched computer retail stores, while other members like Jim Warren founded computer trade shows. When Home Brew was founded it had a regular membership of 500 or so computerphiles, mostly young and male. The purpose of Home Brew (so named because the original members who had computers had assembled them from kits) was to facilitate information-exchange among microcomputer lovers. There were no dues, initiation rites, or bylaws. The typical meeting began with a 'mapping period'—individuals with something to announce, trade, sell, or give away would stand up and identify themselves. Then a 'random access period' allowed like-minded individuals, such as devotees of the Intel 8080 microprocessor, to break up into small groups for a free-flowing discussion. People exchanged computer programs and circuit designs, information

that would in a few years be company secrets. In the mid-1970s Steve Wozniak handed out Xerox copies of his circuit designs for his Apple computer. In return he got peer reinforcement and suggestions for improvement. No one at Home Brew thought that microcomputers would become a competitive industry.

## Decentralization and "Disrespect"

When it comes to innovation, small as we have seen, is more beautiful than even we had ever imagined. Virtually *all* successful innovation—in innovative or noninnovative companies, in the factory as well as in the world of new products and services—comes from or is markedly abetted by a skunkwork. So the issue is not the *validity* of the skunkwork as a center of innovation: skunkworks are it. The issue is, simply, *quantity:* have you got enough of them to win within a world of twenty-to-one (or worse) odds against new product or service success?

An ancillary point is this, which we've already discussed in part: the language in the air at 3M is "big ends from small beginnings." PepsiCo talks incessantly about giant businesses that came from $500 investments. Innovative companies publicly (and ceaselessly) preach that a little team can make a giant contribution. President Ken Olsen, in a speech to his Digital colleagues summarizing ten years of development success and failure, commented (and it's become a drumbeat theme for DEC since) that not a single substantial, commercially successful project had come from an "adequately funded team." They'd always come, he said, from the scrounging, scrapping, underfunded teams. We want to emphasize that such public discussion (repeated endlessly) encourages people to believe that it's just as important to be a part of a tiny team as to be assigned to the giant, highly visible, "bet the company" team. In fact, perhaps it's more important. (Subsequent promotion of those who took small-team chances will help confirm the rumor.)

The context of innovation is about respect for the reality of the innovation process: the need for lots of tries, lots of failures, lots of scrounging, but *always* action. It's also, therefore, about disrespect. One thoughtful commentator put it this way: "We need the confidence necessary to show disrespect for our own institutions." He had been talking about HP's late-sixties decision to decentralize radically before the move was required by market forces; he viewed that as the prime reason HP had flourished, while his company, once a shoulder-to-shoulder HP peer, had stagnated. J&J's Chairman Jim Burke expressed the same sentiment: "I view my role as saying no to those who would re-centralize things. As soon as any trouble arises, the tendency is, 'Let's bring it back in [to the center] so that we can oversee the fix.' That's the kiss of death." Gordon McGovern's recent radical decentralization of

Campbell Soup has the same logic: "We first broke the business into [fifty-two] manageable parts, multiplied the number of people running to an opportunity and with the wherewithal to get things done. We then established with these people a concept which is flexible and rich and open-ended, so they can go out and grab parts of it that we at the top *wouldn't even imagine.*"

J&J, IBM (in their new Independent Business Units), Kollmorgen and Gould, among others, give divisions and groups their own boards of directors. The objective is to keep the corporate staff from fouling up the autonomous operations. It's the ultimate wisdom: to know that you are *not* smart enough *not* to intrude *in*appropriately, and hence to create a protective shield *explicitly* aimed at insulating your operators from *you*. IBM puts it this way: The number one task of the IBU is *not* to follow the corporate planning process. Ore-Ida, working with our colleague Bob Waterman, has instituted an internal entrepreneur program, which is rapidly paying big dividends. The *publicly* avowed purpose: "to short-circuit the system." We'll go into more detail on this in chapter 17; here we focus on the extent to which debureaucratization, and an atmosphere in which circumventing the bureaucracy is the norm, are crucial to innovativeness.

Fighting City Hall is not easy, and requires constant vigilance. As Burke says, the tendency is always to slip into the centralizing, consolidating, "Fix it with a PERT diagram" mentality. David Ogilvy merits putting in the last word: "Make sure you have a Vice President in Charge of Revolution, to engender ferment among your more conventional colleagues." How's *your* "purposeful disrespect" IQ?

---

### "Decentralization and Disrespect":
### Some Questions—and Things to Do Now

· We talked before of disrespect by honoring terms like cheating. This section covers, in part, a more formal set of traits. Do you "show disrespect" (1) by the establishment of two- to three (or ten- to twenty)-person skunkworks in *direct* competition with other of your (typically more formal) activities, (2) by fostering decentralization and explicitly *fighting* efforts to centralize after failures, (3) by creating boards of directors or other formal-sounding boards to explicitly "short-circuit" the central planning system and protect fragile small-team innovative efforts from premature or overly extensive central prods? Do you consider such devices—think about this and talk about it with colleagues—as essential or as signs that you "really aren't organized well enough?" (Look at the most innovative parts of your company or the most innovative companies in your business. See if you observe a greater prevalence of these or like devices.) Do you consider such devices as the "luxury" of a giant company, or can you imagine them or a semblance of them in your $25 million division, your three-store operation? (We observe that this process should best begin at the $2 to 3 million mark. At the very latest!)

• Do you and your colleagues view your role (especially toward innovation) as a facilitator's role, as opposed to the role of a planner/arranger? Have you visited the spaces of your new project teams a half-dozen times in the last two months? Have you, upon the occasion of or immediately following the visit, done *three* or more specific mundane things to clear Mickey Mouse hurdles out of the team's way? (All functions *should* be in on this. It is wholly legitimate/useful for the accountant, MIS, and personnel person to see her or his role in *exactly* the same way the operator does.) As part of this analysis, go visit a team or two and ask them if you are facilitating, if other departments are facilitating or barrier-building or—worst of all—treating the team with benign neglect (i.e., subjecting it to "merely" the same rules as everyone else). Finally, plan such a facilitation visit in the next *ten* days; set as a specific objective the removal of a minimum of *five* tiny irritants.

---

## "Nurturing" Champions and Creating Heroes

A successful Bell Labs executive describes his job: "First and foremost, I walk around, I try to remove the petty irritants that impede action. Some team needs $4,000 for a personal computer; I don't want them to go through a six-month capital-appropriation drill. I give 'em the money. Somebody needs the support of a manufacturing engineer for two weeks. I find one."

The companies *best* organized *formally* for innovation (e.g., HP, 3M, J&J, Raychem, Kollmorgen) understand best the need for the interference runners. A 3M executive notes: "The real shortfall is nurturers of champions." And that's from 3M, where every formal procedure and structure is already aligned to maximize innovation.

But it's not enough to sanction cheating, to run interference for champions. Once your rule-breaking, system-short-circuiting team has brought home the bacon, it's vital to *label* them heroes. And it's important to get it straight in the minds of the rest of the organization: to celebrate them as heroes because they got a win *and* because they got it by breaking the rules. Moreover, wild-eyed dreamers need not apply. The innovator/cheater—i.e., the champion/team/skunkwork that brings home the bacon—is, above all, utterly pragmatic. As David Ogilvy says (re advertising): "If it doesn't sell [the product] it isn't 'creative.'" We find that effective product/service developers are pragmatists and exploiters of others' ideas. They are mechanics and tinkerers, with a raging thirst to see the idea work.

Most vital is to nurture champions and create heroes in all phases of innovation. In a discussion with a pharmaceutical company's research managers, we distinguished between two distinct phases of product development: "discovery" and "all the rest." Discovery is the high visibility part. It is a pragmatic business, but does have pure science as its basis. It's the stuff of Nobel Prizes and articles in *Science*. "All the rest" is the "last 90 percent" of the process—clinical tests, approvals and the like. Some companies treat this "last

90 percent" as mechanical and bureaucratic, the work of clerks and automatons. Yet it turns out that a "passionate champion" of this latter sequence of events can cut more time from the total process than can the genius of the discovery phase. For instance, he or she can drum up support for the drug among the members of the medical establishment, push and cajole the clinical testers. All in all, such champions can often reduce the normal clearance time by as much as 75 percent, if they energetically pursue their tasks. A few companies in the industry (which is traditionally marked by a belief in the pure-scientist-as-hero) are wise enough to treat the tail end of the process as equal in importance to the "head." They go out of their way to create a special hero class for those who drive through the "last 90 percent" with alacrity. Moreover, the "last 90 percent" heroes are put on pedestals as high as—or higher than—those of the pure scientist who had the "Eureka" breakthrough in the discovery phase. Similarly, the marked respect at 3M and HP for the whole development team (accountants as well as scientists or engineers) is intended to create a host of heroes among the oft ignored support functions that, in fact, are the real key to timely commercial success.

## Incentives—for All Hands

3M is a galaxy of heroes. However, heroes who bring in successful $10 million products are touted nearly as loudly as those with successful $200 million winners. Hewlett-Packard is awash with mini-hero success stories. Surprisingly, much of the momentum for constant innovation can be badly stifled when the rewards for innovation get too big. The $100,000 award creates a superstar syndrome. The subtle message is "Only a few people can do it." 3M, HP, Milliken, Wal-Mart, Raychem, Domino's, Dana, The Limited, et al. believe that a large share of the population can and should be innovating— regularly. Winners, big and small, are touted to the skies, but principally via nonmonetary compensation. It seems an iron law: When the rewards structure gets too lumpy (marked by sporadic, big hits), people start hiding things to enhance the probability of their getting the credit and the big one. Sharing, cooperation and emergence of a bunch of tiny, cooperative teams are unintentionally stifled, remarkably quickly.

The innovative companies tend to be innovative from stem to stern. Hewlett-Packard is innovative in the new product area. It encourages skunking to an extreme degree. But you find just about as much skunking going on as well in MIS, personnel and in the factory. An HPer described an occasion when engineering had developed an unwieldy design for a major board. When it got to the factory, one of the manufacturing people realized the incipient problems. His idea? We'll go off, on a brief after-hours bootleg project, and build it differently. His boss's response? Essentially a wink. The complex design failed in the real world of the factory. But the generic tendency to bootleg at HP (in all functions) meant that a better design was instantly available from the wings.

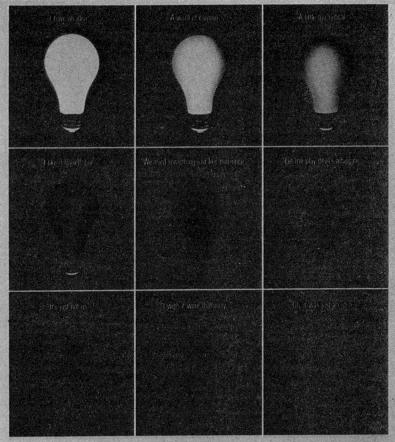

## Champions, Heroes, Incentives for All Hands
### Some Questions—and Things to Do Now

• Are you and your colleagues "hero creators?" Do you, even when it makes you grit your teeth a bit, hail the pain-in-the-neck champion? Do you focus on modest heroism (i.e., lots of mini-heroism)? Do you reserve your top plaudits for the pragmatist-champion, the person(s) *not* involved in the dramatic part of the project, but whose obsessions with the nuts-and-bolts phases may have cut the cycle time most significantly? How (and how regularly), very specifically, do you "post" such acts of heroism? Is everyone, at all levels and in all functions, aware of *exactly* what you think heroism is? Are you sure? Ask. (Developing a program to bring "implementation heroes" or "pragmatist heroes" to the surface and reward them won't be all that easy. It isn't done often, and they are usually less visible—or less findable—than the buyer/research scientist. You will have to mount a treasure hunt of sorts. All can participate—this hunt can be as visible/valuable as the ultimate award. I.e., the headline might read: "An all-out search is being mounted to find the *real* heroes of the 2632AN-3 project.")

• Is your definition of innovation limited in any way? Of creativity? Do you consider a minor procedural invention by the receptionist to be true creativity? Think about it—long and hard. Our observation is that the best are "size blind"/"function blind." They reward as frequently, as publicly and as vociferously the tiny innovation as they do the giant one.

• Is your award-for-innovation structure (assuming you have one) skewed in the direction of monetary rather than nonmonetary rewards? A few big lumps of money rather than many small lumps? Money for individuals rather than money for teams? If the lion's share of your effort is not going into the second part of these three questions, you are probably blunting your effort. (Remember, attention is the key. Quality senior-officer time spent at an obviously caring, somewhat lavish blowout costing $75 a head for three-hundred "support group innovators" is worth more than $250 surreptitiously added to the paycheck—with FICA, federal, state and city withholding.)

---

Barber's chairs. Sidling over. Cheating. Disrespect. Praising failure. Creating heroes of rule breakers. The managerial and leadership task implied by all this is not an easy one. As one manager said, "It's a thin line between discipline and chaos. But that's what we get paid for."

# 12

# The "Smell" of Innovation

JUST HOW DO you know when your company "smells" of innovation? Here are twenty-three ways:

1. Inaction is *not* tolerated, period! I.e., managers at all levels look harshly askance at phrases like these: "We need more staffing," "We need more data," "Form a committee to look into it," "We coulda gone further, *but* purchasing [etc.] didn't get thus and such for us on time." The most common question is "What have you gotten done in the last 24 to 48 hours?"

2. "Try," "Test," "Quick and dirty," "Get me two [as opposed to 22 or 220] data points and then let's move ahead" are much more common than "Let's get a group together to analyze this," "Let's not be too hasty," "What do X and Y and Z [and L and M and N . . . ] think about it?" (Listen very carefully to—perhaps quantify—the routine queries and modes of agenda item disposal at formal and informal get-togethers.)

3. This is common: "Why don't you and Joe [in marketing] and Bill [in manufacturing] and Ann [in sales] get together and bring in those two guys from ZZ division *this afternoon* and figure something out? And, yeah, call Dan [customer], maybe, too. He'd have something to contribute. Let me know what you *did*." This is not: "Let's charter a committee and get A and B and C and D to contribute. We'll have E chair it, so that his boss's boss doesn't get his nose bent out of joint. And plan on a formal review with the principals in about eight weeks."

4. Failure is not only tolerated but learned from. We hear this: "Wow, that was a really interesting problem that manufacturing had scaling up the XYZ subassembly. We [engineering] really got caught with our pants down. But it looks like we learned A and B and C. Can we get back to them with a reworked design by tomorrow?" And this: "Boy, the focus group really pounced on that new packaging. Maybe we ought to get another group in. Though I'm inclined to say we flat out blew it. Let's get the gang together this evening and see if we can modify it to respond to those comments, or

whether we ought to scrap it and try something else." We don't hear this: "Those SOB's in manufacturing didn't give it a fair shot. I'm not going back to my boss and tell him just yet. I know it's a sound design. We'll get some analysis together and we'll confront them at Thursday's senior staff meeting. We can't let them go on pulling this BS. I told the boss it was a good design, ready to go. And as far as I'm concerned, it still is. Make sure young Dave in your shop doesn't blow the whistle on this."

5.   Failures are well-known parts of the background of the star performers, those promoted several times. They talk openly and regularly about "my biggest embarrassment," "my top ten foul-ups of '85" (while making it clear that they kept on trying until they got it right). They are not known by phrases like these: "a good presenter," "keeps his head in until all his ducks are lined up with all the players," "never really blew one in the course of the long march to the head of the division," "I don't think he's ever made a mistake."

6.   The lion's share of the Hall of Fame consists of new product/service champions who are known to have fought through thick and thin (including many rancorous battles with corporate) to bring an idea to market. They are also known to be a tiny bit flaky, yet persistent as all get-out.

7.   Despite an avowed tolerance for a bit of eccentricity, practical team playing is revered. That is, the Hall of Fame champions are seen as people who despised corporate politics, policies and staffs, yet were marvels at practical coordination and had a masterly ability to recruit top-flight teams and to cadge time and space and other resources from all parts of the organization (usually unofficially) to work on their exciting project.

8.   Invention with customers (inside user for, say, an MIS or accounting project; regular commercial customer for product/service development) is considered normal. People outside the sales/marketing area are encouraged to engage directly in creative customer contact. Customers are regular members of problem-solving teams (i.e., the organization is accustomed to having them around—in focus groups, for early trials with partially completed products; in pre-design or pre-scale-up brainstorm sessions).

9.   "Innovation for innovation's sake" is to some degree rewarded at all levels and in all functions. Regular celebrations are held for receptionists, loading-dock teams, accounting sections who create something new or who break time-honored rules or traditions to enhance their performance creatively, and such enhancements are a major component of the routine evaluations of all people.

10.   The physical layout (everywhere) encourages chance and informal communication, especially cross-functional communication. Teams are readily formed, then immediately given temporary (semi-isolated) team space. Numerous social and informal events are aimed specifically at enhancing cross-functional and cross-divisional communication.

11.   It is considered normal (almost required) for all hands, especially designers/buyers/brand managers/lending officers/engineers, to devote 10 to 20 percent of their time to bootleg projects. Moreover, it is a plus for others to help

out those bootleggers. (It is rewarded, not considered a distraction.) The boss has a formal or semiformal system for keeping track of whether or not his people are bootleggers. He *consciously* and *regularly* rewards thoughtful and clever bootlegging, even if it results in a dry hole and a little broken bureaucratic china.

12.   Most of the stories told to new hires or related by senior management focus on innovating, somewhat crazy champions, bootlegging and other forms of corporate-beating, scrounging resources, getting semi-illicit help from other functions, providing semi-illicit help to other functions. The stories paint the average manager as a bit of a rascal.

13.   It is considered more valuable (at an early stage in one's career) to get on a little team working on a modest (but wholly "owned") project than it is to "look good" on a trivial tidbit associated with the company's or division's or department's big (but more routine) project. Senior heroes are not those who oversee masses of resources (i.e., empire builders). Rather, they are those who leave cushy jobs to take on small but vital future-oriented problems or projects.

14.   Quick-hit, small-team (five to ten or even fewer), spur-of-the-moment activity is seen as the normal problem-solving mode, as opposed to "Throw resources at it."

15.   Senior (and middle) managers repeatedly show *open* disrespect for their own procedures and structures, regularly encouraging others to subvert the rules.

16.   When news of an incipient skunkwork surfaces, the knee-jerk tendency is to wink or smile ("There goes Amy again"), rather than to cut it off at the knees "before it starts working at cross purposes with the ABC team [i.e., the officially designated team]."

17.   Well over half of top management (the top twenty-five) has one or more "painful innovative successes" in their background. That is, top management and innovation go together.

18.   It is normal for product or service developers to intrude on the orderly functions e.g., operations/manufacturing—i.e., it is routine for a new product developer to disturb a manufacturing operation to get his or her new prototype worked on. The "tiebreaker" in making decisions is always facilitating product development.

19.   Insistent championing is so revered that some champions are promoted even though they aren't supermanagers. Again, the "tiebreaker": having "done it" (brought a product or service to market) counts for more than a good administrative record. Conversely, "He doesn't make waves" is the kiss of death.

20.   There is a conscious effort to give a solid charter to a small team and then to keep their funding low and deadline pressure high. That is, management cultivates a sense of lean, practical no-nonsense urgency.

21.   Milestone/PERT charts are limited to a tiny handful (a dozen, say) of practical, signal accomplishments on which one makes a blood oath to deliver

(e.g., "Ship first prototype by September 18"). Vast lists of five hundred to one thousand milestones are unknown.

22.  Some product/service and development team overlap is tolerated. Duplication, cannibalization and noncompatibility are not automatically the enemies.

23.  The company "smells" of its products. Bragging, display and demonstration (in every nook and cranny) is endemic.

As in our discussion of "smell" of the customer, we do not suggest that all top-flight innovators exhibit all these traits with equal vigor. But this list, garnered entirely from empirical observation, will serve, we hope, as a benchmark for a frank assessment of the innovativeness of any organization.

## Some (More) Good Reading on Innovation

Three books do a superb job of capturing, in a global way, the notion of the messy world of innovation. The first, cited extensively in our chapter on "The Mythology of Innovation," is *The Sources of Invention* (2nd ed., W. W. Norton, 1970), by John Jewkes, David Sawers and Richard Stillerman; it includes fifty-eight delightful case studies on major and minor twentieth-century innovations in the United States and Europe. *Readings in the Management of Innovation* (Pitman, 1982), edited by Michael Tushman and William Moore, includes classic articles from leading thinkers in the field, such as Brian Quinn, Jim Utterback and Eric von Hippel, again consistent with the framework provided in "The Mythology of Innovation."

Three very readable books are superior studies of individual examples of the messy, human, emotional world of innovating: Nicholas Wade's *The Nobel Duel* (Anchor/Doubleday, 1981), the story of the race between Roger Guillemin and Andrew Schally for the Nobel prize in medicine, James D. Watson's *The Double Helix* (Atheneum, 1968), his personal account of his and Francis Crick's discovery of the structure of DNA, and *A Feeling for the Organism* (Freeman, 1983), by Evelyn Fox Keller and W. H. Freeman, on the exciting and largely unappreciated fifty-year career of eventual Nobel Prize–winning biologist Barbara McClintock.

The life of skunks has generally gone unrecorded. However, Tracy Kidder's *The Soul of a New Machine* (Atlantic Monthly/Little Brown, 1981) is the alpha-to-omega story of a successful Data General skunkwork that has a bearing on virtually every skunkwork we have observed in industries of all sorts. Gerhard Neumann's *Herman the German* (Morrow, 1984) is the autobiography of the mechanic turned World War II Flying Tiger turned multibillion-dollar aircraft engine business developer for General Electric.

Finally, a couple of more "formal" books on what we call the "context of innovation": Rosabeth Moss Kanter's *The Change Masters* (Simon & Schuster, 1983) nicely describes the setting in which innovation is either fostered or inhibited. Somewhat more specialized is Gifford Pinchot's *Intrapreneuring* (Harper & Row, 1985); it looks at the specifics of developing internal entrepreneurship in the corporation.

# FOUR

## People, People, People

Now you hear this. Take good care of those people in that speech of yours. In this room are the finest 1,200 people in this country. They deserve the best you can give.
—Dave Thomas, Wendy's founder,
  on the occasion of a speech by Tom Peters to Wendy's franchisees

"PRODUCTIVITY through People" was Tom's favorite chapter in *In Search of Excellence*. Little did he realize that it barely scratched the surface. The power of ownership of the job has become overwhelmingly clear in the last three years, as has the giant gap between those who believe that the average person will be his or her best if given the chance and those who think the opposite.

The "smell" of the customer and the "smell" of innovation have nothing to do with some grand design. They have to do with a thousand tiny things done a little bit better—serving the customer (guest) courteously, honorably, and with distinction; inducing the champion/skunk within almost all of us to come to the fore.

To achieve distinction on either of these dimensions, then, requires not sleight of hand by geniuses but the commitment to excellence (quality, service, make it better/innovation) by everyone. In short, people are the unmistakable base.

How sad! By 1980, as the strategists view had come to hold sway over the minds of business (and public sector) chieftains and their advisers, "people stuff" had come to be looked at as "soft." But though business schools may deny it, and corporate leader after corporate leader may neglect it, "they," the people in the remote distribution center in Dubuque or Fairbanks, the people cleaning the streets, schooling the young or frying the burgers are what it's all about, what it has always been about, and what it always will be about. Make no mistake about it. "Techniques" don't produce quality products, educate children, or pick up the garbage on time: people do, people who care, people who are treated as creatively contributing adults.

This section consists of three chapters. We begin by looking at the beliefs that managers hold about people. The gulf between those who believe in the humanity of the clerk and those who don't is enormous. From philosophy we turn to "ownership": does the average person view himself or herself as in command, as listened to, as a vital part of the business (city staff, school) or not? We conclude with an essay about celebration (chapter 15, "ApplauseApplause"). To be human is to be sad, to be glad; to participate fully is to care. Celebration of that caring (manifest—or not—in a host of ways, by every person, every day) is not a footnote; it's at the heart of the success we've observed in organizations from Apple to People Express, from Milliken to The Limited.

We'd ask one favor: before you start to read what follows, find a private room or a lonely tree beside a lake. We ask some very personal questions about what you believe (or don't) about people. A bit of sober self-assessment is pretty much a must if this section is to be of value.

# 13

## Bone-Deep Beliefs

BERT SNIDER, who runs Bourns, a profitable mid-sized instrument maker, is appalled: "Why, some of [my] new secretaries don't even know what a precision potentiometer is." Why should they? you ask. What is Bert getting at? Nothing less than the dignity of every member of the Bourns "family," the expectation that everyone understand and be an informed part of the business—including the newest of newly hired secretaries. And for Tom Beebe, former chairman of Delta Airlines, for John McConnell of Worthington Industries, for Ren McPherson, former chairman of the Dana Corporation, for Bill and Vieve Gore of W. L. Gore & Associates, for Max DePree of Herman Miller and Tom Monaghan of Domino's Pizza, for Bob Swiggett of Kollmorgen, Stew Leonard of Stew Leonard's and Dave Thomas of Wendy's, the story is the same.

How starkly Bert Snider's attitude stands in contrast to our all too common experience. Tom listens as the president of a $600 million company opens a meeting of several hundred of his people. His vice presidents, naturally enough, are sitting in a neat little row—the first row, of course—in the auditorium. He looms high above them on the podium. He begins his speech: "We've had a good year." Looking down at his vice presidents, he adds, "and I want especially to thank each of you for what you've achieved in your divisions, and I also want to thank the rest of you"—with a sweep of his arm—"who have contributed as well, many not in this room." Tom's stomach turns.

After a speech to business school alumni at Cornell, we are approached by the onwer of an old, mid-sized Northeastern business "You're naïve," he says. "Look, these communities are made up of second- and third-generation union families. They just don't care, don't give a damn, about work, especially about quality." No wonder, we think. No wonder he has problems.

The enemy lurks in our minute-to-minute behavior—and in our language. A chief operating officer of a retailing operation pulled Tom aside to explain why in the midst of reorganizing the company to sharpen the focus on merchandising, he was, contrary to tradition, filling most buyer jobs from outside the company: "Look, to tell the truth, you don't have to be all that bright to run a store." Self-fulfilling prophecy! If the senior folks, even in their most secret confabs, state (and believe) that you "don't have to be that bright," the word will somehow ooze out and spread throughout the organization. (And "Since we ain't that bright, why put out?" will follow in its stead as surely as the night follows the day.) We talked in an earlier chapter of "thinly disguised contempt" for the customer. What is this but "thinly disguised contempt" for the people of the organization?

We've also discussed something we call the "1,000 percent factor," how a group of hundred turned-on people can do the same work, faster and of higher quality, that several thousand are unable to accomplish. This chapter, too, is about the 1,000 percent factor.

## "Believe It or Not"

John McConnell, chairman of Worthington Industries, runs a steel company with no corporate procedure books. Instead, there's a one-paragraph statement of philosophy, a Golden Rule: Take care of your customers and take care of your people, and the market will take care of you. Hard to believe, isn't it? But it turns out he's not alone. Bob Swiggett of Kollmorgen: "It's all about trust and the Golden Rule." Tom Monaghan, of Domino's Pizza (and new owner of the 1984 world chamption Detroit Tigers), says, "Pay attention to the Golden Rule, and the world is yous." Mo Siegel of Celestial Seasonings and, yes, old Tom Watson, Sr., of IBM also hold to the Golden Rule. Steel. Electro-optics. Pizza. Computers. And all of them say it's "just" the Golden Rule.

Tom first met Tom Beebe, the recently retired Delta Air Lines chairman, on a flight from Atlanta to Dallas in early 1983. It was not long after twenty-five thousand Delta employees had banded together, in the midst of the 1981–83 recession, to give the company $30 million to buy a new airplane. Tom asked Beebe about it, a little unbelievingly to tell the truth: "What *is* all this about your people buying you a plane?" Beebe began to describe what had happened, in particular the rolling out of the plane onto the tarmac in Atlanta, with a bright red ribbon wrapped around it. There was wonder in his voice. His eyes misted over. Tom Beebe was sixty-eight then, had been forty years in the industry— and he was not jaded one iota. Only moments later he introduced Tom to Delta's recently retired chief pilot. Upon retirement, the fellow had taken full-page ads in the morning and evening Atlanta papers to thank Delta management for a great career!

Here's Max DePree of Herman Miller describing his lovely "theory fastball," derived, in essence, from the fact that Sandy Koufax (the great Dodger baseball pitcher) wouldn't have been worth a hoot without a catcher who could handle that hot fastball. Max says, "Although Herman Miller has become *famous* because of its star pitchers—its designers—we have only been *successful* because of the outstanding catchers who produced and sold their designs." And more Max (this one *is* hard to believe, in a world where it sometimes seems that the only goal is short-term profit improvement): "My goal for Herman Miller is that when people both inside and outside the company look at all of us, they'll say, 'Those folks are a gift to the spirit.'" A gift to the spirit, indeed! And how does Max put this philosophy into practice in his (highly profitable) operations? Obviously, in a hundred ways, but at the head of the list is a bill of rights, what he calls "A Person's Rights." They include: "the right to be needed, the right to understand, the right to be involved, the right to a covenantal relationship [with the company],* the right to affect one's own destiny, the right to be accountable, and the right to appeal." At the heart of it is Max's all too rare understanding of the role of management: "The common wisdom is that American managers have to learn to motivate people. Nonsense. Employees bring their own motivation. What people need from work is to be liberated, to be involved, to be accountable, and to reach for their potential." Leadership as the liberation of talent, rather than restraint by rule, is a common theme in all our winning enterprises.

Bill and Vieve Gore of W. L. Gore & Associates don't talk about "employees" or "workers." They have only "Associates." And the Associates in the organization are bound together by the Gores' four principles: "fairness, which controls destructive dissension; freedom, which allows associates to experience failure; commitment, the power behind the desire to succeed; and "waterline" or discretion, which reduces the chances for behavior that could damage the company's reputation and profitability." (See p. 350 for more.) And what do the Gores think about the result? Says Bill: "I think my Associates are changing the world." And he really does. With a warm September sun shimmering on the Hudson, Tom listens to Bill talk for a couple of hours about his people. Bill thinks that the set of people he's gathered in Newark, Delaware and at his many other locations are the most special people in the world (move over, Dave Thomas). He fervently believes that their way of working together is creating a new wave in the United States.

"I think my Associates are changing the world." That's the depth of commitment that's missing when you hear "and I want to thank the 'other' people, too," or "third-generation union families don't care." There are no "other people" for Bill and Vieve Gore. They assume that all people are capable of caring and contributing *if* management cares and believes in them. Every one of their Associates is right up front—changing the world. Every one of their associates would be expected, as at Bourns, to know exactly what a precision potentiometer is well before the conclusion of his or her first day on board. Of course everyone must know: unless you understand the business, how can you be a full partner in pushing it (and yourself) forward?

Bill and Vieve Gore couldn't even imagine the kinds of statements people make to us time and time again: "But be honest, Tom/Nancy. You *know*

---

*DePree makes a distinction between a contractual and convenantal relationship. The former, he argues, is legalistic and formal. The latter is based upon "shared commitments to ideals, values and goals."

there are 30 percent who would rather *not* know what's going on." In contrast, Swiggett of Killmorgen (quoted in *Inc.*, April 1984): "The leader's role is to create a vision, not to kick somebody in the ass. The role of the leader is a servant's role. It's supporting his people, running interference for them. It's coming out with an atmosphere of understanding and trust—and love. You want people to feel they have complete control over their destiny at every level. Tyranny is not tolerated here. People who want to manage in the traditional sense are cast off by their peers like dandruff . . . . We preach trust and the golden rule."

Jimmy Treybig left Hewlett-Packard to found Tandem Computer. It makes a fine machine. But its superior reputation is based, above all, upon the extraordinary level of service that has allowed it to compete with IBM effectively from the start—in IBM's traditional markets. At the core of it is Treybig's philosophy: "(1) all people are good; (2) people, workers, management and company are all the same thing; (3) every single person in the company must understand the essence of the business; (4) every employee must benefit from the company's success; (5) you must create an environment where all the above can happen." Simple, to the point, and, unfortunately, rare.

Bim Black revitalized Teleflex, a $150 million applications engineering company (sophisticated valves, control systems, coatings), by installing a vigorous, decentralized entrepreneurial style in a formerly hidebound organization. A strong people philosophy was at the heart of it:

—People are people . . . not personnel.

—People don't dislike work . . . help them to understand mutual objectives and they'll drive themselves to unbelievable excellence.

—The best way to really train people is with an experienced mentor . . . and on the job.

—People have ego and development needs . . . and they'll commit themselves only to the extent that they can see ways of satisfying these needs.

—People cannot be truly motivated by anyone else . . . that door is locked from the inside; they should work in an atmosphere that fosters self-motivation . . . self-assessment . . . and self-confidence.

—People should work in a climate that is challenging, invigorating, and fun . . . and the rewards should be related as directly as possible to performance.

—When people are in an atmosphere of trust, they'll put themselves at risk; only through risk is there growth . . . reward . . . self-confidence . . . leadership.

Renn Zaphiropoulos heads up about a billion dollars' worth of Xerox's office systems business. Until recently he ran Versatec, a tremendously successful Xerox subsidiary, which he founded. He has lived the Versatec philosophy, and in 1983 he codified it into a written document. It begins: "There is basically one killer [of] successful and productive symbiosis, and it is contempt. Contempt tarnishes someone's self-image. It is also a deadly blow to a person's ego. Criticism should not include contempt. The most commonly practiced crime in industry today is a fundamental insensitivity toward personal dignity. False fronts are one way of displaying contempt. Private parking places are contemptuous towards those who do not have them." Amen! We believe that private parking spaces are a near-motral sin—along with the executive dining room, and, heaven help us (and they're still around), the executive washroom. As a thirty-five-year veteran of the automotive industry, who runs a substantial piece of North American manufacturing for one of the big three, said to us: "I've never seen people working in a factory angry because they were making nineteen thousand dollars while the plant manager was making seventy thousand dollars. What makes them furious, what demotivates and demoralizes, is that slushy, January twenty-sixth morning, when they arrive for their shift at five-forty-five A.M. They park their car one hundred yards away, amidst the muck and dirt and slush. And then they wander in, finally entering cold and wet through the door that's right next to the plant manager's empty parking spot. That's what certifies them as non-full-scale-adult human beings." Right on! It's the accumulation of little slights that kills—kills the spirit (and with it the possibility of excellent performance).

"Now, come on," you're probably saying. "Are these people for real?" We've asked the same question, over and over again. But the evidence keeps coming in. Even as we are drafting this essay a story appears in *USA Today* (May 16, 1984). Monolithic Memories is a $200 million company in the violently competitive semiconductor business. It just about went bust two or three years ago. In fact, it was so hopeless that the board didn't even bother to bring in a turnaround artist. They just took their vice president for finance and figured, what the heck, he couldn't make it any worse, and since he was a finance guy, he might even help smooth the way as the company went out of business. Now Monolithic Memories is about the fastest growing company in that tough industry. The man responsible: Monolithic's president, Irwin Federman, an accountant raised in Brooklyn. To what does he attribute the turnaround? "Revitalization of the human spirit saved this company."

And across the sea at Marks & Spencer the story is exactly the same. How does the then chairman, Marcus Sieff, begin his speech at a 1982 conference of chief executives in Tylösand, Sweden? "They asked me to give a talk today on 'industrial relations.' I can't do it. I only know about 'human relations.' I've never met an 'industrial.'" The chairman's first stop whenever he visits any Marks & Spencer store is the washroom! Says he: "If the washroom isn't good enough for the people in charge [of the corporation], then it's not good enough for the people in the store."

Respect for all people. Respect is caring and trust. Respect is presence: Can you respect people at a plant if you don't visit the plant (and them) regularly? Of course not. But many, it would seem by their actions, don't understand that. In the winter of 1983 Tom visited Sweden again, and talked with a fellow who runs a mid-sized company that distributes electrical and plumbing parts. He had taken over as general manager when the company was on its way down the tubes and had turned it around in just eighteen months. His focus: Teach people to believe in themselves again; teach them self-respect. To put it into practice, he did something that was unexpected. He started spending time, at the rate of 150 days a year, in the field. The company was a major employer in the smallish town it occupied, and the press got on his case for his odd behavior: "This is a bleeding company. Why aren't you out there 'managing'?" (The assumption being, we suppose, that "managing" means sitting in the office sharpening pencils and doing stategic planning.) His response: "If I don't go to the field, if I don't treat the field as important, and being out there is the only way I can show that it's important, then why should I expect people in the field to think that they're important?" Why, indeed? The people in the plants of Milliken and Company, peppered throughout the South, think that they're the cat's meow in their communities and in the industry. And where do you find sixty-nine-year-old Chairman Roger Milliken at least a third of the time? Out in the plants, talking to his people, down on his knees fiddling with the machinery. If you don't demonstrate that you think it's important, why should the people who are *there* think it's important? They shouldn't. They don't. It's leading by inspiration, by simple example, by showing respect instead of contempt via the executive parking spot. Says Joe Schultz, a successful Lockheed manager: "I have only one rule: You can do anything I do." That may just about say it all.

---

### "Bone-Deep Beliefs": Some Questions—and Things to Do Now

• Spend some contemplative time on this. Alone, with a colleague, in a small group, think about team/group/organizational highs and lows in the past. What has marked the highs and lows in terms of people beliefs? Those of the leader? Of peers for each other? Picture (yes, visually) two or three exceptional bosses: what characterized them (especially, again, their people beliefs)? Repeat for one or two bad bosses.

• Spend some time on this, too: Become a "real time" expert. Visit a top performing store, youth league soccer team, Girl/Boy Scout troop. Talk to/observe the coach/manager. What do you feel/see/hear about their people beliefs? (This is *expensive* in terms of time. But what of it? If you are serious about your chosen profession as a manager/leader, how better could you spend your time? A manager, at any level and in any organization, is a "career leader." Yet few spend *any* time systematically observing/studying leaders. We should.)

• What is your contempt/respect IQ? Ask your secretary, colleagues, a trusted subordinate (it won't be easy to do). Are there any little (usually unintended) ways that you've fallen into the trap of expecting undignified subservience? (Remember, the little ways are *most* important.)

• The $64 question: Do you *really* believe the person on the loading dock is just as important/more important than the buyer/product designer/copy writer? If you do, do you show it? How (name twenty ways in five minutes)? If you don't believe it (welcome to a large club), will you do us the favor of thinking about it? Alone. With colleagues. (We don't spend much/enough time examining our people philosophy, even though all of us—who would dare not?—give lip service to the "people first" conventional wisdom.)

• Does everybody who works for you know what your equivalent of a precision potentiometer is? Are you sure? When did you last ask? Can *everyone* cite last quarter's sales and profit figures? The change from last year/last quarter? Describe the last three new products/services launched? Describe the strategy in twenty-five words or less? If not, why not? More important: when's the last time you asked?

• Do you have a written people philosophy, a bill of rights? If not, have you ever tried to draft one? If so, is it boilerplate, or could most people recite it? (If you can't answer the last question, ask.)

• Do you show respect by spending 25–50 percent of your time wandering the shops, back rooms, loading docks? At all hours? If not, why not?

---

### The Bottom Line: A Better Bottom Line— and a Gulf That's Vast

At the outset, we think it's terribly important to set one common misunderstanding aside. This book is about serving customers (or students or patients or citizens) well, providing superior-quality products and services, constantly innovating to come up with new products and services and programs at an unprecedented rate. In other words, we're talking about hard-nosed, bottom-line-oriented management. (Or a better urban environment, a more effective school.) This section on people, too, is about hard-nosed performance improvement.

Among the forty-three companies analyzed in *In Search of Excellence*, we know the Hewlett-Packard Company better than any other. And we can state directly and unequivocally that Hewlett-Packard is the toughest darned setting we've experienced! There's no question about it, it's even downright mean. As our colleague Bob Le Duc said, "HP is the toughest environment I've ever worked in, and I started as field engineer with SOCAL [Standard Oil of California]. They [HP] give you the tools and then they expect results." And that, we think, is *exactly* the point.

The HP's of the world give you the tools and train the daylights out of you; they get rid of the Mickey Mouse regulations that sap your time and stand in the way of top performance; they provide simple and clear and unchanging measures of performance; the expectations are fair and real. And then what have they done? They've done the very worst thing you can do to a living human being: they've created a "No excuses" environment. If you don't get "it" done, that's your problem. In other words, through humane and people-oriented management (leadership) they've created a pragmatic, no-nonsense, performance-oriented organization.

There are leaders who believe in people. They believe all people will contribute if given the chance—and if the Mickey Mouse is kept out of the way, and if the objective/vision is clear and unchanging. Someone asked us whether we though such leaders would win their jobs by election—if, in fact, that was the way it was done. And, by contrast, whether the leaders of the companies that are not so well run would not be elected. We didn't have an answer, obviously, though we suspect that in both cases it would be yes. But what's clear is this: You can order the average person who reports to you to come to work five days a week and work his or her eight-and-a-half-hour day. But you cannot order anyone to perform in an excellent fashion—"excellent" meaning courteous, creative. Excellence, by its very definition and at all levels, is a purely voluntary commitment. It ensues only if the job is sincerely "owned." Soft (trust, care for people) is hard (dollars, a well-run city).

There is nothing really new here; trust, care, respect are hardly new ideas. But what borders on the new, to us, is the gulf, in language and intensity of deed, between the Sniders, Beebes, Gores and the others— the lip-service givers, the generators of subtle contempt (by omission much more than commission).

It's not merely that we found some "people people." It's that we found some incredible human beings. We watched Ren McPherson closely in the course of a four-day conference (the first ever Skunk Camp, in September 1984). He wears his passion on his sleeve. And his anger. Sometimes it comes out via a sharp tongue: "Goddammit, there you go again, Tom. Not 'Do this or that for your people'! They aren't 'your people.' No! No! No! No! You don't own 'em. Don't you see? It's this subtle stuff." At times even a sharp tongue failed him—he would bury his face in his hands for long moments in frustration. It was then that we felt the vastness of that gulf.

## Integrity, One More Time

To live the people message, to live leader-as-servant, requires total integrity. Not too long ago, Tom spent time with a Northwestern company that has a week-long gala (called Appreciation Week) in the middle of the summer—to celebrate the fact that they're alive, well, making nifty products that their customers like. Big tents are erected on the lawn among all the facilities, and all people are given extra time off at lunch each day to socialize, enjoy a beer and barbecue. All the offices are open—even the lawyers' and accountants'—and each small unit creates a display describing what its department is up to and how it contributes to the whole. One part of the shindig features an old-fashioned carnival dunking machine, where you throw a ball at a target. At carnivals, when you hit the target, a pretty girl is dropped into the water. Here, instead of the pretty girl, the executives of the company take their turns sitting in the dunking machine. It was the idea of the bright, aggressive and caring manager of this $75 million outfit. Tom thought it was terrific. But the manager revealed that it had caused a great deal of consternation among the senior ranks. Several had complained that "they'd lose their dignity if they were dunked." Dignity? If a three-piece suit with a buttoned vest is the only proof of importance and is all that allows you to "maintain control," then

*"Help! I'm trapped in an executive vice-president!"*

• • •

Drawing by Handelsman; © 1975
The New Yorker Magazine, Inc.

heaven help us. And if it is beneath executives' dignity to be dunked, who would they suggest be dunked in their stead? A "lower level" pretty girl with no dignity to lose? You see the problem.

The boss of Nissan's remarkably successful manufacturing plant in Smyrna, Tennessee makes a habit—without fail, even when dignitaries from afar are present—of wearing the company-issued coveralls to work. We, frankly, have a bias in this direction. Either you're part of the team or you're not part of the team. We don't think the people who work in the plant would expect you to wear coveralls when you make a sales call on a customer, but if you're not comfortable trooping the line—or sitting in your office—in the same kind of clothes your people wear, then you really aren't part of the program. And while there are indeed managers who would look ridiculous in a pair of coveralls, and it's probably best that they not wear them, we wouldn't bet two cents on their ability to run a truly distinctive manufacturing operation.

You don't lose your dignity if you're dunked, or if you wear coveralls. And if you believe in people, you likewise don't lose your dignity if you admit mistakes. The managers of a sizable aircraft producer had made a dumb mistake about parking lots, wiping out a convenient one in order to install some new equipment (that really didn't need to go there). They had, with good reason, gotten most everybody riled up, and the top team had spent hours trying to figure out how to wiggle out of the mess they'd gotten into. Then the manufacturing boss came up with an idea, simple and to the point, and acted on it without telling the rest of the group: he reversed the stupid decision, then heralded the mistake and the remedy on the front page of the company newspaper. To admit screwing up to a fare-thee-well and then having the sense to fix it, and fix it promptly, demonstrates not only self-confidence but the depth of your confidence in others. Conversely, you are being contemptuous of your people if you believe that they can't handle the thought of the top team making a mistake. After all, they are the ones who must live most intimately with your day-to-day, year-to-year mistakes.

Be confident in your beliefs. Live them with integrity. Remember that the "small stuff" is all there is. It's a pretty tough message. If your convictions about people aren't all that clear and strong, then it's tough to be confident and consistent. Maybe that's the secret, for good or ill, after all.

# 14

# Ownership!

TOM AND BOB WATERMAN discussed the Dana Corporation in *In Search of Excellence*. In the last three years we have gotten to know Dana's former chairman, Ren McPherson, much better. This story grows on us as we learn more of it. On the facing page is an advertisement of Ren's that ran for several months in *Fortune, Forbes* and *Business Week:* "Talk Back to the Boss." Dana, an axle manufacturer based in Toledo, Ohio, was once described by its own chairman as having "the rottenest product line ever granted by God to a Fortune 500 company"; for the 1970's it ranked number two in return on total capital among the entire Fortune 500, and though battered along with the rest of the automotive and trucking industry in 1979–81, it has made a remarkable comeback. McPherson's guiding principle was simple: "Turn the company back over to the people who do the work."

The key was the radical decentralization of the personnel, legal, purchasing and financial departments. The reasoning was simple. For instance, per McPherson: "Centralized purchasing *always* looks good on paper, and virtually never works as planned in reality. Yes, we've got some areas where, in theory, we need to purchase centrally in order to get a volume-based price break: certain steel shapes, transportation, energy, and so on. But look, I want my ninety store managers [his term for factory managers] to sign up for their quarterly objectives. And I don't want them to come in ninety days later and say, 'Ren, I would have made it, *but* the guy in purchasing didn't get my steel on time and I had to short my top two customers. Maybe next quarter . . . ' I won't accept that. See, I've got the ultimate weapon. I've got ninety very bright factory managers. If seven of them know they need to get together to buy a certain steel shape and get a price break, well, they'll get together. They don't need a corporate daddy to tell them when or how to do it."*

---

*Besides, field people readily know how to "beat" corporate types, and abrogate the benefits of paper centralization. An AT&T manager recalled a time when some purchasing function was centralized. The fellows in the field switching stations started to get shorted (causing service to deteriorate) as a function of the new central group's

A Dana executive vice president in a speech made in the late summer of 1982, in the depths of the 1981–83 recession, puts it this way: "We have no corporate procedures at Dana. We threw the books away in the late sixties. We eliminated reports and sign-offs. We installed trust."* Trust! Trust and treating people as adults: During the recession Dana had to lay off ten thousand people. Once a week management sent an extensive newletter to every employee's home, including those who had been laid off. It talked about where the layoffs had been, what the prospects were, and, even more boldly, where the next layoffs *might* occur. What was the result of this up-front approach? There was one indicator that McPherson takes particular pride in. Before the layoffs 80 percent of the employees owned stock in the company, the result of a voluntary stock-purchase program. At the height of the layoffs, the percentage of employees owning shares edged *above* 80 percent, and included all ten thousand people who had been laid off.

While we were working on this chapter, Tom gave a talk that stressed measuring customer satisfaction directly, and then evaluating people on it (see chapter 6), noting that all seem to agree that the procedure would be valuable but few do much about it. Subsequently he got into a discussion with a manager, who said, "But how do we measure customer satisfaction in a meaningful way for the machine operator in the factory?" Not knowing the industry, Tom shot back, "Why don't you *ask* the machine operators what the right measure is? After all, they're closest to it." The manager paused for a moment, and then said, "That's a great idea. You know, we don't naturally do that sort of thing around here—ask people, that is." About three weeks later we got a lovely two-page letter from him. He had asked, he said, "and the ideas were terrific. A couple of people [on the line] even visited a few customers, on their own, to talk about it with them." Efforts were now under way, he added, to collect data in accordance with several of the suggestions. "You hit a sore spot. We've got to get out and do this more," he concluded.

We were both delighted and frustrated: delighted that he did it, *but* why is *asking* such a novel approach for so many? Why in the world would you expect people in a plant to get excited about their "comparative differential negative variance in scrap rate" (vis-à-vis a competitor) when you never share any information about scrap rates with them in the first place? Why in the world would you expect them to be interested in comparative plant profitability if you never tell them how they're doing? Why, indeed? We wonder

---

system-wide inventory minimization program. No dummies they: Subsequently, each time they ordered they'd ask for one or two more than they needed. Pretty soon they had reestablished illicit field inventories. Moreover, since the field was no longer graded on inventory level, they obtained a larger local supply than under the precentralization regime. Inventory climbed, and eventually the experiment was abandoned.

*Don Estridge, president of IBM's Entry System Division (the PC maker), uses virtually the same language: "We don't need 'checks and balances.' We need trust."

# TALK BACK TO THE BOSS.

It's one of Dana's principles of productivity.

Bosses don't have all the answers. The worker who does the job always knows more about it than his boss. But all that he knows can't be used unless he's free to talk about it. Especially to his boss.

At Dana, bosses listen. It's part of what we call humanistic management, giving people the freedom to work well, to grow and to share the rewards.

You can see the results in our productivity. It's more than doubled in the last 7 years.

Productivity alone doesn't produce profits. But we're balancing our output of parts for the vehicular, service and industrial equipment markets we manufacture for. So, as well as increasing productivity, we've improved our earnings year after year.

And that's not bad for a bunch of people who talk back to their bosses.

Dana Corporation, Toledo.

**PRODUCTIVE PEOPLE**

that our people don't seem interested in the well-being of the business—and yet we have never told them what the hell the well-being of the business is.

What we're talking about here is a phenomenon that we've come to call "all people as 'business people.'" Making everybody part of the strategic information stream of the business; making everybody an owner. Ed Carlson, former chairman of United Airlines, used to talk about countering the NETMA (Nobody Ever Tells Me Anything) factor. McPherson believes that all should know where the next layoffs are coming from. Treybig of Tandem makes sure that the entire staff, including the newly hired secretaries, has a copy of the complete strategic plan. New secretaries at Bourns are expected to know what a precision potentiometer is (and care about it), not because of any technical need associated with their job, but because they're considered full-scale members of the Bourns team. People who are part of the team, who "own" the company and "own" their job, regularly perform a thousand percent better—often many thousand percent better—than the rest. Treat all people as business people and they do become business people—fully involved in the bottom-line orientation of the business and committed to its success.

The illustration below is a calling card: "Sarah Clifton, Supreme Commander." We'll get to Sarah in just a moment. She holds the key to ownership. But allow us to backtrack, and in fact repeat a brief analysis from *In Search of Excellence.* It was buried in an obscure corner. It now occupies a front-row center seat in our thinking: it's at the heart of the issue of ownership.

*In Search of Excellence* recounted an experiment in which an industrial psychologist brought a bunch of adult subjects to a lab, supposedly to take part in an investigation of garden-variety industrial hygiene, focusing on the effects of noise on productivity. All of them were given some difficult puzzles

to solve and some rather dull proofreading to do; while they attempted these two chores, a raucous audio tape consisting of one person speaking Spanish, two people speaking Armenian, a mimeograph machine running, a chattering typewriter and street noise ran in the background. Half the subjects were given a button they could push to suppress the noise. The other half were not. The results? As you might expect, those with buttons to push solved five times more puzzles and made one-quarter as many proofreading errors as those who had no button. The news was that never once (and the experiment was repeated several times) did *anyone* ever push his or her button. The mere fact that people *perceived* that they had a *modicum* of control over their destiny—the *option* of pushing the button—led to an enormous improvement in performance. The power that can be unleashed as a result of "mere" ownership (or even the *perception* of it) is awesome!

Let's quickly get away from the industrial psych lab and proceed to the real world: Edison, New Jersey, site of a Ford Motor Company assembly plant. A while back they began an experiment that parallels the one from the lab (and also resembles some Japanese factory techniques). Every person on the line in the huge facility was given a button that he or she could push to shut down the line—quite a gutsy move on the part of the plant manager. The results we're sharing occurred during the first ten months of the experiment (the results since then have been consistent with those at the start). To begin with—no surprise here—Edison, New Jersey, is *not* like an industrial psych lab! People *did* push their buttons at Edison. To be precise, they shut the facility down twenty to thirty times per *day!* The ameliorating news is that the average shutdown lasted only about ten seconds, time enough to make a quality adjustment, a tweek, a twist, a turn, to tighten up a nut or bolt. Now, twenty to thirty shutdowns of about 10 seconds each add up to about 200 to 300 lost seconds a day, essentially unnoticeable. Indeed, productivity in the plant did not change. Three other indicators, however, are worthy of note. The number of defects per car produced dropped during the first months of the experiment from 17.1 per car to 0.8 per car. The number of cars requiring rework after they had come off the end of the line fell by 97 percent. And the backlog of union grievances at any point in the facility plummeted from an average of well over 200 to an average of less than 12.

Moreover, the change in language and attitude was as extreme as the numbers. One old pro on the line commented, "It's like someone opened the window and we can breathe." Or, describing the foremen under the new team-based approach: "They're no longer policemen, but advisers." And along with the opened-up atmosphere came exactly the things you pray for: the side benefits of ownership that are probably at least as significant, if not more so, than the quantifiable indicators. Story after story emerges of the following sort. There had traditionally been difficulties with seat-cover installation. A line employee worked up a method using Saran Wrap in appropriate places to increase slipperiness and thus make it easier to set seat covers. He did the *entire* experiment on his own, at home. He then brought the results to work and shared them with his colleagues. Are we talking about the American automotive industry? Yes, we are. (Similar experiments in Ford's truck plants in Louisville, Kentucky, have been just as successful.)

Now back to Sarah Clifton and her calling card. Sarah worked for W. L. Gore & Associates. She began as a secretary-bookkeeper in one of Gore's twenty-eight factories. Bill Gore doesn't stand on formality. There are no titles whatsoever in the company. Sarah was to go to a meeting in Phoenix to talk about W. L. Gore. She ran into Bill, on one of his many visits, a couple of weeks before the event. "I'm going to this meeting, Billy," she said, "and they're going to want to know who I am. What do I do?"

"Well, Sarah, that's up to you," Gore replied. "What do you want to be?"

"Beats me."

"Well, how about 'Supreme Commander'?" Sarah agreed. Sarah is an "owner" of W. L. Gore & Associates in the deepest sense of that word.

Some go to extremes to ensure not only a sense of ownership but stock ownership as well. Like Dana's McPherson, Publix Super Market's George Jenkins passionately beieves that all employees should own shares in the corporation so that they are "working for themselves." So determined was he that he "even gave a raise to the ones who didn't have the money to buy in." Now, that's putting your money where your mouth is!

Ownership. How can we capture the drama, the power of people who have just a *bit* of space and control? Perhaps the best way to bring it to life is through a series of vignettes, small and large. They are but a handful of the stories we've collected about performance of the Ford/Edison sort—not improvement by a percent or two here or there, but a remarkable response to apparently minor opportunities.

SAS. We previously described the turnaround that Managing Director Jan Carlzon brough about at Scandanavian Air Systems. Here's a tiny piece of the story, per Carlzon: "The objective was to become the number one on-time airline in Europe. I couldn't figure out how to do it. I nosed around trying to determine what group [of people] should be most responsible for it. Finally I unearthed a group that seemed to be as close to the heart of the matter as I could find. I called the fellow who ran the shop and said, 'What will it take to make us the number one on-time airline in Europe? See if you can answer that for me. Come and see me in a couple of weeks and tell me if we can do it.' A couple of weeks later he set up an appointment to see me. He came in, and I said, 'Well, can we do it?' He responded, 'Yes, we can. It will take about six months, and it's going to cost you a million and a half dollars.' I immediately cut him off. It would have been a bargain at five times the price! 'Fine,' I said. 'Get on with it.' He was taken aback: 'Wait, I've got my people with me and a presentation for you. We want to show you just how we're going to do it.' 'I don't care,' I said. 'Go ahead and do it.' To make a long story short, about four and a half months later he called me in with the advance information on the past month's on-time performance. Sure enough, he had jacked us into first place. But that wasn't the only point of his call. He had more: 'And you get half a million of that million and a half dollars back. It only cost us a million.' Now here's my point. If I'd gone down to him, put my arm around him, and said, 'Look, I want you to make us the number one on-time airline in Europe. I'm going to give you two million dollars. I want you to do such and such.' Well, you *know* what would have happened! He would have come back to me six months later and said, 'Well, we've done what you asked, and we've made some headway. We're not quite there yet. It's just going to take another ninety days or so. And it's going to cost another million dollars. And so on.' That's what would have happened. That's the game. But not this time. He asked for some money, and I gave him what he asked for. And he delivered."*

*Quad/Graphics.* An article titled, "Management By Walking Away," *Inc.* (October 1983) reports on successful Quad/Graphics: "'We don't believe that responsibility should be that defined,' [CEO] Quadracci explains. 'We think it should be *assumed* and *shared*. Nothing should ever be "somebody else's responsibility." Anybody who sees that something needs to be done ought to assume responsibility for doing it. Our people shouldn't need me or anybody else to tell them what to do.' The fact is, Quadracci often *refuses* to tell his employees what to do. For example, when Quad/Graphics' shipping department needed greater back-haul revenue to finance expansion of the trucking fleet, Quadracci handed each of his drivers the keys to one of the company's Peterbilts [trucks]. From now on, he told them, they were owner-operators—partners in a new division called DuPlainville [Quad/Graphics headquarters] Transport, Inc.—and it was their duty to make the rigs profitable on return trips. When the truckers asked what they should take on the back-hauls, Quadracci shrugged, 'How should I know? I don't know anything about driving an 18-wheeler. I'm not going to carry your loads.' With that, he turned and walked away." Amen!

*Trust House Forte.* Goldsmith and Clutterbuck's *The Winning Streak* reports:

> That there can be autonomy in a centralized organization is borne out by THF's experience in Paris, when it acquired the three grand hotels, the George V, La Tremoille and the Plaza-Athenée.
>
> The unions of the three hotels had campaigned vociferously against a foreign takeover, parading in their chef, bellboy and waiter uniforms outside the hotels to attract public attention. Having won control, Forte discovered that managemment in the Plaza-Athenée had effectively

*A colleague who consults in Japan relates a similar tale: "It was the biggest difference I noticed. In the U.S., if ten people submit proposals and you only have funding for five, what you usally do is fund all ten at fifty percent of what was asked. So when a problem arises, the fellow can lay it on the higher-ups: 'They only gave us half of what we wanted.' In Japan, they'd say no to five groups and yes to five groups. Then the five yes groups have got a problem: They got what they asked for. Now they've got to deliver."

abdicated, leaving the day-to-day running of the business to the union. In one of those flashes of insight that distinguish the entrepreneurial genius from the normal businessman, Forte offered the post of managing director to the shop steward, who happened to be chief concierge.

The choice was not as irrational as it might have appeared. In analysing the problems of the hotel, it quickly became clear to the THF representative in Paris that the head concierge had a clearer idea than anyone else of what needed to be done.

The new managing director introduced a regime of remarkable employee participation, quite unlike anything found elsewhere in THF. An employee consultative committee took over the handling of lateness, absenteeism and other disciplinary matters. An incentive scheme was worked out under which the employees shared with THF all profits above 5 per cent of turnover. In return, the labour force was reduced by 20 per cent. Profits rose dramatically to three and a half times the level on acquisition. The remaining employees saw their annual income double over a five-year period.

*Tupperware.* Ownership involves the enhancement of pride, pride in ourselves and our close associates. Each of Tupperware's several hundred distributorships has a weekly program called Rally. At Rally, each Tupperware salesperson, during a ceremony called Count Up, marches up front to applause when the amount of their sales for the week is read off (e.g., when "three hundred dollars to five hundred dollars" is read out, you march up if you had sales of $319 for the week). "Count Up" continues until only the week's top five salespersons are left. For them the procedure is different. They come to the front of the room, where there's a giant blackboard. Each walks up to the blackboard and signs her name. End of story. Is that it, you ask? No. But it's *exactly* what we mean by ownership. To sign your name on a big blackboard in front of your peers is the essence of ownership.

*Sunset Publications.* Ownership means being involved, in *any* way, in the business. Sunset Publications develops cookbooks. Each recipe for a Sunset cookbook is tried in the company's test kitchens in Menlo Park, California— by a half-dozen employees selected from a sign-up list. That's no big deal, you say—but your're wrong! There are, literally, hundreds of people in line to be recipe testers. And the list includes the most senior as well as junior people, people who simply want to be a part of the "live" process. It's a kick to read a cookbook and realize that a recipe, being sent out to a host of customers, is *only* there because you tested it and said it was okay. It's a little thing. Or is it?

*Alpine Electronics* (high-end car stereos) general manager Reese Haggott was taken by the Sarah Clifton story. He didn't go the "Supreme Commander" route, but he did issue each person in this sizable company calling cards (and personalized note pads). The cards had the person's name and the appropriate department—e.g., Joe Doaks, Quality Control, Alpine Electronics. Reese was delighted with the results, and adds, "But it makes so much sense, you know. Remember when you got your first calling cards [we do]? It was a really big deal. 'Hey, I'm real,' you know." Yes!

*IBM.* Tiny things, even from the granddaddy of it all. An IBMer, a twenty-five-year veteran, hands us his business card. It is the first business card we have seen from an IBMer who has been there for more than twenty-five years. On the calling card is a beautiful blue shield with a gilt edge and gilt embossed printing. It's a printed reproduction of his twenty-five-year pin. It reads "IBM. Twenty-five Years of Loyal Service." Big deal? No. Just another "little way" in which IBM says, "Thanks for the twenty-five years of service." And they want you to be able to share it with everyone you come in contact with. Genius!

*Markem* of Keene, New Hampshire, has a calendar. Peppered throughout are quotes. Bartlett's? No. Hemingway? No. Michael Jackson? Not even. How about Markem employees: "A full year of quality thoughts from Markem employees to inspire our finest performance [from the cover]." Sample: five to ten days a month are marked by quotes—e.g., January 15, 1985: "Quality is a celebration of commitment."—Barbara Yoerger. Or this from George Scott, April 23, 1985: "The priceless ingredient in every product is the honor and integrity of the person who makes it." Or this, on August 2, 1985, from Jim Lawrence: "Quality is always working one step beyond your best." Ownership!

*People Express.* Not only has this exceptional airline shattered every record in the book for growth by "respecting people and giving them a good deal," it has established a unique way for its more than three thousand full- and part-time people to work together: Every employee is a "manager"— those who would be termed "flight attendants" on other airlines are "customer service managers" at People Express; in other airlines' cockpits you'll find pilots, but at People Express you'll find "flight managers." And everywhere you look, you find not employees but owners. Everyone in a permanent position is a shareholder. Don Burr, president, CEO and founder of People Express, comments in a Harvard University Case Study: "I guess the single predominant reason that I cared about starting a new company was to try and develop a better way for people to work together. . . . that's where the name People Express came from, as well as the whole people focus and trust. . . . It drives everything we do. I'm not a Goody Two-shoes person, I don't view myself as a social scientist, as a minister, as a do-gooder. I perceive myself as a hard-nosed businessman, whose ambitions and aspirations have to do with providing goods and services to other people for a return."

The airline started out with no hierarchy, and still operates with no vice presidents, no supervisors and no secretaries. Everybody answers the phones and takes care of his or her own correspondence. Everybody works more than one job: People Express calls it "cross-utilization." Flight managers may fly one day and work in the Newark, New Jersey, headquarters the next; customer service managers also take reservations; the six managing officers (the airline's founding group) also work in-flight, as customer service managers, or on the ground, checking baggage or helping customers board.

Don Burr's two favorite words are "awesome" and "empowerment." What the people at People Express have accomplished is "awesome;" what people need is to be "empowered," not managed.

---

### Training Manual

A retailer, who had run a store for six or seven years, personally conducted all the training; she correctly thought it was a vital function. As the store grew to seventy-five employees (with retail's typical high turnover, though hers was far below average), the task became almost impossible. She began to write a training manual, and was thinking about appointing someone to assist her as training manager. But that sounded bureaucratic to her, so she shifted gears and decided to ask her best people in each area if they would like to do some of the training. Would they ever! She was astonished by the outpouring of enthusiasm. Old hands signed up for even the most inconvenient shifts to train a newcomer. It became a major distinction to be chosen/allowed to train. And that enthusiasm—and talent—had been all there, lying untapped, during the prior two years, when the task had been getting beyond her control. Moreover, she readily admitted, "The quality of the training has gone way up, mainly as a function of the enthusiasm the new 'trainers' bring to it."

---

*Baltimore Orioles.* Tom was born in Baltimore and is a loyal Oriole fan. The Orioles are well over a hundred wins ahead of the number two team in major league baseball over the last twenty-five years. Yet, until a couple of years ago, they always ranked twenty-sixty out of twenty-six major league teams on the salary scale—i.e., they were at the very bottom, and hence a "no-name" team. The unique factor in the Baltimore system is that all twenty-five players on the roster actually play, and twenty-five no-names playing as a team are, it turns out, a winning team.

*Los Angeles Raiders.* Tough-guy owner Al Davis, according to an article in the *New York Times* (September 2, 1984), is *loved* by his players yet almost universally hated by the other owners (and not just because he has by far the best won/loss record in the NFL over the last twenty-five years). The *Times* explains why:

He gives his players the impression he cares about them. Chandler, the retired wide receiver, tells the story, about a discussion with Davis for a new contract after Davis had acquired him in a trade from the Buffalo Bills. Chandler had distinguished himself for ten years with the Bills.

When they traded him to the Raiders, he felt betrayed. Yet he figured that this would be as good a time as any to cash in.

"I decided that I would go in and ask Al for a lot of money," Chandler said. "The first thing he told me was, 'You're a great receiver. If you had been here your whole career, you'd be going into the Hall of Fame. I've wanted you since you were a senior in college, but we always had Fred Biletnikoff. Now, about the money. There's no way I can pay you more than I'm paying Cliff Branch. Cliff's been with me nine or ten years; he's done a lot for the organization. Loyalty is important to me, more important than anything else.'

"So he paid me the same as Cliff, which was less than I had asked for. But, you know, I came out of that meeting feeling great. Before when I had negotiated for a new contract, the team always made me feel like a $C^+$ player. But they expected you to play like an A player. That wasn't the case with Al. I remember thinking, 'This guy thinks I'm a great player.' When I left his office I couldn't wait to show him he was right." . . .

"It means they're not always in your face," said Dave Casper, the tight end whom Davis traded to the Houston Oilers in 1980 and who resigned this summer [1984] after he was released by the Minnesota Vikings. "If you treat players like dogs, they turn into dogs. That doesn't happen here."

"It means they don't try to turn a team of 45 players into Raiders," said Chandler. "The team is 45 individuals who become the Raiders."

And it means tolerating the unusual nature of many players who have come and gone over the years. . . .

"The don't nitpick you to death here or hammer you all the time," said Lyle Alzado, the defensive lineman who played for Cleveland and Denver before he became a Raider in 1982. "I've been places where a guy would be fined $200 for being one minute late to a meeting and the team would embarrass you by announcing it at a meeting. Here, they treat you like an adult until you prove that you're not."

---

### Butter Sculptures

A tough industrial enterprise in Ireland has a couple of dozen facilities, each with about seventy-five to two hundred employees. One of the managers proposed that once every several months each facility should have an "open house," featuring a garden-variety cafeteria meal for each of their people and members of their families. It was to be held in the canteen at the factory. The results? Amazing on every score. The manager reports that "the people in the canteen [the work force there] are not exactly looked upon as the most creative in the world. They're held in some contempt, frankly. But you wouldn't have believed how they responded to this. I remember, in place after place, seeing an outpouring the likes of which I wouldn't have dreamt. It was more like coming to dinner at a fine hotel in Dublin. Massive, beautiful, extremely elaborate butter sculptures were created. It was a delight to behold." And he is further amazed by the reactions of the families: "It was astonishing. In some cases it was the first time in over a dozen years of employment that families had ever been to the facility, had ever seen where their husband or wife or son or daughter worked." He adds that the goodwill (and productivity) that have been garnered is substantial. Such small things, such big payoffs!

---

Mervyn's, the shining star in Dayton-Hudson's tiara, yields a marvelous example of "autonomy by accident." Or at least we call it "by accident." One of the issues in retailing today is that the merchant/buyer element tends to dominate the stores. In other words, company after company has taken the sense of ownership away from the stores. It hurt Sears, especially, in the late seventies; once-proud store managers became second-class citizens (bureaucrats going through the motions to respond to Chicago) and they did all sorts of things, intentional and unintentional, to express their ire. Well, Mervyn's too, is forced to deal with the real world, a world of fast-changing fashion tastes that requires a fairly centralized buying organization. The buyers put together "programs," and the store people execute them. Now a term commonly used to denote a program is a "rounder." "Rounder" is short for a "round rack," the rack that displays an array of skirts, sport coats or what-have-you in a store. The Mervyn's buyer organization, under energetic leadership, has really gotten on with the programs. In fact, buyers have outdone themselves. They've outpaced the stores: "We have 105 programs and only 70 rounders per store." The result? Despite Mervyn's best-laid plans, the store managers still have a lot of flexibility! That is, they have the wherewithal to execute only 70 programs, but 105 have been ordained from on high. So what do they do? They do what they think is best with what they have (70 rounders). Their power to make decisions thus remains high. And what does that mean, in turn? A sense of ownership. Store managers who still think they run their stores (and do) are the blessed norm.

---

### Productivity in Research

A department administer in a research hospital came up to Tom after a seminar he gave for the Association of Western Hospitals. Her story was an involved one, but it boiled down to just a couple of sentences. About a year before, with each of her groups she had taken a new tack on managing. "My approach was to tell people in the department, 'Do whatever you want to as long as it's legal and within the budget.'" She said that she'd provided virtually no guidelines beyond that. The results? "I was astounded. Research productivity in the department, in terms of papers produced and accepted for publication, for instance, increased by a factor of *six!* And all within less than a year. I still can't believe it. Do you think the ownership phenomenon is really that potent?" Yes.

*Seattle First* (Seafirst), the bank, got in a lot of trouble, principally with some inappropriate energy loans. The response of the new top team, following a Bank of America bailout, was to go back to their knitting, to seek to become, again, a premier regional bank. A basic problem, in addition to a shaky loan portfolio, was a wholesale sense of demoralization throughout the work force. The new chairman, Dick Cooley, came up with an inventive program to counter it, and make some money besides. He divided the entire staff of the bank into nine hundred teams—teams from everywhere: receptionists, people in MIS, those in the various operations departments, as well as loan officers. High visibility contests were run with one target: Bring in new accounts. The effect was spectacular—$500 million in new accounts in ninety days! More significant in terms of the long-term reinvigoration of the institution, the contest winners seldom came from the "right" places—i.e., from the lending departments. In fact, the topmost team came from the MIS department; they thought it was terrific to have a chance to go out and sell business—to their friends, to their neighbors. Ownership!

In *Baltimore*, Mayor Schaefer has launched a host of programs aimed at enhancing citizen ownership. For instance, last year he "sold" potholes to citizens for Valentine's Day. For $35 ($5 for students and senior citizens) you "bought" a pothole. The city patched it and painted a heart on the finished product; then they sent a card with a picture of your repaired and Valentined pothole to the loved one of your choice. The program was a smashing success. The mayor also insisted that communities, even destitute ones, buy into urban improvements. Richard Ben Cramer in *Esquire* (October 1984) reports an exchange between a vocal community group and the mayor:

"What are you going to do?" they demanded.
Schaefer: "Wait a minute. What are you going to do?"
"What do you mean? We're not supposed to do it."
Schaefer's chins tucked, and his eyes started shining. "You want a playground?"
"We are *entitled* to playgrounds."
"You gonna maintain it?"
"We can't maintain it."
"Then . . . we're not gonna build it."
Pretty soon he started demanding that the neighborhood group buy the swings, or the jungle gym. "It'll cost you $1,000," he'd say. "I don't care if you gotta sell cookies. Just get it." If there was no neighborhood group, they had to make one. Then hold the bake sales. Then buy the swings. Pretty soon, in a couple of neighborhoods, then a half dozen,

then a few more, people stopped to show him their playgrounds. They showed him how they'd changed the city's plans to make it more like they wanted it. And they showed where they wanted the city to put a recreation center for the older kids. Could the city kick in part of the money?

Even the [Irish] *Post Office* ... A very aggressive retailer has taken on a collateral duty as chairman of the Post Office in Ireland. For St. Patrick's Day in 1984 the Post Office did something very special: each local branch sent St. Patrick's day cards to their subscribers—a card that was signed by all the people at the branch. The chairman, a real pepper-pot, couldn't be more enthusiastic: "Typical were the clerks I run into in central headquarters. Before, I'd ask them what they do, and I'd get, 'I'm a clerk.' Now I ask and they reply, proudly, 'I work for the Post Office.' They're no longer ashamed. It's pride. Pride is everything, you know." We didn't know when we started. But we're beginning to learn.

---

## Ownership: MBWA with Customers

The *Wall Street Journal* (December 12, 1984) reports from Sparrows Point, Maryland:

> When Robert Felts's supervisor at Bethlehem Steel Corp. here asked him to visit a customer, the veteran line operator jumped at the chance. But there was one problem: The client was in East Texas, and Mr. Felts had to fly for the first time in his life.
>
> "I didn't like that. And they put me on four planes to get me there," he recalls with a shudder.
>
> Mr. Felts's adjustment is only a small part of a general upheaval in traditional management-labor roles in the country's basic industries. Increasingly, management is turning to hourly workers for help with problems formerly handled only by field engineers and select executives. Employees like Mr. Felts are calling on customers and, in some instances, even visiting foreign competitors to determine firsthand how their own products stack up. ...
>
> [G]eneral manager *John G. Roberts* is largely credited with starting the employee visitation program. "Management still has to make the tough economic decisions. But these are easier to make when employees understand the issue and also trust management," he says.
>
> The Sparrows Point main office is also educating its work force about the steel market by distributing a weekly business news roundup throughout the plant. A recent issue reported that foreign steel was getting a 31% share of the domestic steel market in July and August.

The program seems to be working. For line operators here, the priority for years was to churn out so many tons of steel each hour with quality a secondary concern. But that changed for Tony DeLuca, a mill worker, during a recent trip to a client. "A foreman there said, 'You guys at Sparrows Point are garbage rollers,' and that really hit my pride," he says. Other steelworkers recall how they were jolted after seeing defects in Bethlehem sheet steel show up in their customers' products.

"You're especially aware when you go to warehouses of customers and see all that foreign steel wrapped up in pretty packages," says steelworker Greg Blackenship. "We know what we're doing now. Before we were just rolling steel."

Customers say they generally appreciate the visits, which let them air grievances with workers who are actually responsible for the product. The visits also show the supplier's commitment, they add. Dale Aulthouse, a purchaser for High Steel Structures Inc. in Lancaster, Pa., a big Bethlehem client, says he was ready to switch to a competitor because Sparrows Point management apparently wasn't heeding his complaints about flaws in Bethlehem's steel plate.

A visit by Sparrows Point plate workers, he says, was a "last-ditch effort." When the steelworkers saw the problem their defects were causing, they were "practically in tears," Mr. Aulthouse says. The defect was resolved overnight.

*H. H. Robertson*, a highly profitable UK specialty steel producer: According to the *Financial Times*, November 14, 1983, "Efficient production is not the whole story. Robertson's managing director, Cliff Dyer, felt a year ago that the company was missing orders it should have won and decided to use a radical organizational tool to change things. He developed the 'ginger group' program. Each group is ad hoc and formed for a specific project, or likely order. It comprises the key people concerned, irrespective of rank in the company. Thus, design, sales, production, cost accounting and purchasing might all be asked to join, often with junior people brought in. The system has broken down interdepartmental barriers, producing a fluid, creative approach that Dyer describes as 'analog' [organization]—as opposed to the 'digital' organizational structure with segregated functions with formal communications between departments which bogs down many managements." Let people have the tools—and watch out. The results have been smashing.

*Monarch Marking*, principally a maker of labels for retailers, has a bunch of exciting programs. One involves their smallest division, which sells labels for industrial use—e.g., tag wires in an aircraft's electronics area. Until the new boss took over, the division had been in a state of rapid decline in an apparently decrepit market, falling from $9 million in sales to $4 million in a three-year period. As of late 1983, the new man's been in charge for about two years; sales—in the face of the recession of 1981–83—had vaulted to $23 million. What's going on? A hopped-up organization with everybody involved. For instance, once a week there's a series of "partnership meetings" for all hands. Everyone participates. Everyone is treated as a full-scale business person and partner. Everyone goes out and visits customers—regularly. The leap from $4 million to $23 million in sales has not come via one or two superproducts; it's come from an outpouring of tiny products. Most were developed by the most unlikely people, and in the most unlikely places once intensive customer contact (listening and inquiring) by all hands was begun. All participate and all have come to feel responsible for serving even better the customers they have. Tiny things: for instance, a flashy letterhead (pride, again!). The manager even made a trip to Las Vegas for the sole purpose of picking up some old silver dollars (he could have obtained them via courier, but he made the trip personally as a symbolic gesture). Now, when something good happens (some small success), he gives out one of those precious silver dollars.

---

### Paint and Potties

A tough old nut, sporting a close-cropped crew cut in the 1980's, ran the Buffalo, New York, foundry for General Motors. He turned it around—and in just eighteen months. The secret? He began with a bucket of paint and an innocent query, "Is there any reason why a foundry can't be white?" There wasn't. And it mattered to his people. An officer at Memorex, and another from Hewlett-Packard, both with exceptional records, apply the same "magic." Colleagues say of each: "Whenever he arrives someplace, he always begins the same way— paints it up. Makes it a place you'd be proud of."

And the potty part? We mentioned before that Marcus Sieff of Marks & Spencer speaks often of having the washrooms up to snuff. Ed Carlson, the UAL turnaround genius in the early seventies, also preached the importance of clean washrooms—if they're not clean enough for you (the honcho), then they aren't clean enough for your people. A. Ray Smith turned the minor league Louisville Redbirds into a sparkling winner at the gate. His formula? Clean washrooms—"a place you'd be proud to take the family." And after a Dayton, Ohio, speech to Hewlett-Packard customers sometime back in which Tom had been talking about "bone-deep belief in people," the seventy-year-old-plus (he'd estimate) manager of several foundries outside of Cleveland came up to him, pulled him aside and said, "I liked what you said. But you were much too abstract. It's clean washrooms. Start by cleaning up the washrooms. If the goddamned place stinks to high heaven and looks like hell, if you wouldn't piss in it yourself, where's the pride, where's the care going to come from? How do you preach pride in product with any

> credibility at all when the smell from the head seeps onto the shop
> floor? Too goddam few people understand that. You tell 'em that."

What is the common denominator of this series of stories—stories that range from the Irish Post Office to an Irish canteen, from embossed lettering on an IBM calling card to "partnership meetings" in a forgotten division, from the sale of potholes to the citizens of Baltimore, to signing your name on a blackboard or testing a recipe? Ownership. Being a full-scale business person/partner, inexorably involved in a hands-on way in the output of the organization, particularly output directed toward customers for those not used to customer contact. Pride. Enthusiasm. Redefinition of a mundane job (e.g., working in the canteen) in a way that turns the performer of a "routine" task into a valued expert. Recognition and respect, in a host of small ways, especially for seldom acknowledged people and functions. Being part of a charged-up group with a pragmatic goal, sufficient resources and a fair time frame in which to achieve it, but no handed-down-from-on-high approach to getting there. The chance to set yourself apart as a winner.

These stories are also about integrity and guts. Integrity in that the leaders we've mentioned here believe in the capacity of people. Integrity in that they give recognition and opportunity, but not in a gimmicky or frivolous way. Chairman Bill Lane and his colleagues at Sunset have encouraged recipe testing not as a "gimmick" to involve people, but because they sincerely believe that their people can perform a genuine service. Guts in that these leaders are giving up control in not specifying the steps to the goal and in resisting the impulse to step in, to retract the grant of ownership opportunity before a fair effort has been made—one that will invariably include missteps along the way.

And what are the stories *not* about? They are *not* about expensive programs. Our friend Jim Kouzes conducted a seminar for engineering managers a while back. After a discussion of issues such as the granting of autonomy and ownership, one of his engineer-manager students summed it up: "All this [stuff is] free. And it works."* These are not tales of exotic programs, involving plans that take months. They are tales that result from the application of plain common sense in pursuit of giving people ownership of their jobs. You could start on any one tomorrow, or this afternoon.

> ### Quality for Your People's Sake
>
> Want superior quality? Courtesy? Pride transmitted to the customer
> via enthusiasm and care?

---

*Actually his student said "All this shit's free." And our friend Jim put it on a T shirt, of which we were early, proud recipients.

Davgar Restaurants (a successful Burger King franchisee with fifteen outlets) uses Heinz ketchup, rather than a second-rate substitute. They use butter instead of margarine. Is there a clear market advantage? Why, heavens no. They don't even tell their customers they're doing it. Nutty? No to that, too. They say, "Our people know they are serving the best. In a hundred ways they transmit their pride to our customers."

Delta Airlines cleans up all their *ground* equipment with a passion, according to a former manager—yet no customer ever sees it. Why do they do it? "It makes you [their support people] feel part of a quality effort."

Being the best by a country mile makes your own people feel like allstars. And allstars usually rise to the occasion, perform like allstars. "Treat me C−," says one employee, "and you'll get a C− effort. Treat me as an A+ and you'll get an A+, or at least my very best effort."

---

### "Ownership"
### Some Questions—and Things to Do Now

• Review the stories we've just told. Talk with colleagues at all levels, in all departments, and collect similar cases within your own group/division/company. Briefly write up fifteen to twenty-five of them. Look for the common variables: manager attitudes, team leader, problem to be solved. What can you learn? Do you allow autonomy or create small, self-sufficient problem solving teams, à la SAS, H. H. Robertson, Quad/Graphics? Do you enhance ownership via tiny marks of pride as do Sunset, Tupperware, IBM, the small retailer? Do you look to hiving off little divisions (instead of cutting them off) à la Monarch? Do you ensure that operators— à la Mervyn's—still have "space" left in their jobs? Analyzing these cases is serious business. A full day or two, at a minimum, could be usefully spent on this subject, with a group of ten to fifteen colleagues. The end product might be a detailed, thirty- to sixty-day plan to experiment with some efforts like these. The plan should also include a plan within a plan to get *all* managers (1) to search for examples like these, and (2) to develop their own plans for rapid experimentation.

• What is the status of information availability at the lowest levels in the organization? Is detailed comparative information on each unit's performance available to all? Are ten to twenty important output indicators, updated at least weekly, available to *everyone*—indicators that go from the individual to the team to the corporate level? When you develop new indicators, do you ask—at the *lowest* level—for guidance and ideas? For starters, does everybody at least receive and understand the annual report?

• *Stop:* another big request for a commitment is coming! Take a first or second-level supervisory job in three areas that are critical to you. Spend two days with each of the three supervisors, "shadowing" them and extensively debriefing them. (Better yet, take on a supervisor's shift for one full week—preferably an off-hours shift.) Write up a ten- to fifteen-page description of what the job is like, focusing on constraints and Mickey Mouse versus output orientation. (Or get two or three colleagues to join you in this effort. After your "shadowing" or performing the job, go off-site for one and a half to two days and do the same analysis on butcher paper.) In any event, pass the analysis back to the supervisors and have them grade you on it. Then get together with them and a half dozen of their colleagues and spend one day assessing your analysis and developing a game plan for "first step" thirty-day changes to enhance ownership of the jobs you looked at and similar jobs.

• Find 50 (!) little marks of respect—of the Sarah Clifton/IBM calling card and Tupperware blackboard variety—in use in your organization. Can you? Can you find 25 *new* ones introduced in the last *six* months? If not, . . .

• Find 50 (!) little marks of *dis*respect. (E.g., language, facilities, restricting information, demeaning rules, blatantly exhibited perks for senior people, "little" differences in benefits.) If you come up short, keep trying. They're there! Next: Eradicate some (five within the first ninety-six hours after the exercise). Repeat the exercise once every three or six months.

These exercises constitute hard work, and lots of work, especially if viewed as "in addition to" work. We contend, however, that this is the "it," not the "in addition to." Ownership is pivotal in achieving superior quality, service and innovation, and there can be nothing more important. If you *disagree*, try to explain why (to yourself, and to your people).

---

### The Basics of Ownership

Our good friend Julien Phillips brought the following to our attention from the *Wall Street Journal* (February 8, 1984):

> Medical-supply companies plan to introduce a patient-controlled analgesic device in the U.S. hospital market this year. A few hospitals, including the University of Kentucky Medical Center in Lexington, are testing the infusion pumps. What is different about the pump is that it gives patients some control over their own pain medication. Currently, hospital staff members can be pretty stingy with painkillers. Fear of an overdose or addiction means "physicians tend to under-prescribe, then nurses tend to under-administer," says Terrence Murphy, a professor of anesthesiology at the University of Washington pain clinic in Seattle. "No great harm is done. The patient is just a lot less comfortable than he might be."
>
> Not only do patients control pain better with the pump, they use *less* painkiller to do it. In one test, patients recovering from abdominal surgery were randomly assigned either shot therapy or pain pumps. The patients on the pumps used 31.5% less painkiller

than the patients getting shots. Mr. Lonnie Weddington, a patient in Kentucky, says that even though pain medicine was available from his pump every six or eight minutes, he used the pump rarely.

Researchers say that's not surprising. Certain psychological dimensions of pain are eliminated simply because the pump is there, they say; when a patient knows he has a way to control pain, he actually hurts less. Because they hurt less, patients on the pump are "more willing to cough, get up and do all the other things that are needed post-operatively," says Eulene Boyle, a nurse at the University of Kentucky Medical Center's intensive-care unit. In theory, Dr. Bennett says, patient-controlled analgesia reduces recovery time after surgery, but studies have yet to prove that. The patient-controlled analgesic device saves nurses a great deal of time. A nurse at a Chicago hospital says that normally she has to open a double-locked cabinet, sign a medicine sheet and account for every bit of painkiller each time she gives a shot.

People who oppose the pump aren't convicted it's safe to give a patient control over narcotics. One head nurse at a Chicago hospital says flatly, "I wouldn't have it on my floor." She fears patients might become dependent on the pump. "Fear of dependence or addiction is incredibly overblown," says Arthur Lipman, professor of clinical pharmacy at the University of Utah. "People in pain aren't junkies looking for a fix." He says that at the University of Utah medical facility, where the pump is being tested, patients "go off the machine at least as soon as they go off the shots." The second big concern is accidental overdose. But Dr. Bennett of Kentucky says the pump's design makes both overdoses and addiction nearly impossible. After the pump delivers a small dose of the narcotic, the patient is "locked out" of the pump for as long as the doctor has decided beforehand. If the patient presses the button during a lock-out period, no painkiller is delivered.

The simple story here *is* our story. Ownership, the promise of it. Ownership, the nonabuse of it (patients use 31.5 percent *less* painkiller). And, sadly, predictable resistance to it. To allow ownership is risky— to the nurse or any manager. Pain relief for patients is a major "perk" for the nurse (nurse as savior). Likewise, *telling people how to do their job* is a "perk" for managers at all levels, and thus ownership is a threat to what is traditionally the essence of the manager's job.

## The Issue of Scale (Again)

In our discussion of customers and innovation, we observed small groups producing higher quality, more personalized service and faster innovation than larger entities. It turns out that scale—small scale, via team organizations and decentralized units—is a vital component of top performance. The bottom line: ownership is inevitably lost in big groups.

What does "ownership" look like when the *whole* organization is involved? There's no better place to go for an answer than to W. L. Gore & Associates. It's the home of Sarah Clifton, Supreme Commander. It's the home of Bill and Vieve Gore: "We can't run the business. We learned over twenty-five years ago to let the business run itself. Commitment, not authority, produces results." Bill Gore calls the "structure" of the company a "lattice organization." Everybody depends on everybody else. He adds, "Certain attributes of the lattice can be defined: no fixed or assigned authority, sponsors rather than bosses, natural leadership defined by followership, person-to-person communication, objectives set by those who 'must make them happen,' tasks and functions organized through commitments. We don't manage people here, People manage themselves." And boost themselves, too: "People promote themselves here. They promote themselves every time they take on a new responsibility, every time they get a big sale, every time they come up with a new invention. We have a lost of heroes around here." (In fact, he refers to the whole process as "creating heroes.")

"We organize ourselves around voluntary commitments." Do they ever! When you come on board W. L. Gore & Associates, you aren't given an assignment at the outset. You *find* an assignment. You try a bunch of jobs, in any area you think might fit. You actively seek a "sponsor," because no one stays on permanently unless he or she finds a sponsor. Bill calls it the "mentoring system." The sponsor is responsible for your development and, with other sponsors, for your ongoing evaluation, compensation, etc. How many years until you become a sponsor? If you're a natural leader and people gravitate to you, you could become a sponsor in thirty, sixty or ninety days. It's happened. The winners end up being sponsors for many and being sponsored by many. Significantly, your worth is assessed principally by your peers—a hard group to deceive.

A while back Tom was talking about Gore with a sophisticated audience. After the speech an executive from another company came up and pounded him on the shoulder: "It's true. But you understate. [We've heard it so many times—we talk about the remarkable turnaround at Ford in Edison, New Jersey, and somebody visits there and sends us a detailed letter saying that we understated.] My daughter was hired off the street by the Gores. She came up with a neat idea, and within just thirty days of hiring she had been given more than three thousand dollars to play with. It might not work out and she knows that. But she also knows that if she does a decent job she need not fear failure. I'd also add that she's had no business experience, but that she's already become a mentor to some in her group. This has *all* happened in four months. They mean what they say."

The issue that we want to focus on with the Gore story is the issue of teams and scale. In a word, ownership and commitment, pride and enthusiasm, and an "all people as business people" attitude are virtually impossible in a giant, overly specialized organizational unit. Bill Gore is a hard-nosed scientist; he was a senior research executive at Du Pont when he left to found his company with Vieve over twenty-five years ago. He believed in the efficiencies of scale, and he initially let his factories grow like wildfire to achieve those efficiencies. He's backed off now, and backed off radically. These days Bill Gore illustrates what he means by optimal size with complex charts and graphs. But originally he learned his lesson through tough observation of what was going on. He says: "As the number [of people in one of his facilities] approaches two hundred, the group invariably turns into a crowd in which individuals grow increasingly anonymous and significantly less cooperative." Now the Gores almost religiously limit the size of their facilities to 100 to 150 people.

We regularly observe that such "small" plants, which do not pass any tests for "efficiencies of scale," outperform the bigger ones time and again. Milliken & Company maintains that the "right" number is about 100. 3M says 200 to 300 is the limit, and HP and Digital Equipment say no more than 300 to 400. Emerson Electric and Dana limit the size of their plants to about 500. GM now says that if it ever builds anything new, the limit will be around 300, while for Volvo the magic number is 500 or less. None of these is a number derived from theoretical science; rather, each is based upon years of experience with the failure of giant operations to live up to their promised (on paper) performance levels.

The essence of ownership is giving people some space. And the corollary that almost automatically goes with it is that it is smaller organizational units that make it possible to do so.

---

### Rush Week

That's right, "rush week"—fraternity/sorority jargon. The unparalleled growth of People Express had resulted in over 4,000 people on the payroll by late 1984. Senior management became concerned that the earlier zest might begin to wane. Their solution was to "reorganize" into teams of 200 to 300 people. The teams were to be roughly consituted around aircraft types (e.g., 737's, 747's). Each team would do its own scheduling within some general parameters.

The remaining issue was how to divvy up team membership. People's managing officers hit upon the rush-week theme. Each team captain would set up a recruiting booth in the crew space at Newark Airport's North Terminal (the location of company headquarters) and sign up volunteers. It was as simple as that. And it worked. Team captains (i.e., People executives) manned the booths and resorted to all sorts of inducements in the course of the week, especially as one team's membership surged ahead of another's. New recruits had their pictures taken with their new team captain. One team sent off to a Houston restaurant (many of People's senior people are Houston refugees) for special

Nachos. By Wednesday the pace was feverish, and even the initially reticent pilots were joining in the frenzied competition.

The net result was a gigantic running start for the new form of organization—and confirmation of the bedrock principle of ownership and involvement at People Express, even in the face of increasing numbers.

## Teams

Japanese corporations have very large manufacturing facilities in many instances. But their distinctive trait is the team. The focus is on groups of ten to twenty people (they're called "sections" in Japan) that are given exceptional autonomy; the American experience in dependence on teams, though not so widespread, is just as decisive. The Gores believe in teams. And so do two other very special people to whom we'll now turn—Bob Swiggett of the Kollmorgen Company, and Bill Creech, recently retired commanding general of the U.S. Air Force's Tactical Air Command (TAC). All three cases exemplify the vital importance of the sense of ownership that goes with small turned-on teams. More significantly to our mind, all three leaders are hard-nosed rationalists who have come to their conclusions almost unwillingly. Gore, as we've seen, was a senior scientist at Du Pont. Swiggett is an MIT-trained engineer, and Creech is an Air Force warrior-bureaucrat. Yet they have caused *revolutions* in organizations ranging in size from $250-million-a-year W. L. Gore & Associates through $400-million-a-year Kollmorgen to TAC, with tens of billions of dollars in assets. Each had a bias that said centralization, consolidation and efficiencies of scale are vital. Each changed that view. Their odysseys, then, are as important as the outcomes themselves.

The Kollmorgen story is an exciting one. A manufacturer of printed circuits, DC motors and controls, and electro-optic devices, Kollmorgen had some fine early successes, and with the successes came complications in manufacturing (apparently inevitable), and also the opportunity to take advantage of efficiencies of scale. Led by the Swiggett brothers, Bob and Jim, the company proceeded down the path of more centralization, more automation. By the late sixties, they were ready to install what was called the IBM System 70: state-of-the-art computer-driven factory control. In Bob Swiggett's words, "We were going to put this business on line, real time. We were going to know where every part was. We were going to have scheduling. Loading algorithms. We were smart. We weren't willing to trust our gut." And install the system they did. The result? Bob Swiggett explains: "Statistically we got what we wanted. But the foremen became preoccupied with their printouts instead of our customers." Quality deteriorated, schedules weren't met, and the company plunged downward. Disaster loomed.

Salvation, it turned out, lay in the company's files from the recent past— data from a bunch of unheralded efforts that had involved a fruitful team approach to rapid product development and manufacturing. After the early success, Kollmorgen had found it had become the new big guys in the printed circuit business; suddenly small guys started doing to Kollmorgen what Kollmorgen had done to the big guys of a generation before: moving faster, listening better and being more adaptive to customer needs. As a partial solution, Kollmorgen had created what was called the Proto [prototype] Department, which regularly accomplished in one week the product modifications and advances in manufacturing that it took the main-line part of the organization fully ten weeks to complete. (Remember the 1,000 percent factor?) "The Proto guys," says Bob Swiggett, "had one game, to satisfy the customer. The others were playing departmental games, like who has the best score for efficiency. The customer was just a job number."

The Proto "method" had been used on numerous occasions, whenever crisis demanded it, but though the results had always been positive, the team efforts had been perceived as "one off" activities, anomalies (it's a common engineer's bias). Now, however, as overall disaster approached, Bob Swiggett recalled the past and considered turning to the teams in a wholesale fashion. The idea was to organize the entire company into small production/product/customer-oriented teams. Team Manufacturing was to replace the System 70. System 70 would be scrapped.

Team Manufacturing was installed in 1968. In a six-month period—"a chaos of empire shattering," says Swiggett—the organization was transformed into a structure consisting of six teams of seventy-five persons each. The results were dramatic. Within the same six months, Kollmorgen's output per employee more than doubled, and on-time delivery to customers rose from less than 60 percent to well over 90 percent.*

Now, nearly fifteen years later, the teams are embedded in numerous small divisions (in effect, a second layer of teams that are highly autonomous profit centers. The objective? That each division be "strong enough to go public." New divisions are created regularly—as needed, with little fanfare—in an approach reminiscent of 3M's. Each has its own board of directors to both guide it and insulate it from distracting corporate intrusions.

The focus on the contribution of each person in the organization extends with astonishing uniformity throughout Kollmorgen's world. Tom had the opportunity to meet with the head of its Irish operations. Now Ireland is hardly the home, in general, of vigorous, new-wave management. And yet the Kollmorgen organization of Ireland is a joy to behold, looking more like Apple in Cupertino, California, than like its neighbors. Tom's first opportu-

---

*In the April 1984 issue of *Inc.* Lucien Rhodes describes a trip Bob Swiggett made to the Harvard Business School shortly before Kollmorgen made the shift to Team Manufacturing: "He packed his bags and went to Harvard to consult 'the world's leading guy on control.' Said Swiggett, 'I talked for quite a while. He was very patient. Then he said, "Here you are in the modern age with computers, control theory, and you just spent two hours on how you want to abdicate your responsibility. Forget this team manufacturing stuff."'" Fortunately, Swiggett went his own way.

nity to speak with the head of the operation came at a very proper dinner (among the guests was the Prime Minister of Ireland). "There are two exceptional people I'd especially like you to meet when you visit us," said the "boss" of Kollmorgen/Ireland. The design engineers or the like, Tom supposed. No. The first was "the fella who cleans up the washrooms. He'd stand in a group like this as a man of extraordinary integrity." The other was a person who had been with the company for a long time and who now ran the supply room.

So strong is the emphasis on the team and the development of the whole person in this man's operation that young men and women in the town where Kollmorgen/Ireland is headquartered are spurning college to go, instead, to what they've dubbed Kollmorgen College—the training program that has been installed in the organization. Our colleague gets his greatest pleasure from turning young men and women fresh off the streets into responsible contributors. The payoff? The real new-product heroes (each division of Kollmorgen, even overseas, is wholly responsible for the generation of its own set of new products) are a couple of unschooled eighteen-year-old tinkerers: "They"ll grab hold of those ideas [from the formal, "scientific" product developers], and quicker than a wink turn them into practical prototypes. It's my eighteen-year-olds that are doing the real work." As our colleague was saying this, Tom was reminded of a couple of similar stories from Japan. The head of Mitsubishi Electric states that the most innovative research in his company (very sophisticated) has come from some recent high school graduates, "with many fewer preconceptions than the rest—and a willingness to listen before they act." And at Kyocera Corporation, which makes 70 percent of the ceramic packages for semiconductors, the chairman talks ceaselessly about "maximizing the output from the 50 percent person," the average person in the company's employ. His secret weapon: *teams!* An article in the April 16, 1984, issue of *Business Week* reported that "the corporation is divided into groups of 10 to 20 employees, in a system that president and founder Kazuo Inamori calls 'amoeba management.' Each group keeps separate accounts and is expected to make a profit, measuring production and value against cost." Kyocera has been voted the best-managed company in Japan.

Teams and ownership work miracles for Gore. They work for Kollmorgen. For Kyocera. But do they work in a truly giant organization? Well, when Tom returned from the visit to Ireland during which he met the head of Kollmorgen/Ireland, awaiting him was a delightful four-page letter from an unexpected source: General Bill Creech, the four-star general who commanded the United States Air Force's Tactical Air Command (TAC) until October 1984. Amazingly, Creech's story sounds a lot like Bill Gore's and Bob Swiggett's and Kazuo Inamori's.

We've seen in chapter 4 (pp. 48–49) something of the turnaround at TAC—an organization of 113,000 people. Central to that not so minor miracle was Creech's realization that the Air Force (like most of the rest of

America's organizations—schools, hospitals, private corporations) had been ill-served by the "centralization/consolidation disease of the 1960's," which he calls "dehumanizing." Centralization, he says, "creates functional 'stove-pipes,' long on management theory and short on overall mission responsibility. Centralization wants one thing of a type, not many. There's little or no stress on competition. Centralization prizes 'one-of-a-kind,' not 'competitive' sub-elements. . . . The theory was that if you had all the inputs [the so-called functional stovepipes], the output would 'take care of itself.'" While Creech talks ceaselessly about the importance of leadership, he also believes that leadership can't do it all: "Even the best leaders get submerged and stymied in organizations that are highly centralized, highly consolidated." His solution was to shift from the highly centralized and specialized (input-driven) structure he inherited to an output-focused organization he called POMO (Production-Oriented Maintenance Organization). And with it in place, the remarkable reversal occurred. Keep in mind that he had no "outside" help. He had (1) no more people, (2) no positive change in weapon systems mix (i.e., no easier-to-maintain planes), (3) fewer parts available, and (4) a work force with *less* experience than had been available, on average, during the previous ten years. You can't just explain the change away by any set of external factors.

What is the POMO magic? It's quite simple—some might say it's obvious. First and foremost, management's focus was shifted from the higher level (input-based) unit—the wing—to the lower level (output-oriented) unit—the squadron. Each "production unit" (squadron)—shades of Kollmorgen's team manufacturing or Kyocera's teams—now does its own scheduling. It has its own decentralized computers, much to the dismay of the central MIS people (just as in industry). Squadron-versus-squadron comparison numbers are readily available, and intense squadron-versus-squadron competition has been introduced. Though the Air Force always deploys or fights as a squadron, the centralization logic of the sixties and seventies had led to squadrons literally being abolished. Colorful aircraft tail markings were not allowed. Squadron patches were forbidden. Even the fabled 94th, the Eddie Rickenbacker squadron, disappeared—history, unit pride and all. Now the colorful pennants, tail markings and arm patches (along with mugs, ties, tie tacks, T-shirts and a host of other paraphernalia) are back, and sprouting up everywhere.

Many other things happened in the wake of the change in organizational philosophy. Maintenance was reorganized; the decentralized squadron became self-sufficient. Parts were made available on the flight line. (In an Air Force dominated by "efficiences of scale" there had been one depot, no matter how many miles it was away from the flight line. Unfortunately, this led to frequent non-sorties because there were no parts available.) Creech's motto was "Organize as you will fight." He wanted his "squadron supervisors to train as wartime leaders." Previously his NCO's "had evaluated themselves by the thickness of their carpets." MBWA was introduced: "I insisted that specialists of all skills get back to the flight line." Other terms were "cross-utilization," "on-scene supervision" and "immediate [parts] availability."

But the reincarnation of the squadrons wasn't even the half of it. Creech went yet a level lower: the long-neglected support people in maintenance and supply became his obsession. First he created coherent aircraft maintenance units (AMU's) at the squadron level. The units were given decent facilities, in contrast to the second-rate quarters previously accorded them. Tiny details counted: Artwork (done by the men) was hung in the facilities (previously it had been implicitly assumed that only pilots cared about such things); one AMU now has a self-executed wall mural on the history of aviation. The maintenance and supply people were given recognition. The NCO in charge of an aircraft is now a "dedicated crew chief"; highly visible bulletin boards inside and outside an AMU facility include pictures of that AMU's dedicated crew chiefs—always next to their planes. The team leaders/dedicated crew chiefs are now directly in charge of their people's evaluation. (Previously evaluations were done way up the line by an officer unfamiliar with the outfit.)

The output of the AMU's is highly visible. Walls are dotted with sizable charts showing trend lines with key readiness and quality-improvement indicators. The most vital are posted on big boards outside the unit, visible to all who drive by (i.e., all one's competitive peers). Competitions among supply and maintenance units have been introduced. In fact, each wing has a sizable trophy room wholly devoted to trophies and plaques won only in supply and maintenace competitions. Regular award banquets for supply and maintenance people are now commonplace.

Thus the "least" of activities are now heralded and the subject of competition. General Creech even instituted a semiannual base-by-base "drive-by" (a takeoff on the spectacular aircraft "fly-by"), a triumphant parade of pickup trucks, jeeps, parts trailers and other support vehicles. Top-management attendance (i.e., base commander et al.) is 100 percent.

Does this ownership stuff count for much? Well, you have the overwhelming statistics from TAC, Kollmorgen et al., to support the point. But perhaps the last word, and the best, comes from one of Bill Creech's noncommissioned officers. The general asked him what the difference was between the old, specialist organization and the new organization, in which the plane and the sortie are the "customer," where the supervisor ("designated crew chief," remember) "owned" the plane. The NCO's to-the-point reply: "General, when's the last time you washed a rental car?" We think that may say it all. None of us washes our rental cars. There's no ownership. And there's no ownership if you're a specialist, no matter how well trained, if you're responsible only for two square feet of the right wing of a hundred planes. Only whole planes fly. Only "owners," especially in competition and with flags flying, will go all out to make a whole plane fly. Creech had, pure and simple, made that NCO a proud owner—with (and this is vital, too) the wherewithal to get the job done.

One last point, as we move beyond TAC and Kollmorgen and our focus on teams: the speed of the transformations. Many ask, "How long does a turnaround take?" A $50 million outfit (then), Kollmorgen, had a revolution in results in six months. The Creech revolution—in a $35-billion operation—

was well under way in a year, and remarkable results were evident after just two years. To build a sustaining new "culture" may (will) take decades, but to get a running start—with dramatic changes in output—takes only months.

---

### Creech's Laws

General Creech, as he prepared to turn over his command in the fall of 1984, published a set of fifteen "organizational principles." Here they are:

1. *Have a set of overarching·principles and philosophies. Have an overall theme and purpose.*

2. *Use goals throughout*—goals at all levels, from crews to senior command. There should be darned few of them—in general, paperwork should be kept to a minimum—and they should be clearly achievable—i.e., most people should end up as winners.

3. *Measure productivity at several levels.* But "don't strangle in paperwork." Also: "Micro-information should not be used to micro-manage [that is, it should be used primarily to spur peer-versus-peer competition]." All information should be "oriented to the product"—i.e., the aircraft sortie.

4. *Create leaders at many levels.* With this goes a plea to "get leaders [e.g., dedicated crew chiefs] where the action is. Staff supports the line. Not vice versa."

5. *Match authority and responsibility and instill a sense of responsibility.* "Ninety-nine percent will accept responsibility if authority goes with it," and authority should always be product (i.e., aircraft)-oriented, not function-oriented. "I'm not wild about accepting responsibility without authority," says the general. "Why should my people be?"

6. *Set up internal competition and comparison where feasible.* "Reward success" is the key corollary. The resultant pressure is high: "Nobody wants to report that his unit is last, month after month."

7. *Create a climate of pride.* "Instill individual dignity. Provide challenge and opportunity to each. Intangibles matter."

8. *Create a climate of professionalism.* "Esprit is the critical measure."

9. *Educate, educate, educate.* By means, first and foremost, of regular feedback.

10. *Communicate, communicate, communicate.* Do not depend on the formal hierarchy; skip down several levels—regularly.

11. *Create organizational discipline and loyalty.* This is vital, but will inevitably "stifle initiative." Hence, specific devices must be in place to lead people to disregard the system and reward initiative.

12. *Provide everyone with a stake in the outcome.* Make each job meaningful. Reward good performance (lavishly) in all areas.

13. *Make it better.* Create a sense of individual and organizational worth. Create an "optimistic organization." Provide a climate for continuous change. Above all: "The leader is not just a scorekeeper and steward. He is responsible for creating something new and better."

14. *Make it happen:* "Vigorous leadership at all levels is the key." The leader is at once responsible for creating "the dynamic spark" and simultaneously "working the details" that make it happen.

15. *Make it last.*

---

We talked of Edison, New Jersey, where the Ford Motor Company gave a shut-down-the-line button to each of its people. We talked about Sarah Clifton, Supreme Commander. But the magic of Ford at Edison is not just—or even primarily—the button. It's Phil Staley trooping the line, it's his pride and enthusiasm and zest. And in addition to decentralization, unit flags, intense competition and crew ownership of the aircraft/sortie/customer, the story of Bill Creech's turnaround at TAC is likewise the story of intangibles that go beyond team structure per se. Read Creech's Laws again. Note the emphasis on pride and enthusiasm. "You need pride," Creech says. "There are no poor outfits—just poor leaders." As additional evidence, he provides a homely example, from another service—the Navy's helicopter carrier *Iwo Jima*. In a remarkably brief period it went from "worst to first" in its squadron, he reports. The "magic" used by the commanding officer? "You know how he did it? He had the crew paint the whole damned ship from one end to the other. He started preaching pride."

---

### More than a Label

In their discussion of unsuccessful companies in the chapter called "Success versus failure" in *The Winning Streak*, Walter Goldsmith and David Clutterbuck vividly illustrate the importance of the trade names that give people (at every level) their working identity:

When Jaguar was renamed 'large car assembly plant number one', its founder, Sir William Lyons, marched into the boardroom and removed his portrait from the wall. He had no intention of presiding, even on canvas, over the undermining of the principles of grace, pace and space on which he had built the company and its reputation.

John Egan, the sixth chief executive in eight years, describes what happened: 'In 1975 an attempt was made to subjugate Jaguar, along with other marques such as Rover, Land-Rover, Triumph, Austin Morris, MG and so on, under the ill-fated Leyland Cars umbrella.

'At one stage Jaguar flags at the entrance to the factory were torn

> down. Only Leyland flags were allowed to be flown on the prem-
> ises and telephonists were threatened with disciplinary action if
> they answered callers with "Good morning. Jaguar Cars." Instead
> they were supposed to say, "Good morning. Leyland Cars," and if
> any further address was needed, "Large assembly plant number
> one." Worse still, the then two constituent factories of Jaguar were
> put into two quite separate organizational units within Leyland—
> the Power and Transmission Division and the Body and Assembly
> Division—hardly an appropriate fate for one of the most famous
> marque names in the world motoring industry.
>
> 'Sir Michael Edwardes' . . . genius was to recognize immediately
> that no progress was possible unless famous marque names were
> re-created as a focus for group and individual loyalty.'

It's so important not to get off track in this chapter, especially in this section on teams. Because teams can work only if the leader believes in his or
her people. And that belief, perhaps surprisingly, tends to be best reflected
in a focus on the mundane sources of pride—a newly painted ship, or the
butter sculptures that appear when people are allowed to celebrate, for their
families, in their facility. Some will move to decentralization/teams, but then
fail to give the team leaders the tools to do the job; not believing in them,
they don't trust them with parts on the flight line or responsbility for scheduling. And this is probably worse than making no change—it smacks of
hypocrisy, among other things.

So it's paint and potties.* It's stimulation through competition. It's fun and
enthusiasm. General Creech is thoughtful about it. He says he's been accused
of merely created a five-year "Hawthorne effect."† He adds, "If you wish to
call it a 'Hawthorne effect,' then so be it." We agree with him. So be it. But
we'd go further—much further. We think the best leaders are, perhaps above
all, perpetual creators of Hawthorne effects. Sam Walton, the Wal-Mart boss,
makes the opening of every one of his stores—over seven hundred now—
exciting and different from the one before. The $64 question—and the gut-

---

*And more: Staley's turnaround in Edison features a strong dose of additional fans
and watercoolers—and the removal of time clocks. A dramatic Western Electric
plant turnaround features extra pay phones in the coffee-break areas, awnings over
the doors to keep out the rain, and lights in the parking lot.

†The Hawthorne studies in Western Electric's bank wiring rooms in the thirties
revealed that simple attention paid (e.g., by management) led to dramatic productivity increases. For instance, in an examination of the effects of industrial hygiene,
lighting levels were increased. Not surprisingly, productivity increased. When the
experiment was completed, the lights were turned down. To the researchers' surprise, the productivity went up again, not down. Many more experiments were done
to corroborate this finding. All added up to the same thing: Pay attention, stimulate
the system, and effectiveness increases.

wrenching issue—all of us must face as leaders is: Are we, as Mr. Sam (Walton) is, capable of creating yet another Hawthorne effect after the seven hundredth opening? Of making our teams into excited, turned-on, prideful, enthusiastic, competitive owners of the job, responsible for the output, wholly aware of *all* the statistics and information that affect the enterprise? Of making the organization an exciting place to be?

---

### "Teams":
### Some Questions—and Things to Do Now

• Seriously consider a radical restructuring (whether you are in charge of twenty-seven or seventy-five or seventy-five thousand) into a team-based organization. Begin by going back into your own history—personal and professional. Look at the things that worked—athletic teams, Girl/Boy Scout troops, army squads, college groups, alumni fund-raising—and the work environment. Do you find any pattern? if so, take the next step and begin to codify the supporting devices: à la TAC, did the unit have the full wherewithal to get on with the job? Was unit competition a part of it? Were flags, pennants and other symbols of pride part of it?

• If this is a serious endeavor (as we think it ought to be), have ten to twenty people at various levels perform the same analysis. Then go off-site for a day or two (or a long weekend) and assess the data—personal and professional.

• Look at some first steps (read the account of Sam Neaman and McCrory's in chapter 10): Can you start the team process *somewhere?* It need not be a likely or highly visible place. E.g., can you, as did the retailer described on page 00, construct a team of pros to train others in a critical skill? Can you form a SWAT team of MIS people to actually *help* a small facility somewhere? Following the H. H. Robertson example (see page 227), can you form a few multifunction service teams in a group to help problem/opportunity customers? Can you give a team the charge to "somehow" make better use of a facility or asset à la Quad/Graphics and the back-haul (see page 219)? Two cautions: First, don't take on too much too soon. The would-be leaders (if this is foreign stuff) will take lots of coaching (your time), and you don't want this to be viewed as a flash in the pan. We're suggesting, à la Swiggett, that you think of it as a way of life. Second, make sure the team has a thirty- to sixty-day output objective; above all, we are *not* talking about landing a new prime customer, adding a new service, installing a new (up and running, debugged) support system.

• Finally, the usual caution: This is a big deal! We are suggesting action, but also sober and serious reflection, about the way you organize for results. If this reflection comes *easy*, either you've already done it or you haven't dug deep enough. You've got to go through some form of the marathon runner's wall of pain on this, we suspect.

## More on Trust: We Has Met
## the Enemy and It Is Us

The story up to this point has been positive, the story of the enhancement of individuals, of flag-bearing teams and small units. The negative side is that we are our own worst enemy; that is, we get in our own way. Actually, it's worse: It's a double-negative story. Not only do we get in our own way, but we don't mean to. In other words, there is little stupidity, little irrationality, little malicious intent among us. It's rules, in fact, that trip us up and strip our Sarah Cliftons or NCOs of the sense of ownership—rules that invariably were instituted for sound, rational reasons.

Thoughts of Sarah Clifton forced themselves into our consciousness soon after we were called upon to assist an Eastern aircraft manufacturer with a $750 million operation. The problem was quality. After some study, our decision was to focus all our energy on but a single topic—the life and times of the first-line manufacturing supervisor in a several-thousand-person manufacturing organization. We determined to take that one job and tear it apart, second by second, minute by minute, hour by hour, to answer the question: What's it *really* like to be a first-level manager in this place? The procedure involved an intensive, seventeen-hour-a-day, four-day-long off-site retreat with the top twenty people and two of us. This is typical of what we found: The first-line supervisor was responsible for some twenty-five to thirty-five people, and had $1 million at least, and often up to $4 million worth of capital equipment, under her or his control. And yet, characteristically, this supremely responsible individual didn't have the authority to buy an $8.95 can of paint to clean up his or her people's work space. An "owner"? Hardly. He or she was responsible for the quality of the product, for the company's number one asset, its people (twenty-five or more of them), and several million dollars' worth of capital, but was not *trusted* with $8.95 unless the facility manager signed off on it. As one small businessperson said, "We make people responsible for all that's important, then we treat them like children, and then we're utterly dismayed when they turn around and behave and respond like children."

In this case, we decided to do something about the situation. At the end of a lengthy day's deliberations we agreed to give that first-line supervisor $25 in unquestioned spending authority. You may laugh at the lack of largesse (as many have in many groups), but that's not the punch line. After the fateful decision was made, one vice president raised his hand and said, "I want to go on record, before we do this, as saying that you know and I know what they're going to do with those twenty-five bucks—they're going to go out and buy handguns." (And you wonder why the quality wasn't so great!) So we face-tiously suggested another solution. "Leave it at $8.95, if you wish," we said. "We'll make but one suggestion. Write the rule if you must—for reasons of control, etc.—but add a little parenthetical expression in *red*, at the end:

'We're doing this because we don't trust you.' If you can stomach that language, then leave the proposed rule in."

It is claimed that such demeaning rules are necessary to ensure "fiduciary responsibility." But although a forty-three-year-old, high-school-educated, first-line manufacturing supervisor may not know the nuances of fiduciary responsibility all that well, she or he surely is an expert on the meaning—exactly—of the word "trust." And trust—make no mistake about it—is what it's all about.

We could bore the reader with the full contents of a four-inch-thick file folder labeled "The 8.95 syndrome." Instead, we'll mention just one other example. A plant manager for a Big Three auto maker in Europe employs three thousand people in a major urban center (it makes him the biggest employer in the city). He was solicited a while back to supply musical instruments for a school band. The cost would have been a few hundred dollars. But he had to write Detroit for approval, which took weeks. He couldn't say yes on the spot. Talk about revealing someone's powerlessness to his peers and people and the community! Talk about demeaning! Talk about demotivating!

Such abominations can—and do—happen. in the very best of companies. We spoke earlier about Renn Zaphiropoulos and his concern for individual dignity. In 1984 Tom went through a presentation with him that included the $8.95 paint-bucket analysis, and they and several of Renn's people were sitting around his office afterwards. They decided—and it attests to Renn's integrity (and guts) that he agreed—that they'd run an on-the-spot check. Three or four of his people from the secretarial pool, the copier room and so on were called in and asked to come up with the most demeaning regulation they could name. What an eye-opener! The procedure for leaving a $1 IOU in petty cash to buy stamps and the form required to purchase more than five pads of paper were nothing short of gruesome. Renn was stunned. And that's the point. The very best of us are shocked at how quickly the web of individually trivial but cumulatively demeaning Mickey Mouse can spread.

Sometimes assaults on ownership do seem to border on the malicious, though even then, malicious is not exactly the right word. It's more likely frustration or thoughtless insensitivity. After a daylong seminar, we talked to a fellow who runs a middle-sized (about six hundred employees) timber-products wholesaling and retailing operation. He had just taken a tough strike. In the midst of the strike there had been some incidents of apparent arson—a couple of small fires, one of which almost destroyed a $15,000 facility. Now, what such actions prove, in our view (and in the view of most with whom we've shared this story), is that most of life's phenomena follow bell-shaped curves. That is, given a cast of six hundred, you will probably find one or two real turkeys. We have not a shred of sympathy for the arsonists. Neither, naturally, did the manager of the operation in question. But his response was, nonetheless, wholly inappropriate—the worst imaginable, we believe. Because when the strike was over, he did the one thing that might indeed turn 20 percent of the workforce into potential arsonists. He instituted draconian inspection procedures—essentially going through the pockets of his people as they entered the facilities to work, to see if they had lighters or matches. And in so doing, he severely and unnecessarily alienated the 598 out of 600 who were *not* arsonists. He treated the 598 like children or worse—like criminals. In such ways do we all too regularly shoot ourselves in the foot (or heart).

There comes a special time when we weep at the $8.95 paint-bucket (and band-instrument and pocket-inspection) stories. During the course of a several-days-long program with some presidents of small companies, we spent a pleasant afternoon over a bottle or so of wine talking about their experiences with allowing their people a little bit more control. There's one story that we remember particularly clearly. This executive, we'd judge in his late fifties, was coming late to this subject of treating people with respect. The experiment he launched consisted of taking a couple of his facilities—an old plant and a foundry—and giving them $2,000 a month apiece to spend any way they wished. There were only two strictures: the plant manager could not sit on the committee that decided on the nature of the expenditure, and the composition of the expenditure committee had to mirror the proportion of managerial to nonmanagerial people in the facility's population. He recalled the first month of the experiment. He'd granted the $2,000. The likely nature of the expenditure had been the subject of much flippant chatter among the senior people, several of whom thought our friend was a bit batty ("They'll buy handguns"). What *did* the people in those old facilities choose to do? Well, one group took the $2,000 and built a memorial garden outside the plant. It honored past members of the work force who, over the course of several decades, had died in industrial accidents and in foreign wars.

Yes, these are the same beings of a lower order who are not responsible enough to spend $8.95 wisely. Yet, given $2,000, what do they do with it? Buy handguns? No, a memorial garden for former colleagues. And that *is* the nature of the average human being in the work force, if given an opportunity to shine.

---

### Two "Knockout" Factors—
### and What to Do about Them

Again and again in our seminars, two hurdles to achieving a people/ownership orientation, in the sense talked about here, arise. "Sure, *I* believe this stuff," says the division general manager (or big-company CEO), "but the unions get in the way." And: "Sure, *I* believe this stuff, but I can't bring first-line supervisors along. They are so threatened by enhanced 'ownership.'"

Let's take unions. First, we agree. Unions *do* get in the way. The question is why? We aren't sure we buy very often (ever?) the "*My* hands are clean, *theirs* are dirty" argument. We are in agreement with pollster Daniel Yankelovitch, Walt Kelly (in *Pogo*) and Gary Bello of Clark Equipment, who said, respectively: "The work ethic [in America] is alive and well, urgently wishes to express itself, and is hobbled at every turn by management"; "We has met the enemy and it is us"; "Management gets *exactly* the work force it deserves, not one iota more and not one iota less."

In a nutshell, we think *you* are the problem. There is no doubt that unions, nationally and on a company-by-company basis, vary greatly. For instance, Ford's great progress on employee involvement in the early eighties was spurred on in part by a lucky happenstance: the advent of a new Ford industrial relations VP and a new head of UAW at Ford with no Ford history. Neither carried bad prior baggage to the table. Principally, however, we agree with Ren McPherson, the former Dana head. *The* issue, he states adamantly, is management getting *its* house in order. One of his former colleagues added, "Look, let's take [union] work rules. They're awful. Right? Well, I'll tell you the union-contrived work rules pale by comparison with the crap we used to send out from the executive offices and try to enforce through the foreman." Amen. Look ahead to chapter 17, on debureaucratizing. We observe the possibility of a 95 percent-plus reduction in bureaucracy—even in the Army. Management, unlike foreign policy, is ripe for unilateral disarmament; let's clean up our act first.

An advance in management-union relations began, belatedly, to happen on another dimension in the 1981–83 recession. For the first time in memory, cuts in middle management occasionally matched (or, in rare instances, exceeded) layoffs on the line from a percentage standpoint. Yet this promising start was, we believe, generally inadequate. It is a rare company that couldn't enhance its management by cutting yet another 25 to 75 percent of its horribly bloated middle management. Again: "Let's get our own house in order" is the message.

Finally, it's important to *persist* if progress is to be made. We believe that the attitude of *people*—i.e., the work force—toward quality and productivity are *the* issue in steel and autos. Yet a recent analysis we made of public speeches by auto executives finds *people* missing. Automation, unions, unfair competition and that old devil Washington still win the word-count prize by a country mile. But if you listed to, say, Ren McPherson or Phil Staley of Ford or Bob Strammy of GM or Bill and Vieve Gore, you find the insistent theme is people. Tom has known Ren McPherson well for five years, and still has no idea what his views are on automation, because McPherson doesn't talk about it. We think, then, that most who view unions as the problem don't view people as the solution, to begin with. They don't really, deep down, believe that "stuff" is worthy of no. 1 priority status. And sure enough, they reap less than superb union relations as one reward.

And what of that other objection—recalcitrant first-line supervisors? To begin with, we agree. First-line supervisors are threatened by enhanced ownership on the line. Their traditional control vehicles are thrown out; they must transform themselves from order givers to cheerleaders and facilitators. The problem is major, and the solution to it is that the response must be major as well. In the hell-bent and sometimes faddish plunge into increased participation and ownership, we often skip over the role of the supervisor. Shop-floor or back-room operations teams are trained in group problem solving, but the supervisor is ignored. Such a situation will inevitably come back to haunt you.

Our ultimate solution is radical, but must be stated. We see little need, over the long haul, for the traditional first-line supervisor. Team leaders (temporary or permanet) selected by the work group are proving a brilliant alternative. But we won't belabor that here, for the issue in this brief section is what to do if you do have traditional supervisors. Our answer is threefold: training, careful use of new promotion opportunities and separation.

First, training. The supervisor is being asked to change, and change radically. You must provide excessive help. Expensive and extensive retraining is a must. It was at the heart of McPherson's reason for setting up Dana U., his pride and joy. And, of course, the key to superb training is not leaving it to the trainers. If the issue is big (and it usually is) and if it is the block to performance improvement (and it usually is), then senior management must be involved in the program's design and delivery. It's simply far too important—especially the element that deals with supervisorial training—for the frequently second-rate training department. (While a good bit of the substance of this book is related to this issue, you might turn at this point to the chapter on "Coaching" for some more detailed suggestions.)

Second, use promotion wisely. When a new first-line supervisor job opening comes up, don't get overwhelmed by an attack of (largely appropriate) sympathy for an old hand who played the game well by the old rules. Promotion is the swiftest and clearest signal of altered priorities to vast numbers of people. First promotion must go to those who are learning fastest to play the game by the new rules. Anything less spells delay or disaster. (See also chapter 16, "Leading toward Excellence.")

Finally, separation. If your training is sound and intense, if you set out clear new expectations and if you live up to them, then (and only then) the time will come when you can separate those who can't or won't play by the new rules. And you must. Our only caveat here is fairness. Did you really give the old hand a good shot? And this fairness issue always falls on the senior managers' shoulders. Did you preach the new way but inadvertently fail to practice it in a thousand tiny acts, thus giving hopelessly mixed signals to the shop floor? Unfortunately, that is most often the case.

Finally, another word of warning: following our guidelines—all which we have learned from others, the real people pros—not only will *not* make life easy but will not even make the problems go away rapidly! Often as not, even the most enlightened new boss—e.g., division general manager—is fighting decades of tradition. Expect a five- to-ten-year struggle at a minimum. Progress, we observe, from colleagues at Ford, TAC, Milliken et al. can come almost overnight. Victory, however, is elusive.

---

A pithy summation on the issue of demeaning regulations—and it speaks clearly to the matter of nonmaliciousness—comes from a senior manufacturing person at IBM. "Our systems are the scar tissues of past mistakes," he says. Ah, yes. And each layer of that scar tissue—the initial system that was developed—made perfectly rational sense when created. Yes, each layer is rational, or microrational. Every line on every form makes sense—taken alone. It's the thousands of lines taken together that, unintentionally, add up to a macro-illogic (the same macro-illogic based on micro-logic that General Creech so successfully fought at TAC).

How does sense deteriorate into nonsense? Suppose you have a dozen facilities (stores, distribution centers, plants, bank branches, or what have you). There's a fire in one of them. You put together a SWAT team of your best people to analyze why it occurred. They do a super job (you can depend on it—after all, they're your best and brightest). They come up with a 35-page report, concluding with 42 recommendations about what to do to avoid the problem in the future. The recommendations are without exception solid and sound. As a responsible leader, you want to make sure that *everybody* can take advantage of this wisdom. So you pass it along, in the form of hard-and-fast rules, to *all* of your twelve facilities. Great (so far). And then a major computer failure occurs in another location six weeks later. Another bright and aggressive SWAT team is instantly mounted. Another 30-page (more likely 300-page) report and another 26 (or 86) recommendations. Again, all sound. Again, everyone should have the opportunity to take advantage of this wisdom. Again, 26 "recommendations" (or at least 20) are added to the rule book. At the end of five, or ten, or, heaven help us, seventy years, the Sarah Cliftons of the world are trying to work according to 950-page rule books. That's when we get in trouble. Ownership is reduced to about zero.

The systems come to take on a life of their own. The systems end up having little to do with what we are trying to accomplish. Tiny distortions are added by each person who holds the job (in accounting, purchasing, MIS). These are the ten things George wanted to measure when he was the accounts receivable person, or Ellen when she was the reports person for this part of the bank. A senior manufacturer from the Northrop Corporation stated it nicely: "Our systems get detached from the way people build a plane. Systems, after all, are supposed to mirror and abet the way things are done, are supposed to make things easier. Yet the systems, so often, don't look like the creature that we are attempting to build."

And one other point. As the head of several top Hickory Farm franchisees said to us, "Let's call them what they are. They aren't rule books. They're *excuse* books. Nobody reads the damned things unless there's a screwup. And then they only read them to figure out who to blame the foul-up on." Amen! Tom was an officer in the Navy for five years. They say the Navy is run by U.S. Navy Regulations. Tom, to this day, has yet to read the first word of Navy Regulations. And he never will—that is, unless the Navy tries to come back and accost him for some horrible misdeed of twenty years ago. Then he'll read them. You bet. And his objective? You've got it—to figure out whom he can blame the sin on!

Dee Hock, the former chairman of the highly innovative Visa organization, puts it this way: "Substituting rules for judgment starts a self-defeating cycle, since judgment can only be developed by using it. You end up with an army of people who live by rote rather than reason, and where reason cannot be depended upon." Above all, we desperately *want* people to exercise judgment. We want maximum "creativity"—from the person handling the mail, in the PBX room, on the loading dock. And we do mean creativity. We want that person on the loading dock to be alert for a box that has a toe mark where it inadvertently got kicked. And we want him or her to have the "ownership" (both the care and the power) to do the right thing when that box comes along—i.e., cast it aside. We want the PBX operator to feel a sense of ownership and to behave creatively *whenever* a call comes in—to break his or her back, just a little bit, to respond courteously to a difficult/impolitic/irritable query, to take an extra forty-five seconds to try to direct the caller to the right person. *That* is creativity! As one manager commented, "Creative design teams are a dime a dozen. A well-functioning, well-oiled and creatively courteous PBX room or loading dock crew is as rare as a smog-free day in Los Angeles." A nice epilogue is provided by former HEW Secretary John Gardner: "Don't let form triumph over spirit."

---

### "The Enemy Is Us":
### Some Questions—and Things to Do Now

• Analogous to our aircraft manufacturers and $1 IOU vignettes, conduct two levels of analysis. First, in depth. Select one to four critical "hourly" or first-line supervisory jobs. Collect as much information as possible on "how it feels to live there" (e.g., interviews, anonymous questionnaires, collection of all the procedural material that governs the job, performing the job for two shifts). Have four or five colleagues do the same thing. Spend *two full days*, preferably off-site, going through your analysis in detail. What does it tell you in general? Specifically? Then, make long- and short-term action plans—both remedial and proactive. Begin, during the two days, by taking twenty *concrete* actions (e.g., decidedly *not* "Form a committee to cut paperwork by 20 percent") that reduce demeaning irritants. Set up a plan to continue this process, with you directly in charge (no delegation). Proactively, set in place a process to review future procedures with an eye toward minimizing the demeaning ones (again, you as boss must be *directly* in charge). Take the results of the off-site and review it with the affected people. (The odds are that they will be delighted that you tried, but appalled by how little you still know. But it *is* a start.) Plan to involve them directly in future rounds.

• The second level of analysis is less in depth, but just as important. For this one, call a group of twenty-five together (all the same level—e.g., hourly, then first-line supervisors; other variations are mixed levels, new hires with ninety or fewer days' experience, etc.). Have each one offer up "the most demeaning and annoying rule/regulation/form/procedure with which I must live." (This takes guts.) Then change something, on the spot, relative to at least 50 percent of the ideas; promise rapid action (within ten working days) on the rest. Repeat the exercise regularly; perhaps form regular councils to offer up ideas.

(At a third level, more casually, develop a planned habit of spending one hour every three weeks with one randomly chosen person—an MIS new hire, a new dispatcher; repeat, more informally, the "most demeaning rule" exercise—and act on it.)

The suggestions above are not in any sense a "best approach" to attacking the issue. They all do, however, contain two elements that are musts for any such effort: (1) you must dig into the detail, and (2) you and you alone must then *act* on what you find. (Interestingly, regardless of your level—second-level supervisor or vice president, you will find, we guarantee, much more than you think. Our experience is wholly consistent on this point: Once you allow yourself to really get into the process, you will discover vast avenues for improvement within your purview.)

---

# 15

# ApplauseApplause

TO TALK ABOUT people, we've focused on philosophies, on ownership, on teams and on the pernicious effects of petty rules. Now we turn to a subject that is most conspicuously absent from management textbooks: Fun, Zest, Enthusiasm. (All three words deserve to be capitalized.) All of us learn how to enjoy things before the age of six. And then we observe joy later on—among the members of the county's top Girl Scout cookie-selling troop and the city's top youth league soccer team, at the top Limited store, the top Wang sales branch and in the bakery crew at Stew Leonard's "Disneyland of Dairy Stores." But all too often our instinct for zest is driven out of us by our formal education, especially professional education. Life, and surely life in organizations, is not supposed to be fun.

We've often commented that we have a secret hypothesis (it's one that we don't wish to test, since there's a good chance that we're wrong). The hypothesis is that over the entrance to the Harvard Business School (or the business/professional school of your choice), there's a giant stone lintel. Deeply inscribed in the granite are the following lines: "All ye who enter here shall never smile again. American business/education/etc. is damned serious stuff!" And yet time and again, whether the evidence is the unit flags on the flight line at TAC or the smiles on the faces of the people at Nordstrom, we've observed that winners are people who have fun—and produce results as a result of their zest.

The Limited is as fast-growing (and profitable) a big company as exists anywhere. It prides itself on a remarkably lean corporate staff. Yet on the staff of The Limited Stores is a full-time manager of nonmonetary compensation and incentives. One of her products? A lovely magazine called Applause-Applause. It comes out every two weeks, and it praises, by name and with pictures, the actions of a minimum of about five hundred people. That's what we call celebration. The holder of the job, Lynn Buckmaster-Irwin, says, "I

The chapter title was blatantly lifted from The Limited biweekly magazine of the same title.

consider a new contest a week to be a minimum." There's always something going on at The Limited. Fun, zest, enthusiasm—and unparalleled results.

We've seen some extravaganzas in the way of celebrations. We've attended a Tupperware celebration, and a celebration of the IBM Golden Circle, which honors the top 3 percent of its sales force. We've seen film footage of Mary Kay's galas. Talk about shows! The Limited Stores has a doozer, too, in a class with the best. It has an annual celebration for its top 100 store managers (out of about 800). They are invited to the annual President's Club meeting; it always takes place in August, in Vail, Colorado. It's a gala. The highlight is the presentation of awards. The 100 managers to be honored are brought to the top of a mountain on a chair (ski) lift. There, at the mountaintop, the awards ceremony takes place, with video cameras recording every second of it. A memorable occasion, to put it mildly. And the film? It's instantly sent around the entire Limited Stores system.

Think big! We talked about the Scandinavian Air System (SAS) and its remarkable (1981–83) turnaround. What a prize Managing Director Jan Carlzon gave his people. At Christmas in 1982, all sixteen thousand SAS employees received a gold watch. Moreover, there was a lavish, three-country blowout (SAS is owned by Sweden, Norway and Denmark). There were several thousand people at each party. A ride home in a private limousine was provided to each person at the end of the night. That's a celebration!

Think big, even if you're small(er). Oxford Software is a $10 million company based in New Jersey. It had a lot of growth, a lot of profit, and passed a big hurdle—the $10 million mark—in 1983. In January 1984, Chairman Judd Shenker decided to celebrate. He took *all* 125 employees (that's right, including the clerks from the mail room and the receptionists) to Acapulco for four fun-filled (and work-filled) days. Memorable!

---

### The Spirit of the Thing

The spirit of the thing lives in the details.

—Mies van der Rohe

Raychem's record of innovation is virtually unmatched in American industry (as are its margins). Nonetheless, the senior team began to fret about some incipient calcification about three years ago. They decided to do something about it.

Each year, Raychem's top officers head for Pajaro Dunes, in Watsonville, California, an exclusive housing development at the north end of Monterey Bay, for a three-day retreat and strategic review. The year 1981 was no different. Same quarters as always. Same players (there had been almost no turnover among the top team in the twenty-five years of the company's existence).

For the opening afternoon meeting, Chairman Paul Cook began with a strategic overview. It stressed changes in the environment, the tough constraints on all sides. It wasn't doom and gloom, but it was hardly upbeat, either. Then Cook stopped, virtually in mid-sentence, and almost shouted (about his own presentation), "What a bunch of BS." He said it was time for a reassessment. Time to take a radical second look at the company. Time to scrape off the barnacles and begin anew.

The dozen or so participants were stunned, and even more so when the next sound was that of helicopters hovering over the house and then landing on the beach (no small feat, since clearance from about five agencies was required). The whole bunch was herded out of the house with virtually no explanation. They were asked to take with them the Sony Walkman that each had been given as a memento upon arrival.

At sunset the helicopters took off and headed across Monterey Bay and down the Pacific toward Big Sur. Each passenger was asked to turn on his Walkman and plug into the aircraft's sound system. The strains of Bach blended with the Pacific sunset, and with Paul Cook's voice. He explained that the next few days would be different. That the constraints were off. It was all to symbolize a new beginning, a new look. He set out a handful of concise, memorable (and challenging) goals for growth and innovation.

The helicopters landed, and a startling three days of intense exchanges and exotic fanfare began. The meetings had traditionally consisted of rather dry presentations by the managers to Cook and President Bob Halperin. This time, a dozen presentations had been written by Cook and Halperin themselves. They led each discussion. No sacred cows were left untouched.

The days were also broken up in a number of ways. One day, on a walk down to lunch, the team hiked past the Pfeiffer Big Sur parking lot. There stood two elephants! Each had a giant pennant affixed to it trumpeting one of the (concise and memorable) goals that Cook and Halperin were using as themes for the meeting (and, indeed, for the next ten years). Another evening was Sheik of Araby night. Raychem's top bunch (almost all engineers) dressed up in splendid Arabian costumes; one highlight of the evening was a camel race! Live camels, of course (four of them), and (of course) each bedecked in a blanket with one of the new goals inscribed on it. (And, again, their presence requiring fancy footwork through many a regulatory maze.)

There was a host of little touches as well. A daily "newspaper" was put together between the hours of midnight and 4:00 A.M., then delivered; it highlighted memorable business and nonbusiness events of the previous twenty-four hours. On the last day an impressive videotape of the three days was shown (all events had been filmed).

The result? A group that had grown a bit too complacent, a bit too familiar with each other, passed an emotional watershed. Three years later the event was still referred to in the course of everyday decision

> making, and many of the little events were regularly recalled to invoke
> the "spirit of the camels and elephants meeting."

We spend a good bit of time giving presentations at company meetings of
all sorts. We are above all impressed by the attention and intensity with
which IBM, SAS, The Limited, Mary Kay et al. approach theirs. Clearly they
consider them "strategic"—we think that's the right way to put it. Another
way: Muck up a Golden Circle—even as a vice president at IBM—and
you've had it. In a million tiny ways, IBM—and The Limited et al.—show
that the event is not a distraction from normal routine. This is an "it," a
serious (as well as fun-filled) main event of the year.

---

### A Very Golden Circle

IBM celebrates, lavishly, the success of the top 80 percent of its sales
force. All attend gala Hundred Percent Club multiday meetings. But
the show for the top 3 percent, the Golden Circle, is something else. It
tends to be at an exotic site—Bermuda or Majorca, for example.

Every detail is taken seriously. (As a "service provider"—i.e.,
speaker—Tom has never been through such a mill: you either agree to
a host of demanding requests, from the 35-mm slide format and
rehearsal schedule to arriving exactly on time days ahead of time, or
you can forget it.) The daily "shows," says an Emmy Award–winning
producer who attended a 1984 Golden Circle, are "Broadway caliber."
Speakers tend to be those who have recently performed exotic deeds.
The meeting Tom attended featured a fellow (who was on the cover of
the then current *National Geographic*) who had discovered an old
sunken ship in the Arctic Sea. The other featured speaker had recently
led the first expedition to go around the earth the "wrong way"—via
the two poles.

Small acts of celebration were impressive. About ten of the Golden
Circle participants had made twenty Hundred Percent Clubs in the
course of their career. Interspersed in the goings-on were film clips of
them and their families, about five minutes long each, showing their
home, hobbies—e.g., skydiving—and so on; the films were "production
quality," no expense spared.

It's difficult to describe all the special touches, from the handsome
name tags to the short films, put together in twelve hours, featuring the
prior afternoon's recreational activity. The show was simply first-class
and all the attendees (even the speakers!) felt as if they had been part
of a memorable event.

And there's one more thing: top IBM management was present
throughout, and presided over a massive and spectacular black-tie

awards banquet. How can we impress upon you the difference in approach between IBM or The Limited and so many of the corporate "celebrations" we attend? Alas, most give the celebration lip service, and then delegate it way down the line, showing up for a one-day-out-of-four cameo appearance.

(Incidentally, the lavishness of Golden Circles is not a luxury of IBM's current positive cash flow. Mr. Watson, Sr., was known in 1915 as a "collector of salesmen," and the lavishness preceded by decades IBM's ability to pay.)

There's no limit to celebration—large or small. We've come across all sorts:

• The facing page exhibits samples from the new *Quality News* from the Paul Revere Companies (insurance). Shown are some recent headlines and the scoring systems and awards program. Also note the lovely—and bizarre—team names. No, it's not against the Ten Commandments to have fun! (Even in insurance).

• Paul Revere again! Our friend Pat Townsend reports: "We have begun the PEET program. It stands for 'Program for Ensuring that Everybody's Thanked.' The system is this: Each Monday morning, each of the seven members of the executive committee, including the president, gets his PEET sheet. It lists three quality team leaders along with some highlights of what their team has been up to of late. It also notes who visited this particular team leader last, and when. The executive committee has made the commitment to find at least five minutes for each of their assignments some time during the week."

• In response to *In Search of Excellence*, a service group at Digital Equipment discussed enhancing the morale of the company's operation through hoopla. Said a senior and somewhat "traditional" manager several months later: "It was the best thing we've done in years. For one thing, the entire senior staff dressed up as reindeer to sing Christmas carols to the troops. Boy, did they get a kick out of it. It was the talk of the halls for weeks. I was amazed."

• The head of a 15-person accounting department in a little electronics firm came up to Tom after a speech: "Wow! Hoopla is it. I've gotten into the habit of finding, *at least once per week*, an event of *some* sort to celebrate. It can be somebody's birthday, but preferably—and we've gotten good at finding these—some positive accomplishment at work. The celebration doesn't need to be dinner at an expensive restaurant, it can be a box of doughnuts. But we celebrate. And it does work! The morale of the place has turned around in just three months." (Hawthorne effect? You bet. The issue? Keep it up. How long? No more than forty or fifty years.)

• A manager of several small facilities in the South decided to cut back the workweek from five days to four for several months. The objective was to

## Here's how the Quality Recognition Program works...

### Bronze Award

When a team meets the qualification criteria for the Bronze Award, each team member receives a Bronze cloisonne lapel pin which recognizes each team member's contributions to "Paul Revere Quality."

### Silver Award

When a Quality Team reaches the Silver A̲ each team memb̲ Silver-plated la̲ off his or he̲ Revere Q̲ each Q̲ rec̲ s̲

### Gold Award

When a Q̲ reaches t̲ each te̲ Gold̲ B̲

The Paul Revere Companies
Our policy is quality

## Names of new Bronze Team Members —

**FAFFANOOSE:** Virginia Quitadamo, Barbara Lyseth, Madeline Crocker, Martha Baker, Alfreda Owens, Elizabeth Young, Diane Buthen, Gloria Steele, Evelyn Mercon, Rita Desroches, Dorothy Gonyea, Carmella Monfreda, Dorothy Olen, Janet Mercon, Marrion Lamarche. **PAT'S POURRI:** Pat Townsend, Selma White, Ray Perkins, Sally Hanscom, Mary Gablaski, Rick Perez, Marybeth Lucey, Evie Frederickson, Karen Todd, Cheryl Alderman, Kathy Gaucher. **YTILAUQ:** Mark Reger, Jane Dornings, Timothy McNamara, Sandy Schiltz, Donna Euwart, Gerry Rochon, Robert Murphy, Ray Martinez, Beverly Labrie, David Moorefield, Diane ̲ Andonian, Nellie ̲ Paula Bechard, ̲e, Doreen Evans, ̲en Ricciutti, Julie ̲ith Malyonowski, ̲rg, Lynda Hadley, ̲ Linda Pilsdey̲

## Cooperation Breeds Quality

In order to improve the morale of the clerical staff and the sales force in the̲ Supervisor Donna To̲ grams. One provides̲ clerical staff who displ̲ who make an effort at̲ A recognition plaque̲

## Seven-Up Gold

Straight to Gold! Orv Miller and his Quality Team, the *Seven-Ups*, received their Bronze, Silver, and Gold pins all at once from Aubrey K. Reid.

How'd they do it? Orv credits the fact that the Quality Has Value process "allows non-management people to get involved." A decision was made to remove some phrasing from the Voluntary Accident Program for AVCO Corporation — phrasing that had been the cause of some expensive lawsuits in the past.

## More Teams Bronzed

Twenty-three additional Quality Teams had attain̲ Bronze status by March 28, and have been reco̲ by the company with individual ̲ member.

One of these, the *"Gophers"* dec̲ ty, by adopting the strategy of think̲ the time, and never doing anything̲ tions. Team leader Bette Ostenf̲ members of the *Gophers* "now feel̲ this company; that they count and th̲ feel more a part of the Paul Revere̲ to weekly meetings, the team also h̲ ment" Quality meetings, because̲ something will make a difference, it̲ to talk about.

Regina Prentiss and Bette Spe̲ sions," and their team goal is to ob̲ in the department. Everything they discuss and improve upon leads to this goal. Everyone is excited because "they themselves are doing the changing and implementing, so they feel more important and better about themselves."

**OCTOBER GOLD TEAMS: Audrey Arrington** and *Systems-Addicts*, **Tom Junell** and *Mr. T's Team*, **Janet Burns** and *The A Team*, **Gary MacConnell** and *ISD Mgmt*, **Ken McNulty** and *Ken's Kost Kontrollers*, **Marrion Lamarche** and the *All Stars*, **Jayne Bryce** and *Lucky 13*, **Bette Ostenfeld** and the *Gophers*, **Shirley Salah** and *Shirl's Girls*, **Marge White** and *The Mighty Eight*, **Loxle Woodcock** and *Supply-We Deliver*, **Barbara Harper** and *B's Guys and Dolls*, **Irene Liberty** and *Liberty Belles*, **Sally Freeburn** and the *Support Team*, **Isabella McKinlay** and *George's Candi-Kanes*, **Pat Dicesare** and *Renewal Crediting*, **Kay Roberts** and *Special K's*

Quality News

spend the fifth day figuring out how to make the facilities better places to work. Some of the things that came out of the discussions amazed us (and him). In one of his oldest facilities, there was an energetic boss who led the way by building a"potato shack." She took a small unused shed in the back of the plant, and turned it into an eating facility and recreation area. People got heavily involved. It made all the difference in the world to morale—and productivity.

• In a textile factory the factory manager came up with an ingenious solution to a problem. He wanted to buy new, fairly expensive chairs for each of his on-line people (for their workstations). He decided to delay the buy, and in a remarkable fashion: anybody who exceeded the target output per hour and then some (about a 25 percent premium) for a month would "win" a chair. The chair was awarded in a unique way: the plant boss brought the chair to his own office, then the line person came and sat down in the chair, and the boss rolled him or her back out to the workstation.

• Executive recruiters would like as not be near the top of anyone's list of "stodgy" types—they seem to get paid in part for being stodgy. Virtually the best of the bunch is Russell Reynolds Associates, where a special routine is practiced. One year Russ Reynolds went to Paris and bought old French taxicab horns (they're quite beautiful) and had one placed in each of his offices. Now, whenever a job is placed, the horn is blown. Ceremonially. Even executive recruiters can celebrate!

We've come to label these celebrations, both small and large, the "technology of enthusiasm," and we chose the word "technology" for a particular reason. When it comes to production or backroom operations, we're capable of analyzing problems thoughtfully. When it comes to marketing, we can quick as a wink generate analyses by the ton. But when we talk about rewarding, enthusiasm, celebrating, and the like, the eyes usually glaze over. What we're suggesting is that you can be just as thoughtful, just as meticulous and systematic in developing programs that substantially boost the enthusiasm in your organization, as you are when you test-market your new widget.

The Rolm Corporation (recently acquired by IBM) has been a remarkably profitable and fast-growing company, successfully challenging the giant AT&T in the PBX market. A Rolm officer put it this way: "The leader is not a devil's advocate. He is cheerleader." Cheerleader, indeed. Cheerleading is not merely legitimate; it's at the core of most successful organizations. It always has been. We've noticed it, in sports teams and the like, since we were kids. Now let's apply it, as the best have, to business and other organizations.

We've talked of Tom Monaghan, the Domino's Pizza (and Detroit Tigers) boss. Tom, we're proud to say, is a fan of *In Search of Excellence*. In fact, when Tom (Peters) first met him, he pulled out the little black notebook that is his business bible and said that he had the eight main points from the book written down in it. Then he apologized! "I hope you won't think I've committed a sacrilege," he said. "but I've changed it a little bit." How? He had added his own ninth point: "Have fun."

## Eight Common Questions about
## Celebrations—and
## Some Answers

1. *Can you have too many prizes, or banquets, and thereby cheapen the whole process?*
Yes and no. One award is too many if it isn't given with conviction and for generally perceived merit. But if these two attributes (conviction and merit) are in place, the sky is the limit. Paul Revere's quality program includes team awards (e.g., bronze, silver, gold) for various levels of accepted suggestions. Soon teams began to go beyond gold. So now it's double bronze, double silver, etc. An Apple manufacturing manager has a trinket bag in her desk. When something good is done, the doer gets a trinket. A Milliken manufacturing manager is a former football player. A common football award, for a lineman, is a gold star permanently affixed to the helmet (e.g., for an unassisted tackle). He uses the same device at Millken to great effect. He's comfortable with it, and believes in it. It shows. It works.

Do you have any talented sailor friends? Go into their home and you'll find, unfailingly in our experience, a big trophy case in the living room, or close to it. They may be bankers or brokers, but they can never get too many loving cups. And they never tire of showing them off.

2. *But isn't it hard to design meaningful awards for people other than, say, salespeople (based on sales dollars) or engineers (based on patents registered)?*
No. Or, rather, yes. It *is* harder, since we have so underexercised our imagination in this area. But it can be done. Anywhere. Each Milliken department has a scoreboard posted for all to see. In one instance it may note "X days since an order-entry error," in another, "Y days since a below-standard order was produced." One trick here: the people closest to the job know the job best, *and* its impact on others, so have them specify the standards for achieving the award. Our experience is that they will be tougher on themselves than a manager would be, *if* it is clear to them that the objective is not to subsequently use the standards against them (punish them for not achieving a certain standard), and if it is clear that management is sincere in its approach to the program.

3. *How do you get secretaries, loading-dock teams, etc. involved in "big" events where celebrations of company successes are in order?*
Invite them! It may come as a surprise, but there is no iron law that says (1) celebrations can't be held for support functions or (2) support people can't be feted at sales banquets. Milliken marketing meetings include the whole team—every support function. Bill Creech at TAC, remember, held regular banquets and awards nights for his supply and maintenance teams.

4. *But engineers (accountants, bankers) don't go for this stuff, do they?*
Try them! The parties at MIT are as festive as at any other school, and the

singing is just as loud. In professional societies, the desire for recognition is as great as at Mary Kay. We are all suckers for brass bands and pats on the back.

5. *But I don't feel right rushing around with balloons in my hand. What do I do?*

First, we suspect that over time you can come to feel right. We've seen it happen among the macho, "Not me" pilots at People Express and the engineers at Raychem and the manufacturers at Milliken. But if you don't feel right, don't do it. Do something that feels appropriate. A friend, an executive, is a bibliophile. When something special occurs, he gives out a carefully selected first edition of a fine book. Many recipients aren't bibliophiles, yet it is clear that he has personally invested time and trouble in selecting the gift. Even those who read no more than the *Reader's Digest* are unfailingly touched.

6. *But isn't there a role for punishment, the negative stuff, as well as rewards and celebrations?*

The answer is twofold. First: there is a role for punishment—minor to major—when continuous poor performance merits it. Second, however: the celebration serves a dual purpose, for it is a strong, indirect "punishment" to those who do not win accolades. The best "awarders"—IBM, Tupperware, Mary Kay, Milliken—provide awards to almost all who participate in their programs ("showing up" awards). But just as clearly, they provide special awards to the top 60 percent, 25 percent, 5 percent, 1 percent. Failing regularly to be in the "top 60 percent," especially in situations where one is surrounded by one's peers, is a powerful stimulus to better performance—without being labeled as a loser. As one senior manager puts it, "You quickly get tired of walking out of group celebrations with 'honorable mention.'" (We'd hasten to add, though, that the honorable mention *is* valuable. It's a lot better than "no show.")

7. *How do I convince my boss that we ought to spend possibly hundreds of thousands of dollars on a single bash for, say, our salesforce?*

Beats us! No short-term cost/benefit analysis will provide justification. You simply must believe in people and believe that people like to be around one another and share one another's successes. Sorry. We have never had a shred of luck with our clients on this. We think that if you could smuggle that reluctant dragon into an IBM or Limited celebration, you could make a believer out of him or her. Short of that, we're stymied, too.

8. *What should the average prize be? What's the role of money?*

For one thing, people will work eighteen hours a day for months for a T-shirt if the context is meaningful and the presenter is sincere. For another, big cash awards can be horribly disruptive, leading to "Hide the idea," "Screw the other guy" and "Don't help *them*" behavior. We observe that small gifts or sums of money and equal gifts (monetary or otherwise) to *all* members of a team are the most effective. Put simply, I will be delighted with your $250 award, provided that awards are plentiful and I can picture myself winning one too. I will be resentful of your $1,000 or $3,000 award, especially if such awards are granted infrequently. I'll figure I was just as deserving as those who received them, especially if I think I aided you in any tiny way (the tiniest of assists leads to a wholesale feeling of "He couldn't have done it without me").

## Integrity, Again!

Throughout this section of the book we have come back again and again, explicitly and implicitly, to integrity. It is nowhere more important than in this matter of applause and celebration. Tom Monaghan didn't learn about zest at the Harvard Business School. He learned it from life, and his endorsement of joy and celebration comes from within.

Now, there is a chance that our quieter friends could view this section with alarm. In part, that's the point! You can't fake this stuff. People have great built-in BS meters, they've been through the mill before. If you don't believe it, if you're behaving in an even slightly manipulative fashion, they'll see through you in a flash. On the other hand, we do think you can learn to appreciate the power (and beauty) of *genuine* celebration. At least you can let those who *are* comfortable begin now. Watch what happens. You may (we predict you will) be pleasantly surprised. We'd also reiterate that celebration and extroversion are not handmaidens. Jan Carlzon is a consummate showman. Tom Monoghan is actually quite shy. Yet both exude zest and excitement and involvement. And both really *care*. They celebrate because they genuinely appreciate what their people have accomplished. It's plain as day from the gleam in their eye and the genuineness of their greeting.

## Some (More) Good Reading on People

There is a vast number of books on "managerial psychology," but on the issue of ordinary people working in organizations we find few works in any field to be enlightening. There are a couple of remarkable exceptions. Our favorite, with nothing a close second, is Robert Townsend's *Further Up the Organization* (Knopf, 1984). It's succinct. It's plausible (Townsend turned Avis around years ago). And it's right on target (we think).

More encyclopedic is *The One Hundred Best Companies to Work For in America*, by Robert Levering, Milton Moskowitz and Michael Katz (Addison-Wesley, 1984). The book consists of one hundred vignettes of fine companies—from the grocery business to the computer business, with every stop in between; many are also profiled in our book.

Mary Kay Ash's *Mary Kay on People Management* (Warner, 1984) is a personal saga of people management from which anyone can learn. There's a tendency by some to write it off as "a bunch of new-to-the-work-force-women-conned-by-pink-Cadillacs." Wrong! The toughest truck dealers around could learn invaluable lessons from Mary Kay if they were willing to open their ears.

James Fallows's *National Defense* (Random House, 1981) is not a "people management book," but it fills the bill better than any we know on the "people" issues involved in debureaucratizing; we use several chapters in our seminars to show in graphic terms how sensible, reasonable human beings responding to the real world can get themselves into hopeless, irrational tangles.

Finally, we would recommend a subscription to *Inc.* Its profiles on business persons leading $50–500 million enterprises, virtually one a month, are a constant source of inspiration to us.

# FIVE

## Leadership

The leader must have infectious optimism. . . . The final test of a leader is the feeling you have when you leave his presence after a conference. Have you a feeling of uplift and confidence?
—Field Marshal Bernard Montgomery

Make it fun to work in your agency. When people aren't having any fun, they don't produce good advertising. Encourage exuberance. Get rid of sad dogs who spread doom. What kind of paragons are the men and women who run successful [advertising] agencies? My observation has been that they are enthusiasts.
—David Ogilvy, Ogilvy on Advertising

# 16

## Attention, Symbols, Drama, Vision—and Love

"ALL BUSINESS IS show business." Those words were uttered by Jan Carlzon, of the Scandinavian Air System (SAS). We agree. All business *is* show business. All leadership *is* show business. All management *is* show business. That doesn't mean tap dancing; it means shaping values, symbolizing attention— and it is the opposite of "administration" and, especially, "professional management."

As we said at the beginning of this book, for the last twenty-five years we have carried around with us the model of *manager* as cop, referee, devil's advocate, dispassionate analyst, professional, decision-maker, naysayer, pronouncer. The alternative we now propose is *leader* (not manager) as cheerleader, enthusiast, nurturer of champions, hero finder, wanderer, dramatist, coach, facilitator, builder. It's not a model of what might be, or a prescription for the impossible. We've learned it in real-time, from people who've done it in glamour industries and those who've won in extremely adverse situations—in low-growth or no-growth industries or the public sector. We've learned it from Bill Hewlett of Hewlett-Packard; from Steve Jobs of Apple; from Buck Rodgers and Don Estridge of IBM, from Jim Treybig of Tandem. Others we've learned so much from are Bill and Vieve Gore of W. L. Gore & Associates; Roger Milliken of Milliken & Co.; Ren McPherson of the Dana Corporation; Jan Carlzon of SAS; Frank Perdue of Perdue Farms; Sam Walton of the Wal-Mart Corporation; Willard Marriott (Sr. and Jr.) of the Marriott Corporation; Sam Johnson of the S. C. Johnson Company; Jim Rinehart, former General Motors hero at Packard Electric and now chief executive officer of Clark Equipment; Bob Stramy, a GMer who launched the new Livonia, Michigan, Cadillac engine plant; Phil Staley, plant manager of Ford's Edison, New Jersey, assembly operation. And Mayor William Donald Schaefer of Baltimore and General Bill Creech of the Air Force. From all these people we've learned nothing about magic. We've learned, instead, of passion, care, intensity, consistency, attention, drama, of the implicit and explicit use of symbols—in short, of leadership.

## Attention

We think our colleague Bob Waterman said it first: "Attention is all there is." Ren McPherson, who made the key to the turnaround he guided at Dana "turning the company back over to the people who do the work"—that is, the first-line people—adds: "When you assume the title of manager, you give up doing honest work for a living. You don't make it, you don't sell it, you don't service it. You don't stand on the loading docks in the cold, or sit in the PBX rooms answering the phones hour after hour." Putting the two statements together, we say that as long as the manager doesn't do "honest work" (and we agree), the only thing he's got left is using his calendar, his day-timer, to pay attention to what's important.

Ah! How do we make this tough? How do we make it complicated enough to seem plausible? Attention *is* all there is. We're coming out of a twenty-five-year period during which managers were said (by all the consultants and teachers) to be powerless, confounded by multiple stakeholders, multiple constituencies, swirling and uncontrollable "external forces" and trapped in the middle—whether the manager was chairman (trapped between the EPA, an angry board and the Japanese) or first-line supervisor (trapped between the union's grievance committee and middle management). We think this is nonsense. The manager is shockingly powerful. Remember when you were a nineteen-year-old on your first job? You darn well knew what your manager (who was probably all of twenty-two) ate, and when his eating habits changed. You were a manager watcher par excellence. We all were. Managers are powerful. People pay attention to the obsessions (or—and here's the rub—lack of them) of managers.

Attention is all there is. Milliken & Company has long been way ahead of the pack, even the Japanese, in the manufacturing technology of textiles. The source of their prowess? Here's an example. Once every three or four years there's a show of textile machinery from all over the world. In 1984 it was in Milan, Italy. The average sizable company sent four or five people for three or four days. Roger Milliken sent a hundred and fifty of his people for the full ten days! He accompanied them. At the end of each long day of wandering the floors, they had a three- or four-hour meeting that usually lasted way past midnight to swap ideas. Roger Milliken wouldn't misspend a single penny knowingly. He's hardly extravagant. Yet he *is* extravagant when it comes to his strategic obsession—keeping Milliken's plants at or ahead of the state of the art.

Sam Walton has accumulated a personal fortune well in excess of $2 billion (said *Forbes* in 1984) while boosting the Wal-Mart Corporation from $40 million to over $6 billion in a decade (with equity returns staying near 40 percent). He thinks retailing is all about stores (an almost novel idea in the systems-and-merchandising-dominated 1980s). Years ago, Mr. Walton began making a point of visiting every one of his stores at least once a year; that was when he had only eighteen. The number by early 1985 was close to seven hundred fifty; and he was still visiting each one at least once a year! And hitchiking with Wal-Mart Trucks across the country, greeting each store manager and spouse by name at annual meetings, wandering down to share doughnuts at 2:00 A.M. with his people in the distribution centers. Do the store people know he's interested? You bet!

Bill Hewlett constantly wandered the engineering spaces at Hewlett-Packard, as did Barney Oliver, his head of R&D for forty years. Today, though neither is any longer an active duty, a twenty-four-year-old student at the Stanford Business School (a cooperative engineering student from Hewlett-Packard) can still say, "Believe me, each and every one of us [the eighty thousand people on the payroll] thinks that Bill or Barney is likely to stop by our desk any minute and ask about the prototype we're working on." Absurd! But repeated time and again, in other places. The McDonald's franchisees expected Ray Kroc within the hour even when they knew he was in the hospital.

Terry Deal and Allan Kennedy, in *Corporate Cultures*, recount this story about the present chairman of the General Electric Corporation:

> When Jack Welch was an up-and-coming group executive, he had a special telephone installed in his office with a private number which was made available to all the purchasing agents in his group. If an agent ever got a price concession from a vendor, he could phone Welch and the call would come in on his telephone. Whether he was making a million-dollar deal or chatting with his secretary, Welch would interrupt what he was doing, take the call, and say, "That's wonderful news; you just knocked a nickel per ton off the price of steel." Then, straightwaway, he'd sit down and scribble out a congratulatory note to the agent—a profoundly messy and ambiguous motivational procedure. But Welch not only made himself a hero by the symbolic act, he also transformed each and every purchasing agent into a hero, too. [Later, Deal and Kennedy go on to analyze what went on.] Welch could have attacked the problem of high costs in a number of ways. He could have appointed a task force to study the problem and come up with solutions. Or he could have hired consultants to do the same. Or he could have reassigned his best managers to head up the purchasing function. What he chose to do was install a telephone in his office. Suppose no one called? Suppose people called but the impact on purchasing costs was negligible? It took courage to pursue such an unconventional, culture-reinforcing approach to the problem—the courage to trust others in the culture to do the right thing!

Extraordinarily successful Seattle Seahawk coach Chuck Knox would doubtless identify with the Welch story. A large part of the (positive) reversal of Seahawk performance between 1982 and 1984 was moving from the bottom of the heap to the top in "turnover ratio." (That is, they used to lose many more fumbles than they took from opponents, and have many more passes intercepted than they intercepted.) In a late 1984 TV interview, Knox gave what was, in his view, a prime reason for the shift: "I began starting every practice with a five-minute drill on some aspect of turnovers. I just wanted them [the team] to focus, each and every day, in some way or other, on the importance of the turnover deal." Just five minutes. But constant— and up front—repetition. I.e., attention.

Tom spent an exciting day with Kelly Johnson, founder of the original Skunk Works at Lockheed. Beyond the imposing outcomes that Johnson achieved lies an even more impressive story, one that includes chapters like this. In our rather extensive experience with big development projects we've found that the major development issue is invariably manufacturing scale-up. That's a semitechnical way of saying that the engineers (designers) seldom if ever talk to the manufacturers (builders), and vice versa. So Tom asked, in the course of a wide-ranging discussion, "Mr. Johnson, how did you beat the manufacturing scale-up issue? How did you solve the problem of getting the manufacturers to talk to the engineers?" His response? "What problem?"

"Well, sir," Tom began, "in every *other* company we know it's a major problem."

"It's not a big thing," he said. "At about six-thirty A.M. most every morning I'd get the manufacturing supervisors together and let them moan about what the engineers had done to them during the last twenty-four hours. Then at seven A.M. I'd get all the engineering gang together and let them jaw about what the manufacturers had done to them. At seven-thirty, for about a half an hour, no more, we'd get 'em all together, decide what the problems were, and what we'd do about them now." He concluded: "If you do that sort of thing, five or six days a week, fifty or so weeks a year, for forty years, all those problems you talk about go away." Indeed!

Or, consider this. A major tire company follows standard industry procedures: cosmetically defective tires (not ones that would cause safety problems) are put on sale at a radical discount. There's even a name for them—"blemmies" (from blemish, of course). The company is running a 6 percent "blemmie" rate. A new person becomes honcho. He finds this unacceptable: "Let's discontinue the discount sales," he says. But nothing much happens; after all, it's a time-honored tradition, dating back decades. The people don't really believe him. Then he heads out to a plant and spends two full days there, in shirt sleeves, slicing up blemmies with a carving knife. Mysteriously, in a multithousand-person operation, the blemmie rate plummets the historically immutable 6 percent level to 1 percent in a matter of weeks, and it never goes back up.

## Who Gets Promoted:
### An (Unsung) Attention Getter

Calling promotion an "unsung" tool may surprise some. It surprises us, to tell the truth. But it expresses an honest observation. Perhaps the

best and clearest signal of what's important, what is being paid attention to, especially in times of change, is who gets promoted, when and
for what. Yet as Tom's former colleague at McKinsey, the renowned
Arch Patton, once stated, "Promotion is *the* most underutilized managerial tool."

If an organization is not tiny (having, say, thirty or more people on
the payroll), promotions occur regularly—at least three or four a year,
in even the very small outfit. The issue? Will you use promotion con-
*sistently*, to tell a consistent story about values and priorities (or shifting
priorities if apropos)?

So often in times of change we (all too understandably) waste a promotion to reward a loyal soldier who performed honorably under the
old scheme or value set. Now, we are all in favor of rewarding loyal
soldiers. But do it with a raise or a medal signifying a fine and loyal past,
not with a relatively scarce promotion that singularly signals your colleague's fit with the (new) value set and course for the future.

There are two additional points worthy of note in this connection.
First, we urge senior bosses to get heavily involved in making and cer-
tifying promotions, even three or four or more levels down. It was said
that GM's legendary Alfred Sloan would often miss policy meetings but
never a personnel meeting. And with a 250,000-person outfit at the
time, he would regularly spend three or four hours on the appointment
of a chief engineer in a small facility. He viewed such time (attention)
as his most significant contribution to the enterprise—i.e., it was his
primary means of signaling certain concerns. (How different from most
of today's organizations, where promotions even two levels down are
rubber-stamped by a boss who simply notes that "the process"—often
ungainly and mechanical—has been followed.)

Second, promotion is a wonderful tool for the *non*chairman, a marvelous way (the best we know) to sow the seeds of revolution from other
than the very top. The best way to instill your agenda is via numerous
unsung promotions to the first and second levels. You can quietly, in
only a few years, create a substantial new look. General Bill Creech, for
instance, is open about having nurtured a large group of fellow "enemies of consolidation and centralization" and having seeded them in as
many vital command slots as possible throughout the Air Force.

Promotion *is* attention. We suggest you not allow even one of these
inevitably offered up (yet still scarce) opportunities to go to waste.

It's "just" a matter of paying attention. You might not know what your
priorities really are; you might not even remember what breakfast cereal you
eat. But your people know. The problem is that your people *do* pay attention

to you! We were once called in to work with a company that was having a terrible problem: the chairman was determined to enhance entrepreneurship, but the message was not getting through. As consultants we spent a lot of the chairman's money reanalyzing his strategy, checking his structure and job descriptions, and dissecting each one of his business subsystems (capital budgeting and the like). They all looked great, aimed at the right target. Out of sheer desperation, we looked at the only other thing we could think of left to look at—his calendar, the way he spent his time. We looked at the meetings he attended, and did a detailed content analysis of the agenda over a period of several months. We looked at the visits he made and the people he talked to and the order in which he talked to them while at a site. He was even kind enough (or brave enough) to allow us to run a phone log on him for several months. The net? He was "Mr. Entrepreneurship"—in the speeches he made on the Fourth of July—but he spent barely 3 percent of his total time on his presumed objective. His attention wasn't there. And his people knew it.

Another project, with a major construction company, revealed a similar problem—one that was amenable to an obvious solution. The company, which was run by engineers (who liked to talk about engineering problems), had gotten badly overextended in new overseas areas. Yet a detailed, minute-by-minute (for months) analysis of the agendas of top management's weekly meetings suggested that about 80 percent of their time was spent *not* talking about overseas implementation issues, but about the nuts and bolts of the engineering problems, with which they felt more familiar (and which they apparently had more skill dealing with). Over a twelve-month period meeting agendas were shifted until 70 percent of management's attention was focused on implementation. And things changed radically.

How does change come about? First, and not so obvious, it's a matter of the *quantity* of attention paid to the matter at hand rather than the quality, odd as that statement may sound. When the senior folks (at the store level, the department level, the division level or the corporate level) start to focus on a newish "it" (entrepreneurship, overseas implementation), then the rest of the organization starts to pay attention to "it." And what gets attended to gets done. Thus, if you want to focus on quality, focus on quality, *period*. If you haven't focused on quality a lot before, you won't know exactly what to talk about at first. Conversations will drag, will be abstract. It doesn't matter a whit. Everybody will eventually get the drift—that you're focused on quality (and *not* some other, former priority—an equally important message). It doesn't have to be a *good* conversation about quality, just a conversation about quality. In some fashion, pay significant attention to the blemmies, and *somehow* the blemmie rate goes down. Not because of a specific program you invented, but because of the energy that comes to be focused on "it."

There it is again: "the mere Hawthorne effect." Productivity goes up "merely" because attention is being paid to people and not because some mechanical (real) improvement (like brighter lights) has been installed. And they're right! Hawthorne it is. But "mere"? No!

## Attention as Symbolic Behavior

Attention *is* symbolic behavior. One difficulty we find in dealing with this subject stems from baggage that comes along with the word "symbolic" for the hard-nosed, rational manager. Somehow, given the macho jargon of Western management theorizing, describing an executive's behavior as "symbolic" suggests something other than the "tough-minded stuff of decisive strategic decision-making." But symbolic it is. As a result of our "symbolic" attention—symbolic of our concern and our priority—others become engaged. (And let us pointedly remember, symbols—paying attention—are all the manager, who doesn't drive a forklift, has.) So it is with Marriott's reading of the complaint cards, Milliken's concern with the factory, Perdue's obsession with the hairs on a chicken wing and quality in general. The annual day-timers of these leaders (observed in retrospect) are simply (not "merely") the *only* valid measures of the concerns they have, concerns that will eventually lead to down-the-line promotion or demotion, favor or disfavor.

Mars, Inc., executives make a fetish of physically attaching every administrative facility to a factory, furnishing the facilities in Spartan fashion, prominently displaying next to the desk the white coats to be worn without fail in going into the factory. Truth be known, those few dozen white coats don't really have a whole lot to do with either the spotlessness of the factory or the Mars quality record. And yet they have everything to do with it. They make it crystal clear what the primary concerns of top management are.

Experts agree that the only thing that distinguishes mankind from the rest of the planet's creatures is our use of language and reasoning power—i.e., the manipulation of symbols. Leadership (management) *is* symbolic behavior, whether your're talking about Martin Luther King's trek to Selma, Alabama, or Jack Welch's special phone for purchasing agents. And that's all it is—not because symbols constitute a "good" variable to manage, but because they're the *only* variable we have at our command, whether we recognize it as such or not.

Now, this is at once a very good news story and a very bad news story. Good news, because it doesn't involve capital spending—every second is an honest-to-gosh "symbolic opportunity." Bad news because of *exactly* the same fact: *Every* minute *is* a symbolic opportunity. It's an opportunity that you consciously or, more likely, unconsciously choose to grasp or squander. What's the old man (or supervisor) interested in? Who's he talking to? What are the changes since yesterday? Why's he talking to Dick about that, rather than Jim? What do the marginal notes on the memos look like? Who's he chewing out now? Why? How come Harriet got a pat on the back for her presentation and Dave didn't get one for his? How come he chose white paint instead of blue? It was quality last week, now he's off on costs—and it's only three days later. We knew it wouldn't last. Remember—again—that the manager can't really *do* anything much of value. He can only suggest (symbolize) what's important by the way he behaves. And the myriad *subcon-*

*scious* actions, those that end up as marginal notes penned on memos, are *more*—much more—important cumulatively than so-called strategic decisions. So you're in favor of quality. So you make a couple of "strategic" decisions to reinforce that, spending a bit of capital on robots. So what? The quality message will get across only if it ends up as marginal notes penned on memos day after day, year after year.

---

### Attention: Turnarounds

Substantial turnarounds are few and far between. Not surprisingly, each involves a strong leader, a leader who is obsessive about paying attention to his theme. SAS's Jan Carlzon finds no opportunity too small to hammer on the service theme. You can't get him to talk about airplanes. He talks about passengers. He focuses on the language: SAS is no longer an "asset-oriented business" but a "service-oriented business," no longer an "airplane-oriented business" but a "customer-oriented business," no longer a "technically oriented and financially oriented business" but a "market-oriented business." The stories he tells are stories about mundane service improvements. That's it: minute by minute, day after day.

Ren McPherson, architect of the remarkable Dana turnaround, we've described, is the same way. People—that's his theme. He gives but one speech on management, regardless of setting. It focuses on the enhancement of productivity in manufacturing through people on the line, period. There is no way you could miss it.

Andy Pearson, as chief operating officer at Pepsico, was, along with Chairman Don Kendall, the guiding light behind the extraordinary PepsiCo turnaround. SAS turned toward service, Dana turned toward increasing manufacturing productivity through turned-on people, PepsiCo turned toward enhancing entrepreneurship. And Pearson was another broken record. No matter what the PepsiCo audience, he was always jawing about action, about test markets: "What are you up to?" "What's been going on in your test market in the last ninety-six hours?" At a dinner (a social occasion nominally), the subject, sure as can be, became not baseball or philosophy or $150 million capital expenditures but what was going on in the test markets for Pizza Hut, La Petite Boulnagerie, Frito-Lay.

Most senior corporate officers are broad-minded, with eclectic interests and lots of different things to talk about. Not Frank Perdue, who talks solely about chicken and its quality. Not Debbi Fields, who talks about her cookies. Not Ray Kroc, who talked about Quality, Service, Cleanliness, and Value. Herman Lay (Frito-Lay founder) was a broken record on the subject of the perfect potato; Bill and Vieve Gore are the same about their "Associates," and so is Roger Milliken on textile tech-

nology. The turnaround artists—Carlzon, McPherson, Pearson et al.—
are the same: one-track minds, obsessive.

---

It all adds up to this: *Every* system, *every* seating arrangement, *every* visit
is symbolic behavior. Questioning routines; What's the first question the boss
invariably asks? Market-oriented people ask about marketing. Financially oriented people ask about finance. (DuPont people ask about safety!) Want to
change your strategic emphasis? Determined shifts in time-honored questioning habits can be a big part of it. Seating arrangements. Who gets invited to
what kinds of meeting? In "staff-oriented" organizations, a disproportionate
share of staff gets invited to meetings. Want to take the emphasis off staff?
Quit inviting staff people to meetings! Visits: Who gets visited, in what
order? What functions first? Junior or senior people first? How much time is
spent with what level people in which functions? The word gets around—at
approximately the speed of light (some argue faster).

Got a problem? Symbolize your concern by paying obsessive attention to
it. In a straightforward, no shortcuts fashion. Put time on it, and on all appropriate players, year in and year out, decade in and decade out. The remarkable cleanliness of Disney's parks is merely a matter of a lot of people trying
to do cleanliness better. The secret is, they don't sell gum in the parks! Disney
is a thousand people dreaming up a thousand thousand "no gum" ideas.

---

### Attention:
### Some Questions and Things to Do Now

*Analysis*

1.   Review your calendar, if you keep one in detail, for the last year, the last
90 days in more detail, the last 30 days in great detail. What does it tell you
about your (1) substantive priorities, (2) MBWA proclivities—visits, in the
office or out?

2.   Repeat no. 1 for your chron file: What do your replies to your correspondence tell the world? (Don't be defensive. Do it privately.) They may tell the
world that you're busy with 46 conflicting priorities. *All* are legitimate. But
maybe you can do better in the future. Cut it to 43? or 10? How about two?

3.   Repeat no. 1 for your visits (MBWA). Whom do you visit at a site? In
what order? Is there a regular pattern? What does that tell you about your
priorities?

4.   Repeat no. 1 for your phone log.

5.   If no. 1 through no. 4 fail for lack of data, plan to accumulate this data for
the next 30 to 90 days, starting today.

6.   Get a colleague to note carefully remarks/queries at a series of meetings

over the next 7 to 14 days. What do you ask/talk about? About service? About factories? About financials? (Don't assume, when analyzing the data, that the "financial focus" was "just because it was budget time." We are *all* broken records. We create, subconsciously in the main, opportunities to ask about our pet topics. Believe it!)

*Next Steps*

Treat no. 1 through no. 6 as studies in *variable* behavior. You *can* redo your calendar, your visitation pattern, your phone focus, your meeting routines. It will be damned hard work! (Stopping smoking or shedding twenty pounds permanently is child's play by comparison.) It necessarily—or best—begins by having the analysis of the past in front of you. Redo the calendar, to the tune of *only* 10 percent (2 days) next month. Rework *one* visit routine. Make a note of *one* variation in meeting routine. Enlist, if you can, a trusted colleague to work through this with you. To do so is not a sign of weakness. This is not kid stuff. This is the "it" of strategic skill development.

---

And that leads us to our next subject: symbol *management*, and the leader (manager) as dramatist. Each one of these symbol-using activities (which is what they are) is a minidrama. It has nothing to do with Theory X or Theory Y, extroverted personalities or introverted personalities. It has to do with the economical (symbolic, dramatic) use of time—the economical use of each and every phone call, the order of each and every item on the agenda of every minor meeting.

## Attention Plus:
## Symbols and Drama

Symbols and drama. We've mentioned Renn Zaphiropoulos's feelings about private parking spaces. When, in early 1984, he assumed a more senior position within the Xerox group, he walked into his new office and asked his secretary-to-be where the nearest hardware store was. She told, him, of course. He proceeded to make a couple of phone calls. Then he took off, with an executive assistant in tow, for the hardware store. Upon arriving, he took two crisp twenty-dollar bills out of his wallet, bought two one-gallon cans of black paint and a paint brush. He returned to the office. And then, in front of his office building, the chief executive stripped off his coat, rolled up his sleeves, opened a paint can, and while the cameras rolled (the two phone calls had summoned the video people) he began to paint out the labels on the executive parking spots. Symbolism? You bet. "Strategy" in action? You'd better believe it!

Symbols. Drama. Our colleague Jim Kouzes recounts the following. Corning Glass had focused its energies on decorative glass for most of its history.

Now it was faced with a declining market. Arthur Houghton was the newley appointed chief executive officer. He wanted to move Corning toward higher technology. His approach? He went down to the warehouse containing some of the most beautiful glass Gorning had ever produced (it was lying fallow in inventory). He had a sledgehammer with him. He proceeded to smash several million dollars' worth of glass into smithereens. He wanted to make it clear that he was up to something new. He did!

General Bill Creech, architect of the turnaround at TAC, has a superb sense of symbols and the dramatic. On an inspection visit soon after he took over he came across a supply office in disrepair, the epitome of the second-class status to which supply people had been relegated (and the issue toward which he was directing so much energy). The supply sergeant, a fifteen-year veteran, occupied a government-gray chair with a torn back (mended with electrical tape) and only three casters—the fourth leg was propped up on a block of wood. Creech ordered his aide to have the chair boxed and sent to TAC's Langley, Virginia, headquarters. Soon thereafter the general held a major ceremony. The three-star general—Creech has four stars—who headed logistics was "awarded" the chair, and told that it was now *his* chair, until the supply operation was cleaned up.

An executive came up to us after a meeting with a McDonald's competitor. He had worked at McDonald's for quite a while some years back, and remembered a time when founder Ray Kroc had gotten irritated because his crew chiefs (shift managers) weren't, in his opinion, spending enough time out at the counter with the customers: "He sent an order around. It was a while back, you know, when the tables and chairs were wooden. The order was to be executed immediately (and it was): 'Saw the back off each manager's chair.' Ray figured that might keep them a little less comfortable while desk sitting." Apocryphal or not, it's a tale that reveals the importance of keeping in touch at McDonald's. And it's still told—pointedly—today.

A Nordstrom brother was out on one of his regular store inspection tours. He visited a shoe department. Wandering into the back room, he noted that there were lots of gaps along the shelves (indicating stockouts, and Nordstrom's, above all, prides itself on customer-satisfying "overstock," by others' standards). He asked the clerk why the gaps were there. "Don't worry," the young man replied, "I've got them on order." He produced the order forms as proof. Nordstrom picked up the order forms, rolled each one up carefully, walked over to the back-room shelves, and placed the appropriate forms in the empty spaces. "Why don't you wrap these forms around the customers' feet if they ask for the out-of-stock items?" he said, and walked out. That night after work the young man raced to the nearest warehouse to pick up replenishment stock. The (symbolic) story lives today!

Entrepreneurship can also be spurred by symbols. GE was singled out as the paragon of strategic thinking for fifteen years (the entire history of the high-visibility strategy movement, in fact). We noted earlier that when Jack Welch became chairman in 1981, one of the first things he did was dismantle much of the strategic planning staff. Welch hadn't given up on strategic thinking. Rather, he sent it back to where it belongs—to the strategic business units and divisions. In addition to breaking up the central staff, he accomplished a major (symbolic) change in the location of strategy review, which used to be full-dress affairs held in corporate headquarters in Fairfield, Connecticut. The staffs were invariably the heroes of the hour (overwhelmingly outnumbering the line), and sharpshooting among staffs was rampant. Welch simply moved the strategic reviews to the field. Immediately the "heroes" were making their case on *their* turf. Small point? No, a big one.

Drama. Real-life drama. Set your mind in that direction.

Domino's Pizza lives by and owes its phenomenal success to its 30-minute (maximum) "We deliver anywhere" pledge. Domino's Pizza Distribution, therefore and logically enough, must *never* allow a franchise to run out of dough. "Shutting a store down" is the number one sin. It nearly happened a while back, and Distribution President Don Vlcek got a call telling him about the probable disaster. His ready response (in a low-margin business): "Charter a plane. Get it there!" Charter they did, get it there they did.* In another instance, Vleck's lieutenant, irrepressible young Jeff Smith, did have a store shut down for lack of dough. He went out and bought a thousand black arm bands and his whole team wore them in mourning for quite a time afterwards. The message, at Domino's, is clear—and memorable.

And again (with planes, no less). Stew Leonard's, as we noted, is Frank Perdue's biggest single-store customer. Stew wanted to change his chicken-packaging technology a while back, and Frank's people were the only ones expert in the new techniques. So Frank, without a second though, sent two Lear jets up to Connecticut to fetch fifteen of Stew's chicken packers down to Salisbury, Maryland, for schooling at Perdue Farms' headquarters.

What is such behavior? "Real"—to a point. "Symbolic"? Dramatic? All of those. The stories of Vlcek and the charter, Smith and the armbands, and Perdue and the Lears will be remembered ten years from now, likely thirty years from now, and every time they're told the message will be reinforced: Domino's Distribution *means* franchise service; Perdue Farms *means* quality and customer service. It's at the very heart of the culture/value/strategic strength transmission process.

We believe that in a slightly less dramatic form, "charter opportunities" quite literally occur five hundred to five thousand times a week. Remember, every opportunity to meet with thirty people (or one person) is an opportu-

*From time to time we get rebuttals to this: "But you can't afford to deliver the average load of dough by plane!" Of course not. And, indeed, Vlcek had to make up the charter fee by cutting back somewhere else to meet his profit targets. The point is that the story transmits graphic evidence about exactly what comes first, what the "tie-breaker" is, about just how far you *must* go to live the *chief* strategic value of the institution. (And if you have to go that far, then you're saddled with the issue of how to find the money; but at the time of decision, the story teaches "Think customer first, budget second.")

nity to let them know exactly what's on your mind. Every casual conversation is interpreted endlessly. Every tiny change on your calendar is an indicator of the importance (or lack of it) you assign to a given activity. And such power is available way down the line, not only to Fortune 500 CEO's or the entrepreneur-owners of $20 million companies. When you are nineteen, the "boss," that twenty-two-year-old, is God.

If you choke on that idea, more power to you—as a decent human being. We're glad you don't regularly think of yourself as a deity. But still, listen (and recall your own experience). Whether you are twenty-two and a first-line supervisor or the CEO, your every action is watched, and watched closely and charted by "your" people. Inconsistencies are noted. Small deviations are the subject of intense Kremlinology. Patterns are assessed and updated daily, if not more frequently. Stories are remembered for years. It might not make you comfortable, but you know darned well it's true.

Drama also has a number of other connotations. SAS's Jan Carlzon, remember, stated that "all business is show business." Stew Leonard has turned shopping into an event. Carl Sewell has done the same with car buying. A. Ray Smith, in the midst of decline all around him, has made the Louisville Redbirds into a minor league team outdrawing many of the majors; the edge, as we noted, is clean rest rooms and a show every night. Little Scandinavian Design has founded "Scandinavian Design University" to teach "stage direction." Tupperware, The Limited, Mary Kay Cosmetics, and IBM unabashedly stage dramatic events to motivate their people. Even "conservative" Milliken & Co. stages regular Fabulous Bragging Sessions (see pages 304–307).

We are emotional creatures. We feel pride, we feel slights. Our life *is* a drama to each of us. The winners are institutions and leaders that own up to that reality and live with us as humans—not as automatons.

## Language

Attention and symbols and drama are about signaling, of course—about the creation of a "language of attention." Language is fundamental. Sometimes it is specific words. Disney, McDonald's, Gore, Wal-Mart, Dana and People Express eschew "worker" or "employee" in favor of "cast member," "crew member," "associate" and "person." At People everyone is a "manager." Disney calls every customer "guest."

The conscious use of certain words is a vital form of paying attention. And we all get the opportunity to choose our vocabulary. We all call our people or our customers *something.* But do we all use the opportunity to use labels to shape new and positive and strategically important ways of seeing things? (It's especially crucial here to keep in mind the matter of integrity. To shift from "employee" to "associate" means nothing unless you treat each person as a respected peer rather than a hired hand. On the other hand, if you do believe your clerks are associates/peers/self-managers, then using the word is yet another—and significant—mark of respect.)

## Stories

In talking of Domino's Pizza and Perdue Farms, we have introduced the role of stories. There's a lot of psychological literature that we could bring to bear on our discussion of this; *In Search of Excellence* covered some of it. It turns out that human beings reason largely by means of stories, not by mounds of data. Stories are memorable, stories about real people doing real things. Remember Ray Kroc's visit to a McDonald's franchise in Winnipeg? He finds a single fly. Even one fly doesn't fit with QSC&V (Quality Service, Cleanliness and Value). Two weeks later the Winnipeg franchisee loses his franchise. You'd better believe that after this story made the rounds a whole lot of McDonald's people found nearly mystical ways to eliminate flies—every fly—from their shops. Is the story apocryphal? It doesn't really matter. Mr. Kroc *did* do things *like* that.

Just as Forrest Mars has done things *like* throwing candy bars at his officers after finding a single miswrapped one on a candy counter. A former Mars manager recounts the tale—to him as fresh as if it had happened yesterday— of Mr. Mars visiting a chocolate factory in mid-summer. He went up to the third floor, where the biggest chocolate machines were placed. It was hotter than the hinges of hell. He asked the factory manager, "How come you don't have air conditioning up here?" The factory manager replied that it wasn't in his budget, and he darn well had to make budget. While Mr. Mars allowed as how that was a fact (the fellow had to make budget), he nonetheless went over to a nearby phone and dialed the maintenance people downstairs and asked them to come up immediately. He said, "While we [he and the factory manager] stand here, would you please go downstairs and get all [the factory manager's] furniture and other things from his office and bring them up here? Sit them down next to the big chocolate machine up here, if you don't mind." Said our Mars colleague: "The guy figured out that it was probably a pretty good idea to air-condition the factory, sooner rather than later. Mr. Mars told him that once that had been completed, he could move back to his office anytime he wanted." The stories are memorable. They teach. And they're a darn sight more efficient than policy manuals!

A Procter & Gamble manufacturing manager remembers a call in the middle of the night. It came from a district sales manager, soon after this fellow (now a fifteen-year vet) had become a manager: "George, you've got a problem with a bar of soap down here." Down here, George explains (in 1983), was three hundred miles away. "George, think you could get down here by six-thirty this morning?" Our informant adds, "It sounded like something more than an invitation." And, finally, he concludes, "After you've finished your first three-hundred-mile ride through the back hills of Tennessee at seventy miles an hour to look at one damned thirty-four-cent bar of soap, you understand that the Procter & Gamble Company is very, very, serious about product quality. You don't subsequently need a detailed two-hundred-page manual to prove it to you." We suspect this story is true or close to it. The point is, our friend believes it. He repeats it. It lives. (And if P&G were not living the quality message, day in and day out, such stories would either not exist or not be regularly transmitted.)*

---

### The Impact of Stories
### A Study

A colleague, Alan Wilkins, studied the impact of stories told in two companies with very different track records in the same industry. The first company was a strong performer and sustained its growth; the second had suffered severe setbacks for the past five years. Could the stories told in each have affected performance? Wilkins says yes. In the high-performing company, managers placed clear emphasis on their management philosophy (the "high story" company); 98 percent of the stories told were favorable to the company's interests. In the "low story" company, only about 50 percent of the stories were favorable. The basic business philosophy in the high story company was overwhelmingly clearer to all employees—managers, technicians, secretaries—than in the low story company. Wilkins discovered that the managers in the low story company confused their people on priorities, while their counterparts in the high story company "had close to a passion for [consistently] communicating a philosophy."

Wilkins concluded that some kinds of stories were powerful ways to motivate, teach and spread enthusiasm, loyalty and commitment; others served an equally powerful purpose: to perpetuate cynicism, distrust and disbelief. Themes that hindered performance included "sinking ship" stories (this company is inept, failing, unable to cope in a changing environment, what's the use?); "trickster" stories (this world is sinister and the only way to survive is to live by your wits; you're on your own, buster); "unjust company" stories (the system is unfair, managers can't be trusted); and "rule" stories (recounted as a way to establish or justify rigid rules rather than to share a perspective). Unlike the helpful variety, these stories tend to encourage sabotage (how to hurt the company), destructive competition among groups or individuals (deliber-

---

*Even as this chapter was being written, a P&G manager at a seminar told us that he became a believer when he saw an hourly P&G employee at a Jiff peanut butter plant bring a shopping bag full of jars of Jiff to work. The fellow had noticed while shipping that the labels on the Jiff in the store had been mounted off kilter and he had been *unable* to leave them there, so he had bought them all, assuming P&G would pay him back. Indeed they did. "You'd have had to see it to believe it," our friend said. How many others do you suppose he's told that story to?

ately encouraging noncooperation, asking only "What's in it for me?"),
and high turnover ("I give up; I'd be better off someplace else").

So if you come across close at hand such stories as those described
above listen carefully; don't dismiss them as ridiculous and untrue. The
stories may not be factual, but that's wholly beside the point. What is
valuable about them is that they reveal underlying beliefs or doubts
people feel but are unwilling to confess to you directly. So take the time
to lean in and listen close. Care about the stories you hear and treat
them as the crucial company heartbeats they are. In fact, the drift of
stories over time is arguably the single best measure of corporate
vitality.

Following the first layoffs in decades, the tone of stories of all sorts
throughout one company turned sour. Suddenly every policy was interpreted through a new lens; management was seen as uttering double-
talk. Such a problem is not a "morale problem." It's a strategic problem
of the first order. Quality decline soon matches "morale" decline. Stories are so powerful that a decade's work can be undone in six weeks.
And, sadly, it may take years (and/or a change in management) to undo
the damage.

The storytelling, per se, is vital. In the innovation section we noted the
way a Honeywell officer explains how he enourages skunkworks: "I never tell
my people to cheat. I just go down and chat with them. I merely describe to
them what I did when I was a young man their age."

Once you realize the importance of stories, you can begin to think of yourself, in part, as a story-trail creator. Domino's Pizza Distribution, again: Don
Vlcek recalls the speed and impact with which a certain story traveled
through his system. He was visiting a distribution center. He noticed some
unacceptably lumpy dough. As he tells it, "The quality wasn't right. We
couldn't let it go out. I stopped, I rolled up my sleeves and I worked with the
local team to fix the procedure. In twenty-four hours, the news had traveled
twenty-five hundred miles! I got a call from one of my centers on the other
side of the continent: 'Don, we heard about what you did. That's great. That's
the kind of commitment to quality we need. We're behind you out here.
We'll redouble our efforts.' You had to have been there to believe it." No,
Don, we do believe it. Your tale has too many parallels to be coincidence.

Stories as pictures. How do we say this, get this right? We follow, remember, by example. King's march to Selma, Gandhi's march to the Ganges,
Mao's "long march": none had much strategic—"hard"—significance. And
yet each played a significant part in changing the face of a nation—the United
States, India, China. USC's Warren Bennis describes Jim Rouse, city builder
and rebuilder, at work, talking about teaching: "I wanted them to understand
my vision. They'd come to me with plans. I'd correct the plans. They'd come
back. It would be worse. This went on three or four times. Finally, when they
came to see me again, I had plane tickets. Go visit [X] and [Y], look at it. It's

what I mean! It worked." Bennis adds a corroborative note about Robert Redford (in the role of director) as he began shooting *Ordinary People*. He called his crew, gave them an audiotape of Pachelbel's "Kanon," and said, "Ride around until you see a place that *feels* and *looks* like this *sounds*. That's where we'll begin." And a successful banker says, "A relationship with a customer is more than return on assets. I can feel a relationship when it's right. My job is to transmit that picture to my people: 'This [X, Y, Z] is what a good relationship looks like.'"

---

### Stories and Changing Focus

Stories—or their absence—are most important at times of change. HP, DuPont, Raychem are attempting to shift focus somewhat from research/technical excellence to market/customer service excellence. Traits enhancing the former are currently enshrined in stories of all sorts. Traits desirable for achieving the latter are not—almost by definition. That is, HP has few or no Hall of Fame members who drive through sleet, snow and mud to deliver a seventeen-cent part. (IBM has a host of them, on the other hand.) HP's Hall of Famers, instead, beat down the barriers of physical science to develop a splendid new product in record time. Developing—partly spontaneously and partly through guidance—a revised or enhanced Hall of Fame (especially one that includes the factory floor and the MIS center) is arguably *the* most vital step in any major change. Quite simply, the new or modified thrust is not credible until there is a tapestry of legends to support it.

---

"Soft is hard" is what it's all about. We act as if the hard (tough) stuff were the formal rule book. That is *exactly* wrong. The hard stuff is the Mars story about air conditioning. The values of any organization live most humanly through stories, pictures. If we are serious about ideals, values, motivation, commitment, we will pay attention to the role of stories, myths, pictures of our vision. Bill Moore of Recognition Equipment calls it "seeing the glory." (Business people, do us a favor right now. Picture what it would be like to be served well on a flight. Translate that picture into your own company. You're on your way!)

---

### Symbols, Drama, Language Stories:
### Some Questions—and Things to do Now

*Analysis*

1. Do you use symbols naturally? Dissect the last two or four visits you've made, the last two or four meetings in your office, the last two or three committee meetings you have attended. Have you consciously and in detail managed the settings: who gets invited, seating arrangements, order of agenda

items, content of agenda items, location of meeting? If not, why not? Each is an opportunity to symbolize (or not) strategic concerns.

2.   Do you have a conscious and well-thought-out process for managing your involvement in the rewarding process? Do you select factories to visit, sales branches to visit, workstations to visit so as to signal your approval for specifics on their performances? If you do (nice going!), do you go the next step and personally involve yourself in the selection and format for the awards/ rewarding process?

3.   Check the number of hourly people with whom you've come in close (more than ten-second "How are you") contact with. What's the number/ occasion? Does it adequately reflect your concern with issues of quality, service, cost reduction? Do you consciously balance the number of hourlys versus the number of supervisors?

4.   Have you a spontaneous or planned vehicle for learning about real-life "mini-dramas" of customer service or innovation excellence (not the $7 million contract but the $7,000 one)? Do you collect and use those stories of real-life, down-the-line winners in your discussions with senior executives? With lower-level people?

5.   Have you ever done a "language audit" (casually is good enough)? How are employees described? (Customers? Customer problems? Persistent champions?) Does your (and your colleagues') language show passionate pride in the institution, its products, its people, its customers? If not, why not?

6.   Are you aware of the "top three" stories making the rounds of your organization today? How do they depict you and your colleagues? What do they disclose about your perceived interests?

7.   Take one recent visit. Dissect it, minute by minute, starting in the planning phase. If you were a man from Mars (or an hourly in the Podunk plant), how would you interpret the whole affair? What values and concerns would it reveal/reinforce—e.g., as a function of whom you visited, in what order, and exactly what you talked about with whom?

*Next Steps*

Again, each of the items above is about "cheap" (except in terms of time) variables. You can manage any of them. The objective is to get your minute yet closely observed actions in line with your (doubtless) noble objectives. Select any of the seven and begin to work on modest 5 percent changes in the pattern this week.

---

*Attention, Symbols, etc: When It All Fits*
*Du Pont and Safety*

Du Pont's safety record is seventeen times better than the chemical industry average, and sixty-eight times better than manufacturing as a whole. The fixation on safety at Du Pont goes back to the early days of the company, over one-hundred-eighty years ago, when it began as an explosives maker. This fetish spills over to produce and sustain excellence in manufacturing—and quality. That, along with Du Pont's almost equally strong devotion to research and development, is the foundation of the company's almost singular record of success.

Du Pont's fetish provides a marvelous opportunity to see all the levers—stories, language, attention—pointed in one direction. Safety is pervasive at Du Pont, defying all formal categorization. In fact, when we were talking about this notion with a senior DuPonter, he said, "It's important that you not spend too much time looking at the formal attributes, the procedures, the structures. The pervasiveness goes so far beyond that." Well, what are the symbols? Where do you see them? In the annual report, which unfailingly includes, early in the document, a major section on safety, with extensive statistics (this we've never seen before in any other annual report). Virtually every meeting, regardless of the subject matter, begins with a report on safety. Any accident, no matter how minor, must be reported instantly; the report is automatically on the chairman's desk within twenty-four hours after the accident occurs. In addition, the chairman receives an accident report from the entire $35 billion system every day.

But even all this fails by a long shot to convey the depth of commitment. At the time of our discussion in the summer of 1984 there had been a recent and relatively minor accident somewhere in the system. Our informants tell us that Chairman Ed Jefferson (remember, he's running a $35 billion business) came back to it on three separate occasions in the course of two consecutive executive meetings, irritated that it should have happened and determined to find out why.

Du Ponters are as obsessive about *off*-the-job accidents as they are about on-the-job accidents. Naturally, this obsession results in the posting of the customary "Drive safely" signs, but—much more significantly—it also affects the annual evaluations of every unit manager, no matter how senior. In 1984 a directive went out through the system refocusing on off-the-job safety. The cause wasn't anything so grand as a rash of fatal traffic accidents; it was a rash of minor athletic accidents—e.g., a few twisted knees in summer softball games—that led to time off the job.

It goes further. Much further. Senior managers readily acknowledge that, indirectly but surely and swiftly, incentive compensation and evaluation are *radically* affected by any accident that might occur—so much so that one twenty-five-year hand comments: "If I had to choose between losing a major account and taking a minor on-the-job lost-time accident, it would be easy. I'd prefer the loss of the account."

Du Pont initiates a high visibility program to improve manufacturing quality, quality in the marketing organization, quality in various departments. It is meant to be pervasive. One thing is left out: safety. Why?

Safety is far too important to be part of a "mere" program. Safety is beyond such seasonal vagaries.

In the halls of the Hotel Du Pont, across the road from the company's headquarters, Tom heard two Du Pont people chatting. They were talking about a meeting on safety they had just attended. Now, we've spent many days in many halls in many hotels across from many corporate offices, and that was the first time either of us had ever heard the word "safety."

A walk past the marketing communications department (marketing!) yields more confirmation. What's exhibited outside? Evidence of product or customer successess? No. There's a glass display case containing all sorts of safety gear that can be bought—for the employee's home. Flares, signs, to put up behind your car if you have an accident, first-aid kits and the like. You simply can't travel more than twenty feet in any direction at Du Pont without running into the safety message.

The result has been enviable: the safety record itself and a massive spillover into the entire area of product quality and manufacturing technique. The real point of this brief discussion, however, is what holds it all in place. The focus on customers at IBM is a function of many formal procedures; at Du Pont the same is true of safety. But more significant by far is the explicit and regular *attention* paid to the "it" of the company in ways that one just doesn't see in other organizations. "It" pervades the language and stories of people at all levels: the for-certain notion that one would rather lose an account than confront even a minor accident. Is this stuff—symbols, attention, language, stories—powerful? Take a trip to Wilmington and listen to the Du Pont story. You'll never ask the question again.

## Preaching the Vision

Attention, symbols, drama. The nuts and bolts of leadership. More is called for than technique. You have to know where you're going, to be able to state it clearly and concisely—and you have to care about it passionately. That all adds up to vision, the concise statement/picture of where the company and its people are heading, and why they should be proud of it. The elements of a successful vision, we believe, lurk in our sections on Customers, Innovation and People, tailored of course to your organization's specific circumstances. The issue here, in our discussion of leadership, is not, then, the substance of the vision, but the importance of having one, per se, and the importance of communicating it consistently and with fervor. Bill Moore took on the presidency of Recognition Equipment when it was near death's door. In just a couple of years he turned it around. In an interview published in the "Speakout Series" (1983) of the *Electronic Engineering Times* he speaks eloquently on leadership:

- The leader's got to have vision of where he plans to take the company.

- [He] has to be able to *dramatize* that vision for his organization.

- If there is one role the CEO should play, it is that of "chief salesman."

- Too often a chief executive hesitates to get up and perform the role of cheerleader or stem-winder.

- Simple and direct communication should be the watchword. When you get caught up in the planning fetish, you make the business much too complicated for the average person to understand.

- As most of us know, it's rare that one can ask the question "What are you trying to do in this company?" and get the same answer from the guy on the production end as you get from the guy in marketing. But if you keep it simple and direct, you have a chance to achieve that consistent understanding.

- I think we'd all be better off if we spent more time articulating our corporate plans and less time on perfecting them.

Vision, then, comes first. General Walter Ulmer, unconventional and highly effective U.S Army combat commander: "The essence of a general's job is to assist in developing a clear sense of purpose . . . to keep the junk from getting in the way of important things." Bourns CEO, Bert Snider: "The CEO's prime task is teaching his people what the company is all about and then getting them to teach their people. . . . It seems that a lot of CEO's don't appear to have a clear vision of what their company is about. All the ruckus about strategic planning can be reduced to a very simple idea: knowing exactly what you want to do with your company. Then you convey that." Successful Casa Bonita (restaurants) founder Bill Waugh: "My main job as president is to share the values and business philosophy. . . . The value system has to be taught through more than just manuals and reciting the values. It has to be taught through example."

Even if you're small, vision—and the teaching of it—comes first. Hamburger U. Dana U. Disney U. When we think of the top corporate training schools, we think of the unabashed culture shaping of IBM, Disney, McDonald's, Dana, Marriott et al. Yet Apple opened Apple University at an early date. They wanted to teach the Apple values—and Apple's special brand of enthusiasm—on their own turf, in their own way. We mentioned that Scandinavian Design, a modest (in size) but immodestly successful retailer of furniture, launched Scandinavian Design University early in its history. Its objective is to unabashedly teach the company's culture and generate enthusiasm: "Stage direction, lighting, theatrics, excitement. It's the way we do things."

Most will agree that Ronald Reagan has done an astonishing job on this dimension. A *New York Times* (October 14, 1984) report suggests that the magic is exactly vision, belief and dramatization: "He [an effective president] must embody a dream and values. . . . He [Reagan] is a true believer. He repeats [his simple dream] again and again because he believes every word of it. . . . [He has a] gift for narrative and storytelling. . . ." (The *Times* said all this with some implicit criticism, but read Bill Moore, et al. again: vision and communication of that vision through attention, symbols, drama, are the key, *not* perfection of plan.)

The Reagan phenomenon raises a point often overlooked: the empowering vision will inevitably be one that stresses the positive (e.g., "America's back"). Invariably, the effective visions—from People Express's Precepts to Apple's Values to Johnson & Johnson's Credo (see p. 332)—stress contribution to customers and community, growth of every employee in the company, constant seeking of the new (innovation), striving for top quality. The most effective visions tap the inherent pride that resides in virtually the entire population.

On the other side of the coin, the successful visions are also realistic, within grasp. The most effective leaders from all walks of life—the classroom, the battlefield, the corporation—have set down challenging *but achievable* visions. In the worst of times, one can always strive for doable minor improvements. Bernard Montgomery and George Patton inherited dispirited armies in North Africa. Both began their campaign by focusing on internal discipline—housekeeping, uniform maintenance, physical fitness. The avowed objective was to teach their soldiers that they were winners, could accomplish things. Nothing is more demoralizing and ultimately useless than an unachievable vision.

## Concocting a Vision

Visions cannot be "concocted"! Many ask us, "How do I go about writing up my values?" The implicit question is, "What formula did General Johnson use to develop the J&J Credo?" There is none, of course. It must come from the market and the soul simultaneously. It must be felt passionately before it's published. People Express has had remarkable success, in the face of extraordinary growth, in transmitting their "Precepts." However, it is clear that the now written precepts are a passionate (and market-wise) expression of the implicit values that were within Don Burr when he founded the company. The precepts are sharper; but the unarticulated vision was there much earlier.

A vision must always, we observe, start with a single individual. We are wary, to say the least, of "committee visions." That does not mean (and again the People Express experience is confirming) that a major team effort of rewriting and buy-in should not ensue. It usually should. But the raw material of the effective vision is invariably the result of one man's or woman's soul-searching. Time for soul-searching can indeed be put aside—and should be. But above all, this process is not amenable to straightforward analysis and group process techniques.

Finally, visions are not just for presidents! From a Ford plant in Edison, New Jersey, to a Crown Zellerbach paper plant in St. Francisville, Louisiana, and Domino's Pizza Distribution Company we find clear and effective visions at lower levels of organizations—down to single clinics and classrooms and five-person accounting departments. If the vision is at odds with the central view of things, executing it will be tougher, no doubt of it. However, we continually find pockets of excellence in the worst of companies—and pockets of superlative performance in the best; most are marked by a leader (at any level) with a vision that is clear and compelling.

## You Can't Have It All

"Attention is all there is." I.e., if you want to create a constantly innovative environment, you must pay close to full-time attention to innovation.

Now, here's the rub: full-time attention to innovation means, by definition, less than full-time attention to customers (the other of our two bases for lasting distinctive performance). The implication is clear: you can't have it all!

This issue first arose when many interpreted the *In Search of Excellence* message as meaning that the forty-three exemplary companies scored "perfect 10's" on all 8 "basics" presented in the book. This, of course, is not so. IBM is awesome on customer service, and a bit bureaucratic at the innovation game; HP is the reverse. P&G scores top marks on the quality angle of customer closeness, but has also slowed a step on innovation; in roughly the same industry, PepsiCo has the reverse imbalance.

To survive in business (or in running a school, a city) you must score at least C+ at all aspects of business: financial controls, customer service, innovativeness, etc. We do, however, find that A+ behavior on all the key dimensions is a virtual impossibility. Moreover, to even seek A+ behavior on all major dimensions causes confusion as to just what the real number one priority is. Seeking to "get better" on all dimensions is fine (e.g., IBM's third of three precepts—excellence in execution), but seeking unmatched multidimensional greatness is not fine.

In fact, we bridle at corporate philosophy statements that say "Be the best at *everything*"—lowest cost producer, most innovative producer, highest value added producer, all-segment coverage, etc. Philosophies, we observe, are worse than useless if they constitute an undoable charter; they become pipe dreams or worse, a form of hypocrisy. (Again, let us be clear. A "program of the year" for 1985–86 to "focus on innovation" is fine, even if you're an IBM. It means "Let's improve." But the program must not conflict, at the deepest level, with the three basic IBM precepts, which clearly call slavish customer service the king, the ultimate tie-breaker. We saw a classic example of a company that understands itself in this regard. As noted, when Du Pont launched a major "quality" program, *safety* was not included. Why? Safety, the Du Pont sine qua non, is *too important* to be part of a "mere" program.

The issue best comes to life, as always, via mundane example. Raychem and HP (see pp. 173–174) gladly shut down a manufacturing line to fiddle with a prototype. Terrific, we say. It's near the heart of their skill as remarkably rapid innovators. But guess what? Such behavior translates into less reverence (than at a P&G or IBM) for meeting shipment schedules. Likewise, the IBM slavish devotion to making things smooth for customers gets in the way of HP-like innovation.

This issue is a devilish one. You can take bits of our advice in each chapter, apply them now and, we are certain, things will get better. But relative to the hoped-for towering distinction and dimension of clear uniqueness, think twice before taking on all the challenges/opportunities we present.

Finally, note that this discussion has not involved people. People are the "exception" (but not really, as we will see in a moment) to the rule. Either of the strategic distinctions (customers, innovation) rests upon a bedrock of belief in the dignity and worth and creative potential of each and every person in the organization. Thus IBM's "customers first" philosophy rests upon their precept number one—respect for the individual. Likewise, HP's "innovation first" philosophy rests foursquare upon the "HP Way" of treating people.

## . . . and Love

In an article in the August 1984 issue of *Texas Monthly,* reporter Joe Nocera wrote: "Several years ago Trammell Crow was invited to speak at the Harvard Business School. After his speech, the floor was opened for questions. 'What is the secret of your success?' asked one of the students. 'Love,' said Trammell Crow."

You have to have a vision, and you have to care—passionately. During a February 1984 seminar a young man, an undergraduate at Utah State University, asked Tom what he thought the most important criterion for career success might be. He clearly wanted a systematic answer. Tom turned and went to the board and wrote, in foot-and-a-half-high letters, one word: "Passion." That is, you gotta love what you do, you gotta care. Mr. Marriott, Sr., could not have read those complaint cards for fifty-six consecutive years if he had not loved the hotel business. Ray Kroc was serious: "You've gotta be able to see the beauty in a hamburger bun"; all his stories are hamburger stories—love stories about hamburgers, really. Debbi Fields, founder of the wildly successful Mrs. Fields Cookies, says, "I am not a businesswoman, I'm a cookie person."

Love translates into joy. Donald Trump (of Trump Tower in New York City and New Jersey Generals fame) has Broadway's Flo Ziegfeld and builder Bill Zeckendorf as role models because they created "glamour and pageantry" and "brought joy to what they do." Observe a meeting of a thousand Tupperware distributors, men and women. They are unabashed enthusiasts. They have fun doing what they're doing. They enjoy each other's company and success. Bill Moore says of the turnaround at Recognition Equipment: "I can't overemphasize the role of enthusiasm in making this process work."

---

### Love in the Cooking

In an interview in the October 1983 issue of *Northwest Orient* magazine, André Soltner, of Lutèce in New York, one of the world's premier restaurants, puts it this way: "I am more than thirty years a chef. I know what I am doing and each day I do my absolute best. I cook for you from my heart, with love. It must be the same with service. The waiter must serve with love. Otherwise, the food is nothing. Do you see? Many times, I will leave my kitchen and go to the tables to take the orders myself. It starts right then and there. That feeling the customer must have is relaxation. If not, then his evening is ruined. Mine, too, by the way. How can he love, if he's not relaxed? People ask me all the time what secrets I have. I tell them there is nothing mysterious about Lutèce. I put love in my cooking and love in the serving. That is all."

---

Even garbage! Len Steffanelli runs San Francisco's Sunset Scavengers, the widely acclaimed model of an excellent garbage company in a giant industry. Steffanelli loves his garbage as much as Steve Jobs loves his [Apple] computers. Visit Steffanelli's office. Look at the mementos (e.g., a collection of ceramic pigs and garbage cans). Listen to him. He cares. (The flip side, of course, was aptly expressed to us by a service company executive. "If you [the executive] don't even love your product," he said, "why would you expect your people to?" Why, indeed?)

Successful North American Tool & Die's chairman, Tom Melohn, talks with Nancy. She asks him what he looks for in a prospective employee. Melohn scribbles something on a table napkin, hides it momentarily, and asks Elli Parrnelli, the office manager who makes the hiring decisions along with Melohn, what she looks for. She answers without hesitation: "Someone who's a caring person." Nancy adds that as Melohn looks at Parrnelli and nods his agreement, his eyes are filled with tears.*

---

*Ah, sadness and cynicism! Nancy used this vignette in an article for a New York–based magazine. It was cut from the final copy with the editor's cryptic note: "Too emotional."

Vince Lombardi, the Green Bay Packers legendary coach, didn't shy away from caring either. He spoke to an American Management Association group shortly before his death: "Mental toughness is humility, simplicity, Spartanism. And one other, love. I don't necessarily have to like my associates, but as a man I must love them. Love is loyalty. Love is teamwork. Love respects the dignity of the individual. Heartpower is the strength of your corporation."

## Empathy

We have found no more eloquent source on what it means to care than this from a speech given a number of years ago to the Armed Forces Staff College by a former commander of the U.S. Army's blood-and-guts 101st Airborne, the late Lieutenant General Melvin Zais:

> I will stop providing you with pearls of wisdom and I will elaborate on one. The one piece of advice which I believe will contribute more to making you a better leader and commander, will provide you with greater happiness and self-esteem and at the same time advance your career more than any other advice which I can provide you. And it doesn't call for a special personality, and it doesn't call for any certain chemistry. Any one of you can do it. And that advice is that you must care. . . .
>
> How do you know if you care? Well, for one thing, if you care, you *listen* to your junior officers and your soldiers. Now, when I say listen, I don't mean that stilted baloney that so many officers engage in and stand up to an enlisted man and say, 'How old are you, son? Where are you from? How long you been here? Thank you very much. Next man.' That's baloney. That's form. That's pose. I can remember when I asked my son, when he was a cadet at West Point, how he liked his regimental commander, and he paused awhile and with that clean-cut incisiveness that most midshipmen and cadets evaluate people, he said to me, "He plays the role." Wow! That was damning! "He plays the role." And I noticed this officer in later life, and he postured a great deal, and he always stood with his knees bent back, and he always turned one toe out, and he always wore special little things around his collar. And, you know, he always turned sideways, and I knew what he meant when he said, "He plays the role." Well, I'm not talking about that kind of stuff. I'm talking about listening, . . . listening . . . 'cause the little soldier won't come out and tell you that everything's all wrong. He'll be a little hesitant. If you ask him if he's getting along all right and he just shrugs, he's getting along lousy. If he's not enthusiastic in his response, there's something wrong. You better dig a little deeper.
>
> To care, you must listen. You care if you listen to him [your soldier]. *Really* listen to him! You care if you *really* wonder what he's doing on his off-duty activities. When you're about to tee-off on Saturday after-

noon, when you're at the club at happy hour, if you're wondering, if there's a little creeping 'nagging in the back of your head, "I wonder, I wonder what the soldiers are doing." Do you do that? What are the airmen doing? What are the sailors doing? Where do they go?

You care if you go in the mess hall, and I don't mean go in with white gloves and rub dishes and pots and pans and find dust. You care if you go in the mess hall and you notice that the scrambled eggs are in a puddle of water and twenty pounds of toast has been done in advance and it's all lying there hard and cold, and the bacon is lying there dripping in the grease and the cooks got all their work done way ahead of time, and the cold pots of coffee are sitting on the tables getting even colder. If that really bothers you, if it really gripes you, if you want to tear up those cooks, you care.

It's little things. When I was in Vietnam, a quartermaster captain was bragging to me about the ice cream that they made at Camp Evans and were taking out to the soldiers at the fire bases. And I said, "That's great." And he said, "Sir, would you like to see where we make it?" And I said, "Yeah, I'd like to, very much." And I went there and they had these machines and it was pouring out into these gallon containers. And he was very proud. He said, "We get it out there every day." And I said, "That's great." I said, "What do you carry it out there in?" He said, "Oh, these containers." I said, "Yeah, but how do the soldiers eat it? You know, they're all in little dugouts. They're not all lined up in the mess hall. They don't have mess kits out there and things like that." He said, "I don't know, sir." I said, "I know how they eat it. They pass that damn thing around and they stick their fingers in it and each one grabs some. Get some Dixie cups and send them." He said, "Dixie cups?" I said, "Yeah, Dixie cups." . . .

And I can't make you do this. But you really, you really need to like soldiers. You need to be amused at their humor, you need to be tolerant of their bawdiness, and you have to understand that they're as lousy as you let them be, and as good as you make them be. You just have to really like them and feel good about being with them.

Finally, the general quotes from a newsletter he had written while commanding the 101st Airborne:

You cannot expect a soldier to be a proud soldier if you humiliate him. You cannot expect him to be brave if you abuse and cow him. You cannot expect him to be strong if you break him. You cannot ask for respect and obedience and willingness to assault hot landing zones, hump backbreaking ridges, destroy dug-in emplacements if your soldier has not been treated with respect and dignity which fosters unit esprit and personal pride. The line between firmness and harshness, between strong leadership and bullying, between discipline and chicken, is a fine line. It is difficult to define, but those of us who are professionals, who have also accepted a career as a leader of men, *must* find that line. It is because judgement and concern for people and human relations are involved in leadership that only men can lead, and not computers. I enjoin you to be ever alert to the pitfalls of too much authority. Beware that you do not fall into the category of the little man, with a little job, with a big head. In essence, be considerate, treat your subordiniates right, and they will literally die for you.

## Personality: Roadblock to Success?

Is there a certain kind of person who alone can exhibit the leadership traits we have described and praised? The wonderful answer is no. Or, nearly so. That is, the leaders we've learned from are neither unfailingly extroverted nor unfailingly introverted. They are visionaries, but then, as Jan Carlzon (SAS) says, the visions are often quite garden-variety: "We had a vision: to be the 'businessman's preferred airline for Europe.' But everyone else has had that vision. The difference was, we executed."

Ah, there's the key. These leaders seem to pay *equal* attention to soaring ideals ("a gift to the spirit"—Max DePree; "the perfect potato"—Herman Lay) *and* the details of execution (Rodgers of IBM: "Above all, we want a reputation for doing the little things well").

Tom once wrote a short column for the *Wall Street Journal* entitled "Ideas, Plans and Actions." It suggested that the best leaders were comfortable moving back and forth between (or working simultaneously with) the highest abstractions (visions, ideas) and the most mundane details (minute-to-minute actions). Even their language illustrated the point. Ren McPherson, Marcus Sieff and Jan Carlzon talk of vision, but invariably illustrate their visions with stories of a specific first-rank person at the retail counter, on the line or in the Podunk factory.

Many (Walton of Wal-Mart, Carlzon of SAS, Watson of IBM, Mary Kay Ash of Mary Kay Comestics) did/do see "all business as show business." Yet a Stanford student chided Tom severely for using that phrase. "It cheapens the whole process," he said. "Look," Tom replied, "it's not *my* fault. I'm using Watson's and Carlzon's *exact words*." That leads, indirectly, to our last point. All of life *is* show business. Our life, to each of us, is a spell-binding drama, and we play, day in and day out, the lead role. Time and again, we are put upon, are not fully appreciated or loved, are misunderstood. Thus, we would argue that the specialness of Perdue, Gore, Staley, DePree, McPherson, Melohn and Walton is that each allows (encourages) humanness, the very essence of it, to pervade his organization. Each creates "places to go," "places to be." Commitment, passion, zest, energy, care, love, and enthusiasm can be readily expressed. And unashamedly so. And that *is* their distinction.

If you're not quite there, getting there takes some nerve. It *does* mean letting go of paper control, the comfort of ten staff reports before acting, before siting a rest room. But we urge that every manager give it a shot. Start with a two-week stint on the graveyard shift at a customer facility. Start with a graveyard shift in your own operations department. Goethe said that in order to understand the world it's necessary to select an *Eckchen*, a small corner of it, for contemplation. We sorely need, in managing our enterprises, to get beyond our almost total dependence on committees, staff, reports, and rules. We need desperately to select an *Eckchen*, to begin to get back in touch. We need to begin (again?) to depend, instead, on people—the power of commitment, ownership, verve, zest, enthusiasm, celebration, and love.

Take a look at your calendar—now. Are you *living* your proclaimed priorities—when it comes to people, to quality, to innovation, to service? Have you painted out a parking spot today? Have you held a celebration? Have you eliminated at least one unnecessary rule or form? Have you responded to a customer's complaint or query? Have you shared doughnuts on the loading dock at 2:00 A.M.? If no to all the above, you're out of touch. You're not living values connected to sustainable strategic excellence, no two ways about it. And there's *nothing* to stop you, darn it. No Capital Appropriations Committee is in your way. Only you stand in your way, you and the vestiges of the management theories that we and others have foisted on you in the past, "proving" to you that you should—instead of buying doughnuts at 2:00 A.M. for the distribution center team (as Sam Walton does)—hunker down, call in the staff and review yet another 600 clever overhead transparencies. We're sorry. We were wrong. Terribly wrong. But you should have known better! Now is the hour.

# 17

## Transformations and Enhancements: Small Wins, Debureaucratizing and Pockets of Excellence

Attention. Symbols. Drama. Language. Stories. Vision and love. These are the stuff of effective leadership, much more so than formal processes or structures. But another thread needs to be pulled into this tapestry. In discussing strategic distinction, we argued that it is, above all, built upon a base of one thousand things done just a bit better. Subsequently we suggested that such a strategy leaves no choice: the thousand little things will come only from "ownership" at all levels of the organization, from the executive suite to the newest hire on the loading dock.

Missing in all this is any practical suggestion on how to move methodically toward a systemwide overhaul. We gave advice on shifting calendar content, on listening to customers, on supporting good tries that end in failure. But just how do you get the whole thing started? Our answer is the *small win* (and a system for generating a *string of small wins*) and debureaucratizing (that is, consciously policing, nipping in the bud, or rolling back the excessive regulations—and regulators—who get in the way of ownership). Thus these two tools constitute opposite approaches in a sense: building winners and ownership and adding momentum, on the one hand (small wins); and keeping people from becoming losers or disenfranchised on the other (debureaucratizing). We find both are essential elements of either enhancement of already good performance or transformation of an unsatisfactory situation.

### Small Wins: The Efficient Path to Success

In some respects this represents a new tack. In most respects it doesn't. Our focus when it comes to initiating change and leading it is unfailingly on the mundane, the trivial, taking advantage of the typical nine-minute act that Professors Henry Minzberg and John Kotter find so characteristic of the general manager in *The Nature of Managerial Work* and *The General Managers*, respectively. That we tout "Small is beautiful" should come as no surprise.

Let's be concrete. We want to offer an example, one that we now use as the primary vehicle for teaching implementation in our executive seminars (the ones known as Skunk Camps). It's the story of Sam Neaman and McCrory's told in Isadore Barmash's *For the Good of the Company.** Neaman was brought into the ailing McCrory's chain in the sixties by Chairman Meshulam Riklis. His background included experience as a garment manufacturer in Europe and owner of a steel plant in Mexico. Here he describes his start:

> I had no [formal] authority, but here was my opportunity. It was a store that had lost money. I wanted to know what it took to make a good store, so I said to John [the store manager], "Look, we are going to form in this store a group of people, a team, and you'll be the quarterback. You and they will visit all the competition in town and write up what you find. You'll check out merchandise and write it up. Every evening you'll hold classes with a blackboard and will have a consultation with everyone. I want to know the sum total or our know-how by taking a sampling of a group of people dedicated to finding out what they can do thinking together. For weeks they studied the store. The had a tough time agreeing with each other, but they did. The spirit was sky-high; excitement was beyond description. Why? For the first time they were given a chance to express themselves as individuals and as a group, each one giving the best that he knew. Not a nickel was spent. Every change was made from what we had in the store. Floors were changed, aisles widened, walls painted. It was a new store, a pleasure to the eye.
>
> What put that store across? They knew they had to visit all the competition and then visit our store with a cold eye. They applied what they learned. Up till then, they had to look at the eyeball of the boss and guess what it was he wanted. All I did was ask them to use their senses and their heads, and I got a damn good store.
>
> Over the next two years, it reduced its losses and then started making money. After all the hustle and bustle, the whole company became aware of it. The chairman and his entourage came running to see what was happening. Now everybody jumped on the bandwagon. Now everybody wanted a district—every vice president, the executive vice president, even the chairman. . . .
>
> Show the people a way. That's what I did. I even had a place to send everyone. Indianapolis. "Go to Indianapolis. Go there, look at the store, and learn. It was put together by people like you, using spit and polish and only their own normal talents." A little while later, in the home office, I changed the pattern. To a variety-chain vice president, who was

---

*The McCrory's example was used in *In Search of Excellence* to illustrate the general point about experimentation, but was never analyzed. We have vaulted it into a preeminent position; here we subject it to intense analysis.

in charge of buying, I said, "All right, Joe, you don't have to go to the Midwest. Do me an Indianapolis right here in New York. You have seen it can be done. But I don't want you to copy it. We will keep Indianapolis as a sort of school." I told him to give me his version of a good variety store in Flushing. Well, several weeks later he invited me to the store and I found one of the most beautiful retail stores I have ever seen. I immediately invited a few others to see it. You would never have believed that this horrible store could be the attraction of the neighborhood and the jewel of the company. Sales began rising right away, and the store became our best in New York. But what it also did was to challenge the other home office executives to go out and do an Indianapolis. As the parent company began to brag more and more, I extended the variations, I used the idea of the Indianapolis stores as a visual aid, getting the people to bring it into shape, then bringing others to see what they did. This became a substitute for writing memos or giving instructions on the phone. Instead, I said, "Come look and see. This is the new company—nothing else is—this is it!" I instructed every district [10 to 15 stores] that it must have its own model store. Every district manager would have to reflect all his knowledge in one store and from that "Indianapolis" improve all the stores in his district. The idea caught on like wildfire. They did it evenings, Sundays, holidays. The Sundays became big shindigs with beer and food provided by the store's restaurant manager. They had the year of their life getting the chain in shape, all 47 districts.

Before analyzing this, we want to answer the question, "Why listen?" McCrory's long-term record is arguably not worth emulating. But true though that might be, the fact remains that the results represented by this brief vignette are exceptional. Sam Neaman was a miracle worker. His efforts with some six-hundred stores led to a remarkable increase in profitability in a short period of time. It was a personal clash with the headstrong Riklis that led to a breakup between the two, and dashed hopes for the project Neaman had so auspiciously begun.

We will break our analysis into two parts. First we want to talk about Indianapolis as a simple experiment. Then we will talk about the experimenting process per se. Indianapolis is, in the scheme of things, a "small win," or to put it better, a small win made up of many even smaller wins. What are its attributes?

## The Small Win: Doability

Above all—and this theme runs through our whole discussion of leadership, subtly and sometimes explicitly—the small win is about *doability*. It's about tasks (and subtasks) that can be done by "real people." Mr. Neaman turns the average performer into a star. Or, better stated, he *allows* the average performer to *find* that there *is* a star within him. He began with a single store. Moreover, it wasn't a high visibility store. It wasn't being looked at under a microscope by top management as the "experiment." Neaman trundled off, without portfolio, and dug around for several weeks, observing the ins and outs of the McCrory system. And then he happened upon Indianapolis. He had learned enough to be ready to take a next step. But he didn't begin with a call to the architects, a plea for capital expenditures for a new store. He didn't begin with an arrogant, brash "Throw the existing turkeys to the wolves" attitude. He began with the idea that the people in this store were all worth saving; they had simply been misled. (Tom Watson, Sr., took that same view with the disheartened and disoriented C-T-R [Computing-Tabulating-Recording] Company, which he inherited in 1912. He didn't fire people. He said they had the stuff within them to become winners. It's been the approach of IBM ever since.) It was *their* show. He told people to go out and *look* at the local competition. Not do competitive analysis in the "on paper" (abstract, sterile) sense, but have real people (e.g., the woman who sells purses at McCrory's in Indianapolis) go out to the store next door and take a look at the counter where the same goods are being sold. (As one senior manager said to us, "I'll bet, and it would pretty much hold for us, it was the first time that anybody like that had really taken that kind of a look at a competitor.")

Then Sam introduced one heck of a routine. *All* hands gathered together *every* evening—five evenings in a row each week—to look at what they had learned that day, to talk about it, to debate what it meant. Real-time feedback, based on real-time collection of tactile data. Not systematic market research, but *real* people collecting *real* impressions about *real* things about which (it turned out—as it always does) they knew a lot. Neaman knew who the experts were: the people in those underled McCrory stores who hadn't been allowed out or hadn't had the motivation to go out, who had not been asked their opinion in years, if ever. His focus was on the tangible. Not *analysis* of purse departments, but *visits* to purse departments. How do *they* display the merchandise? The vehicle and process, the nightly meeting, was vital. It wasn't easy. Doubtless the discussions were forced or stilted at first. People had gone through twenty-five years of learning *not* to talk, *not* to speak up. How did he get them to speak up? He did it by putting them to work in areas where they were legitimately expert. He didn't tell them to expound a retail philosophy. He told them to talk, in nuts-and-bolts terms, about something they understood—their twenty-five square feet of turf. (The words of Dana's Ren McPherson echo in our ears: "When I'm in your twenty-five square feet, I'd better listen.")

So the focus was on doability, tangibility, *speed* (24-hour feedback, low budget, real people talking about actual experience). No staff or "experts" were allowed to meddle. *Self-anaylsis* was essential.

Neaman's wonderful term is "guided autonomy." The "guided" part was based on his clear vision. Not a clear vision in terms of shelf-display algorithms. But a vision such that he would *know* when he had a "beautiful store." It was perhaps mystical, maybe Zen-like, but certainly real to him. And he rapidly made the *possibility* of it real to others. And the autonomy? (It sounds a lot like "ownership.") The group of locals—"People like you, using spit and polish and only their normal talents" were his words—was to figure out how to get from here to there. He gave them spirit: beer busts on the weekend, yes, but mainly a purpose. It was *their* game, *their* store to fix, *their* store to build. The company was in trouble. There was no capital available. They weren't going to get $2 million to build a spanking-new store. Lamenting the fact that Penney's had a better nationwide distribution system wasn't going to do them a bit of good. They had to figure out a way to turn the store around—on their own. He was rigid in only one thing. He clearly dictated the outline of the process, the daily feedback sessions based upon analysis of real-time data. So the three pillars were *vision*, ("guided") *autonomy* and a rigid real-time *process*.

A "learning system" is vital. Learning is an inadequate word; a constellation of terms like real-time, momentum-building is better. And make sure the learning "system" or process encompasses (and generates) many small wins. Get people to make daily assessments; then act on those assessments. (Incidentally, the small-win, quick-feedback process actually *generates* practicality. Go out once a year with a call for suggestions, or focus on the few big $5,000 awards, and you reap what you sow: big, largely impractical suggestions. Develop a system that "demands" a suggestion a week and process it in a few days and, lo and behold, you induce practical and implementable suggestions—e.g., a new way to hold a welding iron.)

Consider another pair of words: *opportunity* and *constraint*. Managers, according to the consultants and the academics, are "constrained." Neaman, said, in effect, "The heck with constraints." He got his people to look at that Indianapolis site and the Indianapolis process as an *opportunity*: "Figure out what *we* (you) can make of this."

Finally, an "experiment" does not have to be a present or future event. Interestingly, it can have happened in the past. Here's how it works. At Hewlett-Packard, most managerial skills—R&D, manufacturing, etc.—are taught by a vehicle called "best practices." The best practitioners are sought out and a composite of their work patterns (not rules) is used as a model. An IBM officer, assigned the task of being the quality "czar" of a division, took the same tack. Frustrated by his inability to define quality based upon textbook analysis, he sought out the "best receptionist" and so on; these real-time models became his operational definitions of top quality. Such devices need not be the province of superstars alone. In our experience, the *worst* of organizations have top performers, worthy of emulation. Thus a marvelous way to "save steps" and get on with a new program is to ferret out bits of good news from the past: e.g., one receptionist who does the job well. Though these obviously must soon be matched by new good news, they should at least help you to hit the ground trotting.

## Ownership and the Small-Win Process—
## Natural Diffusion

Let's move to the small-win process per se. Here's where the true genius of Neaman shows itself. What was Neaman's trick? We think, above all, it was *patience*, the fact that he wouldn't let people *copy* Indianapolis. Neaman said others could come and *look* at Indianapolis, *visit* Indianapolis, *touch* Indianapolis, *feel* Indianapolis, but they could *not* copy Indianapolis. Indianapolis became a model, a symbol, a story, a small win. It was, moreover, a tangible example, and therefore what was most important—given the way humans process information—was that it was *real*. A staff-generated book on "how to do an Indianapolis" would *not* have been real.

This point is vital because it touches on the single most important reason why most new programs fail. Many—ranging from quality circles to rejuvenated factories—do develop an Indianapolis, one shining star that's touted because of some powerful and extraordinary champion. But then there's a horrible tendency to say, "Boy, oh boy. We've got a winner. Let's take advantage of it—*now!* Let's write down *exactly* what happened at Indianapolis. Let's write it up as a case study. Let's turn it into a book, a procedures book." What you're saying, of course, is: "Let's shove it down the throat of each of the leaders of the five-hundred ninety-nine other stores." By doing so, you kill the fatted calf because the magic, it turns out, isn't the *specific* techniques of Indianapolis; it's the sense of *ownership* and *commitment* so patiently developed—allowed to develop—within the Indianapolis operation/context.

At the Dana Corporation, Ren McPherson's vision of "turning the company back over to the people who do the work" was his own form of guided autonomy. McPherson hammered away on productivity, ranted and raved about it, lived it—his calendar vividly illustrated what *his* priority was. But he didn't *tell* his people what to do. In fact, he made his central staff's mission the exact opposite of what the staff's mission usually is. At Dana, staff ceased to be enforcers. They became leaders of a natural diffusion process. That is, they became people who went out on the road to find good-news stories and to tell other people about them. They were *not* to suggest explicitly that what worked in Toledo ought to work in Dayton, but simply to tell the people in Dayton what happened in Toledo—and let them learn from it if they could, if it made sense in *their unique* setting. Now the staff *did* become "experts." They became experts in diffusion. They became experts in exposing people to other people's experiments. And, in two annual Hell Weeks, success stories were swapped with memorable intensity.

Eschewing "participation through mandate" is, of course, basic of what Neaman did. After a successful "Indianapolis" became visible, he then unearthed an aggressive headquarters person who volunteered to "do" a Flushing. And then a few more came aboard. He let the process take its course. He nudged, to be sure. But he nudged by providing people access,

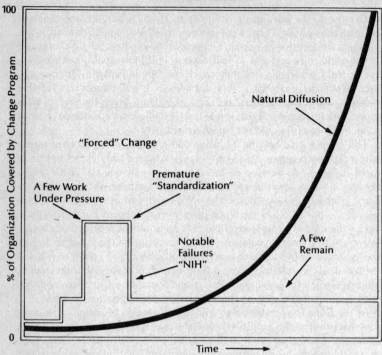

the opportunity to become excited. He did not mandate. The process took a long time. The people who were impatient after seeing the startling Indianapolis success were doubtless dissatisfied. They wanted to sweep the Indianapolis experience through the system; the result would undoubtedly have been an out-and-out disaster. There would have been some initial change for the better, to be sure, but things would soon have leveled off. The upshot: just one more program shoved down the throats of the operators by a smart-aleck corporate staffer, one more great hope shattered by year's end.

We've drawn up a conceptual chart to illustrate the McCrory phenomenon. The overall point is that the natural diffusion process, albeit slow at the start, is a process that is ultimately more efficient—*and faster*—than the one following the principle of "Change by mandate." You nudge a program into existence—i.e., cause/create an Indianapolis. Then, having decided to go the "Force it" route, you send in the staff. You draw up a manual—mandate it. People do, indeed, listen. There are additional successes. But because the program has been mandated, two things happen. Commitment is vitiated (NIH—Not Invented Here—at work), and there are some failures (because Indianapolis was unique—each location is). Soon the vultures descend (in all change programs, the vultures are close at hand): "See? See? I told you Indianapolis was a fluke. Great market. Dumb guy in charge before. Neaman's the only reason it happened. He forced it." The skeptics (always far outnumbering champions in the early days) have a field day. And the program peters out. A little of the good is left, but the system in general returns to rest close to where it was before.

Now let's look at the alternative to the mandate: natural diffusion. The start is usually painfully slow, an exponential curve, as pictured. Finding the second and third "champion" (inducing him or her to come out of the woodwork) is often agonizing. But then the diffusion process begins to take hold, and the champions (even including skeptics, who are unfailingly good "straw-in-the-wind watchers"; more on that later) queue up. Failure is by and large avoided because near champions—who are committed and ready—are the early proponents; they make it happen. Then as news of their results spread, there are more and more successful experiments to learn from in a nonthreatening situation. The odd conclusion, of course, is that the natural diffusion path turns out to be *more* efficient, speedier. Those who said "we haven't got the time to wait for volunteers to surface" are ultimately proved wrong.

We want to stress that natural diffusion does not stand in the way of planned forums (à la Milliken's Fabulous Bragging Sessions, discussed on p. 304) or a traveling staff with videotapes spreading good news (à la Dana). In fact, these devices constitute exactly what *can* be a consciously managed "technology of diffusion" aimed at maximizing the speed of spreading the word and maximizing peer pressure. But what is maximized by management is, precisely, diffusion—not a forced march.

After Flushing (success no. 2) was completed, Neaman did indeed go another step in turning up the flame under the "guiding" process. But the increased heat was wholly consistent with his guided autonomy model. Remember, he had forty-seven districts of ten to fifteen stores each. He insisted (now that he had demonstrated, via Flushing, that Indianapolis was not a fluke) that each district have its own "Indianapolis." Each of the forty-seven was to have one model store among the ten to fifteen. He assumed at this point that a district boss could find at least *one* would-be champion among his branch managers. And from those (one in ten to fifteen), the natural diffusion process would flow again, stepped up in pace a bit. And so it happened.

Let's shift focus to these vital champions for a moment. The single most important piece of advice we think we can offer to would-be major-change managers is the following: For heaven's sake, go after the easy stuff first! What's the thrill of beating your head against a brick wall? Sam Neaman found *someone* he could work with at Indianapolis. Then he found someone else who was ready to roll, who did Flushing. Then he sought one in fifteen (one per district): These were the champions, the handful of people who, even in the worst of circumstances, in the most bureaucratic and stifling environments, *do* want to get on with "it" urgently. In our experience such champions *always* exist. So begin with the people on the ten-yard line. Give them a big push to help go the last ten years and score a touchdown. It's absolutely vital. What a previously defeatist system needs most is momentum and a handful of believable successes and new role models. What it needs is to understand that there *can* be winners. What it needs is to see that there are incipient champions who *can* be successful in this (previously) stodgy environment. Mr. Indianapolis became a champion. Mr. Flushing became a champion. Then the one in ten to fifteen became champions.

The chart on the facing page illustrates this. We find that in any system there are some "lunatic" champions out on the fringe. They'll unfailingly do their own thing, often successfully. But, perhaps surprisingly, they really aren't the heart of the systemwide change process, as we've described it. Why? Because they'll always be considered lunatics by their peers, decidedly *not* "just like you and me." The fact that they behave strangely—albeit effectively—is of little comfort to the rest of the gang. But what we want desperately is the next group, the group that we view as between the five- and the fifteen-yard line. They're about ready to charge. They're energetic. They're would-be champions/skunks. They haven't yet been wholly beaten down. Push *them* to be the champions of the Indianapolises, or Flushings, or of the first store in each district. They, by dint of their location on the distribution, are *not* lunatic fringe. They are not *quite* "just like you and me." But they decidedly *are* plausible, credible role models. And then, once there are a few credible wins and winners in the system, and once we've been smart enough to celebrate them (yet not force the example they set down others' throats), *then* the next group will catch on. They are, say, the next 20 percent of the distribution—they are seducible, still far from being hardened skeptics. *Now* you do have the ball rolling! The key is *always* to go after the next bunch of the nearly converted. Proving that the true skeptics are indeed truly skeptical achieves nothing, except that you've dented your pick and probably permanently diminished your credibility (and failed to appreciate the vital importance of building a fragile momentum).

(An odd thing does frequently occur. The most hardened skeptics are *not* the last to come on board. Straw-in-the-wind watchers that they are, the hardened skeptics—the laggard tail of the normal distribution curve—will often jump on the bandwagon as momentum builds and progress appears to be more than fleeting. It's the center of the distribution, the neither angry nor particularly seducible bunch, that is more likely to climb on last.)

And the job of senior managers in all this? Go back to the previous chapter. They're in charge of the *symbols*. In charge of finding and nurturing that original Indianapolis into being, and making darned sure *it* doesn't fail. You need that first small win, and you need it desperately. To this end, spending a *full* year of your life on a "trivial" Indianapolis, just one store out of six-

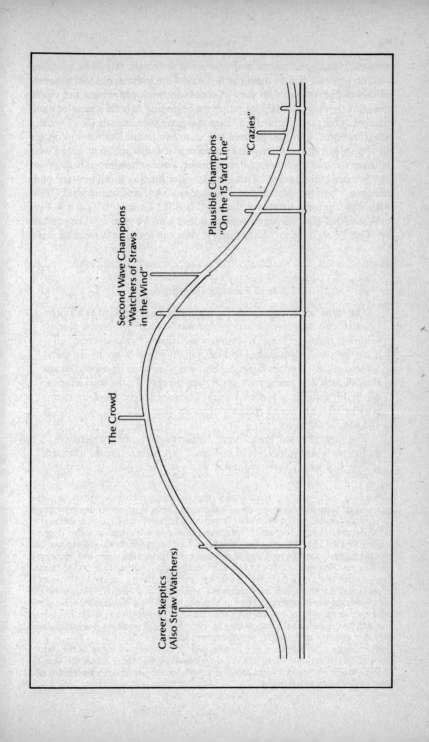

hundred, is likely the highest and best use of your time. (Similarly, spending a *month* planning how to make the first *day* of the Indianapolis trial a success is likely the best use of your time.) Others will think you're nuts; but you're managing (leading) the delicate process of beginning to build a winning environment. (One sage commented: "Beginnings are such delicate times.") After that (successful) start you become historian. Symbolist. Dramatist. You get out the video camera when there's a success at Indianapolis, or at the next Indianapolis. You are noter, poster, publicist, visible cheerleader, hero anointer. "See our Indianapolis?" This is a *picture* of the way it can be—and your colleagues ("just like you and me") have done it. As Sam Neaman said, "This *is* the new company—nothing else is—this is it." Look at it. Touch it. Feel it. Watch that film. See those people on that film. They're just like you and me. They're no different. They made it. You can make it. We can all make it.*

---

### Milliken's Fabulous Bragging Sessions

The turnaround story (albeit from a strong running start) at Milliken bears a striking resemblance to Neaman's routine. Success stories, resulting from the "quality through participative management" program the company launched in 1980, rapidly began to accumulate, and forums called Fabulous Bragging Sessions were then developed to aid the diffusion and momentum-generating process. At the sessions, people by the bale swap success stories. They are indeed fabulous, exemplifying all we've been saying about ownership, small wins, celebration and natural diffusion.

The idea emerged from Roger Milliken's continuing frustration at finding nifty new programs in one plant that hadn't diffused to others where they were clearly applicable. He was wise enough to know that

---

*There's a great deal of psychological theory, relating both to individuals and groups, that supports the observations we've made here. With respect to individuals, psychology focuses on the overriding importance of commitment, if motivation is to be sustained, and of the quick feedback associated with human-scale, tangible achievements. The literature on resistance to change (in both individuals and groups) suggests that the best way to overcome it is taking tiny steps, and, moreover, working on the positive ("we can do something right"), rather than trying to confront negative feelings directly. "Social comparison" theory speaks to the critical importance of competition between peers, and systematic research focuses on the exceptional power of stories ("little knots of meaning")—e.g., Indianapolises—as the most significant way of transmitting information. The dominant strain in current learning theory heralds the importance of role models; the small win is exactly about the rapid creation of plausible, positive role models.

At the organizational level, the most powerful theories now speak to the importance of "organizational learning." What we've talked about here, under the heading of Sam Neaman's "guided autonomy," is a model for the textbook paradigm of efficient organizational learning.

even though his last name was Milliken, the one way to make sure they would not diffuse was to *tell* plant A to take on a technique he'd observed in plant B. (Shades by Neaman, to be sure.)

So the Fabulous Bragging Sessions (more formally, Corporate Sharing Rallies) were born—out of the notion that it was essential to get people together somehow to share war stories. Here are some of the elements, some of the things Milliken's people have learned along the way:

1.  Frequency. *Corporate* Fabulous Bragging Sessions are held every ninety days. Held less frequently and the momentum is lost. More frequently and they eat up too much time, even by Milliken's tolerant (on this dimension) standards. Each session lasts almost two full days.

2.  Structure. In the course of the two days a hundred or more teams will present ideas or success stories. Teams will come from any of Milliken's scores of facilities, and may travel several hundred miles to make a five-minute presentation. Attendance at the sessions is wholly voluntary (the practical limit has been the size of the facility). Several hundred people usually show up, and many more are waiting in the wings.

3.  Few "rules." Milliken President Tom Malone did have to install three. First, no negatives. Plain and simple, no criticism of any team's presentation is allowed (this reminds us of the Gores, who quite literally outlaw the term "devil's advocate" at W. L. Gore & Associates). The second rule is that there is no such thing as a "big" idea or "small" one. Ideas are evaluated on their quality, and a fine idea that brings in a small savings in a clerical department is considered as much a winner as an idea that generates a giant improvement in a factory. Third and finally, "I coulda done it [done it better], *but* . . . [e.g., but MIS wouldn't help out]" is not allowed. You are responsible for making your "it" happen, period.

4.  Themes. Each quarter's bragging session has a major "theme." One time it's sales enhancement. Another time it's quality enhancement, or what Milliken calls its "center-cut program" (a program through which they attempt to surpass their customers' quality standards by 70 percent or more). The next quarter it's cost reduction. All in all, the sessions rotate through about a half-dozen themes, around which all the presentations at any session are focused.

5.  Tangible objectives. Each improvement is to be reported with a quantitative outcome indicator, but the quantitative indicators are not "audited" by any outsider to the group. Honesty is up to the presenting team. As Malone says, the last thing people are likely to do around their peers is inflate an outcome. "They'd BS me at the drop of a hat," he notes, "but not each other."

6.  Voting. Milliken wants to make sure that teams/people don't "win" just on the basis of clever presentation. So several criteria have been developed for voting on projects. One of them does focuses on the qual-

ity of the presentation, but the rest stress various aspects of the idea per se. (Malone asserts that peers are exceptionally tough on one another. After the early sessions he found himself voting almost all presentations "excellent." Peers, however, did not.)

7. Everyone a winner. While several ascending grades of awards are given to those who have the outstanding presentations, everyone and every team goes home with a framed certificate simply for participating. Moreover, there's a subtle ritual that Malone engages in which speaks a thousand words. He usually finds an outside speaker to come in for a couple of hours very near the end of the session. During that time Malone and his colleagues are hard at work, signing and framing every award certificate. The grand finale is an awards ceremony, during which, on the spot, each participant is handed (by Malone or chairman Roger Milliken) his or her framed and signed certificate.

The corporate Fabulous Bragging Sessions at Milliken are only one element, albeit the most dramatic, of Milliken's extraordinary quality enhancement program. In addition, sharing/bragging sessions are held within each facility prior to each quarterly corporate extravaganza; Malone visits scores of these as well. Teams with top ideas may end up presenting several times: once or twice within their facility, at the corporate sharing session, and to the corporation's senior management group. Each corporate president's council meeting, in fact, is kicked off by several stellar teams making presentations.

The effort is by "all hands." In each facility the secretaries and loading-dock bunch will likely form teams, as will the people running the giant weaving machines. Malone reports that it was tough at first to figure out how to get the sales and marketing people involved (a common lament of those who are working quality circle programs and their kin), how to move them beyond the traditional role of the salespersons-as-Lone Rangers. Nonetheless, he decided to plunge ahead, and the results have been gratifying. The salesperson is made "chairman" of a CAT (Customer Action Team) that includes participants from various supporting disciplines. Very tough targets—for instance, to double sales with a particular customer within ninety days—are set. "Doesn't this mean that the team goes after 'small' customers?" "You bet," Malone says. "But getting the involvement and getting the point across that such objectives can be set and met is what it's all about, after all, isn't it?"

Another intriguing element in Milliken's program is the extent to which it has come to include a "bottom-up push." As you might guess, some old-school supervisors didn't exactly leap aboard. To Milliken's delight, these supervisors' people ganged up on them: "We want to present. Why can't we? Everyone else is. We want to go to the Spartanburg Session." Time and again the reluctant dragons were dragged in from below.

It's vital to note here that the ongoing personal attention (quantity and quality) paid to the quality program by Roger Milliken, Tom Malone and the senior Milliken team is the crucial ingredient that's absent in most similar programs. Most quality drives are kicked off with great gusto and then lose momentum. There are several reasons. Flagging attention is one. Another is the fact that most focus only on the so-called substance (some dramatic outcome), not the *process* necessary for sustaining all-hands commitment to the goal. Milliken's program, at the end of four years, is *still* picking up steam. Much of the reason is the continued energy directed at the process generating and sustaining momentum—the Fabulous Bragging Sessions and all that surrounds them.

### The Management Role in Small Win-Induced Transformations— a Summary:

• Ferret out would-be champions and would-be sites for first and subsequent experiments.
• Sanction experiments "caught in midstream" or just getting under way.
• Sanction the notion of experimenting.
• Label the experiment a success (if warranted), or a part of the experiment a success; "toast" the results in notable ways and become chief publicist of partial and wholesale experimental success(es).
• Buffer new experiments and would-be champion-experimenters from intrusive staff, not only those obvious stiflers who have an apparent need to say no, but also those who *like* what they see and want to prematurely pry (for good and well-intended reasons).
• Arrange peer pressure (competition, visits, publicity) that is rapidly transmitted to people in similar settings.
• Work hard to keep the NIH phenomenon from arising; for example, as Neaman did, by allowing no exact replicas or premature (forced) implementation of ideas.
• Be sure that first or early champions cannot be denigrated as "crazy" (as nonplausible role models) and that first successes are not distinguished by extraordinary environmental circumstances (somebody builds a ninety-story office building right next to an old store).

### The Small-Wins Process: Some Questions—and Things to Do Now

*Analysis*
1.   Review a priority program dealing with enhancing a strategic skill, especially one that's stalled. Are you taking on the world, or have you identified a potential champion and a potential "Indianapolis"? If yes, is your Indianapolis site marked by "Sam-like" traits: (1) not of such darned high visibility

that all eyes are upon it, (2) your obsessive attention, (3) doable/visible positive outcome within the next 90 (30? 15?) days? Try again. Are you really committed to making the Indianapolis a success? Are there any (be honest, now) higher priorities on your agenda? Do you know the "real people" in your Indianapolis well enough to be able to answer this question and predict the outcome?

2. The process: Do you have one? How are you recognizing Indianapolises? How do you seek them out? Support them? Hide them from probing bureaucrats? Do you celebrate with real fanfare? How often? Is your staff still focused on "cop tasks," or are they aimed at "managing the diffusion process"? Do you have an explicit, well-planned, thoughtfully construed process for conducting Fabulous Bragging Sessions/Hell Weeks? How often do you get your "experimenters" together? (If the answer is less often than once every three weeks, think about it.)

3. What is your visitation record re those experiments? Last 120 days? Last 15 days? Last week?

4. What, explicitly, have you done to publicize/reward/give prizes to your new heroes? Are heroes credible?

5. How "public" are you with your support of the experiments? Are you on videotape? Do you unfailingly (i.e., at every inappropriate opportunity) speak, in story form, of early successes?

6. When's the last time you talked to a "champion"? If "over forty-eight hours ago" is the answer, why so long?

7. How do you keep your finger on the pulse re how many of your colleagues/subordinates are starting their Indianapolises? Is it prevalent? If not, why not?

8. Do you (and colleagues) regularly talk about the Indianapolises in your organization?

*Next Steps*

Pick one important program, seek out an Indianapolis demonstration activity to get it off stall. Look for a would-be champion "on the ten-yard line," not a skeptic (even if the champion is ranked "too low," according to the formal structure). Within the next 5 to 10 days, say, plan for inducing an Indianapolis with some results in the next 30 to 45 days. Talk with your colleagues about urging one Indianapolis into being in each of their top priority/opportunity areas.

---

### Marv's Meetings: Small Wins, Big Outcome

Cross-functional noncommunication is at the heart of most management problems. It is the genesis of the matrix structure—so beautiful on paper (it solves all those nasty communications problems) but invariably horrendous, at least in practice. Well, let's just take a look at one more place with obvious cross-functional problems and look at their (definitely nonmatrix) solution. We work from time to time with the Northrop Corporation's $1.5 billion Aircraft Division, where the materiel/purchasing function is run by Marv Elkin, whom we introduced earlier. The materiel/purchasing function is important in any organization, but in the world of advanced avionics and the like it's especially important—probably 70 percent of the cost of the aircraft comes from outside purchases. Well, different functions don't talk to one another—*anywhere*. In hospitals the nurses don't talk to the doctors. In banks the lenders don't talk to the operations people. As we said before, in industrial companies the engineers don't talk to the manufacturers. Salesmen everywhere are seen to be self-serving blow-hards. And, of course, *nobody* talks to the purchasing guy!

Elkin, however, has found a way to beat the rap. What is it? Oh, oh, is it b-o-r-i-n-g. He has a bunch of programs going. They are called FIN-MAT, TECH-MAT, Q-MAT. So what does that jargon mean? The first, FIN-MAT, is a team that involves supervisors from the finance area (FIN) and the materiel (purchasing) area (MAT). In the second, TECH stands for technology; in the third, Q stands for the quality organization. FIN-MAT simply means that the finance people *meet* with—i.e., talk to—the materiel people. What could be simpler? Or rarer? It works this way. Sometime in 1983 Elkin got the idea that the best way to overcome the seemingly God-given barriers would be to have people meet and learn to appreciate each other. So he got together with the head of finance and suggested that they take about thirty people—the top fifteen managers in each area—and go off-site for two or three days "just to discuss things." They did. It was a revelation for all involved: each found out the other function was made up of human beings with reasonable objectives. An agenda of doable cooperative tasks began rapidly to emerge. At least as important, people got to know others, so they could call on them as colleagues, not adversaries, when a problem came up. They decided to continue the dialogue. They went off-site once a month. ("It's hard to do a 'Gotcha' on a guy you've been drinking beers with once a month," Elkin says.) At last count, they had been doing so for fourteen consecutive months.

Well, it's working! Now they'd never think of abandoning it. They no longer go off-site; that was, Elkin admits, "a con": "It's the only way I know to get 'em away from the phones." He adds, "Now that they've gotten used to the program, we can do it on premises. Moreover, the program was at first dictated. That is, I insisted that my people go, and [the finance person] did the same. Now, as the program is well under way, we've made it voluntary." What's the result? Has attendance dropped off from thirty to four die-hards? To the contrary: Elkin was so pleased with the process and the results that he decided to do the same

thing with technology people, and then with the quality group. Hence
TECH-MAT and Q-MAT. Each has followed the same course.

Now, what's the big deal? None, we suppose. But let's look at it again.
There are a bunch of factors at play here. The first one obviously is
leadership. Elkin was bound and determined to make it work. He paid
attention. Second, as discussed in the Neaman case, he looked for an
"easy opening": namely, the finance man, who was a solid individual
who believed the same things Elkin did. Elkin didn't go after the most
recalcitrant fellow; he went instead after the colleague who was the
most sympathetic. Third he (they) didn't really have any objective other
than "making things better." The meetings weren't for the purpose of
browbeating or "getting *your* [the other guy's] act together." Fourth,
the effort was marked by *intensity* and *persistence*. Once a month.
Month in and month out. When will they be "finished"? Never, we
presume (hope). And they do, too.

## Degrees of Winning

The small-win theme prevades this book—expecially the extensive discussions of "ownership" (in the section on People). This is because we know of
no other sure fire way to generate momentum and create a winning tradition,
especially when a turnaround is required, than through small wins that turn
all hands into winners—*and at their own pace.* Winning is a key word.
Almost all of us believe we're winners. Tom and Bob Waterman reported a
study in *In Search of Excellence* that suggested that almost 100 percent of us
think ourselves in the top 1 percent of the population on cooperativeness, in
the top 25 percent on leadership; and even when an objective skill is the
subject—i.e., athletic talent—about 75 percent of us put ourselves in the first
quartile. Yes, almost all of us think we're (very) hot stuff. Yet most of our
organizations go out of their way to disconfirm that daily.

We're not talking about a Pollyana's world view here. Mars, Inc., is hardly
a "soft" company, yet every person gets a weekly 10 percent bonus—including the president (in a $6 billion company)—if she or he comes to work on
time each day! And, yes, it *is* quite an accomplishment to get up five mornings in a row and show up on time with the car's battery run down and the
latest bout of German measles about to set in.

Most of the companies we think highly of proceed according to what we
call a "degrees of winning" principle rather than a "degrees of losing" one.
Moderately good performance is touted. It's true at Tupperware, Disney,
McDonald's, Mary Kay Cosmetics, The Limited Stores, Mars Inc., Milliken,
Stew Leonard's, People Express and Hewlett-Packard. Even IBM. IBM works
like the devil to make sure that fully 80 percent of its sales force is successful.
Now, of course, it does offer special recognition for the top 3 percent—the
members of the Golden Circle. But more important, to our minds, is the fact

that fully 80 percent are celebrated as members of the Hundred Percent Club.

### Creating Winners:
### Are "They" Ready?

We hear the following time and again: "Many companies are now highly centralized and autocratic. You recommend, almost without caveat, radical decentralization and greatly enhanced doses of autonomy. But isn't it true that some people aren't ready for it immediately? Or ever?"

That is, are people ready to do an Indianapolis? There are two sides to the answer. The first is to acknowledge that the problem does exist. Speaking of the encouragement of numerous, sometimes duplicative product-development teams at Hewlett-Packard, a division general manager says, "We can only allow the apparent chaos because of the bone-deep belief we all share in superior product quality and the way in which people should be treated." Indeed, we do, flatly, find that there is little worse than creating autonomous teams willy-nilly, before beliefs to guide the teams is clear.

There is, then, a necessary order: values first, autonomous teams second. For instance, Campbell Soup, as we noted, is undertaking radical (for them) decentralization right now. But before launching the transformation, Chairman Gordon McGovern took all his senior colleagues through a lengthy and agonizing reappraisal of the company's value system, in which respect for quality stands out at the very top. Johnson & Johnson may have the most radically autonomous units of any company we've investigated. At the same time, it has as rigorous, regular and tightly articulated a value-review process as any we've observed—an annual, intense review of its credo called the Credo Challenge. Also, J&J's Statement of Strategic Direction is clearly autonomy-guided-religiously (almost literally)-by-the-Credo. (See chapter 18, on coaching)

The same line of reasoning holds for individuals as for teams. The creative party giving of the autonomous Tupperware salesperson becomes "magic" only because she is "overtrained" in the Tupperware Way before ever being allowed to conduct her first house party. That is, Tupperware ensures beyond a reasonable doubt that the first independent try will indeed result in a small win. Likewise, the "harshness" of, say, IBM's full liability policy (salespersons are docked out of *salary* for prior commissions earned on IBM equipment that is removed from a customer's premises while that customer is one of their accounts) only works as well as it does (and does not create nightmarish conditions) *because of* the superb training that salespersons receive. That is, they are "ready"—fully prepared—to deal with their tough environments. We, in fact, have become great fans of the IBM, Tupperware or Disney sort of "boot camp." Substantial autonomy without prior training "overkill" is sure prescription for disaster.

The important flip side of the "Don't give them premature autonomy" issue is widely misunderstood. First, most people *are* responsible—*now*; are ready for far more autonomy than we commonly suspect. (Neaman's story is fine evidence.) It's also essential to note that it is not a fair or symmetrical world. The analyst's bias, albeit unintentional, is almost always on the side of "They're not ready yet." And the analyst is dead right! The new general manager, the superbly prepared Tupperware house party giver and the Disney ticket taker alike will make a host of mistakes early in the game. The only way to be fully "ready to be there" is to have been there—a classic catch-22.* So one must be terribly careful not to allow "They're not ready yet" to hold sway forever.

The early days following the granting of enhanced autonomy, then, no matter how well planned, will always be marked by minor—and often major—glitches. However, the experience we've had with scores of people who have granted increases of autonomy is that in almost every instance—and here's another rub—if it's done with goodwill (a genuine belief that it will work), the results are positive. Most managers, if they've given it an honest go, are literally shocked at the amount of responsibility that units and teams with a new sense of ownership take on and the speed with which they take it on. In fact, much of the "problem" arises because teams do so well, making it readily apparent to the supervisor that he is less needed than he thought!

## Debureaucratizing

We spend 30 percent of our days in off-site senior management meetings. At each, it seems, some fair share of the time is spent railing against unnecessary bureaucracy. And it should be. We have said that there are only two paths to lasting strategic dominance: constant innovation and superior customer service. Further, each is wholly dependent not upon mystical techniques but upon ownership—i.e., the creative contribution of each person in the organization. And what most gets in the way of ownership—on the loading dock, in the mail room? Unnecessary bureaucracy. So, logically, inescapably, cleaning up the bureaucratic junk must be the number one strategic priority.

At each meeting we attend, top management promises to do something "serious" about it; maybe even something quantitative: "Cut the paper by 25 percent." And then they appoint a low-level committee to carry out this so-called prime directive. By doing so, they ensure that next year at this time nothing will have happened.

If you're gonna do it, you gotta do it! (Profound, eh?) No ifs, ands and buts. The Newsweek cover story of August 1984 illustrated this point in even the heartland of bureaucracy. General Walter Ulmer, who has no stomach for bureaucracy, reduced "several feet of local regulations [theretofore perceived as unalterably imposed by higher-ups] to less than two inches." In the pro-

---

*This reminds us of the old saw: Good judgment is the product of experience; experience is the product of bad judgment.

cessed-steel industry, Worthington Industries' John McConnell, Sr., never had corporate policy manuals to begin with. As a young man working for other companies, he decided that policy books and rules restrict rather than guide. If he ever had his own company, McConnell determined to treat people the way he would have liked to have been treated as an employee. The Worthington Industries philosophy fits on one small card, and reads simply: "We treat our customers, employees, investors and suppliers as we would like to be treated." Period.

Remember Ren McPherson, who in 1969 produced a one-page operational philosophy statement to replace Dana Corporation's hefty collection of corporate policy manuals? Add Marcus Sieff of Marks & Spencer, who began his tenure as managing director by taking a one-year "sabbatical," as he calls it. He spent the entire period, with virtually no exception, reducing the company's paperwork. He eliminated 80 percent of it, or, he judges, 27 million pages a year. Sieff brought that year to a memorable close by piling the 5 tons of useless paper into a massive heap, striking a match, and hosting a company-wide bonfire.

---

*General Principles for Operation*
*Simplification at Marks & Spencer:*

1. Sensible approximation—the price of perfection is prohibitive.
2. Reporting by exception (only when absolutely necessary).
3. Manuals—no attempt is made to legislate for every contingency and every eventuality. (Before simplification there were thirteen instruction manuals, and now there are two small booklets: *Guide to Staff Management* and *Store Regulations*).
4. Decategorization—people have been removed from water-tight compartments and placed in general categories.
5. People can be trusted, so checks can be eliminated. This, in turn, saves time, staff and money, and leads to increased self-confidence and a sense of responsibility among staff. Control can be effectively exercised by selective and occasional spot checks, which are usually more satisfactory and productive and certainly less costly than a whole series of permanent control systems and continuous routine checks.

---

A friend at Hewlett-Packard concurs. Since a major body of sound psychological research has reached the conclusion that we can hold only a half-dozen things in mind at once, our friend insists that his assistants never use more than half a dozen measurement parameters when they measure something. He says, "Look, I want everyone to be a businessperson. That means everybody—the most junior clerk—has got to understand how the business works, totally. So we only measure half a dozen things. People become familiar with them, can see how they interrelate, how they vary as a function of what we're up to. If some smart-aleck young analyst comes along and wants to complicate it, I say, Fine. Five measures are the maximum. Do you want to prove to me that you have two better measures? Don't bother. You just go ahead and add your two, but then get rid of two existing ones. We simply won't let the total go above five."*

## Control Is Not a Form

We had just been through another discussion of Willard Marriott Sr.'s habit of reading complaint cards. An executive in a mid-sized health care firm piped up: "Control is not administration. It's not control via forms. It's *exactly* those fifty-six years of card-reading." Control? Formal? Informal? A former Marriott regional vice president, once a property manager, adds: "It may be 'informal control' to you, but it's got teeth. Mr. Marriott's habit meant that you had one hundred forty property managers working twenty-eight-hour days, fifteen-month years, to make sure that the old man had a very, very, very light reading load!" Du Pont, as we noted, demands that all accident reports be on the chairman's desk in Wilmington, Delaware, within twenty-four hours of the occurrence. Control is the knowledge that someone who is interested and cares is paying close attention.† Real and effective control comes from a *small* number of *simple* rules (or measures) that are *directly* consistent with the organization's vision. Mr. Marriott Sr.'s complaint-card reading is perfectly consistent with his and Bill Jr.'s vision of Marriott's hotels as those that best serve the customer.

Even when one does feel the pressing need to venture in the direction of "rulism," it need not mean the 175-page manual. In fact, there need not be anything "ordered" at all. Hewlett-Packard—(and IBM to a lesser extent)— runs almost every aspect of the company according to so-called best practices. There isn't a rule book. Instead, HP captures the best ways of doing things— for the receptionist, the design engineer, the manufacturing foreman. They actively collect these best practices and put them together in what we like to call "storybooks," chockablock with hard-edged examples of how real people ("your peers") best perform common tasks in accordance with the "HP Way."

Milliken and Company has taken the same route. In their effort to improve

---

*Goldsmith and Clutterbuck made a similar point in *The Winning Streak:* "One immediate observation of most of our successful companies, which contrasts with many unsuccessful companies, is that they try hard to keep central controls to a minimum. . . . That doesn't mean that the controls are lax. Quite the opposite, in fact. As a general rule, it seems that the fewer controls exercised by the centre, the more strictly line managers are expected to adhere to them."

†The ultimate: in Singapore, strongman Prime Minister Lee Kuan Yew reads the quarterly grade transcripts of each young man and woman the state has sent to the university on a special fast-tracking program to prepare for public service. "Do your homework" takes on special meaning, via this "informal" review!

customer listening skills, most units have launched several experimental programs. They want to share results widely, yet abhor excessive rules; moreover, they don't want to shove one person's/groups's experience down another's throat (see the preceding chapter). So they've taken to constructing a master binder. Stories (good-news outcomes—usually small—of successful experiments) are collected and regularly added to the binder. What a lovely alternative to a 300-page rule book in bureaucratese on "how to listen to customers," put out by a "genius" (or a committee of geniuses) on a corporate marketing staff!

A small retailer, running a $4 million store, invented a similar routine. Her objective was to describe to new employees how the store did business and what it stood for. She tried to write a rule book, but that wasn't the way she really wanted to run the store, and besides, the thing immediately began to get lengthy—fifty pages before she had batted an eye. So she chose an alternative approach. She got all of her people together, some seventy-five, on about five occasions. She had them submit their best stories, orally or in written form, about when they were most proud of the way they had presented themselves to their customers and fellow employees. Those stories, edited down, formed a thirty-page booklet of "examples of how we do things." They are the heart of the company's training program, and constitute both its philosophy and its book of rules. Moreover, the document is a *living* one: people are proud to add to it, to get their examples into it, and so they constantly offer up new material. (Lo and behold, the store has a problem with the length of "the book" because people keep adding stories—or "rules"!)

---

### It Takes Guts

We have never seen a form or manual that couldn't be reduced by 50 to 75 percent. But it does take *guts* to give up on the paper. Paper is a form of security, and something *is* lost when it's given up, something that must be replaced by mushy old trust (abetted by prior training and development). And it takes guts of another sort, as well: A friend runs a forty-person establishment. Someone was fired (for, it seems to us, just causes), and for a while it appeared that the separated employee might file a suit, which, though frivolous, would have been expensive and time-consuming to defend. One day her lawyer sat our friend down and took her through the routine she *must* follow, he said, in order to avoid such eventualities in the future. It turned out that if she followed through exactly, she would have to accumulate an FBI-like dossier on each of her people. She refused flatly, because to do so would be in complete contradiction to the people-oriented philosophy behind her fine and spirited (and profitable) business. "I'd rather be sued and lose than become an undercover agent spying on our people" was her conclusion. And it took guts.

## Control Is Not a Form: Some Questions—and Things to Do Now

• Anti-Mickey Mouse Brigade I: This afternoon or tomorrow stop in on a first-line person (this will take about one-half hour). Ask him or her what the dumbest form/dumbest rule/dumbest report/biggest minor irritant is in the daily routine. What are you going to *do* about it? (Can you get rid of it/revise it on the spot? You likely can.) Repeat the exercise once per week for ten weeks. Repeat once per month—forever. Have your assistants (and/or your secretary) do the same thing (and perhaps empower them to act on what they find). Variations: Purposefully mix visits to more senior first-line people and to the most junior (week 1, 2 or 3 impressions are invaluable). Try it outside your area of responsibility—you and a colleague supervisor (or VP) can probe each other's area usefully.

Report on it: Post a big scoreboard on "Mickey Mouse removed." How about an anti-Mickey Mouse Hall of Fame for those who remove the "dumbest rule/form/etc."—best (i.e., worst) of the month, year. Blue ribbon, red ribbon, gold awards for ten forms demolished, silver for five. And a meeting with the president for twenty-five! (Why not?)

• Anti-Mickey Mouse Brigade II: Repeat the above with a team focus: e.g., get teams together to decide on the "three dumbest and most amazing rules." Etc. (Our experience shows this *does* work. First-line people have an acute and fair sense of what's needed and what's not, and will rarely propose removal of useful rules/forms, unless we've been keeping them in the dark and not telling them what we're up to in the first place.)

Caveat: This process *will* work. Beware. It snowballs. If you're not serious, you will be overwhelmed. Backing off is high hypocrisy.

• Report in the Annual Report—quantitatively—on progress made in debureaucratizing!

• Consider replacing a large share of your precedure books with "best practices" books. Or highlighting a strategic program (à la Milliken) with a "significant recent wins" book.

• Pencil in 10 percent of your calendar time to work directly on anti-Mickey Mouse activities. Do *two* things *today*. Do *two* things tomorrow. Do a minimum of five this week.

## What Gets in the Way:
### Staff Size, Layers

One of the regular rejoinders we get to all this is, "I'm really a good guy. We do all this Mickey Mouse only because the EEO or OSHA requires it." But the fact is that while the EEO, OSHA and others *do* obligate us to do some reporting, our overzealous, overstaffed middle managements tend typically to take a fairly simple request for a report and turn it into a 97-line requirement for information from all the company's operating units. And another fact is that you can invariably (and this is said after four years' experience in Washington) drive a Mack truck through any regulation. Yes, *something* is required, but seldom what staffers, justifying their existence as "OSHA experts," tell us is required.

The most important deterrent to debureaucratizing is often simply the layers of staff that get in the way. Moreover—worst of all—it's the layers of *intelligent* staff. One division general manager of a smaller concern notes: "The problem is, the [central] staff guys are *smart*. If they were dumb, and if they asked dumb questions, we could ignore them. But they're smart, and they ask smart questions, smart questions that can tie us up for days, if not weeks and months. And if it were just one request, that would be fine, but it's multiple staffs, with multiple centers of intelligence, asking multiple series of smart questions that really keep us from getting the job done." Every line on every form and every form itself has a "champion" just as tenacious as any "product champion," who believes that life itself revolves around that particular packet of data.

There is, then, a lot that can be said for simply cutting staff. We find so many companies that do so much better with so many fewer people. Our journey through the terrible recession of 1981–83 was peppered with stories of company presidents who had cut their staffs, often by up to 80 percent. The only noticable difference in output, they'd tell us time and again, was *better* staff work. Said one, "I went to every management development course that came along. It seemed that each one would encourage me to add a specialist to help me with some task at which I was deficient. My dad, a wise soul who had founded the company, shook his head every time I'd add another one. Brother, was he right. We find that we're living a lot better— more effectively as well as more efficiently—without seventy-five percent of them."

The other piece of improvement is fewer layers. It makes decision-making simpler and faster. But a word of warning: Right after a reduction in layers too much will be bucked upstairs for decisions. You'll be appalled. But if you have the guts to refuse to decide—i.e., the guts to buck the decisions right back down—the system will soon learn that you are serious. The prime benefit of flat organizations is what we call their "self-defense" properties. That is, *none* of us is smart enough to keep our hands out of our subordinates' business. But if the span is wide (at least twice as wide as you think wise is a good rule of thumb), then you simply don't have enough hours to interfere, though most of us try desperately to do so at first. Flat structure, in a word, automatically breeds ownership, whether you like it or not. "But what if 'they' aren't ready?" We dealt with that one in the preceding chapter. They usually are—and in any case in the flat organizations your role shifts dramatically from monitor/decider to coach/teacher/developer (see chapter 18). The issue, it turns out, is this: Are *you* ready? Because your new number one

objective—like it or not—*must* be getting "them" ready once you've decided
to make your move.

---

### "Upside Down" or "Right Side Up"?

How do you draw your organization chart (if you feel you must have
one)? "Right side up?" or "upside down?" "Huh?" you ask. Look at this
one:

> ## CUSTOMERS

> First-line people who design, make, sell and
> service products for customers.

> First-line people in direct support of first-
> line people who support customers.

> Other

An "upside down" organization chart, to be sure. "No," screams Ren
McPherson (we can still hear the echo in our ears). "The other
[standard] one's 'upside down.' This one's 'right side up.'" McPherson
introduced us to the reversed chart. He used it at Dana. We've since
come across them at Wal-Mart, Nordstrom and SAS, all fine
performers.

The "reverse" chart is a simple depiction of business success. The
customer comes first. Our first-line people in line functions who support
him come next. Below them come first-line people in support functions
(MIS, accounting, personnel). Finally management (called "other"
here).

We don't necessarily suggest you adopt some version of this chart.
To do so willy-nilly could be gimmickry of the worst sort. The four

companies we mentioned live for their customers and first-line people; given that, the chart is a fine confirmation and reinforcement.

The few illustrations we provide aren't meant to serve as specific advice for anyone. But they *do* suggest that there are *radically* different approaches to organizing—i.e., more than one way to skin a cat. In *In Search of Excellence* it is noted that Ren McPherson had been able to reduce the corporate staff at Dana from 600 to 150 while the company was simultaneously growing from $1 billion to $3 billion. In 1984, several years after his departure, the staff is down to the low eighties, and the layers of management, which he reduced from eleven to five, remains at five. Similarly, *The Winning Streak* reports that British Steel's then Chairman Ian MacGregor began his realignment efforts there by cutting central staff from over 1,000 to 170, and moving them from a "Taj Mahal" in London to a very modest situation.

But let's take an even more extreme example: Mars, Inc., is a complex business: sixty divisions, almost two-thirds of its sales overseas. Divisions are allowed to compete openly with one another. Moreover, each one of those sixty divisions faces tough outside competitors. In other words, it's a prototypical multi-industry, multisegment, multiproduct, multinational enterprise. It's a clear case, in a characteristically low-margin business, of a situation commonly believed to require strong centralized control—"checkers checking checkers," as a frustrated chemical-company colleague puts it. Yet somehow Mars runs a highly profitable $6 billion enterprise with a corporate staff of just twenty officers and twenty secretaries (in a nondescript building without a sign on it, at the end of a road that you can barely find *with* a map, in McLean, Virginia).

Or, yes, an even *more* extreme example: Nucor Steel, based in Charlotte, North Carolina. Chairman Ken Iverson manages to run a $552 million company (as of 1984—with a five-year return on shareholder's equity of over 23 percent) with a corporate staff, including secretaries, of less than a *dozen!* And make no bones about it, Iverson sees his lean form as perhaps his most vital strategic weapon. He was asked a while back what he could do if he were called upon to run one of the giant steel companies. His immediate response: "The biggest hurdle would not be the union. It would be the management with its deeply ingrained method of operation—all those layers. You'd have to tear it all apart and start over again."

Part of the issue *is* sheer numbers. Mars, Nucor, Dana et al. have fewer people on their staffs. But numbers may be a less significant part of it. At least as important is *where* these staff people are. At Dana, for instance, very few of the victims of the reduction from six-hundred to eighty-five were laid off. Instead, they were given the opportunity to go to where the action was—to the plants. Mars doesn't necessarily have fewer accountants per dollar of revenue. The accountants are where they can best support the company as businesspersons—in the plants, in the small divisions. A funny (nice) thing happens. Remember one of our themes: "All people as business people." Accountants (lawyers, etc.) *can* learn to act as members of a profit-making team, not just as referees or cops. A senior controller in retailing was able to get about 75 percent of his people out of corporate headquarters. "Time and again," he said, "I would send them out to the field for close to permanent duty, as part of a 30- or 40-person profit-making team. Once they became full-scale members of the team, and I made it clear that the primary dimension of their evaluation would come from what that profit-center boss thought of them, then suddenly they became business people—not just 'accountants.'"

All this is easier said than done, of course. In headquarters-focused companies, the sole objective is to reduce the number of feet between you and the chairman. Most big companies, sadly, fall into this category. Decentralizing only works effectively—and attracts the best people to the field—when the reward system (e.g., subsequent promotions) starts to say "to be in the boondocks is to win." At HP, Citicorp, GE (today, under Jack Welch), the unmistakable be-all and end-all is creating "wins" as far from headquarters as possible. And implicit in this fact is a reward structure based on "good deeds performed," wherever, rather than "a good presence" close to headquarters.

---

### Staff as Support

January 1, 1984, was independence day for seven regional companies—the remnants of the Bell System. One, say most experts as of the end of 1984, has fared better than the rest (though most have done well): U.S. West, the Denver-based regional.

Above all, it's said, U.S. West is more aggressive, more entrepreneurial. We know at least one reason for it. Each of the seven regions (which made up the twenty-two former operating companies of the Bell System) got a "bonus" upon formation: 3,000 central-staff people from the old AT&T central apparatus. Most organized them as AT&T had, as centralized operations. U.S. West did not. It stuck by CEO Jack McAllister's "rule of 100." The staff of U.S. West would not exceed 100, period. Such an iron law was mandatory, he felt, to induce the decentralized entrepreneurship he cherished.

So what do you do with the other 2,900? The answer was simple (to McAllister). Form a wholly owned support subsidiary consisting of the 2,900. Moreover, keep the U.S. West central staff out of the act. Have the subsidiary chaired (on a rotating basis) by the head of one of the three decentralized operating companies that the 2,900 are designed to support (the other two operating company heads constitute the rest of the "board"). Thus McAllister took a giant step toward (1) enhancing incipient but fragile entrepreneurship (by keeping the central staff very lean—100 for a $10 billion business) and (2) putting support people in clear support of those whom they are supposed to support (the three line operating companies). So simple. So rare.

### "Staffs"/"Layers":
### Some Questions—and Things to Do Now

• We don't want to suggest a "study" on optimal staff size. You will do what is appropriate when you think it necessary. We would suggest a "pre-first step." Become a student of spans of control and staff size. Seek out some organization in your industry (and outside it) known for especially lean staffs and flat organizations. Visit them, see how they survive. Try to begin to observe other ways of life. This is a big deal. It's worth your investment.

• Consider relocation of staff, even on a temporary basis. Check back in your experience to times when "staffies" have been assigned as full-time members of business-unit teams, with evaluation coming from the business-unit leader. Did it affect their behavior? Did they become more "business-oriented"? If so, as we suspect you'll find, consider an experiment with several accountants, etc., going out to a field unit (under the field leader's control) for three to nine months. Revisit the results and consider more sweeping changes.

---

## Pulling It Together:
## Pockets of Excellence

And if I'm not chairman or division general manager? Or even if . . . ? This is a book for chief executives and a book for first-line supervisors. It is a book for Fortune 100 executives. And for those who run garages and corner stores. The two strategic distinctions—superior customer service/product and constant innovation—are the key for CEO and supervisor. What makes his or her outfit unique on these dimensions is a valid question for Chairman Jack Welch of GE, Stew Leonard of Stew Leonard's and the head of an accounts-receivable section in a $20 million division of a $100 million company. The lessons of leadership are available to anyone and amenable to instant action.

So—if you're not chairman, we suggest subversive acts. Don't answer the mail from headquarters. It works! The logic is this: if we are even half right when it comes to the power unleashed via ownership (see chapter 14), then giving people in your unit some room will likely—and quickly—result in substantial improvement in performance. It's your best defense. People with the best store, sales branch, department, crew are seldom fired for lousy paperwork. Ren McPherson said of his own odd practices on the way up: "I came close to being fired six times [the first time for sharing results—e.g. profitability numbers—with all the people in his plant, at the time an unheard-of act of ownership enhancement]. But when they came right down to it, they had a tough time firing the fellow with the top performing outfit." A former IBMer, then a market forecaster, tells another story that's apropos: "One Sunday I was doing some repair projects around the house when it occurred to me that most of the people providing me with data were subsequently not promoted, or left. The best seldom answered my queries. I talked to my boss about it the next day, and he replied, 'Of course. To get to the top of the heap, they [the best] spend more time with customers and have little patience with bureaucracy. Once they are on top of the heap we're hardly going to ding them, except perfunctorily, for tardy paperwork. Only the marginal ones, scared for their jobs, are slavish devotees of requests from headquarters. They're petrified of accumulating the tiniest black mark."

---

### Oil or Paper?

A colleague in Kuala Lumpur reports on a bureaucratic insurrection. Years ago the head of Royal Dutch/Shell Malaysia had had enough. He gathered up a vast stock of requests sent out to him by Shell headquarters. He knew the board was meeting in The Hague. He hopped a flight and went there unannounced—highly irregular behavior in general, and even more irregular given the staid nature of that board. He arrived at the meeting, and, for all practical purposes, barged in. He opened the suitcase on the spotless, orderly table and dumped out thirty pounds of forms, asking as he did so, "Do you want me to fill these out or hunt for oil?" We have no report of the immediate reply. However, we do know that the Malaysian boss did go on to head the Royal Dutch/Shell Group, and to lead it through a necessary and profitable overhaul.

---

Insurrections don't always lead to eventual promotion to the top. But they surely can lead to a dramatic performance improvement in a part of the organization. Our evidence is clear. Even if the company is not an exciting one, we observe *pockets of excellence*. Excellence is what you, the supervisor (or vice president), create on your turf. We see great factories in rotten manufacturing companies, super buyer areas and great stores in moribund retailing establishments, a fine and aggressive specialist/lending operation in an unduly conservative bank. It can be done and it is done. The principal tools are the small win—semi-surreptitious creation of Indianapolises à la Sam Neaman, or Westborough, Massachusetts, basement bunches à la Tom West's Data General skunkwork in *The Soul of a New Machine*; and debureaucratizing—creating a void in an otherwise oppressive and constricted system.

In this we are *not* Pollyannas. The fact that your store (or department within a store) is great does not mean the qualities that make it so will spread to the rest of the company. Major overall corporate transformations tend to be top-down, not bottom-up. But that is no excuse for not getting on with it among your people.

---

### Small Win as Demonstration

"It's so tough to convince top management of the rightness of the 'new way' [Whatever it is]." Top management got there through pragmatism. Logic will seldom be decisive to them, even yours. Demonstration may be. A small win is a demonstration. Don't fight City Hall! Do it. Demonstrate it. (Via your own Indianapolis.) We don't believe in fighting, especially old pros. We do believe in the process of demonstrating that alternatives are possible.

There is one guaranteed "win" from all this: you'll feel better about yourself! Serving customers, innovating, celebrating, inducing ownership and local heroism through a string of small wins and by cutting out the Mickey Mouse is likely to be a damn sight more satisfying than being a "good steward" of one part of an aging and stultified bureaucracy. We think it's important to picture yourself looking in the mirror at age fifty (or thirty-five, or sixty). What will you see? "A good steward"? One who "did his forms well and made good presentations"? Or something a little more exciting?

We dwell on this last point because of a sense of sadness. We recently ran into an executive vice president of a $10 billion company. This fellow ran a $3.5 billion portion of it. And yet his direct response to our remarks was, "But *I* can't do anything. The chairman is flatly opposed to most of the things you speak about." Had it been the first time it had happened, we could have written it off. But it was more like the forty-first.* How sad! *Not* "how sad that the chairman opposes." But "how sad that this fellow [in his mid-fifties] *perceives* that he can't do anything about it." Perhaps pitiful is a better if harsher term. (And then there is the chairman who can't do "it" because of the government, the securities analysts or the board.)

It *can* be done. Mayor Schaefer has done it with a city. Bill Creech did it in the Air Force. Phil Staley did it with an old Ford plant. And the accountant we described on p. 256 did it with an accounts-receivable section in a stodgy company.

---

*Two of the saddest came from the public sector. Both concerned MBWA. A city manager of a town of 500,000 said, "The supervisors would think I'd lost my marbles [if I spent 50 percent of my time doing MBWA]." We referred him to the actions of Mayor Schaefer of Baltimore. A county school superintendent uttered virtually the same words, suggesting painful consequences from the reaction of his board if he were to start wandering the schools.

# 18

## Coaching

*Virtually every day, a couple of the engineers in my section get calls from competitors inviting them out to lunch to talk about their futures. A key aspect to my job, obviously, is to keep this group motivated, enthusiastic. . . . The best managers are the ones whose people want to get up in the morning and work for them. The secret is making it clear to your people that you care, that you're really interested in them as individuals. They need to know that you appreciate their efforts and that their accomplishments are recognized.*
　　*—Hewlett-Packard Research & Development section manager*

*Perhaps if there has been one failing within our organization over the years, it is that we haven't tried to dispel the notion that our success comes out of a computer. It doesn't. It comes out of the sweat glands of our coaches and players.*
　　*—Tom Landry, head coach, Dallas Cowboys*

*Has the leader a right to mold and shape? Of what use is aging, experience, and wisdom if not to be the leaven for those who are younger? Of what use is pain if not to teach others to avoid it? The leader not only has the right; if he is a leader, he has the obligation.*
　　*—Harry Levinson, The Exceptional Executive*

THERE IS NO MAGIC: only people who find and nurture champions, dramatize company goals and direction, build skills and teams, spread irresistible enthusiasm. They are cheerleaders, coaches, storytellers and wanderers. They encourage, excite, teach, listen, facilitate. Their actions are consistent. Only brute consistency breeds believability: they say people are special and they treat them that way—always. You know they take their priorities seriously because they live them clearly and visibly: they walk the talk.

The trick is demonstrating to people, every day, where you want to take your organization. It begins with a shared understanding of purpose, made real and tangible through consistent "mundane" actions. It's being amazingly consistent that counts, ignoring the charge (which will be leveled) that you are a broken record. Some of the brightest and best-trained managers we know miss the boat entirely on this score. Once they've said it, they've said it, is their feeling. But the only thing that convinces people that you really care, that you take personally your commitment to them, is unflagging consistency. And it is a commitment: for instance, virtually all the best-performing organizations believe in promotion from within their own ranks. At the 275-store Publix SuperMarkets chain everyone on the retail side of the business (including the company's officers) started his or her career bagging groceries.

Fine performance comes from people at all levels who pay close attention to their environment, communicate unshakable core values, and patiently develop the skills that will enable them to make sustained contributions to their organizations. *In a word, it recasts the detached, analytical manager as the dedicated, enthusiastic coach.*

Coaching is face-to-face leadership that pulls together people with diverse backgrounds, talents, experiences and interests, encourages them to step up to responsibility and continued achievement, and treats them as full-scale

"I understand you've learned some new tricks
since you were here last."

•   •   •

Drawing by C. Barsotti; © 1981
The New Yorker Magazine, Inc.

partners and contributors. Coaching is not about memorizing techniques or devising the perfect game plan. It is about really paying attention to people—really believing them, really caring about them, really involving them. New Orleans Saints coach Bum Phillips observes: "The main thing is getting people to *play*. When you think it's your system that's winning, you're in for a damn big surprise. It's those players' efforts."

To coach is largely to facilitate, which literally means "to make easy"—not less demanding, less interesting or less intense, but less discouraging, less bound up with excessive controls and complications. A coach/facilitator works tirelessly to free the team from needless restrictions on performance, even when they are self-imposed.

In these next few pages we will talk about some of the most vital aspects of coaching: visibility, listening, limit-setting, value-shaping, skill-stretching. To develop one's skill in these areas is not easy; it does not often come naturally and must be worked at. But, oh, the rewards that can follow! Think back on your career, starting as far back as elementary school. Almost all of us can name a handful (but only a handful) of superior coaches—teachers, sports or nonsports activity leaders, bosses—who have contributed disproportionately to our development, almost as if they had laid a magic hand on you. They drew from within you a best that you couldn't have conceived of.

Tom remembers two such people. The first was Ned Harkness, who led almost anti-athletics Rensselaer Polytechnic Institute to NCAA titles in hockey and lacrosse. He became Tom's lacrosse coach at Cornell after the tragic death of the former head coach. Tom had played the sport, as all good Baltimoreans do, since age six. Yet his skill grew more under Harkness in a week or two than it had in the prior decade. Harkness knew his stuff—was technically commanding. But much more important, he instinctively (it seemed) knew his players' limits. He pulled you to those limits (which in Tom's case were well short of stardom) and beyond, but never pushed you to discouragement. And, above all, you knew he cared, cared individually about what was going on in your head as you faced tiny (and not so tiny) defeats and exhaustion, as well as occasional victory.

Tom's other all-star coach was Dick Anderson, captain of a Navy Seabee (construction) batallion to which Tom was assigned as an ensign in 1966. Again, the result was the same: almost instant growth and flowering. Dick was a demanding taskmaster (all the best coaches are), but he was demanding because he cared (you could feel it and smell it) and because he was hell-bent on cajoling the best from you, a best you didn't even know you had. Also, as in the Harkness case, he had a fine sense of limits. He pushed and nudged, and occasionally ranted and raved. But just as zealously he guarded you against a big fall and religiously avoided pushing you too far.

Moreover, when his somewhat irreverent charge (Tom) would run afoul of those above him, Anderson, an avowed breeder of skunklike instincts, would be there, quick as a wink, to protect him vigorously from the bureaucrats above (and then he'd chew Tom out unmercifully in private for having played his hand so awkwardly).

## The Manager as Teacher

The Center for Creative Leadership in Greensboro, North Carolina, has long been associated with emerging perspectives on the subject of leadership. As part of the Center's Research Sponsor Program, successful managers were asked to talk about their best teachers. In most cases, they turned out to be a former boss. The following were the most frequently mentioned characteristics of these managers-as-teachers.

• They counseled. *They gave younger managers constructive advice and feedback. They used younger managers as sounding boards.*

• They excelled. *Whether in finance, production or marketing, these managers were the best in some aspect of their business.*

• They gave exposure. *They made sure that the work and accomplishments of young managers were seen. They opened doors for them.*

• They provided latitude. *They gave young managers the freedom to try, the courage to fail. They involved them in important tasks.*

• They were tough taskmasters. *They challenged; they demanded excellence.*

Nancy encountered her first bona fide coach shortly after her college graduation, in an unlikely setting. Robert Liberman, a research psychiatrist who ran a unique and innovative treatment center in California, was Nancy's first boss when she was a member of his research team. Bob was, above all, a superb teacher. A soft-spoken man, he never ranted or raved, but made his presence felt quietly and always supportively. He particularly urged people to reach for "firsts"—acting on a new idea, writing a difficult article, organizing and leading new staff-training programs, working with a new patient—and devoted enough time, usually daily, to make sure that the "first" wouldn't be the last. If a staff member doubted his or her ability to work successfully with a new patient, Liberman would take the time to sit down with him or her and rehearse the first meeting in detail, asking questions, encouraging, nudging, listening, even role-playing the part of the patient. When that first meeting finally came, he would show up just before, to offer a word or two of encouragement, and again after, to ask how things had gone, and to spend time debriefing the meeting if the staff member wanted him to. He had the gift of being around when you needed his help the most—and not around when you needed to go it on your own. He was a master momentum-maker.

It's because of the profound effect of these coaches on our lives, and the profound effect our research suggests great coaches can have on organizations as well as individuals, that we will push you to examine this topic with us. It may seem that coaches can have but a tiny number of charges or protégés, but, surprisingly, they have the ability to affect many people. A few years back, Tom was with a group of about twenty-five McKinsey partners from all over the world. They were being led through an exercise to identify top coaches in their McKinsey careers. The number who identified the same two or three people, in this 1,000-consultant, 175-partner operation, was startling. Just a few had affected so many, often in the deepest ways.

## Coaching by Wandering Around

At Herman Miller, the superb office furniture company, there's a term called "roving leadership." Chairman Max DePree describes roving leaders as "those indispensable people in our lives who are there when we need them." DePree goes on: "Roving leadership is the expression of the ability of hierarchical leaders to permit others to share ownership of problems—in effect, to take possession of a situation. It demands that we be enablers of each other." Coaching is the process of enabling others to act, of building on their strengths. It's counting on other people to use their own special skill and competence, and then giving them enough room and enough time to do it.

Coaching at its heart involves caring enough about people to take the time to build a personal relationship with them. Easy to say, tough to do. Relationships depend on contact. No contact, no relationship. The best coaches know this: they lavish time and attention (occasionally to their personal detriment)—time and attention that others never quite get around to spending on a consistent basis—on people. They also make sure people see enough of one another to impart a vital sense of continuity, momentum and urgency, and to focus attention on the long term. They find reasons every day to get the whole team together—hundreds at times, à la Kelly Johnson or Gerhard Neumann—and to underscore the point that "we're all in this together for the long run, so we damn well better do what we can to help each other out." Armchair coaches and Monday-morning quarterbacks, on the other hand, wait until the opponent has scored and only 37 seconds remain on the clock before they step in or get people together. But by then it's too late. Coaching is a real-time endeavor. Former Purdue football coach Alex Agase puts it this way: "If you really want to advise me, do it on Saturday afternoon between one and four o'clock. And you've got twenty-five seconds to do it, between plays. Not on Monday. I know the right thing to do on Monday."

You have to be there when games are played, and the only way to do that is to do it. Plan to spend the lion's share of your time out of your office, not behind your desk. Show up in your team's floor space. Better yet, move your desk there. That's what all Milliken bosses, up to and including division presidents, are encouraged, none too gently, to do. Listen. Spread rampant enthusiasm and pride. Encourage tries. Get the whole group together often—say, every day.

Participating directly—seeing with your own eyes and hearing with your own ears—is simply the only thing that yields the unfiltered, richly detailed impressions that tell you how things are really going, that give you the minute-to-minute opportunities to take another couple of steps toward building trust, toward making room for people to innovate and to contribute, and toward making your strategic priorities clear. It's the awesome power of personal attention, and it is communicated in one way only: physical presence.

Coaching is tough-minded. It's nurturing and bringing out the best; it's demanding that the team play as a team. And should it finally become clear that there are prima donnas who won't forgo the "I" in favor of "we," you have to handle that one, too—by letting them go. The chairman of a giant, multidivisional aerospace company that manufactures integrated systems made it clear that divisions must cooperate if long-term customer relations were to be maintained. The boss of his most profitable division retorted that the top spot on the short-term dollar scorecard protected him against all the "'Love thy neighbor' bullshit," as he ungently put it. The chairman had had enough. The fellow was sacked, and given less than twenty-four hours to be off the premises.

## Coaching, Contribution and Career Mazes

Coaching goes far beyond the short-term need to help someone learn the mechanics of preparing a budget and selling a proposal up. It is the principal means through which people learn what makes their organization tick, what it stands for, and how they can contribute to it over time. *Perhaps surprisingly, the more elbowroom a company grants to its people, the more important on-the-job coaching becomes.* Hewlett-Packard, W. L. Gore & Associates and People Express have crafted distinctive environments that do without the traditional "career path" structures found elsewhere. In these organizations we find instead "career mazes"—loosely defined hierarchies and wide-open fields of opportunity for people to develop skills, contribute directly and receive recognition. Such companies demand that people focus not so much on the climb to the top, and encourage them instead to keep their eyes on making a sustained personal contribution to producing, selling or servicing products, and to building the spirit and commitment of all hands—and this holds for people at all stages of their careers and in every job category. A middle manager in Hewlett-Packard's oldest manufacturing division describes the difference in focus: "I'd been managing a fifty-person department for about a year, and I was thinking about my next step. I'd just turned thirty; a lot of my friends from school were running bigger operations in their companies. I think I'm as capable as they are, and I guess it started to bother me. So the next time I saw my boss I told him about my concerns, asked him what I could do to move up. He thought about it for a minute, and his answer surprised me. He smiled and said, "What's your hurry? The best way to move up here is to do the best you can with the job you've got. I know it takes time to get used to the way we do things here, but trust us a little bit. Pay attention to how you can contribute now; have fun! That's the way people move up.' And the funny thing is, he was right. I realized he always took the time to lend a hand, help me out. In fact, everyone seemed to be aware of what I was working on, how I was contributing. HP just takes a real interest in people. They assume you're here for the long run, and they personally give you the help and feedback you need. They don't leave it to somebody else."

## Coaching as Value-shaping

Every coach, at every level, is above all a value-shaper. The value-shaper not only brings company philosophy to life by paying extraordinary attention to communicating and symbolizing it, he or she also helps newcomers understand how shared company values affect individual performance.

### Shaping Values

Effective shared values are a well from which come leadership and the ways customers and colleagues appraise your company and its products and services.

Johnson & Johnson articulates its business principles in a document called "Our Credo," reproduced on page 332. It clearly sets out the company's responsibility to customers, employees, communities and stockholders. First given to employees in 1947, these guiding principles have been renewed over the years, in part through Credo Challenge meetings. Chairman Jim Burke comments:

> A generation later, in 1975, some of us became concerned as to whether, in fact, we were *practicing* what we preached.
> ⋅ We had become a large and complex corporation, with well over 100 companies around the world, each with its own separate mission. In corporate headquarters we were concerned that the Credo perhaps had greater meaning to us than to those who were ultimately responsible for managing our various businesses around the world.
> So we tried an experiment. We invited twenty-four of our managers from the United States and overseas here for a meeting to challenge the Credo. I opened the meeting with the observation that the document was hanging in most of our offices around the world. If we were not committed to it, it was an act of pretension and ought to be ripped off the walls. I challenged the group to recommend whether we should get rid of it, rewrite it, or commit to it as is. The meeting was a turn-on, a genuine happening, as these managers struggled with the issues that the Credo defined. What we discovered was that we had a set of guiding principles far more powerful than we had imagined.
> This was the beginning of a series of Credo Challenge meetings to include all of our key management from around the world. Dave Clare, our president, and I chaired these sessions over the next three years. The basic philosophy is unchanged. Many words stayed the same; others were changed substantively, some just modernized. Some of the respon-

sibilities were expanded to take cognizance of a much more complicated world.

[Then, on September 29, 1982], . . . we learned with a terrifying suddenness that inexplicably someone had chosen one of our products—Tylenol—as a murder weapon. Thus began what was to become for us an unremitting nightmare, and one that required literally dozens of people to make hundreds of decisions in painfuly short periods of time. Even when we had time for careful consideration, most of our decisions were complicated, involving considerable risk, and we had no historical precedent to rely on.

As you know, we have received much praise for our handling of the "Tylenol Affair." Certainly we are proud of the heroic job done by our people at McNeil Consumer Products and all of those from their sister companies who worked so tirelessly to help them during those difficult weeks. However, all of us at McNeil Consumer Products and Johnson & Johnson truly believe that the guidance of the Credo played the most important role in our decision-making. Ask yourselves, with a statement like that, if we had any alternative but to do what we did during the Tylenol tragedy. Ask yourselves how the Tylenol consumer, the Johnson & Johnson employee, the public, the stockholder would have felt. What would your attitude today be toward Johnson & Johnson if we hadn't behaved the way we did?

And, of course, the important thing that the Tylenol affair reaffirmed is the intrinsic fairness of the American public. A remarkable poll by the Roper organization taken three months after the tragedy showed 93 percent of the public felt Johnson & Johnson handled its responsibility either very well or fairly well. *But* the public also gave very high marks to the Food and Drug Administration, the law enforcement agencies, the drug industry in general, *and* the media! The public knew that all of these institutions were working—together—and in their interest! And what did *our* customers do? They gave us back our business. A year ago tonight we had but a fraction left of one of the most valuable consumer franchises ever built. Our latest Nielsen, taken in July–August [1983] shows Tylenol has regained over 90 percent of the business we enjoyed prior to the tragedies.

Burke's words are exhilarating—to us. To many they will seem like flowery nonsense. "Surely," many (most?) say, "there's more to J&J than that." There is—and there isn't. Yes, J&J has a structure (albeit a very loose one) and tough reporting standards. Yet J&J *is* that Credo. We have gone out of our way to corroborate the Tylenol story, talking to media investigators who were on the scene, lawyers, lower-level J&J employees. All had been impressed by the strength of the institution (though it was devastated by the tragedy per se). "Seeing" a value live—at J&J, IBM, People Express, Apple, HP, Gore—is remarkable, yet will always remain impossible for the skeptic and cynic.

# Our Credo

We believe our first responsibility is to the doctors, nurses and patients,
to mothers and all others who use our products and services.
In meeting their needs everything we do must be of high quality.
We must constantly strive to reduce our costs
in order to maintain reasonable prices.
Customers' orders must be serviced promptly and accurately.
Our suppliers and distributors must have an opportunity
to make a fair profit.

We are responsible to our employees,
the men and women who work with us throughout the world.
Everyone must be considered as an individual.
We must respect their dignity and recognize their merit.
They must have a sense of security in their jobs.
Compensation must be fair and adequate,
and working conditions clean, orderly and safe.
Employees must feel free to make suggestions and complaints.
There must be equal opportunity for employment, development
and advancement for those qualified.
We must provide competent management,
and their actions must be just and ethical.

We are responsible to the communities in which we live and work
and to the world community as well.
We must be good citizens — support good works and charities
and bear our fair share of taxes.
We must encourage civic improvements and better health and education.
We must maintain in good order
the property we are privileged to use,
protecting the environment and natural resources.

Our final responsibility is to our stockholders.
Business must make a sound profit.
We must experiment with new ideas.
Research must be carried on, innovative programs developed
and mistakes paid for.
New equipment must be purchased, new facilities provided
and new products launched.
Reserves must be created to provide for adverse times.
When we operate according to these principles,
the stockholders should realize a fair return.

*Johnson & Johnson*

## Look in the Mirror First

How can you reduce the risk that your actions contradict your stated values? The first step (again and again) is to appraise honestly and critically the way you spend your time. This theme pervades every chapter in this book. We revisit it here because coaching is made up of actions, not words. You will unfailingly see your behavior reflected in that of your team: they *see* what's really important to you. Look for the *tiniest* inconsistencies (the tiniest are the *most* important, it turns out): Do you sit in your office talking about quality, yet spend the bulk of your time on factory visits reviewing inventory levels? Take an unflinching look at what your calendar says about what really matters to you. Like it or not, that's the sincerest—and only—measure. And the reason (again, it's absolutely vital to the whole issue of leadership) is this: any closely held value, no matter how well concealed (even from yourself), inevitably prompts action that is consistent with it, because *all* your people are boss watchers, boss students, boss anthropologists of the first order. If you say innovation is important but you don't tolerate the minor missteps that inevitably go hand in glove with innovation, your true priority will be as evident as if it were emblazoned on banners and streamers. If you preach trust but impose demeaning limits on purchasing authority—e.g., the ability to buy office supplies or the $8.95 bucket of paint—your people get the message in a flash.

Take the time to judge how well your hard work furthers your company's core values and expresses your beliefs. (And we do mean *hard* work. Almost all managers *do* work hard. Few are slothful in our experience. Yet most squander their effort through inconsistency.) Look for the ways you trip yourself up—how you get in your own way without meaning to. It will help you anticipate where problems and setbacks will likely occur in the coaching process.

## Doing the Right Thing: Trust and Integrity

*Shaping values for others means attaching more importance to integrity than skill:* even if people don't know exactly how to do something, if they do know precisely where their bosses (and their company) are coming from, they can rely on *themselves* (and you can rely on them) to affirm that direction in day-to-day activity. Trust (proffered by one's own boss) and integrity of vision is learned only by example, not from procedure manuals, training courses or Labor Day speeches. It's learned when the off-hours chatter, belly up to the bar, reflects the same respect for the individual as the carefully crafted speech. Effective value-shapers protect their company's integrity at all costs, at all times. They are unmerciful when it is betrayed. Yet the hardest part is mustering the courage to give others a chance to "do the right thing" in the first place. *If* you've communicated shared values, acted consistently, *and* provided training and coaching, you won't need to intervene so often to "fix" things. Your people will keep their promises *if* you keep yours.

Where we find integrity and trust, we also find aggressive cooperation. The best coaches spend as much time developing the team's ability to believe in what each member can contribute as they do working with individual players. It sets the tone for the way people should aim to work together, and trust evolves in the process. When everyone is headed in the same direction, there's every reason for team members to trust one another, every reason to anticipate innovative action and creativity.

### The Coach as Storyteller

Nothing reveals more of what a company really cares about than its stories and legends—i.e., its folk wisdom. We've seen (in chapter 16) that leaders use stories to persuade, symbolize and guide day-to-day actions; there's simply nothing better than a story to tell people what they really want to know about "how things work around here," or to illustrate the right thing to do in a given situation. They can lend believability and impact to a company's philosophy (in fact, they are almost the only routes to believability)—they will highlight, with lightning speed, any gaps between what a company says it values and what it actually holds dear. That is, you are simply as good or as bad, as consistent or as inconsistent, as your stories. You can like that or not. You can ignore it or manage and guide it. But it *is* a fact.

Stories engage. They help put current decisions and events into an overall framework that is readily understood, and they embellish a company philosophy in a unique way. The common memory created by swapping tales imparts a sense of tradition and continuity, and sparks interest as nothing else can. Listening to a company's stories is the surest route to determining its real priorities and who symbolizes them. At L. L. Bean and Nordstrom, the stories are about customer service. At Publix Super Markets and People Express they're about pride of ownership, and at Perdue Farms, Maytag and J. M. Smucker, about quality. Stories are a rich, colorful tapestry that illustrates what's most important to the organization; effective value-shapers use stories to convey the successes and the mistakes so that others can learn from them, and to build enthusiasm and involvement.

### Coaching Opportunities

#### One-Idea Club

Stew Leonard (of Stew Leonard's dairy store) solicits his people's ideas regularly. One unique way is via regular visits to competitors. There aren't many stores that compete with Stew across the board, but sometimes he will come across an interesting department like one of his (e.g., bakery goods), or an interesting store in another business (e.g., a florist). When he does, even if it's three hundred or four hundred miles away, he's likely to grab fifteen of his people (including hourly people, even very recent hires) and hop into the 15-person van that he uses for just such occasions.

Off they go to Stew's challenge to join the One-Idea Club. The issue? Who will be the first to come up with *one* new idea for Stew's gleaned from the competitor's outfit? Next, can *everyone* come up with at least one new idea? (It *must* be implementable immediately upon returning home.) That's almost all there is to it—but not quite. Even though Stew Leonard's is at the top of the heap, none of his travelers is allowed to talk about anything that Stew's does better than the competitor they're visiting. The point is for each person to find at least one thing that the competitor does better than Stew's. "It's so darned easy to fall into the trap," Stew says, "and grouse that 'Those guys don't know what they're doing with this, or that.' We have a rule. We just don't allow that. You should be able to find at least one thing that the competitor does better. Often as not it'll be a tiny thing. But that's the way *you* get better." The new ideas gleaned are communicated throughout the store in the company newsletter, *Stew's News.*

The parallel to Sam Neaman's routine is close. Keys include: self-analysis, hourly-person-as-expert, eyeball analysis, looking for the small and the immediately doable, a vehicle for swapping notes (the van ride in this instance), rules about the process (e.g., the "no derogation" rule), and an overall approach that is, again, guided autonomy. And it works!

---

What's Stew up to? He's teaching, leading, coaching. He's turning everyone into a fully empowered expert in retailing and competitive analysis, into an owner, into a winner, and into an enthusiast ("We can make it better" and "Wow!" are Stew's two favorite expressions).

Coaching isn't limited to what you personally teach. What can you lead your people to learn from customers, suppliers and colleagues in other parts of the company? How can you take advantage of day-to-day opportunities as part of your coaching game plan? The list below is a starting point:

—Have people regularly attend meetings they wouldn't ordinarily (e.g., concerning unfamiliar specialties—accountants to marketing and vice versa) to gain firsthand exposure to other colleagues' work.

—Start your own One Idea Club inside or outside the company.

—Have your team observe you in real time as you handle customer complaints, make formal presentations, wander around.

—Rotate people through other jobs and functions, with temporary—but real (i.e., having palpable output)—assignments; e.g., set an objective of having every team member able to perform everyone else's job.

—Encourage enrollment in continuing education programs and participation in your best internal training programs and classes; make sure implicit penalties for "being away from the job" are not levied.

—Have your people co-lead company courses and seminars.

—Spring for memberships in professional associations.

—Encourage people to make presentations on their projects inside and outside the company, especially to other functions and divisions.

—Get people to serve on temporary multifunction task forces (volunteer them to others, on a non-quid-pro-quo basis).

—Invite colleagues at all levels in other departments to spend time with your people to explain what they need from your group (and encourage them to invite your people to visit them).

—Follow Roger Milliken's example (see p. 266) and send one hundred fifty of your people, not just two or three, for the full ten days of a trade show.

—Invite someone from another department or company (e.g., a customer or vendor) to work in your department for a while.

Every opportunity to involve people in the business in its broadest sense is a coaching opportunity, and none is too small to overlook. If learning a new skill is important to your team's success, focus on it. Use every device you can think of to facilitate learning.

Caution: Most will not volunteer for out-of-sight assignments because they assume (stories, again) that out of sight is out of mind. Through your evaluation of your people and by seeding a few (positive) stories of your own, you must demonstrate by action that to engage in these nonroutine activities is a short- and long-term plus.

### Look in the Mirror Again

We told you this was important! A colleague says, "The best coaching opportunity is getting people involved with how you do your own job, showing them how what you do gets you a little further toward a goal. I had a boss once who used to set aside a little time every day for 'coaching.' He'd talk about the importance of quality, all the right things. But then he ran into trouble. As soon as he finished 'coaching,' he'd go back to 'doing his real job.' So if it was time to ship products, and if there was pressure to get the products out the door, he'd press to do it, even if the product was scratched or damaged. To him, 'coaching' and 'doing his job' were two different things. It didn't take us long to figure out what really mattered to him. He'd talk a great game, but the one he played was totally different. He couldn't understand why our product-quality record wasn't terrific, since he talked quality a lot. He didn't realize that we paid more attention to how he handled quality issues in his own job than to what he said in his 'coaching' sessions."

A familiar story, this. To your team, you are your enacted priorities, no more and no less. The mundane, minute-to-minute choices you make as you do your own job are the most powerful teachers. Your people won't miss a beat. So look in the mirror again. You are coaching all the time, like it or not; on and off the field you set the example that others will follow. Do you walk the talk?

---

### Leadership and Expertise

Leadership and expertise, or the perils of professional management. The boss of Domino's Pizza, Tom Monaghan, can flip a pizza with the best of them. Don Vlcek, president of Domino's Pizza Distribution Company (the dough providers), is a Grade A dough maker. David Ogilvy, throughout his career, would return to copywriting, and he's a fine writer. At the age of seventy-eight, McKinsey's legendary leader, Marvin Bower, is still a new-business generator—and per hour spent, there's none better (he recently brought GM into the fold). In a word, walking the talk is massively enhanced if you are "of the business," as a good friend puts it. Living the basic values—e.g., people, customers— does come first. But, frankly, it only becomes coherent and full of life for your people if you understand what the context is. "The astute professional manager can manage anything" has been the common litany. "Nuts," we say. "To know is to be credible" is more correct. But to know is *not* enough: supercoaches know the business—are expert— *and* live the more abstract values passionately. Neither is sufficient alone.

---

## Five Coaching Roles

How do you know what approach to take in coaching? What to emphasize? What to leave alone for the time being? Where do you start?

An HP marketing manager observes that "to coach well, you have to be flexible. What works with one person doesn't with someone else. It depends on knowing the person and understanding the situation." In short, sometimes coaching is not coaching but counseling, or sponsoring, or confronting, or educating.*

---

*We want to acknowledge Robert Dyer's pioneering work in this area, for contributing so much to our thinking on this subject, and for being one of the first to conceive of coaching as a collection of roles.

It's a paradox. Writer John McPhee observed of Deerfield's legendary headmaster Frank Boyden that his values were simple, yet it took a complex person to live simplicity in an ambiguous world. That is, the great coaches, as we've said, live simple values. But the art is to bring these simple values to life for each different person with whom one comes in contact and whom one attempts to influence.

### Educating, Sponsoring, Coaching, Counseling and Confronting

We want to be very concrete. In our work with exceptionally talented leaders and coaches, we've discovered that they make dozens of intuitive judgments daily about how to work with their people. Sometimes they focus on removing barriers to performance. Other times they immerse themselves in a situation and exert a great deal of influence on the way it turns out. There are times when they help people work through personal or performance problems, and there are times when the only requirement is to provide straightforward information. In some situations the coach is the dominant figure, while in others the team practically forgets he or she is there.

It turns out that successful coaches instinctively vary their approaches to meet the needs of this person at this time, or that group at that time. They perform five distinctly different roles: they educate, sponsor, coach, counsel and confront. Each approach is executed with the intensity we have come to expect, always toward the same goal: to facilitate learning and elicit creative contributions from all hands to the organization's overarching purpose. Let's take a closer look at the five roles. We summarize the hallmarks of each before digging into the roles individually.

---

### EDUCATE

#### TIMING
When goals, roles, or business conditions change
To orient a newcomer · When you are new to a group
When new skills are needed

#### TONE
Positive, supportive
Emphasis on learning and applying specific new knowledge

#### CONSEQUENCES
New skills acquired · Confidence increases
Perspective on the company or organization is broadened

#### KEY SKILLS
Ability to articulate performance expectations clearly
An eye for recognizing real-life "learning laboratories"
Ability and willingness to reinforce learning

---

We appreciate the special inventive contribution of HP's excellent management trainer, Pat Lingen, to the material in this chart.

## SPONSOR

### TIMING
When an individual can make a special contribution
To let an outstanding skill speak for itself

### TONE
Positive, enthusiastic
Emphasis on long-term development and contribution to the company
Future focus · Polishing, fine-tuning

### CONSEQUENCES
Showcase for outstanding skill, contribution
Greater experience · Promotion

### KEY SKILLS
Debureaucratizing · Dismantling barriers to performance

Ability to develop collegial relationship
Willingness to let go of control
Willingness to provide access to information and people

## COACH

### TIMING
For special encouragement before or after a "first"
(e.g., first-customer visit, first board meeting)
To make simple, brief corrections

### TONE
Encouraging, enthusiastic · Preparatory, explanatory

### CONSEQUENCES
Enhanced confidence, skills, better performance

### KEY SKILLS
Ability to express genuine appreciation · Ability to listen

## COUNSEL

### TIMING
When problems damage performance · After educating and coaching
To respond to setbacks and disappointments and speed recovery

### TONE
Emphasis on problem solving · Positive, supportive, encouraging
Structured · Two-way discussion

### CONSEQUENCES
Turnaround · Enhanced sense of ownership and accountability
Renewed commitment

### KEY SKILLS
Willingness to listen · Ability to give clear, useful feedback

---

## CONFRONT

### TIMING
Persistent performance problems are not resolved
An individual seems unable to meet expectations despite educating
and counseling
An individual is failing in his or her current role

### TONE
Positive, supportive · Firm
Clear focus on need to make a decision and time at which decision
will be made
Calm

### CONSEQUENCES
Reassignment · A chance to succeed in another position
Current job is restructured, responsibilities curtailed · Dismissal

### KEY SKILLS
Listening · Ability to give direct, useful feedback
Ability to discuss sensitive issues without overemotionalizing them

---

## Educating

When Ren McPherson wanted to enhance productivity at Dana, one of the most important things he did was to insist that entire divisions—each, say, a 1,500-person operation—get together at least quarterly to share corporate operating results, to keep up with developments throughout the corporation. As we pointed out in our chapter on ownership, McPherson acted upon the assumption that all, including the new hire of eight days ago—have the potential to be a full business partner if he treated them that way. If we can get people involved on a weekly, monthly or quarterly basis, we can encourage them to see themselves as a real part of the organization—in both its successes and stumbles.

---

### Dana Corporation's Forty Thoughts to Put into Practice

Dana, under the leadership in the 1970's of Ren McPherson and today of chairman Gerry Mitchell, added an important chapter to the book on American management. As noted, one of McPherson's first acts as chairman was to reduce the company's existing policy manuals to a one-page operational philosophy. In the mid-1970's that single page was culled to become "The Dana Corporation's 40 Thoughts"—not by the chairman but by a group of Dana employees acting entirely on their own initiative. They wanted to make it even easier for everyone at Dana to read and remember what made the company tick. The "40 Thoughts" are still vital to Dana's remarkable productivity:

Remember our purpose—to earn money for our shareholders and increase the value of their investment · Recognize people as our most important asset · Help people grow · Promote from within · Remember—people respond to recognition · Share the rewards · Provide stability of income and employment · Decentralize · Provide autonomy · Encourage entrepreneurship · Use corporate committees, task forces · Push responsibility down · Involve everyone · Make every employee a manager · Control only what's important · Promote identity with Dana · Make all Dana people shareholders · Simplify · Use little paper · Keep no files · Communicate fully · Let Dana people know first · Let people set goals and judge their performance · Let the people decide where possible · Discourage conformity · Be professional · Break organizational barriers · Develop pride · Insist on high ethical standards · Focus on markets · Utilize assets fully · Contain investment—buy, don't make · Balance plants, products, markets · Keep facilities under 500 people · Stabilize production · Develop proprietary products · Anticipate market needs · Control cash · Deliver reliably · Do what's best for all of Dana

Now reflect on this for a moment. We observe (and commend to you) that educating is *not* principally about jamming techniques down the neophyte's throat, whether the neophyte is a new hire, new manager or new vice president. The prime education is "You belong," "You can contribute." Once that message is genuinely transmitted, and absorbed, *then* the "technique-learning process" can be shortened by 60 to 90 percent, for there is suddenly the will to learn.

So leaders-as-educators treat every person—full time, part-time and temporary—as a full-fledged team member (for reasons of profitability and performance as well as humanity). They facilitate the sense of belonging (ownership) by providing a full complement of training, free access to information about how things are going throughout the company, and by making performance expectations clear, consistent, simple and concrete. Even industries that face cyclical and seasonal manufacturing problems can use the educating role to affirm the full-partner status of their people, regardless of their tenure.

Educating well ("overeducating" by most of the world's standards) at the beginning—bringing newcomers into the organization and making them a part of it in a short time—is the bedrock for sustained creative contributions. Educating is not about giving instructions. It's acting on a deep-down belief in the potential of every person to contribute, over time, by providing the tools, the elbowroom and frequent, concrete, believable feedback about progress. It means giving people a chance to experiment a little bit from the start and to learn the difference between mistakes and disasters, between satisfactory and exceptional.

## When Should You Educate

—When you want to introduce a newcomer—at any level—to your organization, philosophy and way of doing business.
—When people need specific information that will enable them to contribute as fully involved partners day to day.
—When performance expectations are unclear.
—When people need information about changing goals, strategies, roles or responsibilities.
—When people successfully apply their current skills and want to concentrate on expanding their ability.
—When you want people to learn a specific skill.
—When company business values are misinterpreted, ambiguous or unobtrusive.

## Educating the Newcomer

At North American Tool and Die, based in San Leandro, California, on-the-job education begins with the *interview* process! Candidates are asked to spend two or three days working (with pay) to see where they would best fit in. During that time the candidate learns about the precision machine parts business, meets most of the company's eighty people, gets hand-on exposure to several jobs, and is immersed in the North American way of doing things. President Tom Melohn meets with every recruit, often for an hour or more, to answer questions and to talk about what he believes in: profitable growth, sharing the wealth and having fun. Hiring decisions are reached by consensus, and the candidate is given equal voice. "If the person will fit in with our way of doing things, he or she knows it after those two days," Melohn observes. "Then they can't wait to go out and start on something. We want to get people involved from the very beginning; we want them to know that's important to us."

So the best education processes begin long before the hiring decision is made: each interview or plant tour is an opportunity to make your priorities clear and understandable, to reinforce expectations, and to get the newcomer involved in the whole of the business. We met Donna Ecton, vice president of administration at Campbell Soup Company, when we researched the best companies for women for *Savvy* magazine's June 1984 cover story. Campbell scored high on our list, and so did Donna's approach to her new position (she had come to Campbell from Citibank): she had spent her first quarter working in the company's processing plants, "packing pickles, working the graveyard shift, eviscerating chickens, and listening to people." In less than a year, she had worked at every one of the company's ninety operating units. The (senior) newcomer's investing time in getting to the roots of the business is oh so rare.

## Training and Beyond

Educating the newcomer often begins with a formal orientation program. The best firms focus on the company's history, evolution, current product lines, business philosophy, how each individual contributes to the organization's success. The newcomers are unfailingly taught by top management. Intel President Andy Grove says his new-hire orientation teaching is his most significant contribution to the $1.2 billion company. The entire top team at People Express devotes four to eight hours a week to in-house classroom orientation. They believe it is the best way to ensure that People traditions do not become attenuated in the face of incredible growth. But the real orientation begins when the newcomer starts his or her new role and depends on peers and managers to do the lion's share of the educating on the job. Harry Levinson, in *The Exceptional Executive*, enhances the theme:

> Although always imperative, the need for closeness is most crucial at the beginning of a relationship with the organization. It is at this point that people become "attached," and the attaching process must take place at a time when they are most confused about the new job and the strange organization. They are more heavily dependent then than at any other time in their organizational careers. Unless someone takes them in hand, they literally cannot begin their work, let alone become part of the organization.
>
> An adequate orientation reduces anxiety. Much of the turnover among newly employed people is due to their concern that they might fail, their feeling of desertion about being left to 'muddle through,' and their impression that no one really cares about them.

One more point, one more time: all the training in your power to provide won't matter a whit unless you believe the individual *wants* to contribute, and unless you give him or her a chance to contribute—creatively—from the start. The first step is to make this belief crystal clear. Make it tangible and believable through concrete example and by encouraging early participation.

Experience is still the best teacher. At HP, newcomers are often invited to sit on temporary task forces convened to address a particular issue, resolve a problem or streamline a system. It's a way to draw people in immediately and to convince them that the company is dead serious about wanting their participation and full contribution in the most complex business decisions. The beauty of harnessing brief, practical task forces as educational opportunities is that they build in real accountability without excessive risk. The odds overwhelmingly favor the newcomer's successful contribution—the group is kept small but diverse, the group is focused on a particular task, and is held responsible for contributing to a fully implemented solution. It's a small slice of organization life that showers full-scale responsibility on newcomers.

As a newcomer to HP, Nancy was a member of a small, multifunctional task force formed for the purpose of reviewing, redesigning and implementing a new performance evaluation system throughout the company. The six-person group was made up of two senior people from operating divisions, a representative from the sales regions, a corporate senior vice president and two senior personnel managers. Meetings were held regularly over a three-month period, each lasting half a day; minutes were published and distributed the same day.

The real work of the task force, however, was done between meetings, when the members worked with managers from all over the company to incorporate their "best practices"—particularly innovative approaches or effective solutions developed in a division or region and worthy of company-wide attention—into the task force recommendations (see chapter 17). Here the real learning occurred: Nancy spent a considerable amount of time with line managers in HP divisions and regions, was exposed to a broad cross section of the company's business, and learned firsthand how the HP Way is put into action at the operating level, where it counts. These meetings were first-class testing grounds for a newcomer's impressions and ideas. Almost every conversation would yield some new information: "Oh, we wouldn't do it that way here." "Why not?" "Well, because the HP Way is different. Here, we do it this way, because equity is so important...." A better education couldn't be designed. Accountability was also an important feature of the experience, and felt most acutely when task force progress and result were reported to line and senior managers. This was a no-nonsense occasion, when the expectation that the task force produce real results was evident.

Pritchard Services Group, now a successful $325 million diversified health services company in the UK, was originally best known as a cleaning company. Despite its size, Pritchard regularly takes on cleaning contracts that other companies would consider too small to bother with. The reason? As reported in *The Winning Streak*, these contracts provide a superb training ground for inexperienced managers, who can make mistakes and learn from them without excessive risk, and who can develop the practical entrepreneurial skills and mind-set that breathe life into this large corporation.

## Educating the New Manager

Somehow it's easier to imagine educating individual contributors than to think in terms of following the same approach in educating newly promoted managers to perform well in their roles. Take a minute or two and review the "Educating the Newcomer" section, replacing "newcomer" with "new manager" as you go. Our point is simple: new managers, though now responsible for others' welfare and destiny, need the same clear expectations about performance and accountability, *and* the chance to make mistakes through hands-on experience. New managers need to know and work from corporate objectives, know how to work with their new teams and more experienced managers, know how to build peer relationships and how to resolve conflicts. Educators can exert tremendous positive influence on new managers' development *if* they will recognize the obvious early confusion and at the same time the unparalleled opportunity to mold behavior. It's easy to rationalize leaving new managers alone to fend for themselves under the rubric of "hands-on experience," but we believe strongly that this is a mistake and a tragic waste precisely because what's being inadvertently taught is that managing (leading) effectively is not the special skill we know it to be. When we say in effect "Well, you know your job, so go manage," the implicit message is that there's nothing more to it, that any dummy (who's made it this far) can do it, that if you're uncomfortable it's because you're weird. Let's be blunt: how many new managers are given the same level of training in "shaping corporate values" as they were given when they were learning engineering or fashion buying? The latter was the subject of four years (or more) of collegiate training and big doses of corporate refurbishment. The former nets two weeks of training at the most, and yet the skills to be assumed and the responsibility (i.e., for corporate value maintenance and transmittal) are awesome. (Incidentally, this is an area where IBM has shone brightly: new manager training, which (1) begins with a refocusing on values, and (2) is *never* delayed due to "job exigencies" is expensive, intensive and superb.)

### When Everyone's a Newcomer: Culture Shock

In baseball: The major league umpires threaten to walk out again only minutes before the fifth and final game in the battle between the Chicago Cubs and the San Diego Padres for the National League pennant. The team members are introduced, the national anthem is sung; there are no umpires. At last the men in blue appear, reporting to work without a contract. Later in the game, the attorney for the Umpires Union, Richie Phillips, comments to a television reporter, explaining the umpires' presence: "I trust Peter Ueberroth [the new commissioner of baseball and arbitrator for the binding arbitration the umpires agreed to in their negotiations just before the 1984 World Series]." Phillips speaks of trust not once but three times in a thirty-second interview. And Ueberroth, for his part, is equally confident. "We'll settle before the Series," he says calmly, optimistically—and it is a promise, not a threat.

In electronics: During the 1981–83 recession, Kollmorgen Corporation, like so many others, was forced to lay off hundreds of people. But the company believes in commitment—they wanted these people back and they wanted them to know it. So Kollmorgen did an unusual thing: Each week every Kollmorgen division manager held "news conferences"—open forums to which everyone, including those who had been laid off, was invited. The news conferences drew standing-room-only crowds, and each week division managers were asked to explain exactly what the company was doing to get their people their jobs back. The managers shared every bit of information they had, including what progress had been made and where the next layoffs might occur. Trust and truth in real time—giving the people all the information even when it is the hardest thing imaginable to do—is the heart and soul of educating.

When conditions change, new standards must be set, new skills learned, new roles taken, old records broken. Educators are essential at these times, to point the way, to articulate progress, and to share what was previously considered unsharable. It's as much a new beginning—a new mind-set—as any newcomer faces. In fact, though our topic here is education, the deeper theme, again, is trust. Peter Ueberroth gained it quickly by prior reputation and by acting in an unheard-of, new fashion—genuinely listening to both sides—and he can lose it just as quickly. Kollmorgen earned it through years of consistency and through openly sharing all news—regularly. Both used trust and mutual respect as the basis for timely action in a crisis. Trust is always important, but never more so than in times of rapid change.

## Accountability and Support

The education process works when it is characterized by accountability and unwavering support. People need to know exactly what their roles are and what results they are expected to produce. They need to see that mistakes are allowed and expected as a part of learning. The effective educator prefers a bit of daring and persistence to unimaginative perfection, and supports learning by paying vigilant attention to each successful (and unsuccessful) try. Progress is recognized and reinforced every tiny step of the way.

The need for support and active guidance in the learning process is well understood by anyone who remembers what the first few weeks of a new job (supervisor of the cleaning crew or vice president) are like: strange, confusing, uncertain and, all too often, lonely. Harry Levinson underscores the point: "Despite its importance, the most glaring deficiency in contemporary organizational functioning is the almost universal inadequacy of support. This is evident in the repetitive response to a simple question. If one asks people in almost any organization, 'How do you know how well you are doing?' 90 percent of them are likely to respond, 'If I do something wrong, I'll hear about it.' Too often this topic is discussed as if praise were the answer; it is not. What people are saying in such a response is that they do not feel sufficient support from their superiors. Praise without support is an empty gesture." Support is reflected in real, active help in accomplishing work, in providing training, in full disclosure of information about the company's financial health and key measures of output, and in the conviction that trust and confidence is reciprocated between leader and newcomer. Exerting pressure to perform without giving such support is hopelessly destructive, and all too common.

The educator role requires the ability to:

• Articulate *consistent* performance expectations and objectives.

• Find a "learning laboratory"—task forces; real but low-risk projects—where practical experience can be acquired without heavy penalties or losses.

• Give balanced, believable, timely feedback about the specifics of day-to-day performance so people know where they stand and how they're doing.

• Provide access to all information that people need to be full partners in the enterprise—and then some.

• Explain (most effectively by storytelling) the difference between an acceptable performance and an exceptional one.

• Spend enough time to be a useful facilitator and source of support.

• Give meticulous attention to planning the education process.

• Confident educators do one thing more. They have lived their values with integrity and transmitted those values; the newcomer, new manager or person faced with crises has thus been exposed to bedrock. Given that, the exceptional educator inculcates flexibility. In the terms of our innovation section, he or she encourages skunking and "cheating." He or she is intolerant of "I could have done it, but . . ." That is, the educator has taught the values so well that he or she expects (demands, really) that the newcomer or new manager bend silly rules to get the job done. This is the ultimate subtlety in the education process.

---

## Educating:
### Some Questions—and Things to Do Now

• How well do you educate newcomers? Go ask the last three people you hired about their respective orientations. Were they treated as colleagues and team members? (Collect specifics from them.) Or ignored (i.e., treated as students going through a required mill)? Was your organization's philosophy communicated clearly? (How can you tell?) Did they receive support and clear guidance? Did they develop a sense of accomplishments early? (If so, how?) Did you (as chief orienter) point out how to approach various people in the organization, what the barriers to action are and how to deal with them, what idiosyncrasies exist in the company and how to respond to them? Did you spend enough time, personally, with the newcomers to listen to their first reactions and to reinforce your guidance accordingly? What changes would *they* make in the way they were introduced to the organization? Incorporate their suggestions into the orientation program, but—much, much better— build them into the way you work with all newcomers.

• Here comes a big request: Share information vital to your business or organization—Annual Reports, Quarterly Reports, monthly operating results, measures of weekly or daily quality performance, comparative performance (among divisions or units)—with everyone on your team, to the lowest level. Do all hands know, on a *weekly* basis, how their group is performing according to the ten or fifteen most important measures of output? How it stacks up with other groups? Do they know what the measures mean and how they were arrived at and why?

• Devote one week to judging your organization's health by tuning in to its stories. This is best done when you are out of your office, wandering around, listening. (If you are new to MBWA, be aware that it will take some time before people share stories; such self-disclosure depends on long-standing trust.) Lead company seminars; it's one of the best ways to hear, firsthand, what the group has to say about their company's beliefs and philosophy. Try to understand why the beliefs persist (e.g., "Nobody listens to salespersons around here," or "Manufacturing can do no wrong"). What kinds of examples (stories) are used to support their beliefs about how your organization runs? Do the beliefs and stories reflect your own impressions? If not, why not?

• Facilitate getting information across organizational or departmental bounds quickly by scheduling same-level management staff meetings to occur within twenty-four hours of each other, every week. Instead of staff meetings that pop up on an apparently random basis throughout your organization (i.e., at times convenient for each individual group but inconvenient for the organization as a whole), scheduling same-level meetings in tandem means that everyone knows when information is being shared and has access to it much faster. For example, the general manager of a Hewlett-Packard division holds his meeting with his seven functional managers on a Monday morning; they, in turn, meet with their own teams Monday afternoon, and their staffs, meet with their groups by Tuesday afternoon. As a result, the 2,000-person division is fully and consistently informed on a routine basis within forty-eight hours of the general manager's meeting.

• Volunteer to teach in your organization's new-hire orientation program. Participate at least once a month, for three or more hours.

• Give new *staff* members hands-on orientation experiences by having them spend at least a week working alongside line operators and providers of direct customer service within their first month on board. Request that they write a short (no more than two pages) summary of what they learned from the experience.

• Spend some contemplative time on this question: Does your orientation or newcomers serve to "tame" them or prepare them for long-term contribution? The former emphasizes controlling, limiting and restricting; the latter assumes the newcomer is a highly useful resource for innovative ideas and new approaches. What does your orientation say about your beliefs?

---

### What's So Special about You?

Information sharing, as we've said time and again, is an extraordinarily sensitive topic. It shouldn't be! "But there will be leaks" was a rejoinder we heard recently, relative to a discussion about sharing detailed operating information with supervisors. Our nasty response took these two tacks. First, "Oh yeah? And where do most leaks come from? Vice presidents. Ever hear of a leak from a maintenance supervisor?" Second, "And why should a forty-six-year-old, nineteen-year vet on the line have any more inclination to leak than you, a thirty-eight-year-old, six-year vet department head?"

Obviously, there are some few areas of information—e.g., acquisition-related, pre-patent application—where secrecy is called for. Other than that, it is a "simple" matter of trust: You've either taken care in recruiting and developing people, and thus trust them, or you haven't. This strong view, which we hold deeply, doesn't even include the most practical rejoinder to pro-secrecy arguments; namely, there are few important facts that competitors can't get a pretty good fix on by legitimate and legal means. With rare exceptions, the result of most stringent secrecy programs we've observed is mainly to restrict desirable intra-company information flow.

---

## Sponsoring

Sponsoring makes it possible for people to take charge of their environments after they've received a full complement of training and encouragement. Sponsors grant practical autonomy by removing obstacles to performance; sponsoring assumes that the key skills are already in place and have only to be applied.

The key to sponsoring is not to grant too much autonomy too soon and thereby invite failure rather than pride in steady achievement. Although we find that it is much more common to underestimate what people can handle than to overestimate, this point is nonetheless too important to overlook. It's just as bad to give so much room that people feel abandoned as not to give enough. They'll observe that you are out of touch with reality, that you don't understand what they can actually accomplish without your support and personal leadership. They'll conclude that you don't care if they get beaten up unnecessarily. And, of course, they'll be dead right. Sponsoring is not the all too common lack of attention masquerading as "giving people room to grow."

Sponsoring is personally *guided* autonomy—and you're the chief guide. Although somewhere near the heart of sponsoring is letting go of the impulse to overcontrol the situation, it never means letting go of the individual.

## The Sponsor's Commitment

Everyone at W. L. Gore & Associates has a sponsor, and often more than one, depending on the scope of the Associate's interests and responsibilities. Sponsorship is the pivotal concept in the Gore "lattice" organization, (see page 205).

The sponsor's role is defined within the context of Gore's four guiding principles. Successful participation as an Associate (and sponsor) depends on observing and perpetuating them:

1.  Fairness. Each of us will *try* to be fair in all dealings—with one another, with our suppliers, with our customers, within our communities, and with all the people with whom we have transactions or agreements. Fairness is seldom clearly defined, but if a sincere effort is made by all, it generates a tolerance that preserves good feelings among us.

2.  Freedom. Each of us will allow, help, and encourage his or her Associates to grow in knowledge, skill, the scope of responsibility and the range of activities. Authority is gained by recognized knowledge or skill. It is a power only of leadership, not of command.

3.  Commitment. Each of us will make his or her own commitments—and keep them. No Associates can impose a commitment on another. All commitments are self-commitments.

We organize our enterprises—projects, functions and work of all kinds—through commitments. Therefore, a commitment is a serious matter, amounting to a contract that must be fulfilled.

4.  Waterline. Each of us will consult with appropriate Associates who will share the responsibility of taking any action that has the potential of inflicting serious harm on the reputation, success or survival of the enterprise.

The analogy is that our enterprise is like a ship that we are all in together. Boring holes above the waterline is not serious, but below the waterline, holes could sink our ship.

Sponsors at W. L. Gore & Associates voluntarily take a specific, personal interest in the activities, well-being, progress, accomplishments, personal problems and ambitions of the people he or she sponsors. Sponsors help newcomers get started and vigilantly follow their progress. Sponsors also take the lead in compensation decisions, an especially important role because everything at Gore is done in teams, and the results may not be clear until months or years later. Sponsors, acting together in small committees, evaluate the relative contribution of comparable groups of Associates, and act as positive advocates for the value of each person's individual contribution to the enterprise.

## Sponsors and Mentors

Sponsoring and mentoring. The difference may appear to be merely semantic, given conventional usage, but we believe it's useful to differentiate. We called this trait mentoring at first, but then discarded the word for two reasons. First, mentoring has been gobbled up by the psychologists; it's become an "in" word. Who knows what they mean? Second, and more significant, "mentoring" has come to suggest cult-of-personality problems: e.g., the Bill Agee–Mary Cunningham fiasco. If the mentor dies, the mentored one(s) die also: e.g., "Reed's people" versus "Theobald's people" at Citicorp in 1984. (Reed became chairman, at the end of a two-person race, and his "people" quickly came to receive a lion's share of the top slots.) Sponsoring is broader. We steal it unabashedly from Bill and Vieve Gore. The sponsor at Gore is not only responsible for an Associate's development "down" (e.g., practical skill-building), but also responsible for "selling" an Associate laterally and up—i.e., sponsorship occurs wholly within the context of the *organization's* philosophy and needs. Mentoring, often as not, deteriorates into a "Follow *my* flag" relationship.

## When Should You Sponsor?

—You assess an individual's ability as consistently high or exceptional.
—You want to prepare someone for promotion or increased responsibility.
—Your main focus is to fine-tune already good technical, administrative and leadership skills and performance.
—Exposure to other areas of the company is necessary to broaden experience.
—You want to alert your colleagues to a promising performer.
—You want to enable people to contribute without stifling them.

## The Sponsor Relationship

Sponsoring reflects your direct responsibility for guiding and developing in new contexts the particularly strong skills your people possess. Building on strength is key. Warren Bennis's new study of leadership isolates five factors that mark superb leaders. At the top of the list: they build on strengths rather than focus on weaknesses.

Sponsorship should start early, and almost all superb senior leaders have been superb sponsors throughout their careers. They have understood that the best leaders follow that easy-to-state, hard-to-follow (because ego will be ego) folk wisdom: Promote people who are better than you, then watch them shine as they make you look good. (David Ogilvy cemented this notion symbolically. Upon promoting someone to the position of office manager at

Ogilvy & Mather, Ogilvy would send the new manager a wooden Russian matryoshka doll from Gorky—the kind that opens to reveal a smaller doll inside, which in turn opens to reveal another. Inside the smallest, the new manager will find this message: "If each of us hires people who are smaller than we are, we shall become a company of *dwarfs*. But if each of us hires people who are bigger than we are, we shall become a company of *giants*.")

The result of the work of the clever and committed sponsor is that when he or she reaches a senior position, all elements of the organization are seeded with his or her talented charges; change of focus thus becomes much more rapidly and effectively achievable.

## What Sponsorship Is Not

Sponsoring can be many things, but the following are the antithesis of sound sponsorship.
—Encouraging an individual to become too dependent on you.
—Using the sponsoring role to control rather than to guide and to support performance.
—Shielding people from mistakes or bad news (i.e., dishonesty).
—Telling an individual what he or she wants to hear.
—Becoming involved in the personal decisions an individual must make.
—Applying the sponsor role only to people just like you, avoiding those with different backgrounds or professional goals.
—Confusing sponsoring with parenting.
—Pitting your people against one another in the name of "healthy competition" or survival of the fittest.

Again, we'd stress the difference between the mentor (as popularly conceived) and the sponsor. Sponsoring is the best way of rapidly pushing talented performers to achieve. It is the very core of effective management/leadership development. If you are wise, you will push your most talented charges out into green fields and expect to reap a reward only indirectly, over time. Mentoring, we observe in the real world, often deteriorates into hoarding and, eventually, backbiting politics as "Jones's candidate" contends with "Smith's candidate."

## Positive Sponsorship

Positive sponsorship deals with helping people become sensitive to but not enslaved by—a fine balance—your company's norms and prevaling philosophy. The skills addressed in sponsoring are much more subtle, for the most part, than those you address in other coaching roles, because sponsoring assumes that you are moving beyond raw skills and abilities that are already substantially developed and applied. It may, then, focus on the gentle arts: knowing when to shut up, when to stop digging into a problem, when to give in and when to stand and fight, and knowing the limits of skunklike behavior. Many managers refer to these as "street smarts," the kind of understanding that develops over time and cannot be learned in classrooms. The role of sponsorship is to acknowledge unabashedly the subtle norms and to push your best and brightest to come to understand them, take them into account, and use them to achieve.

A fair share of sponsoring—again—involves making philosophy and core values explicit. The best sponsors sit down with an individual to discuss a particular decision and show why it was chosen over other alternatives, or why a course of action turned out to be a mistake. (At Gore & Associates, this consultation involves several sponsors for critical "waterline" issues.) Others spend time talking about how they approach their own jobs with an eye to highlighting the reasoning that underlies decisions.

We have devoted such substantial space to this role because effective leadership is, after all, no more than developing other leaders who both cherish the organization's philosophy (if it is a sound one) and yet test it and adapt within it at every opportunity. An organization is as good as the consistency and vitality of its leadership cadre. Almost without exception the most effective leaders at the top are those who started early looking for others to sponsor. When they were department heads in a single retail store, they were determined to look for a would-be superstar to follow in their footsteps. In fact, they were confident of promotion from the start, and were wise enough to realize that their path to glory lay in creating a swath of newly anointed heroes in their wake.

Sponsoring takes time—lots of it. The wise realize that it is the only surefire path to success. (And even if success does not surely follow, at least—no small thing—one can look back on a slate of people developed and enhanced. In the deepest sense—when the light goes on over the mirror—who could ask for more?)

### Profile of a Good Sponsor

Like the other four development tasks, sponsoring requires constant attention. Short spurts of attention won't help, but the following will:
—Treating people as colleagues.
—Being on the lookout for opportunities to help people learn and experience other jobs and new responsibilities.
—Making company norms and philosophy explicit and understandable; helping people understand them (their power *and* their limits) within the context of their current activities.
—Regularly discussing an individual's career plans and goals with him or her in the context of recent accomplishments and pratfalls.
—Not being threatened by an individual's exceptional skill or ability.
—Desperately and passionately wanting your people to succeed.

To live this profile takes guts, above all. The gutsiest move imaginable (whether you are a first-line supervisor or chairman) is to give an only somewhat junior person the encouragement and opportunity to push his or her substantial skills to the limit. It *is* scary. It *is* threatening. It is also the *only* path to development of a truly talent-rich organization.

---

### Sponsoring:
### Some Questions—and Things to Do Now

• There is only one exercise for sponsoring. Do your managers take the kind of broad, sincere interest in people that the sponsors at W. L. Gore & Associates do? How about you? Could you describe the especially strong skills that each of your people possesses? When does each of your people sparkle the most? With whom do they work the best? What experiences does each of your people find the most rewarding? (Sponsoring is tailored to each individual's strenghs—not providing the same collection of experiences for everyone alike.) Take the time to answer these questions for each of your people. Put together a real development plan for each person and sit down to discuss what each wants to achieve, what his or her ambitions are. A paper program is not enough!

---

## Coaching

### *Is There a Leader in Your Company?*

In an open memorandum to the "outside directors and trustees of all the organizations not in the Fortune 1000", Robert Townsend, author of *Further Up the Organization*, posed one question: "Ask yourself if you have a leader as a CEO." Do you have a leader in your company?

| LEADER | NON-LEADER |
|---|---|
| Carries water for people. | Presides over the mess. |
| A coach appealing to the best in each person; open door; problem-solver and advice-giver; cheerleader. | Invisible—gives orders to staff—expects them to be carried out. |
| Thinks of ways to make people more productive, more focused on company goals; how to reward them. | Thinks of personal rewards, status, and how he or she looks to outsiders. |
| Comfortable with people in their workplaces. | Uncomfortable with people. |

| LEADER | NON-LEADER |
| --- | --- |
| No reserved parking place, private washroom, dining room or elevator. | Has them. |
| MBWA (manages by wandering around). | No MBWA. |
| Arrives early—stays late. | In late—usually leaves on time. |
| Common touch. | Strained with blue collars. |
| Good listener. | Good talker. |
| Simplistic on company values. | Good at demonstrating his command of all the complexities. |
| Available. | Hard to reach from below. |
| Fair. | Fair to the top; exploits the rest. |
| Decisive. | Uses committees, consultants. |
| Humble. | Arrogant. |
| Tough—confronts nasty problems. | Elusive—the artful dodger. |
| Persistent. | Only when his own goodies are at stake. |
| Simplifies (makes it look easy). | Complicates (makes it look difficult). |
| Tolerant of open disagreement. | Intolerant of open disagreement. |
| Knows people's names. | Doesn't know people's names. |
| Has strong convictions. | Vacillates when a decision is needed. |
| Does dog-work when necessary. | Above dog-work. |
| Trusts people. | Trusts only words and numbers on paper. |
| Delegates whole important jobs. | Keeps all final decisions. |
| Spends as little time as possible with outside directors, outside activities. | Spends a lot of time massaging outside directors. |

| LEADER | NON-LEADER |
|---|---|
| Wants anonymity for himself, publicity for his company. | The reverse. |
| Often takes the blame. | Looks for a scapegoat. |
| Gives credit to others. | Takes credit; complains about lack of good people. |
| Gives honest, frequent feedback. | Info flows one way—into his or her office. |
| Knows when and how to fire people. | Ducks unpleasant tasks. |
| Weeds the garden. | Likes to get bigger and more complex. |
| Goes where the trouble is to help. | Interrupts people in crisis and calls them to meeting in his or her office. |
| Sees growth as by-product of search for excellence. | Sees growth as primary goal. |
| Has respect for all people. | Thinks blue collars and pink collars are lazy, incompetent ingrates. |
| Knows the business, and the kind of people who make it tick. | They've never met him or her. |
| Honest under pressure. | Improvises, equivocates. |
| Looks for controls to abolish. | Loves new controls. |
| Prefers eyeball to eyeball instead of memos. | Prefers memos, long reports. |
| Straightforward. | Tricky, manipulative. |
| Consistent and credible to the troops. | Unpredictable; says what he thinks they want to hear. |
| Admits own mistakes; comforts others when they admit them. | Never makes mistakes; blames others; starts witch hunts to identify culprits. |
| No policy manuals. | Policy manuals. |
| Openness. | Secrecy. |
| Little paperwork in planning. | Vast paperwork in planning. |

| | |
|---|---|
| Promotes from within. | Always searching outside the company. |
| Keeps his promises. | Doesn't. |
| Plain office. | Lavish office. |
| Thinks there are at least two other people in the company who would be good CEO's. | Number one priority is to make bloody sure no one remotely resembling a CEO gets on the payroll. |
| Focused to the point of monomania on the company's values and objectives. | Unfocused except on self. |
| Company is No. 1. | Self is No. 1. |
| Sees mistakes as learning opportunities. | Sees mistakes as punishable offenses. |

You *now* know more about leaders and leadership than all the combined graduate business schools in America.

You also know whether you have a leader or an administrator in your CEO's office.

There are subtle differences between coaching and sponsoring. Coaching teaches people how to contribute and participate as active, full partners; sponsoring begins when outstanding skill has begun to speak for itself.

Effective coaching means creating winners, keeping the faith in the thick of turmoil, building momentum, finding tiny glimmers of light (to reinforce) in the midst of darkness, building on the strength that ninety-nine out of a hundred have.

We've learned about coaching from participants in our seminars. Here's what they've said about the characteristics of good coaches:

Challenges me to do my best.
Sets a good example.
Never divulges a confidence.
Explains the reasons for instructions and procedures.
Helps me polish my thoughts before I present them to others.
Is objective about things.
Lets me make my own decisions.
Cares about me and how I'm doing.

Does not seek the limelight.

Won't let me give up.

Gives personal guidance and direction, especially when I'm learning something new.

Is empathetic and understanding.

Is firm but fair.

Keeps a results orientation.

Makes me work out most of my own problems or tough situations, but supports me.

Lets me know where I stand.

Listens exceptionally well.

Doesn't put words in my mouth.

Is easy to talk to.

Keeps the promises he or she makes.

Keeps me focused on the goals ahead.

Works as hard or harder than anyone else.

Is humble.

Is proud of those managers he or she has developed.

Gives credit where credit is due.

Practices MBWA.

Never says "I told you so."

Corrects my performance in private.

Never flaunts authority.

Is always straightforward.

Gives at least a second chance.

Maintains an Open Door Policy.

Uses language that is easy to understand.

Lets bygones be bygones.

Inspires loyalty.

Really wants to hear my ideas, and acts on them.

Lets me set my own deadlines.

Celebrates successes.

Is open and honest.

Doesn't hide bad news.

Gives me enough time to prepare for discussion.

Is enthusiastic.

Follows through.

Is patient.

Wants me to "stretch" my skills.

Gives me his or her full attention during discussions, won't be distracted.

Has a sense of humor.

Handles disagreements privately.

Reassures me.

Makes me feel confident.

Tells me the "whole story."

Says "we" instead of "I."
Makes hard work worth it.
Can communicate annoyance without running wild.
Is courageous.
Insists on training.
Is a stabilizing influence in a crisis.
Gets everyone involved.
Wants me to be successful.
Is optimistic.
Operates well under pressure, or in a rapidly changing environment.
Has a reputation for competence with his or her peers.
Has a good understanding of the job.
Is tough and tender.
Believes we can do it.
Sets attainable milestones.
Communicates philosophy and values.
Is perceptive—doesn't require that everything be spelled out.
Has a strong sense of urgency.
Preserves the individuality of his or her team members.
Thinks and operates at a level above that expected.
Wants to make the organization the best in the industry.
Is willing to act on intuition; believes feelings are facts.
Empowers us.
Is there when we need him or her.
Enjoys his or her job.
Likes to spend time with us.

This list has one stunning characteristic: there is absolutely nothing new on it. Leaders want to do all these things. Most get distracted by the technical aspects of their job. They don't get around to it. New managers find that time spent doing those things "doesn't feel like work." No leader practices all these traits all the time. What they best do (usually intuitively, because most leadership training is so shoddy) is realize that these are the "it." Effective leadership *is* full-time people development. Moreover, it doesn't take an extroverted personality, or special flair or a flashy style, to coach well—it only takes consistent attention and vigilant action. In coaching, the name of the game is execution.

## When Should You Coach?

—When you assess an individual's administrative, technical or leadership ability and performance as moderate.
—When you want to encourage people to discover what they can do by "pushing" themselves.
—When you want to develop teamwork.

—To express confidence and support.
—When recognition and credit are due for innovativeness.
—When reassurance is all that's needed for successful performance.
—When you want to develop each individual's skill and foster individual performance.
—To celebrate the accomplishments of a team or an individual.

---

### Demanding PepsiCo Is Attempting to Make Work Nicer for Managers

*The Wall Street Journal,* October 23, 1984, reports:

Can PepsiCo Inc. become a nicer place to work without losing the edge that has helped make it a highly profitable, $8 billion food and soft-drink company?

Its management thinks so. Although PepsiCo prizes the fast pace and demanding standards that make it so competitive, it worries about battle fatigue in the ranks. Says Andrall E. Pearson, the company's president: "We probably attract people who give ulcers, rather than those who get them."

Accordingly, PepsiCo has decided that a bit more back-patting and hand-holding are in order—but not so much, mind you, that standards slip. The time is ripe to focus on such "soft stuff," Mr. Pearson explains, because the company has recently rebounded from a financial slump. Wall Street is touting its stock and earnings are headed for record levels.

But the principal motivation came last spring, when two surveys of PepsiCo's top 470 executives turned up some troubling job alienation. Many managers complained that they didn't feel cared about as people, that they didn't know enough about what was happening in the company as a whole, and that they weren't told how they were doing in their jobs.

As a consequence, Mr. Pearson told executives at a big May meeting in the Bahamas that they need to give more feedback and demonstrate a "real interest" in subordinates.

Although the company doesn't claim to have made enormous strides in six months, it has started tinkering with a corporate environment that is often criticized for encouraging individualism at the expense of the collective effort. . . .

PepsiCo will try to convince its solid achievers that it cares about them as well as its fast-track stars. It will try to better inform such employees of specific career paths to promotion, and limit job changes to those that are necessary.

In addition, the company wants to emphasize the value of coaching and training, management traits that aren't rewarded now. In the future, promotions and pay will be based partly on how well an executive furthers the development of subordinates.

According to J. Roger King, the new head of personnel, PepsiCo hopes to accomplish all this without sending managers to "sensitivity" training courses. "There are a lot of workshops where you dip people in and bring them up clean," Mr. King says. "I call it the bathtub theory of training. Two hours later they're dirty. It doesn't work because you can't take it to the workplace."

Instead, he favors on-the-job changes that, while slight, may change attitudes and behavior. In the past, for instance, January bonus checks have been distributed with a handshake but few words. This year, the employee's supervisor will review performance and try to explain precisely what determined the size of the bonus.

At annual merit-increase reviews, the company will be more specific in showing what kinds of behavior are rewarded. The forms for such reviews have been rewritten: Instead of dwelling on generalities, they now ask how a manager is doing daily, how effectively he is planning for the long term, what he is doing to develop subordinates, and how his own personal development is progressing.

## After the Turn-On, What?

Each summer, thirty thousand Mary Kay consultants convene in Dallas, Texas, for a "seminar"—an extravaganza by any standards. There are countless awards. Applause floods the Convention Center. Mary Kay Ash steps to the stage and addresses the sea of people before her. She urges, cheers, directs, pushes, advises and convinces virtually all of the thirty thousand consultants that they can go out and do anything.

This is coaching, to be sure, although many managers dismiss such grand-scale events as "mere" theatrics or show business. We've said that all business *is* show business—yes, a matter of symbolizing and shaping values and beliefs. After the turn-on of the big event, what? How does coaching work day to day, minute to minute?

### Support (versus Praise)

Coaching does include praise—expressing approval or admiration, applauding, commending and lauding small (and large) victories. No coach can build a successful team without dipping into these reserves. But warm words of reassurance are not enough. Coaching is the act of helping the team withstand the tough times and the inevitable setbacks along the way, maintaining momentum, and building small successes into a solid track record. Support is shown by the personal commitment of the coach, proven through his or her stubborn, imaginative interest

(not just friendliness or congeniality) in helping each individual progress. Support is sometimes proven through direct intervention—when
a talented individual strays off track and want (needs) forthright, active,
palpable help or more information. At other times, the most supportive
act is to stay out of the way, allowing people to discover for themselves
how best to handle a situation: quiet but assertive trust that they will
overcome difficulty is the essence of support. Praise *without* support is
mere platitude.

Coaching is ongoing leadership, frequently unobtrusive. We like the
imagery of former Stanford basketball coach Dick DiBiaso. He calls it "floor
coaching": the coach as part of the team, observing, making notes, critiquing
play, offering suggestions for improvement, challenging, working *for* the
team, alongside. It's a subtle process. A former IBMer stresses the point:
"Coaching isn't always noisy and obvious. The best coach I ever had used to
come around and ask, 'How's such and such going?' or 'What do you think
the customer wants?' Those questions were perfectly aimed. I'd leave those
little meetings believing I'd come up with the answers. Only later did I realize
that he directed my attention with those questions of his, used them as rud-
ders to steer me in a certain direction. He never once came out and told me
what to do; he led me there and made me feel like I'd figured it out on my
own. He was never impatient, or too busy to listen. But I think what I appreciated about him most was that he never asked me to do something I didn't
have the ability to do, even if I didn't realize it. He knew me well enough to
judge my reach; that was his credibility. If he had put me in situations where
I failed, I would have doubted *his* ability as a coach more than mine as a
player. I knew he wanted me to succeed and that we could count on each
other. After talking with him, I felt empowered."*
As vital a point here as any is "He never asked me to do something I didn't
have the ability to do." Coaches stretch you to your limit, a limit often
beyond what you thought possible. *Great* coaches stretch you *exactly* to that
previously unknown limit, but no further. Because their chief concern is turning you into a successful person, to have you experience *some* stretch and *lots*
of success, to build momentum and enthusiasm for further accomplishment.
General Douglas MacArthur said he learned one thing, above all, from his
almost equally celebrated father, a Civil War hero: "Never give an order that
can't be obeyed." I.e., the ultimate loss is to push your people beyond their
capacities. Business's classic "stretch target" more often than not leaves us
appalled. It's stretch for stretch's sake, creating "can't win" situations (read

---

*This IBM account is hardly random. IBM is the rare institution that views leader-
ship (and coaching) as teachable, and goes about doing so with a vengeance. Moreover, while "developing subordinates" is a new wrinkle in PepsiCo's formal evaluation process, it is the paramount success criterion for IBM managers at all levels.

"creating losers"). IBM's sales goal negotiation process, on the other hand, is great. It's tough, but the manager is marked down badly if his or her people aren't successful (i.e., if they are allowed to commit to too much). He or she is paid, says IBM, to get it roughly right—stretch, to be sure, but not excess.

Mary Kay Ash, in her book *Mary Kay on People Management*, reprises the "stretching" theme with her account of a telephone call from a "consultant", (her term for Mary Kay field people) in Michigan, who was not doing well in her business.

> We talked for a while, and I finally told her, "Here's what we're going to do. We're going to have a special contest just for you. I want you to book ten beauty shows for next week, and after you've held them, I want you to call me back and tell me how you did."
>
> "Ten shows?"
>
> "That's right," I answered. "I want you to call each hostess in your datebook, and say that you just talked to Mary Kay. Tell her that I've established a contest for you, and then let her know how much you want to win it. Finally, ask her to be a hostess for next week." Based on what she told me, I knew her problem: she was giving only one or two beauty shows a month. I also knew that former hostesses would be the most receptive to her request, giving her a better chance to book more beauty shows. With enough exposure, I felt she would do well. She just needed to gain confidence.
>
> At the end of the following week she called me back to report $748 in sales. Although it was not among the highest sales recorded that week, it was by far a record for her. Even though she hadn't booked all ten shows, she was elated and seemed to have snapped out of her depression.

Educating supplies the knowledge and training needed to perform. Coaching guides that performance in real time, shapes it, refines it, carries it forward, makes it matter. No more detached, cynical naysayers, but people who operate from feelings, who inspire others, who count on their teams to perform, who see that performance is rewarded and appreciated. Coaches know they will never have perfect information and they act anyway. They take one step, try something, move forward to listen and encourage.

---

I would like to suggest that in a day when so much energy seems to be spent on maintenance and manuals, on bureaucracy and meaningless quantification, to be a leader is to enjoy the special privileges of complexity, of ambiguity, of diversity—but especially the opportunity to make a meaningful difference in the lives of those who permit us to lead.

—Max DePree, Herman Miller, Inc.

## Coaching:
## Some Questions and Things To Do Now

• Reflect on this: alone, or with a colleague, or in a small group, think about team, group or organizational highs and lows in the past. What has marked the highs and lows in terms of people beliefs? Those of the leader? Of peers for each other? Picture (yes, visually) two or three exceptional coaches/bosses: What characterized them (especially again, their people beliefs)? Repeat the exercise for one or two bad bosses.

• Do you show substantial *support* for your team (as opposed to using praise or pressure alone)? How do you think your team members would evaluate your willingness to understand their problems and to do something about them (recall Mary Kay Ash's tangible support for the sidetracked consultant)? Evaluate how much real support you provide for your team. Think of at least three occasions when you applied pressure to perform, but without support; three times when you provided praise without support; and three times when you provided support and praise or pressure. How did the consequences of each approach differ? Why? Which approach was the most successful? Least successful?

• Visit a store, department, company or other organization that you particularly admire, and observe the manager/leader/coach very carefully. What does he or she do that enables the other people to perform? Plan to spend at least two or three hours observing. Do the same at the next sporting event you attend: Watch the coaches. Football, basketball, swimming or soccer are all good choices with plenty of opportunities to watch coaches in action. (Better yet, take a week "off" and attend a pro football summer camp—practices are usually open. Watch a Don Shula of the Miami Dolphins work with his staff and players.) How do they interact with their teams? When do they work with an individual? How does the style vary from one person to another? How does the coach behave during time-outs and during play? Make this a systematic study. Write down your impressions along with two or three ways you can apply them in your interactions with your team. (I.e., so you want to be a great leader? *Study* great leaders. Devote time to it. After all, whether as supervisor of the night maintenance crew or chairman of the board, your career *is* leadership. Have you studied it as you studied accounting? Physics? If not, why not?)

• Do you, de facto, know what your team expects from you as a coach? Ask each person individually how they want to work with you as a leader/coach. Do your impressions of their ability coincide with theirs? If not, is this a surprise? Or do patterns develop—e.g., do you tend to overfocus on administrative responsibilities and underfocus on helping your team members expand their skills or trying them out in new areas?

• Do you define coaching as showing up when there are problems? Do your people feel that they hear from you only when something has gone wrong? Ask two or three of your team members this question (it will be hard to do).

• Do you have an Open Door Policy? (I.e., do people use the open door?)

• Do you show up to provide real-time encouragement before an important event for one of your team members? And after to find out how it went?

• Find twenty-five little behaviors of yours that show you care about your team, that convey genuine respect and care beyond lip service. Be specific.

• Find twenty-five little behaviors that show indifference to your team (welcome to a very large club). You may not intend to communicate noncaring or noninvolvement, but your team members are the best judges. If you aren't sure, ask one or two of your team to help you (this can be very tough but extremely helpful).

• Follow Donna Ecton's example (VP, Campbell's Soup, then at Citicorp) and infuse your team with enthusiasm by renaming a company district or territory, e.g., from District 12B South (who can take pride in a name like that?) to the Superstars or other name that you and your team devise. Create symbols to go along with the name, and use it the way professional athletic teams use their colors, names and mascots to generate ownership and care.

---

### To Scream or Not to Scream

Indiana basketball coach Bobby Knight rants and raves—in practices and at games. And wins. San Francisco Forty-niner Coach Bill Walsh is so cool and collected that he is regularly called "cerebral," "the professor." He wins. Both are respected by their players. Both have an extraordinary degree of compassion for their players, albeit exhibited in almost diametrically opposing ways.

This is not the place to review the thousands of papers and monographs written about leadership and personality. It is, however, the place to underscore again that we observe that no one personality type is associated with coaching and leadership success. We do believe that compassion, empathy and a belief in the ability of the average team member is a must. But this belief can come in wrappers of all descriptions.

## Counseling

Problems arise. They fester. They must be fixed. "Tough-minded" managers take pride in "stepping up to the plate on tough personnel issues." Yet most, we find, stink as counselors. For counseling is about frankness *and* (equally) about compassion. It is the acid test of whether you really live up to the spirit of the "belief in people" you doubtless espouse. Poor counseling—too early or too late, too harsh or too soft, too perfunctory or dragged on forever—puts your beliefs on display as nothing else does.

It is April 24, 1984, and Herman Miller's Max DePree addresses the Annual Scanlon Plan Associates Conference in Raleigh, North Carolina. His themes are leadership, followership and, particularly, "ownership." DePree characterizes ownership, above all, as full-scale *accountability*, reaching for one's potential and "taking full possession of a situation," including sharing the ownership of problems. Counseling is the delicate but vital leadership role that leads people to seek and accept accountability.

All people have the *right* to know where they stand, "to be accountable," in Max DePree's words. This means your caring enough to let someone know in a timely fashion when performance is off track. It takes self-confidence and skill to lead people to recognize problems, as well as successes, in a constructive way. But as a veteran manager said to Nancy recently, "It's downright cruel to allow people to flounder when you can see what's happening and you don't do anything to turn it around. There's no excuse for that kind of insensitivity. None."

---

### The Art of Listening

Mary Kay Ash describes how she handled a personal problem of one of her executives:

> Sometimes listening by itself may not be enough—some people must be prodded if you are to find out what they're thinking. But a word of caution: Be subtle, or you'll come across as being intrusive. Sometimes a thin line separates invasion of privacy from concern and interest. With this in mind, when I sense a problem, I'll ask a question or two, then be quiet and listen for a response. Sometime ago, for instance, the work habits of one of my executives, whom I will call "Bill," began to falter. He had always submitted his reports promptly, but for several consecutive weeks he had been arriving at the office late, at the committee meetings he had contributed very little—all of which was quite uncharacteristic of him. One day while he was in my office explaining why a report was late, I decided it was time to have a heart-to-heart talk with him. I stood up from my desk and walked around to pour him a cup of coffee.
>
> "How do you like your coffee?" I asked.
>
> "Black would be fine."
>
> I put his cup on the table in front of the sofa and sat down. He automatically sat down beside me. "Bill," I said, "you're one of our

key people, you've been with us for twelve years, and I feel we have become good friends in that time."

"I feel that way, too, Mary Kay," he said in a soft voice.

"I'm concerned about you, Bill. You've always been so conscientious about your work that we've come to depend upon your contributions. But lately you just haven't been yourself...."

He didn't respond, so I stopped talking and took a sip of coffee. He seemed tense, and I offered to pour some more coffee for him. "No, that's all right," he answered.

"Is something wrong at home?" I asked.

His face grew red, and after a few moments he nodded his head.

"Is there anything I could do to help?"

He proceeded to tell me how upset he was because his wife's doctor had discovered a tumor on her upper back—and he wanted to tell me because he knew it was affecting his work. I'm certain it was necessary for him to release his bottled-up feelings; we must have talked for over an hour. He seemed to feel much better at the end of the conversation, and later his work improved immensely. While I didn't solve his personal problem, it was good for the two of us to talk about it.

Just how far a manager should go in discussing an employee's personal problems is something only the individuals involved can determine. I don't think a manager can work with a person day in and day out and not develop some sort of personal relationship.

The counseling role at its best leads people to understand and overcome problems that get in the way of top-notch performance. It's a question of always taking the time—now. Some problems turn out to be no more than small glitches and can be solved in fifteen minutes; many others will be the predictable result of incomplete information or simple misunderstanding. Others will require months of intermittent effort to unleash the potential of someone whose superior skills are shackled by an unwillingness to be a partner or team player. Counseling is *overkill* in all these situations.

## When Should You Counsel?

—When an individual has a solid track record but isn't performing as well as usual.

—When performance isn't improved by educating or coaching.

—When an individual asks for your help to solve a personal problem.

—When an individual is "stuck," unsure about how to proceed.

—When people are having trouble coping because your organization is growing very fast or is experiencing major change.

—When an individual used to success experiences failure or disappointment and seems unable to bounce back, especially after his or her role has been broadened by promotion.

## Counseling and Major Change

In a volatile environment marked by economic turbulence or fundamental change, even the very best will stumble before finding their sea legs. The same is true in industries that undergo major technological revolutions every few years as a matter of course. Counseling provides needed support and stability at these times by helping people discover how they can continue to contribute to their organization as it rolls with the punches; it also prepares people emotionally for the uncertainty to come. Even positive change needs to be facilitated by the willingness to counsel: Reducing bureaucracy to give each individual more freedom and a real stake takes some getting used to. Staff layers are reduced and real accountability replaces the "way we've always done it around here." It may sound like an unadulterated good. But it feels like a whole new ball game, and people have the right to expect sustained support and clearly articulated goals.* Counseling at its best can help people move through a period of change with their self-respect intact, which in turn can speed up the entire pace of change dramatically.

## The *Right* to Counsel

Before you take on the counseling role, ask yourself if the situation really calls for it. The first step is to give the individual a reasonable chance to turn things around under his or her own power, with your wholehearted support, without your interference. Counseling is *not* meddling—"involvement without the right or an invitation." Too soon is as disastrous as too late. You have the right to counsel when and only when you're invited, or performance problems threaten to undermine an individual's ability to contribute over time in spite of conscientious education and coaching. The right to counsel is *earned* by your demonstrated and repeated willingness to educate and coach first. If you pass that tough first test and the problems persist, it's time to extend a purposeful hand: "I want you to be effective, and I know that you want to be effective. Let's see how we can work together to achieve that."

---

### A Counseling Sequence

What follows is a counseling approach that we've learned from the collective experiences of Hewlett-Packard, Gore & Associates, People Express and Dana managers. Their problem-solving model is charac-

---

*GM confronted this during the early days of the 1984 merger with Ross Perot's EDS. The nonbureaucracy of EDS came as such a shock that hundreds of GM's senior MIS department people sought out unions as a buffer from straightforward transfer to EDS.

terized by the kind of care, sensitivity and respect for people that we see reflected in everything they do. Its unique attribute is the combination of hardheaded practicality (putting the organization first, as you must do for the sake of others) and compassion.

## Preparation

Getting ready to counsel has mainly to do with defining the key issue as you see it: improving working relationships, bringing slipped project schedules back into line, improving customer-service track records. Develop a focus on objective behavior and measurable results that the individual *can do something about*. Hazy interpretations are always misunderstood, and are rarely, if ever, very helpful. Worse, they betray a sincere desire to help by making you appear out of touch with real achievements as well as real setbacks.

## Schedule the Meeting

Some times are better than others for a counseling discussion. Counseling is a promise you must keep: Don't squeeze it between staff meetings. Don't cancel your first two tries. Pick a time when you both can give it your full attention, but do it during working hours. Conducting a counseling meeting after hours over a drink doesn't work. Superior counseling is not a warmed-over negative innuendo or two eased in between beers.

Top-notch counselors have very strong feelings about how much advance notice to give someone they will counsel. In a nutshell: not much. The reason? "People usually know when things aren't going well, even if they haven't asked for help," comments one manager. "You don't tell them on a Friday that you want to meet on Monday or Tuesday. Do you know what kind of a weekend they're going to have trying to second-guess what's on your mind? I'd want to be treated with more courtesy than that." The recommended alternative: ask the individual early in the day if he or she can meet with you that afternoon.

## State the Problem

The counseling process begins with a face-to-face discussion that you open with a brief, straightforward statement of why you wanted to meet. At this point you don't have to agree on the problem—just that you have something to talk about. This is not the time for drama. Open the discussion, and then listen.

## Listen

The most important part of counseling is listening. Nothing matters so much as your full attention. See what you can learn. Face up to a hard question: How have *you* contributed to the problem situation? A manager who's been there comments, "It's tough to admit that you're part of the problem. It's easy to convince yourself that you've been coaching just right. But you've probably gone too fast or too slow, maybe held on too tight. If you listen, you'll find out." What's at the root of the problem?

### When the Problem Is Personal

Counseling requires special sensitivity and genuine respect when the problem is personal in nature: family troubles, illness, alcohol or drug abuse, money problems. It can be tough to know how to help in situations like these, whether your interest will be seen as interference (it usually is) or your reserve mistaken for callousness (it usually is). Reassure the individual that you want to do what you can to help; be sure that people know what outside resources are available (e.g., counseling support, financial counselors or advisers). An empathetic ear and an open door may be the most genuine signs that you care.

### Put Together an Action Plan on the Spot

Once you know where you're headed, build the means to get there. What needs to happen, and when? What will your role be? Do you both agree? Before the meeting ends, set up another one to check on how things are going, to see how you can help and support progress.

### What Counseling Is Not

Counseling has boundaries that must be respected. Counseling is not:

—An opportunity for you to practice psychiatric therapy.
—A one-shot activity.
—An off-the-cuff discussion.
—Punitive.
—Solely concerned with personal problems.
—The Personnel Department's business.
—An opportunity to review an individual's whole life.
—A one-way mini-lecture by the counselor.
—A brief, hurried activity.
—Intended to solve all an individual's problems.

### Profile of a Good Counselor

How well do you perform the counseling role? The following characterize a good counselor:

—Is easy to talk to.
—Listens well.
—Helps people solve problems but does not overcontrol.
—Shows empathy when discussing problems.
—Is receptive to feelings.
—Can keep a confidence.
—Is perceptive in recognizing when help is needed.
—Wants people to do well.
—Builds self-esteem and confidence.
—Is interested in what the other has to say, not just what he or she wants to hear.
—Takes the other seriously.
—Is willing to spend time.
—Is receptive to the idea of others.

—Gives the other his or her full attention.
—Encourages another try.

In the "People, People, People" section we stressed ownership almost exclusively. In the customer and innovation sections, we stressed top-to-bottom attention to the customer's perception and inculcating the right to fail (a prime precursor to regular innovation). All three of these bases for distinctive performance emanate, more fundamentally, from genuine trust, care, respect and integrity on the part of leaders at all levels. Not mollycoddling, but sincere respect for the potential of the person.

The chief indicator of wholesale respect by you (the boss) for me (a person) is your willingness to give unabashedly of yourself as a counselor. It is via the act of counseling—a tremendous commitment on the part of every manager—that one best sees the willingness to take care and give respect beyond lip service.

No one disagrees: "All problems are people problems." Yet few put their calendars where their mouth is. Counseling meetings are delayed time and time again in the less effective companies. Failure to devote genuine concern and energy to counseling isn't a major black mark when senior managers evaluate junior managers. "Oh, boy, we waited too long, again [to address a problem]" is the common hallway lament in the mediocre performers. At IBM, if you wait too long, your days, to be blunt, are numbered. IBM says in a hundred ways, "Put the time in, *now*."

Like most of our "common sense" traits, this one, too, takes time. Even, heaven help us, time away from MBWA with customers and the shop floor. Nonetheless it may be the most distinctive mark of the star performer. Counseling, done with genuine care, *is* respect. Without it, the trust that breeds true ownership—throughout the entire organization—is simply not possible.

---

### Counseling:
### Some Questions—and Things to Do Now

• Think back and reflect on the first major setback you experienced in your career. How did your boss handle it? What was (or wasn't) done to make you feel stronger and wiser, rather than weaker and less confident? How specifically can you learn from your own experience and apply it tangibly with your team members? What would you do differently as a counselor from the ways you were counseled earlier in your career? What would you do the same ways? Why?

• If yours is a company in an industry that undergoes dramatic changes in short periods of time, have you adequately protected your people from its volatility by being aware (very closely aware) of the skills, achievements, talents and weak spots each person possesses (essential if your are to help an individual develop a long-term career)? If you can't describe, in detail, each person's skills and vulnerabilities, sit down within the week and talk at length with each of your team members. A large part of successful counseling is keeping up with potential problems before they arise, and protecting people from unexpected shocks or setbacks. Listen to what your people tell you. Review their performance records. What skills can be highlighted and stretched? What areas need to be strengthened? How can you help people stay in front of technological or industry changes rather than play "catch up" later? (P.S.: You *can* find the time. Our friend Marty Davidson, of the highly successful Southern Pipe and Supply, has an annual 45-minute meeting, on the road, with each of his *five hundred* employees, in forty locations.)

• Reflect again on your own career. What obstacles were the most difficult for you to overcome? Why? How can your experience be applied as you work with your team?

• When you counsel an individual, do you show respect for him or her by listening more than talking and advising? (If you said yes, try again. Are you sure? Most of us think we're good listeners, but aren't.) Do you treat the problem as important? Do you try to help the individual organize his or her feelings and impressions?

• Do you overprotect people so they cannot accept full ownership of situations (including problems)? Have you tried to hide or soften bad news? Do you encourage overdependence on you as a result? What do you imagine would happen if you gave clear, direct feedback about the problematic consequences of a situation?

---

## Confronting

*Don't live with a problem—face it honestly and correct it. Excuses interest no one except our competition. Never tolerate commitments in words instead of in spirit.*

*—Hewlett-Packard group manager*

This comment captures what we mean when we say that HP is a tough, no-excuses environment. Serious problems are taken seriously and addressed cleanly. The company assumes that performance problems can be solved, but only within the context of the HP Way, the company's operating philosophy.

There may come a time when a company has done all it can do to help people turn around a persistent problem. Alternatives have to be faced squarely and honestly. The last-ditch confronting role is for that purpose. It facilitates choice and makes the alternatives crystal clear.

## When Should You Confront?

—When performance consistently falls below expectations or deteriorates.
—When counseling does not resolve problems.
—When an individual seems unhappy and unable to perform in his or her role.
—When an individual's behavior is disrupting a team's performance or contributes to others' decisions to transfer or leave the company.
—When an individual is unable to meet performance expectations even though they are clear and understood.
—When reassignment or termination are the only remaining options.
—When the consequences of continued inappropriate behavior or low performance must be explained.

Confronting low performance is probably the toughest responsibility to carry out, but the alternative, observed all too frequently, is worse. Unaddressed, chronic, serious difficulty not only demoralizes the organization but undermines an individual's confidence and may make it nearly impossible for the person to bounce back. That's the crime of refusing to act, and act quickly. (Quite simply, nothing reduces the manager's credibility faster than the unwillingness to address an obvious problem. Our people rightly ask, "What in the hell is he or she [boss] waiting for?")

## Confrontation Defined

Confronting does *not* mean a tough battle, clash or personal attack, an *unplanned* hostile discussion, browbeating or threatening.* It never means treating people badly. Done by the best, it is in no way an opportunity for a frustrated leader to unload on someone else. Confronting is a form of counseling in which the alternatives and consequences are clear and close at hand. Provided the individual understands performance expectations (i.e., you performed your educator's role well), and provided you have done everything you can (effectively coached and counseled) to foster improvement, confronting can be a constructive, caring response to an individual's chronic low performance—a face-to-face meeting where you bring an individual's attention to the consequences of unacceptable performance, which include reassignment or termination. Confronting recognizes that a change is imperative.

*There is an unexpected benefit of this. We note that "alumni" (who failed to be promoted or were released) of the companies who counsel and confront most effectively end up being among the companies' biggest fans, once the initial pain has passed.

## When Loyalty Isn't Enough

*Inc.* magazine reports in the January 1982 issue:

Warren joined Diemakers Inc. shortly after it was started in 1960. There was only one person working with him when the company gave him the title of die-casting supervisor. But, in the next ten years, Diemakers grew from 40 to 150 employees, and Warren's staff swelled to 6.

Warren was a proud man who worked hard for the firm, and he was only a few years away from retirement. But as his responsibilities grew, Warren had trouble keeping up. Employees began taking their problems to the department's strongest manager, the second-in-command.

"We had a situation that outgrew the individual, and we should have dealt with it directly," says George Spalding, president of the Monroe City, Mo., diecasting company. Instead, Diemakers' management never confronted the supervisor about his limitations. Warren's feelings of frustration and failure mounted until he finally retired. . . .

Why do so many entrepreneurs and managers fail to confront these problems? The most common excuse is that other problems of running the company are more important.

"When you're trying to stay on top of a growing company, you tend to ignore this kind of problem, especially if the employee is at a low level in the organization," says Diemakers' Spalding. "But you can't overlook it because disgruntled people at any level can cause havoc in a company."

The other reason, of course, is the unwillingness to face the pain even if, in the long run, it might make things easier for all concerned.

"Don't kid yourself," said one chief executive. "Confronting a loyal employee about his limited capability makes for a very bad day. But if you can't address these situations, you're in the wrong job yourself. Most chief executives who don't take action think they're being good guys. The truth is you're a lousy guy for doing that."

Once more, this is a vital step beyond lip service in showing true respect for all your direct reports (whether division general managers or down-the-line team members). To allow a problem to fester beyond the limits of good sense exposes you as noncaring. You are not thought sympathetic because you let a problem drag on. (Properly handled confrontation is, of course, an art. Pull the string too quickly and all fear your capriciousness: "There, but

for the grace of God, go I." Pull it too slowly and you demonstrate the lack
of being in touch with your people.)

---

### A Confronting Process

Consider the person who has contributed consistently over time—
the last decade or more—and who is clearly giving the task his or her
full attention, but who recently has been outrun by state-of-the-art technology and is unable to keep up. Or think about the manager who loves
the technical side of his or her work but doesn't like the people side,
and whose team consistently suffers as a result. Consider as well the
person who believes more strenuously in quantification and methodol-
ogy than in paying attention to customers, innovative practices or people—a "forlorn existence," according to Max DePree. Each of these situations might be best handled with confronting, depending on the
answers to a few hard questions:

—Has this person been given every reasonable chance to succeed?
—Have company resources been used well to improve performance?
—Does this person understand what contribution is expected?
—Have you given honest and timely feedback?
—Is it possible to restructure the job to take advantage of this person's
strengths?
—Can this individual contribute to the company in other ways?

Your answers will help you determine whether confronting—to
effect a clear, focused change—is necessary. One manager observes that
"the hardest decision you have to make is when you've done enough
counseling and you have to ask: Have you really worked hard enough?
Was your heart in it? What can my team and my company live with?
The clear-cut decision doesn't exist."

### No Surprises

Except for the rare circumstance that demands on-the-spot action,
the occasion for confronting low performance should never be the first
time an individual realizes that there's a problem. The individual has
the right to know where he or she stands, and to have the means to
judge how serious a problem might become if it is not turned around.
By the time you decide that the time and solutions are limited, you both
should be very familiar with the issues.

### The Discussion

Once you are committed to a course of action, express yourself
directly. Words like "sometimes," "maybe," "sort of" or "a little" confuse and perplex. Your language must convey respect *and* clarity. The
intention to do what is best for the individual, his or her colleagues and

the company should govern what you say. Focus feedback on the value that hearing your comments will have to the recipient, not on the release they may give you.

Be brief: Give only as much feedback as the individual can hear and use. This is not the time to review tiny details of performance or to overfocus on "just the facts." Look the individual in the eye and try to put yourself in his or her place: how would you want to be treated?

Focus on positive alternatives: This is the part of the discussion you have to be precise about before you start. If the individual has a good track record up to now, a reasonable alternative might be to find another role in the company that he or she could perform successfully. When that isn't possible, decide beforehand what arrangements you can make, and stick to them.

At minimum, your feedback in confronting unacceptable performance begins a limited period of reevaluation that may lead to major changes in job focus, so it is never a discussion that is held without very careful thought.

## Paradox—Again

We have urged that you make the time for counseling and confronting, that you not put off the unpleasant meeting. To do so is injurious to all three parties: you, the confronted person, his or her colleagues. Be decisive. But, as we've also said with equal vociferousness, be methodical. And patient: Give every chance. Proceed step by step.

In effect, our advice is paradoxical: Be methodical and patient, but be decisive to be fair to all. We don't apologize for the paradox. Living with it, explaining it, and understanding it is what you get paid for. The "answer" to the paradox is your own (and your organization's) deeply held definition of trust, care, respect, fairness, due process, decisiveness and integrity all rolled into one. No wonder it's so delicate, so vital.

The dilemma is clear: Most of us probably don't think of a counseling meeting delayed a day as a "strategic issue," i.e., as a vital test of integrity (and care, trust, respect, etc.). It is. Our people are people watchers. It is exactly in these delays that the core of our philosophy, which will subsequently impact every strategic outcome, is most on display.

## Confronting:
## Some Questions—and Things to Do Now

• Carefully assess, for all your team members, their capabilities as well as their limitations. Can you anticipate situations where an individual is being outrun or trapped in a job he or she cannot do well—before serious failure occurs? Are you allowing someone to flounder unnecessarily? Pay special attention to those on your team who have recently taken on greater responsibility. How are they doing? Do you see any indication that this new, broad area of responsibility may be beyond the individual's reach? (An outstanding sales representative, for example, may be promoted to sales manager and subsequently fail because he or she liked the specialist role but not the supervisor/leader role.) Are you enough in touch to know who may be faltering in their jobs?

. How can you prepare people for the disappointments that may come their way? (E.g., when a new job isn't as rewarding as it seemed, when someone else gets the promotion, when an individual experiences his or her first failure.) What "shock absorbers" can you tap to help people cope with important changes in their careers before and after they happen? Resist the impulse to accentuate the positive or praise the individual's successes if he or she is, in fact, coping with failure: Allow yourself to hear what the person has to say about the circumstance. Are you comfortable giving people the opportunity to discuss their feelings with you—without fear or excessive embarrassment—about the impending change? If not, why not? Can you accept the individual's feelings and restrictions?

. How can you help an individual facing failure or major job changes to take control of his or her situation as much as possible? How can you engage the individual in joint problem solving?

. Do you find that you have to confront low performance frequently (i.e., is it your most often used approach)? After periods of no contact especially, do you attempt to resolve problems by confronting alone? If you do, consider the cost of your "hit-and-run" behavior, as one colleague so aptly described it. Are people in your department more dependent on you than you would prefer? Do they feel they must check with you before making any decision? (If you don't know, ask them.) If confronting is your most frequent form of contact, one price you pay is that you won't have a capable group who can act independently. Instead, they look to you for direction, even on tiny matters, because they want to avoid your wrath. Does your group experiment a little bit? Try something new? If not, look to your interactions with them. Are you educating? Coaching? Counseling?

---

We have devoted such substantial space to the five coaching roles because we know it to be a very special and powerful form of guidance, one for which there are no substitutes. The best coaches set in motion a continuing learning process—one that, we find, helps people develop a tolerance for their own struggles and accelerates the unfolding of skill and contributions that would not have been possible without the "magic" attention of a dedicated coach. Coaching is *not* a simple rubric. Done well, it is the best a leader can give.

# 19

# Doing MBWA

WE BEGAN WITH the technology of the obvious—MBWA; we explored MBWA with customers, suppliers, MBWA and innovation, MBWA and listening (to customers, as an unparalleled source of innovation), MBWA and leadership. That was introduction. Now we come full circle—to the process of *doing* MBWA. Leading (more so than managing) is a hands-on art. Coaching is the essence of leading—developing those with whom we work. Coaching *is* MBWA (or vice versa, we're not sure which, or whether it matters). This apparently obvious (we said it ourselves) trait/skill/process deserves a closer look.

First, it seems fair, honest, appropriate—and obvious to the many wounded among readers—to begin by saying that MBWA ain't as easy as it may sound! Doing it well is an art. However, it is an art that can probably be learned—and it is clearly unrelated to having an "outgoing" personality. In fact, arguably the best wanderers are the introverts who start with the ability to listen, because listening, and not tap dancing or pronouncing, is at the heart of effective MBWA.

There is a certain inappropriatness, frankly, to our use of the term "MBWA." In a way it makes the physical act of the wandering, per se, seem the most significant point. That is vital—but MBWA as we see it is much more. It is, as we have said, really a code word for all the aspects of leadership we have stressed. That's why it turns out to be so tough.

To begin with, as the effective leader wanders/coaches/develops/engenders small wins, a lot is going on—at least three major activities, usually all at once. They are (1) listening, (2) teaching and (3) facilitating. Listening is the "being in touch" part, getting it firsthand and undistorted—from suppliers, customers and your own people. Varieties of listening was the subject of chapter 2, "MBWA: The Technology of the Obvious." The very act of listening suggests a form of caring. MBWA is also a "teaching" (and "coaching") act. Values simply *must* be transmitted face-to-face. The questioning routines, order of visits and a host of other variables add up willy-nilly to the teaching of values. Finally, the wanderer can also be of direct help! The role of the leader as servant, facilitator, protector from bureaucracy (and bureaucrats) is the third prime MBWA objective. That is, often as not, you'll find a project or team stalled for want of 250 square feet of space in which to build a prototype, or an extra $15,000 travel budget to invite ten would-be customers for a weekend-long evaluation of a projected service. You can relieve the bottleneck on the spot, but only if you're there. As we said, the three roles are usually being performed simultaneously, even in a twenty-minute drop-in visit to a team, accounting group, or what have you.

## Space: Reduced or Enhanced

Let's talk about MBWA as leadership, talk about the art, and talk about the difficulty. For starters, MBWA is all tied up with *delegation*, which we still find to be, by a country mile, the toughest issue in management. Let's consider two people, one of whom (the good guy) we'll mention by name. Both are connected with high tech companies. Both are wanderers. So far so good. But one wanders, and the result is the enhancement of the performance of those with whom he comes in contact. The other is a bull in a china shop; he seems to do about as much harm as he does good.

The "good guy" is a fellow by the name of Barney Oliver, former head of Research and Development at Hewlett-Packard. First, Barney is a brilliant scientist. Second, he's tough as nails, and intellectually demanding. And yet he was the personification of effective MBWA in HP Labs, the heart of its "next bench syndrome," which in turn is the heart of open and participative (albeit tough-minded) communication.

Barney would wander, we are told, with extraordinary regularity. And he'd stop and chat. And, indeed, you had darn well better have something worthwhile to chat about! He'd look at what you were working on and ask the toughest questions imaginable. He didn't shy away from anything. (MBWA *doesn't* mean, then, that most subjects are *verboten*.) He spoke his mind. But the consensus, among twenty-seven-year-olds and fifty-seven-year-olds alike, was that when Barney had finished with you, (1) you'd learned a heck of a lot, of both lasting and short-term significance, and (2) *the project you were working on was still yours*—Barney had not taken away the space, had not in any sense told you what to do or what the next steps should be.

Mr. Bad Guy also wanders in technical spaces. He also knows what he is talking about, and isn't afraid to speak his mind. But when he departs, invariably the consensus is that little is left in his wake. You get the tough-minded dialogue, but the conclusion is his *telling* you, directly or indirectly, almost exactly what you ought to do next (and had better do—given his authority). One blitzed survivor commented, "In six minutes he essentially took away a project that I'd been working on for four months. When he left, it was suddenly his project, not mine."

The important point in the above is the combination of tough-mindedness and space left enhanced (or diminished). Both wanderers are tough. MBWA is *not* about *not* speaking your mind. Good wanderers don't ramble around saying only things like "Howya doin'," "How're the kids?" "Looks like you're doing OK." It's fine to ask about the kids and the spouse if you know there are kids and a spouse (and you should, in fact, find out before you go down and do your wandering). But gee-whiz socializing," per se, is decidedly not the prime objective of MBWA. It's to find out what's going on, to find out what's bugging people, and, indeed, to guide and direct by a questioning routine that conveys your value set—the sorts of things that "are important around here."

But there's a fine line between instilling your value set (via tough-minded, focused questions) and "managing" a project, and it's a line not easy to establish or maintain, because whether you are a first-line supervisor or CEO, your innocent question is so readily turned into a command—a stone tablet delivered from the mountaintop. Superior wanderers set parameters and draw mental pictures of what a good outcome would look like ("dramatizing the vision," as Bill Moore of Recognition Equipment puts it) instead of "suggesting" that "these three courses of action ought to be followed." Superior wanderers leave the "victim" enlarged, not diminished. They give him or her more freedom to try more things—within the parameters of the vision.*

Domino's Pizza Distribution Company president Don Vlcek demonstrated that fine line in the following story. He was on one of his regular field trips, and a supervisor was complaining that in the process of delivering dough to one particular shop, delivery people had repeatedly broken an exposed basement window. Vlcek whipped a $20 bill out of his pocket and said, "Buy some plywood and cover it—permanently." Afterwards, he talked to the supervisor about the episode: "We don't have any rules that prevented you from doing that. I expect you, within reasonable limits, to do what needs to be done." Let's look at what Vlcek did. He "taught" the young supervisor (by "a picture"— i.e., whipping out the $20 bill on the spot) what he ought to be up to—direct problem solving on his own. Yet he left the young man bigger, not smaller: "You do what's necessary and right, and let no Mickey Mouse get in your way." This was hardly a carte blanche to go out and buy Mercedes delivery trucks, but it was *guidance:* space-enhancing advice.†

---

*Tough-minded Tom West, hero of Tracy Kidder's *The Soul of a New Machine*, was a master. He set three or four crystal-clear guiding parameters for his team of youngsters developing a computer at Data General. Then he stayed out of the way, devoting the lion's share of his time to protecting them from corporate interventions. His ultimate genius was in *not* intruding, in the face of awesome outside pressures, during the critical debugging phase (all the more impressive given that debugging was his area of expertise). He left the space for his lads and the subsequent exhibition of the power of ownership to produce results was awe-inspiring.

†This story brings to mind a typical rejoinder we hear: "Show him he can spend $20 on window glass, and tomorrow he'll spend $100 on his girlfriend, if there's no explicit rule book." We believe it's the worst sort of straw man and reveals our interlocutors' complete lack of trust in their people.

### "Space":
### Some Questions—and Things to Do Now

• This will not be easy! If you're up to it, select four or five down-the-line people with whom you've had more or less regular contact. Sit down individually with them and talk about your style, as a space eater or enhancer. (You might have an outside consultant do this for you. It is one of the rare cases when a clinically trained outsider may be helpful.) As a second best, gather a group of two or three trusted peers and spend a half-day talking about how all of you come out on this dimension. (You might try doing the data collection by talking to a trusted colleague's people and getting some feedback on him or her—though it won't be easy.) Alternatively, start your data collection for the future (i.e., now). Have a trusted colleague go with you on your wanders and give you feedback (or have your secretary do so by, say, sitting in on meetings; any setting is fair game).

• Repeat the process for you and your colleagues as a management team. The tone set by the team is at least as important as that set by an individual.

• Suppose you and your team come up as space eaters par excellence, then what? There are some gimmicky aids (gimmicky, but not silly), such as (a) talking last, not first; (b) consciously using "What do you think?" and avoiding "Why don't you try X, Y, Z?"; (c) pushing your "pupils" to give you a detailed narrative, so that they expose their reasoning to *themselves*, with you continually interjecting "And then what did you try?" rather than "Why didn't you do thus and such at that point?"; (d) not forcing them to blame others, via questions such as "Did purchasing get you the parts on time?"; (e) leading them to generate the next steps with indirect (at most) guidance, with queries such as "And what should that fact lead us toward in the way of tests?"; and (f) asking them to stop by and tell you what was tried, or to give you a call, if it would be helpful, when the next step is taken, thus instilling urgency but not forcing a next step or specific milestone. It boils down to thinking ahead some, and trying to replay (ahead of time) what a typical question from you sounds like. (Is it truly a question, merely aimed at stimulating thought? Or is it a piece of rigid "advice"?) Just "thinking about it" is a very useful first step. Few of us do so, regularly or systematically (and even if we do, we readily forget to what degree our innocent *question*—not direction—sounds like a direct order to those ten years or two rungs more junior).

## Frequency

The simplest point to make about MBWA—and the toughest to get most of us to act on—is one that has to do with frequency: If you are not a regular wanderer, the onset of wandering will be, in a word, *terrifying*. Terrifying for you *and* terrifying for those with whom you come in contact (this is true whether you are a first-line supervisor, a small business person or chairman of a Fortune 500 company). Nonwanderers' infrequent forays usually amount to "state visits," prepared for by the "subjects" months in advance, with the result that what one beholds bears no relationship whatsoever to reality. MBWA is decidedly *not* about "state visits." It is a method for keeping in touch, getting real impressions, reinforcing strategic themes. The fact is that the most vital function of MBWA, *listening*, is not accomplished effectively in the "state visit" or "Select the good customer to visit" mode.

Both sides contribute to the problem. Suppose the sales vice president or regional sales manager is going to descend upon a local branch. He tells the top people there five weeks ahead of time. They set up some calls for him, because he thinks he ought to go out on calls. They pick patsy customers, who love the company. He learns nothing. Then he leaves. Two weeks later, routinely, the branch bitches to headquarters about not getting more support. Yet the sales manager's "MBWA experience" has told him that everything is rosy, so what's this about needing an extra $150 worth of tools for each person's kit? All the customers *he* saw were happy as clams.

The best (only?) way to beat the state visit rap is by wandering often, regularly, every day of the year. Barney Oliver was at first a terrifying figure to young and innocent engineers, but the fact that Barney was wandering

On his tenth anniversary with St. Joseph's Hospital in Stockton, California, our friend Executive Vice President Ed Schroeder was presented with this wonderful "MBWA award"—bronzed size-13 shoes!

around a good part of every day meant that eventually they got used to having him around. (It was never easy to have him around, but you did get used to it.) Given the size of HP Labs, and the company's geographic spread, he could hardly be an every-day visitor to every work space. But the real power of the regular wanderer was demonstrated by an amazing comment from a twenty-four-year-old HP engineer: "I know that Dave and Bill and Barney [Packard, Hewlet, Oliver] have been out of active management for quite a while now. But let me tell you, each of the [many thousands of] engineers on HP's payroll still believes today [this was 1983] that any one of the three is liable to stop by in the next five minutes." That's what frequency is all about: expectation, not mere statistical probabilities.

And, yes, it *will* be awkward at first. One president of a small company said, "Well, look, if I make the effort to go down on the shop floor, they [the people down there] have got to make the reciprocal effort and give me honest feedback." Why? Why in the hell should your people be committed to giving you "honest feedback" if your last three visits were to lay people off? So you read *In Search of Excellence* and suddenly you think wandering is a great idea—so what? You can't expect your people to give you a birthday cake the first time out. (Or even the twenty-first.) You *earn* honest feedback. And the main way you earn it is by the frequency of your wandering (and by what you do after you return home—more on that in a bit).

By frequency we mean exactly that. In order to visit each of the over seven hundred Wal-Mart stores at least once a year, Sam Walton takes a minimum of three full days a week; much of the rest of his time is spent visiting distribution centers, riding with Wal-Mart drivers, and visiting suppliers. Robert O. Anderson, Arco's chairman, averaged about five hundred miles a day during his fifteen years as CEO of that company. *Quite frankly, we believe that any supervisor—accounting, first line in the factory, engineering, merchandising, information systems or Fortune 500 CEO—probably ought to be out of the office 75 percent of the time, and in the field (if he or she has multiple, dispersed geographical sites) at least 50 percent of the time.*

And note: Doing away with the state visit doesn't mean that you should be afraid to *advertise* the fact that you are out wandering. The best way to have people think that you might come by is to let them know you are out and about—*listening*—most of the time.

---

### "Frequency":
### Some Questions—and Things to Do Now

• How often are you out of your office? Be specific. Look at your calendar for the last sixty to ninety days. Break it down into meetings, visits and other. Take the meeting component and break it down into formal and informal, making note of the location of each meeting. Go over each in-office/in-headquarters event and ask yourself if it could have taken place as readily on the other person's turf: e.g., why not have the R&D review in the labs, rather than in your office?

Could visits have been used more productively? Look at each. Could one or two (or five or six) brief "walk-throughs" of another field facility or another department have been added?

• Now look ahead sixty days. First, look at booked, must-do events: Can some be held at "their place" rather than "your place"? Look at your currently unprogrammed time; can you put "Don't book" in 25 percent of it, and save the time for spontaneous "wandering"?

• Think about putting a checklist or two in a reachable desk drawer (or even in your wallet). On it (them) note, for instance, your top twenty-five customers, your top twenty-five vendors, twenty-five upcoming milestones for project teams, twenty-five facilities or departments. Systematically plan to "do" two from each list each week (two customer calls, two departmental "drop-ins"). You might even use a desk-top personal computer for this. Have your secretary, if you have one, bug you about the lists (she or he should have duplicates), or even give you weekly gold stars if you get all of your "MBWA 'to dos'" completed.

• Repeat all the above as a team: analysis, meeting location shifts and checklists. Make your *team* MBWA Scorecard a regular (first?) agenda item when you get together for staff meetings. Force group feedback at least weekly.

---

## Trappings of MBWA

Trappings are vital. Anderson's (Arco) routine is highly instructive. Above all, he didn't travel with a retinue. There weren't seven hovering note-takers from staff in attendance, shaking their heads and clucking as they thought he would at forms not filled out appropriately.

The orders or sequence of wandering is vital. Mr. Anderson's habit was to arrive at a district field office and immediately head for an ongoing, routine meeting of junior geologists and geophysicists discussing a minor property. He didn't begin with an hour-and-a-half, behind-closed-doors visit and strategic review with the district supervisor. He hopped in, virtually unannounced, and looked in on whatever was happening at the time. Andy Pearson followed about the same routine at PepsiCo. When he arrived, he'd drop in on a junior assistant brand manager, ask him, "What's up? What's going on?" or stop in on a meeting far down the line that was pretty routine. The bosses came later. A fellow who runs a mid-sized construction company has a similar ritual. One of his vice presidents remarks: "Whenever he arrives at a construction site, it's automatic. He makes a beeline for the crane operators or the welders. The site boss is last on his list." Senior people *will* get their time. They always do. *Starting* at the "lower" levels shows those people the importance you attach to them—that they are not, in fact, "lower" at all, but are vital to the organization.

---

### Bank Wanderer

A manager of several branches of the retail part of Chase Manhattan decided to manage less by form and more by wandering. She didn't tell people when she was going to arrive, not in the state-visit sense, but she did give them a little warning. She'd stop at a phone booth before hitting a site and say, "See you in half an hour." When she arrived she'd go up to somebody in the operations area, look at what he or she was doing, and spend a little time chatting about it. The tail end of the visit would be the branch manager.

---

There are some other, smaller points to be made in connection with the trappings of MBWA. One president of a small business asked us, "What do you wear when you do MBWA?" Our answer? "Whatever feels comfortable." What we mean is that if you're a three-piece-suit wearer, and the vest is always buttoned and the cuffs of your shirts are monogrammed, wandering around in overalls is apt to make you look a bit of a fool. On the other hand, if you can pull it off—i.e., comfortably—we're all for overalls if you're in a plant. We heard a story about a well-run GM plant where the manager was a wanderer supreme. His relationships with his people were terrific. His costume for wandering was almost always the same (what it was, in fact, when he was sitting at his desk—unless the brass from Detroit were about to show up). It was a satin baseball warm-up jacket with the insignia of the UAW local on it; he wore that and a baseball hat pushed back on his head as he ceaselessly trooped around.

It is a little easier to be informal—and to listen—if you can wear informal clothes and not look strange in the process. But there are a lot of jerks who wander around in baseball jackets, so that doesn't mean everything, to put it mildly. And if you are one of the true buttoned-down types, and you are always seen in pictures in the company newspaper wearing a three-piece suit (even on the softball diamond), then don't suddenly head out to the field with a T-shirt on; if you do, people will probably think, "Ah, he's practicing wandering. Been to one of Peters' seminars." And that decidedly is not the point.

---

### "Trappings":
### Some Questions—and Things to Do Now

• Think about the trappings when various people visit you. Analyze two or three recent visits in detail. Do the trappings make a difference? How? What are the smart-aleck remarks you make after visits of higher-ups? Could the visitors have avoided the faux pas that led to your snide assessments? How? Now, turn your attention to yourself (and yourself and your colleagues as a group). To what extent do you manage/think through the "trappings" issue— e.g., order of visits, formality of note taking, clothes? Do you consider this a useful exercise, or low priority, or silly? If you don't take it seriously, ask yourself why. The greatest world leaders have unfailingly been fanatics about trappings.

---

## Maintaining the Chain of Command

Except for the matter of leaving space (or, better yet, enhancing it) the toughest issue in MBWA has to do with abrogation (or not) of the chain of command. A score of points could be made. Quite simply, the best of the MBWAers do not abrogate the chain of command. But wait: Of course they *do*, in a way. Let's not kid ourselves. Wandering down, skipping two or five or six, or, heaven help us, ten layers *is* violating the chain of command. Regardless of your purpose. You're there to hear it firsthand, and you're there to do some teaching firsthand. No bones about it. But there are degrees.

Consider former Chairman Ed Carlson of United Airlines. Soon after taking over the ailing airline, he hit the field, asking very direct questions—in detail, for his objective was to clean up the bureaucratic mess he had inherited. He took endless notes, usually on scraps of paper, and stuffed them into his pocket. He never told people down the line what to do or change, he never fixed what he disliked (unless it was a matter of safety) on the spot. But what he did do—and this is vital—was *promise* that he would get back to people in a very short time (five working days at most). And he promised he would get back with *action*, not the announcement of the appointment of a six-month task force or study group. When he returned to home base, he played it straight: he let the chain of command know what he had found and that he wanted action taken, immediately. Then he initiated correspondence with the down-the-line people he had chatted with on his wanderings, letting them know that something was up, and had his staff check religiously to make sure that action was taken, and taken within the promised time.

Of course an abrogation of the chain of command was involved here. Carlson's unabashed objective was to skip steps, get on directly and rapidly with debureaucratizing, using himself in a highly visible fashion to make his point. (He called it "visible management".) But the implementation was done in a relatively traditional if uncommonly rapid fashion. In sum, to make MBWA credible one must promise fast action and then make damn sure that it occurs within the proposed time frame; but to do so does not mean (or should not mean) impetuously issuing the order to the first-line person on the spot.

Again, frequency is a key issue. The screams about violating the chain of command will be particularly loud at first. Your presence (even if you're a second-line supervisor) is initially awkward. People overlisten to you and overinterpret the subtle inflections in your voice. Many a million-dollar program has been started, or stopped, because of a frown by a division general manager at the wrong second (and because, it turns out, he had a fly land on his nose). And that *will* happen. But it will happen less—this is a simple law of nature—the more you are around. People will figure out what sort of person you are when they've had a chance to be exposed to you. Your managers will come to accept the fact that you're not going to destroy the chain of command only when you repeatedly demonstrate that you won't.

---

### An MBWA Classic

From "The Oldest (and Best) Way to Communicate with Employees," by Roger D'Aprix, (*Harvard Business Review*, September–October 1982):

> In the course of examining the communications of a certain organization, [consultant] Scott Meyers discovered an interesting practice. For some years employees had had a common coffee break during which all coffee machines were programmed to dispense the beverage free. At the same time, a cart carrying free pastries for everyone was wheeled into each area. . . .
>
> At his next meeting with the president, Meyers suggested that he join his people out in the corridor at the coffee bar. The president smiled patiently and said that he couldn't do that. Asked why not, he replied that "it simply wasn't done." Top officers all had their coffee in their own offices dispensed from a mahogany cart. They never mingled with the other employees during breaks. It would have been bad form and might even constitute intrusion.
>
> Meyers persisted, however, and reluctantly the president agreed to try the radical idea. His first attempt was an abysmal failure. He didn't even know how to work the coffee machine. A by-stander, seeing him fumble with coins, walked over and told him the coffee was free. Red-faced, he took the cup in hand and looked for someone to begin a conversation with. No one approached him; employees were clustered in little groups quietly discussing their various concerns and glancing curiously at him. He drank his coffee and walked back into his office.
>
> To Meyers he pronounced the experiment a flop—they wouldn't talk to him. Meyers told him that the problem was two-fold. He made his appearance too formal; instead of wearing his suitcoat, he should have gone out in his shirt sleeves. Moreover, the workers weren't used to seeing him in their area. To make this a fair test, Meyers urged, he must go back tomorrow. At first the president was emphatic in his refusal to subject himself again to such humiliation. Eventually he agreed to try one more time, with his coat off.

This time he got his coffee without incident and screwed up the courage to break into the perimeter of the small gathering. After some conversation about the weather, he asked how things were going and heard some pleasantries from the group indicating that everything was fine.

The following morning, after doing some homework on the current concern of the work force (the opening of a plant in Europe), he raised the subject with the coffee break group and explained the logic behind the decision. He was surprised to find himself in the middle of an animated discussion about the plant.

The next day and the next the president went out to the corridor for his morning coffee. In time, he found himself holding forth on all kinds of company issues with employees, who now felt comfortable enough to air their concerns. The kaffee-klatsches were working so well that he asked his senior staff to begin mingling with their people at coffee time.

A vital subpoint, in connection with this issue, is the necessity of assuring and accomplishing the absolute protection of those who talk with you. The objective is to find out what is going on, to listen especially to the clerks, the MIS gang, the assistant branch manager, the junior buyers and the people on the loading dock. There is a tendency among "real people" (those on the loading dock and in the PBX room) to be frank, interestingly enough. And it is vitally important, especially in a tradition-bound organization, to make sure that the provider of frank feedback isn't shot or exiled to Siberia after your visit. A lot of first-line supervisors don't take too kindly to an hourly person mouthing off to a vice president (or even a third-level supervisor) about the rotten state of the housekeeping ("The toilets stink"). A lot of second-line supervisors don't take kindly to first-line supervisors doing the same thing. So the all-pro wanderers are crystal clear on this point. If they find even the slightest hint that something negative has happened as a result of someone speaking out (and they actively listen to the grapevine to check), the person responsible is fired or demoted or sent to Siberia. The MBWA process rests, foursquare, on absolute integrity. If the integrity is not there, it all becomes a very bad joke. And, once again, the frequency of visits is involved. At first it will be tough enough for people to open up. But once they hear that you wander regularly (50 percent of the time), that you do get back to people quickly, and that you do watch out for the people who have spoken up, then gradually, the process will begin to work.*

---

*This is an extraordinarily thorny issue. We talked with one Fortune 50 president. He wears his integrity on his sleeve, in a company where it's sadly uncommon. People—junior clerks in the Austin, Texas, operation—do open up with him regularly. He is continually astonished at the havoc he creates when he inadvertently lets a clerk's name slip in subsequent conversations with his peers.

Bourns' Bert Snider summarizes nicely: "There's always a chance that a foreman, for example, will think the CEO is screwing things up by getting involved. But I think there's a danger only if the foreman is singing a different song from the CEO. If they're all singing the same song, the CEO is only reinforcing that song in people's minds. If it's a song they've never heard before, then, yes, they'll be confused."

---

### "Chain":
### Some Questions—and Things to Do Now

• Do you have an *exact* routine for getting back to everyone who talks to you? Does it include a harsh (for you) deadline for action—e.g., forty-eight to seventy-two hours? Do you meet your deadline? How do you handle the standard chain of command in asking for follow-up? Do you ensure that they conform to your promised deadline? How do you (if you do) ensure that subtle negative action is not taken against those who speak out (e.g., that snide remarks about "George airing our dirty linen with the boss" don't follow in the wake of a frank exchange about quality with a foreman)? Most important: do you play slavish attention to and "manage" these issues?

---

### Listening, Teaching, Facilitating:
### Some (More) Suggestions

Listening is best done on somebody else's turf. That is why we urge wandering. There are, however, many ways to do it, even on the other person's turf. One is to gather people together in formal question-and-answer sessions. That's not bad. Ren McPherson, the former Dana head, used to do a lot of this, sometimes gathering fifteen hundred people together in the same room and taking questions with all present. It's useful, because the group as a whole takes the measure of the "boss" in this kind of a setting. Is he or she trying to pull the wool over our eyes? Is he or she being straight with us? What is he or she hiding? Why? Small, impromptu get-togethers with cross sections of five or ten people are also helpful. Again, the trick is in the word "impromptu"—the people attending should be picked at the last minute, on the spot. A carefully crafted and preselected group merely sets you up to hear what some supervisor thinks you want to hear. Also vital are wandering the line and going out on calls with sales and service people.

Some other listening rituals: Our colleague Jack Zenger reports that the president of the Syntex Corporation makes a habit of eating breakfast at the same table in the company cafeteria about twice a week. It's well known that he will be there, and that anybody is welcome to come up and sit with him. Note also, however, that nobody came and sat with him at first. Then, probably out of sympathy, a few brave souls ventured to do so. And it's only now—after twenty years—that it has become comfortable. That's MBWA for you!

Bill Moore's turnaround at Recognition Equipment also involved break-fast—a ritual that became known as Biscuits with Billy. Four or five mornings a week he was there in the company cafeteria, to chat with all comers. What did they chat about? Anything, everything, and nothing. His mere presence implied that he wanted to listen and keep in touch. He shared heretofore sensitive data about small gains and small losses, making it clear that every-body was part of the team effort. His self-confidence and frankness conveyed a badly needed "Someone's in charge here" sense to the whole organization. Above all, Moore is neither a time waster nor a "How ya doin'" type. Times were tough and he was taking tough-minded action. So the breakfast vehicle became a vital, frank, and practical daily "state of the corporation . . . and you and me [Moore]" interchange.

Listening is the number one objective of MBWA. Teaching is almost as important, however, and it emphatically does *not* mean telling people what to do (that delicate point again). It does mean telling people in a direct, no-nonsense fashion what it is you think is important about the world—their world and yours. It can as readily be accomplished by the regular pattern of your questioning routine as by a formal speech, but it is a big part of the MBWA process.

Wandering activity is, in this regard (and above all), a golden opportunity. The pattern of your questioning—and variations therein—*will* be noticed and interpreted, have no doubt about it. Everything about what you are up to—your dress, the order in which you talk to people, the things you focus on in your questions, the things you *fail* to focus on—will be, even if you are a regular wanderer, the subject of endless speculation. You have just two choices in the matter: to go about it in an erratic fashion or to go about it systematically. We would highly recommend the latter because it would mean that you will in fact be teaching what you want to teach and not some-thing else.

By systematic we don't mean planning every second of your visit. We do mean making sure that your two or three simple messages are the focus of everything you do: the questioning pattern, the visiting pattern while on the site, etc. Tom followed Frank Perdue around for a day in Salisbury, Maryland, in the summer of 1983. In the course of that day he gave half-a-dozen impromptu talks, always on the same subject—product quality. It is what he's been jawing about for forty years, but he still takes every opportunity, no matter who's the target, to reinforce his point of view.*

On the other hand, we have followed many managers around who squan-der their opportunities. One colleague was involved in a life-and-death qual-ity program: Get it better or lose a $100 million contract renewal. Several solid successes had been chalked up, and more were coming in every day. Yet in the course of a four-department visit, he missed opportunity after oppor-tunity. In one of the four instances he said nothing about quality. In two oth-

---

*And if you knew Frank, you'd know it surely wasn't for Tom's benefit!

ers it was an afterthought. Only in one was quality an up-front topic. In no instance did he attempt to build momentum by giving accounts of the successes in other parts of the organization. Instead he became involved in putting out a series of routine brushfires on a variety of issues. It is not that he wasted time, but that he failed to use the time to hammer home his overarching priority.

In the first chapter in this section we looked at the leader (plant manager or MIS boss) as dramatist. Coaching, teaching and transmitting values, more than any other responsibility of leadership, demand dramatic skills. However, it is vital that the show you put on not be fraudulent in any way, that you do not merely act a part. Your people will judge your integrity. And they will get it right! The smallest inconsistencies or hypocritical acts will be noted. The story is not a wholly negative one, of course. If you do act with total integrity, the MBWA process is the best and, in a sense, the only way in which to truly demonstrate it. That is, your people will judge your integrity by the cast of your eye (Napoleon said, "If you wish to lead people, speak to their eyes"), the firmness of your grip, and a multitude of other little things. You cannot fake it. Nor can you *convey* it except in person. A videotape helps, but it is no substitute for all the millions (literally) of bits of data that we process when we observe a person face-to-face.

There is an important point about communication behind all this. We have had many people, particularly in connection with such MBWAing as a daylong ride-around with a single salesman, say, "Look, it's such low leverage. I have got seven hundred fifty (or seventy-five hundred) people in my company. To spend one day with *one* salesman is too darned expensive." We think such a view is wrongheaded. The worldwide rumor will mill be grinding away *seconds* after that day comes to an end (if not before). Every item of your conversation will be known four thousand miles away about half an hour after it occurs—at the most. As one wise soul said about such visits: "The sound of the old man's voice travels at the speed of light around here." It travels at the speed of light *everywhere*. So the teaching that takes place on that day will not be lost—that is, unless it is lost through your squandering the opportunity.

MBWA's big three are listening, teaching and facilitating; we've talked of the first two and, peripherally, the third. Facilitating is Ed Carlson promising action within about five days after a visit. But even that's somewhat indirect. So what's direct facilitation? A successful senior manager at Bell Labs has it right: "My job? Run the Xerox machine for a team at three A.M the morning their project is due for review. I spend half my time just asking dumb questions: 'What's bugging you?' 'What's getting in the way?' It turns out it's seldom big stuff. It's usually petty annoyances. A small group needed a personal computer, and was being dragged through an almost full-blown capital budget review to get one. I got them one in forty-eight hours. And so on. Running interference and kicking down small hurdles. And, you know, you can only do it if you're out there. Nobody will come to you with this stuff. They think it's 'too trivial' to bother you with! They think they ought to be able to do it themselves. So they'll tie themselves up in knots for a week on some little nit."

The only addendum we have to that is to point out that it's the small stuff that is almost always—because of its cumulative effect—at the heart of major problems. As an IBM systems manager said, "How does a project come to be delayed by a year? One day at a time."

MBWA is not easy, and it shouldn't be easy. Estimating conservatively, we'd bet a thousand variables are at play! We have described only a handful. MBWA exposes you. Your ability to listen is exposed. Your honesty and integrity (or lack of it) is exposed. Your consistency is exposed to the scrutiny of the toughest watchers of all—hourly people. You can bullshit a vice president with ease. But it's almost impossible to BS somebody on the loading dock. They have been there and back. Your vision (or, lack of it) is exposed. Your statements have coherence (or not) relative to the basics of that vision. Jan Carlzon's hammering home his vision of SAS's transformation from a "broker of assets" to a "service company" was and is the theme of a thousand thousand impromptu chats.

Putting major effort and energy into learning MBWA and practicing it is worth the candle, but it won't be easy. In fact, it will be hard. If you haven't done much of it, we can guarantee that the first few days, weeks, months, and perhaps years, will be just plain awful. Few will trust you: "What's he up to?" "How long will it take for this 'wander phase' to pass?"

And ah, yes, how *do* you find the time? You are already busy. You already have forty-seven more legitimate priorities than you can deal with. Maybe you can play a game with yourself. A friend wanted to free 20 percent of his time for wandering. Together we did an analysis of his calendar for the week after next. He had some twenty-nine scheduled meetings; moreover, the phone log revealed that another fourteen people had requested meetings that he'd not been able to squeeze into his docket. The solution was simple: "Dave, cut your meetings to seventeen." His obvious (and reasonable) rejoinder: "Why seventeen?" The rebuttal: "Well, look, you could have had forty-three [the twenty-nine he was going to have plus the fourteen he hadn't been able to schedule], but you only had twenty-nine. Neither the forty-three nor the twenty-nine makes any sense at all as a number. So the seventeen can't make any less sense than the twenty-nine! Right? And it has a nice ring to it, seventeen, doesn't it? It sounds precise, sounds like you've given it a lot of thought."

Who among us can say that our calendar—in any way, shape or form—really makes sense? Perhaps it does reflect, directionally, our strategic priorities. But the set of a week's meetings can hardly be called "optimal." It's mostly random and reactive. And the only way to change it, unfortunately, is to change it. Not through immutable logic, there's none available. But just by doing it. And, perhaps, like our friend Dave, you can at least take some comfort in the fact that the new schedule makes no less sense than the previous one. That we can guarantee you. So what are you waiting for? . . . "Uh, Mr. Arnold, sorry to interrupt your reading, but your ten-forty-five is here."

# 20

# Excellence in School Leadership

... in his valley in western Massachusetts, Frank Boyden, who is 86, continues his work with no apparent letup, sharing his authority by the thimbleful with his faculty, traveling with his athletic teams, interviewing boys and parents who are interested in the school, conducting Sunday-night vesper services, writing as many as 70 letters a day, planning the details of new buildings, meeting with boys who are going home for the weekend and reminding them of their responsibilities to "the older traveling public," careering around his campus in an electric golf cart, and working from 7 a.m. to midnight every day. If he sees a bit of paper on the ground, he jumps out of his cart and picks it up. . . .

In 1966, in *The Headmaster,* author John McPhee wrote those words about Frank Boyden, of Deerfield Academy. Boyden had begun his tenure there in 1902. He had fourteen students, and had induced most of them to come by leaping into a borrowed horse and buggy and heading out to the farms surrounding Deerfield to do hands-on recruitment. Boyden, said McPhee, had "no plan, no theory." He was an "educator by intuition." In one of the seventy letters a day that he wrote in 1953 Boyden stated, while turning down a request to give a speech, "I have no definite topic. I would not quite know how to approach any other than an educational subject, and in my work have just gone ahead from day to day without any particular theory or any particular policy except a real personal interest in the boys, in their work, in their activities. I'm afraid you would be very definitely disappointed in any effort which I might make." In conversations with McPhee, Boyden made the same point: "My philosophy—I can't express it really: I believe in boys. I believe in keeping them busy, and in the highest standards of scholarship. I believe in [creating] a very normal life."

Boyden *did* have a distinct philosophy: for the kids. And everyone had to buy in. The Deerfield faculty had inordinate demands placed upon it. "I'm not running this school for the faculty," said Boyden. "I'm running it for the boys." To achieve his dream, Boyden was omnipresent. In 1902 ". . . he set up a card table beside a radiator just inside the front door of the school building. This was his office, not because there was no room for a headmaster's office anywhere else but because he wanted nothing to go on in the school without his being in the middle of it. Years later, when the present main school building was built, the headmaster had the architect design a wide place in the first-floor central hallway—the spot with the heaviest traffic in the school—and that was where his desk was put and where it still is. . . . If the mood of the student body at large is poor, he will sense it, and when one boy is disturbed, he will see it in the boy's face, and he will think of some minor matter they need to talk over, so that he can find out what the difficulty is and try to do something about it. He has maintained his familial approach to education despite the spread of bureacracy into institutions and industries and despite the increased size of his own school [from 14 boys to over 500]."

While tough on his teachers and demanding exceptional commitment, he gave them almost total freedom to teach as they pleased in the classroom. His philosophy, notes McPhee, was the essence of simplicity. Yet the sensitivity and intensity required to execute it was remarkable. McPhee adds that he was "in the highest sense, a simple man, and he has spent his life building a school according to elemental ideals, but only a complicated man could bring off what he has done, and, on the practical plane, he is full of paradox and politics. Senior members of the faculty, in various conversations, have described him as 'a great humanitarian,' 'ruthless,' 'loyal,' 'feudal,' 'benevolent,' 'grateful,' 'humble,' 'impatient,' 'restless,' 'thoughtful,' 'thoughtless,' 'selfish,' 'selfless,' 'stubborn,' 'discerning,' 'intuitive,' and so on."

Who was this Frank Boyden? He was an original. Or was he? in 1983 Sara Lawrence Lightfoot wrote a book called *The Good High School*, the culmination of years of research, in which she analyzes six schools. Two were tough urban schools, George Washington Carver High School in Atlanta and John F. Kennedy High School in New York City. Two were suburban: Highland Park High School, near Chicago, Illinois, and Brookline High School, in Boston. Two were "elite": St. Paul's School and Milton Academy. In this essay we shall focus on three of the six principals—Dr. Norris Hogans of Carver, Robert Mastruzzi of JFK, and Bob McCarthy of Brookline—the three who face the toughest environments, radically different from Boyden's peaceful valley in western Massachusetts.

We shall attempt to take the framework and findings of *A Passion for Excellence* and apply them to the school setting. To this effort we bring only our commonplace experiences as high school students and a handful of seminars we've held with school administrators; we are admittedly taking a leap beyond our area of expertise, for three reasons. First, school leadership and management are obviously important, and the subject of excellence in education is appropriately high on the national agenda. Second, we were struck as if by lightning by the traits shared by Boyden, Hogans, Mastruzzi, McCarthy, and, say, Ray Kroc, Willard Marriott, Frank Perdue, Tom Watson. As we read McPhee's tale of Frank Boyden, age eighty-six, heading out to his football field in his golf cart late at night, in the rain, to replace the divots that had been dug up during the afternoon's junior varsity game, and as we read about his discussing in great detail with a junior varsity high school coach the unsatisfactory nature of recent postgame receptions, we were struck by the parallel to Willard Marriott's years of reading every complaint card received from a Marriott Hotel guest, to Forrest Mars checking out the displays of M&M's in local candy stores, and to Ray Kroc's ceaseless effort to move quality, service, cleanliness and value one step further at McDonald's.

The third reason stems from the fact that we have regularly been accused of merely rediscovering "common sense"—and the fact that the charge is true, because "common sense" has not been practiced much lately in most of today's businesses. We suspect the same is true in schools, and Sara Lightfoot confirms our suspicions: In most schools, she writes, "Teachers are typically cast in low positions in the school's hierarchy and not treated with respectful regard. In the worst schools, teachers are demeaned and infantilized by administrators who view them as custodians, guardians, or uninspired technicians. In less grotesque settings teachers are left alone with little adult interaction and minimal attention is given to their needs for support, reward, and criticism." Oh, how the bells of familiarity ring. Lightfoot adds that only if teachers are treated as adults, will they, in turn, treat students as adults through "mature and giving relationships." So obvious! And yet it recalls that "obvious" (and sadly unusual) comment from the president of a small company in the private sector: "If you want your people to treat your customers with courtesy, doesn't it follow that you must first treat your people with courtesy?" True. Obvious. And rare. In factory or school, it seems.

## Vision/Symbols/Principal
## as Salesperson

McPhee says that Frank Boyden devoted his life to "developing the character of the school." Lightfoot observes in Norris Hogans a "clarity of vision and purpose." In general, in the six schools she surveyed, Lightfoot notes a "clear authority and vivid ideological stance." At Brookline, Principal Bob McCarthy had his faculty devote an inordinate amount of time to development of a written philosophy; honing the four hundred words required months and months of debate, as the meaning of each semicolon was examined in detail.

---

### *School Philosophy of Brookline High School*

1. *Education Presumes a Climate of Care*

   The schoolhouse must be a kind of home which offers its inhabitants a sense of belonging, of individuality strengthened by expectation, of security born of respect. As in the home, the student should feel known but revered; the teacher, exposed but esteemed. Reason for excellence need not preclude acceptance of human foibles; neither should devotion and understanding be devoid of rigor. Care is by nature compensatory, seeking to provide that which would otherwise be lacking.

### 2. Thoughtfulness Is the Social as Well as the Intellectual Aim of Education

The habit of reflection is the ideal trait of the educated mind, taking for its concern what others may be satisfied to take for granted. Education should foster this habit, should teach us patience in the understanding and construction of ideas. But it should also teach us to consider feelings, to anticipate the probable effect of our actions and words on others, and to temper these when they augur injury. Education is thus forethought rather than afterthought, abiding thought rather than sporadic thought.

### 3. No Style of Learning or Teaching Is Privileged

Learning and teaching are two sides of the same coin. Both rely on a sense of timing, a state of readiness, a heightened sensibility which enables one to see or say or think something not seen or said or thought before. Readiness is achieved in different ways, depending on what there is to be learned. Sometimes it requires painful and protracted effort—thinking, reading, watching, writing, talking, doing. Other times it is attained effortlessly, almost inadvertently. Either way, timing is critical. Knowing how to learn or how to teach is essentially knowing when to press and when to wait. Styles of learning and teaching are characterized by their mix of pressure and patience. Thorough education will expose teachers and students to a range of styles so that they come to know their own.

### 4. Learning Is a Mixture of Pleasure and of Pain

The love of learning is an acquired taste, an addiction for the tart rather than the sweet. To learn is to change, and to change can be both exhilarating and wrenching. As creatures of habit, we must approach learning with trepidation, not expecting those who learn to experience a smooth trajectory of triumphs, nor those who teach to effect unrelieved excitement about their subject. While it is true that what is most easily learned is usually hardest taught, it is also true that love of learning cannot be taught; it can only be exemplified. As is so often averred, teaching requires patience. Let it also be said that what teaching requires, learning must learn.

### 5. Education Examines Not the Individual but the Species

The value of learning lies not so much in its immediate utility as in its generality. Schools are instituted and maintained to serve their communities as havens of learning, not as microcosms of the marketplace. Here students are apprenticed to life in its ideal form, life that is devoted to inquiry, touched by beauty, informed by justice, guided by reason, girded by simplicity, graced by elegance. At the very least, graduates should exhibit competency in the exercise of certain skills—computation, composition—but the aim is to make them literate about the full array of human achievement, so that they will know what it means to do any thing well.

As the best companies are imbued with philosophies, so apparently are the best schools. But the parallel doesn't stop there. Effective and lasting corporate philosophies are in truth about "the obvious" and "common sense." Success lies in the fact that they are lived with intensity. Likewise, the best school philosophies are simple and to the point, as the Brookline statement suggests. Remember that Boyden, who had the clearest philosophy of all, said that he had none except "I believe in boys." Lightfoot discovered that the philosophies in the six schools she observed were, above all, marked by "a universal concern for civility, order, and structure." Bob McCarthy's at Brookline focused on "[developing] a sense of community." High schools (even the good ones) are often marked by a lack of physical and emotional security—on the part of teachers at least as much as students; all six of Lightfoot's school leaders focused first on achieving a sense of security. None took disciplinary infractions lightly, and the toughness was respected by all concerned. McCarthy at Brookline came into a rapidly deteriorating situation. Violence had been on the rise, and was being largely ignored by administrators and faculty, who, Lightfoot reports, would turn the other way and pretend not to see what was going on around them. McCarthy, despite being the model of a delegating and participative manager, nonetheless began his reign by visibly "showing anger." He challenged the "pretense of complacency": "I would not accept breaking up fights as part of my job. I would show those kids how angry I was." Students and faculty alike breathed a long-pent-up sigh of relief when he did.

The philosophy or vision is quickly turned into symbols by the best school leaders. Norris Hogans (who happens to be black) faced an even tougher task than McCarthy at his largely black Atlanta school in a deteriorated neighborhood. Personal presence is the key, Lightfoot notes: "He dominates the school. Hogans is a man of great energy. He walks about the campus in perpetual motion looking severe and determined, always carrying his walkie-talkie. Hogans does not want to be out of touch with any corner of his sphere. There is a sense of immediacy about him, an unwillingness to wait or be held back." It began on day one. Lightfoot observes that "Hogans's first response to the aimlessness and laziness [that he found at Carver] was to show them who was in charge. He started the first faculty meeting with fighting words: 'You're either part of the team or you are not.' Tough standards of behavior and decorum were stressed for the faculty." He also began with an immediate attack via the symbolic—on the shabby physical environment. Lightfoot comments, "The physical environment matched the deteriorating human spirit. Roaches were running around like cats.... There was dirt and filth

everywhere.... The band instruments were all broken up.... Athletic trophies were falling out of the broken glass cabinets! Hogans said incredulously,
'I can't believe no one stood up and screamed about it!'" He took immediate
action to get on with a highly visible cleanup.

All of Lighfoot's good principals are showmen, visionaries, masterly users
of symbols and supersalesmen. Consider Hogans, in perpetual motion, with
his walkie-talkie in hand, or crisscrossing the country with an impressive slide
show promoting the new programs in his school. Some of his faculty, notes
Lightfoot, have suggested that he spends too much time promoting. We suggest that the amount of time he spends is entirely consistent with what we've
learned about leadership. The slide show and the "selling" of the school
everywhere, not merely in Atlanta, have their greatest impact not on the outside world, but on the school itself, as generators par excellence of pride and
self-confidence. Hogans's routine recalls Ren McPherson's "Talk back to the
boss," and "Give them [the bosses] hell" ads in national media, ads directed
mainly to his own people as part of his program of "turning the company
back over to the people." Hogans's salesmanship also takes him into the
Atlanta community, where he has invested huge blocks of time and forged
exceptional relationships. At the heart of the "new Carver" is his Free Enterprise Day. Lightfoot states that "It is a public event that symbolizes Carver's
new image. Vocational education no longer has to be linked with tough and
menial work for people of low status, but can be seen as training for jobs of
choice, skill, and honor. On the cover of the program for Free Enterprise Day
there is a workman's hand 'laying the foundation to success.'" In a remarkable
feat, Hogans talked the Boy Scouts of America into letting all of his boys and
girls become Explorer Scouts. The explorations take place in the world of
work, as each student heads into the community for a work-study program,
proudly wearing the bright white Explorer jackets that Hogan was able to
cadge from his various and obsessively nurtured sponsors.

Mastruzzi at Kennedy is at least as dedicated to showmanship, salesmanship and the use of symbols. He often refers to his school as the "big top,"
and many of his faculty members refer to him as the "master of ceremonies."
Lightfoot delighted in a school plastered from one end to the other with signs
of all sorts focusing on educational excellence. As she carried out her interviewing, Mastruzzi and his senior colleagues had just completed an intense
eighteen-month effort to sponsor and host the New York State Special Olympics; as in the case of Hogans's traveling show, the real aim of this visibility-
enhancing effort was to induce pride *within* the halls of Kennedy.

Like Marriott, Mastruzzi is obsessed. His particular fetish is attendance,
and it is regularly and visibly demonstrated. As in the private sector, he could
be criticized for not having a subtle and sophisticated system for measuring
the quality of his service. But as is the case with Marriott, the energy focused
on a single factor makes it a credible indicator of the success of the school's
endeavors. Computerized attendance records are to schools what computerized accounting systems are to private sector organizations. Yet Mastruzzi

has a hand-done attendance count given to him once a day, within a couple of hours of the opening of school. Lightfoot declares that "his 'fetish' with attendance figures reflects the dual concern for image and essence. High attendance rates are critically important, says Mastruzzi, 'because unless kids come to school, they won't learn.' However, he is equally concerned about the *appearance* of high attendance scores. He believes they are a quick indicator of a school's goodness, a visible and measurable sign. In September 1982, the attendance figures reached 84.5%, and the morning that I [Lightfoot] arrived in early October the principal has just offered his effusive congratulations to the students over the public address system. 'I got on the PA and told them how great they are. They should be rewarded for their sense of responsibility and commitment.'" Free McDonald's hamburgers are given to kids in various classrooms and at various times for particularly good attendance records.

The symbols—vision made visible—are important for the tough schools like Kennedy, Carver, and Brookline. They are just as important for the academies, such as Milton, which Lightfoot also studied. Headmaster Jerry Tieh "admits that his behavior is grounded as much in stylistic, temperamental qualities as in a philosophical stance. 'Style first, then philosophy. I want to set a tone that is permeating the environment. It is not so much a campaign or a clear philosophical view. I want my actions to speak.'" McPhee found the same in Boyden: "Boyden's strategy is best exemplified by his showmanship and his pantoscopic attention to detail. It has been said that a thousand details add up to one impression, and at Deerfield it was the headmaster who added them up. He thought in pictures. Once a picture seemed right, he wanted to keep it that way. Anything that marked it or changed the focus irritated him." McPhee goes on to offer numerous examples of the headmaster's fetish for the tiny and symbolic details that reinforce the image: "A lengthy and expensively produced concert program once arrived from the printer with one name misspelled. 'Miller' had been set as 'Millar.' The headmaster had the program reprinted. He staged basketball games as if he were the manager of La Scala. . . . Once, in the 1920's when Louis Perry, of Exeter, made a visit to Deerfield [at the time Deerfield was a poor second cousin to Exeter] the headmaster assigned each of a number of boys a pose to strike while Perry walked by; one was to be reading busily at his desk, another browsing through a newspaper in a master's living room, a third straightening his belongings. Some boys had two assignments, in the way that spear carriers disappear from stage one moment and return a bit later as messengers or pages."

Boyden simply lived his message: "'If you keep floors and walls nice, it's like having your shoes shined and a clean shirt on.' He has been seen mopping floors. He has the gym floor kept like polished brass and classroom floors polished every day. There was no dirty window panes. 'Bob,' he once said to a coach, 'I was in your locker room after practice today and there was some tape on the floor.'

He was essentially conservative with money, but he will spend any sum to get what he wants. Cut flowers appear regularly in vases all over the campus and there is a single rosebud on each table in the school store. . . . The details have long since added up to a place that is incomparably impressive to the eye. Even the grass is a little greener there, growing in fourteen inches of topsoil, and for many years the headmaster went around with a jackknife digging plantain out of his lawns."

Boyden had one or two fetishes like Mastruzzi's attendance fetish. For his first sixty years as headmaster, until his hearing became too impaired, he personally gave out every grade to every student: "There were no report cards. Each boy had a private talk with the headmaster six times a year and was told where he stood. In these talks the headmaster drew the boys out, getting their reaction to their courses and thus learning where the strength of his faculty was as well. 'Personality counts in teaching at the secondary level,' Boyden said. 'Personality rubs off. The boys are conscious of meeting a colorful and active mind.'" Boyden also believed in keeping in touch via school meetings for all students. And again he did it to a fare-thee-well. How frequent were the meetings? Once per day! From Boyden's world at Deerfield and Tieh's at Milton to Mastruzzi's at JFK and Hogan's at Carver, the message is the same: a crystal-clear and simple vision, the headmaster as chief salesman inside and out, and the constant, blatant, consistent, obsessive use of symbols. It is the foundation on which all else rests.

### Paint

In our analysis we have talked about the "paint and potties" phenomenon. A substantial number of the best business leaders, from factory boss to chief executive, have had a continuing concern about the physical details. People like Ray Kroc, Forrest Mars and a foundry manager from Cleveland contend that getting the (not so little) physical details right sets much of the tone. In the use of symbols by school leaders, we observe the same. Norris Hogans at Carver began with an attack on the roaches. The sparkling white Explorer jackets were another "detail," but a major part of his program to demonstrate new attitudes as well. Frank Boyden was seen at night, in the rain, replacing the divots on the football field, and insisted upon a fresh rose on each table in the school store. McCarthy, at Brookline, had a thing about instantly cleaning up any graffiti. If graffiti are around, discipline is likely to be lax, and learning minimal.

McCarthy's philosophy, once discipline was in hand, was focused on the enhancement of a sense of community. At the heart of it was a participatory Town Meeting structure, involving students and faculty in making decisions on school policy. He also gave greatly increased autonomy to his housemasters, who run 500-person "schools within a school," and symbolized all these major changes with physical "details." Sara Lawrence Lightfoot reports:

Another indication of educational engagement is audible rather than visual. I am surprised not to hear the harsh sounds of bells that indicate the beginning and end of class periods. The day's rhythms appear to be internalized by both faculty and students, who do not rely on the external alarms. Despite the absence of bells, all the classes I visited started easily on time and without much fanfare. The only time when bells are used is to mark the home room period, a largely procedural event. It seems to me that a school that was not serious about education could not proceed without bells. They would be a needed enforcer of student and teacher behavior. Instead, Brookline students show surpirse when I inquire about the lack of bells. Says one to me in mock alarm, "This isn't a prison, you know! We're not Pavlov's dogs!"

Again the specifics of the analogue to industry are eerie. Ren McPherson used virtually the same words to describe the removal of all time clocks at the Dana Corporation as he masterminded its exceptional turnaround. Attention to the physical trappings (visual and audible) are a major part of tone setting and philosophy reinforcement in factory and schools alike.

## Pictures

Related to vision and symbols, and to the use of physical trappings, is thinking in pictures. We regularly find that our best private-sector leaders have a literal picture of their vision. Bill Moore, Recognition Equipment, as we noted, talks about "dramatizing the vision," "seeing the glory." Norris Hogans at Carver believes that "before they can learn, they must be strictly disciplined and mannerly." Thus, when he took over the school—fraught with disciplinary problems and moving toward chaos—he focused on achieving in reality his image of a disciplined school: "Radios and basketballs are confiscated by the vice principals, boys can't wear caps or walk around with afro-combs stuck in the back of their hair, and girls are not allowed to wear rollers in their hair." What Hogans is attempting to achieve, says Lightfoot, is "visible conformity and a dignified presence." Mastruzzi's continued reference to "the big top" gets to the same point. And Boyden of Deerfield thought "in pictures." Once a picture seemed right, he wanted to keep it that way.

There is much talk these days about visualization—it has become almost a separate subfield of psychology—in which the "subject" pictures an outcome (an eventual win) and/or, for example (in athletics), every single step of a race. While none of the leaders we have worked with or read about have used the process scientifically, most seem intuitively to do so. Within their head is a picture of what a positive outcome would look like, and of what the individual components of it are. They attempt to set the picture and, as leaders, to paint it for others. They are, then, as Mastruzzi says, "masters of ceremonies." The private-sector analogue? SAS's Jan Carlzon's "All business is show business."

## MBWA

No matter how often we talk about Managing by Wandering Around, it always seems odd to be doing so. It seems so natural that one should be in touch. But it appears that it's not. After a presentation to hospital administrators, a seminar devoted solely by MBWA, a leader of a small rural hospital came up to us: "But, you know, they don't teach us that in school." We didn't know then, but we're learning.

When we talk with school leaders, the sad nonobviousness of MBWA quickly surfaces. The differences between the superb and the not-so-good teacher, they unfailingly tell us, center on intensity of involvement and empathy. Perhaps the biggest indicator of that is the amount of wandering the teacher does (and, of coure, all that wandering stands for). The involved teacher is constantly pacing the classroom. The noninvolved teacher is most often seen hiding behind the desk. The same thing holds true of vice principals, principals and administrators. Some (most, we fear) just don't seem to be able to find the time to get out. Others (the exceptional ones), with the same clamoring constitutencies on their backs, do. Lightfoot was struck that Norris Hogans of Carver "walks about the campus in perpetual motion." The image of Boyden that seems to have struck McPhee was "the small man in the golf cart." Lightfoot describes Mastruzzi at Kennedy as a very physical person, comfortable with himself: "'He doesn't draw back from you,' says a dark-skinned Black boy who claims that his junior high school teachers were often repelled by and afraid of students of darker hue. 'They'd never touch you. Sometimes I felt like I was diseased ... but I've seen Mastruzzi reach out to all kinds of kids.' The principal's powerful example makes it difficult for others to express their fears or distaste towards certain groups. 'Mastruzzi is not just asking for tolerance among groups,' claims an ardent admirer, 'he's asking for respect and friendship.'"

In our chapter called "MBWA: The Technology of the Obvious," we focused on MBWA with customers, suppliers, one's people. In excellent schools it is the same. Hogans of Carver and Mastruzzi of Kennedy spend huge amounts of time in the community. Boyden of Deerfield wrote seventy letters a day, mainly to alumni, and spent inordinate amounts of time—on the road, in his eighties—with admissions directors and officers of the colleges to which Deerfield sent its boys, and with members of the local community. (As is so often the case, the astonishing consistency of the superb leaders shows up in the tiniest details. McPhee reports, "A Massachusetts state policeman once said, 'The headmaster is the only person of importance around here who calls us all by our first names.'")

Two more Boyden stories illustrate the pervasiveness of his wandering around and his involvement. The first describes the fabled, daily Deerfield Evening Meetings:

> He listens to the noise level in a group of boys and watches the degree of restlessness; he can read these things as if they were a printed page.

This is one reason he believes in meetings that involve the entire school. "You must have your boys together as a unit as least once a day, just as you have your family together once a day," he says. Evening Meeting is a Deerfield custom. The boys sit on a vast carpet in the anteroom of the school auditorium and listen to announcements, perhaps an anecdotal story from the headmaster, and reports of athletic contests and other activities. "Junior B Football beat the Holyoke High School junior varsity 6–0 this afternoon," says the coach of Junior B Football. "Charlie Hiller scored the touchdown with two minutes left in the game." In the applause that follows this one low-echelon athlete gains something, and so does the school. On Sunday evenings, there is a vesper service, or Sunday Night Sing, as it is called, in which the boys sing one hymn after another, with a pause for a short talk by a visiting clergyman or educator. The lustre, or lack of it, in their voices is the headmaster's gauge of the climate of the student body for the week to come, and he accordingly chides them or exhorts them or amuses them or blasts them at Evening Meetings on succeeding days, often shaping his remarks around one of several precepts—"keep it on a high level," "be mobile," "finish up strong,"—which he uses so repeatedly and effectively that the words continue to ricochet through the minds of Deerfield graduates long after they leave the school.

Here is an average afternoon in the headmaster's life:

The headmaster wakes up from his midday nap and decides to take a quick look around the school before lunch. He believes correctly that the more people see of him—students and faculty alike—the more smoothly his school will run. "You won't see any confusion anywhere, I'm sure," he says. (Recently, he was scheduled to go on a complicated journey from Deerfield to Worcester to Chicago and back to Deerfield. He went to Worcester but decided to backtrack to Deerfield. It was 5 p.m. when he reached the campus, and at that time the greatest concentration of students happened to be in the gymnasium. He walked into the gym, stayed two minutes, walked out of the building, and went on to Chicago.) Getting into his golf cart, he shoots at full throttle along Albany Road, which goes through the center of the campus and forms a right angle with the long town street. He loops, twists, drives with his hands off the wheel, dives downhill, shaves trees, goes up the left side of the street into oncoming traffic, and waves and honks to people without regard to obstacles rapidly approaching. He has never actually known how to drive a car, but he used to swirl around Deerfield in an old Pontiac he had, going everywhere at top speed in second gear, because that was the only gear he knew how to find.

Wandering around, staying in touch, keeping out of the office. It's the mark of the superb factory manager, hospital administrator, division manager, city manager and also, apparently, school leader.

## For the Kids

When Peters and Waterman "discovered" the "close to the customer" principle in business, they couldn't have been more embarrassed. How obvious. How trite. We are no longer embarrassed. We now talk about answering the phone, listening "naively" to customers, and the like with the fervor of crusaders. Why? Because we've found that everyone gives lip service to "close to the customer," but few live it with the intensity required to give it any meaning.

In the school world, it seems to us, "for the kids" is an exact analogue. Of course they are the educational target, just as customers must be the object of every manufacturing service operation. But for whose benefit? For the parents'? For the community's? For the nation's? For the school board's? And how many administrators say, "But I know best; I've had the training"? It's the same sweet line that we hear from so many engineers: "But we know best the value fo this feature. The product will sell itself."

Much of the success of school leaders like Mastruzzi and Boyden is in the fact that they really do live "for the kids." Likewise, the magic of any superb teacher, it turns out, is empathy for each child and where each child is in his or her unique development. In our chapter called "Mere Perception" we argue that each and every customer (whether for a jet engine at several million dollars or a hamburger at sixty-nine cents) is different and must be treated differently, must be responded to in his or her own terms. The great companies do so. In the same vein the great teachers and schools do so, and despite the numbers—over five thousand students at Kennedy—they manage to personalize their school's delivery of education.

Bob Mastruzzi at Kennedy views his objective as turning every kid into a winner, a young man or woman who feels that he or she can win. It reminds us of Bill and Vieve Gore at Gore & Associates and Ren McPherson at Dana, all of whom say their objective was to have each of their people be an innovative contributor (and who base evaluations, remember, even of the receptionist, on innovative contributions to the job). Says Lightfoot of Mastruzzi, "His passion seems to be reserved for the kids as he reminds me of the Special Olympics motto, 'you're all winners.' 'I believe that is true for all the kids here at Kennedy,' he says forcefully. 'Each year I tell the faculty to increase their expectations of students. You ask for more and you get more.' ... Hogans is the same. His pet Free Enterprise Day is aimed at getting kids into the community with the understanding that they can be winners.

Moreover, Hogans also emphasizes that being a winner doesn't mean being a doctor or a lawyer; it means doing passionately and enthusiastically whatever work you do. Likewise Mastruzzi:

> Winning has more to do with being a good, caring, and generous person than with visible and lofty achievement. It is an inclusive, rather than exclusive, educational vision—one that does not focus superior or pride-

ful attention on a narrow band of top achievers, or create a school image based on their great successes. Rather, it is a vision that asks for "extra human effort" on the part of *all* students and asserts that they are all equally capable of becoming good citizens. Says Mastruzzi proudly, "There is an unbelievable emphasis on doing something for somebody else." As an example, Mastruzzi points to a now traditional holiday ritual. At Christmastime, Kennedy's students collect hundreds of gifts for needy children. The students wrap each gift and deliver the presents themselves. Last year the presents were given to a home for mentally retarded children, and this year they will probably arrive at an institution for the severely handicapped. The personal attention of gift wrapping and the presenting of gifts is central to the act of giving. It is not a distant, paternalistic gesture. It is an immediate act of charity. Each year the principal offers the same message of charity to the graduating seniors. He rehearses the words to me with great feeling, "I tell them, you need to leave your school with a sense of appreciation for other human beings. That is the primary lesson we teach at this school. I don't care if you are going to Columbia University pre-med, or if you have been tops in our Honors program. If your don't give a bit of yourself to someone else, you are a failure!"

## Kids as Adults

Bob McCarthy at Brookline says it most simply: "I see kids as emerging adults. The more dignity and respect you give them, the more it will come back to you." The single most significant message of *A Passion for Excellence* is this: Treat your people as adults, and they will respond as adults, conscientiously and creatively. Treat them as mindless automatons, treat them with contempt, and they will respond with contempt for you and your product, will respond as automatons. It's as simple as that and as complex as that. It's the obvious again. But it's the obvious that is ignored in schools as well as in the world of goods production and services delivery.

Throughout Lightfoot's analysis there is a contrast between the atmosphere of Brookline, Kennedy and Carver before and after the arrival of McCarthy, Mastruzzi and Hogans, respectively. Before, all three schools were fearful places, with staffs and students distant from one another, standoffish. Now, though all three current principal-administrators are tough as nails and moved quickly to instill discipline and ensure stability, all three staffs feel comfortable, confident, a part of a community, a community in which students are full-time, adult, contributing members—and so do their students. Reports a JFK commentator about Mastruzzi: "He is very physical, very demonstrative, and it affects all of us. Even the kids hold hands in friendship and support.... It's amazing."

The comment is made of Boyden at Deerfield that he did not, as does the traditional headmaster, "see the schoolboy as his enemy." In the same vein,

Lightfoot describes Kennedy's approach to absenteeism: "Instead of searching for reasons why students do not come to school, they believe that the faculty must find ways of getting them there." In other words, instead of student as thief, ne'er-do-well, demotivated urchin, the notion is student as winner, student as full of potential, student as good. Hence, it's the faculty's prime task to make the rewards of coming to school sufficient to induce the student to attend. As we've pointed out before, "Management [the faculty] gets exactly the work force [student body and attendance] it deserves, not one iota more and not one iota less."

Earlier, we made it clear that the Hewlett-Packards of this world are among the toughest environments of all. Remove the excuses (e.g., the bells as McCarthy did at Brookline), get rid of the Mickey Mouse, and suddenly "it" becomes the employee's (student's) responsibility. There's no way to get off the hook. Empathy means care and concern, but it does not mean softness. Treat students as adults, *expect them to respond as adults*, and they will. Lightfoot makes this clear: "By empathy I do not mean something sentimental and soft. As a matter of fact, the empathetic regard of students is often communicated through tough teacher criticism, admonitions, and even punishment." McCarthy comes through as perhaps the most empathetic of Lightfoot's six principals; nonetheless, "[His] first administrative move was to express outrage at the frequent eruptions of violence. He insisted that parents come to witness student punishments. And he developed a disciplinary committee that would respond immediately to acts to transgression." McPhee tells us, "A new boy at Deerfield cannot have been there very long before the idea is impressed upon him that he is a part of something that won't work unless he does his share," and Boyden was clear on the point: "We just treat the boys as if we expect something of them. . . ."

## Autonomy/Experimentation/
## Support for Failure

These excellent principals are tough disciplinarians. And yet they are the grantors of autonomy in the classroom. They facilitate the process of treating students as adults by first treating the faculty as adults.* Mastruzzi is apparently charismatic. But Lightfoot, an able and experienced commentator, thinks his secret is not charisma at all. His faculty's commitment "does not seem to be an expression of idol worship, but a reflection of their connection to a communal process. When people [at Kennedy] refer to 'feelings of connection,' they often talk about the autonomy and independence that Mas-

---

*Talking of philosophies with on California elementary school principal led to this sad comment, "You talk of IBM's first principle [respect for the individual]. Well, I've been in education over twenty years, and I've never seen one school philosophy or district philosophy that even *mentions* the teachers or employees, let alone puts them first."

truzzi permits and encourages. 'He allows a scope, the space to develop our own thing,' says one assistant principal. Another points to the way that Mastruzzi protects his faculty from 'the arbitrary regulations of the central authority. . . . He serves as a buffer between outside and inside. If it weren't for him we'd feel more constrained. We have a great deal of freedom here.' Some observers believe Mastruzzi is able to encourage autonomy among his faculty because of his own deeply rooted self-confidence. 'He is the most secure principal I have ever known. He likes to see strength, not weakness, in the people who work for him,' says a relatively new faculty member who believes there is a 'fair exchange' between the freedom the faculty enjoy and the commitment that Mastruzzi expects."

Supporting good tries that fail is also important to Mastruzzi. Lightfoot goes on: "One enthusiast claims that Mastruzzi not only encourages faculty creativity and autonomy, but he also allows people the room to make mistakes. He is 'forgiving' and believes that people often learn from repairing the damage they have created. The coordinator of student affairs, Pamela Gino, recounts a disastrous story of the first rock concert she organized for students at Kennedy. She had expected a couple hundred students and 800 showed up, many high on alcohol and marijuana. 'A lot of those kids think you can't listen to rock unless you're high. Booze and rock go together.' Not expecting a great number of students, nor their inebriation, Gino had not planned for adequate security; and it became a chaotic, treacherous evening. 'After it all, I felt a tremendous letdown, a real sense of failure,' remembers Gino. 'But I also had learned a lot about how to plan for that kind of event. I knew I could do it better given a second chance.' Mastruzzi greeted her request for a second chance with healthy skepticism and a battery of critical questions, but he allowed her to try again. The second rock concert was a 'great success . . . he's a generous man. He sees failure as an opportunity for change,' beams Gino."

In the private sector a critical attribute of the champion and autonomy-inducing companies is senior administrators who work to "beat the system," even if it is their own system. Mastruzzi at Kennedy is a master: "He spends a fair amount of energy figuring out ways to circumvent policies and directives that, he believes, distort the educational experiences of teachers and students. Even though he finds the external intrusions 'pernicious' he recognizes why they are necessary in a large, diverse city school system. He believes they were established to monitor the poor schools, the ineffective administrators, and the lazy teachers. But in trying to protect against inferior schooling, these 'central authorities' have limited the freedom of the better schools and distorted the essential human encounters that shape education." The source of Mastruzzi's success as a buffer and a shield is his self confidence, the sheer guts to get on with it.

Brookline is the Hewlett-Packard or 3M among this collection of schools. McCarthy, as we have noted, has granted autonomy at all levels. He is uncompromising about disciplinary issues, yet he immediately established a Fairness Committee to deal with the problems. Both students and faculty sit on the committee, and their recommendations for action, notes Lightfoot, "are binding. There are no empty gestures. This is real power and decision-making." In our description of the Raychem Corporation we noted the language that marks the innovative company. In particular, we sat through interviews in which first- and second-line supervisors said things like "people believe they can make anything happen." Similarly, one Brookline housemaster, contrasting McCarthy with his predecessor, says, "with [the predecessor], the housemasters were like lieutenants. The metaphors were very male, very military. . . . But McCarthy has opened the door for housemasters. Lincoln House students are *my* students. I can make all the decisions about them." Lightfoot adds, "and to watch him [the housemaster of Lincoln House] in action, one sees a person with a wide range of responsibilities and tasks. The job does not seem glamorous. His office is functional, cluttered with papers and books, empty of aesthetic expression, and open for people seeking attention and help."

## Family

Bob McCarthy of Brookline says, "I have always found that the more power you give people, the more responsibility they take." His objective is to "create a school structure that will increase the sense of community." Lightfoot notes that "community" is a word that pops up again and again when McCarthy speaks. It similarly dominates the language of Norris Hogans at Carver, Bob Mastruzzi at Kennedy.

In our investigations of organizations in the private sector, time and again we see the unabashed use of the word "family" among those who exhibit a passion for excellence. We sense family feeling at Delta Airlines, at Hewlett-Packard, at Gore: There is no shame in talking about the workplace as a community, as a family. Likewise, Boyden talks about Deerfield as a family, Mastruzzi about creating the conditions of nurturance at Kennedy that are typically found in the family.

In an effective family unit all members are full-scale participants. Boyden had an obsession about ensuring that each student played on athletic teams. A heightened sense of competitiveness? Perhaps, but much more than that. McPhee notes, "When a boy at Deerfield chooses a sport, he automatically makes a team that has a full schedule of games with other schools." That is, everyone is required to participate—but as a full-scale member. Playing time and "making the team" are guaranteed.

## Discipline

In *In Search of Excellence*, "loose-tight" was the awkward term Tom and Bob invented to describe the leadership of their excellent companies. That is, leaders in those companies had simple, crisp and clear visions, but the intensity and clarity of the shared values behind those visions allowed lots of room for autonomy, creative expression, and love, care and empathy. And so it is, it seems, with leaders in schools.

Norris Hogans, thrust into an impossible environment in Atlanta, began with a focus on discipline. He said that it was necessary to establish discipline before learning could ensue. At the same time, he says to his students, "If I didn't love you as I do, I wouldn't do this . . . I wouldn't come down so hard on you. And I won't stand for any negative attitudes. There is no time for that." The example of Boyden, once again, sums it up: McPhee reports:

> Most schools have detailed lists of printed rules, and boys who violate them either are given penalties or are thrown out. A reasonable percentage of expulsions is a norm of prep-school life. Deerfield has no printed rules and no set penalties, and the headmaster has fired only five boys in 64 years. "For one foolish mistake, a boy should not have a stamp put on him that will be with him for the rest of his life," he says. "I could show you a list of rules from one school that is 30 pages long. There is no flexibility in a system like that. I'm willing to try a little longer than some of the other people do, provided there is nothing immoral. You can't have a family of three children without having some problems, so you have problems if you have 500. If you make a lot of rules, they never hit the fellow you made them for. Two hours after making the rule, you may want to change it. We have rules here, unwritten ones, but we make exceptions to them more than we enforce them. I always remember what Robert E. Lee said when he was President of Washington College, which is now Washington and Lee. He said, 'A boy is more important than any rule.' Ninety percent of any group of boys will never get out of line. You must have about 90% as a central core. Then the question is: How many of the others can you absorb?

## Sense-of-the Whole/Rhythm,
## or Passion, Intensity, Enthusiasm

A two-star general who runs a highly effective Wing organization in the Air Force's Tactical Air Command talks of a superbly performing unit as having "rhythm." Boyden of Deerfield says, "The thing I have tried to build is a unity of feeling." Lightfoot talks of the optimism and spirit in the language of the teachers, students and administrators alike at JFK High School. She talks likewise of the sense of "immediacy" when one is around Norris Hogans at Carver. David Ogilvy quotes Howard Johnson, former president of MIT, on great leaders; he says they have a "visceral form of spiritual energy."

We think that most who have written about leadership have missed the boat. We don't know what the essence of goodness is in fast food restaurants or great high schools. But we think the essence of leadership is the same in both: not shortness or tallness, not sweetness or harshness. Such variables are seldom predictors of success or failure. But something else. Vision, energy,

empathy, persistence, passion, attention to detail, a picture of the goal ...
These are not the factors that we have discussed in management for the past
several decades. Yet we believe that they are as amenable to "hard" analysis
as are the themes of MBO and performance appraisal. We just have to start
collecting the right "data."

One must be around that which works, which sings, which has rhythm,
which has passion, which has enthusiasm, before one can understand just how
broad the gulf is between not the winners and the losers (that's defeatist talk)
but things that are humming and things that aren't.

---

### A Personal Note from Tom

After I entered a private junior high school in 1955, my mother took
on a new job—teaching the fifth grade in a nearby suburban elementary
school. It had students from ethnic and socioeconomic backgrounds
other than she had been used to. She taught there—contrary to her initial plans—for almost twenty years, and occasionally I acted as her bum-
bling assistant. The memories are vivid.

First, she was totally involved. She was on her feet all the time (doing
MBWA). There was no reason for her to have a desk, though the school
system provided one. She was never behind it. She paced about the
room, nudging, cajoling, pushing, pressing. Above all, she had a passion
for her students. The letters that she still receives, twenty years later
now, from both good and bad, successful and unsuccessful, attest to that.

Her room was a hotbed of creativity. Everyone was allowed to
express himself or herself with a unique project. At the same time, the
seeming chaos was embedded in a context of extraordinary discipline:
total respect was to be shown by each student for every other student—
or else! No rudeness was tolerated. Not Only did the discipline and
creativity not conflict with each other, but they went hand in glove.
The discipline of care and concern for one another was the necessary
foundation upon which the less venturesome were willing to step out
and try a little bit of something new.

A passion for the material was evident as well. (Joseph Epstein's Masters: Portrait of Great Teachers underscores this point. Above all, each
master teacher is marked by great passion for his or her subject. The
technical excellence—i.e., mastery—is there, too, of course, but it is the
passion which is decisive, which alters the lives of so many students.)
My mother was appalled by the new math (the very best of us are often
appalled by the new twists), but her love of learning knew no bounds.
Certainly I learned more of Maryland's history, one of her special pas-
sions—the school was located halfway between Baltimore and Annap-
olis—and more of an appreciation of where I was within the universe

from working for her as an elementary school assistant than I did in my
private high school.

Nothing is more important to our society, by definition, than the education
of our youth. Nothing in pursuit of educational excellence is more important
than studying the models of things that work. Frank Boyden's Deerfield and
Sara Lightfoot Lawrence's six good high schools—and Tom's mother's fifth-
grade classroom—are models from which we suspect all of us can learn.

### The Marine Corps of Business Schools:
### Pride, Poise and Results

It's 1:00 A.M. as Tom teeters bleary-eyed down the steps of the Cessna
310 in Talahassee, Florida, after completing a long, long day and a
choppy, three-hour flight from Mansfield, Ohio. The poised young man
(all of nineteen) dressed in a well-kept, conservative business suit, greets
him crisply. "I'm Dan Callis, a junior accounting major from Clinton,
Maryland. Welcome to Florida A&M's School of Business and Industry." We've just gotten our first taste of Sybil Mobley's extraordinary
accomplishments as dean of a once unknown black business school, now
the home of four hundred exceptionally talented students (over half
were Merit Scholarship finalists) and first stop on the recruiting trail for
almost all of America's giant corporations.

Dean Mobley decided that the usual business school offerings on deb-
its and credits and the intersection of supply-and-demand curves were
not enough. Business is about social commerce among people; for the
holder of a BS degree who is just starting out, black or white, poise and
confidence are more decisive predictors of a successful future than light-
ning-fast speed with a calculator or PC keyboard.

Thus Sybil's school looks more like a business than a school—beginning with her own office and its reception area. Its accoutrements
include thick carpets and the sort of furnishings more common to the
offices of Fortune 100 chairmen than schoolrooms. Even the names of
student lounges (e.g., the Bull and Bear) are all introduction to business
and business terminology, while the main hallway on each floor of the
new building is named after one of the world's business thoroughfares
(e.g., Wall Street, Threadneedle Street). Each floor/hallway will soon
feature a mural—not "just a mural" but a work of art. The one that
depicts Des Voeux Road, Central, in Hong Kong, already in place, is
exciting—and lavish, a gift from Chase Manhattan Bank. It's all
designed, along with a curriculum that teaches the nuts and bolts and
tenor of business, to turn out students who feel like confident, would-
be winners as they approach the business environment.

Once-a-year internships are another big part of the program. Each student spends a substantial hunk of his or her time each year in a no-nonsense, real-world internship—every one one-crafted by Mobley and her aggressive senior staff. Even more impressive is the day-to-day organization of the students. Each one is assigned to a team, which is organized as a company and involved in recruiting and promoting students as well as accomplishing certain tasks. *Everything* is done by the teams, from the generation of publications to the running of the dorms. (Sybil was adamant about putting the dorms on a profit-making basis. When her student company/teams took over, they quickly saw that the only way to do so was by laying off the custodial staff, with students taking on the chores on a rotating basis. Lay them off they did, and, typically, Dean Mobley got heavily involved in the fracas that ensued. She won, as is her habit.)

One focal point of the teams' effort is the weekly (or more frequent) visits to the school by corporate heavyweights (and others, such as Tom)—each one a grueling and exciting eighteen-hour series of seminars, interviews and speeches orchestrated by the students. Who comes? The managing partner of Touche-Ross preceded Tom by less than seven days. In the last few months the list has included Chairman Jim Burke of Johnson & Johnson, Chairman Jack Welch of GE and Governor Bob Graham of Florida.

One of the student "companies" is wholly responsible, on a rotating basis, for each visit, from airport greeting to departure. Dinner with a dozen students starts things off. As is true throughout the experience, these students are *prepared*. It is not even slight exaggeration to say that they are more ready than the *best* of interviewers Tom has confronted since the publication of *In Search of Excellence*.

The next day begins with a tour. The dean gives lots of running commentary, to be sure, but a student host is a prominent part of every activity. Next, at 10:00 A.M. sharp, you are shepherded into the campus TV facility for your appearance on a student panel show. Called *Today's Leaders Face Tomorrow's*, it is modeled after *Face the Nation*, and is carried locally on a cable network. The questions are not pap, not student-plays-sychophant-with-hot-shot-corporate-chieftain. They are tough. In Tom's case, every article critical of *In Search of Excellence* had been studied with a fine-tooth comb. Every question was hardball! (When a corporate exec is involved, critical reportage and the company's balance sheets are scrutinized in an effort to unearth pointed questions.) If one survives the ordeal, it's on to lunch and the postlunch Forum, where the guest speaks his or her piece for an hour to all students in assembly (remember this happens sixty or seventy times a year). Next, it's on to "wrap-up." Here, twenty-five students, chosen randomly from among the members of the hosting "company," grill you for another hour. Again, the preparation has been awesome; the questions are tough. Again, the setting is vital: the SBI (School of Business and Industry) boardroom, which is no pale imitation of the Fortune 100 model, but the hushed, plush real thing. The twenty-five students who take their seats and proceed to grill a business luminary in this setting are not going to be intimidated by the business world "out there."

It is Sybil Mobley who has made all this happen. Her passion for her task and for her students is palpable. No detail escapes her attention. She exudes energy, on the run, crisscrossing the country in pursuit of support, recruiting, cajoling money from alums. And yet she always has time for a personal tête-à-tête with a student. In her we saw Frank Boyden personified. Her mission is noble. Her results must be seen to be believed.

# 21

## What Price Excellence?

*To fight a bull when you are not scared is nothing. And to not fight a
bull when you are scared is nothing. But to fight a bull when you are
scared—that is something.*

—Anonymous bullfighter

*I seldom think about politics more than eighteen hours a day.*

—Lyndon Johnson

*One is happy as a result of one's own efforts, once one knows the
necessary ingredients of happiness: Simple tastes, a certain degree of
courage, self-denial to a point, love of work, and above all, a clear
conscience.*

—George Sand

A PASSION FOR excellence means thinking big and starting small: excellence
happens when high purpose and intense pragmatism meet. This is almost,
but not quite, the whole truth. We believe a passion for excellence also carries a price, and we state it simply: the adventure of excellence is not for the
faint of heart.

Adventure? You bet. It's not just a job. It's a personal commitment.
Whether we're looking at a billion-dollar corporation or a three-person
accounting department, we see that excellence is achieved by people who
muster up the nerve (and the passion) to step out—in spite of doubt, or fear,
or job description—to maintain face-to-face contact with other people,
namely, customers and colleagues. They won't retreat behind office doors,
committees, memos or layers of staff, knowing this is the fair bargain they
make for extraordinary results. They may step out for love, because of a burning desire to be the best, to make a difference, or perhaps, as a colleague
recently explained, "Because the thought of being average scares the hell out
of me." (Manny, you needn't worry.)

Doing better than average takes tenacious preparation. You need an invigorating purpose you can call your own, one you care enough about to justify

investing your steadfast interest—one that, we hope, makes you happy, because you'll live with it day in and day out. It has to be worth your full attention. It has to be worth the time and effort it takes to master the basics and be diligent on the details, the little things that prove yours is an environment where things happen, where the only thing you like as well as listening is acting without delay, where people are committed to finding a few more ways to get things done the way they want them to be done. The good news? You can start now. The bad news? You'll never finish. As Admiral Hyman Rickover put it, "Good ideas and innovations must be driven into existence by courageous patience." Exactly.

Courage and self-respect are the lion's share of passion: It's hanging in long after others have gotten bored or given up; it's refusing to leave well enough alone; it means that anything less than the best you can imagine really bothers you, maybe keeps you awake at night. It usually means sticking your neck out: daring to give your best shot to something you care about and asking others to do the same *is* self-exposing. It asks you to pick sides, to wear your passion on your sleeve, to take a position and remain true to it even under the scrutiny of an audience, when the wish to please, to be accepted, welcomed, can compromise the clearest inner vision. Passion opens you to criticism, disappointment, disillusionment and failure, any one of which is enough to scare off all but the bravest souls. But the passionate, courageous, self-respecting people we know, when challenges or risks loom before them, regard them as something to be faced. As writer Amy Gross reasoned in her essay on courage, "One person sees a mountain as a mountain. Another takes it personally, as a thing to be climbed, or else. Awful as the climbing might be, the or-else is worse."

---

### Bottom-Linemanship

On the op-ed page of the Sunday, May 20, 1984, issue of the *New York Times*, Norman Lear wrote:

America is suffering from an unhealthy emphasis on success as measured by The Numbers. The tendency to boil the world down into analytic abstractions distorts and oversimplifies the richness of life. It insists upon evaluating the world through ratings and lists, matrices and polls, the bottom line, winners and losers.

Success is not a destination. It is a journey. Robert Louis Stevenson once said, "To travel hopefully is a better thing than to arrive." There is only one arrival in life—and that is at the end of life. All the achievements, the moments of success, are merely milestones along the way.

Television is perhaps the most dramatic example of the failure to continue traveling hopefully. The name of the game for the networks is: "How do I win Tuesday night at 8 o'clock?" When the only criterion for airing the show is how it may rate against the competition in the short term, it isn't good for network business in the long term. And so, despite the threat of audience erosion from the new technologies, we see the networks scrambling—not to innovate, but to imitate, because innovation requires risk-taking, and risk-taking is antithetical to winning in the short term. With painful predictability, the networks putter with the same tired formats, adding more sex here and more violence there—more mindlessness—in an effort to grab the viewers' attention quickly.

If the heads of the three networks were standing in a circle with razors to each other's throats, they could not be committing suicide more deliberately. Just as, it seems clear now, the Big Three were doing all those years ago in Detroit, when they refused to innovate, to build small, fuel-efficient cars; refused to sacrifice a current quarterly profit statement to invest in the future, and meet the threat of the imports from abroad. Or the steel companies, when they wouldn't modernize. Or the labor unions in both industries, when they fought only for added wages and benefits—instead of fighting to protect their members' jobs in the long term.

There are no villains in all of this. It is a matter of climate. The average network programming executive is trapped. Imagine yourself in his job: You wake up and read that your network didn't have one show in the Top 10. Your palms sweat. On your way into the office, you pick up The Wall Street Journal, which now prints an analysis of projected earnings based on ratings. Your network's projected earnings are down. You walk into the office and a warm Xerox copy of last night's overnight ratings is on your desk. You didn't win a single time slot. Now your first appointment of the day is with tomorrow's Rod Serling or Paddy Chayefsky, who has a fresh, innovative idea. You are in no condition to hear a new idea. What you must have, and quickly, is a new version of something that is working on one of the other networks. You are a victim—trapped.

TV must, of course, pay attention to business and prosper economically. But when it overlooks the human essence, that spirit that defies the marketplace and its economic calculus of motives, it does so at its own peril.

... We have been raising generations of children to think that there is nothing between winning and losing. The notion that life has everything to do with succeeding at the level of doing one's best is lost to these kids. If we really believe that we are on this planet for the long term, we will encourage our youth to understand that not everyone catches the brass ring on the carousel of life. The rest of us better enjoy the ride for its own sake, or life has no meaning at all.

Passion doesn't have to be flashy. Garden-variety, everyday passion is the stuff of excellence, the sort of stuff you need when you face the prospect of managing by wandering around, for instance. Being visible takes guts. There you are, a regular person, stepping out from behind your desk, where it's safe. You have to believe that the stepping out is worth the trouble. It does take courage—the ability to face up to difficulty in spite of doubt, the ability to say good isn't good enough, the ability to learn from the losses, to celebrate the successful tries, to resist the impulse to use managing by wandering around as an opportunity to *tell* people how their jobs *ought* to be done, and—maybe most important—to realize that even if you fail the first time, there's reason to try again, that the sting is brief.

It takes some getting used to. From the moment you know it's excellence or bust, you're in for the distance. You'll need a generous supply of both altruism and action to dip into: a passion for excellence goes bad when it relies too much on either. Altruism without the personal drive to make it into something tangible gets stuck, doesn't go anywhere. Action for its own sake can be transmuted into ruthlessness, particularly when a little cynicism is added. Excellence is optimistic. It's believing that something can be done, that it's worth fighting for, worth trusting others to play a part. And there is a benefit: Even recent medical findings suggest that optimism is *good* for you. Duke University Medical Center scientist Redford Williams, while exploring Type A personalities—hard-driving, impatient, relentless folks, thought to be more prone to heart attacks—found that one element stood out as more dangerous than any other: "We suggest that 'cynicism,' better than any other word, captures the toxic element in the Type A personality. We're finding that some components of Type A behavior are far worse than others."

From cookies to computers, real estate to basketball, not a cynic among the winners. We can promise you that they're good at faith, the kind that gets them over inevitable disappointments and setbacks, the kind that propels them when they feel—as they sometimes do—that their small efforts don't count for much, their organization is too brittle, their chief executive officer (or boss) is unsympathetic, their industry decaying. At these times, there is only the passionate belief that something distinctive can be forged nonetheless—if not throughout the organization, then in their tiny part of it: a pocket of excellence. This, they know, can be done. It has been done, in tough places—auto factories, steel mills, retail stores, banks—where handfuls of self-respecting innovators thrive among the bureaucrats.

Consider network television again—that business with the bottom-line, short-term (overnight) focus. Todd Gitlin writes in *Prime Time* (published in 1984) about the hugely successful and distinctive *Hill Street Blues:*

> In network television, even the exceptions reveal the rules. Everything emerges at the end of a chain of *ifs. If* a producer gets on the inside track; *If* he or she has strong ideas and fights for them intelligently . . . *If* the producer is willing to give ground here and there . . . *If* the network

has the right niche for the show . . . then the system that cranks out mind candy occasionally proves hospitable to something else, while at the same time betraying its limits. As Universal Studios executive Jennings Lang once said about the work of the writer Howard Rodman, 'Every department store needs a boutique.' In the early eighties, *Hill Street Blues* was network television's most conspicuous boutique. This intelligent, literate ensemble police series with its rough texture and intertangled plots, its complex mix of crime melodrama and absurdist comedy, was commissioned by the same network executive who brought America *Real People*, *The Brady Brides*, and *Sheriff Lobo*. As the networks scrambled to cash in on the presumed trend toward national discipline, Fred Silverman at NBC wanted a down-and-dirty cop show. But because he assigned the notion to two particular writer-producers at the right moment in their careers; because they were working for the right company; because they caught some of the richness of American life at that moment; because they made the right choices of director, line producer, and cast; and because they took some chances and fought for them, what Silverman got was *Hill Street Blues*, at its best a mature and even brilliant show that violated many conventions, pleased critics, caught the undertow of cultural change, and ran away with the Emmys. Then, in defiance of virtually all predictions, after puny first-season ratings *Hill Street* in its second and third seasons also became NBC's top series hit. . . . *Hill Street*'s achievement was first of all a matter of style. Thirteen principal characters and several other regulars careened through this show, making it, by conventional wisdom, overpopulated. To thicken the plot further, most of the episodes were written in four-show blocks, with at least four major stories running concurrently, each starting at a different moment and often not resolving at all.

Such a pocket of excellence is hospitable to innovative, creative and sometimes risky new ventures. When *Hill Street* was renewed for its second half-season, co-executive producer Greg Hoblit quipped that it was "the lowest-rated show renewed in the history of television." The dogged persistence of the show's creative team—their single-minded focus on delivering a "messy-looking," real-sounding, inventively written television product and their acceptance of its cost—began to pay off.

There will be disagreements with the boss along the way, as there were between the *Hill Street* producers and the network censors, the programming executives, just about everyone. But this was a passionate group. They believed they could do it, believed it could work in their industry. Small pockets can yield sizable rewards.

All the same, sticking with it day in and day out is plain difficult, and not only because of the organizational waves a passionate endeavor can make. Even a pocket of excellence can fill your life like a wall-to-wall revolution.

We have found that the majority of passionate activists who hammer away at the old boundaries have given up family vacations, Little League games, birthday dinners, evenings, weekends and lunch hours, gardening, reading, movies and most other pastimes. We have a number of friends whose marriages or partnerships crumbled under the weight of their devotion to a dream. There are more newly single parents than we expected among our colleagues.

Such profound trade-offs don't have to be a part of the bargain. Lost sleep, some late nights and probably a few weekends do go with the territory. Divorce does not. There is no requirement that the cost of excellence is suffering. But there is also no guarantee that the process will graced by a personal and professional "balance," where things work out nicely on both fronts with little wear and tear on either, thank you. We are frequently asked if it is possible to "have it all"—a full and satisfying personal life and a full and satisfying, hard-working, professional one. Our answer is: No. The price of excellence is time, energy, attention and focus, at the very same time that energy, attention and focus could have gone toward enjoying your daughter's soccer game. Excellence is a high-cost item. As David Ogilvy observed in *Confessions of an Advertising Man:* "If you prefer to spend all your spare time growing roses or playing with your children, I like you better, but do not complain that you are not being promoted fast enough."

Some have built their organizations with the active participation of their families. Stew Leonard's, Marriott, Mrs. Field's Cookies—all are new "family" businesses. When the cost of excellence is shared by husbands, wives, children or grandparents, rewards are, too. The cruel division between the love of work and love of family blurs, softens and bends. In other organizations, family and friends are welcome at all events, including annual organization performance reviews.

When you have a true passion for excellence, and when you act on it, you will stand straighter. You will look people in the eye. You will see things happen. You will see heroes created, watch ideas unfold and take shape. You'll walk with a springier step. You'll have something to fight for, to care about, to share, scary as it is, with other people. There will be times when you swing from dedicated to obsessed. We don't pretend that it's easy. It takes real courage to step out and stake your claim. But we think the renewed sense of purpose, of making a difference, of recovered self-respect, is well worth the price of admission.

# Some (More) Good Reading on Leadership

Quick, go out and get *Leaders*, by Warren Bennis and Bert Nanus (Harper & Row, 1985). Warren is a good personal friend, and has struck gold with this book. His descriptions of forty leaders—from symphony orchestra conductor to movie director to Fortune 500 chairman—focus on the themes that we develop throughout the leadership section here. The six case studies in Michael Maccoby's *The Leader* (Simon & Schuster, 1981) also support our conclusions on the importance of "people-oriented" leadership at all levels.

*Corporate Cultures*, by Terry Deal and Allan Kennedy (Addison-Wesley, 1982) remains the first, most thorough and best description of corporate "culture" we've ever read. It is also exceptionally readable, filled with pragmatic anecdotes of leaders at all levels.

John Kotter's *The General Managers* (Free Press/Macmillan, 1982) is a data-rich analysis of several hundred highly effective general managers. Kotter finds that their success stems from a series of factors seldom discussed in traditional management texts; the ways these leaders deal with information and people are especially consistent with our observations.

For the true student of leadership (and we believe that every manager at every level should be a true student of leadership), there's no better source than James McGregor Burns's *Leadership* (Harper & Row, 1978). In particular, consistent with Warren Bennis's work and ours, Burns speaks of the "transforming leader," one who goes beyond dealing with the day-to-day problems of managing a sizable concern (such as a country) and focuses on the development of a new level of awareness among, often, tens of millions of people.

Finally, we would strongly suggest that the would-be effective leader become a reader of biographies. Ken Auletta's *The Art of Corporate Success* (Putnam's, 1983) is the unusual story of Jean Riboud of Schlumberger, one of the world's most profitable corporations; the portrait is that of a remarkably complex person (in other words, a real-world leader, not one from the world of texts on leadership). Another example is William Manchester's *American Caesar* (Little, Brown, 1978), which provides an extraordinary perspective on General MacArthur; the best part, to our minds, is the account of MacArthur's masterly management of post–World War II Japan (the subtlety of effective leadership has never been made more apparent to us).

# Acknowledgments

NONFICTION AUTHORS who are even half honest with themselves know that the acknowledgments section should be almost as long as the book. If that's true in general, it holds many times over for us. This book is those we've met.

We have listened to a thousand stories, each of which has come from someone who has been thoughtful enough to share an experience with us, to explain it in depth. Virtually all we included were marked not only by hard facts, but also by a genuine enthusiasm and caring on the part of the teller.

In September 1984 our partner Bob Le Duc's first Skunk Camp was held. What a gathering! Bill and Vieve Gore of W. L. Gore & Associates, Stew Leonard and Stew Jr. from Stew Leonard's, Frank and Jimmy Perdue from Perdue Farms, Don Burr of People Express, Tom Melohn from North American Tool & Die, Don Williams from Trammell Crow, Jerry Gallagher from Mervyn's and Dayton Hudson, Tom Malone of Milliken & Co., Ren McPherson from the Dana Corporation, John McConnell, Jr., from Worthington Industries, Ken Schoen from 3M, skunk Ken Stahl from Xerox, Don Vlcek of Domino's Pizza, Manny Garcia from Burger King, Donna Ecton from Campbell Soup, and many others attended. Several special friends couldn't be with us because of crises at the last minute (among them, Karen Strand from the Dana Corporation, Bob Stramy from General Motors, and Phil Staley from Ford). Seldom, if ever, have we learned so much or felt so much.

But that experience is but the tiniest part of all we have benefited from: Getting to know Bill Creech, the four-star general who turned around a huge part of the Air Force. Meeting Dean Sybil Mobley of Florida A&M's School of Business and Industry, who has performed true miracles in transforming an underfunded Southern black business school (she now has everyone from Jim Burke of Johnson & Johnson to Roger Smith of General Motors beating down the door for an opportunity to talk to her students). It's visiting Sweden and finding master showman (by his own admission) Jan Carlzon, who reversed SAS's fortunes; feeling the intensity of his concern for people (on another trip to Sweden) from Marcus Sieff, former chairman of Marks & Spencer.

How lucky we've been! To spend time with today's great entrepreneurs: Lex Wexner of The Limited, Merv Morris of Mervyn's, Dave Thomas of Wendy's, Trammell Crow of Trammell Crow, Tom Monaghan of Domino's Pizza, Roger Milliken of Milliken & Co.

But maybe even these people aren't the most important who've shaped our thinking. Most important are those whose names are absent from these pages. Tens of thousands have attended our seminars. They're often enmeshed in stodgy, bureaucratic organizations. Yet they've had the guts to try again, after years of depression and suppression of their ideas. They're out wandering, and proud of it. Out nurturing skunks. Out celebrating their people's successes.

Inspiration has come from unexpected quarters. We are not fans of the executives who populate the upper floors of most of the Fortune 500 companies. We have become special fans of those, most often in the mid-sized or smaller companies, who are making the American economy grow. Consider the bakers, for example. We met them at a meeting of the American Bakery Association (that's bakers, not bankers, which most people thought we meant when we reported on it). How inspiring! The bakers are down-to-earth business people. They understand about customer service and people—and innovation, too. The bakers, and Peterbilt truck dealers, all 225 employees of the Carl Sewell's Sewell Village Cadillac. Those are the ones who've given us ideas, hope and the courage to speak out about what's important.

How to pinpoint our indebtedness to some? Well, we could mention Don Burr and Bill Gore, who really believe they are creating important new forms of organization, and we believe they are, too. We are convinced by their ideas, to be sure, but above all, by their passion, and by the array of extraordinary people who work with them from whom we've also learned so much. And our minds return time and again to the image of Ren McPherson at our Skunk Camp. Despite the cast of stars scattered around him, whose hearts (and records) are unfailingly on the side of the angels, we would watch Ren bestir himself every forty-five minutes: "Bullshit." Someone (sometimes one of us) had just used the word "employee," rather than "person." And Ren simply wouldn't let it pass. He shouldn't, we shouldn't, and America shouldn't.

On the facing page is the "official portrait" from that first Skunk Camp. The players and their organizations are identified below the picture. Our heartfelt thanks to each and every one of them.

We're often hard on the academics. They have been much kinder to us than we to them. We've been highly critical, often in public. They've been supportive. Tom's close personal friend and colleague at Stanford, Associate Dean Gene Webb at the Business School, has remained a staunch supporter (though tried sorely on many an occasion). There's no way that Tom can thank Gene enough for his steadfastness. Warren Bennis of USC, Jim Kouzes of Santa Clara, Brian Quinn of Dartmouth, Wick Skinner of Harvard, Rosabeth Moss Kanter of Yale, and Andy Van de Ven of Minnesota stand out as

1. Dick Jackson
   *First Georgia Bank*
2. Jake Kerr
   *Lignum, Ltd.*
3. Barry Roach
   *Raychem*
4. Donna Ecton
   *Campbell Soup*
5. Paul Sakamoto
   *Mountain View-Los Altos, CA School District*
6. Sam Tyler
   *The Tom Peters Group*
7. Ren McPherson
   *The Dana Corporation*
8. Bob Le Duc
   *The Tom Peters Group*
9. Manny Garcia
   *Davgar Restaurants*
10. John McCoy
    *Bancone*
11. Melissa Manson
    *The Tom Peters Group*
12. Mara Nieman
    *The Tom Peters Group*
13. Don Williams
    *Trammell Crow*
14. Peter Vaill
    *George Washington Univ.*
15. Pete Mesa
    *Milpitas Unified School District*
16. Kathy Johnson
    *Association of Western Hospitals*
17. Jim Perdue
    *Perdue Farms*
18. Nancy Badore
    *Ford Motor Co.*
19. Don Burr
    *People Express*
20. Frank Perdue
    *Perdue Farms*
21. Bill Benak
    *Levin Metals Corp.*
22. Don Vlcek
    *Domino's Pizza Distribution*
23. Joe Stegmayer
    *Worthington Industries*
24. Ian Thomson
    *The Tom Peters Group*
25. Dale Miller
    *Zenger-Miller, Inc.*
26. Tom Malone
    *Milliken & Co.*
27. Stew Leonard, Sr.
    *Stew Leonard's*
28. Tait Elder
    *Allied Technologies*
29. Ed Prell
    *Bell Labs*
30. John McConnell, Jr.
    *Worthington Industries*
31. Ken Schoen
    *3M*
32. Tony Schulte
    *Random House*
33. Jerry Gallagher
    *Mervyn's*
34. Tom Melohn
    *North American Tool & Die*
35. Tom Peters
    *The Tom Peters Group*
36. Jerry Porras
    *Stanford Univ.*
37. Stew Leonard, Jr.
    *Stew Leonard's*
38. Nancy Austin
    *The Tom Peters Group*
39. Barbara Demere
    *The Tom Peters Group*
40. Bill Gore
    *W. L. Gore & Associates*
41. Vieve Gore
    *W. L. Gore & Associates*
42. Debbie Henken
    *The Tom Peters Group*
43. Ken Stahl
    *Xerox*
44. Debbie Kaplan
    *The Tom Peters Group*
45. Christy Miller
    *The Tom Peters Group*
46. Dee Young
    *The Tom Peters Group*
47. Henry Haskell
    *Kal Kan Foods, Inc.*

special colleagues from academia. They and many others are trying new things in the beleaguered business schools. There's a special category of "miscellaneous friends" ("miscellaneous" only because they defy categorization). One of these is Bob Schwartz of Tarrytown, who is deeply concerned with new forms of managing. His support has meant more than he'll ever know.

And then there are those who have given us courage at exactly the right moment. Tom was down and out after a brush with many too many of the (inappropriately) complacent, publicly advertised "greats" of the Fortune 500. He spent the next day with Chairman Jim Burke of Johnson & Johnson, President Wayne Calloway of PepsiCo, and Don Estridge, who heads the PC division (Entry Systems Division) at IBM. Never has anyone's spirit lifted so fast.

Our partners and cohorts in crime not only have "provided support through the long hours," but have tested, pushed forth and insisted that we *live* the ideas that we talk about. Among them: Stewart Clifford, Linda Devillier, Debbie Henken, Melissa Howard, Debbie Kaplan, Bob Le Duc, Christy Miller, Gail Miller, John Nathan, Mara Neiman, Jeff Newcomb, Malka Rosen, Kathy Swan, Ian Thomson, Sam Tyler, Marilyn Van Wichen, and Dee Young.

And now a word for those who worked directly on the book. Corona Machemer is our editor at Random House. We must do one of two things: either say "thanks" and stop there, or write fifteen pages of tribute. To do less than the latter would severely denigrate her contribution. Corona's technical contribution has been exceptional—what one would expect from a fine editor, and more. Her impeccable sense of organization has been equally thoughtful—again, at some level, what one would expect from a superb editor. What has made the relationship radically different, however, has been her passionate involvement with the ideas we present. This book is about enthusiasm and passion and ownership and pride and care and trust and listening and courtesy and another dozen terms of the same sort. Corona's dedication to what these words represent is doubtless more strenuous than even our own. She has forced us to dig deep to test the strenth and consistency of our beliefs. Time and again she's caught us napping, tested us, and led us to revise what we were doing. The integrity of her work, we believe, shines out from every page. Thanks, Corona. We didn't know such contributions were possible.

Bob Bernstein and Tony Schulte at Random House have made the relationship with our publisher a wholly rewarding one. In the best of worlds one's publisher becomes one's family. That's exactly what's happened at Random House, and we're thankful indeed.

Our technical support at Random House and at home has been more than helpful, and always there when we needed it: thanks to Susan Winn and Linda Dee for getting the whole manuscript together; to Sono Rosenberg for her heroic and masterly copy-editing; to Jo Metsch for her brilliant design work; to Sallye Leventhal, for doing just about anything that had to be done; and to Dee Young, for researching and correcting and her sense of humor.

The book is dedicated to Kate Abbe and Bill Cawley and the skunks. You've read of the skunks. As for Bill and Kate, they've been supportive, yes, but that's the least of it. We both read a lot, and we are inured to the "and thanks to Mary Jo who put up with us when we were cranky" stuff. Kate's and Bill's belief in the possibility of a world in which human beings treat each other decently is what the book is about, what they're about, and what we have tried to live up to. Both Kate and Bill are living demonstrations that you can care about people, care about what you do, and be exceptionally success-ful at it.

We conclude with a tribute to someone that neither of us knew, the late Lieutenant General Melvin Zais, U.S. Army. One of our many unsung sup-porters sent Tom a letter three years ago. Attached was an audiotape of an Army general giving a speech to the Armed Forces Staff College on leader-ship. Unfortunately, in the swirl of things, the letter got detached from the tape, and has been lost. The tape remains, and on a hot summer day in 1983, Tom got around to listening to it. He listened and wept. We now use it at all of our Skunk Camps. You've read some of the words in the book. General Zais's advice is clear: "You must care." To listen to it, a sometimes halting speech by a general who jumped with the 101st Airborne, to listen to him talk of love and care and trust and humility on the part of those who lead still brings on an emotional reaction each time we hear it. Tom Melohn of North American Tool & Die, talking about his people, broke down in front of tele-vision cameras during the filming of our January 1985 PBS special. The inten-sity and passion of Zais and Melohn is inspiring. General Zais, we thank you so much. Finally, our most heartfelt acknowledgment goes out to all of you whom we have not had the opportunity to meet, but who are giving us the most steadfast support by living this message. We trust that we will have the chance to get acquainted with you in the years ahead.

# Acknowledgments

Grateful acknowledgment is made to the following for permission to reprint previously published material:

Thomas Larry Adcock: Excerpt from "They Also Wait Who Stand and Serve," by Thomas Larry Adcock, which previously appeared in *Northwest Orient* magazine, October 1983. Used with permission of the author.

American Psychological Association: Excerpt reprinted from "Small Wins: Redefining the Scale of Social Problems," in *The American Psychologist*, Vol. 39, January 1984, pp. 40–49. Copyright © 1984 by the American Psychological Association. Reprinted by permission of the publisher.

Basic Books, Inc.: Excerpt from *Silicon Valley Fever: Growth of High-Technology Culture*, by Everett M. Rogers and Judith Larsen. Copyright © 1984 by Basic Books, Inc. United Kingdom rights administered by George Allen & Unwin (Publishers) Ltd, London. Excerpt from *The Good School: Portraits of Character and Culture*, by Sara Lawrence Lightfoot. Copyright © 1983 by Basic Books, Inc. Reprinted by permission of the publisher.

Business Week: Excerpt from "Campbell Soup's Recipe for Growth: Offering Something for Every Palate." Reprinted from the December 24, 1984, issue of *Business Week*, by special permission, © 1984 by McGraw-Hill, Inc.

Capistrano Press, Ltd.: Excerpt from Fredonia F. Jacques: "Verdict Pending: A Patient Representative's Intervention" reprinted with permission for World English Language Rights. Garden Grove, Calif.; Capistrano Press Ltd., 1983, pp. 57–58.

Center for Creative Leadership: Excerpt from "Participative Management," by E. J. Cattabiani and R. P. White; *Issues and Observations*, August 1983; © 1983 Center for Creative Leadership, Greensboro, N.C.

Chief Executive Magazine: Excerpt from "The CEO as Champion," reprinted with permission from *Chief Executive* (Spring 1984, No. 27). Copyright © Chief Executive Magazine, Inc., 645 5th Avenue, New York, NY 10022. All rights reserved. Single copy, $7.00.

Crown Publishers: Excerpts reprinted from Ogilvy on Advertising, by David Ogilvy. Text copyright © 1983 by David Ogilvy and compilation copyright © 1983 by Multimedia Publications, Inc. Used by permission of Crown Publishers, Inc.

Dana Corporation: "Dana's 40 Thoughts" reprinted courtesy of the Dana Corporation, Toledo, Ohio.

Dow Jones & Company, Inc.: Excerpts from the February 8, 1984; October 23, 1984; and December 12, 1984 issues of *The Wall Street Journal*. Reprinted by permission of The Wall Street Journal, Copyright © Dow Jones & Company, Inc., 1984. All rights reserved.

Farrar, Straus & Giroux, Inc.: Excerpts reprinted by permission of Farrar, Straus and Giroux, Inc., from *The Headmaster* by John McPhee. Copyright © 1966 by John McPhee. This material originally appeared in *The New Yorker*.

Grosset & Dunlap, Inc.: Excerpt reprinted by permission of Grosset & Dunlap, Inc., from *For the Good of The Company*, copyright © 1976 by Isadore Barmash.

Harvard Business Review: The following excerpts, by Theodore Levitt (except where noted): Excerpt from Chapter 2, "The Globalization of Markets," as adapted in *The Marketing Imagination*, by Theodore Levitt. Copyright © 1983 by The Free Press. "The Globalization of Markets" by Theodore Levitt (May/June 1983). Copyright © 1983 by the President and Fellows of Harvard College; all rights reserved. Excerpt from Chapter 3, "The Industrialization of Service," as adapted in *The Marketing Imagination*. Copyright © 1983 by The Free Press. "The Industrialization of Service" (September/October 1976). Copyright © 1976 by the President and Fellows of Harvard College; all rights reserved. Excerpt from Chapter 4, "Differentiation—Of Anything," as adapted in *The Marketing Imagination*. Copyright © 1983 by The Free Press. "Marketing Success Through Differentiation—Of Anything" (January/February 1980). Copyright © 1980 by the President and Fellows of Harvard College; all rights reserved. Excerpt from Chapter 5, "Marketing Intangible Products and Product Intangibles," as adapted in *The Marketing Imagination*. Copyright © 1983 by The Free Press. "Marketing Intangible Products and Product Intangibles" (May/June 1981). Copyright © 1981 by the President and Fellows of Harvard College; all rights reserved. Excerpt from Chapter 6, "Relationship Management," as adapted in *The Marketing Imagination*. Copyright © 1983 by The Free Press. "After the Sale is Over" (September/October 1983). Copyright © 1983 by the President and Fellows of Harvard College; all rights reserved. Excerpt from "The Oldest and Best Way to Communicate with Employees," by Roger D'Aprix (September/October 1982). Copyright © 1982 by the President and Fellows of Harvard College; all rights reserved. All excerpts reprinted by permission of the *Harvard Business Review*.

IBM Corporation: Advertisement reprinted courtesy of the IBM Corporation.

Inc. Magazine: Excerpt from "The Employee Who's No Longer Useful." Reprinted with permission, Inc. magazine, January 1982. Copyright © 1982, by Inc. Publishing Corporation, 38 Commercial Wharf, Boston, MA 02110.

Johnson & Johnson: Jim Burke's Ad Council speech, and Johnson & Johnson Credo. Reprinted courtesy of Johnson & Johnson.

Little, Brown & Company: Excerpts from *The Soul of a New Machine*, by Tracy Kidder. Copyright © 1981 by John Tracy Kidder. By permission of Little, Brown & Company in association with the Atlantic Monthly Press.

L. L. Bean, Inc.: "The Golden Rule of L. L. Bean," reprinted courtesy of L. L. Bean, Inc.

McGraw-Hill Book Co.: Excerpt from *A Business and Its Beliefs: The Ideas That Helped Build IBM*, by Thomas Watson, Jr. Copyright © 1963 by the Trustees of Columbia University. Used with permission of McGraw-Hill Book Company.

Herman Miller, Inc.: Excerpt from speeches by Max DePree, courtesy Herman Miller, Inc.

The New York Times Company: Excerpt from "Molded in Al Davis' Images," by Michael Janofsky, *New York Times*, September 2, 1984. "Bottom Linemanship," by Norman Lear, *New York Times*, May 20, 1984. Copyright © 1984 by The New York Times Company. Reprinted by permission.

Nordstrom: Advertisement reprinted courtesy of Nordstrom, Seattle, Washington.

Random House, Inc.: Excerpts from *Inside Prime Time*, by Todd Gitlin. Copyright © 1983 by Todd Gitlin. Reprinted by permission of Pantheon Books, a division of Random House, Inc. United Kingdom rights administered by International Creative Management. Material adapted from *The Winning Streak*, by Walter Goldsmith and David Clutterbuck. Reprinted by permission of Random House, Inc. and Weidenfeld (Publishers) Ltd. *The Winning Streak* will be published jointly in the United States and Canada by Random House, Inc., and Not Just Another Publishing Company, Inc.

H. S. Shanlian: Letter reprinted courtesy of Mr. H. S. "Blackie" Shanlian.

The Sterling Lord Agency, Inc.: Excerpt from "Can The Best Mayor Win?" by Richard Cramer. Reprinted by permission of the Sterling Lord Agency, Inc. Copyright © 1984 by Richard Cramer. The excerpt first appeared in the October 1984 issue of *Esquire* magazine.

Texas Monthly: Excerpt from "The Eccentric Genius of Trammell Crow," by Joseph Nocera. Reprinted with permission from the August issue of *Texas Monthly*. Copyright © 1984 by Texas Monthly.

Robert Townsend: quotes from Robert Townsend's Alfred A. Knopf open memorandum on "Leadership."

Travelhost: Excerpt from "The Choicest Potato Chip," by James E. Buerger, Publisher of Travelhost Magazine.

Utah State University School of Business: Excerpt from W. Edwards Deming's speech, "Transformation of Management Needed: Must Remove Deadly Obstacles," reprinted courtesy of Utah State University School of Business, George S. Eccles Distinguished Lecture Series, 1982–83.

Warner Books: Excerpt from *Mary Kay on People Management*, Copyright © 1984 by Warner Books, Inc. Reprinted by permission of the publisher.

# A Guide to Key Concepts

# Index

| | | | |
|---|---|---|---|
| ☐ | THE ONE MINUTE MANAGER Blanchard/Johnson | 0-00-636753-4 | £5.99 |
| ☐ | PUTTING THE ONE MINUTE MANAGER TO WORK Blanchard/Lorber | 0-00-636824-7 | £5.99 |
| ☐ | THE ONE MINUTE SALES PERSON Johnson/Wilson | 0-00-637015-2 | £5.99 |
| ☐ | LEADERSHIP AND THE ONE MINUTE MANAGER Blanchard/Zigami | 0-00-637080-2 | £5.99 |
| ☐ | THE ONE MINUTE MANAGER MEETS THE MONKEY Blanchard/Oncken/Burrows | 0-00-637606-1 | £5.99 |
| ☐ | THE ONE MINUTE MANAGER BUILDS HIGH PERFORMANCE TEAMS Blanchard/Carew/Parisi–Carew | 0-00-637952-4 | £5.99 |

All these books are available from your local bookseller or can be ordered direct from the publishers.

To order direct just tick the titles you want and fill in the form below:

Name: _____

Address: _____

_____

Postcode: _____

Send to: HarperCollins Mail Order, Dept 8, HarperCollins*Publishers*, Westerhill Road, Bishopbriggs, Glasgow G64 2QT.

Please enclose a cheque or postal order or your authority to debit your Visa/Access account –

Credit card no: _____

Expiry date: _____

Signature: _____

– to the value of the cover price plus:

UK & BFPO: Add £1.00 for the first and 25p for each additional book ordered.

Overseas orders including Eire, please add £2.95 service charge.

Books will be sent by surface mail but quotes for airmail despatches will be given on request.

24 HOUR TELEPHONE ORDERING SERVICE FOR ACCESS/VISA CARDHOLDERS –

TEL: GLASGOW 041-772 2281 or LONDON 081-307 4052